READING OLD ENGLISH

WVU PRESS

READING OLD ENGLISH

REVISED EDITION

A PRIMER AND FIRST READER

ISBN (paperback) 978-1-933202-74-7 (alk. paper)

**Library of Congress Cataloguing-in-Publication Data
From the First Edition**

Hasenfratz, Robert. 1957- Jambeck, Thomas. 1936-
    Reading Old English: A Primer and First Reader
    First Edition

p. cm.

      1. English language—Old English, ca. 450-1100—Grammar. 2. English language—Old English,
      ca. 450-1100—Readers. 3. English philology—Old English, ca. 450-1100—Handbooks, manuals, etc.
      I. Title. II. Hasenfratz, Robert. III. Jambeck, Thomas.

IN PROCESS

Library of Congress Control Number: 2005920990

Cover Design by Than Saffel
Interior Design by Than Saffel and 2econdShift Production Services
Typesetting of first edition by 2econdShift Production Services

Contents

Preface

This book focuses on giving you the skills necessary to read Old English quickly and accurately, and while it assumes a minimum of prior linguistic knowledge, it aims to provide a full explanation of a number of grammatical and syntactical nuances that will allow you to read both literary and historical documents with precision. We have written *Reading Old English* with advanced undergraduates, graduate students, and auto-didacts in mind, and have provided a number of graded exercises and readings to guide you through the learning process. For the most part, the book focuses on the reading of prose, providing full editions of Ælfric's *Colloquy* as well as three Old English lives of St. Etheldreda, though many examples from poetry are included throughout the book. Beside the prose pieces already mentioned, the reader includes a short introduction to Old English poetry, a full text of "The Wife's Lament," and substantial excerpts from *Judith* and *Beowulf,* as well as a number of prose and poetic texts relating to Anglo-Saxon book production.

After the opening chapters, almost all illustrative sentences, exercise sentences, and texts for translation have been taken from the surviving corpus of Old English texts, sometimes with slight modifications. For several historical reasons, students today, even graduate students, come to the study of Old English with little background in philology or linguistics. Unlike most other Old English grammars, this one does not assume an in-depth knowledge of historical linguistics or the history of the English language, but instead offers a practical introduction to the reading of Old English with a minimum of technical terminology and a maximum of explanation and practice.

Old English, the form of the English language from roughly 450-1100 C.E., belongs to the Germanic branch of the Indo-European family of languages and thus is most closely related to Frisian, Dutch, and German (its immediate relatives in the West Germanic branch) and somewhat more distantly to those from the northern (Danish, Faroese, Icelandic, Norwegian, and Swedish) and eastern branches (Gothic).

Anglo-Saxon England developed arguably the earliest and certainly the most voluminous vernacular literature of Western Europe in the early Middle Ages. Surviving vernacular texts in Old English cover a broad range: law codes; chronicles; saints' lives and homilies; Bible translations;

heroic, lyric, and religious poetry; translations of Latin patristic and monastic texts; scientific and medical texts; and so on. Given the richness of the surviving corpus of texts, the ability to read Old English should be of interest particularly to students of literature, history, religious studies, and the developing field of translation studies.

How to Use This Book

We have designed this book for both undergraduate courses and graduate seminars. Ideally, the grammar and readings take fourteen weeks to cover, at roughly one chapter per week, students may begin to work on readings in the tenth or eleventh week. Though we have provided a reader at the end of the book (full editions of Ælfric's *Colloquy*, three Old English lives of St. Etheldreda, and a lyric poem, "The Wife's Lament," as well as excerpts from *Judith*, *Beowulf*, The Exeter Book, and the Lindisfarne Gospels), *Reading Old English* might be profitably used alongside a reader or online editions of Old English texts. See *http://english.uconn.edu/readingoldenglish/* for links and additional resources.

Acknowledgments

We are very grateful to Christine Dearden, Daniel Donoghue, Martin Foys, David Johnson, Stacy Klein, Johanna Kramer, Jane Roberts, Andrew Scheil, William Schipper, Jana Schulman, John Sheard, Robert Stanton, and Jocelyn Wogan-Browne, and their students for their many helpful criticisms and suggestions; to our wonderful graduate students, current and former, and particularly to Brandon Hawk and Breann Leake, for helping us improve the book and spot errors; to the staff of the English Department and Medieval Studies Program at the University of Connecticut for all their support and good-humored help; to the University of Connecticut Graduate Research Foundation for its timely and considerable support for our project; and finally to the team at the West Virginia University Press—director Carrie Mullen, former director Patrick Conner, copy editor Stacey Elza, designer and production manager Than Saffel (we can't thank you enough!), production assistant Rachel King, and original typesetters Steve Cannon and Ed Arnold of 2econdShift Productions—for their patience, enthusiasm, and attention to detail.

We are also indebted to the expert attention and keen eyes of our graduate students, particularly Brandon Hawk and Breann Leake, for helping us improve the readings and spot errors in the corrected edition. Our thanks also go to Lindy Brady, Jeremy Deangelo, Joshua Eyler, Wendy Hennequin, Wendy Hoofnagle, Kathryn King, Gregory Hays, Erin Heidkamp, Jon Kotchian, Frederic Lardinois, Katherine Lawson, Matthew McDonough, Amy Mendoza, Michael Mendoza, Frank Napolitano, Katherine O'Sullivan, Suzanne Paquette, Nadia Pawelchak, Andrew Pfrenger, Britt Rothauser, John Sexton, Susan Solomon, Daniella Sovea, Joseph Stephenson, and Michael Torregrossa.

ROBERT HASENFRATZ

I am grateful to Thomas Jambeck for his erudition, patience, and inexhaustible good humor, especially when faced with some of his co-author's crankier moods. Warm thanks also to my friends and colleagues David Benson, Frederick Biggs, Christine Cooper, Irina Dumitrescu, Denis Ferhatović, Jennifer Kenniston, Iris Müller, Cookie Marie Pearce, Melanie Pearce, Penelope Pelizzon, Jerry Phillips, Ann Saunders, Cathy Schlund-Vials, Gregory Semenza, the late and much missed Hans Turley, and Jordan Zweck for their encouragement, help, and support, moral or otherwise.

THOMAS JAMBECK

To my lunchroom colleagues who had no idea what I was up to and as a result offered me no advice at all, but who would be disappointed if they were not mentioned here, my appreciation for their most helpful inattention. To my pal and colleague Roger Wilkenfeld who alone insisted that the world needed another Old English grammar, my sincere thanks for his encouragement and enthusiasm. It has been a pleasure to work with my co-author, Bob Hasenfratz. He has been invariably patient with my errors and kind in his silent correction of the most embarrassing ones. Working with Bob has taught me about the generosity of the true scholar.

To my son Mark David, who at ten years old wrote three books to his father's one, I am always and shamelessly proud of you. To my wife Kathy, who generously took time from her book so that I could write mine, my love, admiration, and devotion.

READING OLD ENGLISH

ABBREVIATIONS

* = when it appears before a word (example: *mouses), the asterisk indicates a hypothetical or supposed form.

1 = first person

2 = second person

3 = third person

acc = accusative

dat = dative

EWS = Early West Saxon

f = feminine

gen = genitive

Gmc = Germanic

IE = Indo-European

inst = instrumental

IPA = International Phonetic Alphabet

L = Latin

LWS = Late West Saxon

m = masculine

ModE = Modern English

n = neuter

nom = nominative

OE = Old English

pl = plural

prehist = prehistoric

PreshistOE = prehistoric Old English

pres = present (tense)

PrimOE = Primitive Old English

sing = singular

WGmc = West Germanic

WS = West Saxon

ONE

Old English Alphabets and Pronunciation

Lesson One: Old English Alphabets

[1] The following chart of English runes and their word equivalents is based on R. I. Page's *An Introduction to English Runes.* 2nd ed. Woodbridge, Suffolk: Boydell P, 1999. The Old English "Rune Poem" provides many of the word equivalences.

When the Germanic invaders arrived in Britain in the early fifth century, they brought with them a runic alphabet of about twenty-four letters. These runes (the Old English word *rūn* means "secret") were designed originally to inscribe relatively short texts on a hard surface such as stone, wood, bone, or metal. The Old English version of the runic alphabet, usually referred to as the *futhorc* from the first six letters of the alphabet,

ᚠ (f), ᚢ (u), ᚦ (th), ᚩ (o), ᚱ (r), ᚳ (c)

changed slightly from its ancestor: it modified the form of some runes, and it added at least seven new letters. Though runes could represent individual sounds like a modern alphabet, each symbol had a word value as well (see the chart below). [1]

Ælfric on Letters Ælfric of Eynsham (ca. 950-ca. 1010), one of the most prolific vernacular prose writers in Anglo-Saxon England, composed arguably the first vernacular grammar of Latin in Europe sometime in the late tenth century, using the Latin grammar of Priscian as a source. Since his students were struggling with the same concepts in Latin as you are in Old English, from time to time we will provide Ælfric's discussion of various grammatical and linguistic phenomena.

De littera: *Littera* is "stæf" on Englisc and is sē læsta dæl on bōcum and un-tōdæledliċ. Wē tō-dælað þā bōc tō cwydum and syððan ðā cwydas tō dælum eft ðā dælas tō stæf-ġefegum and syððan þā stæf-ġefegu tō stafum: þonne bēoð ðā stafas un-tōdæledliċe for-ðan ðe nān stæf ne byð naht, ġif hē gæð on twā.

Concerning the letter: A letter is "staff" in English and is the least (i.e., smallest) part in books and is indivisible. We divide the book into sentences and afterwards the sentences into parts (of speech) and afterwards the parts (of speech) into letter combinations and afterwards the letter combinations into letters: the letters then are indivisible because a letter is nothing if it goes in two.

With the conversion of the Anglo-Saxons to Christianity during the seventh century, missionaries introduced the Latin alphabet. First under the influence of the Irish mission and later under that of the Romans, Anglo-Saxon scribes learned to copy Latin manuscripts using a Roman alphabet modified by Irish monks, usually called "Insular" script (see the chart on page 4 for letter forms of this alphabet). When Anglo-Saxon scribes turned from copying out Latin texts to transcribing English words and later longer vernacular works, they used the letters of this Latin alphabet and their sound values to represent the sounds of Old English. Because we know something of Latin pronunciation, we can approximate with relative confidence the pronunciation of Old English sounds. In some instances, however, English words used sounds that had no Latin equivalent. In these instances, the Anglo-Saxon scribes borrowed or created letters to represent those sounds.

þ, Þ   The *th* sound (whether voiced as in "*th*en" or voiceless as in "*th*in") was represented by þ, known by its runic name *thorn*. (For definitions of "voiceless" and "voiced," see §1.7.2)

ð, Ð   The *th* sound (whether voiced as in "*th*en" or voiceless as in "*th*in") was also represented by the Insular "d" with a light line drawn above the rounded part of the letter: ð. The letter is called an *eth* after its Modern Icelandic name, although the Anglo-Saxons referred to the letter as ð*æt*. The *thorn* and *eth* are used interchangeably for the voiceless and voiced *th* sound in OE.

ƿ, Ƿ   The *w* sound (as in "*w*ing" or "*w*ood") was represented by the rune known as *wynn* (OE *wynn* "joy"). This text, like most modern texts, will use the letter *w* for the *wynn* in order to avoid confusion with the *thorn* symbol.

æ, Æ   The *a* sound (as in "*c*at" or "*b*at") was represented by the Latin digraph æ, later written as the ligature. The æ letter was called an *æsc* (ash) after its runic character which represented the same sound but was written differently as ᚨ.

By the tenth century, another script called Carolingian (or Caroline), a book hand developed by scholars in Charlemagne's court, began to compete with Insular, particularly for the copying of Latin texts. In the tenth and eleventh centuries, some scriptoria reserved the Insular script for vernacular texts and Carolingian for Latin.[2]

[2] For a description of the Insular and Caroline scripts, see the introduction to N. R. Ker's *Catalogue of Manuscripts Containing Anglo-Saxon*. Oxford: Oxford UP, 1957. For several articles relevant to Anglo-Saxon book production, see *Anglo-Saxon Manuscripts: Basic Readings*, ed. Mary P. Richards, London: Routeledge, 1994.

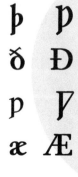

1.1.1 A Crash Course in Anglo-Saxon Paleography

This chart catalogues the most common letter forms found in late Anglo-Saxon manuscripts.

Modern	Insular LC	Insular UC	Carolingian LC	Carolingian UC	Runes (futhorc)	Word-value of the Runes
A	a	Λ	a	A	ᚪ	*āc* "oak; ship made of oak"
B	ƀ	B	b	B	ᛒ	*beorc* "birch"
C	c	C	c	C	ᚳ	*ċen* "pine torch"
D	ð	D	d	D	ᛞ	*dæġ* "day"
E	e	E	e	E	ᛖ (ᛠ = ea)	*e(o)h* "horse" (*ēar* "earth")
F	F	F	f	F	ᚠ	*feoh* "money; cattle"
G	ᵹ	Ᵹ	g	G	ᚷ, (ᚸ = gg)	*ġifu* "gift; sacrifice"
ġ [y]					ᛄ	*ġēar* "year"
H	h	ħ	h	H	ᚻ	*hæġl* "hail"
I	ı	I	i	I	ᛁ	*īs* "ice"
J, io					ᛡ	*īor* "river fish; eel"

CRASH COURSE IN ANGLO-SAXON PALEOGRAPHY *continued*

Modern	Insular LC	Insular UC	Carolingian LC	Carolingian UC	Runes (futhorc)	Word-value of the Runes
K	k	K	k	K	ᛣ	*calc, ćealc* "chalk"
kk, kh					ᛤ	(doubled form of previous rune)
L	l	L	l	L	ᛚ	*lagu* "water; sea; flood"
M	m	M	m	M	ᛗ	*man* "man; human being"
N	n	N	n	N	ᚾ	*nȳd* "affliction"
ng					ᛝ	*Ing* "a heathen god"
O	o	O	o	O	ᚩ	*ōs* "(heathen) god"
P	p	P	p	P	ᛈ (h)	*peorð* "chessman"?
Q	q	Q	q	Q	ʃ (kw)	*cweorð* (formed on analogy with *peorð*)
R	r	R	r	R	ᚱ	*rād* "riding; road"
S	ſ	S	ſ s	S	ᚻ,ᛋ	*siġel* "sun"

CRASH COURSE IN ANGLO-SAXON PALEOGRAPHY *continued*

Modern	Insular LC	Insular UC	Carolingian LC	Carolingian UC	Runes (futhorc)	Word-value of the Runes
T	ꞇ	T	t	T	ᛏ	*Tīw*, "pagan god of war"
U/V	u	U	u(u)/v	U	ᚢ,ᚢ	*ūr* "wild ox"
W	ƿ	Ƿ	w	W	ᚹ	*wynn* "joy"
X	x	X	x	X	ᛉ	*eolh(x)-secg* "reed; sage"
Y	ẏ	Y	y	Y	ᚣ, ᚣ, ᚣ	*ȳr* "bow? gold? horn?"
Z	z	Z	z	Z		
Æ	æ	Æ			ᚫ	*æsc* "ash tree"
œ, e					ᛟ	*ēðel* "home, native land"
th	ð	Đ				*ðæt* "that," abbrev. for *þæt*
th	þ	Þ			ᚦ	*þorn* "thorn"
þæt (abbrev.)	ꝥ					

A Story in Runes The front panel of the Franks Casket (probably eighth century; London, British Museum), depicting an episode from the story of Weland the Smith (a figure in pagan Germanic mythology) on the left and the adoration of the Magi on the right. The runic inscription begins in the upper left hand corner with *fisc flodu*, continuing in the upper right with *ahof on ferg-*, and then down the right side with *-enberig*. The beginning of the inscription thus reads, *Fisc flodu ahof on fergenberig* "The tide bore the fish (i.e., whale) up onto the cliff-bank," telling the story of the whale from whose bones the ivory chest was made.

Lesson Two: Pronunciation　　1.2

The rest of this chapter dwells on many technicalities of pronouncing Old English by giving you some background in phonology. Before starting with this more detailed description of Old English pronunciation, consider the following quick start guide.

THE BRIEFEST POSSIBLE GUIDE TO PRONOUNCING OLD ENGLISH　　1.2.1

CARDINAL RULE

There are *no* silent letters (combinations like *hl-*, *hw-*, and *cn-* are pronounced as they're spelled). The letter *e* at the ends of words should be pronounced like the *a* in Modern English *sofa*—that is, "uh" (the so-called *schwa* sound).

PRONOUNCING ALIEN LETTER FORMS

- Đ, ð (the runic letter *eth*)   =   th
- Þ, þ (the runic letter *þorn*)   =   th
- Ƿ, ƿ (the runic letter *wynn*)   =   w
- Æ, æ (the runic letter *æsc*)   =   a (as in the modern word *ash*).

Most texts regularize *wynn* to modern *w*, though some scholarly editions preserve it.

PRONOUNCING CONSONANTS

- *c* is generally pronounced hard (like modern *k*).
- *g* is generally pronounced hard (like modern *g*).
- *c* and *g* can have alternative pronunciations: *ch* and *y* (respectively), behaving almost exactly as they do in Italian, if an *i* or *e* follows them. In this book when *c* is pronounced like *ch*, and *g* like *y*, both appear with a dot above them (ċ, ġ) (examples: *ċēosan* "to choose" and *ġēar* "year").
- *h* (by itself) in the middle or at the end of the word is pronounced gutturally, as in standard German *Ach!* or *ich*.

PRONOUNCING VOWELS

- Pronounce long vowels (always marked with a macron or long mark) this way:

ā	=	str*aw*	*ādl* "disease"
ē	=	str*ay*	*ēċe* "eternal"
ī	=	str*eet*	*īdel* "idle; empty"
ō	=	str*obe*	*ōþer* "other"
ū	=	str*ew*	*ūp* "up"

- Short vowels (not marked) sound more or less like their counterparts in Modern English, except that short *a* sounds like "ah" rather than the "a" of *apple*.

- *y* (as a vowel) is pronounced like the vowel in French *lune* or German *kühn*.
- By the late OE period, most vowels in final, unstressed syllables are pronounced like *schwa*, that is "uh" (example: *būre* "bower, room"; *ælas* "awls").
- Vowel combinations (diphthongs): pronounce each letter, but blend them quickly together.

ACCENT AND STRESS

- Give most words the stress on the first syllable.
- The prefixes *ġe-* and *be-* **never** take stress, so put the emphasis on the following syllable.
- In verbs with prefixes, the root receives more stress than the prefix—just as in Modern English. Think of this example:

> I always wear an *OVercoat*. (noun)
> The painter must *overCOAT* the old paint. (verb)

DETAILED DESCRIPTION OF OE PRONUNCIATION   1.2.2

GENERAL GUIDELINES

1. All OE letters are sounded; there are no so-called "silent" letters. Hence, both the *w* and *r* in *wracu* "revenge" are pronounced; the *g* and *n* in *gnæt* "gnat," *h* and *l* in *hlinc* "hill," *c* (k) and *n* in *cniht* "boy."

   Similarly, there are no "silent *e*'s" as in Modern English *stone*.

2. Doubled consonants are pronounced "long," that is, are pronounced "double" much as in Modern English compounds: *mad-dog, grab-bag, cat-tail*; compare

GENERAL GUIDELINES continued

for example the Modern English pronunciation of *grabby* (the *b* sound is a short, single *b* sound) and *grab-bag* (the *b* sound is long, that is, doubled). OE examples: *hremman* "to hinder," *biddan* "to ask," *settan* "to place."

3. As in all Germanic languages, the stress in OE generally falls on the first syllable of a word: ***dryhten*** "lord," ***blāford*** "master," ***slǣping*** "sleeping." If a word has an inflectional ending, the first element of the word is stressed and the inflection is unstressed: ***stānas*** "stones" (accusative plural), ***stānum*** "stones" (dative plural), ***gōdes*** "good" (genitive singular).

4. In a compound word usually made up of two nouns or an adjective and a noun, the first element receives the stress; the second element a secondary stress: ***scip-blāford***, "ship master," ***gāst-cofa*** "breast; lit., spirit coffer," ***stān-cnoll*** "stony knoll," ***hwæl-weġ*** "sea, lit. whale way," ***sūþ-stæð*** "south coast," ***hēah-fæder*** "father, patriarch."

5. Prefixes: in words introduced by a prefix, the prefix element is generally stressed; the root element receives a secondary stress: ***ymbe-sprǣċ*** (*ymbe* "about" + *sprǣċ* "talk" = criticism, remark), ***mis-lār*** (*mis* "wrong" + *lār* "teaching" = ill teaching), ***tō-gang*** (*tō* "toward" + *gang* "going" = access, attack).

Exceptions:

(1) The prefixes *ġe-* and *be-* are NEVER stressed: *ġeflit* "strife," *behāt* "promise"; *for-* is seldom stressed: *forġyfnes* "forgiveness."

(2) When the prefix introduces a verb, the stress normally falls on the second element of the word, the root: *wiþ-drīfan* "to drive off," *ofer-brǣdan* "to spread over," *on-wendan* "to change."

1.3   Vowels

OE used seven letters for vowels, written *a*, *æ*, *e*, *i*, *o*, *u*, and *y*. These seven letters represented fourteen sounds; that is, each vowel could be pronounced either as a "long" or a "short" sound. "Long" and "short" refer simply to the duration of the pronunciation of a vowel. (In this text we will distinguish all long vowels from short vowels by a macron over the long vowel, for example: *hām, hārian, nūna.* Anglo-Saxon scribes only occasionally indicated a stressed vowel with an accent mark.) What should be remembered is that the difference between long and short is *phonemic.* That is, the kind of vowel sound distinguishes between two different words that are in every other respect pronounced the same way. Therefore, the long *a* distinguishes *hām* "village, home" from *ham* "under-garment," *hāma* "cricket" from *hama* "dress."

In Modern English there are few instances when we distinguish one word from another by vowel length. Most often, it occurs in dialects that omit a sound and lengthen a vowel to compensate for the omitted sound. For example, in *r*-less dialects, the *r* sound in some words such as the word *park*, for instance, is omitted and pronounced as *pahk*; speakers distinguish the two words, in part, by lengthening the *a* sound in *park* to compensate for the lost *r*. In popular terms, we often speak of the vowel in *fine*, for example, as longer than the vowel in *fin*. But, in fact, that description is incorrect: the vowel in *fine* is a dipththong—that is, a combination of two vowel sounds (see §1.6)—that in *fin* is a simple vowel.

In OE words, vowel length in some instances distinguishes precisely between a vowel that is merely longer in duration, but alike in its formation in every other way (compare long and short [a] and long and short [æ] in the chart below, for example). But in some instances, a long vowel indicates not so much a lengthening of the vowel, but a different quality of formation—that is, it distinguishes between a *tense* and a *lax* sound (see §1.5 for a discussion of *tense* and *lax*). For example, if one were to lengthen the sound of the OE short *i*, it would not yield the OE long *i* sound. Instead, the notion of long and short in this instance refers to a different way of forming the two sounds.

Vowel Sounds   1.4

The vowel sounds will be treated in two different formats. In the first, the OE vowel is listed with Modern English keywords that illustrate its approximate sound. This list will provide the beginning reader a preliminary guide to the pronunciation of OE. In the second (§1.5), we will provide a more technical description of vowel sounds and how they are pronounced, along with the International Phonetic Alphabet. This approach will help the reader understand more clearly the logic of certain sound changes and pronunciation patterns.

1.4.1   OLD ENGLISH/MODERN VOWEL EQUIVALENTS

OE Vowel		Modern English equivalent
a	as in	father
ā	as in	father, but slightly prolonged
e	as in	fetch, met, set
ē	as in	fate, great
i	as in	fit, sit
ī	as in	feet, seen, machine
o	as in	awe, law
ō	as in	foe, rode, road
u	as in	full, put, pull (not cut, putt)
ū	as in	food, rude, ooze
y	as in	French tu, rue
ȳ	as in	French lune, ruse
æ	as in	fat, hat, ash
ǣ	as in	fat, hat, ash, but slightly prolonged

1.5   International Phonetic Alphabet

Understanding OE pronunciation can be simplified if you understand a few technical features of how we form vowels. The following diagram is called the vowel triangle:

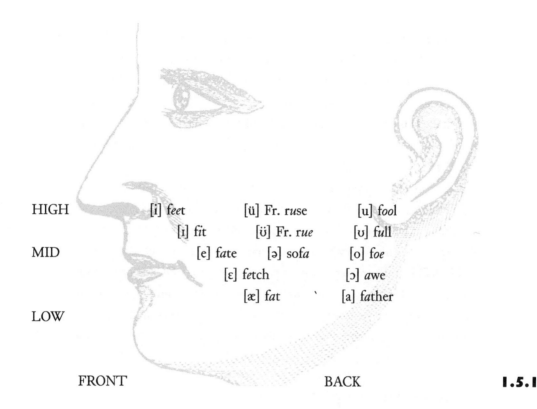

HIGH   [i] *feet*   [ü] Fr. *ruse*   [u] *fool*

             [ɪ] fit   [ü] Fr. *rue*   [ʊ] *full*

MID   [e] *fate*   [ə] sof*a*   [o] *foe*

             [ɛ] fetch   [ɔ] *awe*

             [æ] *fat*   [a] *father*

LOW

FRONT   BACK   **1.5.1**

We include in the vowel triangle the International Phonetic Alphabet (IPA) symbols for each of the vowel sounds that we need in order to pronounce OE, and for that matter, the vowel sounds of most so-called continental modern languages, including Modern English. For each symbol, we have included a keyword from Modern English or French. The IPA sound symbol is always enclosed in the brackets [ ] which indicate that the symbol represents a particular sound, rather than the letter.[3]

    Imagine that the vowel triangle is in the mouth of a speaker; if we imagine also that as the speaker pronounces each of these vowel sounds, he or she opens the mouth more to pronounce one vowel than another, or raises or lowers the jaw, or moves the tongue close to the front teeth or pulls it back from the teeth, we can begin to understand how vowels are formed.

[3] In this book, we employ the modified form of the International Phonetic Alphabet appearing in John Algeo and Thomas Pyles, *The Origins and Development of the English Language* (2005).

For example, if you pronounce the words *fat, fate, feet* in that order, you will notice that your mouth progressively closes; it is more open when you pronounce the word *fat* than when you pronounce *feet*. The reason is simple: as you pronounce the word *feet*, your tongue rises to the roof of the mouth. Because the tongue is attached to the lower jaw, the jaw also rises. Again, if you pronounce *feet* and *fool* in rapid succession, you will notice that with the word *feet* the tip of the tongue touches or nearly touches the front teeth; in the case of *fool*, the tongue pulls back into the mouth. Note, too, that when you pronounce *fool*, your lips are pursed or rounded; when you pronounce *feet*, your lips are unrounded.

Therefore, we can define vowels according to certain characteristics of their formation: we can speak of vowels as having a *vertical* dimension (HIGH, MID, or LOW), or a *horizontal* dimension, depending on whether the tongue moves forward or backward (BACK, CENTRAL, or FRONT), or depending on the shape of the mouth (ROUND or UNROUND). Finally, we can distinguish between vowel sounds by how *tensely* we pronounce the vowel. For example, the vowel sound in the word *feet* is different from the vowel sound in the word *fit* even though both sounds are pronounced in essentially the same position in the mouth (both are high, front sounds); they differ in one aspect: [i] is *tense*; [ɪ] is *lax*.

1.6 Vowels and Diphthongs

1.6.1 VOWELS

IPA Symbol	OE Letter	Modern English Keyword	Phonetic Description
[i]	ī	feet	high, front, unrounded, tense
[ɪ]	i	fit	high, front, unrounded, lax
[e]	ē	fate	mid, front, unrounded, tense

VOWELS *continued*

IPA Symbol	OE Letter	Modern English Keyword	Phonetic Description
[ɛ]	e	fetch	mid, front, unrounded, lax
[ǣ]	ǣ	fat	low, front, unrounded, tense
[æ]	æ	fat	low, front, unrounded, tense
[u]	ū	fool	high, back, round, tense
[ʊ]	u	full	high, back, round, lax
[o]	ō	foe	mid, back, round, tense
[ɔ]	o	fought	mid, back, round, tense
[ā]	ā	father	low, back, unrounded, lax
[a]	a	father	low, back, unrounded, lax
[ə]	diphthongs only	sof*a*	mid, central, unrounded only
[ü]	ȳ	ruse (Fr)	high, central, rounded
[ü̆]	y	rue (Fr)	high, central, rounded

DIPHTHONGS   1.6.2

A diphthong is a combination of two vowel sounds that are pronounced together to form a single syllable. In OE the first vowel element receives the stress; the second element is unstressed. Note the examples below: in both the short and long *ea*, *eo*, and *ie* diphthongs, the second element is pronounced as a *schwa*, that is, the unstressed *a* sound as in Modern English sof*a* or Cub*a*.

Pronunciation	OE Spelling	Modern English Equivalent
[ǣ+ə]	ēa	none
[æ+ə]	ea	none
[i+o]	īo	none
[ɪ+o]	io	none
[e+ə]	ēo	none
[ɛ+ə]	eo	none
[i+ə]	īe	none
[ɪ+ə]	ie	none

1.7   Consonant Sounds

Most OE consonants are pronounced much like their Modern English counterparts. The consonants *b*, *d*, *l*, *m*, *n*, *p*, *t*, *w*, and *x* (that is, the sound pronounced *ks*, as is Modern English *taxi*) are identical in OE and Modern English. Other consonants were pronounced in different ways depending upon their position in a word. To simplify this discussion, we will provide a list of pronunciation rules for consonants. Those rules require some basic information about how consonant sounds are formed; we include that information here simply as a quick reference guide.

1.7.1   Consonants are defined according to three characteristics: *where* they are made, *how* they are made, and whether they have *voice*. We begin with voice.

1.7.2   VOICE

All consonant sounds, like vowel sounds, are made by modifying the breath stream. The breath stream travels from the lungs, up the trachea, and through the larynx which contains the vocal cords. We make the first significant speech sound when we modify the breath stream as it passes through the vocal cords. That is, we either *voice* a sound (like the z sound in the word *buzz*, for example) or we leave the sound *voiceless* (like the s sound in the word *bus*). The z sound in *buzz* is created by a tightening of the vocal cords so that they vibrate as the breath passes through them. This vibration can be felt on the Adam's apple. With the voiceless sound, the vocal cords are relaxed and therefore allow the breath stream to pass through without restriction; no vibration takes place.

> Examples: The *f* in *fat* is voiceless; the *v* in *vat* is voiced; the *th* in *bath* is voiceless; the *th* in *bathe* is voiced; the *t* in *tin* is voiceless; the *d* in *din* is voiced.

CLASSIFYING CONSONANTS 1.7.3

Consonants are further classified by *how* and *where* they are formed, that is, how and where the speaker modifies the breath stream. When the breath stream reaches the throat at the back of the mouth, the speaker chooses to direct the breath stream either through the oral cavity or the nasal cavity. In oral sounds, the velum touches the back of the throat, closing off the nasal cavity and directing the breath stream into the mouth. When the velum retracts from the back of the throat, the opening allows the breath stream to enter the nasal cavity. We will begin with the oral sounds and group the consonants according to six major categories of how a consonant is formed. Each consonant sound begins with the IPA symbol in brackets which is followed by whether the sound is voiced or voiceless and where the modification of the sound takes place.

STOPS: These are consonant sounds in which the breath stream is momentarily stopped and then released.

> [p]   *voiceless bilabial stop*: Examples: *p*in, *p*et, *p*ill, *p*ail, *p*op. (The breath stream is stopped by the two lips pressing together momentarily and then releasing the breath stream.)

[b]   *voiced bilabial stop*: Examples: *b*in, *b*et, *b*ill, *b*ail, *b*o*b*.

[t]   *voiceless alveolar stop*: Examples: *t*in, *t*ab, *t*o, *t*ad. (The tip of the tongue stops the breath stream by pressing against the ridge just behind the upper front teeth, the alveolar ridge.)

[d]   *voiced alveolar stop*: Examples: *d*in, *d*ab, *d*o, *d*ad.

[k]   *voiceless velar stop*: Examples: *c*oat, *k*ick, *c*urb, *c*an. (The back of the tongue stops the breath stream by pressing against the soft part of the roof of the mouth, the soft palate or velum.)

[g]   *voiced velar stop*: *g*oat, *g*et, eg*g*, ar*g*ue, *gh*ost.

FRICATIVES: The speaker makes a narrow opening through which the breath stream is forced, causing friction in the process.

[f]   *voiceless labiodental fricative*: Examples: *f*at, *f*inish, enou*gh*, stu*ff*. (The upper teeth press against the bottom lip, forming a slight opening, through which the breath stream passes.)

[v]   *voiced labiodental fricative*: Examples: *v*at, *v*acuum, *v*arnish, o*v*er.

[θ]   *voiceless interdental fricative*: Examples: ba*th*, *th*in, *th*roat, *th*ink, *th*under, nin*th*, nor*th*. (The tip of the tongue is between the upper and lower teeth, or in some cases, just behind the upper teeth.)

[ð]   *voiced interdental fricative*: Examples: ba*th*e, *th*ine, ei*th*er, *th*en.

[s]   *voiceless alveolar fricative*: Examples: *s*ink, bu*s*, think*s*, i*c*e. (The blade of the tongue forms a slight opening at the alveolar ridge.)

[z]   *voiced alveolar fricative*: *z*inc, bu*zz*, apple*s*, fro*z*en, egg*s*.

[š]   *voiceless alveolo-palatal fricative*: Examples: *sh*ip, *sh*un, men*ti*on. (The front part of the tongue forms a slight opening in the area between the alveolar ridge and the hard palate.)

[ž]   *voiced alveolo-palatal fricative*: Examples: a*z*ure, vi*s*ion, plea*s*ure, fi*ss*ion.

[h]   *voiceless glottal fricative*: Examples: *h*ello, *h*int, *h*uff, *h*op. (The sound is

classified as a fricative because of the very slight friction caused by the vocal cords or glottis, especially when the sound is emphasized.)

AFFRICATES: A combination of sounds in which the first sound is a stop and the second a fricative.

[č] *voiceless alveolo-palatal affricate*: Examples: *ch*in, *ch*ur*ch*, *ch*ap, *ch*oke, *ch*apter. (A combination of the stop [t] and the fricative [š]. The stop [t] is an alveolar. But in this combination of sounds, it anticipates and therefore moves toward the alveolo-palatal area of the fricative [š].)

[ǰ] *voiced alveolo-palatal affricate*: Examples: *g*ym, *j*am, *G*eorge, ra*g*e, fri*dg*e.

LIQUIDS: A frictionless sound that flows (L. *liquidus*, "flowing") around the tongue which presses against the alveolo-palatal area.

[l] *voiced lateral alveolar liquid*: Examples: *l*ove, *l*ook, *l*eve*l*, *l*itt*l*e. (The tip of the tongue "posts" at the alveolar ridge. The breath stream flows around the sides of the tongue.)

[r] *voiced retroflex alveolar liquid*: Examples: *r*ing, e*rr*or, b*r*ing, co*r*al. (The blade of the tongue curves along the palate and the tip bends back [retroflex] at the alveolar ridge. The breath stream flows around the tongue.)

SEMIVOWELS: Represent two sounds: the [w] as in *weather* and the [y] sound as in *yes*. They are very close to the vowel sounds of [u] and [i], respectively. In fact, the tongue position to produce the semivowels is much like its position in the formation of the vowel sounds.

[j] *voiced palatal semivowel*: Examples: *y*our, *y*et, *y*ank.

[w] *voiced velar semivowel*: Examples: *w*inter, *wh*ere, *w*ill.

NASALS: The velum lowers to allow the breath stream to pass through the nasal cavity as well as the oral cavity; in the oral cavity the breath stream is also blocked, forcing the air through the nose. Three nasal sounds are formed: [m], [n], and [ŋ].

[m]   *voiced bilabial nasal*: Examples: *m*achine, *m*ilk, *m*om, sim*m*er. (The lips close and the breath flows through the nose.)

[n]   *voiced alveolar nasal*: Examples: *n*oise, *n*un, *n*orth, sin*n*er. (The tongue stops the breath stream at the alveolar ridge.)

[ŋ]   *voiced velar nasal*: This sound never begins a word in English; its normal position is at the end of a word. Examples: si*ng*, ri*ng*, si*ng*er, bri*ng*. Compare the alveolar nasal [n] in si*n* with the velar sound in si*ng*, or the alveolar [n] in sin*n*er and the velar [ŋ] in si*ng*er

1.8   Old English Consonants

The OE scribe did not use the letters *j*, *q*, *v*, and *z*, and they seldom used the letter *k*. In the following chart, we provide the OE letter, its IPA sound symbol, and a Modern English keyword for ready reference. If more than one sound is possible for an OE letter (as indicated by more than one IPA symbol), we provide a rule to distinguish the sounds.

OE Letter	IPA Symbol	Modern English Keyword
b	[b]	*bob*
c (rarely k)	[k]	*c*urt

Quick Rule: Generally pronounced as [k].
Specific Rule:
1. When it appeared before another consonant: as in OE *cnæpp* "summit," *cræft* "craft," *cwide* "speech."
2. When it appeared before or after a back vowel: as in OE *saca* "foe," *for-cuman* "to come before," *hocor* "insult."

OE Letter	IPA Symbol	Modern English Keyword
ċ	[č]	*ch*ance

Quick Rule: When it appeared next to a front vowel [i, ɪ] or [e, ɛ]. (This text provides an editorial dot over the letter to designate that it is the affricate sound.)

Specific Rule:

1. Initial sound before a front vowel or diphthong: as in OE *ċicen* "chicken," *ċiele* "chill," *ċeaster* "fort," *ċēosan* "to choose."
2. Final sound after [i] or [ɪ], as in OE *misliċ* "various," *iċ* "I," *gālliċ* "lustful, wanton."
3. Medial sound between [i] and another front vowel (as in OE *rīċe* "kingdom," *stiċe* "sting, stitch," *piċen* "of pitch").
4. At the ends of some words which at one time had an *i* in the final syllable: *hwelċ* "which," (WGmc *hwælik > Prehist OE *hwæliċ > OE hwelċ), *swelċ* "such," *bēċ* "book" (WGmc *bōci [dative singular] > Prehist OE *bōċi [the consonant palatalizes before the *i*] > *bēċi [i-umlaut changes root vowel] > OE bēċ).
5. There are instances when a word does not apparently follow or may even seem to contradict one of these "specific rules." For such instances, see Appendix Two, section 18, for advice on how to deal with apparent anomalies.

| d | [d] | *d*ad |
| f | [f] | *f*at |

Quick Rule: When it appeared next to voiceless sounds.

Specific Rule:

1. Initial sound: as in OE *folc-stede* "dwelling place," *for-dōn* "to undo, destroy," *fela* "many."
2. Final sound: as in OE *ġif* "if," *healf* "half," *fīf* "five."

OE Letter	IPA Symbol	Modern English Keyword

3. Before a voiceless consonant: as in OE *swiftu* "swiftness," *eft* "again," *wīf-hād* "womanhood."
4. Doubled: as in OE *wīf-fæst* "married," *offrung* "an offering."

f	[v]	*v*at

Quick Rule: When it appeared between voiced sounds.
Specific Rule:
1. Between vowels: as in OE *hrēfan* "to roof," *lofian* "to praise," *wifel* "weevil, beetle."
2. Between vowels and voiced consonants: as in OE *efne* 'even,' *swefn* 'dream.'

g	[g]	goat

Quick Rule: Generally pronounced as [g].
Specific Rule:
1. Initial sound before a back vowel: as in OE *godcund* "divine," *gadere* "together," *gūð-beorn* "fighting hero."
2. Before a consonant: as in OE *grymm* "grim," *glæd* "glad," *grund* "ground."
3. After the velar [ŋ]: as in OE *grunung* "grunting," *blȳding* "noise," *singan* "to sing."
4. When doubled: as in OE *hogg* 'hog,' *sugga* 'a kind of bird.'

ġ	[j]	*y*es

Quick Rule: When it appeared next to front vowels. (This text provides an editorial dot over the letter to represent the semivowel sound.)
Specific Rule:
1. Initial sound before a front vowel or diphthong (when the first element is a front vowel): as in OE *ġeond* "through," *ġespinnan* "to spin," *ġiefu* "gift," *ġēar* "year," *ġiċċe* 'itch.'

OE Letter	IPA Symbol	Modern English Keyword

2. Final sound of a word after a front vowel: as in OE *weġ* "way," *wīġ* "battle," *dæġ* "day."
3. Final sound of a syllable after a front vowel: as in *bræġden* "crafty," *hræġl-weard* "keeper of vestments."
4. Between front vowels: as in OE *hīġian* "to hie, hasten," *dæġes* "day's," *stiġel* "stile."
5. Sometimes a word does not apparently follow or even seems to contradict one of these rules; see Appendix Two, section 18, for advice on dealing with such anomalies.

g	[ɣ]	(a voiced velar fricative)

Quick Rule: When it appeared between back vowels. A difficult sound to approximate, but you might try pronouncing the voiceless velar fricative [x] sound of German *ach* or *macht* or Scots *loch* but voice the [x] sound.

Specific Rule:

1. Between back vowels: as in OE *dagas* "days," *gagātes* "agate," *āgan* "to own."
2. Between [l] or [r] and back vowels as in OE *burga* "towns," *fuglere* "fowler," *swelgan* "to swallow."
3. Final sound after a back vowel: as in OE *ġenog* "enough," *bēag* "ring," *bōg* "arm."
4. Sound of the second of two adjoining final consonants except [ŋ] as in OE *sorg* "sorrow," *bealg* "swelled."

h	[h]	*h*ot

Quick Rule: Initial sound before front vowels or consonants.

h	[ç]	German ni*ch*t, i*ch*

Quick Rule: Medial sound after front vowels but not between vowels; this is a palatal sound: as in OE *riht* "right," *tiht* "crime."

OE Letter	IPA Symbol	Modern English Keyword
h	[x]	German a*ch*, Scots lo*ch*

Quick Rule: After a back vowel or consonant; this is a velar sound: as in OE *hēah* "high," *sōhte* "sought," *beorht* "bright," *meaht* "might."

l	[l]	*laugh*
m	[m]	*mom*
n	[n]	si*n*

Quick Rule: Everywhere except before a velar stop [g] or [k].

n	[ŋ]	si*ng*, fi*n*ger, li*n*ger

Quick Rule: Before the velar stop [g] or [k]: as in OE *finger* "finger," *drincan* "to drink."

p	[p]	*pilot*
r	[r]	*ring*
s	[s]	si*n*

Quick Rule: Everywhere except between voiced sounds.
Specific Rule:
1. Initial sound in a word: as in OE *slēan* "to kill," *sellan* "to give," *stān* "stone."
2. Final sound in a word: as in OE *wæs* "was," *stānas* "stones," *hūs* "house."
3. Before voiceless consonants: as in OE *nihstiġ* "fasting," *hearp-swēġ* "sound of a harp," *cosp* "fetter."
4. Doubled as in OE *cyssan* "to kiss," *blissian* "to rejoice," *missenliċ* "various."

s	[z]	buzz

Quick Rule: Next to voiced sounds.

OE Letter	IPA Symbol	Modern English Keyword

Specific Rule:

1. Between vowels: as in OE *rīsan* "to rise," *līsian* "to glide," *glæsen* "glassy."
2. Between a vowel and voiced consonant: as in OE *hālsian* "to swear," *puslian* "to pick out," *hlysnan* "to listen."

t	[t]	*tot*
þ, Þ or ð, Ð	[Θ]	*ether*, *think*

Quick Rule: Initial position, final position, and next to voiceless sounds.

Specific Rule:

1. Initial sound: as in OE *þēod* "people," *þegn* "vassal," *þearl* "strong."
2. Final sound: as in OE *tōð* "tooth," *mæð* "measure," *fram-sīð* "departure."
3. Doubled: as in OE *niððas* "men," *moððe* "moth," *cȳðð* "kinship."
4. Next to voiceless consonants: as in OE *sūð-portiċ* "south porch," *stæð-fæst* "stable," *nīð-plega* "battle."

þ, Þ or ð, Ð	[ð]	*either*, *bother*

Quick Rule: Between voiced sounds.

Specific Rule:

1. Between vowels: as in OE *baþian* "to bathe," *cūþa* "relative," *feþer* "feather."
2. Between a vowel and a voiced consonant: as in OE *fæþm* "embrace," *grið-bryċe* "breaking of a truce," *mēþrian* "to honor."

w	[w]	*win*
Letter Combinations		
sc	[š]	*ship*
cg	[j]	*edge*

1.9   Exercises

1.9.1   PRONOUNCING OE VOWELS

Instructions. *Give the appropriate IPA symbol for each of the italicized vowels in the following OE words.*

1. st*æ*l (place) _œ_
2. sc*i*pmann (sailor) _I_
3. r*e*gol (rule, law) _ɛ_
4. sc*ī*ran (to make clear) _i_
5. m*ǣ*le (cup) _œ_
6. s*u*mor (summer) _ʊ_
7. hand-b*ō*c (handbook) _e_
8. f*ō*t-setl (footstool) _o_
9. f*o*x-hol (fox-hole) _ɔ_
10. fr*y*mð (origin) _ʉ_

11. gr*ȳ*tan (to flourish) _ʉ_
12. s*ā*wol (soul) _ɑ_
13. b*u*rh (dwelling) _ʊ_
14. b*ō*ga (bow) _o_
15. f*ǣ*r (peril) _œ_
16. hw*ī*t (white) _i_
17. m*ē*ting (meeting) _e_
18. s*ū*ðerne (southern) _ʊ_
19. m*y*nd (mind) _ʉ_
20. s*e*ġn (sign) _ɛ_

1.9.2   PRONOUNCING OE DIPHTHONGS

Instructions. *Give the appropriate IPA symbol for each of the italicized diphthongs in the following OE words.*

1. þ*īo*wot-dōm (service) _i + o_
2. t*ēo*n (to pull) _e + ə_
3. s*īe*n (sight) _i + ə_
4. m*ea*rc (mark) _œ + ə_
5. tw*eo*lf (twelfth) _ɛ + ə_

6. b*ēa*g (ring) _āō + ə_
7. sc*ie*ld (shield) _I + ə_
8. dr*ēo*pan (to drop) _e + ə_
9. n*īe*d (need) _i + ə_
10. s*io*du (custom) _I + o_

PRONOUNCING OE CONSONANTS

1.9.3

Instructions. *Give the appropriate IPA symbol for each of the italicized consonants in the following OE words. Consult the "Quick rule" and "Specific rule" guidelines to test your answer. Can you explain why you chose the sound symbol that you list?*

[f] or [v]
1. *f*eoh (cattle) ___f___
2. lu*f*ian (to love) ___v___
3. of*f*rian (to offer) ___f___
4. wi*f*el (beetle) ___v___
5. ne*f*a (nephew) ___v___
6. lu*f*u (love) ___v___
7. ste*f*nian (to summon) ___v___

[g] or [ɣ]
8. *g*adrian (to gather) ___ɣ___
9. *g*līdan (to glide) ___g___
10. bo*g*a (bow [weapon]) ___ɣ___
11. folgo*ð* (body of retainers) ___ɣ___
12. būgan (to bow) ___ɣ___
13. hrin*g* (ring) ___g___
14. ho*gg* (hog) ___g___
15. miclun*g* (greatness) ___g___
16. sla*g*a (slayer) ___ɣ___
17. bō*g* (arm) ___g___
18. byr*g*an (to bury) ___ɣ___
19. bur*g* (walled town) ___g___

[h] or [ç] or [x]
20. *h*ēah (high) ___h___
21. hēa*h* (high) ___x___
22. ri*h*tan (to set right) ___ç___
23. tō*h* (tough) ___x___
24. weal*h* (foreigner) ___x___

25. wi*h*t (person) ___ç___
26. *b*ihting (gladness) ___h___
27. se*h*t (agreement) ___ç___
28. scēo*h* (shy) ___x___
29. beor*h*t (bright) ___x___

[n] or [ŋ]
30. *n*iman (to take) ___n___
31. ofe*n* (furnace) ___n___
32. slēa*n* (to strike) ___n___
33. sin*g*an (to sing) ___ŋ___
34. sy*nn* (sin) ___n___
35. wi*n*cian (to blink) ___n___
36. þin*g*ian (to beg) ___ŋ___

[s] or [z]
37. *s*āwol (soul) ___s___
38. hū*s* (house) ___s___
39. mi*ss*an (to miss) ___s___
40. rō*s*en (rosy) ___z___
41. scēad-wī*s* (intelligent) ___s___
42. sū*s*l (misery) ___s___

[θ] or [ð]
43. *ð*ing (thing) ___θ___
44. mo*ðð*e (moth) ___θ___
45. ni*ð*er (beneath) ___ð___
46. swī*ð*-mōd (stout-hearted) ___ð___
47. swī*ð* (strong) ___θ___
48. swī*ð*an (to strengthen) ___ð___

1.9.4   IPA EXERCISE

Instructions. *Fill in the missing IPA symbol in the phonetic transcriptions of the following OE words.*

1. sīþ (journey) [sìθ]
2. mūð (mouth) [muⴱ]
3. dæġ (day) [dæʝ]
4. ēare (ear) [æərə]
5. æppel (apple) [æƥɛl]
6. hlāford (lord) [hlaⱴɔrd]

7. cnīf (knife) [ʞnīf]
8. hnīgan (to bow) [ʜnīgan]
9. hlūd (loud) [hlⱴd]
10. hlēo (protection) [hlɛɔ]
11. ġe-gān (to go) [ɟɛgān]
12. ċild (child) [ʧɪld]

1.9.5   PRONUNCIATION PRACTICE

Instructions. *Read the following OE sentences.*

1. Sum swīþe ġe-lǣred munuc cōm sūþan ofer sǣ fram sancte Benedictes stōwe, on Æþelredes cyninges dæġe, tō Dūnstāne ærċe-biscope.
2. Nū tō-dæġ Godes ġe-laðung ġeond ealne ymb-hwyrft mǣrsað þǣra ēadiġra ċildra frēols-tīde, þe sē wæl-hrēowe Herōdes for Crīstes ā-cennednysse mid ār-lēasre ēhtnysse ā-cwealde, swā swā ūs sēo godspelliċe racu swutelliċe cȳð.
3. Mid þȳ iċ wæs tō him ġe-lǣdd, þā fræġn hē mē and āscode hwæt Alexander sē cyning dyde, and hūliċ mann hē wǣre, and in hwelċre ieldu.
4. Ōhthere sǣde his hlāforde, Ælfrede cyninge, þæt hē ealra Norðmonna norþmest būde.
5. Hē cwæð þæt hē būde on þǣm lande norþ-weardum wiþ þā West-sǣ.
6. Hē sǣde þæt Norð-manna land wǣre swīðe lang and swȳðe smæl.

TWO

Getting Started:
Nouns

2.1   Lesson One: Nouns

Probably the best, and most startling, way to enter the somewhat alien world of OE grammar is through the noun system. We say "startling" because here you will meet, among other curiosities, nineteen different versions of the word *the*. Those familiar with modern German, however, will be on very comfortable ground. The main differences between OE nouns and modern ones are that OE nouns have a relatively robust set of endings (compared to a scant two in Modern English: -*'s* for possessives and -*(e)s* for plurals) as well as grammatical gender (masculine, feminine, and neuter). Though this lesson may look dauntingly long, after you've completed it, you'll have made a major step towards learning to read OE.

ANATOMY OF A SENTENCE

In order to use this book successfully, you must know the basic parts of speech (noun, verb, adjective, adverb, article, preposition, conjunction, and interjection) and what they do. To refresh your memory or to start from scratch, see Appendix One: "A Basic Introduction to Traditional Grammar." For the current lesson, some elementary knowledge of sentence structure is crucial.

The basic structure of a simple English sentence can be mapped as follows (where *S* stands for *subject*, *V* for *verb*, *IO* for *indirect object*, and *O* for *direct object*):

S + V + IO + O

> 1. Grammar gives us answers.
> 2. She wrote him instructions.

Many sentences have no indirect object:

S + V + O

> 3. Grammar gives answers.
> 4. She wrote instructions.

Others have no direct object at all, but only a subject and a verb:

> S + V
>> 5. Grammar exists.
>> 6. She wrote.

To complete this chapter, you must be able to identify subjects, objects, and indirect objects (Appendix One, §1 and §2).

What the Endings Do   2.2

Simply put, the endings (or inflections) on an OE noun give information about how the word functions in a sentence (i.e., whether it's a subject, object, possessor, or indirect object). This information is *crucial* for decoding and translating sentences. Modern English by and large uses word order to relay the same information, though you can still find the shattered archaeological remains of the old inflectional system in the two *s*'s which Modern English speakers add for plural and possessive nouns, as noted above. These two *s*'s are scant left-overs of a much more robust system of signals. OE, in this sense, was a much more redundant language than Modern English since it used word order—much as Modern English does—*as well as* all the added cues of a full system of endings. That's not bad redundancy, but a kind of repetition that ensures the signals will get through. It might be tempting to use OE word order alone to decipher a sentence and to "fudge" the endings—resist that temptation.

Gender   2.3

Like a number of modern European languages, OE had grammatical gender in its noun system: masculine, feminine, and neuter. Though there are some basic correspondences between grammatical gender and real, physical gender (*wer* "man" is masculine; *fǣmne* "maiden" is feminine, and *ċild* "child" is neuter), just as often the concept of natural gender does little good in explaining or predicting the grammatical gender of a noun. Inanimate objects don't have natural gender but are nevertheless assigned a gender, often with no sense of metaphor: a chair can be masculine, a table feminine. Sometimes grammatical gender even contradicts natural gender—for example, the word *wīf* "woman, wife" is neuter while the ancestor of the Modern English word *woman* (OE *wīf-man*) is actually masculine. For English speakers, the sentence, "the train—she is late," may sound like a comic imitation of a European speaking English, but OE uses gender in precisely this way.

Ælfric on the Concept of Gender

De generibus. Æfter ġe-cynde syndon twā cyn on namum: *MASCULINUM* and *FEMININUM*; þæt is, werliċ and wīfliċ. Werliċ cyn byð *hic vir* "þēs wer," *wīfliċ haec femina* "þis wīf." Þās twā cyn synd ġe-cyndelīċe on mannum and on nytenum. Nū ys ġe-cweden æfter cræfte ġe-mæne cyn, þæt is, æġðer ġe werliċ ġe wīfliċ: *hic et haec dives* "ðēs and þēos welega": æġðer byð weliġ ġe wer ġe wīf. *NEUTRUM* is nāðor cynn, ne werliċes ne wīfliċes on cræftspræċe, ac hit byð swā ðēah oft on andġyte, swā swā ys *hoc mancipium* "ðēs wealh," *hoc animal* "þis nyten": ælċ nyten byð oððe hē oððe hēo, ac swā ðēah ðis cyn ġe-byrað oftost to nāðrum cynne, swā swā ys *hoc verbum* "þis word," *hoc lumen* "þis leoht."

Ys ēac tō witenne, þæt hī bēoð oft ōðres cynnes on Leden and oðres cynnes on Englisc. Wē cweðað on Ledyn *hic liber* and on Englisc "þēos bōc"; eft on Leden *haec mulier* and on Englisc "ðis wīf," nā ðēos.

Concerning Gender. In nouns, according to nature, there are two genders (or kinds): masculine and feminine—that is, male and female. [Of the] masculine gender is *hic vir* "this man"; feminine, *haec femina* "this woman." These two genders are natural in human beings and in animals. Now in grammar there is a common gender, that is either masculine or feminine, *hic et haec dives* "this wealthy man or this wealthy woman": either is wealthy, both man and woman. The neuter is neither gender, neither masculine or feminine (in scientific language), but it is often nevertheless understood, just as is *hoc mancipium* "this slave," *hoc animal* "this animal": each animal is either he or she, but nevertheless this gender belongs most often to neither gender, just as is *hoc verbum* "this verb," *hoc lumen* "this light."

It is also to be noted that there are often [nouns with] certain genders in Latin but [which have] other genders in English. We say in Latin *hic liber* "this book" [masculine] and in English *þēos bōc* "this book" [feminine]; again in Latin *haec mulier* "this woman" [feminine] and in English *ðis wīf* "this woman" [neuter], not ðēos "this one" [feminine].

A Few Tips

Knowing the gender of a noun often provides key information on how to decode a sentence. But if you look at most OE nouns completely out of context, you won't be able to tell what gender they have: you must simply look up the gender, indicated by an *m, f,* or *n* (for *masculine, feminine,* and *neuter*) in the glossary entries. For the core vocabulary, you should memorize the gender along with the word and its definition—for the rest, you can be content to look them up. In context (with definite articles and other cues), it's often possible to identify a noun's gender, but more on that later. One last note: In compounds, the word takes the gender of *the last noun* in the combination. The compound *helle-hund* "hellhound" is masculine because *hund* is masculine, though *hel(le)* is feminine.

The Definite Article (the)

Below you will find a chart of the definite article *the*. Though it's a somewhat mind-boggling fact, notice that there are potentially twenty different forms of *the*, corresponding to different genders (feminine, masculine, and neuter), cases (nominative, accusative, genitive, dative, and instrumental), and number (singular and plural). It could be worse, however, if instead of lumping together all the plurals of whatever gender, there were actually separate masculine, feminine, and neuter *plurals* (as there are in Old Norse). Again, those familiar with modern German should feel a bit more at home here.

Though it may not seem like it now, knowing these forms by heart is crucial to reading OE. After you've gone through this chapter thoroughly, **take a few minutes to memorize the chart in its entirety** and refresh your memory from time to time until you know it backwards and forwards. Memorizing the chart takes less than five minutes once you've resigned yourself to doing it. If you are not familiar with the concept of case (*N*ominative, *A*ccusative, *G*enitive, *D*ative, and *I*nstrumental—see the letters along the left-hand side of the chart below), don't worry just yet: case will be discussed thoroughly below (§2.11).

2.5.1   **THE DEFINITE ARTICLE (the)**

Singular	Masculine	Feminine	Neuter	Plural
N	sē	sēo	þæt	þā
A	þone	þā	þæt	þā
G	þæs	þǣre	þæs	þāra, þǣra
D	þǣm, þām	þǣre	þǣm, þām	þǣm, þām
I	þȳ, þon	**	þȳ, þon	**

TIPS: Notice first of all that the masculine and neuter forms are identical in the genitive and dative cases. Secondly, the main area of potential confusion comes with *þā*, which could be feminine accusative singular, plural nominative, or plural accusative (it's also easy to confuse with a very common adverb *þā*, which means "then" or "when"). Note: The definite article can function as a personal pronoun: *sē* = he, *sēo* = she, *þæt* = it.

Notice the similarities between this system and that of modern German, particularly in the genitive and dative cases, with OE *þ* corresponding to German *d*:

THE DEFINITE ARTICLE IN MODERN GERMAN

Singular	Masculine	Feminine	Neuter	Plural
N	der	die	das	die
A	den	die	das	die
G	des	der	des	der
D	dem	der	dem	den

INDEFINITELY. OE has no consistent indefinite article (*a/an*—as in the phrases "*a* pear" or "*an* apple"). You must often supply an "a" or "an" when there is no definite article and the context requires it.

> *Þæt wæs gōd cyning.*
> (That was *a* good king.)

PRONOUN PREVIEW. Though we will introduce you to personal pronouns (*I, you, he, she it, we, you all*, and *they*) in detail in Chapter Seven, they occur so frequently that you should begin to get used to them from the beginning. The personal pronouns are divided into the three "persons" of a hypothetical conversation: the first person (*I* or *we*) speaks to a second person (*you*) about a third person (*he, she, it, or they*). In the chart below, pronouns have two numbers (singular and plural) and four cases (nominative, accusative, genitive, and dative—see §2.11 below).

PERSONAL PRONOUNS: A PREVIEW   2.5.2

1st Person	2nd Person	3rd Person		
Singular		Masculine	Feminine	Neuter
N iċ "I"	þū "you"	hē "he"	hēo "she"	hit "it"
A mē, meċ "me"	þē "you"	hine "him"	hēo / hie "her" hī	hit "it"
G mīn, "my, mine"	þīn "your, yours"	his "his"	hire "her, hers"	his "its"
D mē "me"	þē "you"	him "him"	hire "her"	him "it"
Plural				
N wē "we"	ġē "you all"	hīe "they"		
A ūs "us"	ēow "you all"	hīe "them"		
G ūre, ūser "our, ours"	ēower "your, yours"	hiera, heora "their, heirs"		
D ūs "us"	ēow "you all"	him, heom "them"		

2.6 ## Lesson Two: Main Noun Groups

Not only did OE have an inflected definite article *the*, but the nouns themselves took a variety of endings, also corresponding to gender (masculine, feminine, or neuter), case (explained below), and number (singular or plural). Though OE has several noun classes (declensions), each with its own sets of distinctive endings, we'll focus, for the moment, on the dominant patterns since they account for the overwhelming majority of noun endings you're likely to encounter. You will use the information in these next three charts *every minute* you read OE. After completing this chapter, you **must** learn these endings by heart. For your convenience, a summary of endings is provided in the right-most region of each of the following charts. Note that a double asterisk (**) indicates that the form does not exist and that a single hyphen (-) indicates that there is no ending for the corresponding case and number.

Ælfric on Nouns

Nomen is "nama," mid ðam wē nemnað ealle ðing ægðer ġe synderlīċe ġe ġe-mænelīċe; synderlīċe be aġenum naman: *Eadgarus, Aðelwoldus*; ġe-mænelīċe: *rex* "cyning," *episcopus* "bisceop."

A noun is "name" (in English), with which we name all things either properly (or, specially) or commonly; properly by their own names: *Edgar, Aðelwold*; commonly: *rex* "king," *episcopus* "bishop."

Most grammars of OE refer to these dominant nouns as "strong" (this terminology will be explained at the beginning of the next chapter). For now, it is probably best to think of the following three "strong" patterns as the most basic or regular ones you will encounter.

REGULAR / STRONG MASCULINES: (ġimm "gem") (-a- stem)   **2.7**

	Singular	Plural	Singular	Plural
N	sē ġimm	þā ġimmas	-	-as
A	þone ġimm	þā ġimmas	-	-as
G	þæs ġimmes	þāra ġimma	-es	-a
D	þæm, þām ġimme	þæm ġimmum	-e	-um
I	þȳ ġimme	**	-e	**

REGULAR / STRONG FEMININES: (ġiefu "gift," help "help") (-o- stem)   **2.8**

	Short-Stemmed		Long-Stemmed		Summary	
	Singular	Plural	Singular	Plural	Singular	Plural
N	sēo ġiefu	þā ġiefa, -e	sēo help	þā helpa, -e	-u, -	-a, -e
A	þā ġiefe	þā ġiefa, -e	þā helpe	þā helpa, -e	-e	-a, -e
G	þǣre ġiefe	þāra ġiefa, ġifena	þǣre helpe	þāra helpa, -ena	-e	-a, -ena
D	þǣre ġiefe	þǣm ġiefum	þǣre helpe	þǣm helpum	-e	-um

REGULAR / STRONG NEUTERS: (lim "limb," word "word") (-a- stem)   **2.9**

	Short-Stemmed		Long-Stemmed		Summary	
	Singular	Plural	Singular	Plural	Singular	Plural
N	þæt lim	þā limu	þæt word	þā word	-	-u, -
A	þæt lim	þā limu	þæt word	þā word	-	-u, -
G	þæs limes	þāra lima	þæs wordes	þāra worda	-es	-a
D	þæm lime	þæm limum	þæm worde	þæm wordum	-e	-um
I	þȳ lime	**	þȳ worde	**	-e	**

TIME SAVERS:

2.10.1 # Short and Long Stems

Notice that there are two versions of the feminine (§2.8) and neuter (§2.9) paradigms, the short- and long-stemmed versions, the difference between them a mysteriously missing –*u* (in the nominative singular for feminines and in the nominative and accusative plurals for the neuters). For reasons that we won't go into here, -*u* endings dropped away from long-stemmed nouns. Though this phenomenon has complex causes, it is not that difficult to recognize. Knowing about it can make the job of reading OE much easier and more accurate, since –*u* endings can tell you, for example, whether a neuter noun is singular or plural. If you are reading the *Anglo-Saxon Chronicle*, you'd probably like to know whether the narrative is describing one ship or many ships! A ***long-stemmed noun*** has in its stem (i.e., the trunk of the word with all prefixes and endings taken away) either a long vowel followed by a single consonant (example: *bān* "bone") or a short vowel followed by two or more consonants (example: *brocc* "badger"). A ***short-stemmed noun,*** on the other hand, has a short vowel followed by a single consonant (example: *beð* "bath") and thus retains the -*u* ending. Note that a diphthong (a sound consisting of two vowels) behaves the same way as a single vowel: a short -*eo*-, for example, plus a consonant (example: *eom* "am") is a short stem, while a long -*ēo*- plus a single consonant produces a long stem (example: *bēor* "beer").

Long Stem	Short Stem
long vowel + 1 consonant	short vowel + 1 consonant
short vowel + 2 consonants or more	

Let's take the word *word* as an example. It must be a long-stemmed noun since it has a short vowel (*o*) plus two consonants (*rd*). Since it's a long stem, it takes no –*u* ending in the plural nominative and accusative (see §2.9). Thus, by itself, *word* could be either nominative or accusative in either the singular or plural. Knowing about this phenomenon will help you determine whether a text is talking about one word or several. Context or the definite article may make it clear which is intended (*þæt word* must be singular and *þā word* must be plural), though sometimes in poetry where the definite article is often missing there's no way to tell if the form is singular or plural.[1]

Looking Up

Two minor variations in the basic noun endings might make it difficult to find some words in the main glossary. Fortunately, they should not present any major obstacles.

Syncopate! Some nouns with two syllables may leave out or "syncopate" the second vowel when the noun ending is added—*engel* (masculine) has the following forms: (sing) *engel, engel, engles, engle*; (pl) *englas, englas, engla, englum*, not **engeles*,[2] **engele*, etc.—a good fact to know when you're attempting to look up words in the glossary. See also disyllabic neuters like *hēafod* "head" and *fācen* "deceit" whose plurals are *hēafdu* and *fācnu*, not **hēafodu* and **fācenu*. (See §8.10 and Appendix Two, §13.)

Dæġ / Dagas Alternation. Another slight variation affects some masculine and neuter nouns whose main vowel is an *æ* (see, for example, *dæġ* "day," *fæt* "vat," *bæð* "bath"). Such nouns generally retain the *æ* in the singular forms but have *a* in the plural.

2.10.2

2.10.3

	Masculine		Neuter	
	Singular	Plural	Singular	Plural
N	dæġ	dagas	bæð	baðu
A	dæġ	dagas	bæð	baðu
G	dæġes	daga	bæðes	baða
D	dæġe	dagum	bæðe	baðum

[1] For nouns of more than one syllable, it is generally the last syllable in the stem (i.e., the syllable immediately preceding the ending) that renders the word short- or long-stemmed. Thus, though the neuters *hēafod* "head" and *fācen* "deceit" have long first syllables (*hēaf-* and *fāc-*), their last syllables are short (*-od* and *-en*), rendering both words short-stemmed whose plurals appear with *-u*.

[2] An asterisk at the beginning of a word indicates that it is a form that does not occur naturally in the speech or writing of native speakers.

2.10.4 O-Wo-Jo, A-Wa-Ja

A point of interest: Advanced grammars of OE often classify nouns according to the kind of Indo-European stem type they descended from, and since some important grammars, glossaries, and dictionaries include notations about which stem class the various nouns come from, it may be good for you to know about them (note that the three strong noun charts above have alternative labels). The strong masculine and neuter forms are called *a*-stems, while the strong feminine is classified as an *o*-stem. Slightly confusing is the fact that here the word *stem* refers not to the root (as above), but to the vowel (or syllable) that glues the root to the ending (*stān+a+s*)—here the *-a-* is the stem. Doubly confusing is the fact that these ancient Indo-European stems have been almost completely obscured by various sound changes by the time they arrive in OE, though they appear consistently as *-a-* and *-o-* in Gothic, a Germanic language written down centuries before OE. The minor or "irregular" nouns in Chapter Ten come from different stem classes (*-ja-* and *-wa-* for the masculines and *-jo-* and *-wo-* for the feminines) and show some slight variations from the regular paradigm—not to worry, though.

Exercise 2.1: IDENTIFYING SHORT AND LONG STEMS

1. Label each of the following stems (in the first column) as either long or short.

2. In the second and third columns, give the nominative singular and plural forms of the corresponding word in the first column. You might try a stem-length "scorecard"; that is, starting with the vowel (leave off any consonants before the vowel) assign one point for a short vowel, for a short diphthong, or for any single consonant, but two points for a long vowel or diphthong. If a stem's score is three or more, then it must be long; two or less, and it must be short.

EXERCISE *continued*

[3] See §2.10.3 "Dæg / Dagas Alternation."

	SINGULAR	PLURAL
Examples:		
short scol- "school" of fish (f)	sēo *scolu*	þā *scola*
long bedd- "bed" (n)	þæt *bed*	þā *bedd*
1. *long* land- (n)	þæt _____	þā _____
2. *short* far- "journey" (f)	sēo _____	þā _____
3. _____ hyht- "joy" (f)	sēo _____	þā _____
4. _____ lār- "teaching" (f)	sēo _____	þā _____
5. _____ ġief- "gift" (f)	sēo _____	þā _____
6. _____ rēaf- "plunder, booty" (n)	þæt _____	þā _____
7. _____ ċear- "care, sorrow" (f)	sēo _____	þā _____
8. _____ driht- "troop" (f)	sēo _____	þā _____
9. _____ spell- "news" (n)	þæt _____	þā _____
10. _____ scip- "ship" (n)	þæt _____	þā _____
11. _____ help- "help" (f)	sēo _____	þā _____
12. _____ hūs- "house" (n)	þæt _____	þā _____
13. _____ fæt- "vat, container" (n)[3]	þæt _____	þā _____

2.11   Lesson Three: The Concept of Case

In the noun charts listed in lesson two you'll notice four (sometimes five) abbreviations running down the leftmost column (N., A., G., D., and I.). These stand for the five main cases (or noun roles) encoded into the OE noun system: nominative, accusative, genitive, dative, and instrumental. The genitive (possessive) case is probably the most familiar to English speakers since English has retained an ending (-'s) for it. Each of these cases signals a noun's function, and these are summarized below. It's important that you grasp the concept of case from the beginning since without it you will soon run aground in your everyday reading of OE.

The explanations below provide you with almost all you will need to know about case in OE, and therefore they may seem a little complicated or overwhelming right now. It's best to learn at least the main functions from the very beginning. Plan to turn to this section often as you tackle the coming chapters. If you find yourself completely lost as you read through the following explanations, plan to work through Appendix One: "Basic Introduction to Traditional Grammar".

THE SHORT VERSION: Subjects take the nominative form, direct objects the accusative, and indirect objects the dative. The genitive, as in Modern English, indicates possession (among other things).

2.11.1   NOMINATIVE:

2.11.1.a   MAIN FUNCTION: Marks the *subject* of the sentence—that is, the doer of the action, or the possessor of an attribute

> *Sē æðeling rīdeð onweġ.*
> (The prince rides away.)

2.11.1.b   as well as the *subject complement* (a noun, pronoun, or adjective following a simple *to be* verb)

*Hēo is **sēo cwēn**.*	*Iċ eom **hēo**.*	*Iċ eom **slǣpiġ**.*
(She is the queen.)	(I am she.)	(I am sleepy.)

and direct address.

2.11.1.c

*Þū, **yrþling**! Hū begǣst þū þīn weorc?*
(You, plowman [lit., earthling]! How do you go about your work?)

ACCUSATIVE: **2.11.2**

MAIN FUNCTION: Marks the ***direct object*** or object of the verb. **2.11.2.a**

*Þā þēofas stelaþ **þæt gold**.*
(The thieves are stealing the gold.)

Þā þēofas = nominative (as the doers of the action of stealing)
þæt gold = accusative (as the object or receiver of the action)

ALSO

Object of a Preposition. Certain prepositions always require objects in the accusative **2.11.2.b**
case—these will be labeled in the glossary as *(prep + acc)*. It's impossible to tell by
looking at a preposition which case its object requires. You must simply look it
up. The preposition *þurh* "through" (prep + acc) is such a preposition, and in the
following sentence it transforms *sē tūn* "the town" into its accusative form.

*Hē rīdeð þurh **þone tūn**.*
(He rides through the town.)

Another such preposition is *ġeond* "throughout" (prep + acc)

*Hēo rīdeð ġeond **þæt land.***
(She rides throughout the land.)

2.11.2.c   *Time*. Some statements of time occur in the accusative (without a preposition).

Þone nēxtan dæġ rād hē forþ.
(The next day he rode forth.)

2.11.3   GENITIVE:

2.11.3.a   MAIN FUNCTION: Marks the *possessive*.

*Þā wīcingas of-slōgon **þæs cyninges þeġn.***
(The vikings killed [slew] the king's thane.)

ALSO

2.11.3.b   Of *Replacement*. OE often uses the genitive where Modern English uses an *of* construction. You will meet with this use of the genitive in almost every sentence, so be sure to understand it before moving on. Generally, the way to translate these phrases is to reverse the order of the genitive and its accompanying word and to put an *of* between them. Throughout *Reading Old English*, we will refer to this procedure as the *Genitive Rule.*

Dryhtenes eġe
(the fear of the Lord)

helle grund
(the bottom of hell)

Seaxena cyning
(king of the Saxons)

hūsa mēst
(the greatest [lit., most] of houses)

heofones hrōf   *engla ġedryht*
(the roof of heaven)   (troop of angels)

"Partitive" Genitive. When people or things are described in numbers or units, the unit or "part" often appears in the genitive plural. This specialized use is called the *partitive* genitive:

2.11.3.c

     ān þāra wīfa
     (one of the women)

     *seofon **mīla***
     (seven miles; lit., seven of miles)

Fela. Closely related are certain pronouns like *fela* "many," *ǣlċ* "each," etc., which normally demand a genitive to complete them. They are marked in the glossary with *(+ gen)*.

2.11.3.d

     fela þāra cyninga
     (many of the kings)

     ǣlċ þāra biscopa
     (each of the bishops)

Object of a Preposition. Certain prepositions can require objects in the genitive, though there are very few of these. They will be labeled in the glossary as *(prep + gen)*.

2.11.3.e

     *andlang **þæs smalan weġes***
     (along the narrow path)

2.11.3.f F. *Genitive Objects.* A very small number of verbs, like *bīdan* "to wait for" and *þancian* "to give thanks to," require genitive direct objects. These will be marked in the glossary as (+ *gen*). Normally, almost all verbs take accusative direct objects.

> *Hē bīdeð dōmes.*
> (He awaits judgment [lit., doom].)

> *Hēo þāra ġifena Gode þancode.*
> (She thanked God [dat] for the gifts.)

2.11.3.g *Time.* Some statements of time take the genitive (without a preposition).

> *Hēo rād dæġes and nihtes.*
> (She rode day and night.)

2.11.4 DATIVE:

2.11.4.a MAIN FUNCTION: Marks the **indirect object**. While the direct object receives the action of the verb (*I kicked the ball*), the indirect object can be thought of as the beneficiary of the action (*I kicked him the ball*).

> *Hē ġiefeþ þǣm wīfe þæt bōc.*
> (He is giving the woman the book.)
>
>   or
>
> (He is giving the book to the woman.)

ALSO

2.11.4.b *Substitute Preposition.* OE often employs the dative to signal relationships which Modern English indicates with a preposition. In that sense, the dative functions as a substitute preposition. When nouns occur in the dative *without a preposition*, the best rule is to supply a preposition (often *to* or *by*). Throughout *Reading OE*, we will refer to this procedure as the **Dative Rule**. Note that in poetry, the dative often precedes the noun it is dependent on (see the second and third examples below).

> *His sweord wæs **glēdum** for-grunden.*
> (His sword was ground up *by* the flames. *glēd* [f] = flame)

> ***Gode** lāþ* (*Lāþ* "hateful" is related to modern *LOATHsome*.)
> (hateful to God)

> ***hlāforde** lēof* (*Lēof* "dear, valued" is related to modern *beLOVed*.)
> (dear to the lord)

2.11.4.c

Object of a Preposition. Some prepositions require objects in the dative: *tō* "to" (prep + dat) is a good example.

> *Sē prēost rīdeð tō **þǣm æþelinge**.*
> (The priest rides to the nobleman.)

Dative Direct Object. A few verbs like *helpan* "to help," *folgian* "to follow," and *andswarian* "to answer" require dative direct objects and are marked in the glossary as **2.11.4.d** *(+ dat)*. Normally, almost all verbs take accusative direct objects.

> *Sēo cwēn helpeð **þǣm cyninge**.*
> (The queen helps the king.)

> *Sē prēost folgaþ **þǣm biscope**.*
> (The priest follows the bishop.)

2.11.4.e   *Substitute Possessive (for Body Parts).* Especially with body parts, OE sometimes uses the dative to show possession. Also notice that each of the phrases also has a dative object of a preposition (see §2.11.4.c).

> *þām cyninge on hēafode*
> (on the king's head; lit., [to] the king on head)

> *him on bānum*
> (in his bones; lit., [to] him in bones)

> *þām horse on þām hēafde*
> (on the horse's head; lit., [to] the horse on the head)

2.11.4.f   *Time.* Some statements of time take the dative.

> *hwīlum*
> (at times)

2.11.5   INSTRUMENTAL:

2.11.5.a   MAIN FUNCTION: The instrumental was almost dead in late OE and appears rarely. When it does appear, it acts as sort of a specialized dative, explaining the means of an action. It can often be translated by inserting "by means of" or "with." Sometimes, though, it appears in free variation with the dative with no specialized meaning.

> *Ðy sweorde hē of-slōg hine.*
> (By means of a sword he killed him.)

ALSO

Comparisons. The instrumental often appears with comparative adjectives (for example, "happier," "wiser," etc.) in sentences like "the more the merrier." **2.11.5.b**

> *ðonne hī þȳ ġeornor gode þanciað*
> (when they the more eagerly thank God)

> *No þȳ forhtra wæs Guðlaces ġǣst.*
> (Not at all the more frightened was Guthlac's spirit.)

Object of a Preposition. A very few prepositions demand instrumental objects; the most important of these is probably *mid* "with, along with." **2.11.5.c**

> *mid þȳ folce*
> (with the people)

Time. Some statements of time take the instrumental. **2.11.5.d**

> *þȳ ilcan ġēare*
> ([in] the same year)

> *þȳ þriddan dæġ*
> ([by] the third day)

NOTE: Since instrumental and dative noun endings are identical, only the definite article *þȳ / þon* can indicate the true presence of the instrumental. From this point onward, we will not provide consistently separate listings of dative and instrumental forms.

CASE IN MODERN ENGLISH. Though case is not so intricately marked in Modern English nouns—possessive *'s* is the only survival—the system actually survives today in a simplified form in the personal pronouns, which retain (in the third person) both gender and case markers—nominative: *he, she, it, they*; genitive: *his, her, hers, its,* their, *theirs*; objective (dative and accusative combined): *him, her, it, them.* Other pronouns like *who, whom*—whose days are probably numbered—and *whose* show the same case distinctions. (Of course, even though case isn't often *marked* with endings in Modern English, it does exist nevertheless.)

Ælfric on the Concept of Case

Nominativus ys "nemniendliċ": mid ðām *casu* wē nemnað ealle ðing, swylċe ðū cweðe: *hic homo equitat* "þēs man rīt."

Nominative is "naming": with this case we name all things, just as if you said: *hic homo equitat* "this man rides."

Genitivus is "ġe-strȳnendliċ" oððe "ġe-āgniendliċ": mid þām *casu* byð ġe-swutelod ælċes ðinges ġe-strēon oþþe æhta: *huius hominis filius* "þises mannes sunu" *vel huius hominis equus* "oððe ðises mannes hors."

Genitive is "giving birth to" or "owning": with this case the bringing forth or ownership of each thing is revealed: *huius hominis filius* "this man's son" or *vel huius hominis equus* "this man's horse."

Dativus ys "for-ġyfendliċ": mid ðām *casu* byð ġe-swutelod ælċes ðinges ġifu: *huic homini do equum* "ðisum men iċ for-ġyfe hors."

   Quid das mihi? "Hwæt ġyfst ðū mē?"

   Unum librum do tibi. "Āne bōc iċ ðē ġife."

Dative is "giving, bestowing": with this case the gift of each thing is revealed: *huic homini do equum* "to this man I give a horse."

   Quid das mihi? "What do you give to me?"

   Unum librum do tibi. "A book I give to you."

Accussativus ys "wrēġendliċ": mid ðām *casu* byð ġe-swutelod, hū men sprecað be ælċum þinge: *hunc hominem accuso* "ðysne man iċ wrēġe"; *hunc hominem amo* "þysne man iċ lufiġe"; *hanc rem apprehendi* "þis ðing iċ ġe-læhte."

Accusative is "accusing": with this case is revealed how men speak about each thing: *hunc hominem accuso* "this man I accuse"; *hunc hominem amo* "this man I love"; *hanc rem apprehendi* "this thing I get."

Exercise 2.2: UNDERSTANDING CASE

Instructions. *Identify (in the space provided) the case of the listed words and then the particular function of that case as listed above (see §2.11).*

For your convenience, the gender of the word in question appears immediately after it in square brackets (m = masculine, f = feminine, and n = neuter). Please note that this exercise stresses the MAIN FUNCTIONS of each case. (Spēd þū wel! Good luck!)

Case_____   Case Function_____

1. *Sē fisc swimmeð in ðǣm wætre.*
(The fish [m] swims in the water [n].)

sē fisc   *nominative singular*   *subject*

ðǣm wætre   *dative singular*   *object of preposition*

2. *Sēo cwēn rīxode fiftiġ wintra.*
(The queen [f] ruled fifty winters [m].)

sēo cwēn   *nominative sing*   *subject*

wintra   *accusative plural?*   *direct object*
             genitive plural   *partitive genitive (#)*

3. *Ic eom þæs cyninges scealc.*
(I am the king's [m] servant [m].)

þæs cyninges   *genitive sing*   *possessive*

scealc   *accusative sing*   *direct object*
             nominative sing   *subject complement*

I am þeon
I am servant
both nominative

[4] See §2.11.4.d.

EXERCISE *continued*

4. *Sē scealc fylleð þā drinc-fatu mid wīne.*
(The servant [m] fills the drinking cups [n] with wine [n].)

sē scealc	nominative sing	subject
þā drinc-fatu (§2.10.3)	accusative plural	direct object
wīne	dative sing	~~indirect object~~ object of prep.

5. *Hæfst þū ǣniġ weorc?*
(Have you any work [n]? Do you have any work?)

weorc	accusative sing	direct object

6. *Sēo wæs on ðām temple dæġes and nihtes.*
(She [f] was in the temple [n] day and night.)

sēo (see §2.5.1)	nominative sing	subject
ðām temple	dative sing	object of preposition ~~indirect object~~
dæġes	genitive sing	time
nihtes	genitive sing	time

7. *Sēo stefn andswarode[4] ðām munuce.*
(The voice [f] answered the monk [m].)

sēo stefn	nominative sing	subject
ðām munuce	dative (?) sing	~~direct~~ object

EXERCISE *continued*

8. *Sē cyning hæfde ġe-gaderod sum hund scipa.*
   (The king [m] had gathered about a hundred ships [n].)

   | *sē cyning* | nominative sing | subject |
   | *scipa* | genitive plural | partitive |

9. *On þām īeġ-londe sēo cwēn wæs mid þām cyninge.*
   (On the island [n] the queen [f] was with the king [m].)

þām īeġ-londe	dative sing (?)	substitute + prep.
sēo cwēn	nominative sing	subject
þām cyninge	dative sing (?)	substitute prep.(?)

10. *Hē ġeaf Wyllelme prēoste þæt hūs on Lundene.*
    (He gave William the priest [m] the house [n] in London [m].)

    | *Wyllelme prēoste* | dative sing | indirect object |
    | *þæt hūs* | accusative sing | direct object |
    | *Lundene* | dative sing | object of prep. |

Exercise 2.3: GETTING THE GRAMMAR RIGHT

Instructions. *Fill in the blanks with the appropriate articles and endings (see the charts for the definite article and strong noun forms above): short blanks for endings, long blanks for articles. Assume that these sentences take normal English word order: Subject – Verb – Object. The verbs are glossed in square brackets unless they're pleasantly obvious.*

The nouns in this exercise have the following genders: æþeling (masculine), benċ (feminine), wīf (neuter), hūs (neuter), cwēn (feminine), Hrōðgar (masculine), gold (neuter), hors (neuter), strēam (masculine). The prepositions in *and* on *take the dative case while* þurh *takes the accusative.*

1. _þā_ æþelingᵃˢ (pl) sittaþ [sit] on _þa_ bencᵉ (pl).

2. _sē_ æþelingˣ (sing) sitteþ on _þa_ benċˣ (sing).

3. _þæt_ wīfˣ (sing) sitteð in _þæt_ hūsˣ (sing).

4. _sēo_ cwēnˣ (sing) ġiefeð [gives] Hrōðgarᵉ _þæt_ goldˣ (sing).

5. _þā_ horsᵁ (pl) wadað [go, wade] þurh _þāra_ strēamᵃ (pl).

2.13 Reading II: PRACTICE SENTENCES

Now that you've armed yourself with some key information, you should be ready to read some simplified OE. Because we will not take on verbs until the next chapter, we will gloss verb forms for you in square brackets immediately after they appear. You must determine whether they are singular or plural and add the appropriate verb ending in your translation. *If you're familiar with Elizabethan drama or the King James Bible, you may begin to recognize the verb endings.*

Instructions. *Translate the following sentences with the aid of the vocabulary that follows the reading.* **A friendly warning**: *Word order alone may prove quite deceptive in translating the following sentences. Be sure you understand the grammar of the endings and articles as well as the concept of case!*

1. Sē þeġn findeþ [find] þæt sweord.

   The thane finds the sword

2. Þæt gold swīcaþ [deceive] þone wer.

   The gold deceives the man

3. Þone wer findeþ þæt gold.

   The gold finds the man

4. Sēo fǣmne ġiefeþ [give] þām were þæt gold.

   The maiden gives the man the gold

5. Sē wīfman feohteþ [fight] mid þǣm sweorde.

   The woman fights with the sword

6. Þā cwēne findeþ sē wer.

   The man finds the queen

7. Sēo fǣmne findeþ þone wer.

   The maiden finds the water

8. Þǣre cwēne gold findeþ sē wer.

   The man finds the queen gold

9. Þæs weres gold is miċel.

   The man's gold is great

10. Sē wer findeþ þæt gold mid þǣre cwēne.

    The man finds the gold with the queen

11. Sēo fǣmne gangeþ [go] in þone sele.

    The maiden goes in the hall

12. Þā wīf biernaþ [burn] þone bēor-sele.

    The woman burns the beer hall

13. Þā æþelingas sittaþ [sit] in þām bēor-sele.

    The noblemen sit in the deer hall

14. Bēowulfe sēo cwēn ġiefeð [give] þone bēag.

    The queen gives Beowulf the ring

15. Sē leax swimmeð in þǣm strēame.

    The salmon swings in the stream

16. Wæs [was] sēo hwīl lang.

    Time was so long

2.14 Vocabulary for Reading II

A few conventions here: An (f), (m), or (n) following an entry indicates that it is a noun of the feminine, masculine, or neuter gender. Note that nouns always appear in the nominative case in the glossary. Prepositions—labeled (prep)—often take objects in a particular case, and these are indicated as (+ acc), (+ dat), (+ gen), and so on. Finally, if the OE word has survived into Modern English (henceforth abbreviated as "ModE"), the modern descendant appears in CAPITAL LETTERS. You will find words beginning with aesc (æ, Æ) alphabetized within the letter a, *after* ad *but before* af. *Thorn (þ,Þ) and eth (ð, Ð) appear together after the* t's.

æþeling (m) = nobleman [compare German *edel* "noble"; §2.7]

bēag, bēah (m) = ring, necklace [Yiddish *BAGel* "little ring"; §2.7]

benċ (f) = BENCH [§2.8]

bēor-sele (m) = BEER hall [§2.7]

Bēowulf (m) = Beowulf (a proper name, declined like a regular noun)

cwēn (f) = QUEEN [§2.8]

fǣmne (f) = maiden, virgin [§3.4]

ġēar (n) = YEAR [§2.9]

gold (n) = GOLD [§2.9]

hors (n) = HORSE [§2.9]

Hrōðgar (m) = character in *Beowulf* ["ROGER" in Modern English]

būs (n) = HOUSE [§2.9]

hwīl (f) = time, period of time [§2.8]

in (prep) = (+ acc) INto, (+ dat) IN [§6.15]

lang (adjective) = LONG [§6.7]

leax (m) = salmon [Yiddish *LOX*; §2.7]

micel (adjective) = great, large [§6.1]

mid (prep + dat) = with [compare German *mit*; §6.15]

sele (m) = hall, house [German *Saal* "hall"; §10.11.1]

strēam (m) = STREAM [§2.7]

sweord (n) = SWORD [§2.9]

þeġn (m) = THANE, servant, retainer [§2.7]

þurh (prep + acc) = THROUGH [§6.15]

wer (m) = man, husband; hero [see ModE *WERE-wolf* "man-wolf"; §2.7]

wīf (n) = woman, WIFE [§2.9]

wīf-man (m) = WOMAN [§10.4.2]

Lessons Learned

2.15

Before leaving this chapter you should have . . .
- understood the concept of case (§2.11).
- memorized the definite article paradigm (§2.5.1).
- memorized the strong noun charts (§2.7, §2.8, and §2.9).

THREE

"Weak" Nouns and Regular Verbs

3.1   Lesson One: Weak Nouns

Good news: The nouns you learned in Chapter Two—generally referred to as regular or "strong" nouns—represent about 60 percent of the nouns you will come across in OE texts. On the other hand, *–an* or "weak" nouns, the subject of this chapter, represent about 30 percent. These nouns are easily recognizable, since they take only a few endings, mainly *-an*. Because they represent a large and important class of nouns, you must memorize the following charts. Luckily, there's not that much to memorize.

We have Jacob Grimm to thank (or blame) for the confusing terms "weak" and "strong." In his monumental *Deutsche Grammatik*, a pioneering comparative grammar of the Germanic languages, he labeled a number of very different linguistic phenomena "weak" if they were innovations in the Germanic family of languages (often characterized by separate endings). "Strong" he reserved for the more ancient processes in Indo-European (which involved what he saw as more "internal" and intrinsic processes). Thus "weak" is sometimes no more than a questionable metaphor for "Germanic." It is probably best not to puzzle out any deeper meaning to the terms than that. In fact, some linguists and grammarians prefer more descriptive labels such as "-n declension" (for weak nouns, for example). Since, however, the terms *weak* and *strong* are still widely used, it seems best to retain them here.

As you'll see in a moment, weak nouns have far fewer distinctive endings than the strong nouns, and if you'd like another questionable metaphor to help remember the terms, you could think that because the endings are far less distinctive, they carry grammatical information "weakly." The modern word *oxen* (singular *ox*) is perhaps the only pure survival of this noun class in Modern English.

3.2   Spotting Weak Nouns

Weak nouns are generally very easy to spot in the dictionary, especially the masculines: in the nominative they end in *–a* (no other type of masculine noun ends in *–a* in the nominative) while the feminine and neuters end in *-e*. In the glossary they will be labeled (*weak m, weak f,* or *weak n*).

IDENTIFYING WEAK NOUNS

(1) Masculine nouns have a nominative singular ending in -*a*, such as *cnafa* "boy," *guma* "man," *oxa* "ox," *steorra* "star," and *þēowa* "servant."

(2) Feminine nouns have a nominative singular ending in -*e*, such as *ċyriċe* "church," *eorþe* "earth," *fǣmne* "woman," *nǣdre* "snake," *sunne* "sun," and *tunge* "tongue."

(3) Two neuter nouns have a nominative singular ending in -*e*, such as *ēage* "eye" and *ēare* "ear."

Masculine Weak Nouns (guma "man," cnafa "boy")

	Singular			Plural			Singular	Plural
N	sē	guma	cnafa	þā	guman	cnafan	-a	-an
A	þone	guman	cnafan	þā	guman	cnafan	-an	-an
G	þæs	guman	cnafan	þāra	gumena	cnafena	-an	-ena
D	þǣm	guman	cnafan	þǣm	gumum	cnafum	-an	-um
I	þȳ	guman	cnafan	**	****	****	-an	**

EXAMPLES

Sē guma swingeð þone synfullan cnafan.
(The man beats the wicked boy.)

Sē cnafa swingeð þā synfullan þēowan.
(The boy beats the wicked servants.)

Ðā þēowan þāra cnafena swingon þā oxan.
(The servants of the boys beat the oxen.)

3.4   Feminine Weak Nouns (*ċyriċe* "church," *nǣdre* "snake")

3.4.1

	Singular			Plural			Singular	Plural
N	sēo	ċyriċe	nǣdre	þā	ċyrican	nǣdran	-e	-an
A	þā	ċyrican	nǣdran	þā	ċyrican	nǣdran	-an	-an
G	þǣre	ċyrican	nǣdran	þāra	ċyriċena	nǣdrena	-an	-ena
D	þǣre	ċyrican	nǣdran	þǣm	ċyricum	nǣdrum	-an	-um

EXAMPLES

Sēo hlǣfdiġe fand þā nǣdran in ðǣre ċyrican.

(The lady found the snake [or snakes] in the church.)

Note that *þā nǣdran* can be either singular or plural accusative.

Ðā nǣdran cwǣdon of þǣm steorrum and ðǣre eorþan.

(The snakes spoke about the stars and the earth.)

"Ðā nǣdran habbað tungan," sēo hlǣfdiġe clipode.

("The snakes have tongues," the lady cried out.)

3.5   Neuter Weak Nouns (only these two!: *ēage* "eye," *ēare* "ear")

3.5.1

	Singular			Plural			Singular	Plural
N	þæt	ēage	ēare	þā	ēagan	ēaran	-e	-an
A	þæt	ēage	ēare	þā	ēagan	ēaran	-e	-an
G	þæs	ēagan	ēaran	þǣra	ēagena	ēarena	-an	-ena
D	þǣm	ēagan	ēaran	þǣm	ēagum	ēarum	-an	-um
I	þȳ	ēagan	ēaran	**	****	****	-an	**

EXAMPLES

Sē wītega healdeð þæt ēare tō þǣre eorðan.
(The wise man keeps the ear to the ground.)

Sē hālga guma healdeþ his ēagan on þǣm steorrum.
(The holy man keeps his eyes on the stars.)

Sē dysiġa guma be-tȳneþ þā ēagan and þā ēaran.
(The foolish man closes the eyes and the ears.)

Summary of Weak Noun Endings

3.6

3.6.1

	Singular			Plural		
	Masculine	Feminine	Neuter	Masculine	Feminine	Neuter
N	-a	-e	-e	-an	-an	-an
A	-an	-an	-e	-an	-an	-an
G	-an	-an	-an	-ena	-ena	-ena
D	-an	-an	-an	-um	-um	-um
I	-an	**	-an	**	**	**

Exercise 3.1: UNDERSTANDING CASE AND WEAK NOUNS

Instructions. *In the space provided, identify the case and number of the listed words and then the particular function of that case as listed in §2.11. For your convenience, if the gender of the word is not clear from the context, we provide the gender in square brackets. This exercise stresses the MAIN FUNCTIONS of each case and the forms of the WEAK NOUNS.*

	Case, Number	*Case Function*

1. *Sē guma eteð þone oxan.*
   (The man eats the ox.)

sē guma	nominative, sing.	subject
þone oxan	accusative, sing.	direct object

2. *Ðā oxan etaþ þone guman.*
   (The oxen eat the man.)

ðā oxan	nom. Plural	subject
þone guman	accusative sing.	object

3. *Sēo sunne clyppeð þā eorðan.*
   (The sun embraces the earth.)

sēo sunne	nominative sing (F)	subject
þā eorðan	accusative sing	object

4. *Sē hunta læcceð hīe mid þǣm bogan* [m].
   (The hunter catches them with the bow.)

sē hunta	nominative sing (M)	subject
þǣm bogan	dative sing.	object of preposition

	Case, Number	Case Function

5. *Þā mæsse-prēostas Godes þāra ċyriċena lārēowas bēoð.*

   (The mass-priests of God are the churches' teachers.)

   (lit., The mass-priests of God of the churches teachers are.)

   þāra ċyriċena   genitive plural   posessive

6. *On him sēo byrne scān.*

   (On him the coat of mail shone.)

   sēo byrne   nominative sing.   subject

7. *Ðāra nēdrena slitu wēron dēadliċe.*

   (The snakes' bites were deadly.)

   ðāra nēdrena   genitive plural   posessive

8. *Ðā wæs sē cyning sume hwīle mid ðām flotan [m].*

   (Then was the king some while with the fleet.)

   ðām flotan   dative sing   object of prep.

9. *Hīe næfre his banan [m] folġian[1] noldon.*

   (They would never want to follow his murderer.)

   (lit., They never his murderer follow would not.)

   banan   accusative sing.   object

[1] See §2.11.4.d

Case, Number	Case Function

10. *Sēo sunne scīneþ mid hire scearpan lēoman* [m] *on ðisum middan-ġearde.*
(The sun shines with her bright light on this earth.)

sēo sunne	nominative sing.	subject
lēoman	dative sing.	object of preposition

3.7   Lesson Two: Weak Verbs

Like other Germanic languages, OE has two main categories of verbs—traditionally called "strong" and "weak," though we could just as easily call them "irregular" and "regular" or types "A" and "B." (Again, don't let the terms "strong" and "weak" distract you too much.) The distinguishing feature between these two classes consists largely in how they form the past tense. Strong verbs form the past by changing an internal vowel: take, for example, the Modern English strong verb *to sing* (*sing, sang, sung*); the present tense has an [ɪ] sound as its root vowel; the past tense vowel changes to the [æ] sound while the past participle has a [ʊ]. (More on the past participle in a bit.) Here are some other examples from Modern English: *drive, drove, driven; see, saw, seen; grow, grew, grown; ring, rang, rung.* Grimm labeled these verbs "strong" because this process of internal vowel change (technically called *Ablaut* or vowel gradation) was to his mind an ancient and central process in Proto-Indo-European.

Weak verbs, on the other hand, form the past tense and participle in an entirely different way found only in the Germanic branch of languages: they add a suffix or ending that contains a *-d* or *-t* to the stem of the verb as in the Modern English weak verb *to live* (*live, lived, lived*). Linguists call this *-d* or *-t* a "dental" suffix since both sounds are articulated by the tongue touching near the teeth; thus [d] and [t] are identical in articulation, but [d] is voiced while [t] is voiceless (see §1.7.2). To form the past tense or past participle in OE, first a dental suffix is added to the verb stem and *then,* in the case of the past tense, the endings for person (1ˢᵗ, 2ⁿᵈ, or 3ʳᵈ) and number (singular or plural)—more on these in a moment. The weak verbs are further divided into three sub-classes, all very closely related.

Please note that weak verb classes are designated by Roman numerals (*I, II,* and *III*) while strong verb classes are labeled with Arabic numbers (*1-7*).

Weak verbs constitute almost 74 percent of OE verbs; strong verbs, almost 24 percent; a few irregular verbs, about 2 percent. Thus, learning the weak verb endings by heart is crucial.

Ælfric on Verbs

Verbum is "word," and word ġe-tācnað weorc oððe ðrowunge oððe ġe-þafunge. Weorc byð, þonne ðū cwest: *aro* "iċ eriġe," *verbero* "iċ swinge." Þrowung byð, þonne ðū cwyst: *verberor* "iċ eom beswungen," *ligor* "iċ eom ġe-bunden." Ġe-ðafung byþ, ðonne ðū cwyst: *amor* "iċ eom ġe-lufod," *doceor* "iċ eom ġe-lǣred."

Verb is "word" [in English], and a verb describes an [active] deed, a [passive] suffering, or a [passive] consent. It is a deed when you say: *aro* "I plow," *verbero* "I beat." It is [passive] suffering when you say: *verberor* "I am beaten," *ligor* "I am bound"; it is consent when you say: *amor* "I am loved," *doceor* "I am taught."

Principal Parts of OE Weak Verbs   3.8

In the following charts you will find examples illustrating the several types of weak verbs and their "principal parts" or main forms. The principal parts of OE weak verbs consist of (a) the infinitive (which usually ends in *-an*), (b) the past singular, and (c) the past participle (for example, the *lived* in "I have lived"). In this lesson, you will learn the conjugation of

[1] The internal vowel changes in these verbs are the result of a sound change called *i-mutation*. See §8.11 for details.

Classes I and II—Class III will come later, in Chapter Four. The "classic" forms are regular and reassuring, though the following category of verbs "with internal vowel changes" may seem a bit unsettling: they combine a dental suffix of the weak verbs with an internal vowel change usually associated with strong verbs. It may not be comforting to know that the internal vowel change in these weak verbs comes from a very different source than the internal vowel change in strong verbs (like *sing, sang, sung*). The appearance of the dental suffix (*-d* or *–t*) is what makes them weak.

3.8.1 VERB CATEGORIZATION

Infinitive (Present)	Singular Past	Past Participle
Classic Class I Weak Verbs:		
dǣlan (to share)	dǣlde	dǣled
dēman (to judge)	dēmde	dēmed
fremman (to make)	fremede	fremed
herian (to praise)	herede	hered
hīeran (to hear)	hīerde	hīered
lettan (to hinder)	lette	lett
mētan (to meet)	mētte	mēted, mētt
nerian (to save)	nerede	nered
sendan (to send)	sende	send, sended
settan (to set)	sette	seted, sett
trymman (to strengthen)	trymede	trymed
Weak I Verbs with Internal Vowel Changes[1]:		
bycgan (to buy)	bohte	boht
cweċċan (to shake)	cweahte	cweaht

Infinitive (Present)	Singular Past	Past Participle
sēċ(e)an (to seek)	sōhte	sōht
sellan (to give)	sealde	seald
tellan (to count)	tealde	teald
þenċ(e)an (to think)	þōhte	þōht
wyrċan (to work)	worhte	worht

Weak II Verbs:

āscian (to ask)	āscode	āscod
bodian (to report)	bodode	bodod
clipian (to call)	clipode	clipod
endian (to end)	endode	endod
frætwian (to adorn)	frætwode	frætwod
gad(e)rian (to gather)	gaderode	gaderod
lufian (to love)	lufode	lufod
maðelian (to speak)	maðelode	maðelod
sorgian (to sorrow)	sorgode	sorgod
weardian (to guard)	weardode	weardod
wunian (to dwell)	wunode	wunod

Classes of Weak Verbs   3.9

To avoid some confusion in translating, it is necessary to distinguish between three classes of weak verbs, which (due to historical sound changes) have slightly different endings in a few places.

Class I: As opposed to Class II, most Class I verbs end in –*an*. These verbs fall into two subtypes: (a) verbs with short vowels followed by a doubled consonant (*fremman, lettan,* and *trymman*) or a single *r + i* (*nerian, herian*); (b) verbs with a long vowel (*dēman* or *hīeran*) or verbs with a short vowel followed by two consonants which are usually not doubled (*sendan, bycgan, wyrċan*).

Class II: These verbs all end in -*ian* (see *lufian* as an example). Although Class II verbs are easy to spot, there is one minor problem that may complicate identifying the verbs of this class. Keep in mind that verbs with a short vowel + *r + i* belong to Class I. These verbs (like *nerian* above) may end in -*ian*. Therefore, most verbs that end in -*rian* belong to Class I. There are a few exceptions: *andswarian* (to answer) and *timbrian* (to build), among a very few others, belong to Class II.

Class III: See Chapter Four.

3.10   Weak Verb Endings (Conjugations)

You will notice in the following charts that some verbs may form endings in slightly different ways. For example, the endings signaling tense, containing the [d] or [t] sound, may appear as -*ede,* -*de,* -*te,* while the endings that contain the information about person and number (see below) may also differ slightly among verbs. The differences have to do with various sound changes that influenced these verbs. Because the differences are so slight, we provide the following conjugations with confidence that they will provide you with almost all you need to know to translate weak verbs accurately.

In interests of space, personal pronouns (*I, you, he, she, it,* etc.) will be omitted in the charts below, though the "person" appears as a number running down the left-hand side of the charts. There are three persons: first, second, and third (abbreviated as 1, 2, and 3 respectively). In general, the concept of person is best understood by imagining a hypothetical, and somewhat self-centered, conversation: the first person is the speaker,

I or *we*, while the second person, the one I/we are addressing, is *you*. Finally, the third person—the person or thing being talked *about*—is *he, she, it,* or *they*.

Singular		Plural	
1	iċ "I"	1	wē "we"
2	þū "thou, you"	2	ġē "you"
3	hē, hēo, hit "he, she, it"	3	hīe "they"

For a full discussion of pronouns, see §7.1.

MOOD

3.10.1

The following verb charts are grouped by the following three "moods," representing the speaker's attitude toward the statements in the sentence. Each of the moods requires different endings. Learning how to decode mood will make you a much more accurate translator. Though the discussion of the subjunctive is involved, it is probably best to master the concept of mood now before moving on to the conjugations themselves. If you already understand mood, you may safely skip to §3.11.

1. **Indicative** (the mood for expressing a statement or fact: *The hero **pays** his respects to the king.*)

2. **Imperative** (the mood for expressing a command: ***Do** it! **Save** your money!*)

3. **Subjunctive** (the mood for expressing a wish or desire; an idea that is doubtful or contrary to fact; an obligation or command): Since the subjunctive is a difficult concept for most speakers of Modern English, a somewhat lengthy explanation follows. In general, if you suspect that a verb might be subjunctive, try translating it with a "should" or "might" + the verb.

² Note that in Modern English the indicative and subjunctive plural forms are identical: *swim* and *swim*.

(a)   expressing a wish or desire: *I wish that he **were** here*; compare to the indicative, *He **was** here*; or, *I wish that they **be** happy* (now antiquated); compare to the indicative, *They **are** happy*.

(b)   expressing an idea that is doubtful or contrary to fact: *If I **were** you, I wouldn't do that*; compare to the indicative, *I **was** not you*; or, *If you **be** guilty, I would understand*; compare to the indicative, *You **are** guilty*.

(c)   expressing an obligation or command: *I command that he **go** to the meeting*; compare to the indicative, *He **goes** to the meeting. I expect that she **swim** her very best*; compare to the indicative, *She **swims** her very best.*²

(d)   expressing a call to do something: *Let us **pray*** (OE *bidden wē*).

In these Modern English examples, the verb shows itself to be in the subjunctive mood by adopting a form different from its indicative form. In the case of "to be" verbs, as in the examples in (a) or (b) above, the verb in the present subjunctive is always *be* no matter what the person or number. In the past subjunctive of *be* the verb is always *were* no matter what the person or number. Similarly, with other verbs, as in (c) above, of "an obligation or command," the subjunctive simply uses the infinitive form for all persons and numbers. In most instances, the Modern English subjunctive forms can be traced back, at least in part and with some difficulty, to their OE sources. What is clear in all this is that while the subjunctive is disappearing in Modern English, it was very much alive and well in OE. We list here some of the more frequent uses of the subjunctive in OE:

3.10.1.1   *After verbs of wish and desire:*

> *Nō ðæt ȳðe byð tō be-flēonne —**fremme** sē þe wille—*

> Not at all is [it] easy to escape —**try as he might** he who will—
> (*Beowulf*, ll. 1003-04)

[A more idiomatic translation: "No one may easily escape that (death)—however much he wishes to try." *Fremme* is a weak I, present singular subjunctive.]

After verbs of command, requirement, suggestion, or recommendation: **3.10.1.2**

> *[Hroðgar] sume worde hēt þæt iċ his ǣrest ðē ēst ġe-sǣde . . .*

> [Hrothgar] by a certain word commanded that I first **should declare** to you his regard . . . (*Beowulf,* ll. 2156-57)

[A more idiomatic translation: "Hrothgar asked that I first tell you of his favor toward you." The verb *ġe-secgan* is in the past singular subjunctive.]

After impersonal verbs (see §11.2 for a fuller explanation of impersonals):   **3.10.1.3**

Verbs are "impersonal" when they seem to lack a subject. For such constructions, you must supply an understood subject, usually "it." Certain verbs such as *dafenian* "to be seemly, fitting" and *þynċan* "to seem" often require an impersonal construction. Such verbs will be marked in the glossary with *(impersonal)*. Notice that an *[it]* in square brackets is supplied in the translation (though it doesn't exist in the original):

> *Ūs dafenaþ ðæt wē **wacien.***
> (For us [it] is fitting that we **should stay awake**.)

> *mē ðynċð betre*
> ([it] seems better to me . . .)

Sometimes the *to be* verb can appear impersonally (i.e., without a subject):

> *him **wǣre** bettere*
> ([it] **would have been** better for him . . .)

> *Rīht is þæt prēostas ǣlċe Sunnandæġe folce **bodien**.*
> ([It] is right that priests **should preach** every Sunday to the people.)

In clauses which describe a conditional or contingent situation:

Such clauses often begin with a word (usually a conjunction) which signals that the statement is hypothetical, conditional, etc. A few such words are ***swelċe*** "as if," ***ġif*** "if," ***būtan*** "unless," and ***þēah*** or ***þēah þe*** "though, although":

> *Ġyf mæsse-prēost his āgen līf rīhtlīċe **fadie**, þonne is rīht þæt his wurðscipe **wexe**.*
> (If a priest his own life rightly **lives**, then [it] is right that his honor **grow**.)

3.11   Weak Verbs of Class I

fremman "to accomplish," *herian* "to praise," *hīeran* "to hear," *dēman* "to judge," *sēċan* "to seek," and *sendan* "to send" are conjugated as follows:

WEAK VERBS CLASS I: *fremman* "to do, make," *herian* "to praise"

Infinitive		fremman		herian		Summary	
		Present	Past	Present	Past	Present	Past
Indicative Sing	1	fremme	fremede	herie	herede	-e	-ede
	2	fremest	fremedest	herest	heredest	-est	-edest
	3	fremeþ	fremede	hereþ	herede	-eþ	-ede
Indicative Plural	1, 2, 3	fremmaþ	fremedon	heriaþ	heredon	-(i)aþ	-edon

WEAK VERBS CLASS I: *fremman* "to do, make," *herian* "to praise" *continued*

Infinitive		fremman		herian		Summary	
		Present	Past	Present	Past	Present	Past
Subjunctive Sing	1, 2, 3	fremme	fremede	herie	herede	-(i)e	-ede
Subjunctive Plural	1, 2, 3	fremmen	fremeden	herien	hereden	-en	-eden
Participles		fremmende	fremed	heriende	hered	-ende	-ed
Imperative Sing		freme	*****	here	*****	-e	**
Imperative Plural		fremmaþ	*****	heriaþ	*****	(i)aþ	**
Inflected Infin. (Gerund)		tō fremmenne	*****	tō herienne	*****	-(i)enne	**

WEAK VERBS CLASS I: *hīeran* "to hear," *dēman* "to judge"

Infinitive		hīeran		dēman		Summary	
		Present	Past	Present	Past	Present	Past
Indicative Sing	1	hīere	hīerde	dēme	dēmde	-e	-de
	2	hīerst	hīerdest	dēm(e)st	dēmdest	-(e)st	-dest
	3	hīerþ	hīerde	dēm(e)þ	dēmde	-(e)þ	-de
Indicative Plural	1, 2, 3	hīeraþ	hīerdon	dēmaþ	dēmdon	-aþ	-don
Subjunctive Sing	1, 2, 3	hīere	hīerde	dēme	dēmde	-e	-de
Subjunctive Plural	1, 2, 3	hīeren	hīerden	dēmen	dēmden	-en	-den
Participles		hīerende	hīered	dēmende	dēmed	-ende	-ed
Imperative Sing		hīer(e)	*****	dēm(e)	*****	-(e)	**
Imperative Plural		hīeraþ	*****	dēmaþ	*****	-aþ	**
Inflected Infin. (Gerund)		tō hīerenne	*****	tō dēmenne	*****	-enne	**

WEAK VERBS CLASS I: *sēċan* "to seek," *sendan* "to send"

Infinitive		sēċan		sendan		Summary	
		Present	Past	Present	Past	Present	Past
Indicative Sing	1	sēċe	sōhte	sende	sende*	-e	-de
	2	sēċst	sōhtest	sendest	sendest*	-(e)st	-dest
	3	sēċþ	sōhte	sendeþ	sende*	-(e)þ	-de
Indicative Plural	1, 2, 3	sēċaþ	sōhton	sendaþ	sendon*	-aþ	-edon
Subjunctive Sing.	1, 2, 3	sēċe	sōhte	sende	sende*	-e	-de
Subjunctive Plural	1, 2, 3	sēċen	sōhten	senden	senden*	-en	-den
Participles		sēċende	sōht	sendende	sended, send*	-ende	-t, -(e)d
Imperative Sing		sēċ(e)	*****	send(e)	*****	-(e)	**
Imperative Plural		sēċaþ	*****	sendaþ	*****	-aþ	**
Inflected Infin. (Gerund)		tō sēċenne	*****	tō sendenne	*****	-enne	**

3.11.1 COLLAPSED ENDINGS

Sendan behaves a bit differently from the other weak I verbs in the past tense. As you know, the past tense ending of weak verbs consists of a dental suffix (*-d* or *-t*) and a personal ending (*-e*, *-est*, or *-on*). Verbs whose roots *already* end in a *-d* or *-t* often absorb the following *-(e)d* or *-t* of the past tense ending since the consonants at the end of the verb root and those in the past tense ending are so similar. That's why the past tense of *sendan* has the forms *sende*, *sendest*, *sende*, *sendon* instead of the non-existent, but regular, forms: **sendede*, **sendedest*, **sendede*, **sendedon*. In the past participle, both the regular *sended* and the collapsed form *send* occur in the surviving texts. Similarly, the past tense singular of *fæstan* is *fæste*, not **fæstede*. See §8.10 (as well as Appendix Two, §15.5) for a description of this process in strong verbs.

ANOTHER INFINITIVE   3.11.2

Besides the regular infinitive (usually ending in *-an*), OE had a second infinitive with a *tō* preceding it (as in Modern English, *to be or not to be*): see above *tō fremmenne, tō hīerenne, tō dēmenne,* and the like. Normally, this form will cause you little confusion since it reads very much like the modern infinitive with *to*. However, the ending is of interest in that it combines the regular infinitive ending *-an* with an adjective ending *-ne* (see §6.1.1) for the masculine accusative singular. We should note that the infinitive here acts like a noun, and thus some grammars call it a **gerund** (a verb used as a noun, or more accurately, a verbal used as a noun). The usual ending *-anne* often appears as *-enne*, as it does above in the weak I paradigm.

> *Hē ne ā-blinþ* ***tō ā-sendenne*** *bydelas and lārēowas* ***tō lǣrenne*** *his folc.*
> (He does not cease ***to send*** messengers and teachers ***to teach*** his people.)

–ING FORMS (PRESENT PARTICIPLES)   3.11.3

Modern English forms its present participles with an *-ing,* but OE uses the more ancient ending, preserved in a number of modern European languages, *-end*. A curious side note: Linguists aren't quite sure where *–ing* came from. Either it's an adaptation of a noun ending *–ung* or (less believably) it comes from another language altogether. In Modern English, the present participle plays an important role in forming the so-called "progressive" aspect (describing an act which is still "progressing"): *I am going; I am singing; he is swimming* (see Appendix Two, §3.3). This construction is rare in OE, which normally uses the simple present tense to indicate the progressive idea: *ic gā,* for example, can be translated as "I go" or "I am going." In OE, what look like modern present progressive constructions are often, but not always, translations from Latin.

Cumende *iċ eom tō ēow.*
(I am coming to you.)
visitans . . . vos. (Exodus 3:16)

Native OE texts generally use the present participle as a simple adjective:

Wæs ġe-hwæþer ōðrum **lifiġende** *lāð.* (*Beowulf*, l. 814)
(Each was to the other hateful [while] living.)
(lit., Was each to the other, living, loathesome.)

But see also:

Ac sē æglēċa **ēhtende** *wæs . . . duguðe ond ġeogoðe.* (*Beowulf*, ll. 159-60)
(But the monster was pursuing . . . the old retainers and the young.)

3.11.4 SOUND CHANGES AND CLASS I WEAK VERBS

You've probably noticed in the conjugations of weak verbs, most especially with Class I weak verbs, that some verbs may form endings in slightly different ways. For example, the suffixes containing the [d] or [t] sound may appear as *-ede*, *-de*, or *-te*. The endings that contain the grammatical information about person and number may also differ slightly among verbs. In addition, the stems of some of the verbs change in spelling depending on the tense of the verb or its mood: *fremman*, for example, is sometimes spelled with two *m*'s and sometimes with one *m*. The first person present tense of *fremman* is *fremme*, but the second person is spelled *fremest*, not **fremmest*. The differences have to do with sound changes that influenced these verbs. We offer a brief synopsis of those sound changes in Appendix Two, §15. The synopsis is designed to help you save time in roaming around the glossary looking for the right form.

Weak Verbs of Class II

Bodian "to announce," *lufian* "to love," *āscian* "to ask," and *clipian* "to shout, cry out" are conjugated as follows:

WEAK VERBS CLASS II: *bodian* "to announce," *lufian* "to love"

Infinitive			bodian		lufian		Summary	
			Present	Past	Present	Past	Present	Past
Indicative Sing		1	bodie	bodode	lufie	lufode	-ie	-ode
		2	bodast	bododest	lufast	lufodest	-ast	-odest
		3	bodaþ	bodode	lufaþ	lufode	-aþ	-ode
Indicative Plural	1, 2, 3		bodiaþ	bododon	lufiaþ	lufodon	-iaþ	-odon
Subjunctive Sing	1, 2, 3		bodie	bodode	lufie	lufode	-ie	-ode
Subjunctive Plural	1, 2, 3		bodien	bododen	lufien	lufoden	-ien	-oden
Participles			bodiende	bodod	lufiende	lufod	-iende	-od
Imperative Sing			boda	*****	lufa	*****	-a	**
Imperative Plural			bodiaþ	*****	lufiaþ	*****	-iaþ	**
Inflected Infin. (Gerund)			tō bodienne	*****	tō lufienne	*****	-ienne	**

WEAK VERBS CLASS II: *āscian* "to ask," *clipian* "to shout, cry out"

Infinitive			āscian		clipian		Summary	
			Present	Past	Present	Past	Present	Past
Indicative Sing		1	āscie	āscode	clipie	clipode	-ie	-ode

WEAK VERBS CLASS II: *āscian* "to ask," *clipian* "to shout, cry out" *continued*

Infinitive		ascian		clipian		Summary	
		Present	Past	Present	Past	Present	Past
Indicative Sing	2	āscast	āscodest	clipast	clipodest	-ast	-odest
	3	āscaþ	āscode	clipaþ	clipode	-aþ	-ode
Indicative Plural	1, 2, 3	āsciaþ	āscodon	clipiaþ	clipodon	-iaþ	-odon
Subjunctive Sing	1, 2, 3	āscie	āscode	clipie	clipode	-ie	-ode
Subjunctive Plural	1, 2, 3	āscien	āscoden	clipien	clipoden	-ien	-oden
Participles		āsciende	āscod	clipiende	clipod	-iende	-od
Imperative Sing		āsca	*****	clipa	*****	-a	**
Imperative Plural		āsciaþ	*****	clipiaþ	*****	-iaþ	**
Inflected Infin. (Gerund)		tō āscienne	*****	tō clipienne	*****	-ienne	**

3.12.1   DISTINGUISHING WEAK I FROM WEAK II

Why would you want to distinguish weak I from weak II verbs? In practice, it's important to be able to do so because of the potential ambiguity in the third person singular present tense (§3.11). That is, in Class I, -*eþ* indicates a third person singular present, while -*aþ* is distinctly plural (for all three persons). In Class II, however, -*aþ* represents the third person present *singular*, while -*iaþ* represents the plural. A verb ending in -*aþ* could be either a Class I plural or a Class II singular.

Consider the following sentence:

> *Dēor cunnaþ þæt land.*
> (An animal—or animals?—explores—or explore?—the country.)

Unless you know the verb class (by looking up its infinitive form), you won't be able to tell whether the subject is singular or plural since *dēor* is a neuter noun which looks the same in the nominative singular *and* plural (§2.9). This example is especially ambiguous since *dēor* lacks a definite article (as nouns often do in poetry) which could clear up the mystery. Recall that infinitives of weak verbs ending in *-an* or *-rian* are Class I, while Class II infinitives end in *-ian*.

In this case, a trip to the dictionary reveals that the infinitive form is *cunnian* "explore, investigate," clearly a Class II weak verb; thus, the subject is singular, and we can translate, "the animal explores the country." The plural would have to read:

Dēor cunniaþ þæt land.

Past tense or past participle endings with an *-o-* (sometimes *-a-*) are another clear sign that a weak verb belongs to Class II: *lufode* (Class I: *fremede*), *lufodon* (Class I: *fremedon*), *lufod* (Class I: *fremed*); imperative singulars in *-a* also point to Class II: *lufa* (Class I: *hīer*). Consider the following examples:

*Sē wītega **herede** ðā cnapan.*	Class I
(The wiseman **praised** the boys.)	
*Þā hlǣfdiġan **hīeraþ** ðā lēoþ scopes.*	Class I
(The ladies **hear** the songs of the scop.)	
*Sē guma **maþelode:** "iċ **sende** cnīhtas tō ðām hlāforde."*	Class II/Class I
(The hero **spoke:** "I [will] **send** servants to the lord.")	
*Sē cyning **dēmde** ðone ċeorl.*	Class I
(The king **judged** the freeman.)	

*Wē **lufiaþ** þā cwēne.*   Class II
(We **love** the queen.)

Nere þone hwæl.   Class I
(**Save** the whale.)

Exercise 3.2: WEAK VERB SPOTTING

Instructions. *In the spaces provided, identify the mood, tense, number, and person of the listed weak verbs. Where the verb form has more than one possible answer, identify them.*

	Mood	Tense	Number	Person
1. dēmdest	indicative	past	singular	2
2. āscaþ	indicative	present	singular	3
3. lufodest	indicative	past	singular	2
4. endast	indicative	present	singular	2
5. nereþ	indicative	present	singular	3
6. fremme	indicative	present	singular	1
7. dēmden	subjunctive	past	plural	1,2,3
8. wuniaþ	indicative / imperative	present	plural	1,2,3
9. trymme	indicative / subjunctive	present	singular	1,2,3
10. ðōhton	indicative	past	plural	1,2,3

Reading III.i: THE GOSPEL OF LUKE 1:18-22

The first chapter of Luke recounts the birth of John the Baptist. The following episode describes an angel's visit to Zechariah, the father of John the Baptist who is a priest of the Temple. The angel announces that Zechariah's wife Elizabeth will bear a son whom they should name John.

18: Þā cwæð Zacharīas tō þām engele, "Hwanon wāt iċ þis?[3] Iċ eom nū eald and mīn wīf on hyre dagum forð-ēode." 19: Ðā andswarode him sē engel: "Iċ eom Gābriel, iċ þe stande beforan Gode, and iċ eom ā-send wið þē sprecan, and þē ðis bodian.[4] 20: And nū þū byst suwiende, and þū sprecan ne miht,[5] oð þone dæġ þe ðās ðing ġe-wurðaþ, for-þām þū mīnum wordum ne be-lȳfdest, þā[6] bēoð on hyra tīman ġe-fyllede." 21: And þæt folc wæs Zacharīam[7] ġe-anbīdiende and wundrodon þæt hē on þām temple læt wæs. 22: Ðā hē ūt-ēode, ne mihte hē him tō[8] sprecan, and hiġ on-cnēowon þæt hē on þām temple sume ġe-sihþe ġe-seah. And hē wæs bicniende him and dum þurh-wunode.

VOCABULARY FOR READING III.i (GOSPEL OF LUKE)

Starting with this glossary, words are keyed to the reference number for their corresponding paradigms (charts). Normally, verbs appear in their infinitive form in the glossary, though if the particular verb class has not yet been covered, it will appear as it does in the text along with a simple translation.

(ġe)an-bidian (weak verb II) = to await, wait for, expect [§3.12]

and-swarian (weak verb II) = to ANSWER (+ dat direct object) [§3.12]

ā-send = collapsed past participle of *ā-sendan* (see §3.11.1)

ā-sendan (weak verb I) = to SEND [§3.11]

beforan (preposition + dat) = BEFORE [§6.15]

be-lȳfan (weak verb I) = to BELIEVE (+ dat object) [§3.11]

be-lȳfdest = see *be-lȳfan*

bēoð (verb form not yet covered) = "will be" (future sense) [§4.5.1]

[3] Note that Modern English requires *do* as a helping verb in normal questions: "Do you dance?" rather than "Dance you?" Remember that Zacharias, an old man, has just had some startling news.

[4] *Bodian* is parallel to *sprecan*. Notice the long *ē* in *þē*!

[5] OE often uses the present tense with a future meaning. Translate "þū byst suwiende" as "you will be silent" (lit., "you are being silent").

[6] Translate *þā* as "which" (referring back to *wordum*).

[7] Here the OE retains the Latin ending on the proper noun *Zacharias* (in the accusative case).

[8] Note that the preposition actually follows the object: *him tō* = "to them."

bicnian (weak verb II) = to make signs, gesture (with the hands) [§3.12]

bodian (weak verb II) = to announce, preach [§3.12]

byst (verb form not yet covered) = "are" [§4.5.1]

cwæþ (verb form not yet covered) = "said" [§9.1]

dagum = see *dæġ* (see §2.10.3)

dæġ (m) = DAY (irregular dat pl = *dagum*) [§2.7]

dum (adjective) = DUMB, incapable of speech [§6.1]

eald (adjective) = OLD [§6.1]

engel (m) = ANGEL [§2.7]

eom (verb form not yet covered) = "am" [§4.5.1]

folc (n) = people, FOLK [§2.9]

forþām (conjunction) = therefore, because [§5.1.1]

forð-ēode (verb form not yet covered) = "has advanced" [§4.5.3.1]

(ġe)fyllan (weak verb I) = to fulFILL [§3.11]

God (m) = GOD [§2.7]

hiġ (or *hīe*, pronoun) = they [§2.5.2, §7.1]

him (pronoun) = him or them [§2.5.2, §7.1]

hwanon (adverb) = how, whence, from where [§6.9]

hyra (or *hira*, pronoun) = THEIR [§2.5.2, §7.1]

hyre (or *hire*, pronoun) = HER [§2.5.2, §7.1]

iċ (pronoun) = I [§2.5.2, §7.1]

lǣt (adjective) = LATE [§6.1]

miht, mihte (verb form not yet covered) = "can, is/are able" [§4.3.1]

mīn, mīnum (pronoun) = MY [§2.5.2, §7.1]

ne (adverb) = not [§6.9]

nū (adverb) = NOW [§6.9]

on (preposition + dat) = in [§6.15]

on-cnēowon (verb form not yet covered) = "knew, realized" (pl) [§9.3]

oð (preposition + acc) = until, up to, as far as [§6.15]

(ġe)seah (verb form not yet covered) = "SAW" or "had seen" [§11.1.2-3]

(ġe)sihðe (f) = SIGHT, vision [§2.8]

sprecan (verb form not yet covered) = "SPEAK" [§9.1]

stande (verb form not yet covered) = "STAND" [§9.2]

sume (adjective) = a certain [§6.1]

suwiende = present participle of *swīgian*

swīgian (weak verb II) = to be silent, to become silent [§3.12]

tempel (n) = TEMPLE [§2.9]

tīma (weak m) = TIME [§3.3]

tō (prep + gen, dat, and inst) = TO [§6.15]

ðā (verses 18 and 19, adverb) = then [§5.1.1]

ðā (verse 22, conjunction) = when [§5.1.1]

ðām (definite article) = the [§2.5]

ðās = (pronoun) this [§7.7]

ðe = (pronoun) who; which, on which [§7.5]

ðē (pronoun) = THEE, you [§2.5.2, §7.1]

ðing (n) = THING [§2.9.3]

ðis (pronoun) =THIS [§7.7]

ðū (pronoun) – you, THOU [§2.5.2, §7.1]

ðurh-wunian (weak verb II) = to remain, continue [§3.12]

ūt-ēode (verb form not yet covered) = "went out" [§4.5.3]

wāt (verb form not yet covered) = "know" [§4.3, §4.4]

wīf (n) =WIFE; woman [§2.9]

wiþ (preposition + gen, acc, dat, inst) = WITH [§6.15]

word (n) = WORD [§2.9.2]

wundrian (weak verb II) = to marvel, WONDER [§3.12]

(ġe)wurðaþ (verb form not yet covered) = "happens, takes place" [§8.6]

Reading III.ii: EXETER BOOK RIDDLE #82

The following mini-poem is actually a riddle, one of about ninety Old English riddles in the Exeter Book, one of the four surviving OE poetic codices. Both Symphosius (4th-5th cent.) and Aldhelm (died 709, an English scholar and churchman) wrote Latin riddles, and the genre may very well have been a learned one. In fact we would very likely not know the answer to the following riddle if the solution to a similar Latin riddle had not been included as a title (#94 in Symphosius). Seemingly defeating their own purpose, the Latin collections often include the solutions as titles—no such luck with our vernacular riddles, many of which have baffled generations of scholars.

⁹ *Moniġe* "many" and *snottre* "wise" refer back to *weras* and are thus plural. Be careful to treat *mōde* correctly (see §2.11.4.b).

Though we will look much more carefully at meter later on, you should notice that the OE poetic line is broken into two half-lines (separated by a break or caesura). The two half-lines are held together by alliteration or assonance: the first stressed syllable in the second half-line sets the alliteration pattern. Function words like pronouns, articles, prepositions, etc., very rarely receive stress, which is reserved for "content" words: verbs, nouns, adjectives, etc. At least one stressed syllable must alliterate with the first stressed syllable of the second half-line. Thus, in line 1, the alliterative pattern is based on *w* (*weras*), in 2 on *m* (*mōde*), in 3 on *ē* (*ēaran*), and so forth. (Any vowel can "alliterate" with any other vowel.)

82

Wiht cwōm gongan*   þǣr weras sǣton*   came stalking / SAT (pl)
moniġe* on mæðle,   mōde snottre*;⁹   MANY / wise (pl)
hæfde* ān ēage   ond ēaran twā,   (it) had
ond twēġen fēt,   twelf hund hēafda,
5 hrycg ond wombe   ond honda twā,
earmas ond eaxle,   ānne swēoran
ond sīdan twā.   Saga hwæt* hīo* hātte*.   WHAT / she (referring to
                                                   wiht) /is called

The solution? *Luscus alium vendens.*

VOCABULARY FOR READING III.ii (EXETER BOOK RIDDLE #82)

ān (adjective) = ONE; *ānne* = m acc sing [§6.1]

ēage (weak n) = EYE [§3.5]

ēare (weak n) = EAR [§3.5]

earm (m) = ARM [§2.7]

eaxl (f) = shoulder [§2.8, ModE *AXLE*, German *Achse* "shoulder"]

fōt (m) = FOOT (irregular noun: *fēt* =

dat sing and nom/acc pl) [§10.4]

hand, hond (f) = HAND [§10.6]

hātte (verb form not yet covered) = "is called" [§9.3]

hēafod (n) = HEAD [§2.9]

hrycg (m) = back (part of the human body) (see ModE *RIDGE*, German *Rücken* "back") [§2.7]

hund (n) = HUNDred [§2.9]

mæðel (n) = council, meeting [§2.9]

mōd (n) = mind, heart (see ModE *MOOD*) [§2.9]

on (prep + dat/acc) = ON, onto [§6.16.2]

ond (conjunction) = AND

saga = imperative sing of *secgan*

secgan (weak verb III) – to SAY (see German *sagen)* [§4.1]

sīde (weak f) = SIDE [§3.4]

snottre (adjective) = wise [§6.1]

swēora (weak m) = neck [§3.3]

twā (number) = TWO

twēgen (adjective) = two (TWAIN) [§6.1]

twelf (number) = TWELVE

þǣr (conjunction) = where, to where [§5.1.1]; (adverb) THERE [§6.9]

wer (m) = man, male; person [§2.7]

wamb, womb (f) = belly, stomach (see ModE *WOMB*) [§2.8]

wiht (f) = creature (ModE *WIGHT*) [§2.8]

Solution to the riddle: One-eyed seller of garlic.

Lessons Learned

Before leaving this chapter you should have . . .
- memorized the weak noun charts (§3.3, §3.4, §3.5—see §3.6 for a summary).
- understood the concept of mood (§3.11.1).
- memorized the weak verb endings (§3.11), particularly the present and past indicative.
- learned to distinguish weak I from weak II verbs (§3.12.1).

FOUR

Weak Verbs Class III
and Irregular Verbs

4.1   Lesson One: Weak Verbs, Class III

The third class of weak verbs is set off from the other two by a variety of consonant and vowel changes in the verb stem, making this something of a messy class. The good news is that the class contains only a few verbs, among which are *habban* "to have, to hold," *hycg(e)an* "to think, consider, be intent on," *libban* "to live," and *secgan* "to say." Of these, you should know *habban* by heart: not only is it an important verb in its own right, but it also appears constantly as a helping verb.

4.1.1   WEAK VERBS CLASS III: *habban* "to have," *hycgan* "to think"

Infinitive			habban		hycgan		Summary	
			Present	Past	Present	Past	Present	Past
Indicative Sing		1	hæbbe	hæfde	hycge	hog(o)de	-e	-(o)de
		2	hafast, hæfst	hæfdest	hogast, hycgst	hog(o)dest	-(a)st	-(o)dest
		3	hafaþ, hæfþ	hæfde	hogaþ	hog(o)de	-(a)þ	-(o)de
Indicative Plural	1, 2, 3		habbaþ	hæfdon	hycgaþ	hog(o)don	-aþ	-(o)don
Subjunctive Sing	1, 2, 3		hæbbe	hæfde	hycge	hog(o)de	-e	-(o)de
Subjunctive Plural	1, 2, 3		hæbben	hæfden	hycgen	hog(o)den	-en	-(o)den
Participles			hæbbende	hæfd	hycgende	hog(o)d	-ende	-(o)d
Imperative Sing			hafa	*****	hycge, hoga	*****	-a/ -(e)	**
Imperative Plural			habbaþ	*****	hycgaþ	*****	-aþ	**
Inflected Infin. (Gerund)			tō habbanne	*****	tō hycganne	*****	-anne	**

WEAK VERBS CLASS III: *libban* "to live," *secgan* "to say"   **4.1.2**

Infinitive		libban		secgan		Summary	
		Present	Past	Present	Past	Present	Past
Indicative Sing	1	libbe	leofode, lifde	secge	sæġd(e), sæde	-e	-(o)de
	2	leofast, li(o)fast	lifdest	sæġst, seġ(e)st	sæġdest, sædest	-(a)st	-(o)dest
	3	leofaþ, li(o)faþ	leofode, lifde	seġþ, sæġ(e)þ	sæġde, sæde	-(a)þ	-(o)de
Indicative Plural	1, 2, 3	libbaþ, leofaþ	lifdon, leofodon	secgaþ	sæġdon, sædon	-aþ	-(o)don
Subjunctive Sing	1, 2, 3	libbe	lifde, leofode	secge	sæġde, sæde	-e	-(o)de
Subjunctive Plural	1, 2, 3	libben	lifden, leofoden	secgen	sæġden, sæden	-en	-(o)den
Participles		libbende, lifiende	lifd, leofod	secgende	sæġd	-ende	-(o)d
Imperative Sing		leofa, liofa	*****	saga, seġe	*****	-a/-e	**
Imperative Plural		libbaþ, lifiað	*****	secg(e)aþ	*****	-aþ	**
Inflected Infin. (Gerund)		tō libbanne	*****	tō secganne	*****	-anne	**

TIMESAVERS:
4.1.3

GENITIVE OBJECTS. When *hycgan* means "think about or intend something," its direct object takes the genitive case (see §2.11.3.f). Such verbs will be marked in the glossary with the notation *(+ gen)*.

EXAMPLE:

Ēode swā ān-rǣd   eorl tō þām ċeorle;
Ǣġðer hira ōþrum   yfeles hogode.

(He went thus resolute   the nobleman to the churl;
Both of them to the other   *intended evil*.)

4.1.4   CONTRACTIONS. Instead of contracting the negative *ne* "not" at the end of a verb as Modern English does ("don't," "wasn't," etc.), OE *ne* "not" usually fixes itself to the beginning of certain verbs. Thus, *habban* appears in the negative form *nabban* "not have." This form represents the contraction *ne* + *habban*. The other forms run as follows: present (1, 2, 3) singular *næbbe, næfst, næfþ*; present (1, 2, 3) plural *nabbaþ*; past (1, 3) singular *næfde*, (2) *næfdest*; past (1, 2, 3) plural *næfdon*; present subjunctive (1, 2, 3) singular *næbbe*; present subjunctive (1, 2, 3) plural *næbben*; past subjunctive (1, 2, 3) singular *næfde;* past subjunctive (1, 2, 3) plural *næfden*.

Exercise 4.1: LEARNING WEAK III VERBS

Instructions. *Translate the following Modern English sentences into Old English. For the verbs, consult the appropriate Class III charts above.*

1. The lady had the king's ring. _____

2. The maiden now lives in London. _____

3. A wise man often thinks good thoughts. _____

4. The servant thought about [see §4.1.3] the snakes in the garden. _____

_____

5. As I said before, the army had no joy in battle. _____

VOCABULARY FOR EXERCISE 4.1

Please note that adjectives in the following glossary are pre-packaged with their correct endings.

army = *here* (m) [§10.2.1]

as = *swā* (conjunction) [§5.1.1]

battle = *feoht* (n) [§2.9]

before = *ǣr* (adverb) [§6.9]

HAVE = (use *habban*, §4.1.1)

garden = *wyrt-tūn* (m) [§2.7]

GOOD = *gōde* (adjective) [§6.2.2]

I = *iċ* (pronoun) [§7.1]

in = *on* (prep + dat) [§6.15]

joy = *byht* (f) [§2.8]

KING = *cyning* (m) [§2.7]

LADY = *blǣfdiġe* (weak f) [§3.4]

LIVE = (use *libban*, §4.1.2)

LONDON = *Lunden* (n) [§2.9]

MAIDEN = *mǣden* (n) [§2.9]

no = *nāne* (adjective) [§6.1]

NOW = *nū* (adverb) [§6.9]

OFTen = *oft* (adverb) [§6.9]

ring = *bēag* (m) [§2.7]

SAY = (use *secgan*, §4.1.2)

servant = *cnapa* (weak m) [§3.3]

snake = *nǣdre* (weak f) [§3.4]

think = (use *hycgan*, §4.1.1)

THOUGHT = *(ġe)þōht* (m) [§2.7]

wise man = *wītega* (weak m) [§3.3]

Exercise 4.2: MORE REVERSE TRANSLATION

Instructions. *Translate the following Modern English sentences into Old English. Each sentence represents our translation (and in some cases our adaptation) of an existing Old English text.*

Important Note. *OE does not use forms of* do *to form normal questions as in "Do you have any companions?" Instead, it sounds a bit Shakespearean, "Have you any companions?" In the sentences below, where you encounter such* do *constructions,*

[1] You can translate the object of *thinks about* with a genitive object (see §4.1.3) or with the preposition "about" (see glossary).

eliminate the do *and make the verb that depends on it into the main verb. Forms of* do *that you should eliminate are in boldface italics in the sentences below.*

1. *Do* you have any companion?

    _____

2. The smith says: "Whence (where) *does* the farmer get [use appropriate form of OE *habban* "have"] a ploughshare or a coulter . . . except from my craft?"

    _____

3. What *do* you say, fowler, how *do* you snare birds?

    _____

4. A wise person always thinks about the strife[1] of this world.

    _____

5. Bishop Æðelgār succeeded to the archbishopric after Dunstan, and he (Æðelgār) lived a little while [see §2.11.2.c] after that—only one year and three months.

    _____

VOCABULARY FOR EXERCISE 4.2

about = *ymb* (preposition + dat or acc) [§2.11.4.c, §6.15]

AFTER = *æfter* (preposition + dat) [§2.11.4.c, §6.15]

always = *ā* (adverb) [§6.9]

AND = *and* (conjunction) [§5.1.1]

ANY = *ǣniġne* (m acc sing of adjective *æniġ*) [§6.2.2]

ARCHbishopric = *arċe-stōl* (m) [§2.7]

bird = *fugel* (m) [§2.7]

BISHOP = *biscop* (m) [§2.7]

but = *ac* (conjunction) [§5.1.1]

companion = *(ġe)fēra* (weak m) [§3.3]

COULTER = *culter* (m) [§2.7]

CRAFT = *cræft* (m) [§2.7]

except = *būtan* (conjunction) [§2.11.4c, §6.15]

farmer, plowman = *ierþling* (m) [§2.7]

FOWLER = *fuglere* (m) [§10.3]

from = *of* (preposition + dat) [§2.11.4c, §6.15]

HE = *hē* (pronoun) [§7.1]

HOW = *hū* (adverb) [§6.14]

LITTLE = *lȳtle* (adjective) [§6.1]

live = *libban* [§4.1.2]

MONTHS = *mōnað* (m) [§10.9]

my = *mīnum* (dat sing of pronoun *mīn*) [§7.1]

one = (use Roman numerals): i, ii, iii, iv, v, vi, vii, viii, ix, x

only = *būtan* (preposition + acc) lit., *but for, except* [§2.11.2.b, §6.15]

or = *oþþe* (conjunction) [§5.1.1]

ploughSHARE = *scear* (n) [§2.9]

say = secgan [§4.1.2]

servant = *cnafa* (weak m) [§3.3]

SMITH = *smiþ* (m) [§2.7]

snare, entrap = *be-swīcan* (strong verb 1) [use §3.11]

strife = *(ġe)winn* (n) [§10.11.1]

succeeded to = *fēng tō* (verb form not yet covered, *tō* = prep + dat) [§11.1]

that = *sē, sēo, þæt* (definite article as pronoun) [§2.5]

think = *hycgan* [§4.1.1]

THIS = *þisse* (adjective) [§7.7]

three = (use Roman numerals)

WHAT = *hwæt* (n of *hwā,* interrogative pronoun) [§7.6]

wise person = *snottor* (an adjective, used here used as if it were a noun, here masculine) [§6.2.2]

WHENce, from where = *hwanon* (adverb) [§6.9]

WHILE = *hwīl* (f) [§2.8]

WORLD = *woruld* (f) [§10.11.2]

YEAR = *ġēar* (m) [§2.7]

YES = *ġiese*

you = *þū* (pronoun) [§7.1]

4.1.5   DISTINCTIVE ENDINGS

Though ideally you should know all the verb endings by heart, you can speed up your reading of Old English by having a few distinctive endings especially near the surface of your memory.

-an   Infinitives in Old English, the forms listed in glossaries and dictionaries, almost always end in an *-an*, though they normally do not take a *to* like Modern English infinitives: *to read, to memorize, to suffer*. Infinitives are called *infinitives* because they carry no finite information (person, tense, mood, etc.) to limit them.

-eþ   Though there are other endings for the third person singular (Class II *-aþ*), *-eþ* is distinctively third person singular present tense. It maketh sense, doth it not?

-on   This ending almost always represents the plural past tense (even in strong verbs), though see §4.3 for an important exception.

-anne,   The distinctive ending of the so-called "inflected infinitive" (§3.11.2)
-enne

4.2   Lesson Two: Unusual and Irregular Verb Forms

In this lesson, you'll learn more about some irregular but common verbs and verb endings with an eye to enabling you to translate quickly and accurately.

Preterite(Past)-Present Verbs: 4.3

Besides strong and weak verbs, there is another important, and rather tricky, class of verbs you should know about: preterite-present verbs. In this class belong some important helping verbs (which usually require an accompanying infinitive and denote desire, necessity, etc.—see Modern English *shall, will, must, might, can*, etc.) as well as a few others. They are called "preterite-present" verbs—*preterite*, a Latinate synonym for "past tense"—because their present tenses, confusingly, come from the past tense strong verbs (like *drink, drank, drunk*—see §8.8, for a preview), while the real past tense forms take the regular weak past endings (see §3.11). Though this class of verbs may seem like a diabolical invention to befuddle unsuspecting students, the processes involved were, perhaps not so reassuringly, natural. So, to repeat, preterite-present verbs have a present tense that looks like a strong past tense (*drank*) but whose real past tense is formed like those of regular verbs (**dranked*, with a dental suffix –*d/t*).

We provide below (at §4.4.3) full conjugations of four verbs; the first three appear frequently as helping verbs, and the last is a common verb for "to know": *magan, sculan, mōtan*, and *witan*.

IMPORTANT PRETERITE-PRESENT HELPING VERBS 4.3.1

Infinitive	Present			Past	Pres. Subjunctive
	1, 3	*2*	*1, 2, 3 Pl*	*Singular*	*Singular*
magan "be able, can"	mæġ	meaht	magon	meahte	mæġe
mōtan "be allowed"	mōt	mōst	mōton	mōste	mōte
sculan "must, ought"	sceal	scealt	sculon	scolde	scule, scyle
cunnan "can, be able"	cann	canst	cunnon	cūþe	cunne
durran "dare"	dearr	dearst	durron	dorste	durre

4.3.2   OTHER IMPORTANT PRETERITE-PRESENT VERBS

Infinitive	Present			Past	Pres. Subjunctive
	1, 3	*2*	*1, 2, 3 Pl*	*Singular*	*Singular*
witan "know"	wāt	wāst	witon	wisse/wiste	wite
āgan "own"	āh	āhst	āgon	āhte	āge
ġe-munan "remember"	ġe-man	ġe-manst	ġe-munon	ġe-munde	ġe-myne/mune
þearfan "need"	þearf	þearft	þurfon	þorfte	þyrfe/þurfe
dugan "avail, be good"	dēah	***	dugon	dohte	dyge/duge

Note that the present tense plural forms above have an -*on* ending indicative of the past tense (though they are in fact present tense!). These verbs actually did evolve from the past tense forms of other verbs whose meaning shifted. Since their present tense was formed on the basis of past tense forms, they required new forms for the actual past tense, for which the weak endings were called into service (notice the dental suffixes -*t*- and -*d*- in the true past tense). Below we list the conjugations of the most frequently occurring preterite-present verbs. Since the past tenses follow the regular weak conjugation, we give only the past singular. Please refer to §3.11 for a full conjugation.

TIMESAVERS:

4.3.2.1   NEGATIVES. Some preterite-present verbs show the same kind of contraction for negatives as explained above with *habban-nabban* (§4.1.2). Thus, *witan* "to know" has the negated form *nytan* "not to know." This represents a contraction: *ne* + *witan*. The other forms run as follows—Present: **nāt** (1, 3 sing), **nāst** (2 sing), **nyton** (pl); Past: **nysse, nyste**; Subj: **nyte**.

> *Iċ nāt.*
> (I don't know.)

PRETERITE-PRESENT VERBS, CONJUGATION: **4.3.3**

PRETERITE-PRESENT VERBS: *magan* "may, can," *sculan* "ought to, must"   **4.3.3.1**

Infinitive		magan		sculan		Summary	
		Present	Past	Present	Past	Present	Past
Indicative Sing	1	mæġ	mihte, meahte	sceal	scolde, scealde	-	-t/de
	2	meaht	mihtest, meahtest	scealt	scoldest	-t	-t/dest
	3	mæġ	mihte, meahte	sceal	scolde, scealde	-	-t/de
Indicative Plural	1, 2, 3	magon	meahton, mihton	sculon	sceoldon	-on	-t/don
Subjunctive Sing	1, 2, 3	mæġe, muge	meahte, mihte	scyle, scule	scolde	-e	-t/de
Subjunctive Plural	1, 2, 3	mæġen, mugen	meahten, mihten	scylen, sculen	scolden, scealden	-en	-t/den
Participles		*****	*****	*****	*****	***	***

PRETERITE-PRESENT VERBS: *mōtan* "be allowed, have opportunity to," *witan* "to know"   **4.3.3.2**

Infinitive		mōtan		witan		Summary	
		Present	Past	Present	Past	Present	Past
Indicative Sing	1	mōt	mōste	wāt	wiste, wisse	-	-te

Infinitive		mōtan		witan		Summary	
		Present	**Past**	**Present**	**Past**	**Present**	**Past**
Indicative Sing	2	mōst	mōstest	wāst	wistest	-st	-test
	3	mōt	mōste	wāt	wiste, wisse	–	-te
Indicative Plural	1, 2, 3	mōton	mōston	witon	wiston, wisson	-on	-ton
Subjunctive Sing	1, 2, 3	mōte	mōste	wite	wiste, wisse	-e	-te
Subjunctive Plural	1, 2, 3	mōten	mōsten	witen	wisten, wissen	-en	-ten
Participles		*****	*****	witende	witen	-ende	-en

4.4   Let's Shall

Most of the preterite-present verbs, especially the ones that act as helping verbs, do not have participial or infinitive forms. (Even Modern English lacks such forms as *maying, *caning, *shalling, *to may, *to can, *to shall, *I have mayed, *I have could, *I have should, etc.)

4.5   Some Irregularities: Anomalous Verbs

Some of the most important verbs in OE have irregular patterns. In many cases, these verbs consist of at least two originally separate verbs that have somehow fallen together. In almost every Indo-European language, the *to be* verb appears as something of an irregular jumble. Perhaps frequent use prevents the normal process of regularizing. In any case, you will meet with the following verbs so frequently that memorizing them will allow you to read much faster.

4.5.1   The OE verb *wesan* "to be" is made up of several verbs which were originally separate but fell together to form a "composite" verb. That is why the verbs you see below has such radically different forms as *eom, is, sindon, wǣre,* etc.—because they originally came from different words. To make matters ever so slightly more complex, OE had a second form of the "to be" verb, *bēon,* which coexisted with the composite verb *wesan* "to be" and often has a slightly different meaning.

"TO BE" VERBS: *wesan* "to be," *bēon* "to be"   **4.5.2**

Infinitive		wesan		bēon	
		Present	**Past**	**Present**	**Past**
Indicative Sing	1	eom	wæs	bēo	*****
	2	eart	wǣre	bist	*****
	3	is	wæs	biþ	*****
Indicative Plural	1, 2, 3	sindon, sind, sint	wǣron	bēoþ	*****
Subjunctive Sing	1, 2, 3	sīe	wǣre	bēo	*****
Subjunctive Plural	1, 2, 3	sīen	wǣren	bēon	*****
Participles		wesende	*****	bēonde	*****
Imperative Sing		wes	*****	bēo	*****
Imperative Plural		wesaþ	*****	bēoþ	*****
Inflected Infin. (Gerund)		*****	*****	tō bēonne	*****

TIMESAVERS: 4.5.3

TIME AND BEING. *Wesan* and *bēon* can have slightly different meanings. *Bēon* forms often express the unchanging qualities of a thing, and thus often appear in maxims and proverbs:

Dōm biþ sēlast.
(Glory is [always] best.)

Cyning biþ on-wealdes ġeorn.
(A king is [always] eager for power.)

On the other hand, forms from *wesan* are usually situational. The statement applies to the conditions at hand.

Ofost ist sēlast.
(Haste is best.) −not always but in a particular situation.

4.5.3.b   NEGATIVES. Like *habban*, *bēon/wesan* form contracted negatives by adding an *n* to the beginning of its forms: *neom, nart, nis, næs, nēre,* etc., from *eom, eart, is, wæs, wēre,* etc.

4.5.3.c   MORE ANOMALIES. The following chart gives the forms for four other irregular verbs that occur frequently both in poetry and prose: *dōn* "to do," *gān* "to go," *willan* "to want, desire," and *nyllan* "not to want, not desire."

4.5.3.1   **ANOMALOUS VERBS:** *dōn* "to do," *gān* "to go"

Infinitive		dōn		gān	
		Present	Past	Present	Past
Indicative Sing	1	dō	dyde	gā	ēode
	2	dēst	dydest	gǣst	ēodest
	3	dēþ	dyde	gǣþ	ēode
Indicative Plural	1, 2, 3	dōþ	dydon	gāþ	ēodon

Infinitive		dōn		gān	
		Present	Past	Present	Past
Subjunctive Sing	1, 2, 3	dō	dyde	gā	ēode
Subjunctive Plural	1, 2, 3	dōn	dyden	gān	ēoden
Participles		dōnde	(ġe-)dōn	gānde	(ġe-)gān
Imperative Sing		dō	*****	gā	*****
Imperative Plural		dōþ	*****	gāþ	*****
Inflected Infin. (Gerund)		tō dōnne	*****	tō gānne	*****

ANOMALOUS VERBS *willan* "to want, desire," *nyllan* "not to want, desire"   **4.5.3.2**

Infinitive		willan		nyllan		Summary	
		Present	Past	Present	Past	Present	Past
Indicative Sing	1	wil(l)e	wolde	ny(l)le, ne(l)le	nolde	-e	-de
	2	wilt	woldest	nylt	noldest	-t	-dest
	3	wil(l)e	wolde	ny(l)le, ne(l)le	nolde	-e	-de
Indicative Plural	1, 2, 3	willaþ	woldon	nyllaþ	noldon	-aþ	-don
Subjunctive Sing	1, 2, 3	wil(l)e	wolde	ny(l)le, nelle	nolde	-e	-de
Subjunctive Plural	1, 2, 3	willen	wolden	nyllen, nellen	nolden	-en	-den
Participles		willende	*****	*****	*****	-ende	**
Imperative Sing		*****	*****	*****	*****	**	**

Infinitive	willan		nyllan		Summary	
	Present	Past	Present	Past	Present	Past
Imperative Plural	*****	*****	*****	*****	**	**
Inflected Infin. (Gerund)	tō willenne	*****	*****	*****	-enne	**

TIMESAVERS:

4.5.4   I-MUTATION. Notice the effects of i-mutation (see §8.11) in the second and third person singular present tense of *dōn* and *gān*.

IMPLIED MOTION. *Willan* and *nyllan*, as well as some of the other preterite-present helping verbs, often appear without a verb of motion, which is understood. The Shakespearean "I will away" is a later example.

> *Hīe noldon from him.*
> (They didn't want [to go, depart] from him.)

Exercise 4.3: LEARN TO STOP WORRYING AND LOVE PRETERITE-PRESENT AND IRREGULAR VERBS

Instructions. *In the spaces provided, identify the mood, tense, and number of the listed weak verbs. Where the verb form has more than one possible answer, identify them.*

	Mood	Tense	Person	Number
1. magon	*indicative*	*Present*	*1,2,3*	*Plural*
2. nyllaþ			*1*	

	Mood	Tense	Person	Number
3. willen	_____	_____	_____	_____
4. meahton	_____	_____	_____	_____
5. scyle	_____	_____	_____	_____
6. sindon	_____	_____	_____	_____
7. dō	_____	_____	_____	_____
8. dōþ	_____	_____	_____	_____
9. bist	_____	_____	_____	_____
10. wǣron	_____	_____	_____	_____

[2] The preposition *tō* means something different than it does in Modern English (see glossary).

[3] *ānra ġe-hwelċ* = "each one" (lit., "each of one")

[4] *Swā hwelċ swā* is a phrase—see glossary. In the next phrase the series of *swā's* has a special meaning: see *swā . . . swā* in the glossary. You're not seeing double: *þæt þæt* is a phrase (see glossary).

Exercise 4.4: TRANSLATION EXERCISE

Instructions. *Translate the following Old English sentences into idiomatic Modern English. Underlined phrases and words may require special handling.*

1. Prēostas sindon ġe-sette tō[2] lārēowum **þām lǣwodum folce** [see §2.11.4.b].

2. Iċ ġe-lǣre <u>eallum wyrhtum</u> [see §2.11.4.a] þisne rǣd: þæt ānra ġe-hwelċ[3] his cræft ġeornlīċe be-gā. For-þǣm sē þe his cræft for-lǣtt, sē biþ fram þǣm cræfte for-lǣten. <u>Swā hwelċ swā</u>[4] þū sīe, swā mæss-prēost, swā munuc, swā ċeorl, swā ċempa, <u>be-gā</u> [§3.10.1.2] ġeornlīċe þīnne cræft and bēo <u>þæt þæt</u> þū eart. For-þǣm hit is miċel demm and miċel scand ġif man nyle bēon <u>þæt þæt</u> hē is and <u>þæt þæt</u> hē bēon sceal.

[5] Think carefully about the subject of the first sentence in #4. What does the *-e* on *Gode* indicate? The word *lāreowa* is a genitive plural depending on *on-stal* [see §2.11.3.b]. Don't confuse *mæge* (a verb form) with the noun *mæġ* "kinsman"—the two look almost identical.

[6] *Gāþ* = imperative plural

3. Ond þā cwǣdon hīe þæt him [see §2.11.4.b, depends on *lēofra*] nǣniġ mǣġ lēofra nǣre þonne hiera hlāford, ond hīe nǣfre his banan folgian noldon.

4. Gode æl-mihtigum sīe þanc[5] þætte wē nū ǣniġne on-stāl habbaþ lārēowa [§2.11.3.b]. Ond for-þon iċ þē be-bīode þæt þū dō swā iċ ġe-līefe þæt þū wille . . . þæt ðū be-fǣste þone wīsdōm ðe ðē God sealde þǣr þǣr ðū hine befæstan mǣge.

5. Eft cwǣð sē apostol Iōhannes: "Gāð[6] tō ðǣre sǣ strande, and feċċað mē papol-stānas." Hī dydon swā; and Iōhannes þā on Godes mæġen-ðrymme hī ġe-bletsode, and hī wurdon ġe-hwyrfede tō dēor-wurþum ġymmum.

VOCABULARY FOR EXERCISE 4.4

æl-mihtigum (adjective) = ALMIGHTY [§6.1]

ǣnigne (adjective) = ANY [§6.1]

ānra (adjective) = ONE [§6.1]

apostol (m) = APOSTLE [§2.7]

bana (weak m) = murderer, slayer [§3.3]

be-bīode (verb form not yet covered) = "command" [§8.5]

be-fæstan (weak verb I) = to apply [§3.11]

be-gān (irregular verb) = to begin, practice (note that *be-gā* can be both subjunctive *and* imperative singular) [§4.5.3, variation of *gān* "to GO"]

bēo = see *bēon*

bēon (irregular verb) = to BE [§4.5.1]

biþ = see *bēon* (note that the verb probably indicates the future tense here)

(ġe)bletsian (weak verb II) = to BLESS [§3.12]

ċempa (weak m) = soldier [§3.3]

ċeorl (m) = freeman (of the lowest class), layman, peasant [ModE *CHURL*, §2.7]

cræft (m) = CRAFT [2.7]

cwǣdon (verb form not yet covered) = "said" (past pl) [§9.1]

cwæþ (verb form not yet covered) = "said" (past sing) [§9.1]

demm (m) = misfortune, loss [§2.7]

deor-wurðum (adjective) = precious [§6.1]

dōn (irregular verb) = to DO [§4.5.3]

dydon = see *dōn*

eallum (adjective) = ALL [§6.1]

eart = see *wesan*

eft (adverb) = again [§6.9]

feċċan (weak verb II) = to FETCH [§3.12]

folc (n) = people, FOLK [§2.9]

folgian (weak verb II) = to FOLLOW [§3.12]

for-lǣtt (verb form not yet covered) = "abandons" (present sing) [§9.3]

for-lǣten (verb form not yet covered) = "abandoned, banished" (past participle) [§9.3]

for-þǣm (conjunction) = because [§5.1.1]; (adverb) therefore [§6.9]

for-þon (adverb) = therefore [§6.9]

fram (prep + dat) = by, FROM [§2.11.4.c, §6.15]

gān (irregular verb) = to GO [§4.5.3]

ġeornlīċe (adverb) = diligently, EARNESTLY [§6.9]

ġif (conjunction) = IF [§5.1.1]

god (m) = GOD [§2.7]

ġym(m) (m) = GEM stone [§2.7]

habban (weak verb III) = to HAVE [§4.1]

hī, hīe (pronoun) = they, them [§7.1]

hiera (pronoun) = their [§7.1]

him (pronoun) = HIM or them [§7.1]

hine (pronoun, referring to *wīsdōm*) = "him, it" [§7.1]

his (pronoun) = HIS, its [§7.1]

hit (pronoun) = IT [§7.1]

hlāford (m) = LORD [§2.7]

(ġe)hwelċ (pronoun) = each [§7.8]

(ġe)hwyrfan (weak verb I) = to change, transform [§3.11]

iċ (pronoun) = I [§7.1]

Iōhannes (m) = John (note that the *-es* ending is NOT a genitive singular but part of the name)

(ġe)lǣran (weak verb I) = to advise, teach, give (advice) [§3.11]

lǣwodum (adjective) = unlearned [see ModE *lewd*, §6.1]

lārēow (m) = teacher [§2.7]

lēofra (adjective, comparative) = dearer, more treasured [§6.6]

(ġe)līefan (weak verb I) = to beLIEVE [§3.11]

mǣġ (m) = kinsman [§2.7]

mæġe = see *magan*

mæġen-ðrym(m) (m) = grandeur, majesty [§10.13]

mæss-prēost (m) = PRIEST [§2.7]

magan (preterite-present verb) = to be able, can [§4.4]

man (pronoun) = one, a person [§7.8]

mē (pronoun) = ME [§7.1]

miċel (adjective) = great [§6.2.1]

munuc (m) = MONK [§2.7]

næfre (adverb) = NEVER [§6.9]

næniġ (pronoun) = no, not ANY [§7.8]

nære (irregular verb *ne*+ *wesan*) = [§4.5.3..b]

noldon = see *nyllan*

nū (adverb) = NOW [§6.9]

nyle = see *nyllan*

nyllan (irregular verb *ne*+*willan*) = WILL not, not to want, wish, desire [§4.5.3]

on (preposition) = in (+ dat or acc)

on-stāl (m) = supply [§2.7]

papol-stān (m) = PEBBLE-STONE [§2.7]

prēost (m) = PRIEST [§2.7]

rēd (m) = advice [§2.7]

sǣ (m or f; here, f) = SEA [§10.11.1]

scand (f) = shame, disgrace, SCANDal [§2.8]

sceal = see *sculan*

sculan (pret-pres verb) = must, ought [§4.4]

sē (definite article functioning as pronoun) = he [§2.5, §7.1]

sē þe (pronoun phrase) = "he who"

se(a)llan (weak verb I) = to give [related to ModE *SELL*, §3.11]

(ġe)settan (weak verb I) = to establish, place; *ġe-sette* = past participle (see §3.11.1) [§3.11]

sīe = "be" (present, subjunctive singular form of *bēon*)

sindon = "are," see *bēon*

strand (m) = shore [§2.7]

swā . . . swā (conjunction) = whether . . . or [§5.1.1]

swā (conjunction) = as [§5.1.1]; (adverb) thus, so [§6.9]

swā hwelċ swā (pronoun phrase) = whatsoever [§7.8]

tō (prep + dat) = as, TO, into [§2.11.4.c]

þā (adverb) = then [§6.9]

ðǣr ðǣr (adv + conj phrase) = THERE where [§6.9]

ðǣre (def art) = the [§2.5]

þæt (conjunction) = THAT [§5.1.1]

þæt þæt (pronoun phrase) = "THAT which" [§7.5]

þætte (conjunction) = THAT [§5.1.1]

þanc (m) = THANKs [§2.7]

þe (pronoun) = which, who, that [§7.5]

þē (pronoun) = you, THOU [§7.1]

þīnne (adjective) = your, THINE [§7.1]

þisne (adjective) = THIS [§7.7]

þonne (conjunction) = THAN [§5.1.1]

þū (pronoun) = you, THOU [§7.1]

wē (pronoun) = WE [§7.1]

wesan (irregular verb) = to be [§4.5.1]

willan (irregular verb) = to wish, desire, will [§4.5.3]

wīs-dōm (m) = WISDOM [§2.7]

wurdon (verb form not yet covered) = "were" (past plural) [§8.6]

wyrhta (weak m) = worker [§3.3]

[6] *is hāten* = "is called"

[7] *on þēm* = "in which"

[8] Translate *þā þe* as "those which.

[9] *reades hēowes*: see §2.11.3.b

[10] Here *hȳ* "they" must be the subject, though earlier in this sentence (*hī*) it is the object "them."

[11] *þær* = in that place, not *there* as in the phrase *there* are problems.

[12] *þonne . . . þonne*: when . . . then

[13] Translate *þæt* as "those."

Reading IV: WONDERS OF THE EAST

Wonders of the East, *a predecessor to travel narratives like* Mandeville's Travels, The Travels of Marco Polo, *Richard Hakluyt's* The Principal Navigations, Voyages, Traffiques and Discoveries of the English Nation, *and* Gulliver's Travels *reports on strange human beings and creatures to be found in the territory surrounding the Holy Land. Included in the* Beowulf *manuscript (London, British Library, Cotton Vitellius A.xv.),* Wonders *also appears (with over thirty illustrations as well as a parallel Latin text) in London, British Library Cotton Tiberius B.v. The Latin author of* Wonders *seems to have known* Alexander's Letter to Aristotle, *a putative letter from Alexander the Great to his old teacher on the wonders he encountered in India. This text also appears, translated into Old English, in the* Beowulf *manuscript. Other sources probably include the works of Pliny, Herodotus, and others. As an early example of Westerners conceiving Easterners, this text documents the birth of the exotic as a topos for describing the East.*

Sum stōw . . . is hāten[6] Lentibelsinēa, on þēm[7] bēoð henna ā-cenned, onliċe þā þe[8] mid ūs bēoð, rēades hēowes.[9] Ġif hī hwylċ man niman wile oþþe hyra ō æt-hrīneð, þonne for-bærnað hȳ[10] sōna eal his līċ. Þæt[13] syndon un-ġefræġelicu lib-lāc! Ēac þonne þær[11] bēoð wild-dēor ā-cenned. Þā dēor, þonne[12] hȳ mannes stefne ġe-hyrað, þonne flēoð hȳ feorr. Þā dēor habbað eahta fēt ond wæl-ċyrian ēagan ond twā hēafdu. Ġif him hwylċ mon

Fiery Hens and Eight-Footed Beasts:
An illuminated page from *The Wonders of the East* as preserved in the Nowell Codex (London, British Library, Cotton Vitellius A.xv., fol. 99r), which also contains the unique text of *Beowulf.* Use "A Crash Course in Anglo-Saxon Paleography" (pp. 4-6) to follow the edited texts in the reading.

on-fōn wille, þonne hīera līc-homan hȳ on-ǣlað. Þæt syndon þā un-ġefrǣġelīcu dēor! [14]

Ēac swylċe þǣr bēoð cende healf-hundingas. Þā syndon[14] hātene conopenas.[15] Hȳ habbað horses mana ond eofores tūxas ond hunda hēafdu, ond heora oroð bið swylċe fȳres lēġ.

[14] See §2.5.1.

[15] See the Greek word *Cyno-cephali* "dog headed."

VOCABULARY FOR READING WONDERS OF THE EAST

IMPORTANT NOTE: *In the glossaries that follow (as well as the main glossary in the back of this book) the ġe- prefix is ignored in the alphabetizing of entries. This allows related forms (like* hīeran *and* ġe-hīeran) *to appear together. Also note that words beginning with æ appear under the letter a (after* ad *and before* af), *while words beginning with ð or þ have their own entry after the t's. Glossary tip: y and i(e) are virtually interchangeable in late Old English orthography. Knowing this can save minutes of valuable time.*

ā-cennan (weak verb I) = to beget, bring forth, give birth to; be brought forth, born; be native to a place [§3.11]

æt-hrīneð (verb form not yet covered) = "touch" (with gen, dat or acc object) [§8.4]

bēon (irregular verb, *bēon*) = to BE (*bēoð* = are, *sindon* = are) [§4.5.1]

bēoð = see *bēon*

cennan (weak verb I) = to bear, produce; be born; be native to a place [§3.11]

conophenas = probably a muddled version of *coeno-cephalus* [Greek: "dog" + "head"]

dēor (n) = animal, beast [Ger. *Tier*; §2.9]

ēac (adverb) = also, likewise; Ger. *auch*, ME *eke* [§6.9]

eage (weak n) = EYE [§3.5]

eal (adjective) = ALL [§6.1]

eahta (number indeclinable) = EIGHT, *indeclinable* means NO ENDINGS! The word has an unalterable form.

eofor (m) = wild boar; Ger. *Eber* [§2.7]

flēoð (verb form not yet covered) = "flee" (present plural) [§8.5]

feorr (adverb) = FAR [§6.9]

for-bærnan (weak verb I) = to BURN up [§3.11]

fōt (m) = FOOT (dat sing and nom./acc pl) = *fēt* [§10.4.2]

fȳr (n) = FIRE [§2.9]

ġif (conjunction) = IF [§5.1.1]

habban (weak verb III) = to HAVE [§4.1]

haten (verb form not yet covered) = "called, named" [§9.3]

hēafod (n) = HEAD [§2.9]

healf-hunding (m) = HALF-HOUND or *cynocephalus*, creature with the head of a dog [§2.7]

henn (f) = HEN, chicken [§2.8]

hēow (n) = HUE, color [§2.9]

hī, hȳ (pronoun) = they or them [§2.5.2, §7.1]

hiera (pronoun) = their [§2.5.3, §7.1]

(ġe)hīeran (weak verb I) = to HEAR [§3.11]

hors (n) = HORSE [§2.9]

him (pronoun) = HIM [§2.5.3, §7.1]

hund (m) = HOUND, dog [§2.7]

hwilċ (adjective) = any [§6.2.1]

hȳ = see *hī*

lēġ, līġ (m or n) = flame [§10.11.1]

lib-lāc (n) = witchcraft, magic spell, occult art; see OE *lybb* "poison, charm, drug" and *lāc* "sacrifice" [§2.9]

līċ (n) = body [§2.6.3]

līċ-hama, -homa (weak m) = body, lit., "body-HOME" [§3.3]

mān (f) = MANE [§2.8]

man(n), mon (m) = MAN [§10.4.2]

mid (prep + dat) = with, among [§6.15]

niman (verb form not yet covered) = to take, capture [§8.7]

ō, ā (adverb) = at all [§6.9]

on-ǣlan (weak verb I) = to ignite, set on fire, burn; see modern *anneal* "to temper" and *Hamlet's* "unannealed" [§3.11]

on-fōn (verb form not yet covered) = "to start something, meddle with" [§9.3]

on-līċ (adjective) = ALIKE, similar to [§6.2.2]

oroð (n) = breath [§2.9]

oððe (conj) = or [§5.1.1]

rēades (adjective) = RED (gen sing) [§6.2]

sindon = see *bēon*

sōna (adverb) = immediately, at once [§6.9]

stefn (f) = voice; related to Ger. *Stimme* "voice" [§2.8]

stōw (f) = place, locality; see place names like *Padstow* and *Felixstowe* [§2.8]

sum (adjective) = a certain, SOME [§6.2.1]

swilċe (adverb) = likewise, similarly;
(conjunction) like, just as; as if [§6.9]

syndon = see *bēon*

tūx (m) = grinder, TUSK [§2.7]

twā (numberber, indeclinable) = TWO

þǣr (adverb) = THERE; (conjunction)
where [§6.9]

þæt (pronoun) = THAT, translate here as
"those" [§7.7]

þonne (adverb) = THEN [§6.9];
(conjunction) when [§5.1.1]

un-ġefrǣġelīċ (adjective) = unheard of,
strange [§6.2.2]

wæl-ċyrie (weak f) = witch, sorceress,
VALKYRIE, lit. "chooser of the slain"
[§3.4]

wild-dēor (n) = WILD animal, Ger.
Tier "animal"; *dēor* has narrowed
to identify one particular animal, a
DEER [§2.9]

willan (irregular verb, *willan*) = to wish,
desire, want; will; *willan* requires
a verb in the infinitive form -*(a)n*,
without the modern *to*, which you
must supply [§4.5.3]

Lessons Learned

Before leaving this chapter you should have . . .
- memorized the forms of *habban* (§4.1.1).
- understood the basic concepts behind the preterite-present verbs (§4.3).
- memorized the forms of *magan* and *sculan* (§4.3.3.1).
- memorized the irregular verb *bēon* (§4.5.1) and familiarized yourself with *dōn* and *gān*.

FIVe

Learning How
to Translate

It may seem a bit odd that we're giving you translation tips at this stage since you've been translating sentences happily for the last several chapters. Up to now, though, you've been taking on single sentences that have been chosen and edited for simplicity and illustrative power. In the following chapters, you will tackle stretches of continuous, relatively unmodified prose and poetry.

In essence, the following tutorial aims to show you how to use the paradigms you've been so busily learning. Even if you have had extensive experience reading other languages, the following section should provide some useful review. Though you may not use the techniques outlined below for every sentence, you should plan to fall back on them when you encounter a particularly difficult sentence.

It may seem logical to start translating by looking up the first word in the sentence and working your way sequentially through every word. In fact, especially for beginners, this approach will make your life more difficult than it need be. If you consistently follow the translation steps in the order they're presented here, you should be able to translate even difficult sentences more quickly. The technique works by isolating the backbone elements of a sentence—the clause, then the verb, the subject, and finally other elements of each clause:

Step 1:   Locate clauses.
Step 2:   Identify the verb.
Step 3:   Identify the subject.
Step 4:   Fill in the other elements.

5.1   Step 1: Locating Clauses

Since a sentence can have several clauses, each with its own subjects, verbs, objects, etc., it's important to locate the boundaries between clauses within a sentence so that you can match the right verb with the right subject. *This is crucial for accurate translating.*

Let's start with a few key definitions. It's very important to understand the difference between clauses and phrases. Simply put, a *clause* contains at least a subject and verb, while a *phrase* is a group of related words that function together generally as a single part of speech.

Clauses

I laugh.	(Subject + simple verb)
She reads the book.	(Subject + simple verb + direct object)

Phrases

in the first place	(prepositional phrase: preposition + object)
bright and beautiful	(adjectival phrase: adj + adj)
learning grammatical concepts	(verbal phrase: present participle + object)
exhausted by the ordeal	(verbal phrase: past participle + prepositional phrase)
a book having fallen from the table	(absolute phrase: subject [book] modified by a participial phrase [having fallen] + prepositional phrase)

For our purposes, there are two types of clauses: dependent and independent. Every true sentence requires at least one independent clause (i.e., it must have a subject and verb at the very least and express a complete thought). A dependent clause has at least a subject and a verb, but it cannot stand by itself as a sentence.

Dependent clauses are usually easy to spot—they are often preceded by a subordinating conjunction like *that, if, when, while, until, because, after, before, who, which,* and so on, and have a recognizable subject and verb (at least). Subordinating conjunctions transform independent clauses into dependent ones. (Conjunctions, as their name implies, serve to connect clauses together.)

The king distributes treasure.   independent

***if** the king distributes treasure . . .*   dependent
***until** the king distributes treasure . . .*
***that** the king distributes treasure . . .*
***when** the king distributes treasure . . .*

Though there are other kinds of dependent clauses, we will have more to say about them later.

When you prepare to translate a sentence, you should first locate clauses and their boundaries, perhaps by underlining dependent clauses and putting a box around the main clause or by making a vertical stroke at the clause boundaries—whatever technique works best for you. Keep in mind that dependent clauses can sometimes interrupt main clauses. Consider the following examples, again in Modern English, where the main clause is in a box and the dependent clauses are underlined (with the subordinating conjunctions shaded):

1) While he sits on the throne, the king should distribute treasure.
2) The king should distribute treasure as long as he sits on the throne.
3) The king, while he sits on the throne, should distribute treasure.
4) I believe that the king who sits on the throne should distribute treasure.
5) If he is good, the king who sits on the throne should distribute treasure.

Since independent clauses can be interrupted by dependent ones, it is important to be able to find all the elements (however scattered) of the main clause. Examples 3-5 above have interrupted main clauses, and in 4, a dependent clause is interrupted by yet another dependent clause.

After you've located these boundaries, translate the sentence clause by clause. It's usually a good idea to start with the main (i.e., independent) clause of the sentence and fill in the dependent clauses afterwards.

SUBORDINATION

The following list contains some of the main subordinating conjunctions to look for. Note that some of them are "correlative" conjunctions; that is, they consist of two parts, often separated by several words. Such correlatives are printed below with ellipsis marks (. . .). One of the trickiest things about locating subordinating conjunctions is that a number of them also can function as simple adverbs or prepositions—confusing doppelgangers listed in parentheses in the list below.

Finally, it is useful to recognize that dependent clauses function much like single parts of speech. In general, placing a subordinating conjunction in front of an independent clause can change it into the equivalent of a noun (what?), adjective (which? what kind of?), or adverb (how? when? where? why?). Let's take a subordinating conjunction common in Modern English as well as OE as an example: *that*. This conjunction usually turns the entire clause into the equivalent of a noun. Take the independent clause "it is raining": adding a *that* to the beginning of the clause transforms it into a subordinate structure that functions exactly like a noun, capable of functioning as a subject (That it is raining is undeniable) or object (I do not believe that it is raining).

- *ǣr, ǣr ðon (ðe)* "before" (easy to confuse with the identical adverb "before, previously" and preposition "before")

  Hīe ǣrest tō londe cōmon, ǣr sīo fierd ġe-samnod wǣre. (adverb clause)
  (They first came to land, before the army was gathered.)

  Ǣr ðon ðe sunna on setl ēode, hit wæs cūð and mǣre. (adverb clause)
  (Before the sun went to his seat [i.e., before the sun set], it was widely known and famous.)

- *būtan* "unless, provided that" (easy to confuse with the identical preposition meaning "except")

Ðū scealt cwylmed weorðan, | būtan þū mē sweotollīċe sōð ġe-cȳðe. (adverb clause)
(You will be killed unless you reveal the truth plainly to me.)

- *for þām (þe), for-þon (þe)* "because, for the reason that" (also an adverb, "therefore")

Ðēre burge weard ānne mānliċan ġield of golde ā-rērde, | for þām þe glēaw
ne wæs. (adverb clause)
(The guardian of the city raised up a wicked idol of gold because he was not wise.)

- *ġif* "if"

Hȳ woldon Godwines fierde ġe-sēcan, | ġif sē cyning þæt wolde. (adverb clause)
(They wanted to seek out Godwine's army, if the king wanted that.)

- *hū* "how" (easy to confuse with the interrogative adverb form *hū* "how?")

Þæt wæs wīde cūð | hū hē his dāgas ġe-endode. (noun clause)
(It was widely known how he ended his days.)

Fyrd eall ġe-seah | hū þǣr hlīfedon hāliġe seġlas. (noun clause)
(The whole army saw how the holy pillars of cloud [lit., sails] towered there.)

- *hweðer* "whether"

Sē lǣċe cūðe tō-cnāwan bē his ǣdrena hrepunge, | hweðer hē hrāðe swulte. (noun clause)
(The physician knew how to recognize by touching his veins whether he died quickly.)

- *hwī* "why" (easy to confuse with the interrogative form *hwī* "why?")

  Đā ōþre æt-ēowdon *hwī hīe ðǣr bēon ne mihton.* (noun clause)
  (The others showed why they could not be there.)

- *oð ðæt, oð-ðæt* "until" (easy to confuse with the conjunction *oððe* "or" or the preposition *oð* "until".)

  Hē þǣr wunode *oþ þæt hine ān swān of-stang æt Pryfetes flōdan.* (adverb clause)
  (He lived there until a swineherd stuck him to death at Pryfet's channel.)

- *siððan* "since, as soon as, after" (easy to confuse with the identical adverb meaning "afterwards, then, later")

  Hīe sceoldon helle-þwang habban *siððan hīe ġe-bod Godes for-brocen hæfdon.*
      (adverb clause)
  (They must have the hell-whip [i.e., be damned] after they had broken God's commandment.)

- *swā* "as, as if" *swā swā* "just as, as" *swā . . . swā* "as . . . as" (easy to confuse with the adverb *swā* "thus, so")

  Hī hine þā æt-bǣron tō brimes faroðe, swǣse ġe-sīþas, *swā hē selfa bæd.* (adverb clause)
  (They carried him then to the flood's shore, the dear companions, as he himself [had] ordered.)

Hū sēo þrāg ġe-wāt, ġe-nāp under nīht-helm, *swā hēo nā wǣre!*
(How the time passed, darkened under the covering of night, as [if]
it never were!)

Ne eart þū nā eallunga tō nāhte ġe-dōn *swā swā þū wēnst.* (adverb clause)
(You are not at all brought to nothing [i.e., ruined] as you think [you are].)

Swā *moniġe bēoþ men ofer eorþan,* *swā bēoþ mōd-ġeþoncas.* (adverb clause)
([There] are as many men over the earth, as [there] are thoughts.)

- *þā* "when, since," *þā . . . þā* "when . . . then," *þā þā* "then when" (easy to
  confuse with the adverb *þā* "then" or the definite article *þā*)

Wintra hæfde hē fīf and hund-niġontiġ, *þā hē forð ġe-wāt.* (adverb clause)
(Of winters he had five and ninety [i.e., he was 95 years old], when he
passed away.)

Þā he ġe-fōr, *þā fēng Ċeol tō þām rīċe.* (adverb clause)
(When he departed, then Ceol seized control of the kingdom.)

God þā ġe-swefode þone Adam, *and þā þā hē slēp* *ðā ġe-nam hē ān rib of*
his sīdan. (adverb clause)
(God then put Adam to sleep and then when he slept then he took one
rib from his side.)

Note: This sentence has two main clauses joined by an *and*. Adam is referred to as
"the Adam."

- *þǣr* "where" (easy to confuse with the adverb *þǣr* "there")

  > *Ðis wæs þus cūð tō þām ōþerum scipum þǣr sē cyning wæs.* (noun clause)
  > (It was thus known to the other ships where the king was.)

- *þæt* "that" (sometimes with the meaning "so that") (noun clause)
  > *Þā cwǣdon hīe þæt him nǣniġ mǣġ lēofra nǣre þonne hiera hlāford.*
  > (Then they said that to them no kinsman was dearer than their lord.)

  > *Hīe nāmon mid him þæt hīe hæfdon tō seofon nīhtum mēte.* (adverb clause)
  > (They took [supplies] with them so that they had food for seven nights.)

- *þēah* "though, although, even though," *þēah þe* "though, although" (easy to confuse with the adverb *þēah* "nevertheless")

  > *Þāra Dēniscra wearð mā of-sleġen, þēah hī wæl-stōwe ġe-weald āhton.* (adverb clause)
  > (More of the Danes were slain, even though they had control of the battlefield.)

  > *Þēah þe ġē hine sārum for-sēċen, ne mōton ġē mīne sāwle grētan.* (adverb clause)
  > (Although you may afflict him [i.e., my body] with wounds, you cannot touch my soul.)

RELATIVE CLAUSES. Though a relative clause (beginning with *who, which,* or *that*) isn't headed by a subordinating conjunction as such, it is a dependent clause nevertheless, and the relative pronoun *who, which,* or *that* acts very much like a subordinating conjunction. You will learn much more about such *who* and *which* clauses later on (§7.5), but for now, an example or two should suffice to show the similarities.

Is þēs stede un-ġelīċ swīðe þām ōðrum hām *þe wē ǣr cūðon.* (adjective clause)
(This place is very unlike the other home that we knew before.)

Eart þū sē Bēowulf, *sē þe wið Brecan wunne?* (adjective clause)
(Are you that Beowulf, he who fought against Breca?)

Other subordinating conjunctions: *nymðe* "unless," *þenden* "as long as," *þȳ lǣste* "lest, for fear that," *after, æfter þon* "after," etc. As we have been warning you throughout this section, these conjunctions also have adverbs and prepositions almost identical in form.

A Tip:

It is sometimes difficult to tell a subordinating conjunction from its identical-looking adverbial or prepositional form. One tell-tale sign of a conjunction is that it must come at the beginning of a clause, so if a *þā* occurs several words into a clause (after or between the subject, verb, etc.), it is most likely an adverb "then." If a word like *æfter* (both a preposition and a subordinating conjunction) begins a clause, you should check to see if there is an object to the preposition (*after **the battle***). If anything other than a dative or accusative noun or pronoun follows, the likelihood is that the form is a subordinating conjunction (*after she won*).

A Note on Punctuation: You can often use *punctuation* as an aid for locating clauses in a sentence. For example, a semicolon (;) indicates that there must be at least one independent clause on each side, both before and after the semicolon. Dependent clauses are often set off by commas in some way, while a comma and *and* or *but* often indicate the beginning of a new independent clause.

5.1.2   A PRACTICE RUN

To practice the concepts of this lesson, let's analyze the following excerpts from *Beowulf.* We will return to these sentences at the end of each step, arriving at a complete translation by the end of this chapter. At this stage, though you may get some sense of what the sentence is about, the main goal should be to focus on structure—find the clauses and their boundaries.

> *Fīfel-cynnes eard won-sǣliġ wer weardode hwīle, siþðan him scyppend for-scrīfen hæfde in Cāines cynne.*

In this sentence, at first glance, it seems that the clause following the comma must be a *dependent* one (since it begins with *siþðan* "since, after," a subordinating conjunction). The clause before the comma is a good candidate for the main clause (it has a verb *weardode* and several candidates for subject, but no subordinating conjunction).

> *Hrāðe hēo æþelinga ānne hæfde fæste be-fangen, þā hēo tō fenne gāng.*

In this example, the clause after the comma again seems to be possibly subordinate (because of the conjunction *þā* "when"), while the clause before the comma seems to have a verb *hæfde* and a pronoun which might be the subject, *hēo* "she").

Exercise 5.1: LOCATING CLAUSES

Instructions. *In the following sentences, put a box around what you think is the main clause (even if broken up) and underline dependent clauses, shading any subordinating conjunctions. Consult the Vocabulary for Exercises, page 157, in identifying the words and their parts of speech. At this stage, don't concern yourself with translating the sentences: instead, focus on their structure.*

1. Hrāðe hēo æþelinga ānne hæfde fæste be-fangen, þā hēo tō fenne gāng.

2. Cum nū mid ūs, for-þon þe þū eart ūre wealdend.

3. Brūc, þenden þū mōte, maniġra mēda.

4. Hī ġe-lȳfdon þæt hē mihte miċċlum him fultumian on þām ġe-feohte, for þām
   þe hē ġe-feoht lufode.

5. And Harold cyning ġe-gædrode miċelne scip-here and ēac land-here, for þām
   þe him wæs ġe-cȳðd þæt Wyllelm bastard wolde hider and ðis land ġe-winnan.

6. Ðā iċ þā þis lēoð ġeomriende ā-sungen hæfde, þā cōm þær in tō mē
   heofen-cund wīsdōm.

5.2 Step 2: Finding the Complete Verb

It's a good idea to find the verb first rather than trying to locate the subject; the verb
often gives information about the number of the subject (singular or plural) and also
provides semantic information which might be useful in locating a likely candidate for the
subject (for example, if the verb is *thinks*, then the subject will probably be a singular noun
describing a sentient being). Once you've located clause boundaries and have chosen a
clause to translate, start looking for that clause's verb. In many instances, finding the verb
should be fairly easy: look for a verb with personal and tense endings (-*eð*, -*að*, -*iað*, –*ede*,
-*edon*, etc.). Every main verb must have such "finite" endings; verb forms like participles
(*ġe-dōn* or *gangende*) or infinitives (*dōn* and *gān*) have no finite markers (that is, they carry
no indication of person, number, and tense) and thus can't act alone as a complete verb.

Word order is also helpful in locating the verb. In independent clauses, the verb
usually prefers *the second position*.

*Sēo **gangeð** in þā ċiriċan.*
(She **goes** into the church.)

The verb often gravitates to the second position even when the first word of the clause is not the subject but (let's say) an adverb.

*Þonne **gangeð** sēo in þā ċiriċan.*
(Then she goes into the church.)

Though S-V order is also possible.

*Þonne sēo **gangeð** in þā ċirican.*

If you can find a finite verb and can determine that it has only one part, then you should proceed to Step 3, finding the subject. Make sure, however, that you've located the full verb (the main or finite verb and all its dependent verbs). The following sections will show you what to look for.

Verbs with a Complex   5.2.1

Somewhat trickier are verbs that consist of more than one part (complex verb phrases). Consider the following examples from Modern English:

I *analyzed* the sentence.	verb + past tense marker
I *want to analyze* the sentence.	modal + infinitive
I *have analyzed* the sentence.	have + past participle
I *had been analyzing* the sentence.	have + past participle + present participle
I *was analyzed* by a psychiatrist.	to be + past participle

In all but the first example the verb actually consists of several words. In an Old English sentence, you can't count on the fact that the various parts of the verb will be clustered nicely and neatly together. Fortunately, there are usually only two clear signals that you should look for further parts of the verb: when the finite verb is 1) a *have* or *be* verb (which may be helping or dummy verbs that require a participle of some kind to complete them) or 2) a helping verb like *will, may, might,* or *can* (which in OE usually require an infinitive to complete them).

HAVING AND BEING. In OE, as in Modern English, *to be* (*bēon*) and *to have* (*habban*) can function as regular verbs indicating state of being (*it **is** cold*) and possession (*I **have** a book*) respectively, *or* they can act as helping verbs which require a participle to complete them (*it **is finished**; I **have eaten***). When you see a form of *to be* (*wesan, bēon, biŏ, eom, eart, is, sindon, wæs, wæron,* etc.) or *to have* (*habbe, hæfŏ, hafaŏ, habbaŏ, hæfde, hæfdon,* etc.), your job is to decide whether these verbs are acting alone, expressing ownership and state of being, or whether they are part of a more complex verb structure.

In Old English, the most likely verbal form associated with a *to be* or a *to have* verb is a past participle (usually beginning with *ġe-* and ending with either an *–en,* for strong verbs, or an *–ed/-od,* for weak verbs). If you cannot find a participle, then it is likely that the verb in question is functioning as a main verb and not as a helper or auxiliary verb. In the following two examples, *be* and *have* function as the main verb:

*Hēr **is** fyr miċel.*
(Here is a great fire.)

*Þēos stōw **hafaŏ** nædran.*
(This place has serpents.)

When *have* functions as a helper verb with a participle, however, the result is a verb phrase in the "perfect" (i.e., it describes an action already complete and finished, rather than in progress).

*Hīe **habbað** mē tō hearran **ġe-corene**, rōfe rincas.*
(They, the renowned warriors, have chosen me as leader.)
(lit., They have me as leader chosen, the renowned warriors.)

*Ac hine sār **hafað** mid nyd-grīpe nearwe **be-fongen**.*
(But sorrow has seized him tightly with a coercive grip.)
(lit., But him sorrow has with coercive grip tightly seized.)

*Sē cyning ðæt on-funde, þæt him sē æðeling **ġe-swicen hæfde**.*
(The king discovered that the nobleman had deceived him.)
(lit., The king that discovered, that him the nobleman deceived had)

When *be* functions as a helper verb with a past participle, the result is usually a passive.

*Is mīn flet-werod, wīġ-hēap **ġe-wanod**.*
(My hall-troop, [my] war-band is diminished.)
(lit., Is my hall-troop, warband diminished.)

*Wæs þeah-hwæðere his martyrdōm **ġe-fremmed**.*
(His martyrdom was nevertheless accomplished.)
(lit., Was nevertheless his martyrdom accomplished.)

However, with verbs of motion, *be* functions like a *have* in Modern English to produce a perfect. Remember to translate *be* as the equivalent form of *have* in such constructions.

*Nū **is** sē dæġ **cumen**.*
(Now the day has come.)

Hē is ā-risen of dēaðe.
(He has risen from death.)

**TIMESAVER
5.2.1.1** Weorðan. The verb *weorðan* "to be, become" (a strong verb about which you'll learn more in Chapter Eight) can sometimes act exactly like a *to be* verb in that it takes a past participle.

Þā wearð sē mīhtiġa ġe-bolgen.
(Then the mighty [one] was/became enraged.)

HELPFUL VERBS. Knowing about one other class of helping verbs can make your reading of Old English quicker: verbs such as *can, will, shall, may, must, might,* etc. Traditional grammarians call them *modal auxiliaries*: "modal" because they indicate the *mood* in which the action of the verb takes place (whether in hope, doubt, desire, compulsion, etc.); "auxiliary" because they are helping verbs that can't stand on their own (see Lat. *auxilium* "help, aid"). In Old English, as in Modern English, such verbs must have an infinitive to complete them. The simple rule is that if you find one of these verbs, you should immediately start looking for the infinitive (ending in *-an*, in *-anne,* or more rarely in *-on*).

Hēo wolde hire mǣġ wrecan.
(She wanted to avenge her kinsman.)

Sē engel on-gan ofer-mōd wesan.
(The angel began to be proud.)

Iċ ā-wyrged sceal, þēoden, of ġe-syhðe þīnre hweorfan.
(I, accursed, must, lord, depart from your sight.)

Uton gān on þysne weald.
(Let us go into this wood.)

Notice that in the first three examples above, the infinitive is separated by one or several words from the helping verb. Like the participle, the infinitive may tend to gravitate towards the end of the clause, and that's a good place to start looking.

A list of common modal auxiliaries follows; for each the infinitive, present third person singular, present plural, and past singular forms are listed (§4.3, etc.).

willan, wille, willaþ, wolde "to wish, desire; shall, will"
nyllan, nylle, nyllaþ, nolde "not wish, not desire" (= *ne* "not" + *willan*)
****, *sceal, sculon, scolde* "ought to, must; shall"
magan, mæġ, magon, meahte/mihte "can, be able"
cunnan, cann, cunnon, cuðe "can, be able; know how (to do something)"
*****, *dear, durron, dorste* "to dare (to do something)"
uton/wuton (1 person pres pl only) "let us (do something)"

BEWARE! In general, it may be dangerous to translate these modals directly with their modern meanings. *Sceal*, for example, usually carries the meaning "must, have to," while *wille* usually means "want, wish" rather than indicating the future (*she will go*), and *mihte* does not indicate possibility (*she might go*) but instead usually means "can" (*Hēo mæġ gangan* "She is able to go"). So, be careful.

SOME SMALL EXCEPTIONS   5.2.2

- The infinitive that usually accompanies a modal auxiliary can sometimes be left out if it is a verb indicating motion (*go, rush, fall*, etc.).

*Hēo **wolde** ūt þanon.*
(She wanted [to go] out from there.)

This construction survives in Shakespearean language: "I'll away within these two hours."

- The "to be" verb can also sometimes be omitted, usually when the main verb is a modal auxiliary.

    Hæle sceal wīs-fæst ond ġe-metliċe, glēaw in ġe-hygdum.
    (A warrior must [be] wise and moderate, keen in thought.)

5.2.3   COMPOUNDING THE PROBLEM

Before moving on to some practice sentences, you should keep in mind that any sentence element may be "compounded" or doubled (see examples below), and since Old English poetry prizes artful repetition, such compound verbs, subjects, objects, and so on are a fact every reader of Old English needs to reckon with.

A scribe *reads* and *copies* books. (compound verb—finite verb doubled)
A scribe **must** *read* and *copy* books. (compound verb—infinitive doubled)
The scribe **has** *read* and *copied* the books. (compound verb—past participles)
A *king* and *queen* must protect their warriors. (compound subject)

In looking for the complete verb, be sure to scan through the rest of the sentence looking for doubled finite verbs, infinitives, or participles.

The following sentence contains a string of verbs (boldfaced and underlined), all of which have the same subject:

*Sē āglǣca . . . **ġe-fēng** hrāðe . . . slǣpendne rinc, **slāt** un-wearnum, **bāt** bān-locan, blōd ēdrum **dranc**, syn-snǣdum **swealh**.*

(The monster seized quickly a sleeping warrior, slit [him] suddenly, bit [his] body, drank blood from the veins, swallowed in huge chunks.)

A PRACTICE RUN   5.2.4

To practice locating the verb, let's analyze the following excerpts from *Beowulf* which you analyzed above for clause boundaries:

Fīfel-cynnes eard won-sǣliġ wer weardode hwīle, siþðan him scyppend for-scrifen hæfde in Cāines cynne.

Since there is an independent clause followed by a dependent clause, this sentence should contain *two* complete verbs. In the first clause, *weardode* "inhabited" (a clear past singular of a weak verb—§3.8) seems to be a finite verb standing on its own, while in the second clause *hæfde* "had" is the finite verb. Since *have* can be a helping verb in Old English, it's necessary to look for a past participle (ending in *-en, -od, -ed, -d*). In fact, *for-scrifen* appears to be such a past participle. The complete verb for the second clause, then, must be *hæfde for-scrifen* "had condemned."

Hrāðe hēo æþelinga ānne hæfde fæste be-fangen, þā hēo tō fenne gāng.

This sentence, similarly, has two clauses, and thus should have two complete verbs. In the first clause we again have a *hæfde* "had," and a quick check reveals a candidate for a past participle at the end of the clause: *be-fangen*. The complete verb, then, is *hæfde be-fangen* "had seized."

In the second clause, there is no obvious verb at first glance. The process of elimination is the best bet for finding it: *þā* is a subordinating conjunction and can't be the verb, and *hēo* "she" is a pronoun. The next word, *tō*, seems to be a preposition, and since prepositions *must* have objects, *fenne* would seem to be part of the prepositional phrase *tō fenne*. This leaves *gāng* as the only likely candidate. If you check the glossary, you'll find *gang* as a noun, though the fact that the form here has a long vowel and the noun doesn't should begin to confirm the suspicion that *gāng* is a verb. Since *gāng* doesn't have a typical finite ending (*-e, -eð, -aþ, -ede, -ode, -on,* etc.), the chances are that it's a singular past tense of a strong verb. As it turns out, *gāng* is the past tense singular of *gāngan* "to go," a strong verb, 7th class. The complete verb, then, after all this sleuthing, must be *gāng* "went."

5.2.5   TENSES

Old English uses tenses somewhat differently from Modern English, and to translate a verb accurately and fluently, you should know some of the main differences. For the most part, OE does not have as many complex verb patterns as Modern English does. For example, OE has no systematic way of signaling the future tense and uses the present with an implied future meaning. (Modern English, on the other hand, uses a form of *shall* or *will* + infinitive to signal the future: *she will go*.) Strangely, Modern English does not use the present tense to signal an action that is taking place in present time—it in fact uses the present progressive (*to be* + present participle): *She is going (at this moment)*. Modern English reserves the present tense mainly for actions that occur regularly: *She runs (every day)*. Potentially, then, the OE present tense has three possible translations into Modern English.

Old English	tense		Modern English	tense
hēo gāþ	present	=	she goes (everyday)	present
hēo gāþ	present	=	she is going (now)	present progressive
hēo gāþ	present	=	she will go	future
hēo ēode	past	=	she went	past

Old English	tense		Modern English	tense
hēo ēode	past	=	she was going	past progressive
hēo is ġe-gangen	present perfect	=	she has gone	present perfect
hēo wæs ġe-gangen	past perfect	=	she had gone	past perfect
No OE equivalent			she will have gone	future perfect
No OE equivalent			she will have been going	future perfect progressive

[1] According to Bruce Mitchell, the answer may well lead us into a "jungle of contradictory opinions" (*OE Syntax*, II, § 3734). For the larger issue, see §3724 ff. This text will follow a rather traditional method of analysis.

[2] See *OE Syntax*, II, §3743 ff.

PERCEPTION PROBLEM (accusative with infinitive constructions) 5.2.6

At the risk of overloading you, it may be good to explain an extended verb construction that you will meet with frequently in OE texts. Learning this construction now will save you much pain and wasted time later on.

With certain verbs of perception (*to see, to hear, to perceive, to discover*), of commanding and ordering (*to command, to bid, to order, to ask*), and of permitting (*to let, to allow, to permit*), OE often adds an infinitive construction that can be a bit difficult to decipher.

Modern English has a similar construction: *I ask him to write a letter*. In this sentence the subject of the sentence is *I*; the verb is *ask*. The grammatical problem is how to explain the following clause of words *him to write a letter*.[1] The phrase *him to write a letter* is an infinitive phrase that functions as the direct object of the verb *ask*. Within the infinitive phrase *him* (an accusative form) is the subject of the infinitive *to write*; *letter* is the direct object of the infinitive *to write* (see Appendix One: "A Basic Introduction to Traditional Grammar"). The accusative subject of an infinitive is a common structure in Latin. The influence of the Latin form on OE is a matter of some discussion.[2] But the simple fact is that in OE the subject of the infinitive takes the accusative case.

A similar Modern English construction: *I saw her write the letter*. In this sentence, the subject is *I*; the verb is *saw* (a verb of perception). In this case, the following group

[3] Another way of looking at the construction would be to say that the entire infinitive phrase is the direct object of the main verb *ġe-seah*.

of words is an infinitive phrase that omits the *to* which is the sign of the infinitive in Modern English. That omission is common when the infinitive phrase appears after verbs of perception. As in the earlier example, the infinitive phrase is the direct object of the verb *saw*. Within the infinitive phrase, *her* is the subject of the infinitive *(to) write*; and *letter* is the direct object of the infinitive *(to) write*.

In Old English the construction is similar. Consider the following example:

> *Iċ ġe-seah men gangan.*

Literally, this sentence would read "I saw men go," where *go* is an infinitive. Notice that *men* (an accusative plural) is the object of *ġe-seah* but the subject of the infinitive *gangan*.[3] Another idiomatic translation of the sentence might be "I saw men going," in which case the modern present participle "going" is used to render the OE infinitive *gangan*.

Since your goal in this step is to locate the entire verb phrase, it will be important for you to check for "accusative with infinitive" constructions. The difficulty is that the accusative and infinitive may be scattered throughout the clause. In the following examples, the main verb (in each case, a verb of perception) is underlined, while the accusative and infinitive appear with a gray background; in each instance we provide alternative ways of translating the infinitive.

> *Iċ ġe-hȳrde hine þīne dǣd and word lofian.*
> (I heard him praising your deed and word.)
>
> or
>
> (I heard him praise your deed and word.)

> *Hē þæt wīf ġe-seah on eorð-rīce stondan.*
> (He saw the woman standing on the earthly kingdom.)
>
> or
>
> (He saw the woman stand on the earthly kingdom.)

Hēo ġe-seah þā ā-wyrġedan gāstas beforan hyre standan.
(She saw the cursed spirits standing before her.)

or

(She saw the cursed spirits stand before her.)

ANOTHER WRINKLE   5.2.7

A very similar kind of "accusative with infinitive" construction also occurs with verbs of ordering or commanding, though these constructions can require a bit more care in translation. Typically they begin with some form of the verb *hātan* "to command, order." The accusative with infinitive construction comes next. Consider these straightforward examples:

Hē hēt mē his word weorðian and wel healdan, lǣstan his lāre.
(He commanded me to honor his word and to keep [it] well and to fulfill his teaching).

Hē hēt hīe tō þām sīðe ġyrwan.
(He commanded them to prepare for the journey.)

Another variation on the construction is even more complex, however. In some sentences, the accusative with infinitive construction contains a *passive* infinitive rather than the much more usual active infinitive. Both have identical forms. For example, the infinitive *swingan*, when active, means "to beat, to lash," while *swingan* as a passive infinitive means "to be beaten, to be lashed." It is the context that will allow you to decide whether to translate an infinitive as a passive one.

Hē hēt hīe þā swingan, sūsle þrēagan.
(He commanded her then *to be beaten*, *to be punished* with torture.)

Hēt ðā Hildeburh . . . hire selfre sunu sweoloðe be-fæstan, bān-fatu bærnan.
(Then Hildeburh commanded her own son *to be entrusted* to the flame,
[commanded] the bodies *to be burnt*.)

Exercise 5.2: TRANSLATING ACCUSATIVES WITH INFINITIVES

Instructions. *Translate the following sentences with the help of the vocabulary which follows this exercise. Each sentence contains an "accusative with infinitive" construction. Be sure to decide carefully whether to translate the infinitive as an active or passive one.*

1. Þā hēt hē mē on þysne sīð faran.

   Then he commanded me to go on this journey

2. Ðā hine sēo fǣmne hēt þēostra nēosan.

   Then the woman commanded him to seek out the darkness

3. Byrhtnōð hēt hīe þā hors for-lǣtan.

   Burt commanded them to abandon the horse.

4. Sē hǣðena þēoden hēt hīe hrāðe bærnan.

   The heathen prince commanded them to be quickly burned

5. Beowulf het þa up beran æþelinga ge-streon.

[handwritten: commanding to bear nobleman treasure]

[handwritten: Then Beowulf commanded the nobleman to carry up the treasure]

6. Hē hēt hīe on cwearterne be-clȳsan.

[handwritten: prison to enclose]

[handwritten: He commanded them be locked in prison]

VOCABULARY FOR EXERCISE 5.2

æþeling (m) = nobleman, retainer [§2.7]

bærnan (weak verb I) = to BURN, set on fire [§3.11]

be-clȳsan (weak verb I) = to enCLOSE, lock [§3.11]

Bēowulf (m) = proper name

beran (verb form not yet covered) = "to BEAR" or "to carry" [§8.7]

Byrhtnōð (m) = proper name

cweartern (n) = prison [§2.9]

fǣmne (weak f) = maiden, woman [§3.4]

faran (verb form not yet covered) = "to go" or "to travel" [§9.2]

for-lǣtan (verb form not yet covered) = "to abandon" or "leave behind" [§9.3]

hǣðen (adjective) = HEATHEN [§6.2.1]

hē (pronoun) = "HE" [§7.1]

hēt (verb form not yet covered, past 3 sing) = "commanded" [§9.3]

hīe (pronoun) = "they" (nom) or "them" (acc) [§7.1]

hine (pronoun) = "him" (acc 3 sing of *hē*) [§7.1]

hors (n) = HORSE [§2.9]

brāðe (adverb) = quickly [§6.9]

nēosan (weak verb I) = to seek out, go to (+ gen object) [§3.11]

on (preposition + dat) = in [§6.15]

sīð (m) = journey, expedition [§2.7]

(ġe)strēon (n) = treasure [§2.9]

þā (adverb) = then [§6.9]

þēoden (m) = prince, leader [§2.7]

þēostru (f) = darkness, gloom (often in pl) [§2.8]

þysne (adjective, m acc sing) = THIS [§7.7]

ūp (adverb) = UP [§6.9]

Summary

To summarize the steps for finding the complete verb:

1. If the finite verb consists of only one part, proceed to step 3.
2. If the finite verb is a *to have* or *to be* form (or, a form of *weorðan*) check the rest of the clause (particularly the end) for a past participle. If you can find no participle, then translate the *to be* or *to have* form as the main verb and proceed to step 3.
3. If the finite verb is a modal auxiliary, look for an infinitive. If you can't find an infinitive, you must probably supply a verb of motion or a *to be* verb.
4. If you can't find a complete verb, check to see . . .

- if the verb is the simple past tense of a strong verb. Past tense strong verbs in the singular have no endings and may look like nouns or other parts of speech.

Past Sing	Infinitive
bær	*beran* "to carry"
sōc	*sacan* "to quarrel"
hōf	*hebban* "to lift"
bæd	*biddan* "to ask; pray"
cnēow	*cnāwan* "to know"

- if the verb (either the finite form or the modal auxiliary) carries over from the previous clause to this one.
- if the verb is an implied but missing verb of motion or *to be* verb.

Exercise 5.3: FINDING THE COMPLETE VERB

Instructions. *For the following sentences, list all complete verbs (with translation) in the space provided. Consult the Vocabulary for Exercises, page 157, at the end of the chapter.*

1. Hrāðe hēo æþelinga ānne hæfde fæste be-fangen, þā hēo tō fenne gāng.

    haefde befangen "had seized"
    gang "went"

2. Cum nū mid us, forþon þe þū eart ūre wealdend.

    cum — "come!"
    eart — are

3. Brūc, þenden þū mōte, maniġra mēda.

    mote — are able to

4. Hī ġe-lȳfdon þæt hē mihte miċċlum him fultumian on þām ġe-feohte, for þām þe hē ġe-feoht lufode.

    belive   might greatly   help   in   fight
    he helped in the battle
    ge-lyfdon – believed
    mihte fultumian – might have helped
    lufode – helped

5. And Harold cyning ġe-gædrode miċelne scip-here and ēac land-here, for þām þe him wæs ġe-cȳðd þæt Wyllelm bastard wolde hider and ðis land ġe-winnan.

[handwritten annotations: ġe-gaerole – sarred / waer ġe-cȳðd – was made known / wolde ġe-winnan – wanted to conquer]

6. Þā iċ þā þis lēoð ġeomriende ā-sungen hæfde, þā cōm þǣr in tō mē heofen-cund wīs-dōm.

[handwritten annotations: haesde ġeomriende āsungen – had grieved and sung / cōm – came into me]

5.3 Step 3: Finding the Subject

Essentially, you'll be looking for a noun or a pronoun in the nominative case, one that matches the number (singular or plural) of the "finite" verb (the part of the verb inflected for tense, person, and number) you located in the last step. Remember that you can use the accompanying definite articles and adjective endings to help clarify the case of a noun.

If you can find no recognizable subject, then 1) the subject may be understood (carried over from the previous clause), or 2) the sentence may contain an "impersonal" construction (see §3.10.1.3, §11.2).

Remember that subjects can sometimes be carried over from a previous sentence or clause.

5.3.1 A PRACTICE RUN

Fīfel-cynnes eard won-sǣliġ wer weardode hwīle, siþðan him scyppend for-scrifen hæfde in Cāines cynne.

In the first clause (before the comma), we established in the previous step that the verb was *weardode* "inhabited." There are apparently two possible candidates for the subject: *eard* "home" or *wer* "man." If you check the main noun charts in Chapter Two, you'll see that both these forms could be nominative and both could be singular (demanded by the singular verb *weardode*). Logically, a person (*wer*) can inhabit a place, though it's more difficult to imagine a home inhabiting anything; thus, it's best to assume that *wer* is the subject of the first clause.

In the second clause, we found that the verb was *hæfde for-scrifen* "had cursed." Let's run through the clause word for word for the subject: *siþðan* is an adverb and can't be a subject, while *him* is a dative pronoun. Remember that we're looking for a singular nominative noun or pronoun. *Scyppend* is a noun that could be nominative, so let's set it aside. *Cāines* can't be the subject because it's in the genitive case while *cynne* is similarly eliminated because it's in the dative (see the noun charts). So, *scyppend* is the only likely candidate for the subject of *for-scrifen hæfde*.

Hrāðe hēo æþelinga ānne hæfde fæste be-fangen, þā hēo tō fenne gāng.

For the first clause, the verb is *hæfde be-fangen* "had seized" (a singular verb), so we are looking for a singular nominative noun or pronoun. *Hrāðe* is an adverb and can't be the subject, while *hēo* "she" is a possibility since it can be a feminine third person nominative pronoun (see §7.1 for a preview). On the other hand, *æþelinga* appears to be a genitive plural and *ānne* a masculine accusative singular form (see §6.2, again for a preview)—and thus both are disqualified. Finally, *fæste* is an adverb and cannot be the subject. *Hēo* "she" seems then to be the subject of the first clause.

In the second, *þā* is a conjunction while *tō fenne* is a prepositional phrase, and this leaves *hēo* once again as the only likely subject for the clause.

Exercise 5.4: FINDING THE SUBJECT

Instructions. *For the following sentences, list all subjects and their verbs under the sentences and provide a translation to the right. Consult the glossary at the end of the chapter.*

1. Hrāðe hēo æþelinga ānne hæfde fæste be-fangen, þā hēo tō fenne gāng.

   heo haefde befangen "she had seized" heo gang "she went"

2. Cum nū mid us, forþon þe þū eart ūre wealdend.

3. Brūc, þenden þū mōte, maniġra mēda.

4. Hī ġe-lȳfdon þæt hē mihte miċċlum him fultumian on þām ġe-feohte, for þām þe hē ġe-feoht lufode.

5. And Harold cyning ġe-gædrode miċelne scip-here and ēac land-here, for þām þe him wæs ġe-cȳðd þæt Wyllelm bastard wolde hider and ðis land ġe-winnan.

6. Þā iċ þā þis lēoð ġēomriende ā-sungen hæfde, þā cōm þær in tō mē heofen-cund wīsdōm.

Step 4: Sorting Out the Rest

After localizing the subject and verb, a number of elements could be left over.

FIND THE DIRECT OBJECTS

Let's start with objects. Depending on what kind of verb a clause has, a direct object could be present. Some verbs take direct objects, and others don't (while some may appear either with or without one). Traditional grammarians call verbs that take direct objects *transitive* and those that don't *intransitive*.

Transitive	**Intransitive**
The child kicks a ball.	The child often kicks.
The scholar reads a book.	The scholar reads in the library.
She runs a university.	She runs every day.
*****[4]	He laughs.

[4] No transitive form.

It is important to look for objects right away. To locate them, first try to determine whether the verb can take a direct object or not. If it can, you should scan the clause for any free-standing *accusative* nouns or pronouns. Direct objects almost always appear in the accusative, though as you learned in Chapter Two, some verbs require dative or genitive direct objects (§2.11.3.f and §2.11.4.d). The glossary entry should alert you if the verb takes another case other than the accusative for the direct object. For example:

wēnan (weak verb I) = to expect, look for (+ gen)

If the verb takes something other than the accusative, search for free-standing nouns or pronouns in the case indicated. Once you know the verb and subject, you can construct a question to help you locate any direct objects, or to decide whether or not the verb can be transitive.

Who or What does/do/did SUBJECT VERB (infinitive form)?

EXAMPLES:
(verb = *runs*, subject = *she*)
Who or what does she run?

(verb = *laughs*, subject = *he*)
*Who or what does he laugh?

*Note:Since this question makes no sense, *laugh* must be intransitive.

5.4.1.1   A PRACTICE RUN: THE SEARCH FOR OBJECTS

Fīfel-cynnes eard won-sǣliġ wer weardode hwīle, siþðan him scyppend for-scrifen hæfde in Cāines cynne.

For the first clause, we determined in previous steps that the verb is *weardode* "inhabited" and that the subject was *wer* "man." Converting this information into a question yields *whom or what does the man inhabit?* Scanning through the clause with the aid of the glossary tells us that *Fīfel-cynnes* "monster race's" is a genitive and since *weardian* is not marked + *gen*, it falls out as a possible direct object. The next word *eard* "home" is a possible accusative since it is a regular masculine noun (it could only be nominative or accusative—see §2.7). The glossary confirms that *won-sǣliġ* is an adjective, while *wer* and *weardode* are already eliminated since they are subject and verb. Only *hwīle* is left, and the glossary shows it to be an adverb meaning "at times."

Thus *eard* seems to be a good candidate for a direct object, especially since it answers the question *whom or what does the man inhabit?* "The man inhabited the home."

In the second clause, the verb is *for-scrifen hæfde* and the subject is *scyppend*, giving the question *whom or what did the creator condemn?* A quick check in the glossary reveals that *for-scrīfan* takes a dative object, and there are only two candidates: *him* (see §7.1 for a preview) and *cynne*. Since *cynne* is apparently the object of the preposition, *in*, *him* is the only remaining dative: "The creator had condemned him."

Hrāðe hēo æþelinga ānne hæfde fæste be-fangen, þā hēo tō fenne gāng.

In the first clause, we identified *hæfde be-fangen* "had seized" as the verb and *hēo* "she" as the subject. Converting this information into a question format yields *whom or what did she seize?* As before, *hrāðe*, an adverb, cannot be the object, while *æþelinga* is genitive. Only *ānne* "one" is accusative and thus must be the direct object: "She seized one."

After locating the direct object, the reader must translate unaccounted for dative and genitive forms.

THE DATIVE RULE   5.4.2

The Dative Rule is simple and utterly important. Any time you find a freestanding dative noun or pronoun, you must supply an appropriate preposition with your translation of the noun and pronoun (see §2.11.4.b). (Note: Since you haven't learned pronouns yet, all forms with their cases will be glossed in the vocabulary list.) Of course, you must first decide whether or not the dative form is actually freestanding or not. Here are the situations to eliminate, in which a dative noun or pronoun **cannot** be freestanding: when it is . . .

- a dative direct object required by certain verbs.
- an object of a preposition.

If neither of these can account for a dative form, you should apply the Dative Rule. Examine the following examples:

Hē næs ġe-hende **þām cyninge.**
(He was not near [to] the king.)

Hīe wǣron lēof **Gode.**
(They were dear [to] God.)

Wæs ġe-hwæþer **ōðrum** *lifiġende lāð.*
(Each, living, was [to] the other hateful.)
(lit., Was each to the other living hateful; i.e., Each wanted to see the other dead.)

Frēa wæs **eallum** *lēof, þēoden his* **þeġnum.**
(The lord was dear [to] all, the prince [was dear to] his thanes.)

Heo ne wiste hwæt **þām beornum** *sēlest tō dōnne wǣre.*
(She did not know what would be best [for] the warriors to do.)

Ful oft ġe-bēotedon, **bēore** *druncne, ofer ealu-wǣġe ōret-mecgas.*
(Very often champions boasted, drunk with beer, over the ale cup.)

Secgum *wearð, ylda* **bearnum,** *un-dyrne cūð,* **ġyddum** *ġeomore, þætte Grendel wan* **hwile** *wið Hrōþgar.*
(Therefore [to] men it became, [to] the sons of men, openly known, [by] songs sadly, that Grendel fought [for] a time against Hrothgar.)

THE GENITIVE RULE 5.4.3

Like the Dative Rule, the Genitive Rule applies to freestanding genitives. In almost every instance, a freestanding genitive must depend on another noun, pronoun, or adjective (see §6.1 ff.) and is usually translated with "of" (see §2.11.3.b). Since genitive direct objects or genitive objects of prepositions are rare, you will use the Genitive Rule to translate most genitives you encounter. Essentially, when you identify a freestanding genitive, you must *first* look for the word on which it depends (that word is usually a noun, pronoun or adjective). Translate this base word first and *then* the genitive, with an "of" between them. In the following examples, freestanding genitives appear in **<u>underlined boldface</u>** while the words on which they depend (the base forms) are highlighted in gray.

*Hē bið **man-sleġes** scyldiġ.*
(He is guilty of manslaughter.)

*Swā reordode, **rǣda** ġe-myndiġ, **manna** mildost.*
(Thus spoke, mindful of counsels, the mildest of men.)

***Þāra** ān hēt Iabal.*
(One of them was called Iabal.)

*Īdel stōd **hūsa** sēlest.*
(Empty stood the best of houses.)

*Ðā ferdon Peohtas in Breotone, and ongunnon eardiġan þā norð-dǣlas **þȳses ēa-londes**.*
(Then the Picts traveled into Britain, and began to occupy the northern regions of this island.)

*Adam hæfde niġen-hund **wintra** and XXX ēac.*
(Adam had nine hundred [of] winters and 30 also; i.e., Adam lived to be 930 years old.)

*Hēo wæs swīðe wlitiġ and **wēnliċes hīwes**.*
(She was very beautiful and of comely form.)

Exercise 5.5: APPLYING THE DATIVE AND GENITIVE RULES

Instructions. *Translate the following sentences, applying the Dative and Genitive rules carefully. For genitive constructions, put a box around the base form.*

1. Wurdon þām æðelinge eaforan ā-cende.

   _____

2. Ðām wīfe þā word wel līcodon.

   _____

3. Þæt bið driht-guman un-lifġendum sēlest.

   _____

4. Ġe-līċ wæs hē þām lēohtum steorrum.

   _____

[5] Be sure to look up this word in the glossary, even though it *looks* familiar.

[6] Translate *næs* "(there) was not."

5. Ne eom iċ dēofle ġe-līċ.

_____

6. [Grendel] Heorot eardode, sinc-fāge sel, sweartum nihtum.

_____

7. Moniġ . . . rǣd eahtedon hwæt swīð-ferhðum sēlest wǣre wið[5] fǣr-gryrum tō ġe-fremmanne.

_____

8. Næs[6] ðæs wyrmes þǣr an-sȳn ǣniġ.

_____

9. Hīe ne ahton þǣre spǣċe spēd.

_____

10. On þām sciellum bēoð oft ġe-mētte þā betstan mere-grotan ǣlċes hīwes.

_____

[7] A subjunctive: translate "will have."

11. Ne þearft þū nō wēnan þæt ðā wlitegan tungol ðæs þēow-dōmes ā-ðroten weorðen[7] ǣr dōmes dæġe.

_____

12. Swā bið scinna þēaw, dēofla wīse, þæt hī þurh dyrne meaht duguðe be-swīcað.

_____

Vocabulary for Exercise 5.5

ā-cennan (weak verb I) = to bring forth, give birth to, be born [§3.11]

ǣlċes (pronoun) = "of each" (m gen sing of the pronoun *ǣlċ* "each") [§7.8]

ǣniġ (adjective) = ANY [§6.1]

ǣr (conjunction) = before, ERE [§5.1.1]

æðeling (m) = nobleman [§2.7]

agan (preterite-present verb) = to own, possess, have [§4.3.1]

ahton = see *agan*

an-sīen (f) = presence, sign [§2.8]

ā-ðroten (verb form not yet covered) = "grown weary or tired" [§8.5]

bēon (irreg verb) = to BE [§4.5.1]

bēoð = see *bēon*

be-swīcað (verb form not yet covered) = "deceive, trick" (pl) [§8.4]

betstan (adjective) = BEST (superlative form of *gōd* "good") [§6.8]

bið = see *bēon*

cōm (verb form not yet covered) = "came" [§8.7]

dæġ (m) = DAY [§2.7]

dēofol (m or n) = DEVIL [§2.7, §2.9]

dōm (m) = judgment [§2.7]

driht-guma (weak m) = troop-man, warrior [§3.3]

duguð (f) = body of noble retainers; people, men [§2.8]

dyrne (adjective) = "secret" (f acc sg) [§6.1]

eafora (weak m) = son, offspring [§3.3]

eahtian (weak verb II) = to consider, deliberate [§3.12]

eardian (weak verb II) = to inhabit, make a home in [§3.12]

eom = see *bēon* [§4.5.1]

fǣr-gryre (m) = sudden terror [§10.2.1]

for-ġeald (verb form not yet covered, past singular) = "paid for" or "rewarded" (+ gen = "for") [§8.6]

(ġe)fremman (weak verb I) = to do, undertake [§3.11]

gangan (verb form not yet covered) = "going" (an infinitive acting in conjunction with *cōm*) [§9.3]

Grendel = a monster in *Beowulf*

hē (pronoun) = HE ([§7.1]

Heorot (n) = the name of Hrothgar's hall in *Beowulf*

hī (form not yet covered) = they (3 nom pl, personal pronoun) [§7.1]

him = them (3 dat pl, personal pronoun) [§7.1]

hīw (m) = form, appearance, shape; color [§2.7]

hwæt (pronoun) = WHAT [§7.5, 7.8]

iċ (pronoun) = I [§7.1]

lēan (n) = LOAN, compensation [§2.9]

lēoht (adjective) = LIGHT, bright [§6.1]

(ġe)līċ (adjective) = ALIKE, similar (to) (+ dat) [§6.1]

līcian (weak verb II, + dat object) = to be pleasing, be pleasant [§3.12]

meaht (f) = MIGHT, power [§10.11.2]

mere-grota (weak m) = pearl, sea-GROAT [§3.3]

(ġe)mētan (weak verb I) = MEET, find (*ġe-mette* = past participle; see §3.11.1) [§3.11]

moniġ (pronoun) = MANY (nom pl) [§6.1]

ne (adverb) = not [§6.9]

niht (f) = NIGHT [§2.8]

nō (adverb) = not at all [§6.9]

oft (adverb) = OFTen, frequently [§6.9]

on (preposition) = (+ dat) ON, in, among; (+ acc) onto, into [§6.16.2]

rǣd (m) = counsel, advice [§2.7]

sciell (f) = SHELL, shell fish; oyster [§2.8]

scinn (n) = spectre, ghoul, evil spirit [§2.9]

sel (n) = hall, house [§2.7]

sēlest (adjective) = best (superlative form of *gōd* "good") [§6.8]

seofona = SEVEN (genitive pl of the number *seofon*) [§6.1]

sinc-fāge (adjective) = "treasure-decorated, decorated with treasure" (n acc sing) ([§6.1]

steorra (weak m) = STAR [§3.3]

spǣċ (f) = SPEECH, talk [§2.8]

spēd (f) = capacity, power; means [§2.8]

sum (adjective) = "one" or "a certain (person)" [§6.1, §7.8]

swā (adverb) = thus, SO [§6.9]

sweart (adjective) = dark [see ModE *swart*; §6.1]

swīð-ferhðum (adjective acting as noun) = "stout-hearted, brave (ones)" (dat pl) [§6.1]

tō (infinitive marker) = TO

tō (preposition + dat) = TO [§6.15]

tungol (n) = star [§2.9]

þā (adverb) = then [§6.9]

ðæs (adverb) = afterwards, thence [§6.9]

þæt (conjunction) = THAT [§5.1.1]

þearft = see *þurfan*

þēaw (m) = habit, custom, way of behaving [§2.7]

þēow-dōm (m) = service (to God) [§2.7]

þurfan (pret-pres verb) = to need, be obliged to [§4.3.1]

un-lifiġendum (adjective) = "UNLIVing, dead" (dat sing; originally, a present participle) [§6.1]

wæs, wǣre = see *bēon*

wel (adverb) = WELL [§6.9]

wēnan (weak verb I) = to believe, imagine [§3.11]

weorðe (verb form not yet covered) = to be, become; have (with verbs of motion) [§8.6]

wīse (weak f) = way, manner, fashion [§3.4]

wið (preposition + dat) = against, as a remedy for [§6.15]

wīf (n) = woman [§2.9]

wlitegan (adjective, nominative pl) = bright, beautiful [§6.1]

word (n) = WORD [§2.9]

wurdon (verb form not yet covered) = "were" (past pl) [§8.6]

wyrm (m) = dragon [§10.11.1]

A PRACTICE RUN:
THE SEARCH FOR FREE STANDING DATIVES AND GENITIVES   **5.4.4**

Fīfel-cynnes eard won-sǣliġ wer weardode hwīle, siþðan him scyppend for-scrifen hæfde in Cāines cynne.

> In the first clause *fīfel-cynnes* is a clear genitive while *Cāines* in the second clause also appears to be genitive (check the charts in Chapters Two and Three). In both cases, the Genitive Rule applies: for *fīfel-cynnes*, *eard* is the base form and the translation would run "the home of the monster-kin," while *cynne* is the base for *Cāines* and should be translated as "the kin of Cain."

Hrāðe hēo æþelinga ānne hæfde fæste be-fangen, þā hēo tō fenne gāng.

> In the first clause, *æþelinga* appears to be a genitive plural. There are two candidates for the base form: *hēo* "she" and *ānne* "one." The first gives "she of the nobles," and the second "one of the nobles." The second of these seems more likely.

PULLING IT ALL TOGETHER   **5.4.5**

You are now ready to put all the elements of the clause together. After translating the verb, subject, objects, freestanding datives and genitives, some elements (mainly adverbial) will be leftover: adverbs, prepositional phrases, etc. In your translation, be sure to align freestanding datives or genitives with the elements they belong to and attempt to produce a sentence that sounds idiomatic in Modern English. That is, do not be afraid to rearrange the word order for better sense.

Exercise 5.6: SORTING OUT THE REST

Instructions. *Translate the following sentences with the glossary provided.*

1. Hrāðe hēo æþelinga ānne hæfde fæste be-fangen, þā hēo tō fenne gāng.

2. Cum nū mid ūs, forþon þe þū eart ūre wealdend.

3. Brūc, þenden þū mōte, maniġra mēda.

4. Hī ġe-lȳfdon þæt hē mihte miċclum him fultumian on þām ġe-feohte, for þām þe hē ġe-feoht lufode.

5. And Harold cyning ġe-gædrode miċelne scip-here and ēac land-here, for þām þe him wæs ġe-cȳðd þæt Wyllelm bastard wolde hider and ðis land ġe-winnan.

6. Þā iċ þā þis lēoð ġeomriende ā-sungen hæfde, þā cōm þǣr in tō mē heofen-cund wīs-dōm.

Vocabulary for Exercises

æþeling (m) = nobleman, retainer [§2.7]

ānne (adjective & numeral) = ONE,
a (the nominative form is *ān,*
while *ān-ne* is a masc acc sing)
[§6.1]

ā-sungen (verb form not yet covered) =
"SUNG" (past participle) [§8.6]

be-fangen (verb form not yet covered) =
"seized" (past participle) [§9.3]

bēon (irreg verb) = to BE [§4.5.1]

brūc (verb form not yet covered) =
"enjoy!" (imperative sing + gen
object) [§8.5]

cōm (verb form not yet covered) =
"CAME" (past sing) [§8.7]

cum (verb form not yet covered) =
"COME!" (imperative sing)
[§8.7]

cyning (m) = KING [§2.7]

(ġe)cȳðan (weak verb I) = to make
known, inform [§3.11]

ēac (adverb) = also [§6.9]

eart = see *bēon*

fæste (adverb) = firmly, steadFASTly
[§6.9]

fenn (n) = FEN, marsh, moor [§2.9]

(ġe)feoht (n) = FIGHT, battle [§2.9]

forþon (þe) (conjunction) = because, for
the reason that [§5.2]

fultumian (weak verb II) = to help, assist
[§3.12]

(ġe)gædrian (weak verb II) = to GATHER,
bring together [§3.12]

gāng (verb form not yet covered) =
"went" (past sing) [§9.3]

ġēomrian (weak verb II) = to grieve,
mourn [§3.12]

habban (weak verb III) = to HAVE [§4.1]

hæfde = see *habban*

Harold (m) = Harold Godwinson

hē, hēo, hit (pronoun) = HE, she, IT
[§7.1]

heofen-cund (adjective) = divine, of a
heavenly nature [§6.1]

hī (pronoun) = they or them (nom or
acc) [§7.1]

hider (adverb) = HITHER, to that place
[§6.9]

him (pronoun) = HIM or them
[§7.1]

hrāðe (adverb) = quickly [§6.9]

iċ (pronoun) = I [§7.1]

in (adverb) = IN [§6.9]

land (n) = LAND, country [§2.9]

land-here (m) = LAND-army, infantry [§10.2.1]

lēoð (n) = song, poem [§2.9]

lufian (weak verb II) = to LOVE [§3.12]

(ġe)lȳfan (weak verb I) = to beLIEVE [§3.11]

magan (pret-pres verb) = to be allowed, be able [§4.3]

maniġ (adjective) = MANY [§6.1]

mē (pronoun) = ME [§7.1]

mēd (f) = reward, MEED [§2.8]

miċċlum (adverb) = greatly, very much [§6.9]

miċel (adjective) = great, large [§6.1]

mid (preposition + dat) = with, along with [§6.15]

mihte = see *magan*

mōtan (pret-pres verb) = to be able, have the power (to do something) [§4.3]

nū (adverb) = NOW [§6.9]

on (preposition) = (+ dat) in, ON; (+ acc) into, onto [§6.16.2]

scip-here (m) = SHIP-army, fleet [§10.2.1]

sē, sēo, þæt (definite article) = the [§2.5]

þā = (adverb) then, at that time [§6.9]; (conjunction) when [§5.2]

þǣr (adverb) = THERE [§6.9]

þæt (conjunction) = THAT [§5.1.1]

þām = see *sē*

ðis (pronoun) = THIS [§7.7]

þenden (conjunction) = as long as [§5.2]

þū (pronoun) = you, THOU [§7.1]

tō (preposition + dat) = TO [§6.15]

ūre (pronoun) = OUR [§7.1]

ūs (pronoun) = US (dat pl) [§7.1]

wæs = see *bēon*

wealdend (m) = ruler, leader [§10.10]

willan (irreg verb) = to want, wish, desire (with infinitive) [§4.5.3]

ġe-winnan (verb form not yet covered) = "to conquer" [§8.6]

wīsdōm (m) = WISDOM [§2.7]

Wyllelm bastard (m) = William the Bastard (a.k.a., the Conquerer)

Reading V: WONDERS OF THE EAST (2)

The Wonders of the East:
A page from *The Wonders of the East* as preserved in the Nowell Codex (London, British Library, Cotton Vitellius A.xv., fol. 100r). The manuscript was damaged in a fire at Ashburnham House in 1731.

[8] Translate *þā* as "who" (see §7.5.3).

[9] A definite article acting as a pronoun. Translate as "them" (referring to the fish).

[10] a subjunctive plural

[11] a subjunctive plural

[12] a subjunctive plural

On sumum lande bēoð men ā-cende, þā[8] bēoð on lenge syx fōt-mǣla. Hī habbað beardas oþ cnēow sīde, and feax oð hēlan. *Homodubii* hȳ syndon hātene—þæt bēoð "twī-men"—and bē hrēawum fixum hȳ lifiað and þā[9] etaþ. *Capi* hātte sēo ēa in þǣreilcan stōwe þe is hāten *Gorgoneus*—þæt is, "wæl-kyrging." Þǣr bēoð cende

5   ǣmetan swā micle swā hundas. Hȳ habbaþ swelċe fēt swā græs-hoppan. Hȳ syndon rēades hēowes and blāces hēowes. Þā ǣmettan delfað gold ūp of eorþan from foran nihte oð ðā fiftan tīd dæges. Þā men þe tō þon dyrstige bēoð þæt hī þæt gold nimen,[10] þonne lǣdað hȳ mid him olfendan, meran mid hyra folan ond stēdan. Þā folan hȳ ġe-sǣlað ǣr hȳ ofer þā ēa faren.[11] Þæt gold hīe ġe-fǣtað on þā meran ond

10 hȳ sylfe on-sittað ond þā stēdan þǣr for-lǣtað. Þonne þā ǣmettan hȳ on-findað ond þā hwīle þe þā ǣmettan embe þone stēdan ā-bysgode bēoð, þonne þā men mid þām merum ond mid þām golde ofer þā ēa farað. Hȳ bēoð swā hrædlīċe ofer þǣre ēa þæt men wēnað þæt hȳ flēogen. [12]Sēo Nīl is ealdor fullicra ēa, and hēo floweð of Ēgypta lande. And hī nemnað þā ēa *Archoboleta*—þæt is hāten "þæt micle wæter."

15 On þyssum stōwum bēoð ā-cende þā miclan mænego olfenda. Ðǣr bēoð cende men, hȳ bēoð fīftēne fōta lange and hȳ habbað hwīt līċ and twā neb on ānum hēafde, fēt and cnēowu swȳðe rēade, and lange nōsa and sweart feax. Þonne hȳ cennan willað, þonne farað hȳ on scipum to *Indeum*, and þǣr hyra ġe-cynda in woruld bringaþ.

Latin original: In aliqua nascuntur homines statura pedum .vi. barbas habentes usque ad genua, comas usque ad talos, qui *Homodubii* appellantur et pisces crudos manducant. Capi fluvius in eodem loco appellatur *Gorgoneus* ibi nascuntur formicae statura canum habentes pedes quasi locustae rubro colore nigroque fodientes

5   aurum et quod per noctem fodiunt sub terra profertur foras usque diei horam quintam homines autem qui audaces sunt illud tollere sic tollent apud camelos masculos et foeminas illas quae habent foetos autem trans flumen gargulum alligatos relinquunt et camelis foeminis aurum inponunt illae autem pietate ad suos pullos festinantes ibi masculi remanent et illae formicae sequentes inveniunt

10   eos masculos et comedunt eos dum circa autem eos occupatae sunt foeminae
     transeunt flumen cum hominibus sunt autem tam veloces ut putes eos volare.
     Nam Nilus est capud fluviorum et per Ægiptum fluit quam Ægipti Archoboleta
     vocant quae est aqua magna in his locis nascitur multitudo magna elephantorum.
     Nascuntur et ibi homines habentes statura pedum xv corpus habentes candidum
15   duas in una habentes capite facies rubra genua naso longo capillis nigris cum
     tempus gignendi fuerit suis navibus transferuntur in Indiam et ibi prolem reddunt
     (*De Rebus in Oriente Mirabilibus*).

Vocabulary for Reading V: *(WONDERS OF THE EAST 2)*

Though some strong verbs appear below, assume for now that they take the same present

tense endings as the weak verbs, Class I.

ā-bisġian (weak verb II) = to BUSY,
    occupy [§3.12]

ā-cennan (weak verb I) = bear, give birth,
    be born; be native [§3.11]

ānum (adjective) = ONE [§6.1]

ǣmette (weak f) = ant [§3.4]

ǣr (conjunction) = before, ERE
    [§5.1.1]

Archoboleta = proper name

bē (preposition + dat) = BY, by means of
    [§6.15]

beard (m) = BEARD [§2.7]

bēon (irreg verb) = to BE [§4.5.1]

blāc (adjective) = BLACK, dark [§6.2.2]

bringað (verb form not yet covered) =

"BRING" or "bring forth" (present
    plural) [§8.6]

Capi = river name

cennan (weak verb I) = to bring forth,
    give birth, reproduce; be native to a
    place [§3.11]

cnēow (n) =KNEE [§10.3.2]

(ġe)cynd (n, f) = KIND, nature, origin
    [§2.8, 2.9]

dæġ (m) = DAY [§2.7]

delfað (verb form not yet covered) = to
    "DELVE" or "dig" (present plural)
    [§8.6]

dyrstiġ (adjective) = adventurous,
    DARing [§6.1]

ēa (f) = river (usually indeclinable except

in the dat pl) [§10.4.2]

ealdor (m) =ELDER; chief, greatest, foremost thing or person [§2.7]

Ēgypt (m, n) = proper noun EGYPT [§10.11.1]

embe, ymbe (preposition + acc, dat) = around, about, in regard to [§6.15]

eorðe (weak f) = EARTH [§3.4]

etað (verb form not yet covered) = "EAT" (present pl) [§9.1]

farað (verb form not yet covered) = "travel" or "FARE" (present pl) [§9.2]

(ġe)fǣtan (weak verb I) = to load, cram, stuff [§3.11]

feax (n) = head of hair, hair [§2.9]

fīftan (adjective) = FIFTH [§6.1]

fīftēne (indeclinable num) = FIFTEEN

fisc (m) = FISH (plural = *fixas*) [§2.7]

flēogen (verb form not yet covered) = "are flying" (present pl subjunctive) [§8.5]

flōweð (verb form not yet covered) = "FLOWs" [§9.3]

fola (weak m) = FOAL, colt [§3.3]

foran (preposition + dat) = beFORE [§6.15]

for-lǣtað (verb form not yet covered) = "abandon" or "leave behind" (present pl) [§9.3]

fōt (m) = FOOT [§10.4.2]

fōt-mǣl (n) FOOT-measure [§2.9]

from (adverb) = FROM [§6.9]

fullicra (adjective, gen pl) = FULL, complete; large, main [§6.1]

Gorgoneus = place name

græs-hoppa (weak m) = GRASS-HOPPer [§3.3]

habban (weak verb III) = to have [§4.1]

hāten (verb form not yet covered) = "called" or "named" [§9.3]

hātte (verb form not yet covered) = "is called" [§9.3]

hēafod (n) = HEAD [§2.9]

hēow (n, also spelled *hīw*) = HUE, color [§10.3.1]

hēlu (weak m) = HEEL [§3.3]

hīe (pronoun) = they or them (also appears as *hȳ*, *hī*, and *hīo*) [§7.1]

hiera (pronoun) = their [§7.1]

Homodubii (m pl) = DUBIous HUMans, human-like monsters [Latin]

hrædlīċe (adverb) = quickly [§6.9]

hrēaw (adjective) = RAW, uncooked [§6.1]

hund (m) = dog, HOUND [§2.7]

hwīl (f) = time, hour, WHILE; *þā hwīle þe* = "for the time which, while" [§2.8]

hwīt (adjective) = WHITE [§6.1]

hȳ = see *hīe*

hyra (pronoun) = their [§7.1]

ilcan (adjective) = same [§6.1]

in (preposition + dat) = IN [§6.15]

Indeum (proper noun) = INDIA

is (irreg verb) = see *bēon* [§4.5.1]

(ġe)lǣdan (weak verb I) = to LEAD, take [§3.11]

land (n) = LAND, country [§2.9]

lange (adjective) = tall, LONG [§6.1]

leng (f) = LENGth, height [§2.8]

libban (weak verb III) = to LIVE [§4.1]

līċ (n) = body [§2.9]

mænego (f) = multitude, MANY [§10.7]

mann (m) = MAN, person [§10.4.2]

mere (weak f) = MARE [§3.4]

miċel (adjective) = large, big; great [§6.1]

mid (preposition + dat) = with, along with [§6.15]

neb (n) = nose, face [§2.9]

nemnan (weak verb I) = call, NAME [§3.11]

Nīl (f) = (proper noun) Nile

niht (f) = NIGHT [§10.4.2]

nimen (verb form not yet covered) = "(should) take" (subjunctive pl) [§8.7]

nōsa (f) = NOSE [§10.6]

of (preposition + dat) = OFF, from [§6.15]

ofer (preposition + dat/acc) = OVER [§6.15]

olfende (m or f) = camel [apparently a form of Lat. *elefantem*; §3.3, 3.4]

on (preposition + acc/dat) = ONto (+ acc), on (with dat) [§6.15]

ond (conjunction) = AND

on-findaÐ (verb form not yet covered) = "discover" or "come upon" (present pl) [§8.6]

on-sittaÐ (verb form not yet covered) = "SIT ON" or "mount" [§9.1]

oþ (preposition + acc) = to, as far as; until [§6.15]

rēad (adjective) = RED [§6.1]

(ġe)sǣlan (weak verb I) = to tie; German *Seil* "rope" [§3.11]

scip (n) = SHIP [§2.9]

sē, sēo, þæt = definite article [§2.5]

sīde (adjective) = broad, ample, large; wide [§6.1]

sīde (weak f) = SIDE [§3.4]

siex (indeclinable num) = SIX

stēda (weak m) = (male) camel; STEED [§3.3]

stōw (f) = place [§10.3.3]

sum (adjective) = a certain, SOME [§6.1]

swā (adverb) = as , so, thus, therefore
(*swā . . . swā = as . . . as*) [§6.9]

sweart (adjective) = black, dark [§6.1]

swelċ, swilċ (adjective) = such
(*swelċe . . . swā = such . . . as)* [§6.1]

swȳðe (adverb) = very, completely [§6.9]

sylfe (pronoun) = themSELVes [§7.6]

syx (indeclinable num) = SIX

tīd (f) = time; hour, TIDE; see
Christmastide, Yuletide; [§10.11.2]

tō þon = see *þon*

twā (indeclinable num) =TWO

twēo-mann (m) = lit. doubt MAN, or
a doubtfully human creature; OE
twēo "doubt, confusion" is related to
twā "TWO." Having doubts means
not being able to decide between
two alternatives. See the phrase "to
be of two minds" about something.
[§10.4.2]

þā = see *sē*

þā = (adverb) then [§6.9]; (conjunction)

when [§5.1.1]

þǣr (adverb) =THERE [§6.9]

þæt (conjunction) = THAT, so that
[§5.1.1]

þæt = (definite article) [§2.5]

þe (pronoun) = who, which [§7.5]

þyssum (pronoun) = THIS [§7.7]

þon (adverb), *tō þon* = to that extent
[§6.9]

þonne (adverb) = then [§6.9];
(conjunction) = when [§5.1.1]

ūp (adverb) = UP, UPward [§6.9]

wæl-kyrging (f) = VALKYRIE; witch
[§3.4]

wæter (n) = WATER [§2.9]

wēnan (weak verb I + gen or acc) = to
imagine, believe, think, fancy; hope,
WEEN [§3.11]

willan (irreg verb) = want, desire [§4.5.3]

woruld (f) = WORLD [§10.11.2]

Lessons Learned

Before leaving this chapter you should be able to . . .
- recognize the difference between clauses and phrases (§5.1).
- translate a sentence using the sequence described on the opening page of the chapter.
- apply the Dative Rule (§5.4.2) with confidence.
- apply the Genitive Rule (§5.4.3) with confidence.

SIX

Adjectives and Adverbs,

Prepositions

6.1 Lesson One: Adjectives

Like nouns, OE adjectives have case, gender, and number endings which agree with the case, gender, and number markers of the nouns they modify. Knowing how to decipher the adjective endings will add accuracy to your reading of OE and often make it easier to spot the gender of the noun it modifies. At first the following charts might look like a swarm of new endings to memorize. Luckily, though, most of the adjective endings mirror those you've already learned, so the process of memorization should be *much* easier.

Notice that the following two charts are almost identical except that (like the nouns you learned in Chapter Two) long-stemmed adjectives leave off *-u* endings (in the feminine nominative singular and in the neuter nominative and accusative plural). See §2.7 for a review.

6.1.1 STRONG ADJECTIVES (Short-Stemmed) *til* "good, useful"

				SUMMARY		
	Masculine	Feminine	Neuter	Masculine	Feminine	Neuter
Singular						
N	til	tilu	til	–	-u	–
A	tilne	tile	til	-ne	-e	–
G	tiles	tilre	tiles	-es	-re	-es
D	tilum	tilre	tilum	-um	-re	-um
I	tile	*****	tile	-e	*****	-e
Plural						
N	tile	tile, -a	tilu	-e	-e, -a	-u
A	tile	tile, -a	tilu	-e	-e, -a	-u
G	tilra	tilra	tilra	-ra	-ra	-ra
D	tilum	tilum	tilum	-um	-um	-um

STRONG ADJECTIVES (Long-Stemmed) *gōd* "good"   **6.1.2**

	Masculine	Feminine	Neuter	SUMMARY Masculine	Feminine	Neuter
Singular						
N	gōd	gōd	gōd	-	-	-
A	gōdne	gōde	gōd	-ne	-e	-
G	gōdes	gōdre	gōdes	-es	-re	-es
D	gōdum	gōdre	gōdum	-um	-re	-um
I	gōde	*****	gōde	-e	*****	-e
Plural						
N	gōde	gōde, -a	gōd	-e	-e, -a	-
A	gōde	gōde, -a	gōd	-e	-e, -a	-
G	gōdra	gōdra	gōdra	-ra	-ra	-ra
D	gōdum	gōdum	gōdum	-um	-um	-um

In reviewing these two charts of adjective endings, you will do well to keep the definite article in mind (see the definite article paradigm §2.5). Notice that the *–ne* ending for the masculine, accusative singular form corresponds to the *–ne* of *þone* (the matching definite article). Also notice that the *–re* endings in the feminine singular genitive and dative forms mirror *–re* of the corresponding article form *þǣre*, etc. The only exception is that *–um* on an adjective could be dative *singular* as well as plural.

TIMESAVER

6.1.3   ADJECTIVES ENDING IN *-U*. Some adjectives have a final *-u* or *-o* that is not an ending but part of the adjective stem. In such words, the *-u* changes to an *-o* before consonants but to a *-w-* before vowels. Take *ġearu* "ready, prepared" as an example:

| | Masculine | Feminine | Neuter | SUMMARY | | |
				Masculine	Feminine	Neuter
Singular						
N	ġearu -o	ġearu -o	ġearu -o	-	-	-
A	ġearone	ġearwe	ġearu	-ne	-e	-
G	ġearwes	ġearore	ġearwes	-es	-re	-es
D	ġearwum	ġearore	ġearwum	-um	-re	-um
I	ġearwe	*****	ġearwe	-e	**	-e
Plural						
N	ġearwe	ġearwe, -a	ġearu	-e	-e, -a	-u
A	ġearwe	ġearwe, -a	ġearu	-e	-e, -a	-u
G	ġearora	ġearora	ġearora	-ra	-ra	-ra
D	ġearwum	ġearwum	ġearwum	-um	-um	-um

6.2   "Strong" and "Weak" Adjectives

In OE, adjective endings take two forms depending on their grammatical context—weak or strong. If an adjective is preceded by a definite article (*the*), a demonstrative pronoun (*this, that*), or a possessive (*her, his, your*, etc.), it takes the so-called "weak" endings (weak because the preceding word carries most of the grammatical weight, allowing the adjective to carry a weaker load). Adjectives appear with "strong" endings if they carry the grammatical load themselves—i.e., if they are not preceded by an article, demonstrative, or possessive, or if they appear by themselves after a *to be* verb (*the gift is good*).

Here follows the weak adjectival endings. Again, before despairing that you must learn two sets of adjective endings, keep in mind that the weak adjectives correspond almost exactly to the weak noun endings that you've already learned (see §3.6.1).

WEAK ADJECTIVES   6.2.1

	Masculine	Feminine	Neuter	SUMMARY Masculine	Feminine	Neuter
Singular						
N	gōda	gōde	gōde	-a	-e	-e
A	gōdan	gōdan	gōde	-an	-an	-e
G	gōdan	gōdan	gōdan	-an	-an	-an
D	gōdan	gōdan	gōdan	-an	-an	-an
Plural						
N	gōdan	gōdan	gōdan	-an	-an	-an
A	gōdan	gōdan	gōdan	-an	-an	-an
G	gōdra, -ena	gōdra, -ena	gōdra, -ena	-ra, -ena	-ra, -ena	-ra, -ena
D	gōdum	gōdum	gōdum	-um	-um	-um

The following examples should help you begin to recognize the different environments   **6.2.2** in which weak and strong adjectives normally occur.

sēo gōde eorðe   weak
(the good earth)

gōd eorðe	strong
([a] good earth)	
tō þām gōdum mannum	weak
(to the good men)	
to gōdum mannum	strong
(to good men)	
Sē leornað þā gōdan lāre.	weak (see §2.5.1)
(He learns the good teaching.)	
miċelu weorc	strong
(many works)	

Note: The adjective *miċel* is a short stem (because the last syllable is short), and thus it retains the –*u* ending, but *weorc* (n) is a long-stemmed noun and thus drops the –*u*.

Þæt wæs weorc gōd.	strong
(That was a good work.)	
Iċ hæbbe mihte miċel.	strong
(I have great power.)	
waldend þone gōdan	weak
(the good ruler—lit., ruler the good)	

Note: Sometimes the adjective follows the noun it modifies, as in the last three examples.

Adjectives sometimes function independently as nouns, and when they do, you must add   **6.2.3**
a noun like *one, man, woman,* or *person* to your translation.

Sēo hāliġe spræc ofer hēanne weall.   weak
(The holy [woman] spoke over the high wall.)

Hē for-lēt þone gōdan.   weak
(He abandoned the good [man].)

Ġe-seh þā . . . hāliġ hāliġne.   strong
(Then the holy man saw the holy man.)
(in context: St. Andrew saw St. Matthew.)

Þonne bēoð þȳ hefigran heortan benne, sāre æfter swæsne.   strong
(Then are the heart's wounds the heavier, pains for the dear [one].)
(i.e., . . . pains for the death of the dear one.)

A lightly regularized passage from a homily by Ælfric illustrates the weak and strong   **6.2.4**
forms nicely:

Ġif þā scēap bēoð gōd þonne bēoð gōd hyrdas.   strong / strong
(If the sheep are good then the shepherds are good.)

And of þām gōdum scēapum cumað þā gōdan hyrdas.   weak / weak
(And from the good sheep come the good shepherds.)

And ealle ðā gōdan hyrdas syndon under Crīste þe is sē gōda hyrde.   weak / weak
(And all the good shepherds are under Christ who is the good shepherd.)

Exercise 6.1: RECOGNIZING STRONG AND WEAK ADJECTIVES

Instructions. *Translate the following sentences with the vocabulary provided. To the right of each sentence, indicate in the first column whether the adjective* gōd *is strong or weak, and in the second what gender, case, and number the adjective possesses.*

	Weak/Strong	Gen/Case/Num

1. Þæt sweord is gōd.

   The sword is good .

   strong — neut/nom/sing

2. Sē cyning is gōd.

   The king is good .

   strong — m/nom/sing

3. Sēo is on gōdne weġ. (see §2.5.1)

   She is on a good path .

   ~~weak~~ strong — m/acc/sing

4. Yfele æþelingas ne sindon [are] gōde.

   Evil noblemen are not good .

   Strong — m/nom/plur

5. Hē sitteþ on þǣre gōdan benċe.

   He sits on the good bench .

   weak — f/dative/sing

	Weak/Strong	Gen/Case/Num

6. Sē cræftiġa hereþ [praise] þā gōdan ġiefe. _weak_ _f/acc/sing_

The skillful one praises the good gift.

7. Gōde æþelingas feohtaþ [fight]. _strong_ _m/nom/plur._

Good noblemen fight .

8. Þǣre gōdan cwēne ġiefu wæs yfelu. _weak_ _f/gen/sing_

The good queen's gift was evil .

9. Þæs gōdan cyninges ġiefa sindon [are] yfele. _weak_ _m/gen/sing (?)_

The good king's gifts are evil .

Provide grammatical information for
the adjective *yfel* in numbers 4, 8, and 9.

	Weak/Strong	Gen/Case/Num

4. _strong_ _m/nom/plur._

8. _strong_ _f/acc/sing_

9. _strong_ _f/acc/plur._

VOCABULARY FOR EXERCISE 6.1

You have not yet tackled strong verbs, but for the purpose of this exercise, assume that they take the same present tense endings as the weak verbs that you encountered in Chapter Three—an assumption which is thankfully true. From this point on, adjectives will appear in regular entries.

æðeling (m) = nobleman, retainer [§2.7]

benċ (f) = BENCH [§2.8]

bēon (irregular verb) = to BE [§6.5.1]

cræftiġ (adjective) = skillful, knowledgeable [§6.1]

cwēn (f) = QUEEN [§10.11.2]

cyning (m) = KING [§2.7]

feohtan = FIGHT, do battle against [§8.6]

ġiefu (f) = GIFT [§2.8]

gōd (adjective) = GOOD [§6.1]

hē, hēo, hit (pronoun) = HE, she, IT [§7.1]

herian (weak verb I) = to praise, compliment, extol [§3.11]

is = see *bēon*

ne (adverb) = not [§6.9]

on (preposition) = (+ dat) ON, in; (+ acc) onto, into [§6.15]

scop (m) = singer, minstrel, poet [§2.7]

sē, sēo, þæt (definite article) = THE [§2.5]

sindon = see *bēon*

sittan = to SIT [§9.1]

sweord (n) = SWORD [§2.9]

weġ (m) = way, path [§2.7]

yfel (adjective) = EVIL, bad [§6.1]

6.3 Participles as Adjectives

You are probably used to thinking of participles, if you think of them at all, as part of the verb system. They can, however, function as adjectives as well as verbs. When the participle functions as an adjective, it is said to be a *verbal*, that is, "like a verb" in that it has the form of a verb, but with the function of an adjective.

In the simplest cases, participles behave exactly like regular adjectives, appearing generally before the nouns they modify and taking the appropriate adjectival endings (strong or weak):

*Ac Petrus æt-ēowede þone **ġe-blētsodan** hlāf þām hundum.*   (weak m acc sing)
(But Peter showed the blessed loaf to the dogs.)

*Sē cyning sende þūsend **ġe-wǣpnodra** manna.*   (strong m gen pl)
(The king sent a thousand armed men.)

You may sometimes find these participial adjectives in the glossary as independent entries, but for the most part, you will be able to locate them only by looking up the main verb from which they are formed. For example, *ġe-blētsodan* "blessed, sanctified" would appear under *ġe-blētsian* "to bless" (a weak verb of the second class).

When participles appear in verb phrases, they appear sometimes with—and sometimes without—strong adjective endings (see §6.1).

When the helping verb is a form of *to be*, the result is usually a passive sentence in which the participle agrees with the subject (in the following examples participles appear in boldface, adjectival endings are underlined, and the antecedents to the participle appear in a box):

*Þonne his gatu **be-locenu** bēon, þonne nime hē his cǣga.*   (n nom pl)
(When his gates are locked, then he should take his key.)

*Sēo un-ġesǣliġe sāwl byð fram Gode **for-lǣtenu**.*   (f nom sing)
(The wretched soul is abandoned by God.)

When the helping verb is a form of *have*, the result is usually an active sentence in the "present perfect" (denoting an action already finished). In such sentences the past participle agrees in case, gender, and number with the *object* of the verb if there is one:

*Þū mē hæfst **ā-frēfredne**.*   (The speaker must be a male!)
(You have comforted me.)

ðā hē hīġ *hæfde* ealle *ā-myrrede* . . .   (acc pl)
(when he had scattered them all . . .)
(lit., when he them had all scattered . . .)

Hīe þā hæfdon heora sīð-fæt *ġe-feredne.*   (m, n acc sing)
(They then had traveled/completed their journey.)

Just as often and perhaps more frequently, however, participles appear with no apparent adjectival ending at all.

Þæt ġeat *bið* **be-locen.**   (no ending)
(The gate is locked.)

Sāwl *prūtes bið* **for-lǣten** *fram Gode.*   (no ending)
(The soul of the proud is abandoned by God.)

Hē *sceal bīon* **ā-frēfred.**   (no ending)
(He must be comforted.)

Eorðe *wæs* **ā-myrred** *þurh þā flēogan.*   (no ending)
(The earth was laid waste by the flies.)

Exercise 6.2: PARTICIPLES AS ADJECTIVES

Instructions. *In the following sentences, take the infinitive in parentheses, and 1) turn it into a past participle (by adding the appropriate participial ending: -ed for weak verb I and -od for weak verb II), 2) add a slash and then a version of the same participle with* *the appropriate adjectival ending (see §6.2.1) and insert into the slot provided, and finally 3) translate the resulting sentence in the space provided. Note that the past participial endings –ed– and –od– are short stems and require the endings associated with short stemmed adjectives in §6.1.1.*

(bærnan)   Þā scipu wǣron *ge-bærned / gebærnedu* _____.

The ships were burnt. _____.

1. (trymian)   Sē alwalda hæfde engel-cynna tīen¹ _____.

_____.

2. (laðian)   Wē sind tō þǣre heofonlican Hierusalem _____.

_____.

3. (sendan)   In carcern ðū bist _____.

_____.

4. (lettan)   His sīð-fæt wæs _____.

_____.

5. (martyrian)   Hī wurdon on þyssum dæġe wuldorfullīċe_____.

_____.

6. (hīeran)   Þonne ġe-wearð sēo stefn _____ of heofonum.

_____.

7. (ġearcian)   Hē hæfde ealle his ðing (pl) _____.

_____.

8. (smirian)   Sē cyning bið _____ mid ele.

_____.

9. (dǣlan)   Hīe hæbbað ðæt yrfe rihtlīċe _____.

_____.

10. (trymian)   Ealle þīne wegas bēoð _____.

_____.

VOCABULARY FOR EXERCISE 6.2

al-walda (weak m) = all-ruling (one), the
Almighty [§3.3]

bærnan (weak verb I) = to BURN, set on
fire [§3.11]

bēon, bīon (irregular verb) = to BE [§4.5.1]

carcern (n) = prison [§2.9]

cyning (m) = KING [§2.7]

dæġ (m) = DAY [§2.7]

dǣlan (weak verb I) = to share, divide,
DEAL out [§3.11]

eall (adjective and pronoun) = ALL, every
[§6.1, §7.8]

ele (m) = OIL [§10.11.1]

engel-cynn (n) = order, rank of angels
[§10.2.2]

ġearcian (weak verb II) = to prepare,
supply [§3.12]

habban (weak verb III) = to HAVE,
possess, hold; (helping verb for
perfect constructions: *habban* + past
participle) [§3.13]

hē, hēo, hit (personal pronoun) = HE, she,
IT [§7.1]

hī, hīe, hȳ (pronoun) = feminine nom / acc
singular OR plural nom / acc; see *hē,
hēo, hit* [§7.1]

heofon (m, f; often plural) = HEAVEN;
the heavens, the sky [§2.7, §2.8]

heofonliċ (adjective) = HEAVENLY [§6.1]

hīeran (weak verb I) = to HEAR [§3.11]

Hierusalem = Jerusalem

in (preposition) = (+ dat) IN, on; (+ acc)
into, onto [§6.16.2]

laðian (weak verb II) = to invite, call,
summon [§3.12]

lettan (weak verb I) = to hinder, prevent;
LET [§3.11]

martyrian (weak verb II) = to MARTYR,
torture (to death) [§3.12]

mid (preposition + dat) = with, along
with, among; with respect to [compare
German *mit*; §6.15]

of (preposition + dat) = from, OFF [§6.15]

on (preposition) = (+ dat) in, ON;
(+ acc) into, onto [§6.16.2]

rihtlīċe (adverb) = RIGHTLY, properly,
virtuously, correctly [§6.9]

scip (n) = SHIP [§2.9]

sendan (weak verb I) = to SEND [§3.11]

sē, sēo, þæt (definite article, adjective, or
pronoun) = the; that (one), that (thing)
[§2.5, §7.7]

sīð-fæt (m, n) = journey, voyage [§2.9]

sind = see *bēon*

smirian (weak verb I) = to anoint, rub with oil (as part of a ritual) [see ModE *SMEAR*; §3.11]

stefn (f noun) = voice [compare German *Stimme* "voice"; §2.8]

tīen (number) = TEN [§2.8]

tō (preposition + dative) = as, TO, into, until [§6.15]

trymian (weak verb I) = to strengthen, establish [§3.11]

þēs, þēos, þis (pronoun, adjective and pronoun) = THIS [§7.7]

þīn (adjective) = your, THINE [§7.1]

ðing (n) = THING, possession [§2.9]

þonne (adverb) = then, immediately [§6.9]

ðū (pronoun) = you, THOU [§7.1]

þyssum = see *þēs, þēos, þis*

wǣron, wæs = see *bēon*

weġ (m) = WAY, path [§2.7]

(ġe)wearð (verb form not yet covered) = "was" [§8.6]

wuldor-ful-līċe (adverb) = gloriously [§6.9]

wurdon (verb form not yet covered) = "were" [§8.6]

yrfe (n) = inheritance, legacy; property [§10.2.2]

6.4   Lesson Two: Comparative and Superlative Forms

Like Modern English adjectives, most OE adjectives can be intensified by adding comparative (*-er*) and superlative (*-est*) endings: *fast, faster,* and *fastest*. For OE, these endings are, reassuringly, *-ra* and *-ost* (*fæst, fæstra, fæstost*). In Modern English, most multi-syllabic adjectives take *more* or *most* instead of the endings *-er* and *-est* (*more beautiful* and *most beautiful* rather than the non-existent **beautifuler* and **beautifulest*).

Old English has no such distinction: ALL adjectives, no matter how many syllables, Take the *-ra* and *-ost* endings.

Ælfric on
Adjectives

Sume synd *ADJECTIVA*, þæt synd ðā ðe bēoð ġe-īhte tō ōðrum namum and ġe-tācniað oððe herunge oððe tǽl: *justus* "rihtwīs," *injustus* "un-rihtwīs," *bonus homo* "gōd man," *malus homo* "yfel mann."

POSITIVUS is sē forma stæpe: rihtwīs.
COMPARATIVUS ys sē oðer stæpe: rihtwīsre.
SUPERLATIVUS is sē ðridda stæpe: ealra rihtwīsost.

Some [words] are adjectives, which are those that are added to other nouns and signify either praise or blame: *justus* "just," *unjustus* "unjust," *bonus homo* "a good man," *malus homo* "an evil man."

The positive is the first step: "just."
Comparative is the second step: "more just."
Superlative is the third step: "most just of all."

Comparative + Personal Ending   6.5

Keep in mind, however, that these intensified adjectives often have two endings: first, the intensifying endings *-ra* or *-ost,* and *then* the regular strong or weak adjectival endings. Comparatives (*-ra*) always take weak endings, even if there is no preceding article, demonstrative, or possessive. Superlatives (*-ost*) function normally with either the strong or weak forms as the context demands. After the comparative or superlative endings come the regular endings for case, number, and tense that you learned above. Sometimes these layered endings can be a bit tricky. Consider the following two examples:

Þæt wæter wæs **biterre** *ond* **grimre** *tō drincanne þonne ǽniġ ōðer.*
(The water was bitterer and more horrible [lit., grimmer] to drink than any other.)

Note that in this example, the adjectives *biterre* and *grimre* are comparatives (the base forms are *biter* and *grim*). In the case of *biterre*, the second *r* indicates the comparative (the first *r* is simply part of the word *biter*), while the *-e* is a weak neuter nominative ending (see §6.1.2). The same applies to *grimre*, except that its root ends in *-m*, not *r*.

*Wē libbað on **biterre** ond **grimre** tīde.*
(We live in a bitter and horrible time.)

WARNING: Here *biterre* and *grimre* (though identical in form in the last example!) are *not* comparatives. The *-re* ending is simply the strong feminine dative singular ending (see §6.1.2). It's very important to recognize the difference, something only possible if you know the adjectival endings by heart.

6.6.1   SUPERLATIVES

Superlatives are a bit easier to spot:

*Hē hæfde ġyt ǣnne **lēofostne** sunu.*
(He had still one most beloved son.)

Here, *-ost-* is the superlative ending, while *-ne* indicates the strong masculine accusative singular (see §6.1.2). Note that the same *-ne* ending appears on *ǣn* "one" and that *sunu* "son" takes a *-u* ending in the accusative singular because it belongs to a special noun class (see §10.6).

*Hwā mihte his **lēofostan** frēond for-ġietan?*
(Who could forget his dearest friend?)

Here again, the *-ost-* indicates the superlative while the *-an* is a weak masculine accusative singular ending (see §6.2.1).

*mīnra **lēofostra** frēonda sāwole*
(my dearest friends' souls)

> Here yet again, the *-ost-* indicates the superlative, while the *-ra* is a weak masculine genitive plural ending. (Note that *sāwole* is in the feminine nominative plural.)

THAN MARKER   6.6.2

BETTER *THAN* WHAT? Comparatives often require a "than" phrase to complete them. In OE, there are two ways to express this "than" phrase. The first is reassuringly familiar:

*Hēo is swiftre **ponne** iċ.*
(She is faster than I [am].)

Slightly more confusing, however, is the second method, where the dative or instrumental takes the place of *than*:

Mē is hēo swiftre.
([Than] I she is faster.)

COMPARATIVE AS INTENSIFIER   6.6.3

ONE LAST NUANCE. In some instances, the comparative may merely intensify an adjective rather than make a true comparison. Such a function for the comparative is reasonably rare. However, if you encounter a comparative with no real or implied *ponne* phrase or its dative equivalent (see §6.6.2), you may begin to suspect that the comparative is of this type. To translate it, simply add a "very" to the positive form of the adjective.

Irregular Adjectives with Different Roots   6.7

Some adjectives show a vowel change in the comparative and superlative forms and take *-est* rather than *-ost* in the superlative.

Positive	Comparative	Superlative
eald "old"	ieldra	ieldest
ġeong "young"	ġingra	ġingest
lang "long"	lengra	lengest
strang "strong"	strengra	strengest
hēah "high"	hīerra	hīehst

6.7.1   The comparative and superlative forms in the preceding chart show evidence of "i-mutation" (not as alarming as it sounds). That is, the comparative and superlative endings at one time must have had an [i] in them which has since disappeared, and this *i* had the power to change the root vowel. (See §8.11 for an explanation.)

6.8   Like *good*, *better*, and *best* in Modern English, some adjectives in OE have irregular comparatives and superlatives, often from different roots altogether. You must simply memorize the most important of these, though many of them survive into Modern English.

Positive	Comparative	Superlative
lȳtel "little, small"	lǣssa	lǣst
miċel "much; great"	māra	mǣst
yfel "bad, evil"	wiersa	wierst
gōd "good"	betera, sēlra	betst, sēlest

Exercise 6.3: RECOGNIZING COMPARATIVES AND SUPERLATIVES

Instructions. *In the sentences that follow: 1) underline all adjectives and 2) translate the sentences with the help of the vocabulary provided immediately after the exercise. To the right of each sentence, indicate in the first column whether the underlined adjective is positive, comparative, or superlative, and in the second what gender, case, and number the adjective possesses. (Hint: Keep in mind that the comparative always takes a weak ending—see §6.6.)*

Pos./Comp./Sup.   Gen/Case/Num.

1. Sē mōna is <u>swiftra</u> ðonne sēo sunne.

compar   *masc./nom./sing.*

The moon is swifter than the sun.

2. Ič eom <u>lēohtre</u> þonne mōna, swiftre þonne sunne.

compar   ~~weak~~ neuter */nom/sing*

I am lighter than the moon, faster than the sun

3. Lucifer wolde gōdličran ond hēahran stōl on heofne.

positive   comparc   m/acc/sing

Lucifere wanted a more goodly and higher seat in heaven

	Pos./Comp./Sup.	Gen/Case/Num.

4. Iċ nǣfre ne ġe-seah [saw] lāðran landscipe.

POSATIVE
~~COMPER.~~
~~SUPR~~   m/acc/sing

I never saw a more loathsome region .

5. Iċ eardiġe on lāðran landscipe.

POSATIVE
~~COMPER~~   m/dat/sing

I dwell in a more loathsome region .

6. Sēo ġe-seah [saw] þone dryhten lāðra monna.
(Hint: see §2.11.3.b)

lord loath men
POSATIVE
~~COMPER.~~   m/gen/Plrl.

She saw the lords ~~most~~ more loathsome men .

7. Mē is snæġl swiftra.
(Hint: see §6.6.2)

comper   m/dat/sing

~~than~~ The snail is faster than me .

8. Þā æðelingas bēoð him þe lāðran.
(Hint: see §2.11.4.b)

are
comper.   m/dat/sing

The noblemen are the more harmful to him .

Pos./Comp./Sup.   Gen/Case/Num.

[handwritten: From one your woman I am overpowerd]

9. Fram ānre ġingran fǣmnan iċ eom ofer-swīþed.

[handwritten: POSITIVE?]   *[handwritten: F/dat/sing.]*

[handwritten: I am overpowerd by only one younger woman.]

10. Iċ eom māre þonne þēs middan-ġeard, lǣsse
þonne hond-wyrm.

[handwritten: Compar.]   *[handwritten: n/nom/sing]*

[handwritten: I am greater than this earth, smaller than a handworm.]

VOCABULARY FOR EXERCISE 6.3

æðeling (m) = nobleman, retainer
[§2.7]

ān (adjective) = ONE, lone; a/an [§6.1]

bēon (irregular verb) = to BE [§6.5.1]

dryhten (m) = lord [§2.7]

eardian (weak verb II) = to dwell,
live [§3.12]

eom = see *bēon*

fǣmne (weak f) = woman, maiden [§3.4]

fram (preposition + dat) = FROM,
by [§6.15]

ġeong (adjective) = YOUNG [§6.1, §6.5]

ġingre = see *ġeong*

gōdliċ (adjective) = GOODLY, good [§6.1]

bēah (adjective) = HIGH [§6.1]

heofen (m) HEAVEN [§2.7]

him (pronoun) = to him or to them
[§7.1]

hond-wyrm (m) = a kind of insect
(literally, HAND-WORM or
–serpent) [§2.7]

iċ (pronoun) = I [§7.1]

lǣsse (adjective) = LESS [§6.7]

landscip (m) = region, area of land
(ModE *landscape* was borrowed much
later from Dutch) [§10.11.1]

lāð (adjective) = LOATHsome, hateful [§6.1]

lēoht (adjective) = LIGHT, bright; not heavy [§6.1]

Lucifer (m) = the devil (before his fall from grace)

māre (adjective) = see [§6.8]

mē (pronoun) = me [§7.1]

middan-ġeard (m) = earth (lit., MIDDle-YARD or middle earth) [§2.7]

mōna (weak m) = MOON [§3.3]

monn (m) = MAN, male; human being [§10.4.2]

nǣfre (adverb) = NEVER [§6.9]

ne (adverb) = not [§6.9]

ofer-swīþed (adjective) = OVERpowered, conquered (originally the past participle of the weak verb 1 *ofer-swīþan* "to overpower") [§3.11]

on (preposition) = (+ dat) ON, in; (+ acc) onto, into [§6.15]

ond (conjunction) = AND [§5.1.1]

sē, sēo, þæt (definite artical) = THE [§2.5]

(ġe) seah (verb form not yet covered) = SAW (past sing) [§9.1, §11.1]

snæġl (m) = SNAIL [§2.7]

stōl (m) = STOOL, seat [§2.7]

sunne (weak f) = SUN [§3.4]

swift (adjective) = SWIFT, fast [§6.1, §6.5]

þā = see *sē, sēo, þæt*

þe (comparative marker) = THE (as in "*the* bigger *the* better") [§6.4]

þēs (pronoun) = THIS [§7.7]

þonne (adverb) = THEN [§6.9]

þonne (conjunction) = THAN [§5.1.1]

willan (irregular verb) = to want, wish, desire (past sing: *wolde*) [§6.5.3]

6.9   Lesson Three: Adverbs

By and large, OE does not form adverbs the way Modern English does—that is, by adding an *-ly* to an adjective (*slow / slowly, quick / quickly, strange / strangely*, etc.). In fact, the ancestor of *-ly* (OE *-līċ*) was originally an adjectival ending (see OE *gōdliċ* "goodly"). Instead, OE normally added a simple *-e* to an adjective to make it into an adverb. See for example:

Adjective	Adverb
ēċeliċ "eternal"	ēċelīċe "eternally"
dēop "deep, profound"	dēope "deeply, profoundly"
fæst "fixed, firm"	fæste "firmly"
lēas "false, lying"	lēase "falsely, deceitfully"
swīþ "strong, mighty"	swīþe "exceedingly, very; strongly"
scearpliċ "sharp, painful"	scearplīċe "sharply, painfully"
torht "bright"	torhte "brightly"
ān "one, single"	āne "only"

Adverbium is "wordes ġe-fēra," for-ðan ðe hē næfð nāne fulfremednysse, būton hē mid ðām worde bēo. Word ġe-fylð his aġene ġe-tacnunge mid fullum andġyte. þonne ðū cwyst: *scribo* "iċ write," þonne byð ðær full andġyt. *Adverbium* is *bene* "wel." Her nys nā ful andġyt, būton ðū cweðe word ðār-tō: *bene scribo* "wel iċ wrīte"; *bene scribis* "wel ðū wrītst"; *bene scribit* "wel hē wrīt"; . . . and meniġ-fealdlīċe: *male legimus* "yfele wē rædað"; *melius legitis* "bet ġē rædað"; *optime legunt* "sēlost hī rædað," *et cetera*.

Ælfric on Adverbs

An *adverb* is a "verb's (lit., word's) companion," because it has no independence (or completeness), unless it occurs with the verb. A verb fulfills its own signification with a full meaning. When you say, *scribo* "I write," then there is full meaning. *Bene* "well" is an adverb. There is no full meaning here unless you say a verb in addition: *bene scribo* "I write well"; *bene scribes* "you write well"; *bene scribit* "he writes well"; and in the plural: *male legimus* "we read badly"; *melius legitis* "you all read better"; *optime legunt* "they read best," etc.

Keep in mind, though, that an adjective with a case ending might look identical in form to an adverb.

Swīþe rincas feallað. (Strong warriors are falling.)	adjective	(see §6.1.2, masc, nom pl)
Rincas feohtaþ swīþe. (Warriors fight strongly.)	adverb	
Þæt torhte lond is wīd. (The bright land is broad.)	adjective	(see §6.2.1, n, nom sing)
Hē singeð torhte. (He sings brightly.)	adverb	

6.10   Irregular Forms

The adjective/adverb relationship may also be obscured by some adjectives that end in an *-e* naturally.

Adjective	Adverb
clǣne "clean, pure"	clǣne "entirely"
ēaþe "easy, kind"	ēaþe "easily"
þicce "thick"	þicce "thickly"
fæste "quick; firm"	fæste "quickly; firmly"

Interestingly, some of these have survived into Modern English as adverbs without an *-ly* suffix, and since final *-e* was lost in a later period, the adjective and adverb forms are still identical in Modern English:

Adverb	*Adjective*
The rain came down thick.	The thick rain came down.
The car got clean away.	The clean car got away.
The stag ran fast.	The fast stag ran.

In a move to our current system, some adjectives are converted to adverbs by the addition of a *-līċe* suffix.   **6.11**

Adjective	Adverb
blind "blind"	blindlīċe "blindly"
dīegol "secret"	dīegollīċe "secretly"

Some adverbs not formed from adjectives may take other forms (many ending in *-a*), but you can look them up easily (for example, *tela* "well, properly," *fela* "very much, many," etc.).   **6.12**

COMPARATIVE AND SUPERLATIVE FORMS   **6.13**

Like adjectives, the vast majority of OE adverbs take *-or* for the comparative and *-ost* for the superlative forms, but unlike the adjectives, they take no further endings.

Base	Comparative	Superlative
hearde	heardor	heardost
dēope	dēopor	dēopost

6.14   IRREGULAR FORMS

There are some irregular adverbs, as you might expect: the first group forms its comparatives and superlatives from different roots, while the second forms the comparative by a change of vowel (i-mutation—see §8.11) rather than adding an -or.

Base	Comparative	Superlative
lȳtle "little"	lǣs	lǣst, lǣsest
miċle "much"	mā	mǣst
wel "well"	bet, sēl	betst, sēlest
yfle "evilly"	wiers	wyrrest, wyrst
feor "far"	fierr	firrest
nēah "near"	nȳr, nēar	nīehst, nēxt
sōfte "softly"	sēft	sōftost

Exercise 6.4: DISTINGUISHING ADVERBS FROM ADJECTIVES WITH ENDINGS

Instructions. *Translate the following sentences with the help of the vocabulary below, underlining the adverbs and circling the adjectives. Write "Comp." or "Super." above any comparative or superlative adjective or adverb. Since you have not yet studied them, strong verbs are glossed immediately after their appearance, in square brackets [ ] if they are difficult to recognize.*

1. Winter bringeð (swifte) windas.

   <u>Winter brings swift winds</u>.

2. Nū þū in helle scealt dēope ġe-dūfan.

    _____.

3. Þā flot-menn ā-druncon [drowned] on þām dēopan flōde.

    _____.

4. Þā flot-menn suncon [sank] swīðe dēope.

    _____.

5. Hire mīht is ufor þonne heofon & brādre þonne eorðe & dēopre þonne sǣ.

    _____.

6. Sē fisc swimmeð on dēopre sǣ.

    _____.

    (Question: What gender is sǣ in this sentence?)

7. Sē bera hæfþ mē fæste be-fangen [caught].

    _____.

8. Hē on fæstre stōwe lǣdde his folc.

_____ .

9. Þæt wīf is him fæstre. (Hint: See §6.6.2.)

_____ .

10. On sweartre nihte sē ǣglǣca cōm [came].

_____ .

VOCABULARY FOR EXERCISE 6.4

ā-druncon (verb form not yet covered) = "drowned" (past pl) [§8.4]

ǣglǣca (weak m) = monster [§3.3]

be-fangen (verb form not yet covered) = caught (past pl) [§9.3]

bēon (irregular verb) = to BE [§4.5.1]

bera (weak m) = BEAR (the animal) [§3.3]

brād (adjective) = BROAD, wide [§6.1]

brāde (adverb) = BROADly, widely, expansively [§6.9]

bringeð (verb form not yet covered) = "BRINGs" (present 3 sing) [§8.6]

cōm (verb form not yet covered) = "came" (past sing) [§8.7]

dēop (adjective) = DEEP; profound [§6.1]

dēope (adverb) = DEEPly; profoundly, seriously [§6.9]

ġe-dūfan (verb form not yet covered) = DIVE, sink (infinitive) [§8.5]

eorðe (weak f) = EARTH [§3.4]

fæst (adjective) = firm, secure; quick (see ModE color-FAST) [§6.1]

fæste (adverb) = firmly, securely; quickly [§6.9]

fisc (m) = FISH [§2.7]

flōd (m) = FLOOD, sea [§2.7]

flot-menn (m pl) = sailors (sing: *flot-mann*; related to ModE FLOAT) [§10.4.2]

folc (n) = FOLK, people [§2.9]

habban (weak verb III) = to HAVE [§4.1.1]

hell (f) = HELL, place of eternal torment [§2.8]

heofon (m) = HEAVEN [§2.7]

him = him, them (dat 3 sing/pl personal pronoun) [§7.1]

hire (pronoun) = HER (a possessive form) [§7.1]

in (preposition) = (+ dat) IN, on; (+ acc) into, onto [§6.16.2]

is = see *bēon*

lǣdan (weak verb I) = to LEAD [§3.11]

mē (pronoun) = ME (1 dat sing) [§7.1]

miht (f) = MIGHT, power [§2.8]

niht (f) = NIGHT [§10.4.2]

nū (adverb) = NOW [§6.9]

on (preposition) = (+ dat) in, ON; (+ acc) into, onto [§6.15]

sǣ (m or f) = SEA [§10.11.1, 10.11.2]

scealt = see sculan

sculan (preterite-present verb) = must [§4.3.1]

sē, sēo, þæt (definite article) = THE [§2.5]

stōw (f) = place [§2.8]

suncon (verb form not yet covered) = "sank" (past pl) [§8.6]

sweart (adjective) = dark (see ModE SWART) [§6.1]

swift (adjective) = swift, fast [§6.1]

swimmeð (verb form not yet covered) = "swims" (present sing) [§8.6]

swīðe (adverb, intensifier) = very [§6.9]

þā = see sē, sēo, þæt

þæt = see sē, sēo, þæt

þām = see sē, sēo, þæt

þonne (conjunction) = THAN [§5.1.1]

þū (pronoun) = you, THOU [§7.1]

ufor (adjective, comparative) = higher, greater [related to ModE OVER] [§6.1]

wīf (n) = woman; WIFE [§2.9]

wind (m) = WIND [§2.7]

winter (m or n) = WINTER [§2.7 or §2.9]

6.15   Lesson Four: Prepositions

Though you have already learned many of the basics of prepositions in Chapter Two (see §2.11.2.b, §2.11.4.d, etc.), recognizing some of the finer points of prepositional phrases can enhance the accuracy and speed of your reading.

Prepositions (words usually indicating a position in time or space, like *in, under, over, after, before, to, out,* etc.) demand an object, either a noun or a pronoun. As the name "pre-position" implies, prepositions normally appear *before* their objects. Since the nouns or pronouns that follow prepositions are "governed" by the preposition, they are called objects of that preposition. In OE, prepositions require their objects to be in a particular case. For example, *þurh* "through" generally takes an accusative object, while *æfter* "after, according to" usually takes a dative one. As such, these prepositions are marked in the glossary with *(+ acc)* and *(+ dat)* respectively.

> *þurh þæt swefn*   (+ acc)
> (through, by means of the dream)

> *æfter þām wordum*   (+ dat)
> (after the words)

Since the object of a preposition is often a noun, it can carry a full complement of modifiers (adjectives and sometimes other nouns) which may at first make the phrase difficult to decipher, particularly when a modifying noun or noun phrase contains a weak adjective or noun. In the following examples, both prepositions and their objects appear in bold face:

> ***fram** þǣre wiċċan **hūse***
> (from the witch's house)

Here, *hūse* (neuter dat sing) is the object of *fram*, while *þǣre wiċċan* "the witch's" is a weak feminine genitive singular noun modifying *hūse*.

of þǣre ilcan abbudissan **mynstre**
(from that same abbess's monastery)

in þāra æfter-fylġendra cyninga **tīdum**
(in the after-following kings' times)

This phrase means "in the times of the kings who followed after." The object of the preposition *in* is *tīdum* (at the end of the phrase), while *þāra æfter-fylġendra cyninga* is a genitive noun phrase. The adjective *æfter-fylġendra* may be a bit difficult to decipher: it is based ultimately on a verb, *æfter-fylġian* "to follow after." The *-end* ending makes it into a present participle "after-following" and the *-ra* is the genitive plural adjectival ending.

on ðæs lāðestan hǣðenes heaðo-rinces **bēafod**
(on the head of the most hateful heathen's battle-warrior)
(lit., on the most hateful heathen's battle-warrior's head)

The accusative object of the preposition *on* is *hēafod*, again at the very end of the phrase. Sandwiched in between are *two* genitive nouns, one of which modifies the other. The meaning of the phrase is difficult to decipher until the context of this excerpt makes clear that the battle-warrior is the underling of the most hateful heathen.

EXCEPTIONAL. As you've already guessed, there are a few complications, but on the whole they are fairly minor. First of all, some prepositions seem to allow objects in more   **6.16**

than one case, sometimes (but not always) with a change in meaning. For example, the preposition *tō* "to, up to, at, as" could take the accusative, genitive, or dative (with slight changes in meaning).

*Sē cyning **tō þām wītegan** spræc.* (The king spoke to the wise [man].)	(+ dat)	"to"
*Ælfsiġe fōr **tō ðǣm mynstre**.* (Ælfsiġe went up the minster.)	(+ acc)	"up to"
*Sē cyning fōr **tō þāra nīwra scypa**.* (The king travelled to the new ships.)	(+ gen)	"to"
*Hē hit **tō ġiefe** habban nolde.* (He did not want to have it as a gift.) (lit., He it as gift to have wanted not.)	(+ dat)	"as"
*Hē **tō dēofle** wearð.* (He turned into a devil.) (lit., He as devil became.)	(+ dat)	"into"

6.16.1 POST-POSITIONS? Especially in poetry, prepositions can sometimes appear *after* their objects, in some cases separated from them by several words, so be vigilant! In the following examples, the objects of prepositions appear in italic boldface, while the prepositions themselves appear in roman type:

Scedelandum in
(in Sweden)

*Đā cōm **mē** tō, mīn sunu Petrus.*
(Then came to me my son Peter.)

*Þæt wīf **him** cwæð tō.*
(The woman spoke to him.)
(lit., The woman him spoke to.)

EITHER/OR. Some prepositions can take *either* dative *or* accusative objects, where the   **6.16.2**
accusative signals some sort of "motion toward" (into, onto, up to, up under, across to,
etc.), and the dative signals a set state of being or stasis (on, in, under, over, etc.). Though
the concept is a bit difficult, consider the following sentence pairs from Modern English.
The preposition in the first of each pair indicates stasis or state of being (and would thus
take the dative in OE) while the second indicates "motion towards" (and in OE would
take an accusative object).

1. The helicopter hovered over the pond.

   The jetliner flew over the ocean to reach its destination.

2. The fish swam in the tank.   (Though there is motion here—the fish swims—
                                  it is not motion *toward* something.)
   The shark swam into the cage.

3. The key is under the mat.

   The cat leapt out from under the table.

Note that Modern English often changes the preposition slightly to indicate the distinction (*in / into, under / from under*). OE, on the other hand, normally keeps the preposition the same but varies the case of the object. The OE preposition *in* "in" is a perfect example of such an "either/or" preposition: when it takes the accusative it means *into* (motion toward)—when it takes the dative it means simply *in* (state of being). Such "either/or" prepositions will be labeled in the glossary as *(preposition + acc / dat)*.

*Sē cyning eardiaþ **in þām tūne**.*	(dative—state of being, stasis)
(The king lives in the town.)	

as opposed to

*Sē cyning rīdeð **in þone tūn**.*	(accusative—motion toward)
(The king rides into the town.)	

Another example:

*Twælf gatu wǣron **on þǣre ċeastre**.*	(dative—state of being)
([There] were twelve gates in the town.)	

as opposed to

*Ðā æðelingas cōmon **on þā ċeastre**.*	(accusative—motion toward)
(The nobles came into the town.)	

6.16.3   INSTRUMENTAL. Prepositions that take the dative often substitute the instrumental with no change in meaning.

mid þām folce
(with, among the people)

mid þȳ folce
(with, among the people)

Exercise 6.5: PREPOSITIONAL PHRASES

Instructions. *1) Draw a box around the object of each boldfaced preposition, 2) indicate what case the object of the preposition is in (for multiple prepositions, multiple blank lines are provided), and finally 3) translate each sentence in the space provided with the aid of the glossary listed below. Verb forms not yet covered are translated in square brackets.*

Case of Object

1. Hē wæs **mid** ðām cyninge.   *Dative*

    He was with the king.

2. Sē dēofol ġe-fealleð [falls] **on** þæt dēope dæl.   _____

    _____

3. Sē here cōm **in** þā mǣran burh.   _____

    _____

Case of Object

4. Sēo cwēn bryttede welan **in** þǣre wīdan burhe.   _____

_____.

5. Hē spǣtte **on** þā eorðan.   _____

_____.

6. Hē þone rinc feor for-wræc [banished] man-cynne **fram**.   _____

_____.

7. Fēollon [fell] þā þā englas **of** heofnum **on** helle.   _____

_____

_____.

8. Sume men **fram** þāra wyrma slītunge sweltað.   _____

_____.

9. Sēo wolde sūð **ofer** sǣ.   _____

_____.

(Hint: See §4.5.4 and §5.2.2.)

Case of Object

10. Sē wæs cyning **ofer** eall Angelcyn **būtan** ðǣm Deniscan
   dǣle þe [which] **under** Dena on-walde wæs.

_____

_____

_____

_____

VOCABULARY FOR EXERCISE 6.4

Angel-cyn (n) = England, the tribe of the
   ANGLES [§2.8]

bryttan (weak verb I) = to distribute [§3.11]

burh (f) = fortification, castle; town
   [§10.4.2]

būtan (preposition + dat) = except [§6.15]

cwēn (f) = QUEEN [§2.8]

cyning (m) = KING [§2.7]

dǣl (m) = part, portion [Ger. *Teil*; §2.7]

dæl (n) = DALE, valley [§2.8]

Dena (m plural only) = DANES [§10.11.1]

Denisc (adjective) = DANISH [§6.1]

dēofol (m) = DEVIL [§2.7]

dēop (adjective) = DEEP [§6.1]

eall (adjective) = ALL, entire [§6.1]

engel (m) = ANGEL [§2.7]

eorðe (weak f) = EARTH, ground [§3.4]

fēollon (verb form not yet covered) = "fell"
   (past plural) [§9.3]

feor (adverb) = FAR (+ fram = far from)
   [§6.9]

fram (preposition + dat) = FROM [§6.15]

hell (f) = HELL [§2.8]

heofon (m, f, often pl) = HEAVEN; the
   heavens, the sky [§2.7, §2.8]

here (m) = army [§10.2.1]

in (preposition + acc, dat) = (acc) into, (dat)
   in [§6.15]

mǣre (adjective) = famous, illustrious [§6.1]

mann-cyn (n) = MAN-KINd, human beings (as a collective) [§2.8]

men (m pl of *mann*) = MEN [§10.4.2]

mid (preposition + dat) = with, among [§6.15]

of (preposition + dat) = from, OFF [§6.15]

ofer (preposition + acc) = OVER [§6.15]

on (preposition) = (+ dat) ON, in; (+ acc) onto, into [§6.15]

on-weald (n) = power (related to ModE WIELD) [§2.9]

rinc (m) = warrior, soldier [§2.7]

sǣ (m or f, often indeclinable) = SEA [§10.11.1, 10.11.2]

sē, sēo, þæt (definite article) = THE [§2.5]

slītung (f) = bite, sting [§2.8]

spǣtan (weak verb I) = to SPIT [§3.11]

sum (adjective) = SOME, certain [§6.1]

sūð (adverb) = SOUTH [§6.9]

sweltað (verb form not yet covered) = "die" (present 3 plural) [see ModE SWELTer; §8.6]

þā (adverb) = then [§6.9]

þā = see *sē, sēo, þæt*

under (preposition + dat or acc) = UNDER [§6.15]

wela (weak m) = WEALth, riches; happiness [§3.3]

wīd (adjective) = WIDE, spacious [§6.1]

willan (irregular verb, past tense sing.: wolde) = to wish, want, desire (+ infinitive) [§4.5.3]

wyrm (m) = WORM, serpent, snake [§10.11.1]

Camels and a Homodubius:

An illuminated page from *The Wonders of the East* as preserved in the Nowell Codex (London, British Library, Cotton Vitellius A.xv., fol. 101v).

A PUZZLE

The following text describes a way of creating cryptograms (i.e., writing in code). try to translate the instructions and decipher the code. The appropriate words are listed in the main vocabulary for Reading VI at the end of the chapter. HINT: The code works by substituting consonants for vowels. Remember that the Roman alphabet had no separate forms for v, w, or j.

Ðis is *quinque vocales*. Mid þysum fif stafum man mæg wrītan, swā hwæt swā hē wile. Hit is lȳtel cræft, ac þēah man mæg dwelian maniga men mid, ǣġðer ġe wǣre ġe unwǣre.

Cxnnb! Mbgf þx brfgdbn.
Hwæt þks mbgf bfpn.
Kc wfnf þæt hkt nks fõrædf.

Reading VI: WONDERS OF THE EAST (3)

¹ Supply a "that" or "which" after *stōw*.

² i.e., 100

³ literally, "from there [it] is east where"

⁴ See §2.11.4.e.

⁵ *swā is wēn*: literally, "so (there) is an expectation." Translate: "so one might think."

Ciconia in *Gallia* hātte þæt land þǣr bēoð men ā-cende on þrym hēowum, þāra hēafdu bēoð ġe-mānu swā lēona hēafdu, and hī bēoð xx fōta lange, and hȳ habbað miċelne mūð swā fann. Ġyf hȳ hwylċne monnan on þǣm landum on-ġitað oððe ġe-sēoþ oððe him hwilċ man folgiende bið, þonne feor hī flēoð and blōde hȳ swǣtað. Þas bēoð men ġe-wende.

5   Beġeondan Brixonte, þǣre ēa, ēast þonon bēoð men ā-cende lange and miċle, þā habbað fēt and sconcan xii fōta lange, sīdan mid brēostum seofon fōta lange. *Hostes* hȳ synd nemned cūþlīċe. Swā hwylcne man swā hȳ ġe-læċċað þonne fretað hī hyne. Ðonne syndon wild-dēor þā [syndon] hāten *Lertices*. Hȳ habbað eoseles ēaran and sċēapes wulle and fugeles fēt. Þonne syndon ōþere ēalond sūð from *Brixonte* on þām bēoð men būtan

10 hēafdum. Þā habbað on hyra brēostum heora ēagan and mūð. Hȳ syndon eahta fōta lange and eahta fōta brāde.

    Ðǣr bēoð dracan cende, þā bēoð on lenge hund-tēontiġes fōt-mǣla lange and fiftiġes. Hȳ bēoð grēate swā stǣnene swēoras miċle. For þāra dracena miċelnesse ne mæġ nān manna ēaþelīċe on þæt land ġe-faran. From þisse stōwe is ōðer rīċe on þā sūð healfe

15 gārsecges . . . ; þǣr bēoð cende *Homodubii*—þæt bēoð twȳliċe "twi-men." Hȳ bēoþ oð ðone nafolan on menniscum ġe-sċēape and siþþan on eoseles ġe-līċnesse, and hȳ habbað lange sconcan swā fugelas and līþeliċe stefne. Ġif hȳ hwilċne man on þǣm landum on-ġytað oððe ġe-sēoð þonne flēoð hȳ feor. Ðonne is ōþer stōw¹ el-reordiġe men bēoð on, and þā habbað cyningas under [him] þāra is ġe-teald c.² Þæt syndon þā wyrstan men and

20 þā el-reordiġestan. . . .

    Ðanon is ēast þǣr³ bēoð men ā-cende þā bēoð on wæstme fiftyne fōta lange and x brāde. Hȳ habbað miċel hēafod and ēaran swā fann. Ōþer ēare hȳ him on niht under-brǣdað, and mid ōþran hȳ wrēoð him. Bēoð þā ēaran swīðe lēohte and hȳ bēoð swā on līċhaman swā hwīte swā meolc. Ġyf hȳ hwilċne mannan on þǣm lande ġe-sēoð oððe on-

25 ġytað, þonne nimað hȳ hyra ēaran him⁴ on hand and flēoð swīðe, swā hrædlīċe swā is wēn⁵ þæt hȳ flēogen.

LATIN ORIGINAL

Item Liconia in Gallia nascuntur homines tripartito colore quorum capita leonum pedibus xx ore amplissimo sicut vannum hominem cum cognoverint aut si quis persequatur longe fugiunt et sanguine sudent hi putantur homines fuisse.

Trans Brixontem flumen ad orientem nascuntur homines longi et magni habentes foemora et surras xii pedum latera cum pectore vii pedum colore nigro quos hostes rite 5 appellamus nam quoscumque capiunt comedunt. Sunt et aliae bestiae in Brixonte quae Lertices appellantur auribus asininis vellere ovino pedibus ovum. Est et in alia insula in Brixonte ad meridiem in qua nascuntur homines sine capitibus qui in pectore habent oculos et os alti sunt pedum viii et lati simili modo pedum viii.

Nascuntur et ibi dracones longitudinem habentes cl pedum vastitudine columnarum 10 propter multitudinem draconum nemo facile adire potest trans flumen. Post hunc locum alia est regio oceano dexteriore parte . . . ; ubi nascuntur homodubii qui usque ad umbilicum homines speciem habent reliquo corpore onagro similes longis pedibus ut aves lena voce sed hominem cum viderint longe fugiunt. Est et alius locus hominum barbarorum habens sub se reges numero cx; genus pessimum et barbarorum. 15

Ultra hoc ad orientem nascuntur homines longi pedum xv lati pedum x. caput magnum et aures habentes tamquam vannum unam sibi nocte substernunt de alia se cooperiunt et tegunt se his auribes leve et candido corpore sunt quasi lacteo homines cum viderint tollunt sibi aures et longe fugiunt quasi putes eos volare.

VOCABULARY FOR READING VI

ac (conjunction) = but

ā-cennan (weak verb I) = to bring forth, give birth to [§3.11]

ǣġðer ġe . . . ġe (conjunction) = both . . . and [§5.1.1]

and (conjunction) = AND

be-ġeondan (preposition + acc/dat) = on the other side of, BEYOND [§6.15]

bēon (irregular verb) = to BE [§4.5.1]

blōd (n) = BLOOD [§2.9]

brād (adjective) = BROAD, wide [§6.1]

bregdan (verb form not yet covered) = "join together" or "solve" [§8.6]

brēost (m, f, or n pl) = chest; stomach, mid-section [§2.7-9]

Brixonte = proper name for a river

būtan (preposition + dat) = without [§6.15]

cennan (weak verb I) = to bring forth, give birth to (past participle = "born") [§3.11]

Ciconia = proper name

cræft (m) = skill, art; trick [§2.7]

cunnian (weak verb II) = to attempt, try (imperative sing = *cunna!*) [§3.11]

cūþlīċe (adverb) = certainly, clearly, evidently [§6.9]

cyning (m) = KING [§2.7]

draca (weak m) = dragon, fire-DRAKE [§3.3]

dwelian (weak verb II) = to deceive, lead astray [§3.12]

ēa (f) = river [§2.8]

ēage (weak n) = eye [§3.5]

eahta (number & adjective) = EIGHT [§6.1]

ēalond (n) = isLAND [§2.9]

ēare (weak n) = EAR [§3.5]

ēast (adverb) = EAST [§6.9]

ēaþelīċe (adverb) = easily, without difficulty [§6.9]

el-reordiġ (adjective) = foreign, of strange speech, barbarous [see OE *el-* "strange, ALien" + *reord* "language"; §6.1]

eosel (m, f) = ass; donkey [§2.7]

eð-rǣde (adjective) = "easy to READ" [§6.1]

fann (f) = a winnowing FAN (usually a broad shovel or a wide basket used to toss grain into the air in order to separate it from the chaff) [§3.4]

(ġe)faran (verb form not yet covered) = "travel," "FARE" (infinitive) [§9.2]

feor (adverb) = FAR [§6.9]

fēt = FEET (m acc 3 pl of *fōt* "foot") [§10.4.2]

fīf (number) = FIVE

fīftiġ (n) = FIFTY

fīftyne (number) = FIFTEEN (+ partitive gen §2.11.3.c)

flēoð (verb form not yet covered) = "FLEE, attempt to escape" (present 3 pl) [§8.5, §11.1]

flēogen (verb form not yet covered) =
"are flying," "would fly" (present 3 pl
subjunctive) [§8.5]

folgian (weak verb II) = to FOLLOW
(+ dat) [§3.12]

for (preposition + dat) = FOR, because
of [§6.15]

fōt (n) = FOOT (the body part); foot
(unit of measurement) [§10.4.2]

fōt-mǣl (n) = FOOT-measure [§2.9]

frettan (weak verb I) = to devour,
consume, gobble up [§3.11]

from (preposition + dat) = FROM, away
from [§6.15]

fugel (m) = bird, FOWL [§2.7]

Gallia = proper name

gārsecg (m) = ocean, sea [§2.7]

ġe . . . ġe (correlative conjunction) =
whether...or [§5.1]

ġif, ġyf (conjunction) = IF [§5.1.1]

grēat (adjective) = GREAT, tall, thick,
massive [§6.1]

habban (weak verb III) = to HAVE,
possess [§4.1]

hand (f) = HAND [§10.6]

hāten (verb form not yet covered) =

"called," "named" (past participle)
[§9.3]

hātte (verb form not yet covered) = "is
called" (present 3 sing) [§9.3]

hē, hēo, hit = HE, she, IT (pronoun)
[§7.1]

hēafod (n) = HEAD [§2.9]

healf (f) = HALF, side, region [§2.8]

heora, hyra = their (3 gen pl personal
pronoun) [§7.1]

hēow, hīw (n) = HUE, color [§2.9]

hī, hȳ = they (pronoun) [§7.1]

him (pronoun) = them (dat 3 pl pronoun,
dat direct object of *folgiende*) [§7.1]

him (pronoun) = themselves (reflective)
[§7.4]

hit = see *hē, hēo, hit*

Homodubii = proper name, Latin for
"doubtful or ambiguous humans"

Hostes = proper name, Latin for
"enemies"

hrædlīċe (adverb) = suddenly, nimbly [§6.9]

hund-tēontiġ (number) = one HUNDred

hwæt (pronoun) = WHAT [§7.6]

hwilċ, hwylċ (adjective) = any [§6.1]

hwīt (adjective) = WHITE [§6.1]

hyne (pronoun) = him (m acc 3 sing [§7.1]

iċ (pronoun) = I (nom 1 sing) [§7.1]

in (preposition) = (+ dat) IN, on; (+ acc) into, onto [§6.16.2]

(ġe)læċċan (weak verb I) = to catch, seize, LATCH onto [§3.11]

land (n) = LAND, country [§2.9]

lang (adjective) = LONG, tall [§6.1]

leng (f) = LENGth [§10.11.1]

lēoht (adjective) = LIGHT, shining [§6.2.2]

lēon (m) = LION [§2.7]

Lertices = proper name

līċ-hama (weak m) = body [§3.3]

(ġe)līċnes (f) = LIKENESS [§2.8]

līþeliċ (adjective) = soft, gentle, LITHE [§6.1]

lytel (adjective) = LITTLE, small, simple [§6.1]

magan (pret-pres verb) = to be able, can, have the power (to do something) [§4.4]

maġe = *mæġe* (subjunctive sing of *magan*)

man (pronoun) = one, a person [§7.8]

man (m) = MAN, person [§10.4.2]

(ġe)māne (adjective) = MANEd, with a mane [§6.1]

maniġ (adjective) = MANY [§6.1]

men = men, people (nom pl of *man*) [§10.4.2]

mennisc (adjective) = human [§6.1]

meolc (f) = MILK [§2.8]

miċel (adjective) = great, large [§6.1]

miċelnesse (f) = greatness, size [§2.8]

mid (adverb) = with it [§6.9]

mid (preposition + dat) = with [§6.15]

monna (weak m) = MAN, person [§3.3]

mūð (m) = MOUTH [§2.7]

nafola (weak m) = NAVEL [§3.3]

nān (pronoun or adjective) = NONE, no (pronoun + gen) [§7.8, 6.3]

ne (adverb) = not [§6.9]

nemnan (weak verb I) = to NAME, be called [§3.11]

nimað (verb form not yet covered) = "take" (present 3 pl) [see German *nehmen* "to take"; §8.7]

nis = see *bēon*

on (preposition) = (+ dat) in, ON; (+ acc) into, onto [§6.15]

on-ġitaþ, -ġytaþ (verb form not yet covered) = "see," "perceive" (present 3 pl) [§9.1]

oð (preposition + acc) = to, down/up to [§6.15]

oððe (conjunction) = or

ōþer (adjective) = OTHER, another;
second ; ōþer...ōþer = the one...the
other [§6.1]

quinque vocales = Latin for "five vowels"

riht (adjective) = RIGHT, correct [§6.1]

rīċe (n) = kingdom, realm [§10.2.2]

scēap (n) = SHEEP [§2.9]

(ġe)scēap (n) = SHAPE, form [§2.9]

sconca (weak m) = leg, SHANK [§3.3]

sē, sēo, þæt (def article and pronoun) =
the; he, she it [§2.5]

seofon (number or adjective) = SEVEN
[§6.1]

(ġe)sēoþ (verb form not yet covered) =
"SEE," "catch sight of"
(present 3 pl) [§11.1]

sīde (weak f) = SIDE, torso [§3.4]

siþþan (adverb) = afterwards, from there
on [§6.9]

stæf (m) = letter, character (dat pl =
stafum) [§2.7]

stǣnen (adjective) = made of stone, stone
[§6.1]

stefn (f) = voice [see Ger *Stimme*; §2.8]

stōw (f) = place [§2.8]

sūð (adjective and adverb) = SOUTH
[§6.1, §6.9]

swā (conjunction) = like, just like, as
[§5.1.1]; (adverb) so, to such an extent,
thus; *swā . . . swa* = as . . . as [§6.9]

swā hwæt swā (pronoun) =
WHATSOever, whatever [§7.8.1]

swā hwylċ . . . swā (adjective) = whatever,
whoever [§7.8.1]

swǣtan (weak verb I) = to SWEAT,
exude (+ dat) [§3.11]

swēor (m) = pillar, column [§2.7]

swīðe (adverb) = very quickly, very
swiftly [§6.9]

synd, syndon = see *bēon*

(ġe)teald (n) = number, count [§2.9]

twi-men (m pl) = double men, dubious
men [§10.4.2]

twȳliċ (adjective) = doubtful, ambiguous,
belonging to TWO different
categories [§6.1]

þā = see *sē, sēo, þæt*

þā = who, which (m nom 3 pl relative
pronoun)[§7.5]

þǣr = (adverb) THERE [§6.9];
(conjunction) where [§5.1.1]

þæt (conjunction) = THAT [§5.1.1]

þām = which (n dat sing relative
pronoun) [§7.5.3]

þanon (adverb) = from there, from that
place, THENce [§6.9]

þāra = of whom, whose (gen pl relative pronoun) [§7.5]

þāra = see *sē, sēo, þæt*

þās = THOSE (beings) (nom 3 pl of the pronoun *þis*) [§7.7]

þēah (adverb) = nevertheless [§6.9]

ðis, þysum = THIS, these [§7.7]

þonne = (adverb) then, immediately [§6.9] ; (conjunction) when [§5.1.1]

þonon (adverb) = from there, THENCE [§6.9]

þry (adjective) = THREE [§6.1]

þū (pronoun) = you [§7.1]

under (preposition + acc) = UNDER [§6.15]

under-brēdan (weak verb I) = to spread under [§3.11]

un-wær (adjective) = unaWARE [§6.1]

wær (adjective) = aWARe, astute [§6.1]

wæstm (m) = growth, stature, height, form [§2.7]

wēn (f) = belief, expectation [§2.8]

wēnan (weak verb I) = to imagine, expect, guess [§3.11]

(ġe)wendan (weak verb I) = to transform, change (past participle functions as an adjective: "transformed") [§3.11]

wild-dēor (n) = WILD animal [§2.9]

willan (irregular verb) = to wish, want, desire [§4.5.3]

wrēoð (verb form not yet covered) = "cover," "envelop" (present 3 pl) [§8.4, §11.1]

wrītan (verb form not yet covered) = "WRITE" (infinitive) [§8.4]

wull (f) = WOOL [§2.8]

wyrsta (adjective) = WORST (superlative of *yfel* "bad, evil") [§6.8]

Lessons Learned

Before leaving this chapter you should know . . .
- the basic context for "strong" and "weak" adjectives (§6.2).
- the strong (§6.1.1) and weak (§6.2.2) adjective endings by heart.
- how to recognize comparative and superlative forms of the adjective (§6.4).
- the basic functioning of prepositional phrases (§6.15).

SEVEN

Personal Pronouns, Reflexives, Relative Pronouns (Who, Which), Other Pronouns

This chapter will teach you most of what you need to know about pronouns. For efficiency in reading, it's important to know the third person pronouns by heart. You should be able to recognize or look up the rest.

7.1   Lesson One: Personal Pronouns

Unlike its Modern English equivalent, the OE personal pronoun has *three numbers* in the first and second person: singular and plural you know, but OE had a further number called the *dual*. This dual form made it possible to talk about two people—"we two" or "you two" or "us two," etc.—but disappeared during late OE. It is relatively rare in our texts. Note that personal pronouns are so called because they have different forms for each of the three persons (see §3.10).

In the following charts, you should notice that there are generally two forms of the accusative, one which generally ends in -*ċ* or -*iċ* and another which is identical to the dative. Also note the wide variation in spelling especially in the third person plural as well as the third person feminine singular forms (several alternatives are listed below).

7.1.1   FIRST PERSON

	Singular	Dual	Plural
N	iċ "I"	wit "we two"	wē "we"
A	mē, meċ "me"	unc, uncit "us two"	ūs, ūsiċ "us"
G	mīn "my, mine"	uncer "our two"	ūser, ūre "our(s)"
D	mē "to me"	unc "to us two"	ūs "to us"

SECOND PERSON 7.1.2

	Singular	Dual	Plural
N	þū "you"	ġit "you two"	ġē "you"
A	þē, þeċ "you"	inc, incit "you two"	ēow, ēowiċ "you"
G	þīn "your(s)"	incer "your(s)"	ēower "your(s)"
D	þē "to you"	inc "to you two"	ēow "to you"

THIRD PERSON 7.1.3

	Masculine	Feminine	Neuter
N	hē "he"	hēo, hīo "she"	hit "it"
A	hine "him"	hīe, hēo, hī "her"	hit "it"
G	his "his"	hi(e)re "her(s)"	his "its"
D	him "to him"	hi(e)re "to her"	him "to it"

THIRD PERSON *plural (all genders)* 7.1.4

N	hīe, hī, hȳ, hēo "they"
A	hīe, hī, hȳ, hēo "them"
G	hi(e)ra, heora "their(s)"
D	him, heom "to them"

7.1.5   **AGREEMENTS AND DISAGREEMENTS**

Pronouns, of course, stand in the place of nouns, and the nouns to which the pronouns refer back are called their *antecedents*. Generally, OE uses pronouns in much the same way Modern English does. If the pronoun's antecedent is an inanimate object or an animal of no discernable sex, OE tends to prefer the neuter pronoun *hit* "it," while with nouns like *wīf* "woman," which are grammatically neuter but refer to the physically and culturally feminine, OE prefers the *natural* gender.

> *Sēo **bōc** cōm tō ūs and wē ā-wendon **hit** on Englisċ.*
> (The book came to us and we translated it into English.)

> *Þæt earme **wīf** andswyrde and cwæð þæt **bēo** wolde tō ċyrcan gān.*
> (The poor woman answered and said that she wanted [to] go to church.)

In a fair number of instances, however, OE pronouns, like those in other languages with grammatical gender, agree in gender with their antecedent nouns, *even when* the noun itself refers to an object with no immediately discernable sex. In the following two examples, the pronouns agree in gender with their antecedents: *bōc* is feminine, while *fisċ* is masculine.

> *Englas brōhton mē āne **bōc**, ac **bēo** wæs swȳðe ġe-hwǣde.*
> (Angels brought me a book, but it [lit., she] was very slender.)

> *Sē **fisċ** ġe-tācnað ġe-lēafan: swā **hyne** swīðor þā ȳþa wealcað swā **hē** strengra bið.*
> (The fish symbolizes belief: the more the waves toss it [lit., him] the stronger it is.)
> (lit., . . . as him more powerfully the waves toss, so he the stronger is.)

PRONOMEN is "ðæs naman speliend," sē spelað þone naman, þæt ðū ne ðurfe tūwa hine nemnan.

> Ġif ðū cwest nū, "Hwā lærde ðē?"
> Þonne cweðe iċ, "Dūnstān."
> "Hwā hādode ðē?"
> "*Hē* mē hādode."

Þonne stent sē "hē" on his naman stede and spelað hine. Eft, ġif ðū axast, *quis hoc fecit?* "Hwā dyde ðis?" Þonne cwest ðū, *ego hoc feci* "iċ dyde ðis," þonne stent sē "iċ" on ðīnes naman stēde.

A pronoun is "representing the name or noun," which represents (or, stands in for) the name, so that you do not need to name it twice.

> If you now said, "Who taught you?"
> Then I would say, "Dunstan."
> "Who ordained you?"
> "*He* ordained me."

Then the "he" stands in the place of his name and takes its place. Again, if you asked, *quis hoc fecit?* "Who did this?" Then (if) you said, *ego hoc feci* "I did this," then the "I" stands in the place of your name.

The definite article (*sē, sēo, þæt*—§2.5) can also function as a personal pronoun.

Hēo fongeþ fixas ond hēo eteð þā.
(She catches fish and she eats them.)

Sē rīdeð forþ.
(He rides forth.)

7.1.7   When personal pronouns follow their verbs immediately, the verb sometimes takes a reduced set of endings in the present tense (particularly in the first and second person plurals), so that the normal endings *-aþ* or *-iaþ* become *-e*.

*Myċel **habbe wē** ġe-synegod.*	normal form: *habbaþ*.
(Much have we sinned.)	
*And hwæt **wille ġē**?*	normal form: *willaþ*
(And what do you want?)	

Exercise 7.1: PERSONAL PRONOUNS

Instructions. *Translate the following sentences into Old English (refer to §3.11 for verb endings and to §5.2.5 for the use of tenses):*

1. I love him. (*lufian*)   *ic lufie hine*

2. She loves her.   _____

3. They love them.   _____

4. She is giving them the box.   _____

5. You (sing.) are giving her the sword. _____

6. I am giving you (pl.) pain. _____

7. Give (imper. sing.) me the book! _____

8. Give the box to us two (dual)! _____

VOCABULARY FOR EXERCISE 7.1

book = bōc (f) [§10.4.2]   *LOVE* = **lufian** (weak verb II) [§3.12]

box = **ċist** (f) [see German *Kiste* "box"; [§2.8]   *pain* = **sār** (n) [§2.9]

GIVE = **ġiefan** (strong verb 5) [§9.1]   *SWORD* = **sweord** (n) [§2.9]

POSSESSIVE   7.2

Personal pronouns in the genitive, though they can occasionally function as pronouns proper, most often act like adjectives, modifying a noun. In the few cases where they act as pronouns, you should translate them using what you already know about the genitive case (see §2.11.3.b-f) and supply an "of."

Hīe **his** eġe habbað.   PRONOUN
(They have fear of Him.)

> *His* is a genitive pronoun dependent on *eġe* "fear, awe."

Hīe hlystaþ **his**.   PRONOUN
(They listen to it.)

> The pronoun *his* is the neuter genitive direct object of *hlystaþ*, which requires a genitive object.

Þæt ēower fela ġe-seah.   PRONOUN
(Many of you saw that.)

> Here *ēower* is a genitive dependent on *fela* "many."

Næfre iċ māran ġe-seah . . . ðonne is ēower sum.   PRONOUN
(I never saw a larger [warrior] than a certain one of you is.)

> Here *ēower* is a genitive pronoun dependent on *sum* "one, a certain."

wine mīn   ADJECTIVE
(my friend)

> Here the adjective *mīn* follows the noun it modifies, a common position.

hæleð mīn sē lēofa   ADJECTIVE
(my beloved hero)

> Literally, "hero mine the beloved."

Wolde hire bearn wrecan.   ADJECTIVE
([She] wanted to avenge her child.)

Nū iċ ēower sceal frumcyn witan.   ADJECTIVE
(Now I must know your lineage.)

> Note that the verb *sceal* "must" comes between the adjective *ēower* and the noun it modifies, *frumcyn*—this kind of construction occurs mainly in poetry.

When they are used adjectivally, the genitives of first and second person pronouns (*mīn, þīn, ūre, ēower, uncer, incer*) and an old reflexive pronoun *sīn* "his, her, its" take strong adjective endings (see §6.1.1, 6.1.2). Note that all of the possessives considered here are long-stemmed; that is, they have a long vowel in the stem of the word or a short vowel followed by more than one consonant; therefore, they follow the strong declension for long-stemmed adjectives (and thus are -*u*-less in f sing and neuter plural—see §2.10.1).

Ġe-sette **mīnne** *hyht on þeċ.*
([I will] set my joy on you.)

> Note the strong m acc sing adjectival ending -*ne* on *mīn-ne*: see §6.1.1.

Þonne bēoð **ēowere** *ēagan ġe-openode.*
(Then your eyes [will] be opened.)

POSSESSIVE PRONOUNS, THIRD PERSON

Happily, the third person singular and plural possessive pronouns *his, hi(e)re, hiera, hi(e)ra, hēora* were not declined (i.e., they don't take any endings but always appear in the forms listed above).

Hē ā-sette his handa ofer **bēora** *ēagan.*
(He set his hands over their eyes.)

Hēo ā-hof **hire** *ēagan upp tō heofonum.*
(She lifted her eyes up to the skies.)

*Ne dorste **his** ēagan up ā-hebban.*
([He] did not dare to cast up his eyes.)

TIMESAVER

7.3   **DATIVES OF POSSESSION**

For whatever reason, OE usually doesn't allow a possessive pronoun with body parts (her head, his foot) but instead prefers a so-called "dative of possession" (to him, to her the head)—this simply means that the dative functions as a shadow genitive in this one isolated environment.

> **Him on bearme** *læ̇ġ mādma mæniġo.*
> (On his lap lay many treasures.)
> (lit., Him on lap lay [of] treasures many.)

7.4   Lesson Two: Reflexive Pronouns

In Modern English a reflexive pronoun is a pronoun that ends in *-self* or *-selves.* It usually appears in a sentence as a direct object, indirect object, or object of a preposition; it is "reflexive" in the sense that the pronoun reflects back or refers to the subject of the sentence. For example: (1) as a direct object: "I could kick *myself* for not studying grammar at an earlier age"; (2) as an indirect object: "She gave *herself* two hours for the journey"; (3) as an object of a preposition: "The dog wanted the bone for *itself.*"

In OE there are no separate forms for the reflexive pronoun: instead, personal pronouns function as reflexives.

> *Sēo sāwol hæfð on **hire** ðrēo ðing, þæt is ġe-mynd, and and-ġit, and willa.*
> (The soul has three things in itself [lit., herself], that is, mind, and understanding, and will.)

Wearþ hine þā on wyrmes līċ.
([He] transformed himself then into [a] serpent's likeness.)

Sē cyning un-hēanlīċe werede hine.
(The king bravely [lit., uncowardly] defended himself.)

Þā ċēap-menn biċgdon þā gōd for him.
(The merchants bought the goods for themselves.)

It's important to realize that in most cases context alone will allow you to distinguish between personal (*him, her*, etc.) and reflexive pronouns (*himself, herself*, etc.). In the last three examples, it would be possible to translate *hine* and *him* as regular personal pronouns, radically altering the meaning of the sentences. Thus, narrative context (the number of actors and how they interact) is crucial for translating such pronouns accurately.

[He] transformed *him* then into a serpent's likeness.

The king bravely defended *him*.

The merchants bought the goods for *them* (or, *for him*).

VERBS WHICH REQUIRE A REFLEXIVE   7.4.1

Some OE verbs require a reflexive object. (Such verbs will be marked "+ *reflexive*" in the glossary entries.) Some Modern English verbs function in a similar way (think of the verbs *to avail* and *to betake*, which require reflexive objects: *to avail oneself of something, to betake oneself to leave*). For the most part, however, OE reflexives accompanying verbs often aren't translated into Modern English. Certain verbs that describe emotions or mental states, for example, often take the reflexive.

*Hēo **hire on-drǣdeþ** helle wītu.*
(She fears hell's torments.)

> The reflexive *hire* is not translated, but has the sense "for herself."

*Ðā on-gān hēo **hire onemn-þrōwigan** þæs ealdan witan staðol-fæstnysse.*
(Then she began to sympathize with the steadfastness of the old wise man.)
(lit., Then she began to sympathize in herself . . .)

> Again, the reflexive *hire* cannot be translated. The verb *onemn-þrōwigan* "to sympathize" literally means "to suffer along side of" and thus is probably a translation of Latin *com-passio*.

Verbs of motion like *hwearfan* "to turn, go, move about," *wendan* "to WEND, turn," and *ġe-cierran* "to turn," for example, also often take reflexive objects that cannot be easily translated.

***Hwearf him** þā tō heofonum hāliġ drihten.*
(The holy Lord went to the heavens.)
(lit., Turned himself then to the heavens holy lord.)

*Þonne **wendeð him** Sanctus Pētrus þanon fram þēre helle-dura.*
(Then Saint Peter turns away from the door of hell.)
(lit., Then turns himself Saint Peter away from the hell-door.)

*Godes wer **him** eft ġe-cierde tō his mynstre.*
(God's man went back to his monastery.)
(lit., God's man turned himself back to his monastery.)

Another example: The verb *mētan* "to dream" generally takes a reflexive object. In addition, *mētan* reverses the subject-object assumption of Modern English in a strange way. Where today a person dreams a dream, in Old English a dream dreams a person.

> *Iċ swefna cyst secgan wylle, hwæt **mē ġe-mætte** tō midre nīhte.*
> (I want to tell the choicest of dreams, what I dreamed in the middle of the night.)
> (lit., I of dreams choicest to tell wish, what to me dreamed in middle night.)

ONE LAST WRINKLE. One of the most common verbs requiring a reflexive object is the verb *ġe-wītan* "to go, depart." Not only does *ġe-wītan* generally require a reflexive object, but it also often requires a second verb (always an infinitive). Perhaps the most literal way to translate such constructions is to render them with the archaic verb "betake," which takes a reflexive in (relatively) Modern English as well as an infinitive: "she betook herself to go." A more modern translation of *ġe-wītan* would be "leave" or "depart," though with this verb the reflexive object cannot be translated: "she left to go." See the following examples:

> *Ġe-wāt him þā sē hālga heofonas **sēċan**.*
> (The saint betook himself [or, departed] to seek the heavens [i.e., he died].)
> (lit., Betook himself then the saint heavens to seek.)

> *Ġe-wāt him on naca **drēfan** dēop wæter.*
> ([He] betook himself [or, departed] into the boat to stir up the deep water [i.e., to sail].)

> *Ġe-witon him þā **fēran**.*
> (Then they left.)
> (lit., [They] betook themselves then to go.)

Exercise 7.2: POSSESSIVE AND REFLEXIVE PRONOUNS

Instructions. *Translate the following sentences with the aid of the glossary provided. In the blanks to the right give full grammatical information in the first column and in the second indicate whether the pronoun is functioning as PRONOUN, ADJECTIVE, or REFLEXIVE.*

	Gram. Info.	Function
1. Hēo hine swīðe lufode.	3. f sing nom	pronoun
	3. m sing acc	pronoun

She loved him very much .

| 2. Hēo him fultumað. | hēo _____ | _____ |
| | him _____ | _____ |

_____ .

| 3. Wē þeċ blētsiað. | Wē _____ | _____ |
| | þeċ _____ | _____ |

_____ .

| 4. Hēr sceal mīn wesan eorðliċ ēþel. | mīn _____ | _____ |

_____ .

| 5. Nis þæt ēower sīð. | ēower _____ | _____ |

_____ .

	Gram. Info.	Function

6. Ġyrede hine Bēowulf corl-ġcwǣduiii.   hine_____   _____

_____ .

7. Ne on-drǣd þū ðē.   þū _____   _____

ðē _____   _____

_____ .

8. Hēo hire hām ġe-wāt fram Affrica-lande.   Hēo _____   _____

hire _____   _____

_____ .

9. Hire þā Adam andswarode.   Hire_____   _____

_____ .

10. Wende hine wrāð-mōd þǣr hē þæt   hine _____   _____

    wīf ġe-sēah.   hē _____   _____

_____ .

11. Nǣfre iċ mē on-drǣde[1] dōmas þīne.   iċ_____   _____

mē_____   _____

þīne_____   _____

_____ .

[1] on-drǣde = present tense with future sense.

VOCABULARY FOR EXERCISE 7.2

Affrica-land (n) = AFRICA [§2.9]

andswarian (weak verb II) = to
   ANSWER (+ dat object) [§3.12]

blētsian (weak verb II) = to BLESS
   [§3.12]

dōm (m) = judgment (see ModE
   DOOM) [§2.7]

eorl-ġewǣde (n) = EARL-WEEDs, noble
   attire; i.e., armor [§2.9]

eorðlič (adjective) = EARTHLY [§6.1]

ēþel (n) = home, dwelling [§2.9]

fram (preposition + dat) = FROM, away
   from [§6.15]

fultumian (weak verb II, + dat or acc) =
   to help, come to the aid of [§3.12]

ġyrwian (weak verb II) = to equip;
   prepare, make ready [§3.12]

hām (m) = (dat singular: *hām*) HOME,
   dwelling [§2.7]; (adverb) home,
   homewards [§6.9]

hēr (adverb) = HERE [§6.9]

lufian (weak verb II) = to LOVE
   [§3.12]

nǣfre (adverb) = NEVER [§6.9]

on-drǣdan (weak verb I) = to fear,
   DREAD (+ reflexive) [§3.11, §7.4.1]

(ġe)seah (verb form not yet covered) =
   "SAW" (past 3 sing) [§11.1]

sīð (m) = journey, exploit; time [§2.7]

swīðe (adverb) = very, very much [§6.9]

þǣr (conjunction) = THERE, to where
   [§5.1.1]

(ġe)wāt (verb form not yet covered) =
   "departed," "went"; "betook himself"
   (+ reflexive, + infinitive; past 3 sing)
   [§8.4, §7.4.1]

wendan (weak verb I) = to WEND, turn,
   go (+ reflexive) [§3.11]

wesan (irregular verb) = to be [§4.5.1]

wīf (n) = woman [§2.9]

wrāð-mōd (adjective) = angered, in a
   WRATHful MOOD [§6.1]

7.5 Lesson Three: Who/Which (Relative Pronouns)

First things first—a relative pronoun (*who, whom, whose; which, that*) introduces an entire
clause which interrupts or follows the main clause and provides further information about
a noun or pronoun in that main clause. (It is called a "relative" pronoun because it always

relates back to or explains a noun or pronoun that appears earlier. See Appendix One, §4.2.)

The sentence *that* you see before you has a relative clause in it.

In this example, the main clause (interrupted) is in a box while the relative clause is underlined, with the relative pronoun in ***bold italics***. As you can see in the examples below, the relative pronoun can take on any function of normal nouns and pronouns within a sentence. It can be a subject, direct object, object of a preposition, and a possessive adjective.

She is a person *who* understands grammar.   SUBJECT

She is a person *whom* others respect.   DIRECT OBJECT

She is a person in *whom* we trust.   OBJECT of PREPOSITION

She is a person *whose* integrity is above suspicion.   POSSESSIVE ADJECTIVE

OE has no separate system of relative pronouns as Modern English does (*who, whom, whose; which*). Instead it can signal a relative pronoun in three basic ways: 1) with the unchangeable word þe "who, which," 2) with a combination of definite article + þe, or 3) with the definite article alone (acting as a relative pronoun). The first alternative is the easiest to spot and translate since, happily, the relative particle þe NEVER accepts gender, case, and number markers but remains its reassuring old self: þe. That means that when confronted with þe you simply choose the appropriate translation demanded by the context: "who," "whom," "to/for whom," "which."

With the second alternative, however, things get a bit more complicated precisely because the relative pronoun *does* carry markers for gender, case, and number that you must learn to interpret. It's crucial to understand that a relative pronoun introduces a clause that interrupts and modifies a noun in the main clause, and the relative pronoun is a kind of linch-pin or junction between the two clauses. In Modern English, the relative pronoun takes its case only from its function *within* the relative clause, *not* its function in the main clause, at least according to prescriptive grammarians.

> She will give the book to ***whoever*** <u>writes the best essay</u>.

> She will give the book to ***whomever*** <u>she deems worthy</u>.

Note that in Modern English, the decision to use *who* or *whom* depends on the function of the relative within its own clause (underlined in the preceding examples), *not* on its function in the main clause. In the first example, *whoever* is the subject of the relative clause and therefore is in the nominative or subjective case, while in the second *whomever* is the object of the verb *deems* and thus takes the objective case. Some speakers of English might be inclined to use *whomever* in the first example because it appears to be the object of the preposition *to*. In traditional grammar, though, the object of *to* is the entire relative clause not the single word *whoever*. In learning how to decipher some Old English relative pronouns, you'll need to be able to analyze how the pronoun functions within its clause.

THREE ALTERNATIVES

Old English forms the relative pronoun with . . .

7.5.1   THE INDECLINABLE PARTICLE *þe* "who, which"

The easiest to translate. Simply choose "who," "whom," "whose," or "which"—the pronoun that fits into the context of the sentence.

Note that *þe* "who, which" is easy to confuse with *þē* "you, thee." (Once you remember, though, that *þē* "thee" has a long vowel while *þe* "who, which" has a short one, the two should be relatively easy to distinguish.)

þæt wīf **_þe wēfeð_** . . .
(the woman who weaves . . .)

On-gān him winn ūp ā-hebban wið þone . . . waldend, **_þe siteð on þām hālgan stōle_**.
([He] began to raise up a battle with the Lord, <u>who sits on the holy throne</u>.
[Note that *him* is an untranslated reflexive that might be rendered with "for himself, from himself."])

Is þēs...stede un-ġelic swīðe þām ōðrum hām **_þe wē ǣr cūðon_**.
(This place is very unlike the other home <u>which we knew before</u>.)

A DEFINITE ARTICLE (*sē, sēo, þæt*) + the particle *þe*   **7.5.2**

This construction isn't essentially much different from the first (§7.5.1), since *þe* also acts here in an identical way as the relative pronoun. However, the definite article preceding the relative can be a bit tricky to translate. First of all, it's a good idea to translate such a construction literally: "she who, he who, that which, those who," etc. That is, take the definite article portion as a kind of demonstrative and then add the relative ("that one which" or "that thing which") or a pronoun ("he who," "she who," "it which," "they who," etc.)

The main difficulty is that the first part of the construction (the definite article) sometimes takes its case from the relative clause, but sometimes from the main clause. In the examples below, main clauses appear in boxes while relative clauses are <u>underlined</u>. Note that the relative pronouns might come within the sphere of either or both of these clauses. Fortunately, this alternation isn't random—there are some observable patterns.

- When the definite article portion is in the nominative, the entire relative pronoun is always the *subject* of the relative clause.

  Wæs sē grimma gǣst Grendel hāten . . . , sē þe mōras heold.
  (The grim spirit was called Grendel, he who held the moors.)

  Eart þū sē Bēowulf, sē þe wið Brecan wunne?
  (Are you the Beowulf, who [lit., he who] fought against Breca?)

  Fēleþ sōna mīnes ġe-mōtes, sēo þe mec nearwað, wīf wunden-locc.
  (The woman with braided hair, she who nears me, feels immediately my contact.)
  (lit., Feels immediately my meeting, she who nears me, woman braided-locked.)

- When the definite article is in any of the other cases, it might take its case from either the relative clause (as in Modern English) . . .

  Ān æl-mihtiġ god is þone þe Bartolomēus bodað.
  ([There] is one almighty God, him who Bartholomew preaches about.)

  Þæt is sēo fǣhðo and sē fēondscipe ðæs ðe iċ wēn hafo.
  (That is the feud and the hostility of which I have an expectation.)

  > It is important to apply the Genitive Rule to ðæs ðe and supply an "of"
  > (§2.11.3.b, §5.4.3.)

  Þēs brōðor wolde his hwītlas, ðām ðe hē in cumena būre brūcende wæs, in sǣ wæscan.
  (This brother wanted to wash his blankets, those which he was using in the hostel [lit., strangers' bower], in the sea.)

> Here *brūcan* "to use, enjoy" takes a dative object, *ðām ðe*, though elsewhere it usually takes a genitive object (§2.11.4.d).

. . . or (more frequently) from the main clause. Note that in the following examples the definite article belongs to the main clause (indicated with a box) while the *þe* belongs to the relative clause (underlined):

Hē þā ġe-hyrde hēah-gnornunge þ̄ēra *ðe ġe-bundene bitere w̄ēron.*
(He then heard the deep groanings *of those who* were bitterly bound.)

> Again, it is important to apply the Genitive Rule to *þ̄ēra* and supply an "of" (§2.11.3.b, §54.3.)

Mihtiġ drihten syleð eallum mēte þ̄ām *þe his eġe habbað.*
(The mighty lord gives food *to all those who* have fear of him.)
(lit., Mighty lord gives [to] all food, [to] those who his fear have.)

> Similarly, apply the Dative Rule to *þ̄ām* and supply a preposition (§2.11.4.b, §54.2.)

Sē wæs ord-fruma earmre lāfe þ̄ēre *þe þām hēðenan hȳran sceolde.*
(He was the leader of the wretched remnant, [the leader] of that [remnant] which had to obey the heathens.)

Hēo wæs mīnra gylta, þ̄āra *þe iċ ġe-fremede,* ġe-myndiġ.
(She was mindful of my sins, [mindful] of those which I performed.)

Hīe fundon sawulleasne þone *ðe him hringas ġeaf.*
(They found soulless [i.e., dead] him who gave them rings.)

7.5.3   WITH A DEFINITE ARTICLE ALONE, functioning as a **"who"** or **"which."**

> *Rēoteð mēowle,* *sēo hyre bearn ġe-sihð brondas þeċċan.*
>
> (The woman mourns who sees flames cover her child.)
>
> (lit., Mourns the woman who her child sees flames to cover.)

> *Ðonne is sum ēalond* *on þǣm bēoð men ācende* *þāra ēagan scīnaþ* . . .
>
> (Then [there] is a certain island on which men are born whose eyes shine . . .)

> *Ðā cwōm semninga helle gǣst* *þone hēo ǣr ġe-bond ond mid wītum swong.*
>
> (Then came suddenly the demon of hell, whom she previously bound and lashed with torments.)

7.5.4   HEADLESS SENTENCES

Sometimes the relative pronoun functions *as the subject of both the relative and main clauses* (thus they appear below, both inside a box *and* with underlining). This construction is a bit confusing since the main clause seems at first glance to lack a subject. In such cases, it's often best to translate the relative clause first.

> *Hrēoh bið þonne* *sēo þe ǣr gladu wæs.*
>
> (She who was formerly glad will be sorrowful then.)
>
> (lit., Sorrowful is then she who before glad was.)

> *Wel dēð* *sē ðe* *unwitigum styrð mid swinglum.*
>
> (He who motivates the ignorant with lashes does well.)
>
> (lit., Well does he who the ignorant motivates with lashes.)

> *Beald bið* *sē ðe* *on-byreġeð bōca cræftes.*
>
> (Bold is he who tastes the power of books.)

> Note: *on-byrġian* "to taste" takes a genitive object—in this case, *cræftes*.

Mē is eal lēofast **þæt** *þē lāþost is.*

(What is most hateful to you is most preferable to me.)

> Note: When *þæt* functions as a relative pronoun, be sure to translate it as *what*, not *that*.

Exercise 7.3: RELATIVE PRONOUNS

Instructions. *In the following exercise, 1) underline all relative clauses, 2) put boxes around the main clauses, 3) double underline the relative pronoun, and 4) translate the sentences. Review the three ways of signaling a relative pronoun discussed above.*

1. Iċ lufie þone þe mē lufað.

   I love him (or, that person) who loves me .

2. For eallum þyssum ġe-dyne, ne mæġ sēo sāwl ā-wæcnian sēo þe wæs āne niht on helle.

   _____ .

3. Sēo myċċle ċiriċe þonne, sēo þe þǣr on middum stondeþ, is ufan open and unoferhrēfed.

     _____.

4. Hī ġe-nēosodon ðā hālgan ċirċan on þǣre wæs þæs wuldorfullan Stēphanes ġe-mynd.

     _____.

5. Sē ðe ne lufað his brōðor þone þe hē ġe-sīhð—hū mæġ hē lufian God?

     _____.

6. Eugenīa mid wōpe ġe-spræc hire twēġen cnīhtas, þāra naman wǣron Protus and Iacinctus.

     _____.

7. Ðā ġe-gaderodon ðā þe on Norðhymbrum būgiað [būan] sum hund scypa.

     _____.

8. Ðā cwōm wundorlicu wiht ofer wealles hrof, sēo is eallum cūð.

_____ .

9. On þǣre ēðel-tyrf, niððas findað gold, þæs þe ūs secgað bēċ.

_____ .

10. Gregorius spræc tō his dēacone, þām wæs nama Pētrus.

_____ .

11. Sē cyning, þām sē wudu līcode, hēt ðæt teld ā-slēan.

_____ .

VOCABULARY FOR EXERCISE 7.3

ān (number and adjective): ONE, a/an [§6.1]

ā-slēan (verb form not yet covered) = "to strike," "erect," "set up" (infinitive) [§11.1]

ā-wæcnian (weak verb II) = to AWAKE, revive [§3.12]

bēċ = see *bōc*

bēon (irregular verb) = to BE (past pl: *wǣron*) [§4.5.1]

bōc (f) = BOOK (nom plural: *bēċ*) [§10.4.2]

brōðor (m) = BROTHER [§10.5]

būan, būgian (weak verb III) = to dwell (in),

inhabit [§4.1]

ċirċe (f weak) = CHURCH [§2.8]

cnīht (m) = boy, young man; servant [§2.7]

cūð (adjective) = known, well-known [§6.1]

cwōm (verb form not yet covered) = "CAME"
(past 3 sing) [§8.7]

cyning (m) = KING [§2.7]

dēacon (m) = DEACON, minister (late Latin
loan) [§2.7]

(ġe)dyne (m) DIN, noise [§10.2.1]

eall (adjective & pronoun) = ALL, every;
everyone, all people [§6.1, §7.8]

ēþel-turf (f) = home TURF, homeland (dat:
ēþel-tyrf) [§10.4.2]

Eugenīa (f) = proper name [Latin form]

findað (verb form not yet covered) = "FIND"
(present 3 pl) [§8.6]

for (preposition + dat/acc) = FOR; in spite of
[§6.15]

(ġe)gaderian (weak verb II) = to GATHER,
collect, bring together [§3.12]

god (m) = GOD [§2.7]

gold (n) = GOLD [§2.9]

hāliġ (adjective) = HOLY [§6.1]

hē, hēo, hit (personal pronoun) = HE, she, IT
[§7.1]

hell (f) = HELL, place of torment [§2.8]

hēt (verb form not yet covered) = "commanded," "ordered" (past 3 sing) [§9.3]

hī = see *hē*

hire = see *hē*

hrōf (m) = ROOF; top, summit [§2.7]

hū (adverb & conjunction) = HOW [§6.9,
§5.1.1]

hund (n) = HUNDred, a hundred (+ partitive
gen) [§2.9, §2.11.3.c]

Iacinctus (m) = a proper name [Latin form]

iċ (personal pronoun) = I (1 dat pl: *ūs*) [§7.1]

līċian (weak verb II) = to please, be pleasant to
(+ dat) [§3.12]

lufian (weak verb II) = to LOVE [§3.12]

mæġ = see *magan*

magan (preterite-present verb) = to be
able, to have permission or ability (to do
something) (pres 3 sing: *mæġ*) [§4.4]

mē = see *iċ*

mid (preposition + dat) = with, along with,
among [§6.15]

midd (adjective) = center, middle [§6.1]

myċel (adjective) = great, large [§6.4]

(ġe)mynd (n) = memorial, monument; memory, thought [§2.9]

nama (weak m) = NAME [§3.3]

ne (adverb) = not [§6.9]

(ġe)nēosan (weak verb I) = to seek out, go to,
visit [§3.11]

niht (f) = NIGHT [§10.4.2]

niððas (m) = men, human beings [§2.7]

Norð-hymber (adjective) = Northumbrian; Northumbrian (people) [§6.1]

ofer (preposition + acc) = OVER, from over [§6.15]

on (preposition = (+ dat) ON, in, among; (+ acc) ONto, into [§6.15]

open (adjective) = OPEN, exposed [§6.1]

Pētrus (m) = a proper name [Latin form]

Prōtus (m) = a proper name [Latin form]

sawl, sawol (f) = SOUL, spirit [§2.8]

scip (n) = SHIP [§2.9]

sē, sēo, þæt (definite article & demonstrative adjective / pronoun) = the; that one, that thing [§2.5, §7.7]

secgan (weak verb III) = to SAY, relate, tell about (pres 3 pl: *secgað*) [§4.1]

(ġe)sihð (verb form not yet covered) = "sees" (present 3 sing) [§9.1, §11.1]

spræc, (ġe)spræc (verb form not yet cov-ered) = "SPOKE"; "conversed with," "had a conversation with" (past sing) [§9.1]

Stēphan (m) = proper name

stondeþ (verb form not yet covered) = stands," "stands firm" (present 3 sing) [§9.2]

sum (adjective) = SOME, a certain; (with

number): about, approximately [§6.1]

teld (n) = tent [§2.9]

twēġen (number) = two

ðā (adverb & conjunction) = (adverb): then, at that time [§6.9]; (conjunction): when, since [§5.1.1]

ðā = see *sē*

þēr (adverb & conjunction) = THERE; where [§6.9, §5.1.1]

þære = see *sē*

þæs = see *sē*

þāra = see *sē*

þe (relative pronoun) = who, which, that [§7.5]

þone = see *sē*

þonne (adverb) = THEN [§6.9]

þys, þis (adjective & demonstrative pronoun) = THIS [§7.7]

ufan (adverb) = from above, above [§6.9]

un-ofer-brēfed (adjective) = not ROOFED OVER [§6.1]

ūs = see *iċ*

wæs = see *bēon*

weall (m) = WALL, earthwork; rocky cliff [§2.7]

wiht (f) = creature, being [§2.8]

wōp (m) = cry, scream; WEEPing, crying [§2.7]

wudu (m) = WOOD, forest [§10.6]

wuldor-ful (adjective) = full of glory, glorious   *wundor-lič* (adjective) = strange, marvellous
[§6.1]   [§6.1.]

7.6   Why?: Interrogative Pronouns

The pronouns *who* and *what* appear in questions and hence are called *interrogative*. You may recognize *hwā, hwæs,* and *hwǣm* as the ancient forms of modern *who, whose,* and *whom.*
[Note: Hwā and hwæt can also function as the indefinite pronouns "whoever" and "whatever."]

	Masculine, Feminine	Neuter
N	hwā	hwæt
A	hwone	hwæt
G	hwæs	hwæs
D	hwǣm, hwām	hwǣm
I	hwī, hwȳ	hwȳ, hwon

7.7   This and That: Demonstrative Pronoun

Like the definite article, the demonstrative pronoun *this* is also declined according to case, number, and gender. It can also function as an adjective and thus agrees in gender, number, and case with the noun it modifies. Pronoun: "*This* is difficult." Adjective: "*This* exercise is difficult." It is called a "demonstrative" pronoun because it points out or demonstrates a particular thing (*this, these*).

	Masculine	Feminine	Neuter	Plural
N	þēs	þēos	þis	þās
A	þisne	þās	þis	þās
G	þisses	þisse	þisses	þissa, þisra
D	þissum	þisse	þissum	þissum
I	þ̄ys	***	þ̄ys	***

A number of other pronouns, like *þēs*, can act either as adjectives or pronouns. Some of these pronouns are "indefinite" pronouns. Unlike the demonstratives which specify a particular and known person or thing, indefinite pronouns like *a/an, whoever, whichever, one, a person*, etc. imply not a specific person or thing but *any* person or thing.

Miscellaneous Pronouns *hwilċ* "anyone, someone"   **7.8**

The pronoun *hwilċ* "which" can be either an interrogative pronoun (as in, "Which of you is coming?") or a kind of indefinite pronoun meaning "whoever," "whichever," or "anyone," "anything" (see §7.8.1).

	Masculine	Feminine	Neuter	Plural
N	hwilċ	hwilċ	hwilċ	hwilċe
A	hwilċne	hwilċe	hwilċ	hwilċe
G	hwilċes	hwilċre	hwilċes	hwilċra
D	hwilċum	hwilċre	hwilċum	hwilċum

Pronouns like *hwilċ* are *æġ-hwilċ* "each," *swilċ* "such (a person or thing)," *ælċ* "each," *æniġ* "any." Most of these require a genitive "object" when they appear as pronouns.

> *þāra manna **ælċ***
> (each of the men)

They can also appear adjectively.

> ***ælċ** wīf*
> (each woman)

Several adjectives like *eall* "all," *sum* "one, a certain," and *ān* "one, a single" can act as either pronouns or adjectives.

Old English also has an equivalent of the Modern English indefinite "one" ("one should not smoke"): *mon* "one, a person" which is sometimes easy to confuse with *mann, monn* "man."

> *Lǣran sceal **mon** ġeongne monnan.*
> (One must teach a young man.)
> (lit., Teach must one young man.)

7.8.1   WHATEVER, WHOEVER

One last note: Indefinite pronouns like *hwilċ* are sometimes framed by two *swā*'s in a peculiar construction which adds the sense of "ever" to an indefinite.

hwilċ = anyone	*swā hwilċ swā* = whoever, whatever person (or thing)
hwā = who	*swā hwā swā* = whoever, whatever person
hwæt = what	*swā hwæt swā* = whatever

Reading VII.i PROGNOSTICS

This reading comes from a class of writing known as prognostics, *texts which claim to predict favorable or unfavorable conditions in the future. Roy M. Liuzza's recent study suggests that many prognostic texts, though arguably of pagan origin and sensibility, fit into the atmosphere of the Benedictine Reform (10th-11th centuries), providing "a portrait of monastic culture from the bottom up, not from the top down—not the orderly world of Æthelwold's Benedictine Reform movement but the private world of monastic preoccupation with times and seasons, interior movements and exterior portents, spiritual and physical hygiene, in which 'superstitious' practices existed comfortably alongside orthodox religious devotions."[1]*

Ġif mon bið ā-cenned on Sunnan-dæġ oððe on nihte,[2] swā wer swā wīf swā hweðer hit þonne bið, nafað[3] hē nā mycle sorge, and hē bið ġe-sǣliġ bē his ġe-byrde. Ġif mon biþ ā-cenned on Mōnan-dæġ oððe on niht, hē bið manna gōda[4] ġitsiende and lāð and oft sēoc and hunel. Ġif on Tīwes-dæġ oððe on niht bið ā-cenned, sē bið ǣw-fæst and man-þwǣre and ġe-sibsum and manna lēof. Ġif on Wōdnes-dæġ oððe on niht bið ā-cenned, sē bið scearp on ġe-winne and wær-wyrde and grimful. Ġif on Þunres-dæġ oððe on niht, sē bið ġe-sǣliġ, and wif-mannum lēof, ġif hit wer bið, and wǣpned-mannum lēof, ġif hit wīf bið. Ġif mon bið ā-cenned on Frīġe-dæġ oððe on niht, hē bið ā-wyried fram mannum, and hē yfele cræftas leornað, and hē ǣfre bið yfel-wyrde, and ōðra manna æhte strȳdeð, and bið scort on wæstmum. Ġif mon bið ā-cenned on Sæternes-dæġ oððe on niht, sē biþ dǣda fram,[5] and biþ ealdorman bē his ġe-byrdum; and him bēoþ men æfestgende, ac sē þēah-hwæðre þā costunge þǣra æfestgendra manna hē ofer-swīðeð.

5

10

VOCABULARY FOR READING VII.i

ac (conjunction) = but

ā-cennan (weak verb I) = to bring forth, give birth, be born [§3.11]

æfestiġian (weak verb II) = to become or be envious (of someone = dat) [§3.11]

ǣfre (adverb) = EVER, always [§6.9]

[1] Roy M. Liuzza, "Anglo-Saxon Prognostics in Context: A Survey and Handlist of Manuscripts." *Anglo-Saxon England* 30 (2001): 181-230.

[2] i.e., On Sunday during the day or night.

[3] The present tense signals the future in many of the verbs in this reading.

[4] Be careful: both *manna* and *gōda* are genitive plurals, but *gōda* is the genitive object of *ġitsiende* while *manna* depends on *gōda*.

[5] Note that *fram* is an adjective, not the more familiar preposition (see glossary); be sure to apply the genitive rule to *dǣda* (see §5.4.3).

ǣht (f) = property, possessions (usually pl) [§10.11.2]

ǣw-fæst (adjective) = upstanding, devout [§6.1]

ā-wiergan (weak verb I) = to curse, condemn; outlaw, banish [§3.11]

bē (preposition + dat) = BY, with [§6.15]

bēon (irregular verb) = to BE [§4.5.1]

biþ = see *bēon*

(ġe)byrd (f) = BIRTH, parentage; nature [§10.11.2]

costung (f) = testing; temptation [§2.8]

cræft (m) = skill, ability; deceit, trick, fraud [§2.7]

dǣd (f) = DEED, action [§10.11.2]

ealdor-man (m) = ruler, chief; nobleman [see ModE *ALDERMAN*; §10.4.2]

fram (adjective) = bold [§6.1]

fram (preposition + dat) = FROM, away from [§6.15]

Frīge-dæġ (m) = FRIDAY [§2.7]

ġif (conjunction) = IF [§5.1.1]

ġītsiend (adjective) = greedy for, longing for (+ gen), present participle of *ġītsian*, a weak verb II [§3.12]

gōd (n, pl) = GOODs, property [§2.9]

grimful (adjective) = fierce, violent [§6.1]

habban (weak verb III) = to HAVE; possess, hold [§4.1]

hē, hēo, hit (personal pronoun) = HE, she, IT [§7.1]

hunel (adjective) = wanton, lascivious; impudent [§6.1]

hweðer (indefinite pronoun) = whichever (of two) [§7.8]

lāð (adjective) = hateful, LOATHsome [§6.1]

lēof (adjective) = dear, LOVEd; dear to, loved by (+ dat or gen) [§6.1]

leornian (weak verb II) = to LEARN [§3.12]

mann (m) = MAN, person [§10.4.2]

man-þwǣre (adjective) = mild, gentle, humane [§6.1]

mon (indefinite pronoun) = one, a person [§7.8]

Mōnan-dæġ (m) = MONDAY [§2.7]

myċel (adjective) = great, immense [§6.1]

nā (adverb) = not at all [§6.9]

nafað = *ne hafað*, see *habban*

niht (f) = NIGHT (when it appears in a compound like *Mōnan-niht*, *niht* refers to the night before the specified day) [§10.4.2]

oððe (conjunction) = or

ōðer (adjective) = OTHER; second [§6.1]

ofer-swīðan (weak verb I) = to OVERcome, overpower [§3.11]

oft (adverb) = OFTen [§6.9]

on (preposition) = (+ dat) ON, in; (+ acc) onto, into [§6.15]

(ġe)sǣliġ (adjective) = blessed; fortunate, lucky [§6.1]

Sæternes-dæġ (m) = SATURDAY [§2.7]

scearp (adjective) = SHARP, shrewd; rough, severe [§6.1]

scort (adjective) = SHORT, not tall [§6.1]

sēoc (adjective) = SICK, ill [§6.1]

(ġe)sibsum (adjective) = peace-loving, friendly [§6.1]

sorg (f) = SORROW, pain [§2.8]

strȳdan (weak verb I) = to rob, steal [§3.11]

Sunnan-dæġ (m) = SUNDAY [§2.7]

swā = (adverb) SO, thus, in this way; (conjunction) as; *swā...swā...swā* = whether . . . or . . . or, either . . . or . . . or [§6.9]

Tīwes-dæġ (m) = TUESDAY [§2.7]

þēah-hwæðre (adverb) = however, nevertheless [§6.9]

þonne (adverb) = then [§6.9]

Þunres-dæġ (m) = THURSDAY [§2.7]

wǣpned-mann (m) = man, male, a beWEAPONED person [§10.4.2]

wær-wyrde (adjective) = cautious in speech, aWARE of WORDs [§6.1]

wæstm (m) = growth, stature, form (pl in sing sense) [§2.7]

wer (m) = man, male [see ModE *WEREwolf*; §2.7]

wīf (n) = WOman, female [§2.9]

wīf-mann (m) = WOMAN, female [§10.4.2]

(ġe)winn (n) = profit, gain; war, conflict [§10.11.2]

Wōdnes-dæġ (m) = WEDNESDAY [§2.7]

yfel (adjective) = EVIL, bad [§6.1]

yfel-wyrde (adjective) = EVIL-tongued, accustomed to evil speech or WORDs [§6.1]

[6] Wringing or squeezing is part of the process for making cheese.

[7] The grinding of barley is part of the process for making beer.

Reading VII.ii MONASTIC SIGN LANGUAGE

The following excerpts come from an Old English translation of a Latin guide to monastic sign language (Monasteriales Indicia). *A closely related Latin version was probably composed at Cluny while the Old English translation belongs to the era of the Benedictine Reform (10th-11th centuries) and is included in a manuscript (Cotton Tiberius A.iii) containing copies of the* Benedictine Rule *and the* Regularis Concordia, *a document that lays out liturgical and general monastic practices for the reformed monasteries. The* Benedictine Rule *encouraged silence as part of the contemplative life, particularly during readings at meals: "Let the deepest silence be maintained that no whispering or voice be heard except that of the reader alone. But let the brethren so help each other to what is needed for eating and drinking, that no one need ask for anything. If, however, anything should be wanted, let it be asked for by means of a sign of any kind rather than a sound" (Chapter 38).*

Þās sindon þā tācna þe mon on mynstre healdan sceal þǣr mon æfter regoles be-bode swīgan healdan wile and ġeornlīċe mid Godes fultume be-ġȳman sceal.

1. Ġyf þū lēac habban wille, þonne dō þū mid þīnum fingre, swilċe þū boriġe inn on þīne hand and dō brādlinga þīne hand tō þīnre nāsan, swilċe þū hwæt ġe-stince.

2. Ðonne þū ċȳse habban wille, sete þonne þīne twā handa tō-gǣdere brādlinga, swilċe þū wringan wille.[6]

3. Ġyf þū buteran habban wylle oððe smeoru, þonne strīċ þū mid þrīm fingrum on þīne inne-wearde hand.

4. Bēores tācen is þæt þū gnīde þīne hand on þā ōþre.[7]

5. Ġyf þū meolce habban wille, þonne strocca þū þīnne wīnstran scyte-finger mid þīnre swīþra handa, þām ġe-līċe swylċe þū melce.

6. Ðonne þū fisc habban wylle, þonne weġe þū þȳne hand þām ġe-mete þe hē dēþ his tæġl, þonne hē swymð.

7. Ġif þū ostran habban wylle, þonne clǣm þū þīne wynstran hand, ðām ġe-mete þe[8] þū ostran on handa hæbbe, and dō mid seaxe oððe mid fingre swylċe þū ostran scǣnan wylle.

8. Ġyf þū wæter ġe-nēodie, þonne dō þū swylċe þū þīne handa þwēan wille.

9. Scēarra tācen is þæt þū wecge þīnne scytefinger and þone midemestan on þīnre swīðran hande tō sumum clāðe, swilċe þū hine mid scēarran ċeorfan wille, oððe ymb þīn hēafod, swilċe þū efsian wille.

10. Ðonne þū miċel weax-bred habban wille, þonne strīċ þū mid þīnum twām fingrum on þīne brēost forewearde, swilċe þū dȳleġe, and strȳce þīnne earm and sete þīne hand on þīnes wynstran earmes byġe.

11. Ðonne þū blæc-horn habban wille, þonne hafa þū þīne þrī fingras, swilċe þū dȳpan wille, and ā-wend þīne hand ā-dūne and clyce þīne fingras, swilċe þū blæc-horn niman wille.

12. Feþere tācen is, þæt þū ġe-þēode þīne þrī fingras tō-somne swilċe þū feþere hæbbe and hī dype, and stīere þīne fingras swilċe þū wrītan wille.

[8] Translate *ðām ġe-mete þe* as "in the way which" or, more loosely, "as if."

VOCABULARY FOR READINGS VII.i AND ii

ā-dūne (adverb) = DOWN, downward [§6.9]

æfter (preposition) = AFTER, according to [§6.15]

ā-wendan (weak verb I) = to turn [§3.11]

be-bod (n) = command, decree [§2.9]

be-ġȳman (weak verb I) = to observe, attend to [§3.11]

bēor (n) = BEER [§2.9]

blæc-horn (n) = ink HORN, container of ink [§2.9]

bor(ġ)ian (weak verb I) = to BORE a hole through [§3.11]

brādlinga (adverb) = flat, with the palm spread out [§6.9]

brēost (m, f, or n) = BREAST, bosom; chest, stomach [§2.7, §2.8, §2.9]

butere (weak f) = BUTTER [§3.4]

byġe (m) = bend, curve [§10.2.1]

ċeorfan (verb form not yet covered) = to cut, CARVE (infinitive) [§8.6] *clæmman* (weak verb I) = to CLAM, press [§3.11]

clāð (m) = CLOTH, CLOTHing [§2.7]

clyccan (weak verb I) = to clutch, clench [§3.11]

cȳse (m) = CHEESE [§10.2.1]

dēþ = see *dōn*

dōn (irregular verb) = to DO, act, make; put, place [§4.5.3.1]

dȳleġian (weak verb II) = to blot out, erase (a text) [§3.12]

dȳpan (weak verb I) = to DIP (in ink) [§3.11]

earm (m) = ARM [§2.7]

efsian (weak verb II) = to trim, cut (the hair) [§3.12]

feþer (f) = FEATHER; (quill) pen [§2.8]

finger (m) = FINGER [§2.7]

fisc (m) = FISH [§2.7]

fore-wearde (adverb) = in the front [§6.9]

fultum (m) = help, assistance [§2.7]

ġeornlīċe (adverb) = eagerly, diligently, zealously [§6.9]

ġif (conjunction) = IF [§5.1.1]

gnīde (verb form not yet covered) = "grind" (present subjunctive sing) [§8.4]

habban (weak verb III) = to HAVE [§4.1]

hand (f) = HAND [§10.6]

hē, hēo, hit (personal pronoun) = HE, she, IT [§7.1]

hēafod (n) = HEAD [§2.9]

healdan (verb form not yet covered) = to HOLD, keep (infinitive) [§9.3]

hī = see *hē, hēo, hit*

hwæt (pronoun) = something [§7.6]

inn (adverb) = IN [§6.9]

inne-weard (adjective) = INWARD, inner [§6.1]

lēac (n) = LEEK, onion [§2.9]

melcan (weak verb I) = to MILK [§3.11]

meolc (f) = MILK [§10.4.2]

(ġe)met (n) = manner, way [§2.9]

miċel (adjective) = big, large, great [§6.1]

mid (preposition + dat) = with [§6.15]

midemesta (adjective) = MIDDleMOST [§6.1]

mon (indefinite pronoun) = one, a person [§7.8]

mynster (n) = monastery, MINSTER [see placenames such as *West-minster*] [§2.9]

nāse (weak f) = NOSE [§3.4]

(ġe)nēodian (weak verb II) = to NEED, require [§3.12]

niman (verb form not yet covered) = take, grasp, carry (infinitive) [§8.7]

on (preposition) = (+ dat) ON, in; (+ acc) into, onto [§6.15]

ostre (weak f) = OYSTER [§3.4]

ōþer (adjective or pronoun) = OTHER [§6.1, §7.8]

oððe (conjunction) = OR

regol (m) = RULE, code of monastic laws [§2.7]

scǣnan (weak verb 1) = to wrench open [§3.11]

sceal = see *sculan*

scēarra (f pl) = SHEARs, scissors [§2.8]

sculan (preterite-present verb) = must, be obliged, be bound to [§4.4]

scyte-finger (m) = index finger (lit., SHOOTing FINGER, "bow finger"?) [§2.7]

seax (n) = knife [§2.9]

settan (weak verb I) = to SET, place, put [§3.11]

smeoru (n) = lard or other spread (for SMEARing on bread) [§10.3.2]

stīeran (weak verb I) = to STEER, guide [§3.11]

(ġe)stince (verb form not yet covered) = "were smelling" (present subjunctive sing) [§8.6]

strīċ, strȳċe (verb form not yet covered) = "spread," "rub lightly over the surface," "rub" (imperative sing) [§8.4]

stroċċian (weak verb II) = to STROKE [§3.12]

swīġe (weak f) = silence [§3.4]

swilċe (conjunction) = as if [§5.1.1]

swīþra (adjective) = right (lit., "stronger") [§6.1]

swymð (verb form not yet covered) = "swims" (present 3 sing) [§8.6]

swylċe (conjunction) = just as if

tācen (n) = sign, TOKEN [§2.9]

tæġl (n) = TAIL [§2.9]

tō-somne (adverb) = TOgether [§6.9]

twā (adjective or number) = TWO (+ partitive gen) [§6.1]

þām ġe-līċe swylċe (conjunction) = in a similar way as if, just as if

þām ġe-mete þe (conjunction) = in a similar way as, just as if

(ġe)þēodan (weak verb I) = to join [§3.11]

þēs, þēos, þis (demonstrative adjective, pronoun) = THIS [§7.7] *þīn* (personal pronoun) = your (sing), THINE [§7.1]

þonne = (adverb) THEN [§6.9]; (conjunction) when [§5.1.1]

þrī (adjective) = THREE [§6.1]

þū (personal pronoun) = you, THOU [§7.1]

þwēan (verb form not yet covered) = to wash, clean (infinitive) [§9.2]

wæter (n) = WATER [§2.9]

weax-bred (n) = writing board, WAX tablet [§2.9]

wecgan (weak verb I) = to move back and forth [§3.11]

willan (irregular verb) = to wish, want, desire, WILL [§4.5.3.2]

winestra (adjective) = left [§6.1]

wringan (verb form not yet covered) = WRING; squeeze, press out (infinitive) [§8.6]

wrītan (verb form not yet covered) = WRITE (infinitive) [§8.4]

ymb (preposition + acc) = around [§6.15]

Lessons Learned

Before leaving this chapter you should know . . .

- the singular and plural (but not dual) forms of the personal pronouns by heart, with particular attention to the third person (§7.1.1-§7.1.4).
- how to distinguish reflexive pronouns from personal pronouns (§7.4).
- how to translate the three types of relative clauses (§7.5).

EIGHT

Strong Verbs 1, Classes 1, 2, 3, and 4

8.1   Lesson One: Definitions

In this and the following chapter, you will learn most of what you'll need to know about "strong" verbs. As we mentioned earlier (§3.7), strong verbs change a root vowel to form the past tense and the past participle (see Modern English *grow, grew, grown* and *sing, sang, sung*). Weak verbs, on the other hand, form the past tense and past participle by adding -*d*, -*ed*, or -*t* (i.e., a "dental" suffix) to the root (see Modern English: *walk, walked, walked*; *hear, heard, heard*; and *think, thought, thought*). Strong verbs descend from Indo-European verbs while weak verbs are a Germanic innovation.

The main challenge that strong verbs present to any reader of Old English is that they are generally difficult to look up. Glossaries and dictionaries, as a rule, list only the infinitive form. Of course, when you encounter a word which looks suspiciously like a past tense or past participle of a strong verb, you could simply start at the beginning of the relevant letter in the glossary and scan through the entire section looking for the infinitive. That would be a time-consuming chore to say the least. Later on, if you read texts with the help of fuller dictionaries, you won't be able to block out enough time to roam through page after page of entries. Knowing something about the seven classes of strong verbs can definitely make you a more efficient reader of Old English by allowing you to triangulate more efficiently on the main glossary entry for any strong verb.

(Note: Should you want to consult other grammars, you should probably know that the change in the root vowel in strong verbs is usually called **gradation** or **ablaut,** from a German word meaning to "sound down." For this reason, some grammars refer to strong verbs as **ablaut verbs** and the series of changes in the root vowel as an **ablaut** or **gradation series.**)

8.2   Strong Verb Classes

Old English, like other old Germanic languages, has seven classes of strong verbs; each class is defined by its distinctive vowel series. We list below the seven classes, each with its vowel series and a representative verb. Interestingly, all seven classes originally derived from a single pattern, but a series of complex sound changes produced the seven classes you see below. To the right of the chart, note that each of the classes has a "footprint"—a typical syllable structure in the infinitive form of the verb. This footprint can in many cases help you to identify a strong verb's class just by looking at its syllable structure.

You should be able to locate most strong verbs in glossaries and dictionaries if you know how to use the quick reference chart on the following page: memorizing the seven classes, though it certainly wouldn't harm you, might not be a wise use of your time.

The following chart uses a few new abbreviations: *K* stands for any single consonant, while *V* stands for any vowel, and *pp* for "past participle."

Class	Infinitive	Past Singular	Past Plural	Past Participle	Footprint
1	ī	ā	i	i	ī + K
	bītan "to bite"	bāt	biton	biten	
2	ēo	ēa	u	o	ēo + K
	bēodan "to offer"	bēad	budon	boden	
	ū	ēa	u	o	ū + K
	brūcan "to enjoy"	brēac	brucon	brocen	
3	i	a	u	u	V+n+K, V+l+K
	drincan "to drink"	dranc	druncon	druncen	
4	e	æ	ǣ	o	e + l/r or m/n
	beran "to bear"	bær	bǣron	boren	
5	e	æ	ǣ	e	e + K (K ≠ l/r, m/n)
	cweþan "to say"	cwæþ	cwǣdon	cweden	

Class	Infinitive	Past Singular	Past Plural	Past Participle	Footprint
6	a	ō	ō	a	a + K, e/ie + KK
	faran "to go"	fōr	fōron	faren	
7	ea	ēo	ēo	ea	V of inf = V of pp
	feallan "to fall"	fēoll	fēollon	feallen	
	ā	ē	ē	ā	
	hātan "to call"	hēt	hēton	hāten	

8.3   The summary offers a general idea of the seven classes of Old English strong verbs. Because it is a general summary, it obscures the inevitable exceptions that complicate some classes. We will examine these exceptions briefly in the following paradigms. Most of the exceptions are the result of a rich layer of sound changes that at times require more than a brief explanation. Since our goal in this text is to provide you with a hands-on, practical guide to reading OE, we give you enough information to translate a strong verb with some confidence. However, if you wish further information about the how and why of a sound change, we provide that information in Appendix Two.

8.4   Class I Strong Verbs

The vowel sequence of Class 1 verbs is *ī – ā – i – i*. Almost all the verbs in this class are regular, with one sound change producing a single sub-class (see §8.4.1 below). Note also in the example verbs listed below that the infinitive roots in Class 1 strong verbs have a similar structural footprint: ī + a single consonant (see *bīd-*, *bīt-*, *drīf-*, etc.).

Infinitive	Past Singular	Past Plural	Past Participle
bīdan "to wait"	bād	bidon	biden
bītan "to bite"	bāt	biton	biten
drīfan "to drive"	drāf	drifon	drifen
glīdan "to glide"	glād	glidon	gliden
rīpan "to reap"	rāp	ripon	ripen
rīdan "to ride"	rād	ridon	riden
rīsan 'to rise'	rās	rison	risen
stīgan "to climb, go"	stāh[1]	stigon	stigen
(be)swīcan "to deceive"	(be)swāc	(be)swicon	(be)swicen
wrītan "to write"	wrāt	writon	writen

[1] See Appendix Two (§2) on "Verner's Law."

SUB-CLASS OF CLASS I: 8.4.1

Infinitive	Past Singular	Past Plural	Past Participle
snīðan "to cut"	snāð	snidon	sniden
līðan "to travel"	lāð	lidon	liden
scrīðan "to go, glide"	scrāð	scridon	scriden

A SLIGHT COMPLICATION. In this sub-class the past plural and past participle do not show what we would expect as the final consonant of the root form—that is, we would expect snīðan to have a past plural form of *snīðon and a past participle form of *snīðen. Instead, the final consonant of the root form (ð) in both cases changes to d [snidon and sniden]. The shift is due to "Verner's Law" [see Appendix Two (§2)].

8.5   Class 2 Strong Verbs

The vowel series of Class 2 verbs is either $\bar{e}o - \bar{e}a - u - o$ OR $\bar{u} - \bar{e}a - u - o$. Most of the verbs in this class are fairly regular and fall into either of these two subdivisions. One sound change produces a sub-class (§8.5.3). Note that the infinitive forms of this class have a similar footprint: $\bar{e}o$ or $\bar{u}$ + a single consonant.

8.5.1

[2] Some grammars refer to the *u* forms as "aorist presents," that is, a tense expressing a simple past action without any reference to whether that action has been completed or is still going on. The implication is that this group of Class 2 strong verbs adopts the past tense form of an older verb conjugation to use as the present stem of the infinitive.

Infinitive	Past Singular	Past Plural	Past Participle
bēodan "to command"	bēad	budon	boden
brēotan "to break"	brēat	brudon	broden
ċēowan "to chew"	ċēaw	cuwon	cowen
clēofan "to cleave"	clēaf	clufon	clofen
crēopan "to creep"	crēap	crupon	cropen
drēogan "to endure"	drēag	drugon	drogen
flēogan "to fly"	flēag	flugon	flogen
ġēotan "to pour"	ġēat	guton	goten
lēogan "to lie"	lēag	lugon	logen
smēocan "to smoke"	smēac	smucon	smocen

8.5.2   U INFINITIVES[2]

The second group of Class 2 strong verbs has a $\bar{u}$ in the infinitive rather than the $\bar{e}o$ you see in the chart above. Reassuringly, the rest of the vowel series is identical: $\bar{e}a - u - o$.

Infinitive	Past Singular	Past Plural	Past Participle	Pattern
brūcan "to enjoy"	brēac	brucon	brocen	ū + K
dūfan "to dive"	dēaf	dufon	dofen	
lūcan "to lock"	lēac	lucon	locen	
scūfan "to shove"	scēaf	scufon	scofen	

OTHER CONSONANT FORMS   8.5.3

In this sub-class the final consonant of the root form—the *s* in *frēosan* and the *ð* in *sēoðan*, for example—change in the past plural and past participle to *r* and *d* respectively: *fruron*, *froren* and *sudon* and *soden*. The shift is due to "Verner's Law" [see Appendix Two (§2)].

Infinitive	Past Singular	Past Plural	Past Participle	Pattern
frēosan "to freeze"	frēas	fruron	froren	ēo + K
drēosan "to fall"	drēas	druron	droren	
lēosan "to lose"	lēas	luron	loren	
hrēosan "to fall"	hrēas	hruron	hroren	
sēoðan "to boil"	sēað	sudon	soden	

Class 3 Strong Verbs   8.6

Though this class is a bit messy, it rests on the ancient Primitive Germanic vowel series *e – a – u – u*. In Prehistoric OE, several sound changes then modified the vowel series into four separate categories, each with its own footprint.

(a) Verbs in which the root has a short vowel + a nasal [*m* or *n*] + a consonant (*bindan*, *drincan*, etc.). The vowel series in this category runs: *i – a – u – u*.

[3] See Appendix Two (§11), diphthongization by initial palatals.

[4] See Appendix Two (§11), diphthongization by initial palatals.

[5] See Appendix Two (§11), diphthongization by initial palatals.

Infinitive	Past Singular	Past Plural	Past Participle
bindan "to bind"	band	bundon	bunden
drincan "to drink"	dranc, dronc	druncon	druncen
findan "to find"	fand	fundon	funden
(ġe)limpan "to happen"	(ġe)lamp, (ġe)lomp	(ġe)lumpon	(ġe)lumpen
on-ġinnan "to begin"	on-gann, ongonn	on-gunnon	on-gunnen
sincan "to sink"	sanc, sonc	suncon	suncen
singan "to sing"	sang, song	sungon	sungen
swimman "to swim"	swamm, swomm	swummon	swummen
swincan "to work"	swanc, swonc	swuncon	swuncen
þringan "to press"	þrang, þrong	þrungon	þrungen
winnan "to strive, fight"	wann	wunnon	wunnen

(b) Verbs in which the root has a vowel + **1** + a consonant (*belgan*, *delfan*, etc.). The vowel series in this category runs: *e – ea – u - o*.

Infinitive	Past Singular	Past Plural	Past Participle
belgan "to be angry"	bealg	bulgon	bolgen
delfan "to dig"	dealf	dulfon	dolfen
ġieldan[3] "to yield, pay"	ġeald	guldon	golden
ġiellan[4] "to yell"	ġeall[5]	gullon	gollen
helpan "to help"	healp	hulpon	holpen
meltan "to melt"	mealt	multon	molten

[6] See Appendix Two (§2): "Verner's Law."

Infinitive	Past Singular	Past Plural	Past Participle
melcan "to milk"	mealc	mulcon	molcen
swelgan "to swallow"	swealg	swulgon	swolgen
swellan "to swell"	sweall	swullon	swollen
sweltan "to die"	swealt	swulton	swolten

(c) Verbs in which the root has a vowel + an *r* or *h* + a consonant (*beorgan, feohtan*, etc.). The vowel series in this category runs: *eo – ea – u - o*.

Infinitive	Past Singular	Past Plural	Past Participle
beorgan "to protect"	bearg	burgon	borgen
feohtan "to fight"	feaht	fuhton	fohten
hweorfan "to turn"	hwearf	hwurfon	hworfen
steorfan "to die"	stearf	sturfon	storfen
weorpan "to throw"	wearp	wurpon	worpen
weorþan "to become"	wearþ	wurdon	worden[6]

(d) A small group of miscellaneous, irregular verbs:

Infinitive	Past Singular	Plast Plural	Past Participle
breġdan "to brandish"	bræġd	brugdon	brogden
berstan "to burst"	bærst	burston	borsten
friġnan "to inquire"	fræġn	frugnon	frugen
murnan "to mourn"	mearn	murnon	*****

[7] See Appendix Two (§11), diphthongization by initial palatals.

[8] See Appendix Two (§11), diphthongization by initial palatals.

[9] See Appendix Two (§11), diphthongization by initial palatals.

Infinitive	Past Singular	Past Plural	Past Participle
spurnan "to tread down"	spearn	spurnon	sporen
streġdan "to strew"	stræġd	strugdon	strogden
ðerscan "to thresh"	ðærsc	ðurscon	ðorscen

8.7 Class 4 Strong Verbs

The vowel series of OE Class 4 verbs is *e – æ – ǽ – o*, and almost all the verbs of this class follow the series closely. One sound change produces a sub-class (see §8.7.1). The infinitive forms of this class have the footprint of *e* + a single consonant which is either an *l* or *r* (a liquid) or an *m* or *n* (a nasal): *beran, stelan,* etc.

Infinitive	Past Singular	Past Plural	Past Participle
beran "to bear"	bær	bǽron	boren
scieran[7] "to shear"	scear[8]	scēaron[9]	scoren
stelan "to steal"	stæl	stǽlon	stolen
cwelan "to die"	cwæl	cwǽlon	cwolen
teran "to tear"	tær	tǽron	toren
brecan "to break"*	bræc	brǽcon	brocen

*Note that brecan does not have the normal footprint for Class 4 strong verbs and is thus an exception to the rule.

8.7.1 TWO VERBS OF THIS CLASS ARE IRREGULAR

Infinitive	Past Singular	Past Plural	Past Participle
niman "to take"	nam, nōm	nāmon, nōmon	numen
cuman "to come"	cōm, cwōm	cōmon, cwōmon	cumen, cymen

Exercise 8.1: Conjugating Strong Verbs

Instructions. *Consider the ablaut series, the structural patterns, and the exceptions outlined above in each of the four classes of strong verbs. Guided by that information, identify the strong verb class and then provide the principal parts for the following infinitives.*

	Class	Past Singular	Past Plural	Past Participle
1. scēotan (to shoot)	_____	_____	_____	_____
2. helan (to conceal)	_____	_____	_____	_____
3. hrīnan (to touch)	_____	_____	_____	_____
4. springan (to spring)	_____	_____	_____	_____
5. ċeorfan (to carve)	_____	_____	_____	_____
6. būgan (to bow)	_____	_____	_____	_____
7. ġielpan (to boast)	_____	_____	_____	_____
8. scīnan (to shine)	_____	_____	_____	_____
9. ċēosan (to choose)	_____	_____	_____	_____

8.8 Lesson Two: Conjugation of Strong Verbs

In a sea of classes, sub-classes, and exceptions, it should come as something of a relief that all the strong verbs take the same personal endings. Since you will use these endings constantly, you should memorize them. The conjugation of these personal endings is similar to one that you are already familiar with—that of the weak I class of verbs (particularly in the present indicative). We conjugate here a representative verb from each of the first four classes: *bītan* "to bite" Class 1, *bēodan* "to offer" Class 2, *bindan* "to bind" Class 3, and *brecan* "to break" Class 4.

8.8.1   STRONG VERBS CLASSES 1-2: *bītan* "to bite," *bēodan* "to offer"

* For the alternate endings of the second and third person present singular, see §8.10. For the change in the root vowel from *ēo* in *bēodest* and *bēodeþ* to *īe* in *bīetst* and *bīett* or the *e* in *brecest* and *breceþ* to *i* in *bricst* and *briþ*, see §8.11.

** *The second person singular past is formed on the basis of the past plural stem.*

Infinitive			bītan		bēodan		Summary	
			Present	Past	Present	Past	Present	Past
Indicative Sing		1	bīte	bāt	bēode	bēad	-e	-
		2	bītest, bītst*	bite**	bēodest bietst*	bude**	-(e)st	-e
		3	bīteþ, bītt*	bāt	bēodeþ biet(t)*	bēad	-eþ, -t	-
Indicative Plural	1, 2, 3		bītaþ	biton	bēodaþ	budon	-aþ	-on
Subjunctive Sing	1, 2, 3		bīte	bite	bēode	bude	-e	-e
Subjunctive Plural	1, 2, 3		bīten	biten	bēoden	buden	-en	-en
Participles			bītende	biten	bēodende	boden	-ende	-en
Imperative Sing			bīt	*****	bēod	*****	-	**
Imperative Plural			bītaþ	*****	bēodaþ	*****	-aþ	**
Inflected Infin. (Gerund)			tō bītanne	*****	to bēodanne	*****	-anne	**

STRONG VERBS CLASSES 3-4: *bindan* "to bind, tie," *brecan* "to break"

Infinitive		bindan		brecan		Summary	
		Present	**Past**	**Present**	**Past**	**Present**	**Past**
Indicative Sing	1	binde	band	breċe	bræc	-e	-
	2	bindest, bintst*	bunde**	breċest, bricst*	bræ̆ċe**	-(e)st	-e
	3	bindeþ, bint*	band	breċeþ, bricþ*	bræc	-eþ, -t	-
Indicative Plural	1, 2, 3	bindaþ	bundon	brecaþ	bræcon	-aþ	-on
Subjunctive Sing	1, 2, 3	binde	bunde	breċe	bræ̆ċe	-e	-e
Subjunctive Plural	1, 2, 3	binden	bunden	breċen	bræ̆ċen	-en	-en
Participles		bindende	bunden	breċende	brocen	-ende	-en
Imperative Sing		bind	*****	brec	*****	-	**
Imperative Plural		bindaþ	*****	brecaþ	*****	-aþ	**
Inflected Infin. (Gerund)		to bindanne	*****	to brecanne	*****	-anne	**

* For the alternate endings of the second and third person present singular, see §8.10. For the change in the root vowel from *ēo* in *bēodest* and *bēodeþ* to *īe* in *bīetst* and *bīett* or the *e* in *brecest* and *breceþ* to *i* in *bricst* and *bricþ*, see §8.11.

** The second *person singular past is formed on the basis of the past plural stem.*

Lesson Three: Summary of Base Forms

The chart of verb endings listed above demonstrates the following principles governing the way strong verbs are formed:

1. The present indicative, present subjunctive, imperative, gerund, and the present participle take their base form from the ***infinitive stem*** of the verb.
2. The past indicative second person singular, past indicative plural, and past subjunctive take their base form from the ***past plural*** stem of the verb.

3. The past indicative second person singular, the past indicative plural, and the past subjunctive take their base form from the ***past plural*** stem of the verb.

The following information is a bit technical, but if you take the time to understand it, you will find yourself spending less time roaming around the glossary looking for the right strong verb.

TIMESAVERS:

8.10   SYNCOPATION AND ASSIMILATION

In most OE dialects the second and third person present indicative of strong verbs take the endings -*est* and -*eþ*. In the conjugation above, for example, the second and third person of *bītan* is *bītest* and *bīteþ*; of *bindan* the forms are *bindest* and *bindeþ*. However, the one exception to this rule is the West Saxon dialect where the –*est* and –*eþ* endings sometimes occur, but more often undergo one or several sound changes: in the case of *bītan*, for example, the second person ending *bītst* undergoes a single change—syncopation. Syncopation is the loss of a vowel (in this case, the *e* of the personal ending –*est*) between two consonants (in this case, the last consonant of the root [t] and the consonants of the personal ending, [st]). See Appendix Two, §15.4, §15.5.

The third person ending *bītt* undergoes TWO changes, ***syncopation*** and ***assimilation***. First, the vowel -*e*- is syncopated, and the loss of the vowel produces an unusual combination of consonant sounds -*tþ*. Second, those two consonants ***assimilate***, that is, they blend together, one sound becoming similar to its neighboring sound. The process of assimilation can be summarized as follows:

8.10.1   SECOND PERSON

d + st	=	-*tst*	*bīdest > bīdst > bītst*
þ + st	=	-*tst* or -*st*	*scrīþest > scrīþst > scrītst*
s + st	=	-*st*	*rīsest > rīsst > rīst*
g + st	=	-*hst*	*lēogest > lēogst > lȳhst*

THIRD PERSON

d + þ	=	*-tt* (sometimes *-t*)	*bīdeþ > bīdþ > bītt or bīt*
t + þ	=	*-tt* (sometimes *-t*)	*bīteþ > bīdþ > bītt or bīt*
þ + þ	=	*-þþ* (sometimes *-þ*)	*scrīpeþ > scrīþþ > scrīþþ or scrīþ*
s + þ	=	*-st*	*rīseþ > rīsþ > rīst*
g + þ	=	*-hþ*	*lēogeþ > lēogþ > lȳhþ*

Mutating Vowels

One last set of systematic changes shaped the strong verbs signficantly: *i-mutation.* Since it was such a wide-spread process, learning something about i-mutation (as frightening as it sounds) will help to explain not only verb patterns but also noun (§10.4) and adjective (§6.7) patterns as well, so you can find them quickly in the dictionary.

Some basics: [ɪ] as a high front vowel has the tendency to pull vowels in its orbit to a higher more front position (refer to the verb chart below and §1.5). The present tense of strong verbs often shows evidence of i-mutation, but the confusing fact is that the *i* that caused the mutation has utterly disappeared. In Prehistoric OE (that is, sometime between 500 CE and 700 CE), the endings for the second and third person singular indicative present tense were *-is* and *-iþ* (during early historic OE, the second person ending became *-est*). The [ɪ] sound of the endings caused the root vowel to change: as mentioned above, the [ɪ] sound is a high, front vowel sound (see §1.5) that exerts a magnetic pull on the preceding vowel, attracting it to a higher and more fronted sound (a form of assimilation). For example, in the case of a verb like Prehistoric OE *breciþ,* the speaker, anticipating the [ɪ] sound of the suffix, begins to shift the pronunciation of the root vowel (a mid front sound [ɛ]) toward the higher position. In the process, the root vowel shifts from [ɛ] to [ɪ]. Therefore, a verb like *bricþ* would have developed as follows: **breciþ* > [i-mutation] > **briciþ* > [change of *–i–* to *–e–*] > [syncopation] > *briceþ* > *bricþ*.

In the case of *bēodest* > *bīetst,* i-mutation similarly changes the root vowel, the verb developing as follows: **bēodis* > [i-mutation] > **bīedis(t)* > [syncopation] > *bīedst* [assimilation] > *bīetst.*

In the case of *bēodeþ* > *bīet(t),* the verb develops as follows: **bēodiþ* > [i-mutation] > **bīediþ* [change of *–i–* to *–e–*] > **bīedeþ* > [syncopation] > *bīedþ* > [assimilation] > *bīet(t).*

8.11.1   I-MUTATION: TABLE OF SOUND CHANGES IN OE

The vowel triangle described at §1.5 should help you to visualize how the high front sounds—*i, ī,* or *j*—produced the "mutation" in a preceding syllable.

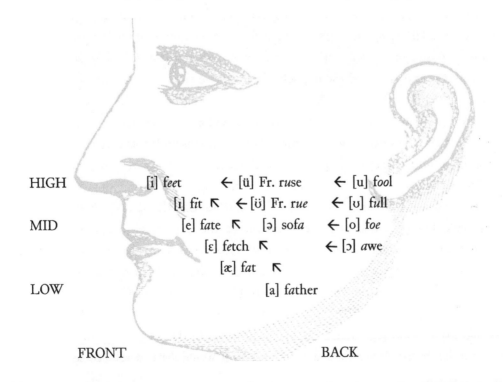

HIGH   [i] f*ee*t   ← [ü] Fr. r*u*se   ← [u] f*oo*l

                  [ɪ] f*i*t ↖   ←[ü] Fr. r*ue*   ← [ʊ] f*u*ll

MID   [e] f*a*te ↖   [ə] sof*a*   ← [o] f*oe*

                  [ɛ] f*e*tch ↖   ← [ɔ] *a*we

                  [æ] f*a*t ↖

LOW   [a] f*a*ther

FRONT   BACK

The working principle of the i-mutation is that the [ɪ] or [i] sound attracts the vowel in the preceding syllable toward the high front position of [ɪ] or [i]. Thus, back sounds like [a], [ɔ], and [o] move forward to the corresponding front sound: [æ], [ɛ], and [e] respectively. The high back sounds [ʊ] and [u] move one position forward to the mid sounds [ʊ] and [ü]. Front sounds like [æ] or [e] rise one position to [ɛ] and [ɪ] respectively.

I-MUTATION: TABLE OF CHANGES FOR WRITTEN OE   8.11.2

Prehistoric Vowel	became	OE Vowel	Example
a (or o) before a nasal	>	e	*mann*, pl *menn* from Prehistoric OE pl *manniz*
a	>	æ	*færð* (3 present sing) from Prehistoric OE *fariþ* (*faran*, to go).
ā	>	ǣ	*bǣt* (3 present sing) from Prehistoric OE *bātiþ* (*bātan*, "to hate").
æ	>	e	*eġe* from Prehistoric OE *ǣġi*.
e	>	i	*bricþ* (3 present sing) from Prehistoric OE *breciþ*.
o	>	e	*mergen* from Prehistoric OE *morgin*.
ō	>	ē	*grēwþ* (3 present sing) from Prehistoric OE *grōwiþ*.
u	>	y	*cymst* (2 present sing) from Prehistoric OE *cumis*.
ū	>	ȳ	*brȳcst* (2 present sing) from Prehistoric OE *brūcis*.

DIPHTHONGS

Prehistoric Vowel	became	OE Vowel	Example
eo	>	ie	*fieht* (3 present sing) from Prehistoric OE **feohtiþ* "fights"
ēo	>	īe	*līehtan* from Prehistoric OE **lēohtjan* "to give light"
ea	>	ie	*fielþ* (3 present sing) from Prehistoric OE **fealiþ* "falls"
ēa	>	īe	*flīeman* from Prehistoric OE **flēamjan* "to put to flight"
io (originally eo)	>	ie	*wierpþ* (3 present sing) from Prehistoric OE **wiorpiþ* "throws"
īo (originally ēo)	>	īe	*stīeran* from Prehistoric OE **stīorjan* "to steer".

Exercise 8.2: UNDERSTANDING THE FORMS OF CLASS 1, 2, 3, AND 4 STRONG VERBS

Instructions. *In the spaces provided, identify the mood, tense, person, and number of the listed verbs. Where the verb form allows for more than one possible answer, provide all of them. Below each form, give the infinitive.*

	Mood	Tense	Person	Number
1. glād	*indicative*	*Past*	*1,3*	*singular*

infinitive *slīdan*

	Mood	Tense	Person	Number
2. smucon	_____	_____	_____	_____
infinitive	_____			
3. swealt	_____	_____	_____	_____
infinitive	_____			
4. wierþ	_____	_____	_____	_____
infinitive	_____			
5. cume	_____	_____	_____	_____
infinitive	_____			
6. beraþ	_____	_____	_____	_____
infinitive	_____			
7. rīt	_____	_____	_____	_____
infinitive	_____			
8. snītst	_____	_____	_____	_____
infinitive	_____			
9. nimeþ	_____	_____	_____	_____
infinitive	_____			
10. sungen	_____	_____	_____	_____
infinitive	_____			

Exercise 8.3: RECOGNIZING SYNCOPATION, ASSIMILATION, AND I-MUTATION

Instructions. *Give the syncopated and mutated forms of the second and third persons, singular present indicative, for the following strong verbs. Refer to the charts on syncopation and assimilation (§8.10.1-2) as well as that on i-mutation (§8.11.2). If the form has more than one correct answer, provide both.*

	Second Person	Third Person
1. glīdan	slītst	slītt, slīt
2. brecan		
3. weorpan		
4. bēodan		
5. brūcan		
6. wrītan		
7. sēoþan		
8. weorþan		
9. beran		
10. snīþan		

Exercise 8.4: TRANSLATION PRACTICE

Instructions. *Translate the following Old English sentences into idiomatic Modern English:*

1. Hē wiste* þæt hē þǣr bād westan windes ond hwōn norþan, ond siġlde þā ēast be lande swā swā hē meahte on feower dagum ġe-siglan.

2. And wē ēac for þām habbaþ fela byrsta and bysmara ġe-biden and, ġif wē ǣniġe bōte ġe-bīdan scylen, þonne mōte wē þæs to Gode ernian bet þonne wē ǣr þysum dydon.

3. Þā tungel-wītegan fērdon æfter þæs cyninges sprǣċe, and efne ðā sē steorra þe hī on Ēast-dǣle ġe-sāwon glād him beforan, oð þæt hē ġe-stōd bufan þām gest-hūse ðǣr þæt ċild on wunode.

4. Ond hiera sē æþeling ġe-hwelċum feoh ond feorh ġe-bēad, ond hiera** nǣniġ hit ġe-þicgean nolde; ac hīe simle feohtende wǣron oþ hīe alle lǣgon . . . .

5. Hēr Æðelstān cyning,   eorla dryhten,
   beorna bēag-ġiefa,   and his brōþor ēac,
   Ēadmund æðeling,   ealdor-langne tīr
   ġe-slōgon æt sæċċe   sweorda ecgum
   ymbe Brūnanburg.

6. Hē bræc ðone bordweall, and wiþ ðā beornas feaht.

7. Ond hīe flugon ofer Temese būton ǣlcum forda, þā up be Colne on ānne iggaþ.

8. Hīe ðǣr þā mid miċelre blīðnesse būton ġe-metgunge þæt wīn drincende wǣron, oð hī heora selfra lȳtel ġe-weald hæfdon.

VOCABULARY FOR EXERCISE 8.4

æfter (preposition) = AFTER [§6.15]

ǣlċ (adjective) = any, EACH [§6.1]

ǣmen (adjective) = uninhabited, deserted [§6.1]

ǣniġ (adjective) = ANY [§6.1]

ǣr (preposition + dat and inst) = before, ERE [§6.15]

æþeling (m) = prince, noble [§2.7]

Æðelstān (m) = Athelstan, King of Wessex, died 939

bād (verb form not yet covered) = "waited for," "awaited" (past sing, + gen object) [§9.1]

be (preposition + dat) = along, by [§6.15]

bēag-ġiefa (weak m) = ring-GIVEer [§3.3]

be-foran (preposition) = BEFORE [§6.15]

(ġe)bēodan (strong verb 2) = to offer (past sing *ġe-bēad*) [§8.5]

bēon (irregular verb) = to BE [§4.5.1]

beorn (m) = man, warrior [§2.7]

bet (adverb) = BETter [§6.9]

(ġe)bīdan (strong verb 1 + gen or acc) = to experience, undergo (something) [§8.4]

biddan (strong verb 5) = to wait for, await (past sing: *bād*) [§9.1]

blīþnes (f) = happiness [§2.8]

bord-weall (m) = shield WALL [§2.7]

bōt (f) = remedy [§2.8]

brecan (strong verb 4) = to BREAK (past sing: *bræc*) [§8.7]

brōðor (m) = BROTHER [§10.5]

Brūnanburg (f) = unidentified fort of Bruna [§10.4.2]

bufan (preposition) = (+ dat) aBOVE, over; (+ acc) on, upon, over [§6.15]

būton (preposition + dat) = without [§6.15]

bysmer, bismer (m, n) = insult, disgrace [§2.7, §2.9]

byrst (m) = loss, injury [§10.11.1]

ċild (n) = CHILD [§10.8]

Coln (f) = the river COLNE [§2.8]

cyning (m) = KING [§2.7]

dagum = see *dæġ*

dæġ (m) = DAY [§2.7, §2.10.3]

dōn (irregular verb) = to DO [§4.5.3.1]

drincan (strong verb 3) = to DRINK [§8.6]

dryhten (m) = lord, leader [§2.7]

dydon = see *dōn*

ēac (adverb) = also [§6.9]

Ēadmund (m) = king of the English (939–46), successor to Æðelstān

ealdor-lang (adjective) = life long, eternal [§6.1]

ēast (adverb) = EAST [§6.9]

ēast-dǣle (m) = EASTern region [§10.11.1]

ecg (f) = EDGE [§2.8]

efne (adverb) = EVEN, just [§6.9]

eorl (m) = nobleman, retainer [§2.7]

ermþ (f) = misery (dat pl: *ermþum*) [§10.7]

ernian, earnian (weak verb II) = to deserve, gain, EARN (+ gen object) [§3.12]

feaht = see *feohtan*

fela (indeclinable adjective) = many [§2.11.3.d]

feoh (n) = money [§2.9]

(ġe)feohtan (strong verb 3) = to FIGHT [§8.6]

feohtende = see *feohtan*

feorh (m, n) = life [§2.7, §2.9]

feower (number) = FOUR

fēran (weak verb I) = to go, FARE [§3.11]

fērdon = see *fēran*

flēon (strong verb 2) = TO FLEE [§8.6, 11.1.2]

ford (weak m) = FORD [§10.6]

for þām (conjunction) = because; (adverb) therefore, for that reason [§5.1.1]

gest-hūs (n) = GUEST HOUSE [§2.9]

ġif (conjunction) = IF [§5.1.1]

glīdan (strong verb 1) = to GLIDE [§8.4]

God (m) = GOD, the Deity [§2.7]

habban (weak verb III) = to HAVE [§4.1]

hē, hēo, hit (personal pronoun) = HE, she, IT [§7.1]

heora selfra (reflexive pronoun) = THEMSELVES [§7.4]

hēr (adverb) = HERE, in this place [§6.9]

hiera = see *hē, hēo, hit* [§7.1]

(ġe)hwelċ (indefinite pronoun with partitive gen) = each, each one [§7.8]

hwōn (adverb) = a little [§6.9]

iggaþ (m) = ISLAND [§2.7]

lǣgon (verb form not yet covered) = "LAY," "lay dead" (past pl) [§9.1]

land (n) = LAND, country [§2.9]

lȳtel (adjective) = LITTLE, small [§6.1]

magan (preterite-present verb) = to be able [§4.3]

meahte = see *magan*

mētan (weak verb I) = to MEET [§3.11]

(ġe)metgung (f) = moderation [§2.8]

miċel (adjective) = much, great [§6.1]

mōtan (preterite-present verb) = must, might [§4.3]

mōte = see *mōtan*

nǣniġ (indefinite pronoun) = NONE [§7.8]

nolde = see *nyllan*

norþ (adverb) = NORTH [§6.9]

nyllan (irregular verb, *ne+willan*) = will not, not to wish [§4.5.3.2]

oþ (conjunction) = until [§5.1.1]

sæċċe (f) = battle, strife, contest [§2.8]

(ġe)sāwon = (verb form not yet covered) = saw (past pl) [§11.1]

scylan (preterite-present verb) = shall, ought to [§4.3]

(ġe)siglan (weak verb I) = to SAIL [§3.11]

siglde see *(ġe)siglan*

simle (adverb) = always [§6.9]

(ġe)slōgon (verb form not yet covered) = "SLAY," "strike," "achieve (by fighting)," "win" (past pl) [§9.2]

sorġian (weak verb II) = to grieve [§3.12]

sorġiende = see *sorġian*

sprǣċ (f) = SPEECH [§2.8]

steorra (weak m) = STAR [§3.3]

(ġe)stōd (verb form not yet covered) = "STOOD" (past sing) [§9.2]

swā (adverb) = SO [§6.9]

swā . . . swā (adverb) = as . . . as [§6.9]

sweord (n) = SWORD [§2.9]

swīþe (adverb) = very [§6.9]

Temese = the THAMES river

tīr (m) = glory [§2.7]

tungel-wītega (weak m) = astrologer, wiseman; see OE *tungol* "star" + *wītega* "prophet" [§3.3]

þā (adverb) = then [§6.9]

þā (conjunction) = when [§5.1.1]

þǣr (adverb) = THERE [§6.9]

þæs (adverb) = afterwards, accordingly; therefore [§6.9]

(ġe)þicgean (verb form not net covered) = to accept (infinitive) [§9.1]

þonne (adverb) = then [§6.9]

þonne (conjunction) = than (+ comparative adjective); when [§5.1.1]

þis (demonstrative pronoun) = THIS [§7.7]

ūp (adverb) = UP [§6.9]

wē = see *hē, hēo, hit*

wesan (irregular verb) = to be, occur [§4.5.1]

westan (adverb) = from the WEST [§6.9]

wīn (n) = WINE [§2.9]

wǣron = see *wesan*

(ġe)weald (n) = power, might, control [compare German *Gewalt* "power"; §2.9]

wind (m) = WIND [§2.7]

(ġe)wit (n) = reason [§2.9]

witan (preterite-present verb) = to know [§4.3]

wunian (weak verb II) = to dwell, remain [§3.12]

ymbe (preposition + acc or dat) = around, about, in regard to [§6.15]

[10] An "impersonal" construction (see §11.2) for which you must supply an implied "it": "if [it] seems to him." Note that the *ġif* can cause the subjunctive (signaling a hypothetical situation, see §3.10.1) to appear in the following clause.

[11] Hint: This word is NOT *bēon* the familiar "to be" verb, but a noun—check the glossary.

[12] A "post-position" governing the object *him* at the beginning of the clause.

Reading VIII.i: PROGNOSTICS 2

Prognostics, as the name suggests, predict the future by examining conditions of the past or present. In the following collection of dream interpretations, some of the connections between dream objects and their significance are fairly transparent, though some are more baffling. In #1, for example, the "honor" predicted for the one who dreams of seeing an eagle is arguably connected with its connection to the aristocratic hunt. But, how the dream of kissing a dead man might betoken a long and successful life (as in #13) is at best an oblique connection. Note that the spelling in this text is sometimes at odds with the more traditional late West Saxon conventions.

1. Ġif mann mǣte, þæt hē ġe-sēo earn on his hēafod ufan, þæt tācnað wurþ-mynt.
2. Ġif him þinċe,[10] þæt hine bēon[11] stikien, þæt byþ, þæt his mōd byþ āstyred fram el-þēodigum mannum.
3. Ġif him þinċe, þæt hē ġe-sēo bēon in tō his hūse flēon, þæt byþ þæs hūses ǣlednyss.
4. Ġif him þinċe, þæt hē fēala penegas finde and ne oþ-hrīne, gōd þæt byþ; ġif hē nymeþ, ne dēah þæt.
5. Ġif him þinċe, þæt his hūs byrnð, miċel blǣd him biþ tōweard.
6. Ġif him þinċe, þæt hē his beard scere, þonne biþ his brocc lȳtliende.
7   Ġif him þinċe, þæt hē ne mǣge yrnan, myċel broc him byþ tōwerd.
8. Ġif him þinċe, þæt hē wiþ cyning sprece, him cymþ ġe-fealiċ gifu tō[12] and gōd.
9. Ġif him þinċe, þæt hē stīġe on hēanne munt, þæt tācnaþ gōd.

[13] Though *singan* is an infinitive, translate it as a verbal noun: "singing."

[14] A reflexive pronoun (see §7.4).

10. Ġif him þinċe, þæt hē dracan ġe-sēo, gōd þæt biþ.

11. Ġif him þinċe, þæt hē hæbbe nīwe scēos, mid brōce him cymþ ġe-strēon.

12. Ġif him þinċe, þæt hē fixas ġe-sēo, þæt biþ rēn.

13. Ġif him þinċe, þæt hē dēadne mann cysse, þæt biþ lang līf and gōd.

14. Ġif him þinċe, þæt hē huniġ ete oððe ġe-sēo, þæt bið angnes.

15. Ġif him þinċe, þæt hē on ċirċean singan[13] ġe-hȳre, myċel gōd þæt tācnað.

16. Ġif him þinċe, þæt hē wiþ his scrift sprece, þæt tācnað his synna forġyfennysse.

17. Ġif him þinċe, þæt his wīf sīe mid bearne, þæt bið gōd swefen.

18. Ġif him þinċe, þæt hē hæbbe hwīt scēap, þæt tācnað gōd.

19. Ġif him þinċe, þæt hē ā-wiht on godcundum bōcum ræde oððe leorniġe, miċel wurðmynt him byþ tō-weard æt Gode.

20. Ġif him þinċe, þæt hē ġe-sēon ne mæġe, lære iċ hine, þæt hē him[14] beorge wið his ēhtend.

21. Ġif him þinċe, þæt hē fela henna ġe-sēo oððe hæbbe, þæt bið gōd.

VOCABULARY FOR READING VIII.i

ǣlednyss (m) = fire, burning, burning down [§2.7]

æt (preposition + acc and dat) = from, on, AT [§6.15]

angnes (f) = anxiety, trouble; pain [§2.8]

ā-styrian (weak verb I) = to move, remove [§3.11]

ā-wiht (indefinite pronoun) = anything, aught [§7.8]

beard (m) = BEARD [§2.7]

bearn (n) = child, son, BAIRN [§2.9]

bēo (weak f) = BEE [§3.4]

bēon (irregular verb) = to BE, to mean, to consist in [§4.5.1]

beorgan (strong verb 3) = to protect [§8.6]

biernan (strong verb 3) = to BURN [§8.6]

biþ, byþ = see *bēon*

blǣd (m) = success, prosperity, riches [§10.11.1]

bōc (f) = BOOK [§10.4.2]

broc (n) = misery, toil, affliction, adversity [§2.9]

byrnð = see *biernan*

byþ = see *bēon*

ċirċe (weak f) = CHURCH [§3.4]

cuman (strong verb 4) = to COME [§8.7]

cymþ = see *cuman*

cyng, cyning (m) = KING [§2.7]

cyssan (weak verb I) = to KISS [§3.11]

dēad (adjective) = DEAD [§6.1]

dēab = see *dugan*

draca (weak m) = DRAGON [§3.3]

dugan (preterite-present verb) = to avail, to be good, to be of worth [§4.3]

earn (m) = eagle [§2.7]

ēhtend (m) = pursuer, persecutor [§10.10]

el-þēodiġ (adjective) = foreign, alien; (here used as a noun:) foreigners, aliens [§6.1]

ete (verb form not yet covered) = "should EAT" (present 3 sing subjunctive) [§9.1]

fela (indeclinable adjective + gen) = many [§6.1]

(ġe)fēaliċ (adjective) = joyous, pleasant [§6.1]

findan (strong verb 3) = to FIND [§8.6]

fisc (m) = FISH (pl = *fixas*) [§2.7]

fixas = see *fisc*

flēon (strong verb 2) = flee, fly from, fly [§8.5]

forġyfennys(s) (f) = FORGIVENESS [§2.8]

fram (preposition + dat) = by, FROM [§6.15]

ġif (conjunction) = IF [§5.1.1]

ġi(e)fu (f) = GIFT [§2.8]

gōd (adjective) = GOOD [§6.1]

god (n) = (pagan) god [§2.9]

god-cund (adjective) = divine, sacred [§6.1]

habban (weak verb III) = to HAVE [§4.1]

hæbbe = see *habban*

hēafod (n) = HEAD [§2.9]

hēan (adjective) = high [§6.1]

henn (f) = hen [§2.8]

hē (personal pronoun) = he [§7.1]

(ġe)hīeran (weak verb I) = to HEAR [§3.11]

him = see *hē*

hine = see *hē*

his = see *hē*

huniġ (m) = HONEY [§2.7]

hūs (n) = HOUSE [§2.9]

hwīt (adjective) = WHITE [§6.1]

(ġe)hȳre =see *(ġe)hīeran*

iċ (personal pronoun) = I [§7.1]

in-to (preposition + dat or acc) = INTO [§6.15]

lǣran (weak verb I) = to advise, instruct [§3.11]

lang (adjective) = LONG [§6.1]

(ġe)leornian (weak verb II) = to LEARN, study [§3.12]

līf (n) = LIFE [§2.9]

lȳtlian (weak verb II) = to lessen, decrease, diminish [§3.12]

mǣtan (weak verb I) = to dream [§3.11]

magan (preterite-present verb) = to be able, MAY [§4.3]

mann (m) = MAN, one [§10.4.2]

miċel (adjective) = much, great [§6.1]

mid (preposition) = with [§6.15]

mōd (n) = mind, spirit [§2.9]

munt (m) = MOUNT, mountain [§2.7]

myċel = see *miċel*

niman (strong verb 4) = to take [§8.7]

nīwe (adjective) = NEW [§6.1]

on (preposition) = ON, in [§6.15]

oþ-brīnan (strong verb 1) = to touch [§8.4]

oððe (conjunction) = or

penegas = see *pening*

pening (m) = penny [§2.7]

(ġe)rǣdan (weak verb I) = to READ [§3.11]

rēn (m) = RAIN [§2.7]

scēap (n) = SHEEP [§2.9]

scēo, scōh (m) = SHOE [§2.7]

scere = see *scieran*

scieran (strong verb 4) = to SHEAR, cut [§8.7]

scrift (m) = confessor [§2.7]

sē, sēo, þæt (definite article) = the [§2.5]

(ġe)sēon (strong verb 5, contract verb) = to SEE [§11.1]

sīe = see *bēon* (*sīe* is a subjunctive)

singan (strong verb 3) = to SING [§8.6]

sprecan (strong verb 5) = to SPEAK [§9.1]

stīgan (strong verb 1) = to ascend, to climb [§8.4]

stikian, stiċian (weak verb II) = to STICK [§3.12]

(ġe)strēon (n) = treasure, riches [§2.9]

swefen (n) = dream [§2.9]

synn (f) = SIN [§2.8]

tācnian (weak verb II) = to beTOKEN, symbolize [§3.12]

tō-weard, tō-werd (adjective) = approaching, coming, imminent [§6.1] *þæs* = see *sē*

þæt (conjunction, introducing clause) = THAT [§5.1.1 and §7.5]

þæt (demonstrative pronoun) = THAT [§7.7]

þincan (weak verb I) = to seem, appear; THINK (often impersonal) [§3.11]

þonne (adverb) = then [§6.9]

ufan (adverb) = from above [§6.9]

wīf (n) = WIFE [§2.9]

wiþ (preposition) = WITH [6.15]

wurþ-mynt (f) = honor [§10.11.2]

yrnan, iernan (strong verb 3) = to run [§8.6]

[15] "Dearly beloved": standard form of address in homilies (lit., "men the beloved").

[16] A subjunctive: "be" or "should be."

[17] A relative pronoun (see §7.5).

[18] Question: Why is *ōðres* in the genitive?

[19] Be sure to apply the Dative Rule to this phrase: *swīðe wependre stemne* (see §5.4.2).

Reading VIII.ii: FROM VERCELLI HOMILY IX

The collection of homilies and poems preserved in the Vercelli Codex (copied sometime in the first half of the 10th century) has a devotional character which often permits some fairly wild imagery. This excerpt and the ones that follow come from a homily on the terrors of hell and owe some of their power to some less than orthodox sources, one of them a lost text in which the devil tells an anchorite all the lurid tortures of hell. Note that this text sometimes substitutes -io- for the more usual -eo-.

Men ðā lēofstan,[15] manað ūs ond myngaþ þēos hālige bōc þæt wē sīen[16] ġe-myndiġe ymb ūre sāwle þearfe, ond ēac swā ūres þæs nēhstan dæġes ond þǣre tō-sċeadednesse ūre sāwle þonne hīo of ðām liċ-homan lǣdde bīo.

Wā bið þām mannum þe bēoð ġe-tēohhode tō ðǣre stōwe, for ðan þǣr is wōp būtan frōfre ond hrēow būtan reste, ond þǣr bið þēowdōm būton frēodōme, ond þǣr bið unrōtnys būton ġe-fēan, ond þǣr bið biternys būton swētnysse, ond þǣr bið hungor ond þurst, ond þǣr bið grānung ond ġēomrung ond miċel wrōht. Ond hī wēpað hēora synna swīðe biterlicum tēarum, ond on heom sylfum bēoð ealle hēora synna ġe-sēne, þā ðe[17] hī ǣr ġe-worhton, ond ne mæġ nān ōðres[18] ġe-helpan. Ac hī þonne on-ginnað singan swīðe sorhfulne sang ond swīðe wēpendre stemne:[19] "Nū wē magon sċēawian ealle ūre synna   10 beforan ealre þysse mæniġo, þēah wē hēo[20] ealle ǣr ġe-worhton." Ne biþ þǣr ġe-sibbes lufu tō ōðrum, ond nis þǣr nǣniġ man þæt þǣr sȳ his scyppendes ġe-myndiġ for ðām sār þe him on-siteð.[21] Ond þǣr bēoð þā sāwle for-ġytene ealre þǣra þe hī ǣr on eorðan ġe-metton.

Sæġeð hit ēac on bōcum þæt sum dēofles gāst sǣde ānum ancran ealle helle ġe-rȳne ond þāra sāwla[22] tintrega. Ond hē wæs cweðende þæt eall þes middan-ġeard nǣre þe māre drȳġes landes[23] ofer þone micċlan gārsecg þe man ænne prican ā-prycce on ānum brede,[24] ond nis þēs middan-ġeard sē seofoða dǣl ofer þone micclan gārsecg, sē mid micclum ormǣtnyssum ealle þas eorðan ūtan ymb-liġeð. Ond lȳtel dǣl is under heofonum drȳġes landes[25] þæt hit ne sȳ mid gārsecge ofer-urnen.

VOCABULARY FOR READING VIII.ii

ac (conjunction) = but

ǣr (adverb) = ERE, before [§6.9]

ān, æn (adjective, indefinite pronoun) = ONE, a/an [§7.8]

āncra (weak m) = ANCHORite, hermit [§3.3]

ā-priccan (weak verb I) = to PRICK, gouge [§3.1]

be-foran (preposition + dat, instr) = BEFORE, in front of [§6.15]

bēon (irregular verb) = to BE [§4.5.1]

biterlīċ (adjective) = BITTER [§6.1]

biternys (f) = BITTERNESS [§2.8]

bōc (f) = BOOK [see §10.4.2]

bred (n) = board, plank [compare German *Brett* "board, plank"; §10.11.1]

būtan (preposition + dat) = without [§6.15]

cweðan (strong verb 5) = to say, "QUOTH the raven" [§9.1]

dǣl (m) = portion, part [compare German *Teil* "part, share"; §10.11.1]

dēofol (m) = DEVIL [§2.7]

drȳġe (adjective) = DRY, parched [§6.1]

ēac (adverb) = also, EKE [§6.9]

eall (adjective) = ALL (usually + partitive gen) [§6.1]

ealre = see *eall*

eorðe (weak f) = EARTH [§3.4]

(ġe)fēa (weak m) = joy [§3.3]

15

[20] *Hēo* refers back to *synna*.

[21] Psalm 6:5.

[22] Be sure to apply the Genitive Rule to *þāra sāwla* (see §5.4.3).

[23] Probably a genitive of respect: "with respect to dry land."

[24] A difficult sentence. Translate, "was not the greater in terms of dry land in comparison to the sea than one might prick a tiny hole in a board." That is, earth's dry land is a mere speck in a sea of terrifying ocean.

[25] The genitive phrase *drȳġes landes* depends on *dǣl* (see §5.4.3 again).

Heaven, Last Judgment, and Hell:
A tinted line-drawing of heaven (top panel), the judgment of the soul (middle panel), and hell (bottom panel) from the New Minster *Liber Vitae* (London, British Library, Ms. Stowe 944, fol. 3r).

for (preposition + dat) = FOR; because of, owing to [§6.15]

for-ġyten (verb form not yet covered) = FORGOTTEN (past participle) [§9.1]

for-þan (þe) (adverb, conjunction) = because [§5.1.1]; therefore [§6.9]

frēo-dōm (m) = FREEDOM [§2.7]

frōfor (f, m) = comfort, consolation [§2.8]

gārsecg (m) = sea, spear's edge? [§10.2.1]

gāst (m) = spirit (good or bad), demon or angel, GHOST [§2.7]

ġēomrung (f) = moaning, grief [ModE *YAMMER*; §2.8]

grānung (f) = GROANING, lamentation [§2.8]

hāliġ (adjective) = HOLY [compare German *heilig* "holy"; §6.1]

hē, hēo, hit (personal pronoun) = HE, she, IT [§7.1]

helle (f) = HELL [§2.8]

(ġe)helpan (strong verb 3) = to HELP (+ dat or gen object) [§8.6]

heofon (m or f) = HEAVEN [§2.7]

heora = see *hē, hēo, hit*

hī, hīe = see *hē, hēo, hit*

hrēow (f) = sorrow, regret, penitence, RUE (as in *you'll rue the day*) [§2.8]

hungor (m) = HUNGER [§2.7]

lǣdan (weak verb I) = to LEAD; take, bring, carry [§3.11]

land (n) = LAND, country, region [§2.9]

līċ-hama, -homa (weak m) = body, (literally) body-HOME [§3.3]

lufu (f) = LOVE [§2.8]

lȳtel (adjective) = small, LITTLE [§6.1]

mæġ = see *magan*

magan (pret-pres verb) = be able, have permission or ability (to do something) [§4.3]

manian (weak verb II) = to remind, exhort, admonish [§3.12]

māra (adjective) = greater, larger; comparative of *miċel* [see §6.8]

meniġu (f, usually indeclinable in sing) = crowd, multitude [compare German *Menge*; §10.7]

(ġe)mētan (weak verb I) = to MEET, encounter [§3.11]

miċel (adjective) = great, large [§6.1]

mid (preposition + dat) = with [§6.15]

middan-ġeard (m) = MIDDle-earth, lit. –YARD [§2.7]

(ġe)myndiġ (adjective) = MINDful (usually + gen) [§6.1]

myneġian (weak verb II) = to warn, mention, remind [§3.12]

nū (adverb) = NOW [§6.9]

nān (pronoun, adjective) = NONE, no; no
    one [§7.8, §6.1]

nǣniġ (pronoun, adjective) = NONE, any
    [§6.1]

nǣre = see *bēon*

nehst, nīehst (adjective, superlative form
    of *nēah*) = NEXT, last, closest [§6.1,
    §6.14]

ofer (preposition + acc) = OVER, in
    comparison to [§6.15]

ofer-urnen (past participle of *ofer-yrnan*)

ofer-yrnan = to over-run [§4.5.3]

ond, and (conjunction) = AND; *ond . . .*
    ond = both . . . and

on-ginnan (strong verb 3) = to beGIN (+
    infinitive) [§8.6]

on-sittan (strong verb 5) = to SIT, seat
    oneself, oppress [§9.1]

ormǣtnys (f) = excess, immensity [§2.8]

ōðer (adjective) = OTHER [§6.1]

prica (weak m) = PRICK, point [§3.3]

rest (f) = REST [§2.8]

(ġe)rȳne (n) = secrets, RUNE [§10.2.2]

sǣde = past 3 sing of *secgan*

sǣġeð = present 3 sing of *secgan*

sang (m) = SONG [§2.7]

sār (n) = SORrow, suffering pain; wound
    [§2.9]

sāwol (f) = SOUL [§2.8]

scēawian (weak verb II) = to see, view, look
    upon, gaze at [compare German *schauen*
    "to look"; §3.12]

scyppend (m) = creator [§10.10]

(ġe)sēne, -siene (adjective) = SEEN, visible
    [§6.1]

secgan (weak verb III) = to SAY; relate, tell
    about, describe [compare German *sagen*
    "to say"; §4.1]

seofoða (num) = SEVENTH

(ġe)sibb (m,f) = kinsman [§2.8]

singan (strong verb 3) = to SING [§8.6]

sorg-, sorh-ful (adjective) = SORRowFUL
    [§6.1]

stōw (f) = place [§2.8]

stemne, stefne (f) = voice [compare German
    Stimme "voice"; §2.8]

sum (adjective, pronoun) = SOME, a
    certain [§6.1, §7.8]

swētnys (f) = SWEETNESS [§2.8]

swīðe (adverb) = very, very much,
    exceedingly; violently, fiercely [§6.9]

sylf, seolf (pronoun) = SELF [§7.4]

synn (f) = SIN, crime [§2.8]

tēar (m) = TEAR; drop [§2.7]

(ġe)teohhian (weak verb II) = to determine, intend, assign; judge [§3.12]

tintreġ (n) = torture, torment [§2.9]

tō (preposition + dat, gen, instr) = as, TO, into, until [§6.15, §2.11.4.c]

tō-scēadednes (f) = separation [§2.8]

þan = see *for*

þe (adverb) = than [§6.9]

þe . . . þe = the . . . than

ðēah (conjunction) = THOUGH, although [§5.1.1]; (adverb) = yet, nevertheless [§6.9]

ðearf (f) = need; profit, benefit; danger, distress [§2.8]

þēos = see *þēs, þēos, þis*

þēow-dōm (m) = slavery, servitude, vassaldom [§2.7]

þēs, þēos, þis (demonstrative pronoun, adjective) = THIS [§7.7]

þurst (m) THIRST [§10.11.1]

under (preposition + dat) = UNDER [§6.15]

un-rōtnys (f) = sadness, regret [§2.8]

ūs, ūre = see *hē, hēo, hit*

ūtan (adverb) = from withOUT, from the outside [§6.9]

wā (interjection) = WOE (+ dat)

wē = see *hē, hēo, hit*

wēpan (strong verb 7) = to WEEP; beweep, bewail, regret with tears [§9.3]

wōp (m) = WEEPing [§2.7]

wrōht (f) = blame, reproach [§2.7]

(ġe)wyrcan (weak verb I) = to perform, do; WORK, [§3.11]

ymbe, embe (preposition + acc, dat) = about, concerning, for [§6.15]

ymb-ligan, -licgan (strong verb 5) = to surround, enclose [§9.1]

Lessons Learned

Before leaving this chapter you should . . .
- **know how to use the master strong verb chart (§8.2).**
- **have memorized the basic verb endings for the strong conjugations (§8.8).**
- **understand the concepts of assimilation and syncopation (§8.10).**

NINE

Strong Verbs II, Classes 5, 6, and 7

Lesson One: Classes 5–7

9.1 Class 5 Strong Verbs

The vowel series of Class 5 verbs is *e – æ – ǣ – e*. Regular sound changes produce two sub-classes (see §9.1.1 and §9.1.2). The infinitive roots of this class have a similar footprint: *e* + single consonant which is not a liquid (*l* or *r*) or a nasal (*m* or *n*): *cweð-*, *drep-*, *et-*, *les-*, etc.

*The change from the expected ð to d in the past plural and past participle forms is the result of Verner's Law. See Appendix 2 (§2).

** See Appendix 2 (§11): The initial palatal ġ changed the simple vowels ē, e, and ǣ (of the original vowel series) to the diphthongs ie, ea, and ēa respectively, a common process. The infinitive forms of these two verbs may have the variant spellings of ġifan and ġitan.

Infinitive	Past Singular	Past Plural	Past Participle
cweðan "to say"	cwæþ	cwǣdon*	cweden*
drepan "to strike"	dræp	drǣpon	drepen, dropen
ġiefan** "to give"	ġeaf**	ġēafon	ġiefen**
ġietan** "to get"	ġeat**	ġēaton**	ġieten**
lesan "to collect"	læs	lǣson	lesen
metan "to measure"	mæt	mǣton	meten
sprecan "to speak"	spræc	sprǣcon	sprecen
swefan "to sleep"	swæf	swǣfon	swefen
tredan "to tread"	træd	trǣdon	treden
wefan "to weave"	wæf	wǣfon	wefen
wrecan "to avenge"	wræc	wrǣcon	wrecen

9.1.1 SUB-CLASS I OF CLASS 5 STRONG VERBS

Infinitive	Past Singular	Past Plural	Past Participle
etan "to eat"	ǣt	ǣton	eten
fretan "to devour"	frǣt	frǣton	freten

These two verbs are irregular in the past singular, using the *-ǣ-* instead of the usual *-æ-*.

SUB-CLASS 2 OF CLASS 5 STRONG VERBS   9.1.2

The infinitives in this sub-class have a short *i* + *KK*, that is, a doubled consonant.

Infinitive	Past Singular	Past Plural	Past Participle
biddan "to ask"	bæd	bǣdon	beden
sittan "to sit"	sæt	sǣton	seten
þicgan "to partake"	þeah	þǣgon	þegen
licgan "to lie"	læġ	lǣgon	leġen

The root consonants have doubled or lengthened (i.e., they have undergone "gemination," indicated in writing by doubling the consonant) when followed by a *j* that subsequently disappeared. (For the interested: the *cg* of *licgan* and *þicgan* is the OE rendering of the original doubling of g to *gg*.) The *j* that caused gemination also produced i-mutation: that is, the *e* of the normal Class 5 verbs has shifted to *i* (see §8.11.1-2). (See Appendix Two [§4] for a discussion of gemination. It influences the conjugation of those weak and strong verbs that undergo the lengthening. See §9.6 for conjugation of Class 5, 6, and 7 strong verbs in which anomalies occur because of gemination.)

Class 6 Strong Verbs   9.2

The vowel series is *a – ō – ō – a*, though a variety of sound changes produces a rather mixed sub-class (§9.2.1). The normal Class 6 verbs have the following footprint: short *a* + single consonant: *bacan, dragan*, etc.

[1] *Scacan* and *scafan* often appear as *sceacan* and *sceafan*. The insertion of the *e* before the usual *a* indicates that the *sc* in OE (developed from *sk* in WGmc) has become palatalized. The insertion of the vowel *e* usually occurs when the following vowel is a back vowel. It is also possible that the singular and plural past tenses *scōc, scōf* and *scōcon, scōfon* and the past participles *scacen, scafen* may also have been affected, depending on the dialect. See Appendix 2 (§9).

[2] *Spanan* may form past tenses by analogy with past tenses of Class 7 strong verbs, see §9.3.

[3] *Standan, stondan* exhibits the WGmc change: *a* before nasal either remained *a* or changed to *o*. See Appendix 2 (§6). [Although the change is not indicated here, *spanan* could also exhibit the *a* to *o* shift.]

[4] In the past singular and plural form *standan* drops the *-n-*.

[5] *Scieppan* is the result of diphthongization by the initial palatal *sc*. See Appendix 2 (§11).

[6] See opposite page.

Infinitive	Past Singular	Past Plural	Past Participle
bacan "to bake"	bōc	bōcon	bacen
dragan "to draw"	drōg	drōgon	dragen
faran "to go"	fōr	fōron	faren
galan "to sing"	gōl	gōlon	galen
grafan "to dig"	grōf	grōfon	grafen
hladan "to load"	hlōd	hlōdon	hladen
sacan "to quarrel"	sōc	sōcon	sacen
scacan[1] "to shake"	scōc	scōcon	scacen
scafan[1] "to shave"	scōf	scōfon	scafen
spanan "to seduce"	spōn, spēon[2]	spōnon, spēonon[2]	spanen, spannen
wadan "to go"	wōd	wōdon	waden
wascan "to wash"	wōsc	wōscon	wascen
standan, stondan[3] "to stand"	stōd[4]	stōdon[4]	standen, stonden

9.2.1 SUB-CLASS OF CLASS 6 STRONG VERBS.

The infinitives of this sub-class generally have a short *ie* (or *e*) + a doubled consonant.

Infinitive	Past Singular	Past Plural	Past Participle
hliehhan "to laugh"	hlōh, hlōg, hlōh	hlōgon	*****
scieppan[5] "to create"	scōp	scōpon	sceapen
sceþþan[6] "to injure"	scōd	scōdon	*****
steppan "to step"	stōp	stōpon	stapen
hebban "to heave"	hōf	hōfon	hafen
swerian "to swear"	swōr	swōron	swaren, sworen

Class 7 Strong Verbs

The vowel series in this class is far from regular. Infinitives may have a variety of root vowels: 1) *ā, a (o)* followed by a nasal (*m* or *n*); or 2) *ea, ēa, ǣ, ō,* or *ē.* However, the class can be divided according to the two possible past tense forms *ē* or *ēo.*

CLASS 7 STRONG VERBS WITH Ē IN THE PAST TENSE

Infinitive	Past Singular	Past Plural	Past Participle
hātan "to order"	hēt, hēht	hēton	hāten
blandan, blondan "to blend"	blēnd	blēndon	blanden, blonden
drǣdan "to dread"	drēd, drǣdde[7]	drēdon, drǣddon[7]	drǣden
lǣtan "to let"	lēt	lēton	lǣten
rǣdan "to counsel"	rēd, rǣdde[8]	rēdon, rǣddon[8]	rǣden
slǣpan "to sleep"	slēp	slēpon	slǣpen

[6] *Sceþþan* is the result of gemination and *i*-umlaut as well as the palatalization of WGmc *sk* to OE sc: WGmc *skæþjan* > WGmc *skæþþjan* > WGmc *skæþþian* > Prehist OE *skeþþian* > Prehist OE *sceþþian* > OE *sceþþan.* See §8.11 for *i*-umlaut and Appendix 2 for WGmc *sk* >*sc* (§9) and gemination (§4).

[7] Note that the consonants in these forms have doubled (i.e., undergone gemination).

CLASS 7 STRONG VERBS WITH ĒO IN THE PAST TENSE

In addition to the *ēo* in the past tenses, this class also consists of verbs in which the stem vowel in the infinitive and the past participle is always the same. We divide this class further into the different stem vowels:

Infinitive	Past Singular	Past Plural	Past Participle
a. blāwan "to blow"	blēow	blēowon	blāwen
cnāwan "to know"	cnēow	cnēowon	cnāwen
crāwan "to crow"	crēow	crēowon	crāwen

[1] In these verbs the infinitive stem differs from the past participle because of *i*-umlaut. In the original Gmc stem of the verb [Gmc *wōpjan* and *hwōsjan*], the *ō* is umlauted to *ē* because of the *j* of the infinitive suffix –*jan* (*i*-umlaut). The past participle form remains *ō* because the infinitive suffix does not appear in the participle. See §8.11, §8.11.1, and §8.11.2.

Infinitive	Past Singular	Past Plural	Past Participle
māwan "to mow"	mēow	mēowon	māwen
sāwan "to sow"	sēow	sēowon	sāwen
b. gangan "to go"	gēong	ġēongon	gangen
bannan "to summon"	bēon	bēonnon	bannen
spannan "to fasten"	spēon	spēonnon	spannen
c. wēpan "to weep"	wēop	wēopon	wōpen[1]
hwēsan "to wheeze"	hwēos	hwēoson	hwōsen[1]
d. bēatan "to beat"	bēot	bēoton	bēaten
hēawan "to hew"	hēow	hēowon	hēawen
hlēapan "to leap"	hlēop	hlēopon	hlēapen
e. fealdan "to fold"	fēold	fēoldon	fealden
feallan "to fall"	fēoll	fēollon	feallen
healdan "to hold"	hēold	hēoldon	healden
wealdan "to rule"	wēold	wēoldon	wealden
f. blōtan "to sacrifice"	blēot	blēoton	blōten
blōwan "to bloom"	blēow	blēowon	blōwen
flōwan "to flow"	flēow	flēowon	flōwen
grōwan "to grow"	grēow	grēowon	grōwen
rōwan "to row"	rēow	rēowon	rōwen

Lesson Two: Conjugation of Strong Verbs

9.4

The following chart of personal endings is similar to that which you have already seen in Chapter 8 (§8.8, strong verb Classes 1, 2, 3, and 4). These personal endings are also similar to those of weak I verbs, particularly in the present indicative. We conjugate here a representative verb from each of the last three strong verb classes: *sprecan* "to speak" (Class 5); *standan* "to stand" (Class 6); *hātan* "to call" (Class 7), and *gangan* "to go" (Class 7).

[1]The alternate endings of the second and third person present singular are the result of i-umlaut (§8.10) and syncopation (§8.11).

STRONG VERBS CLASSES 5-6: *sprecan* "to speak," *standan* "to stand"

9.4.1

Infinitive		sprecan		standan		Summary	
		Present	**Past**	**Present**	**Past**	**Present**	**Past**
Indicative Sing	1	sprece	spræc	stande	stōd	-e	-
	2	spricest, spricst[1]	spræce	stendest, stenst[1]	stōde	-(e)st	-e
	3	spriceþ, spricþ	spræc	stendeþ, stent(t)[1]	stōd	-eþ, -t	-
Indicative Plural	1, 2, 3	sprecaþ	spræcon	standaþ	stōdon	-aþ	-on
Subjunctive Sing	1, 2, 3	sprece	spræce	stande	stōde	-e	-e
Subjunctive Plural	1, 2, 3	sprecen	spræcen	standen	stōden	-en	-en
Participles		sprecende	sprecen	standende	standen	-ende	-en
Imperative Sing		sprec	*****	stand	*****	-	**
Imperative Plural		sprecaþ	*****	standaþ	*****	-aþ	**
Inflected Infin. (Gerund)		tō sprecanne	*****	tō standanne	*****	-anne	**

[1]The alternate endings of the second and third person present singular are the result of i-umlaut (§8.10) and syncopation (§8.11).

9.4.2 STRONG VERBS CLASS 7

Infinitive		hātan		gangan		Summary	
		Present	Past	Present	Past	Present	Past
Indicative Sing	1	hāte	hēt, hēht	gange	gēong	-e	-
	2	hǣtest, hǣtst[1]	hēte	gangest	gēonge	-(e)st	-e
	3	hǣteþ, hāteþ	hēt, hēht	gangeþ	gēong	-eþ	-
Indicative Plural	1, 2, 3	hātaþ	hēton	gangaþ	gēongon	-aþ	-on
Subjunctive Sing	1, 2, 3	hāte	hēte	gange	gēonge	-e	-e
Subjunctive Plural	1, 2, 3	hāten	hēten	gangen	gēongen	-en	-en
Participles		hātende	hāten	gangende	gangen	-ende	-en
Imperative Sing		hāt	*****	gang	*****	-	**
Imperative Plural		hātaþ	*****	gangaþ	*****	-aþ	**
Inflected Infin. (Gerund)		tō hātanne	*****	tō ganganne	*****	-anne	**

9.5 Lesson Three: A Few Exceptions
SUMMARY OF BASE FORMS

The same principles of formation apply to Classes 5, 6, and 7 as to Classes 1, 2, 3, and 4 (see §8.9).

1. The present indicative, present subjunctive, imperative, gerund, and the present participle take their base form from the infinitive stem of the verb (infinitive: *sprecan*; stem: *sprec-*).
2. The past indicative first and third person singular take their base form from the past singular stem of the verb.

3. The past indicative second person singular, past indicative plural and past subjunctive take their base form from the past plural stem of the verb.

SOME IRREGULAR STRONG VERBS

9.6

A few strong verbs of Classes 5, 6, and 7 show some minor differences from other strong verbs. In most instances, the differences are the result of consonant doubling and/or i-mutation caused by the West Germanic –*jan* infinitive suffix. These differences, therefore, appear only in the present tenses, the gerund, and present participle forms. (See above §9.5, #1.) We describe below the present indicative, present subjunctive, present imperative, gerund, and present participial forms only. In the past tense these verbs share the same forms as the other strong verbs. We conjugate here representative verbs *biddan* "to ask" and *licgan* "to lie" from Class 5; *steppan* "to step" from Class 6, and *wēpan* "to weep" from Class 7.

IRREGULAR STRONG VERBS CLASSES 5-7: *biddan* "to ask," *licgan* "to lie," *steppan* "to step," *wēpan* "to weep"

9.6.1

PRESENT TENSE ONLY

Class		5	5	6	7	Summary
Infinitive		biddan	licgan	steppan	wēpan	-an
Indicative Sing	1	bidde	licge	steppe	wēpe[3]	-e
	2	bidest, bitst[1]	licgest, ligst[1]	stepest, stepst[1]	wēpest, wēpst	-(e)st
	3	bideþ, bitt	licgeþ, līþ[1]	stepeþ, stepþ[1]	wēpeþ, wēpþ	-(e)þ
Indicative Plural	1, 2, 3	biddaþ	licgaþ	steppaþ	wēpaþ	-aþ
Subjunctive Sing	1, 2, 3	bidde	licge	steppe	wēpe	-e

[1] These forms have undergone both assimilation and syncopation.

[2] Like the weak verb *fremman*, *biddan* and *licgan* do not have the doubled consonant in the present imperative singular; also, like *fremman*, strong verbs with short stems such as *biddan*, *licgan*, *berian*, and *nerian* have a suffix -*e* in the imperative singular.

[3] The strong verb *wēpan* is conjugated like the weak verb *dēman*.

[2]Like weak verb *fremman*, *biddan* and *licgan* do not have the doubled consonant in the present imperative singular; also, like *fremman*, strong verbs with short stems such as *biddan*, *licgan*, *berian*, and *nerian* have a suffix *-e* in the imperative singular.

Class		5	5	6	7	Summary
Infinitive		biddan	licgan	steppan	wēpan	-an
Subjunctive Plural	1, 2, 3	bidden	licgen	steppen	wēpen	-en
Participles		biddande	licgande	stepande	wēpande	-ande
Imperative Sing		bide[2]	liġe[2]	stepe[2]	wēpe[2]	-e
Imperative Plural		biddaþ	licgaþ	steppaþ	wēpaþ	-aþ
Inflected Infin. (Gerund)		tō biddanne	tō licganne	tō steppanne	wēpanne	-anne

Exercise 9.1: UNDERSTANDING THE FORMS OF CLASS 5, 6, AND 7 STRONG VERBS

Instructions. *In the spaces provided, identify the mood, tense, person, and number of the listed verbs. Where the verb form has more than one possible answer, identify them.*

	Mood	Tense	Person	Number
1. trede	subjunctive	present	1,2,3	singular
2. hlōdon	indicative	past	1,2,3	plural
3. fealden	participle	past	X	X
4. hlætst	indicative	present	2	sing.
5. wadað	ind/imp	present	1,2,3	plur.

	Mood	Tense	Person	Number
6. wrǣce	ind / sub.	past	2, 1,2,3	sing.
7. hielt	ind.	pres.	3	sing.
8. sēow	ind.	past.	1, 3	sing.
9. sweriaþ	ind / imp.	pres.	1,2,3	plural.
10. sitt	ind	pres.	3	sing.

Exercise 9.2: INFINITIVES

Instructions. *For each of the verbs listed in Exercise §9.1, give the infinitive form followed by its strong verb class.*

1. tredan, 5
2. hladan, 6
3. fealdan, 7
4. hladan, 6 ?
5. wadan, 6

6. wrecan, 5
7. healdan, 7?
8. sāwan, 7
9. sworian, 6
10. sittan, 5

Exercise 9.3: TRANSLATION EXERCISE

[1] *Guma* is a variation on *secg* from the previous line: *mæniġ* modifies them both.

[2] present tense functioning in the future sense

[3] *him* = (plural reflexive) "for themselves," "behind themselves"

[4] *On-wenden* is a past participle with *næs* as its auxiliary verb.

[5] *hū* = what

[6] The object of *on-ġinnaŏ dōn* is *þā wierrestan tintegru*.

Instructions: *Translate the following Old English sentences into idiomatic Modern English. Refer to the vocabulary list immediately following the exercise.*

1. Þǣr læġ secg mæniġ
    gārum ā-ġēted,   guma[1] norþerna
    ofer scild scoten.

2. On ǣfenne, hīe hine be-tȳndon on þām carcerne, and hīe cwǣdon him betwȳnum for-ŏon-þe, "ŏisse nihte hē swelt."[2]

3. Þā ridon þæs cyninges þeġnas þider, ond his aldorman Ōsrīc ond Wīferþ his þeġn ond ŏā men þe hē be-æftan him lǣfde ǣr, ond þone æŏeling on þǣre byriġ mētton, þǣr sē cyning of-slæġen læġ, ond þā gatu him[3] belocen hæfdon, ond þā þǣr-tō ēodon.

4. Sē ēadiga Mathēus þā in ēode on þā ċeastre, and hraŏe hīe hine ġe-nāmon and his ēagan ūt ā-stungon. And hīe him sealdon āttor drincan, and hine sendon on carcerne. And hīe hine hēton þæt āttor etan, and hē hit etan nolde, for-þon his heorte næs tō-līesed, nē his mōd on-wenden.[4] Ac hē wæs simble tō Drihtne biddende mid miclum wōpe, and cwæŏ tō him, "Mīn Drihten Hǣlend Crist, for-þon wē ealle forlēton ūre cnēorisse, and wǣron þē folgiende—and þū eart ūre ealra fultum, þā þe on þē ġelīefaþ—beheald nū and ġe-seoh hū[5] þās men þīnum þēowe dōþ. And iċ þē bidde, Drihten, þæt þū mē for-ġiefe mīnra ēagena lēoht, þæt iċ ġē-sēo þā þe mē on-ġinnaŏ dōn[6] on þisse ċeastre þā wierrestan tintregu. And ne for-lǣt mē mīn Drihten Hǣlend Crist, nē mē ne sele on þone bitterestan dēaŏ."

VOCABULARY FOR EXERCISE 9.3

ac (conjunction) = but

ǣfen(n) (m, n) = EVENing [§2.7, §2.9]

ǣr (adverb) = EARlier, ERE [§6.9]

ǣþeling (m) = noble, prince [§2.7]

ā-ġētan (weak verb I) = to destroy [§3.11]

aldor-man (m) = nobleman, ALDERMAN [§10.4.2]

ā-stingan (strong verb 3) = to put out, gouge out [§8.6]

āttor (n) = poison [§2.9]

be-æftan (preposition + dat) = AFTER, behind [§6.15]

be-healdan (strong verb 7) = to BEHOLD [§9.3]

be-lūcan (strong verb 2) = to LOCK [§8.5]

bēon (irregular verb) = to BE [§4.5.1]

be-tȳnan (weak verb I) = to imprison [§3.11]

be-twȳnum (preposition + dat) = BETWEEN, among [§6.15]

biddan (strong verb 5) = TO BID, pray, implore [§9.1]

biter (adjective) = BITTER, painful [§6.1]

byriġ (f dat form of *burg*) = fortress [§10.4.2]

carcern (n) = prison [§2.9]

ċeastre (f) = city [§2.8]

cnēoris(s) (f) = family [§2.8]

Crīst (m) = CHRIST [§2.7]

cweþan (strong verb 5) = to say [§9.1]

cyning (m) = KING [§2.7]

dēað (m) = DEATH [§2.7]

dōn (irregular verb) = to DO, put [§4.5.3.1]

drihten (m) = lord [§2.7]

drincan (strong verb 3) = to DRINK [§8.6]

ēadiġ (adjective) = blessed [§6.1]

ēage (n) = EYE [§3.5]

eal(l) (adjective) = ALL [§6.1]

etan (strong verb 5) = to EAT, ingest [§9.1]

ēodon = see *gān*

folgian (weak verb II + dat object) = to FOLLOW [§3.12]

for-ġiefan (strong verb 5) = to GIVE, grant; FORGIVE [§9.1]

for-lǣtan (strong verb 7) = leave, abandon [§9.3]

for-þon-þe (conjunction) = indeed, for that reason [§5.1.1] *for-þon* (conjunction) = because [§5.1.1]

for-þon (adverb) = therefore [§6.9]

fultum (m) = help [§2.7]

gān (irregular verb) = to GO [§4.5.3.1]

gār (m) = spear [§2.7]

ġeat (n) = GATE [§2.9]

guma (weak m) = man [§3.3]

habban (weak verb III) = to HAVE [§4.1]

healdan (strong verb 7) = to HOLD, keep; (+ reflexive) to behave, act [§9.3]

hǽlend (m) = savior [§10.10]

hātan (strong verb, 7) = to order, command [§9.3]

hē, hēo, hit (personal pronoun) = HE, she, IT [§7.1]

hēton = see *hātan*

brāðe (adverb) = quickly [§6.9]

hū (adverb) = HOW, what [§6.9]

iċ (personal pronoun) = I [§7.1]

in (adverb) = IN, inside [§6.9]

lǽfan (weak verb I) = to LEAVE [§3.11]

læġ = see *licgan*

licgan (strong verb 5) = to LIE [§9.1]

lēoht (n) = LIGHT [§2.9]

(ġe)līefan (weak verb I) = to beLIEVE [§3.11]

mæniġ (adjective) = MANY, many a [§6.1]

man(n) (m) = MAN [§10.4.2]

mētan (weak verb I) = to MEET [§3.11]

miċel (adjective) = great [§6.1]

mīn (personal pronoun) = MY [§7.1]

mōd (n) = spirit, mind [§2.9]

nesan (irregular verb) = not to be [§4.5.1]

niht (f) = NIGHT [§10.4.2]

(ġe)niman (strong verb 4) = to take [§8.7]

nillan (irregular verb) = WILL not, to not want to [§4.5.3.1]

norþern (adjective) = NORTHERN [§6.1]

ofer (preposition) = OVER [§6.15]

of-slēan (strong verb 6, contract verb) = to SLAY [§11.1]

on-ġinnan (strong verb 3) = to proceed, beGIN [§8.6]

on-wendan (weak verb I) = to change [3.11]

rīdan (strong verb 1) = to RIDE [§8.4]

scild (m) = SHIELD [§2.7]

scēotan (strong verb 2) = to SHOOT [§8.5]

scoten = past participle of *scēotan*

secg (m) = man [§10.2.1]

sellan (weak verb I) = to give, give over to [§3.11]

sendan (weak verb I) = to SEND [§3.11]

(ġe)sēon (strong verb 5 contract verb) = to SEE [§11.1]

simble (adverb) = always, continuously [§6.9]

sweltan (strong verb 3) = to die [§8.6]

tintreġ (n) = torment [§2.9]

tō (adverb) = shut, closed [see German *zu* "shut," §6.9]

tō (preposition + dat) = TO [§6.15]

tō-lēsan (weak verb I) = to dissolve, destroy [§3.11]

þā (adverb) = then, at that time [§6.9]

þā (demonstrative pronoun) = those [§7.7]

þǣr (conjunction) = where [§6.9]

þǣr-tō (adverb) = thither, to that place [§6.9]

þe (relative pronoun) = who, which [§7.5]

þeġn (m) = THANE [§2.7]

þēow (m) = servant [§10.2.1]

þider (adverb) = THITHER, there [§6.9]

þū (personal pronoun) = you, THOU [§7.1]

ūt (adverb) = OUT [§6.9]

wesan (irregular verb) = to be [§4.5.1]

wē (personal pronoun) = WE [§7.1]

wierrest (adjective, superlative of *yfel*) = WORST [§6.8]

wōp (m) = weeping, lamentation [§2.7]

(ġe)weorþan (strong verb 3) = to become, come about, happen [§8.6]

[7] See Charles D. Wright, *The Irish Tradition in Old English Literature.* Cambridge Studies in Anglo-Saxon Literature, 6, Cambridge: Cambridge UP, 1993, pp. 189-206.

[8] MS. *heofonas.* The *-as* ending stands for *-es* and is a sign that final unstressed vowels are changing to *schwa* in late OE (especially since they seem to be interchangeable).

[9] The MS. *bylige-* has been regularized to the more usual *belg* "bellows."

[10] Note that *hēora* depends on *ǣġ-hwylċ*, while *ōðres* "the other" is the genitive object of *æt-hrīnan.*

Reading IX: From VERCELLI HOMILY IX (continued)

The following selection, particularly the motif of the "Iron House," is in all probability based on elements of Irish preaching and folklore.[7] Note that the first paragraph, up until the end of the last sentence, constitutes one long subordinate clause: "If . . . and though . . . and though . . ."

And hē, sē dēofol, þā ġyt cwæð tō þām āncran: "Ġyf ǣniġ mann wǣre āne niht on helle ond hē eft wǣre æfter þām of-ālǣdd, ond ðēah man þone gārsecg mid īsene ūtan ymb-tȳnde, ond þonne ealne ġe-fylde mid fȳres līġe ūp oþ ðone heofones[8] hrōf, ond ūtan emb-sette hine þonne ealne mid belgum[9] ond hēora ǣġ-hwylċ ōðres[10] æt-hrīnan mihte,

[11] See §2.5.1.

[12] The following verbs are all in the subjunctive to convey the hypothetical idea of this bizarre scenario "and though this would happen . . ."

[13] MS. *hameron.* Late texts often show some variation in the spelling of final unstressed syllables, probably evidence that unstressed final vowels were leveling to *schwa.* Here, inflectional *m* has changed to *n*, another sound change typical of late OE.

[14] The main clause, finally. Note that *ā-wacode* is probably a past subjunctive.

[15] *Sunnan* and *mōnan* must be genitive singulars (see the following noun phrase); here *þearf* takes a genitive object (see glossary).

[16] See §7.5.2.

5   ond tō ǣġ-hwylcum þǣra belga wǣre man ġe-set ond sē[11] hæfde Samsones strengðe (sē wæs ealra eorð-warena strengest þe ǣr oððe syððan ǣfre ġe-wurde) ond þēah man þonne ġe-sette ān brād īsen þell ofer þæs fȳres hrōf, ond þēah hit wǣre eal mid mannum ā-fylled ond ðǣra ǣġ-hwylċ hæfde ænne hamor on hande, ond þēah man blēowe[12] mid eallum þām belgum, ond mid þām hamerum[13] bēote on þæt īsene þell, and sē līġ brastlode, ne

10   ā-wacode hē nǣfre[14] for eallum þisum, tō ðām wēriġ hē wǣre for þǣre ānre niht-hwīle.

Wā bið þām sāwlum þe on helle bēon sċēolon, for-ðan-þe þæt helle hūs is mid swīðe lāðlicum gāstum ā-fylled! Ac uton wē, men ðā lēofstan, nū wē syndon ġe-gaderode on ðysne drihtenlican dæġ, þæt wē þæs for Godes lufan on ġeornysse sīen, þæt we be-flēon þā helle witu, for þan hit is ðǣr-inne swīðe sārliċ tō wuniganne. Ac uton ġe-ġearwian ūs

15   nū ðā mid inne-weardum ġe-bedum ond mid gǣst-dōme, þæt wē ne weorðen ā-slidene innan þā fȳrenfullan þȳstro þæt synfullum sāwlum is ġe-ġearwod on helle tō-ġēanes. Ac uton þȳdan ūs tō þām ūpliċan rīċe, for-ðan þǣr is þæt wuldor, þæt nǣniġ man ne mæġ mid his wordum ā-secgan ðā wynsumnesse þæs heofon-cundan līfes. Ðǣr bið līf būtan dēaþe ond gōd būtan ende ond yld būtan sāre ond dæġ būtan nihte, ond þǣr bið ġe-fēa

20   būtan un-rōtnesse ond rīċe būtan ā-wendednesse. Ond ne þearf man nǣfre ne sunnan ne mōnan[15] ne nǣniġes eorðliċes lēohtes, for-ðan þǣr is sē ælmihtiga dryhten sċīnendra ond līhtra þonne ealle ōðre lēoht. Ond þǣr ǣfre ā-springað ðā wuldorliċan drēamas ond þā þrymliċan sangas ðām ðe[16] on hyra midlene weorðan mōt. Þǣr bið sē swēta stenċ ond sēo syngalu lufu ond sēo winsumnes būtan ælċere un-wynsumnesse. Ne þǣr ne bið hunger ne

25   ðurst ne ċyle ne bryne ne nǣniġ un-wynsumnes ġe-mēted."

VOCABULARY FOR READING IX

OE orthography has a few shifting dunes. It's best to get used to some of the variations you're likely to encounter. The entries below record the standard Late West Saxon spellings and may differ from the words as you find them in the text. As always, *y* can change places with *i*, but take note of the following correspondences: *y = eo* and *io = eo.*

ac (conjunction) = but

ǽfre (adverb) = EVER [§6.9]

æfter (preposition + dat) = AFTER [§6.15]

ǽġ-hwylċ (adjective or indefinite pronoun, usually + partitive gen) = each [§7.8]

ǽlċ (indefinite pronoun or adjective) = any; each, every (one) (as a pronoun, takes the partitive gen) [§7.8]

æl-mihtiġ (adjective) = ALMIGHTY; (as a m noun) the ALMIGHTY (one) [§6.1]

ǽniġ (indefinite pronoun, adjective) = ANY [§7.8]

ǽr (adverb, conjunction) = ERE, before [§6.9, §5.1.1]

æt-brīnan (strong verb 1) = to touch (often + gen object) [§8.4]

ā-fyllan (weak verb I) = to FILL [§3.11]

ān (indefinite pronoun, adjective) = ONE, a/an [§7.8]

āncora (weak m) = ANCHORite, hermit [§3.3]

ā-secgan (weak verb III) = to speak about, describe [§4.1]

ā-slīdan (strong verb 1) = to SLIDE, slip, fall [§8.4]

ā-springan (strong verb 3) = to SPRING up, break forth, spread [§8.6]

ā-wacian (weak verb II) = to WAKE up [§3.12]

ā-wendednes (f) = change, mutability [§2.8]

be (preposition + dat, instr) = concerning, about, BY [§6.15]

bēatan (strong verb 7) = to BEAT [§9.3]

(ġe)bed (n) = prayer, supplication, Mod. English *bead* derives from the practice of saying one prayer per rosary "bead" [§2.9]

be-flēon (strong verb 2) = to FLEE (l. 13: *be-flēon* = pl subj) [§8.5]

belg (m) = a pair of BELLOWs [§2.7]

bēon = to BE [§4.5.1]

blāwan (strong verb 7) = to BLOW [§9.3]

brād (adjective) = BROAD, vast [§6.1]

brastlian (weak verb II) = to roar, crackle [§3.12]

bryne (m) = BURNing, fire [§10.11.1]

būtan (preposition + dat, instr) = without, lacking [§6.15]

ċiele (m) = CHILL, cold, coolness [§10.2.1]

cwæð = see *cweðan*

cweðan (strong verb 5) = to speak, say, QUOTH [§9.1]

dæġ (m) = DAY [§2.7]

dēaþ (m) = DEATH [§2.7]

dēofol (m) = DEVIL [§2.7]

drēam (m) = joy, ecstasy, mirth; melody, music, song [§2.7]

dryhten (m) = lord, leader; God [§2.7]

dryhtenliċ (adjective) = lordly, glorious, divine [§6.1]

eal (indefinite pronoun, adjective) = ALL [§7.8, §6.1]

ealne (adverb) = always, quite, perpetually [§6.9]

eft (adverb) = again [§6.9]

emb- = see *ymb-*

ende (weak m) = END [§3.3]

eorð-liċ (adjective) = EARTHLY [§6.1]

eorð-ware (*-ware* = m pl; *-waru* = f pl) = EARTH dwellers [§2.7]

(ġe)fēa (weak m) = joy, related to OE *fæġen* "glad, joyful": FAIN would I come [§3.3]

for (preposition + dat) = FOR, because of [§6.15]

for-þan-(þe) (idiom) = (conjunction) because [§5.1.1]; (adverb) therefore [§6.9]

(ġe)fyllan (weak verb I) = to FILL up, derived from OE *ful* "full" with i-mutation [§3.11]

fȳr (n) = FIRE [§2.9]

fȳren-ful (adjective) = FIRey, FULL of FIRE [§6.1]

(ġe)gadrian (weak verb II) = to GATHER [§3.12]

gār-secg (m) = sea [§10.2.1]

gāst, gǣst (m) = spirit, soul; spiritual being (good or evil:), angel, devil [§2.7]

gāst-dōm (m) = spirituality, spiritual devotion; OE *-dom*, as in *Christendom,* [§2.7]

(ġe)ġearwian (weak verb II) = to prepare, equip, make ready (often + reflex., "to prepare oneself,") GEAR up [§3.12]

ġeorn-nes (f) = desire, zeal, industry, YEARNing [§2.8]

ġif (conjunction) = IF [§5.1.1]

God (m) = GOD (note: names for the deity are only very rarely capitalized in manuscripts) [§2.7]

gōd (adjective) = GOOD; (noun) GOOD, good thing, goodness, the GOOD one [§6.1 or §2.7]

ġyt, ġit (adverb) = YET, still [§6.9]

habban (weak verb III) = to HAVE [§4.1]

hamor (m) = HAMMER [§2.7]

hand, hond (f) = HAND [§10.6]

hē, hēo, hit (personal pronoun) = he, she, it [§7.1]

hel(l) (f) = HELL [§2.8]

heofon (m or f) = HEAVEN [§2.7]

heofon-cund (adjective) = celestial, HEAVENly [OE -*cund* = adjective suffix denoting derivation, origin, or likeness, as in *dēofol-cund* "demonic" or *god-cund* "godly"; §6.1]

hit = see *hē, hēo, hit*

hrōf (m) = ROOF, top, apex [§2.7]

hungor (m) = HUNGER [§2.7]

hūs (n) = HOUSE [§2.9]

ield, ieldo (f) = age, old age; from *eald* "old," showing i-mutation [§10.7]

innan (preposition + acc, dat, or gen) = IN, into; from within, within [§6.15]

inne-weard (adjective) = INWARD [§6.1]

īsen (n, also adjective) = IRON; German *Eisen* "iron" [§2.9]

lāðlić (adjective) = LOATHLY, loathsome, hateful, repulsive, horrific [§6.1]

lēof (adjective) = beLOVed, dear [§6.1]

lēoht (adjective) = LIGHT, bright, illuminated [§6.1]

(ġe)lēoht (n) = LIGHT [§2.9]

līf (n) = LIFE [§2.9]

līġ, līeġ (m) = flame; German *Lohe*, "blaze, flame" [§10.11.1]

lufe (f) = LOVE [§2.8]

lufu (f) = LOVE (in 1. 13 appears to be weak, *Godes lufan*)

mæġ = see *magan*

magan (pret-pres) = MAY, be able [§4.3]

man (indefinite pronoun) = one, a person (often translated with a passive) [§7.8]

mann (m) = MAN [§10.4.2]

(ġe)mētan (weak verb I) = to MEET with, encounter [§3.11]

mid (preposition + dat, instr) = with [§6.15]

midlen (n) = MIDst, presence [§2.9]

mōna (weak m) = MOON [§3.3]

mōtan (pret.-pres. verb) = MIGHT, be allowed [§4.3]

nǣfre (adverb) = NEVER [§6.9]

nǣniġ (indefinite pronoun, adjective) = NONE, no [§6.1, §7.8]

ne (adverb) = not [§6.9]; (conjunction) neither, nor: *ne . . . ne* = neither . . . nor [§5.1.1] *niht* (f) = NIGHT [§10.4.2]

niht-hwīl (f) = NIGHTtime, period of a
night [§2.8]

nū (adverb) = NOW [§6.9]

of-ālǣdan (weak verb I) = to LEAD
OFF, to carry off [§3.11]

ofer (preposition + acc) = OVER [§6.15]

ond, and (conjunction) = AND

oþ (preposition + acc, rarely dat) = to, as
far as [§6.15]

ōðer (indefinite pronoun, adjective) =
OTHER [§6.1, §7.8]

oððe (conjunction) = or

rīċe (n) = rule, reign, empire, realm;
power, might, authority; German
Reich [§10.2.2]

(ġe)ryne (n) = mystery [§10.2.2]

Samson (m) = the Biblical strong-man
(see Judges 16:25-30) [§2.7]

sang (m) = SONG [§2.7]

sār (n) = bodily pain, sickness, wound,
SORE place; suffering; SORrow;
(adjective) sad, sorrowful [§2.9]

sārliċ (adjective) = painful, dreadful,
bitter; sad, SORrowful, SORELY
[§6.1]

sāwol (f) = SOUL (acc, dat = *sawle*)
[§2.8]

scīnan (strong verb 1) = to SHINE [§8.4]

sculan (preterite-present verb) = must,
have to [§4.3]

secgan (weak verb III) = to SAY [§4.1]

(ġe)settan (weak verb I) = to SET, place
[§3.11]

sīen = see *bēon*

singal (adjective) = continual, perpetual,
everlasting [§6.1]

sīo = *sēo*

stenċ (m) = smell, fragrance, scent; stink,
odor, STENCH [§10.11.1]

strang, strong (adjective) = STRONG;
strengest (superlative) [§6.1]

strengð, strengðu (f) = STRENGTH
[§2.8]

sunne (weak f) = SUN [§3.4]

swā (adverb) = SO, thus [§6.9];
(conjunction) as; *swa . . . swa* = as . . .
so [§5.1.1]

swēt (adjective) = SWEET, delicious
[§6.1]

swīðe (adverb) = very, exceedingly;
violently, powerfully [§6.9]

syndon = see *bēon*

syn, sīen = see *bēon*

synnful (adjective) = SINFUL, wicked
[§6.1]

syngal = see *singal*

syððan (adverb) = after [§6.9]

tō-ġēanes (preposition + acc, dat) = for, against (as in we prepared "against" their coming); in opposition to, toward (in l. 16, *tōġēanes* appears *after* its object, *synfullum sāwlum*) [§6.15]

tō ðām (idiom) = to that extent, so

þā (adverb) = then; (conjunction) = when; *þā . . . þā* = then...when [§6.9]

þǣr-inne (adverb) THERE-IN, in there [§6.9]

þæs (adverb) = to such an extent, the more; gen sing of *þæt* [§6.9]

þæt (conjunction) = THAT, so that [§5.1.1]

ðām þe = definite article (dat pl) + relative pronoun [§7.4]

þe (relative pronoun, indeclin.) = who or which; source of Modern English *the* [§7.4]

þēah (conjunction) = THOUGH, al-THOUGH [§5.1.1]; (adverb) nevertheless, yet [§6.9]

þearfan, þurfan (pret-pres verb) = to need, have need of (+ gen object) [§4.4.1]

þel, þell (n) = (metal) plate; board, plank [§2.9]

ðēodan, þȳdan (weak verb I) = to join, associate with; come to, be near (note the use of the reflexive pronoun in l. 17) [§3.11]

þēostru, þȳstru, -o (f) = darkness, gloom [§10.7]

þes, þēos, þis (demonstrative pronoun) = THIS [§7.7]

þonne (adverb) = THEN [§6.9]; (conjunction) than [§5.1.1]

þȳdan = see *ðēodan*

þrymliċ (adjective) = magnificent, glorious [§6.1]

þurst, þyrst (m) = THIRST [§10.11.1]

un-rōtnes (f) = sadness, contrition; OE *rōtnes* "gladness" [§2.8]

un-wynsumness (f) = unhappiness [§2.8]

ūp (adverb) = UP [§6.9]

ūpliċ (adjective) = UPper, lofty; sublime, heavenly, celestial [§6.1]

ūtan (adverb) = from the outside, on the outside [§6.9]

utan, wutan = let us . . . (+ infinitive); from the 1st person, pl subj of *wītan*, strong verb 1, "to go" [§8.4]

wā (interjection) = WOE; usually + to be verb and dat: woe be unto them (who) *(ġe)weorðan* (strong verb 3) = to become, get; be, exist (often used interchangeably with *bēon* and *wesan*, but also often in passive constructions); see German *werden* "to become" [§8.6]

wēriġ (adjective) = WEARY [§6.1]

wesan (irregular verb) = WAS [§4.5.1]

wīte (n) = torture, punishment [§10.2.2]

winsumness = see *wynsumness*

word (n) = WORD [§2.9]

wuldor (n) = glory [§2.9]

wuldorliċ (adjective) = glorious [§6.1]

wunian (weak verb II) = to dwell, live, reside; *tō wuniganne* = inflected infinitive; German *wohnen* "live, reside" [§3.12]

(ġe)wurde = see *(ġe)weorðan*

wynsumness (f) = joyfulness, delight, loveliness; WINSOME-NESS, OE *wynn* "joy" [§2.8]

yld = see *ieldo*

ymb-settan, emb- (weak verb I) = to SET about or around, surround [§3.11]

ymb-tȳnan, emb- (weak verb I) = to enclose, surround; OE *tūn* "town" refers to an enclosed city. *Tynan* derives from *tūn* with i-umlaut [§8.11]; OE *ymb=* around, about [§3.11]

Lessons Learned

Before leaving this chapter you should . . .
- be able to recognize strong verb forms from all 7 classes.

TEN

Rarer Noun Forms

10.1   Rarer Noun Forms

Besides the normal noun forms outlined in Chapter Two and the weak or -*an* nouns in Chapter Three, there are a number of irregular noun endings that you should at least know about, even if you don't memorize them. *Before you panic*, you should know that the vast majority of Old English nouns take the regular endings that you have already memorized, and that even the irregular noun forms which follow are often quite close to the "normal" paradigms. Familiarize yourself with the classes in general, but do not attempt to memorize them.

10.2   -E IN THE NOMINATIVE

Let's start out gently. One rarer noun-class has only one difference from the regular paradigm—nouns of this class appear to have an -*e* ending in the nominative singular (even though they are masculine or neuter), though these -*e*'s are part of the word, not case endings. The potentially confusing point is that a final -*e* usually signals the dative singular (for masculine and neuter) and accusative, genitive, *and* dative (for feminine). If the glossary or dictionary shows a final -*e* in the regular entry (i.e., the nominative), you can be sure that this -*e* is not a signal for the dative case, but part of the peculiarity of this class.

These nouns are so similar to the regular noun declensions (the –*a*– stem masculine and neuter nouns and the –*o*– stem feminine nouns described in Chapter Two) that many grammars include them with the regular nouns. In fact, the nouns in this section (technically called –*ja*–, –*wa*–; and –*jo*–, –*wo*– stems) are close cousins to the –*a*– stem and –*o*– stem nouns (§2.10.4). Like the regular declensions these –*ja*– and –*wa*– stems are masculine and neuter nouns that follow closely the paradigm of their –*a*– stem relatives, and the –*jo*– *and* –*wo*– stems are feminine nouns that follow closely the paradigm of the –*o*– stem feminines.

-E IN THE NOMINATIVE—MASCULINES: *hierde* "shepherd," *ende* "end," and *here* **10.2.1**
"army" *(-ja- stems)*

	Singular				Plural				SUMMARY Singular	Plural
N	sē	hierde	ende	here	þā	hierdas	endas	her(i)gas*	–	-as
A	þone	hierde	ende	here	þā	hierdas	endas	her(i)gas*	–	-as
G	þæs	hierdes	endes	her(i)ġes	þāra	hierda	enda	her(i)ga	-s	-a
D	þǣm	hierde	ende	her(i)ġe	þǣm	hierdum	endum	her(i)gum	–	-um
I	þȳ	hierde	ende	her(i)ġe	****	******	*****	*******	–	****

-E IN THE NOMINATIVE—NEUTERS: *rīċe* "kingdom", and *cyn(n)* "kin" *(-ja- stems)* **10.2.2**

	Singular				Plural			SUMMARY Singular	Plural
N	þæt	rīċe	cyn(n)	þā	rīċu**	cyn(n)	–	-u
A	þæt	rīċe	cyn(n)	þā	rīċu	cyn(n)	–	-u
G	þæs	rīċes	cynnes	þǣra	rīċa	cynna	-s	-a
D	þǣm	rīċe	cynne	þǣm	rīċum	cynnum	–	-um

* See Appendix Two, §18 for an explanation of the apparent problem of pronouncing the [g] as [g] before the back vowel.
** Note that a long-stemmed noun like rīċe does not normally take a -u ending (see §2.10.1).

Endings with *-w-*

10.3

Some masculine and neuter nouns end in a *-u* or *-o* in the nominative and accusative singular (something we would normally expect of a feminine noun), but take endings with *-w-*'s in them for the rest of the cases. These nouns developed from Indo-European nouns that had -*wa*- (masculine and neuter) and -*wo*- (feminine) stems between the noun root and ending, still clearly visible below. Luckily, besides the extra -*w*-, the endings themselves are practically the same. (See §2.10.4 for an explanation of stem classes.)

10.3.1   **-W- MASCULINES:** *bearu* "grove, wood" and *hlēo(w)* "protection, lord" *(-wa- stems)*

Singular				Plural			SUMMARY Singular	Plural
N	sē	bearu, –o	hlēo(w)	þā	bearwas	hlēowas	–u, –o	–was
A	þone	bearu, –o	hlēo(w)	þā	bearwas	hlēowas	–u, –o	–was
G	þæs	bearwes	hlēowes	þāra	bearwa	hlēowa	–wes	–wa
D	þǣm	bearwe	hlēowe	þǣm	bearwum	hlēowum	–we	–wum
I	þȳ	bearwe	hlēowe	****	******	******	–we	***

10.3.2   **-W- NEUTERS:** *searu* "contrivance; cunning" and *trēo(w)* "tree" *(-wa- stems)*

Singular				Plural			SUMMARY Singular	Plural
N	þæt	searu, –o	trēo(w)	þā	searu, –o	trēo(w), –wu	–u, –o	–u, –o
A	þæt	searu, –o	trēo(w)	þā	searu, –o	trēo(w), –wu	–u, –o	–u, –o
G	þæs	searwes	trēowes	þāra	searwa	trēowa	–wes	–wa
D	þǣm	searwe	trēowe	þǣm	searwum	trēowum	–we	–wum
I	þȳ	searwe	trēowe	***	******	******	–we	***

-W- FEMININES: *beadu* "battle" and *sceadu* "shadow" *(-wo- stems)*

Short Stems						SUMMARY	
Singular			Plural			Singular	Plural
N	sēo	beadu	sceadu	þā	beadwa, -e	sceadwa, -e	-u	-wa, -we
A	þā	beadwe	sceadwe	þā	beadwa, -e	sceadwa, -e	-we	-wa, -we
G	þǣre	beadwe	sceadwe	þāra	beadwa	sceadwa	-we	-wa
D	þǣre	beadwe	sceadwe	þǣm	beadwum	sceadwum	-we	-wum

-W- FEMININES: *mǣd* "meadow" and *lǣs* "pasture" *(-w- stems)*

Long Stems						SUMMARY	
Singular			Plural			Singular	Plural
N	sēo	mǣd	lǣs	þā	mǣdwa, -e	lǣswa, -e	-	-wa, -we
A	þā	mǣdwe	lǣswe	þā	mǣdwa, -e	lǣswa, -e	-we	-wa, -we
G	þǣre	mǣdwe	lǣswe	þāra	mǣdwa	lǣswa,	-we	-wa
D	þǣre	mǣdwe	lǣswe	þǣm	mǣdwum*	lǣswum*	-we	-wum

* According to *Sweet's Anglo-Saxon Primer*, 9th ed. (Oxford: Clarendon, 1965), p. 13, both *mǣd* and *lǣs* may drop the –w– in the dative plural; therefore, *mǣd* may appear in the dative as *mǣdum* and *lǣs* as *lǣsum*. See also, Campbell, §596-597.

Another declension of feminine nouns—the *-jo-* stems—is nearly identical to the regular feminines (§2.8), except that they never take a –u in the nominative singular, even when the stem is short (see §2.10.1). Nouns in this declension include *byrðen* "burden", *gierd* "twig", *hālignes* "holiness", *synn* "sin", and *wylf* "she-wolf."

	Singular			Plural			SUMMARY Singular	Plural
N	sēo	synn	byrðen	þā	synna, -e	byrðena, -e	–	-a, -e
A	þā	synne	byrðene	þā	synna, -e	byrðena, -e	-e	-a, -e
G	þǣre	synne	byrðene	þāra	synna	byrðena	-e	-a
D	þǣre	synne	byrðene	þǣm	synnum	byrðenum	-e	-um

10.4   Foot-Feet (I-Mutation) Nouns

(Technically known as the ***Root Consonant Stems*** or the ***Radical Consonant Declension***.) These nouns all show evidence of i-mutation (see §8.11). Sometime in the Prehistoric OE period (that is, sometime between approximately 500 CE and 700 CE), the endings for dative and instrumental singular as well as the plural nominative and accusative must have had [i]'s in them (since lost) which caused the vowel in the root of the word to change; how the root vowel changed can be traced below. Remember that [i] was a magnetic vowel which tended to pull other nearby vowels to its position in the high, front part of the oral cavity (see §1.5). For example, in the case of OE *fōt, mann,* and *bōc* in the nominative plural, the mutation would have looked something like this:

PrehistOE nominative sing		Nominative plural		= OE plural
*mann	>	*manniz	>	men
*fōt	>	*fōtiz	>	fēt
*bōc	>	*bōciz	>	bēċ

In all three instances, the suffix *–iz,* which signals the Prehistoric OE nominative plural, includes the high front sound [i]. The [a] in **mann* and the [o] in **fōt* and **bōc* are back sounds. The IPA vowel triangle at §1.5 shows graphically the relationship of the [i], [a], and [o] sounds. In the case of each of these three words, the speaker anticipates the

[i] sound in the plural suffix *–iz*. So, in getting his mouth and tongue ready to say the high front sound, the speaker begins to shift the back sounds [a] and [o] forward and up toward the high front [i].

If we were to graph the mutation by using the IPA vowel triangle, it would look something like this:

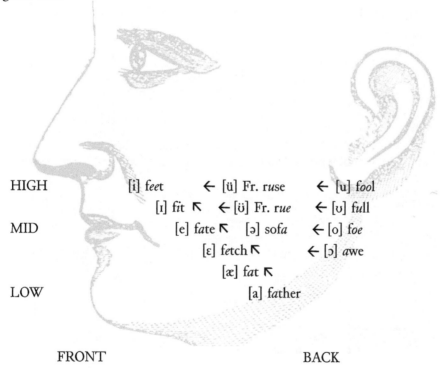

HIGH	[i] *feet*	← [ü] Fr. *ruse*	← [u] *fool*
	[ɪ] *fit* ↖	← [ü] Fr. *rue*	← [ʊ] *full*
MID	[e] *fate* ↖	[ə] *sofa*	← [o] *foe*
	[ɛ] *fetch* ↖		← [ɔ] *awe*
	[æ] *fat* ↖		
LOW	[a] *father*		

FRONT   BACK

In the case of *bōc*, notice that the i-mutation also leads to the palatalization of *ċ* (§1.8, entry *c*). Thus we can see the results of the i-mutation but not the actual [i] that caused it. The cases in which i-mutation occurred are marked with an asterisk (*) below in §10.4.2 and §10.5.

10.4.1   For quick reference only, the following list shows how i-mutation affected the most common vowel sounds. Again, as in the example above, the direction of change is to make the vowels higher and/or closer to the front of the mouth.

Pre i-mutation		Post i-mutation
[a], [o] before nasals	>	[ɛ]
[a]	>	[æ]
[ā]	>	[ǣ]
[æ]	>	[e]
[e]	>	[i]
[o]	>	[e]

10.4.2   **FOOT-FEET NOUNS:** *fōt* "foot," *mann* "man," and *bōc* "book" (root consonant stems)

Singular				Feminine	SUMMARY	
	Masculine				M	F
N	sē	fōt	mann	sēo bōc	-	-
A	þone	fōt	mann	þā bōc	-	-
G	þæs	fōtes	mannes	þǣre bōce, bēċ	-es	-(e)
D	þǣm	fēt*	menn	þǣre bēċ	-	-
I	þȳ	fēt*	menn*	**	-	**
Plural						
N	þā	fēt*	menn*	þā bēċ	-	-
A	þā	fēt*	menn*	þā bēċ	-	-
G	þāra	fōta	manna	þāra boca	-a	-a
D	þǣm	fōtum	mannum	þām bocum	-um	-um

Mother/Father Nouns 10.5

Mother/father nouns are technically known as the *-r-* declension. Whether through domestic trauma or whatever source, several words denoting family relationships and ending typically in *-or* (*mōdor, brōðor, dohtor*) take a very restricted set of endings. Notice the effects of i-mutation in *mēder, brēðer,* and *dehter.*

MOTHER/FATHER NOUNS: *mōdor* "mother," *fæder* "father," *brōðor* "brother," and 10.5
dohtor "daughter"

Singular							SUMMARY	
	Feminine			Masculine			F	M
N	sēo	mōdor	dohtor	sē	fæder	brōðor	-	-
A	þā	mōdor	dohtor	þone	fæder	brōðor	-	-
G	þǣre	mōdor	dohtor	þæs	fæder, -(e)res	brōðor	-	-
D	þǣre	mēder*	dehter*	þǣm	fæder	brēðer*	-	-
Plural								
N	þā	mōdra, -ru	dohtor	þā	fæd(e)ras	brōðor, -ru	-, -a, -u	-, -as, -u
A	þā	mōdra, -ru	dohtor	þā	fæd(e)ras	brōðor, -ru	-, -a, -u	-, -as, -u
G	þāra	mōdra	dohtra	þāra	fæd(e)ra	brōðra	-a	-a
D	þǣm	mōdrum	dohtrum	þǣm	fæd(e)rum	brōðrum	-um	-um

U-Nouns 10.6

These nouns are unusual in that they show a *-u* in the accusative singular and an *-a* almost everywhere else (and thus are easy to confuse with the genitive plural); it is often necessary to look carefully at definite articles and adjectives to find their case. For the distinction between short and long stems, see §2.10.1. *Hand* is the most prominent noun in this class. Remember that long-stemmed *u*-nouns drop the *-u*!

10.6.1   **U-NOUNS:** *sunu* "son," *feld* "field," *duru* "door," and *hand* "hand"

Singular							SUMMARY	
	Masculine			Feminine				
		Short	Long		Short	Long	Short	Long
N	sē	sunu	feld	sēo	duru	hand	-u	–
A	þone	sunu	feld	þā	duru	hand	-u	–
G	þæs	suna	felda	þǣre	dura	handa	-a	-a
D	þǣm	suna	felda	þǣre	dura	handa	-a	-a
Plural								
N	þā	suna	felda	þā	dura	handa	-a	-a
A	þā	suna	felda	þā	dura	handa	-a	-a
G	þāra	suna	felda	þāra	dura	handa	-a	-a
D	þǣm	sunum	feldum	þǣm	durum	handum	-um	-um

10.7   Abstract Feminine Nouns in *-þu/-þo*

(Technically known as the *-u, -o* declension.) Some feminine abstract nouns often derived from adjectives and ending in *-þu/-þo* or *-u/-o* frequently don't take any endings in the singular, but retain the *-þu/-þo* or *-u/-o* throughout. Sometimes, though, they take the normal *-e* endings in the oblique cases (i.e., all the cases but the nominative). They generally do not have plurals at all.

10.7.1   **ABSTRACT FEMININE NOUNS:** *strengþo -þu* "strength" and *bieldu -o* "boldness" are long stem forms while *sacu* "strife" is a short stem (§2.10.1). (*-o-, -u-* stems)

Singular				Short Stem	SUMMARY
		Long Stem			
N	sēo	strengðu, -o	bieldu, -o	sacu	-u, -o
A	ðā	strengðe	bielde	sace	-e
G	ðǣre	strengðe	bielde	sace	-e
D	ðǣre	strengðe	bielde	sace	-e
Plural					
N	ðā	strengða, -e	bielda, -e	saca, -e	-a, -e
A	ðā	strengða, -e	bielda, -e	saca, -e	-a, -e
G	ðāra	strengða, -ena	bielda, -ena	saca, -ena	-a, -ena
D	ðǣm	strengðum	bieldum	sacum	-um

Children Nouns   10.8

(Technically, the *er*-declension.) Some neuter nouns—*ċild* "child," *ċealf* "calf," *lamb* "lamb," and *ǣġ* "egg"—have *-ru* endings in the plural nominative and accusative, but otherwise follow the normal neuter declension (§2.9). Modern English *child/children* is a descendant of this class, though notice the second plural marking *-en* (taken from the descendants of the weak nouns like *oxen*), a curious double plural.

CHILDREN NOUNS: *ċild* "child," *ċealf* "calf," *lamb* "lamb" (er-declension)   10.8.1

Singular				SUMMARY
N	ðæt	ċild	ċealf	lamb	-
A	ðæt	ċild	ċealf	lamb	-
G	ðæs	ċildes	ċealfes	lambes	-es
D	ðǣm	ċilde	ċealfe	lambe	-e

Plural					SUMMARY
N	ðā	ċildru, -ra	ċealfru, -ra	lambru, -ra	-ru, -ra
A	ðā	ċildru, -ra	ċealfru, -ra	lambru, -ra	-ru, -ra
G	ðāra	ċildra	ċealfra	lambra	-ra
D	ðǣm	ċildrum	ċealfrum	lambrum	-rum

10.9 Noun Stems Ending in –þ

Only four nouns belong to this class: the masculines *hæle, hæleþ* "hero, man," and *mōnaþ* "month"; a neuter *ealu* "ale"; and a feminine *mæġþ* "maiden."

Singular				SUMMARY		
	Masculine	Neuter	Feminine	M	F	N
N	sē, hæle, hæleþ	þæt ealu	sēo mæġ(e)þ	-e(þ)	-u	-(e)þ
A	þone, hæle, hæleþ	þæt ealu	þā mæġ(e)þ	-e(þ)	-u	-(e)þ
G	þæs, hæleþes	þæs ealoþ	þǣre mæġ(e)þ	-es	-oþ	-(e)þ
D	þǣm, hæleþe	þǣm ealoþ	þǣre mæġ(e)þ	-e	-oþ	-(e)þ
I	þȳ, hæleþe	þȳ ealoþ	******	-e	-oþ	–
Plural						
N	þā, hæleþ	******†	mæġ(e)þ	-eþ	**	-(e)þ
A	þā, hæleþ	******	mæġ(e)þ	-eþ	**	-(e)þ
G	þāra, hæleþa	ealeþa	mæġ(e)þa	-a	-þa	-a
D	þǣm, hæleþum	******	mæġ(e)þum	-um	**	-um
I	þǣm, hæleþum	******	mæġ(e)þum	-um	**	-um

†Except the genitive plural, no plural forms of *ealu* are attested

Nouns from Present Participles

(Technically known as the *-nd* declension.) All the nouns of this declension describe agents of an action, derived from the present participial form of the verb: *frēond* "friend" (the loving one) from *frēogan* "to love, to free"; *Hǣlend* "savior" (the saving one) from *hǣlan* "to save"; *dēmend* "judge" (the judging one) from *dēman* "to judge"; and *wealdend* "ruler" (the ruling one) from *wealdan* "to rule."

PRESENT PARTICIPLE NOUNS: *fēond* "fiend, foe" and *Hǣlend* "savior" (*-nd* declension)

		Masculine		SUMMARY
Singular				
N	sē	fēond	Hǣlend	–
A	þone	fēond	Hǣlend	–
G	þæs	fēondes	Hǣlendes	-es
D	þǣm	fēonde	Hǣlende	-e
I	þȳ	feonde	Hǣlende	-e
Plural				
N	þā	fēond(as), fiend*	Hǣlend(as), -e	–, -as, -e
A	þā	fēond(as)	Hǣlendas, -e	–, -as, -e
G	þāra	fēonda	Hǣlendra	-a, -ra
D	þǣm	fēondum	Hǣlendum	-um

*The alternative plural *fiend* was affected by i-mutation.

-I- Stem Nouns

This class includes nouns of all genders. The endings for the masculine and neuter *-i-* stems are very similar to those of the regular nouns (that is, the *-a* stem nouns; see §2.7 and §2.9). Similarly, the feminine *-i-* stems follow closely the endings of the regular feminines (that is, the *-o-* stem nouns, see §2.8). Masculine nouns of this declension include: *byrst* "loss," *cwide* "saying," *ele* "oil," *hryre* "fall," and *frēondscipe* "friendship."

Neuters include: *sife* "sieve" and *flǣsc* "flesh." Feminines include: *cwild* "death," *cyst* "best," *dǣd* "deed," *ēst* "grace, favor," and *lēode* "people."

10.11.1 *-I- STEMS* **MASCULINE, NEUTER:** *cwide* "saying," *byrst* "loss," *clyne* "lump," and *flǣsc* "flesh"

	Masculine		Neuter			SUMMARY	
	Short	Long	Short		Long	M	N
Singular							
N	sē cwide	byrst	þæt	clyne	flǣsc	-e, -	-
A	þone cwide	byrst	þæt	clyne	flǣsc	-e, -	-
G	þæs cwides	byrstes	þæs	clynes	flǣsces	-es	-es
D	þǣm cwide	byrste	þǣm	clyne	flǣsce	-e	-e
I	þȳ cwide	byrste	þȳ	clyne	flǣsce	-e	-e
Plural							
N	þā cwide, -as	byrstas	þā	clynu, -o	flǣsc	-e, -as	-u, -o, -
A	þā cwide, -as	byrstas	þā	clynu, -o	flǣsc	-e, -as	-u, -o, -
G	þāra cwida	byrsta	þāra	clyna	flǣsca	-a	-a
D	þǣm cwidum	byrstum	þǣm	clynum	flǣscum	-um	-um

10.11.2 *-I- STEMS* **FEMININE:**

There are very few short stem feminines in the *-i-* stem declension. Most of the feminine nouns went to the regular *-o-* stem declension. See *cwild* "death" and *lēode* "people", below.

	Long Stems			SUMMARY
Singular				
N	sēo	cwild	lēod(e)	-, -e
A	þā	cwild	lēod(e)	-, -e
G	þǣre	cwilde	lēode	-e
D	þǣre	cwilde	lēode	-e

		Long Stems		SUMMARY
Plural				
N	þā	cwilde, -a	lēode	-e, -a
A	þā	cwilde, -a	lēode	-e, -a
G	þāra	cwilda	lēoda	-a
D	þǣm	cwildum	lēodum	-um

As noted in the above paradigms, several of the nouns alternate the older Primitive Germanic ending -e in the nominative and accusative plural with the –as ending (by analogy with the "regular" –a– stem nouns). The retention of the old –e plural ending is especially apparent in the names of peoples: *Dene* = the Danes, *Engle* = the Angles, *Norþanhumbre* = the Northumbrians.

10.11.3

Exercise 10.1: Translation

Instructions. *Translate the following Modern English sentences into OE:*

1. The children went. _____.

2. Those books are larger than this book [is]. _____.

3. The priest dropped the book on his foot. _____.

4. The father's son went with the man. _____.

5. I marvel at the length of the nun's hands. _____.

6. The end of the battle is near. _____.

7. The mother gave her daughter her brother's toy. _____.

VOCABULARY FOR EXERCISE 10.1

battle = *beadu* (f) [§10.3.3]

BOOK = *bōc* (f) [§10.4.2]

BROTHER = *brōþor* (m) [§10.5]

CHILD = *ċild* (n) [§10.8]

DAUGHTER = *dohtor* (f) [§10.5]

DROP = *dropian* (weak verb II) [§3.12]

END = *ende* (m) [§10.2.1]

FATHER = *fæder* (m) [§10.5]

FOOT = *fōt* (m) [§10.4.2]

GAVE = *ġeaf* (strong verb 5) [§9.1]

HAND = *hand* (f) [§10.6]

large = *miċel* (adjective) [§6.1]

LENGTH = *lengþo* (f) [§10.7]

MAN = *mann* (m) [§10.4.2]

marvel = *wundrian* (weak verb II, at = + gen) [§3.12]

MOTHER = *mōdor* (f) [§10.5]

near (adverb) = *nēah* = NIGH [§6.9]

NUN = *nunne* (f) [§3.4]

PRIEST = *prēost* (m) [§2.7]

SON = *sunu* (m) [§10.6]

THAN = *þonne* (conjunction) [§5.1.1]

toy = *pleġ-scyld* (m) PLAY-SHIELD, a particular toy [§2.7]

went = use *gān* [§4.5.3.1]

with = *mid* (preposition + dat) [§6.15]

Exercise 10.2: Translation

Instructions. *Translate the following OE sentences into idiomatic Modern English:*

1. Þā fērdon hīe mid þǣm fierde and þone here metton.

2. In ðisses cyninges rīċe sē ēadiġa ærċ-biscop forð-fērde ond heofonlīċe rīċe ġe-stāh.

3. Witodlīċe Petrus wæs fiscere ǣr his ġe-ċyrrednysse and Mathēus wæs tollere.

4.   . . . wæs¹ þēaw hyra,
   þæt hīe oft wǣron   on wīġ gearwe,
   ġē æt hām ġē on herge . . .

5. "Nū þū meaht ġe-hīeran,   hæleþ mīn sē lēofa,[2]
   þæt ic bealwa weorc   ġe-biden hæbbe,
   sārra sorga."[3]

6. wæs sē grimma gǣst   Grendel hāten,
   mǣre mearcstapa,   sē þe mōras hēold,
   fen ond fæsten . . .

7. Hī būgon þā fram beadwe þe þǣr bēon noldon.

8. Hē ġe-sāwe helle opene ond Satanan, þone ealdan fēond mon-cynnes,
   be-senċedne on þām grundum helle tintreġes.

9. Sē engel cwæþ tō ðām hālgan wīf-mannum, "Ne on-drǣdað ēow. Iċ wāt," hē
   cwæþ, "ġē sēċaþ þone Nazareniscan hǣlend þe for manna lufan ā-hangen wæs."

10. Sē cyning and þā rīcostan men drincaþ mȳran meolc, and þā un-spēdigan and
    þā ðēowan drincað medo.

[2] The word order of this phrase, *hæleþ mīn sē lēofa*, may seem strange to modern ears and eyes, which would probably prefer *mīn lēofa hæleþ*.

[3] *Sārra sorga* is a variation on *bealwa* from the previous line—both are dependent on *weorc*.

VOCABULARY FOR EXERCISE 10.2

ǣr (preposition + dat and inst) = before [§6.15]

Ærċbiscop (m) = ARCHBISHOP [§2.7]

æt (preposition + dat or acc) = AT [§6.15]

ā-hangen = see *ā-hōn*

ā-hōn (strong verb 7, contract verb) = to HANG [§9.3, §11.1]

beadwe (f) = BATTLE [§10.3.3]

bealu (n) = EVIL [§10.2.2]

be-senċan (weak verb I) = to submerge, immerse [§3.11]

(ġe)bīdan (strong verb 1) = wait, endure [§8.4]

būgan (weak verb I) = to flee [§3.11]

(ge)ċierran (weak verb I) = to turn, to convert [§3.11]

cwæþ = see *cweþan*

cweþan (strong verb 5) = to say, speak [§9.1]

(ġe)ċyrrednysse (f) = conversion [§2.8]

drincan (strong verb 3) = to DRINK [§8.6]

ēadiġ (adjective) = blessed, happy [§6.1]

eald (adjective) = OLD, aged, ancient [§6.1]

engel (m) = ANGEL [§2.7]

fæsten (n) = FASTNESS, stronghold [§10.2.2]

fen (n) = FEN, marsh [§2.9]

fēond (m) = FIEND, enemy [§10.10]

fēran (weak verb I) = TO GO [§3.11]

fierd (f) = army (in the *Chronicle*, usually reserved to designate the Anglo-Saxon army) [§10.11.2]

fiscere (m) = FISHERman [§10.2.1]

forð-fēran (weak verb I) = to travel FORTH; depart, die [§3.11]

gǣst (m) = spirit, GHOST [§2.7]

ġe (pronoun) = you (pl) [§7.1]

ġē . . . ġē (conjunction) = both . . . and [§5.1.1]

ġearwe (adjective) = ready [§6.1]

grim(m) (adjective) = GRIM, cruel [§6.1]

grund (m) = DEPTH [§2.7]

habban (weak verb III) = to HAVE [§4.1]

hæleþ (m) = man, hero [§10.9]

hǣlend (m) = savior [§10.10]

hāliġ (adjective) = HOLY [§6.1]

hām (m) = HOME [§2.7]

hātan (strong verb 7) = call, name [§9.3]

healdan (strong verb 7) = to HOLD [§9.3]

hel(l) (f) = HELL [§2.8]

(ġe)hīeran (weak verb I) = to HEAR [§3.11]

heofonliċ (adjective) = HEAVENLY [§6.1]

here (m) = ARMY (in the *Chronicle*, usually reserved to designate the Danish army) [§10.2.1]

herge (m) = see *here*

iċ, wē (personal pronoun) = I, WE (1 dat pl: *ūs*) [§7.1]

lēof (adjective) = dear (§6.1)

lufu (f) = LOVE [§2.8]

man(n) (m) = MAN [§10.4.2]

mearc-stapa (weak m) = haunter of desolate land, MARCH prowler [§3.3]

magan (preterite-present verb) = to be able, can [§4.3]

meaht = see *magan*

medo (m) = MEAD [§2.7]

meolc (f) = MILK [§10.4.2]

mētan (weak verb I) = encounter [§3.11]

monn-cynn (n) = MANKIND [§2.7]

mōr (m) = MOOR [§2.7]

myre (weak f) = MARE [§3.4]

Nazareniscan (adjective) = NAZARENE [§6.1]

noldon (negative form of *woldon*) = see *willan*

nū (adverb) = NOW [§6.9]

on (preposition) = (+ dat) in, ON; (+ acc) into, onto [§6.16.2]

on-drǣdan (strong verb 7) = to fear, DREAD [§9.3]

openian (weak verb II) = OPEN [§3.12]

rīċe (adjective) = powerful, RICH [§6.1]

rīċe (n) = kingdom [§10.2.2]

sār (adjective) = sad, SORrowful [§6.1]

Satana (weak m) = Satan, the devil [§3.3]

(ġe)sāwe (verb form not yet covered) = "saw" "glimpsed" [§11.1]

sēċan (weak verb I) = to SEEK [§3.11]

sorg, sorh (f) = SORROW, pain [§2.8]

(ġe)stīgan (strong verb 1) = to climb, ascend [§8.4]

tintreġ (n) = torment [§2.9]

tollere (m) = tax collector [§10.2.1]

þēaw (m) = custom [§10.2.1]

ðēowa (weak m) = servant [§3.3]

þū (personal pronoun) = you, THOU [§7.1]

un-spēdiġ (adjective used as noun) = POOR [§ 6.1]

wǣron = see *wesan*

wāt = see *witan*

weorc (n) = travail, trouble, distress [§2.9]

wesan (irregular verb) = to be [§4.5.1]

wifman(n) (m) = woman [§10.4.2]

wīġ (n) = war [§2.9]

willan (irregular verb) = to wish, want, desire [§4.5.3.2]

witan (preterite-present verb) = to know [§4.3.3.2]

witodlīċe (adverb) = truly [§6.9]

Reading X: *FROM* **VERCELLI HOMILY IX** (continued)

The devil's report continues with two terrifying descriptions of hell (the first a bit wild, so watch out!). The reading again contains a string of subjunctives (invoked by the hypothetical situation). The very end of the homily appears as the last paragraph.

4 i.e., the name
of hell

5 *nis nān man* =
"(there) is no man"

6 a reflexive (see
§7.4)

7 *þām þe*, a relative
pronoun (see
§7.5.2)

8 with understood
verb of motion
(see §5.2.2)

9 *hē* = the hell
hound; *hund* is a
masculine noun

10 *bidden wē* = "let us
ask" (see §3.10.1,
item 3d)

Ond efne swā myċel swā fram heofones hrōfe is tō þysse eorðan, þonne is leornod on hālgum bōcum þæt sīo hel sīe swylċ twā dēop, and nis nā ðe un-wīdre. Þæt hūs is mid swīðe on-gristliċe fȳre ā-fylled, ond helle hūs hafað forclas miċle. Sē nama[4] is tō ġe-þenċeanne ælċum men būtan hwæs heorte sīe mid dēofles stræle þurh-wrecen. For-þȳ

5 nis nān man[5] þæt hē þanon ā-weġ hine[6] ā-styrian mæġe, ond for ðām is myċel þearf æġ-hwylċum men tō on-wariġanne, þām þe[7] æniġ and-ġit hæbbe oððe wīs-dōmes æniġne dæl, þæt hē þis symle hæbbe on ġe-myndum þā eges-fullan stōwe. For-þan ġif hwylċ man bið on helle āne niht þonne bið him lēofre, ġif hē þanon mōt,[8] þæt hē hangie sēofon þūsend wintra on þām lengestan trēowe ufe-weardum þe ofer sæ standeð on þām hȳhstan sæ-clife,

10 ond sȳn þā fēt ġe-bundene tō ðām hēhstan telgan ond þæt hēafod hangiġe of-dūn-rihte ond þā fēt ūp-rihte, ond him sīġe þæt blōd ūt þurh þone mūð, ond hine þonne ġe-sēċe ælċ þæra yfela þe æfre on helle sȳ, ond hine ælċ ȳð ġe-sēċe mid þām hēhstan þe sēo sæ forð-bringð, ond þēah hine ælċ tor ġe-sēċe þe on eallum clyfum syndon, þonne wile hē eal þis lufliċe þrōwian wið-ðon-þe hē næfre eft helle ne ġe-sēċe.

15 Ēalā, myċel is on bōcum leornod ond hit is sōðliċe eal ġe-sewen; sagað hit þæt on helle sȳ ān hund. Ne meahte hit þæt dēoful þām āncran eall ā-secgan hū myċel þære sāwle wītu bēoð þe tō him bēoð ġe-scyrede. Hē[9] hafað hund-tēontiġ hēafda, ond hē hafað on ælcum hēafde hund ēagena, ond ælċ þāra ēagena is fȳre hāt, ond hē hafað hund-tēontiġ handa, ond on ælċre handa hund-tēontiġ fingra, ond ælċum fingre hund-tēontiġ næġla,

20 ond hȳra is ælċ on nædran wīsan ā-scyrped. Ēalā, mīn dryhten, lāðliċ is hit for ðȳ on helle tō bēonne. Wā ðām sāwlum þe ðær bēon sculon!

Hwæt, wē nū ġe-hȳrdon secgan hwylċ hit is on helle tō bēonne. For ðan wē sculon ġe-swīcan ūra synna ond Gode eāð-mōde bēon mid ælmessum ond mid gōdum weorcum. Ond uton sēcan ūre ċyrċean mid clænnesse ond mid hlūtran mōde, ond bidden wē[10]

25 eāð-mōdliċe bēne þæt wē ne weorðen ġe-tēodde on þā helle wītu. Gif wē þonne swā dōn wyllað swā ūs Dryhten bēden hafað, þonne mōton wē mid Him ond mid his þām Hālgan Gæste wunian in ealra worulda woruld, amen.

VOCABULARY FOR READING X

ǣfre (adverb) = EVER [§6.9]

ǣġ-hwylċ (adjective and pronoun) = each, every [§6.1, §7.8]

ǣlċ (adjective and pronoun) = EACH [§7.8]

ælmesse (f) = ALMS, charity [§2.8]

ǣniġ (adjective and pronoun) = ANY [§6.1, §7.8]

ā-fyllan (weak verb I) = to FILL up [§3.11]

ān (adjective and number) = ONE [§6.1]

āncra (weak m) = ANCHORite, hermit [§3.3]

and-ġit (f) = understanding, insight [§2.8]

ā-scyrpan (weak verb I) = to SHARPEN [§3.11]

ā-secgan (weak verb III) = to tell, relate [§4.1]

ā-styrian (weak verb I) = to STIR, move, raise [§3.11]

ā-weġ (adverb) = AWAY [§6.9]

bēden = past participle of *biddan*

bēn (f) = prayer, request; related to Mod. English *boon* [§10.11.2]

bēon (irregular verb) = to BE [§4.5.1]

bið = see *bēon*

bīdan (strong verb 1) = to ask, BID [§8.4]

biddan (strong verb 5) = to ask, pray, BID [§9.1]

(ġe)bindan (strong verb 3) = to BIND, tie [§8.6]

blōd (n) = BLOOD [§2.9]

bōc (f) = BOOK [§10.4.2]

būtan (conjunction) = except [§5.1.1]

clǣnnes (f) = purity [§2.8]

clyf (n) = CLIFF [§2.9]

ċyrċe (weak f) = CHURCH [§3.4]

dǣl (m) = portion, part, DEAL [§2.7]

dēofol (m or n) = DEVIL [§2.7, §2.9]

dēop (adjective) = DEEP [§6.1]

dōn (irregular verb) = to DO, behave [§4.5.3]

dryhten (m) = lord [§2.7]

eāð-mōd (adjective) = benevolent, of humble MOOD [§6.1]

eāð-mōd-līċe (adverb) = humbly, modestly [§6.9]

ēage (weak n) = EYE [§3.5]

eal (adverb) = ALL, completely [§6.9]

eal (n or adjective) = ALL [§6.1]

ēalā (interjection) = oh!, lo!

efne (adverb) = EVEN [§6.9]

eft (adverb) = again [§6.9]

eġes-ful (adjective) = terrifying, FULL of horror [§6.1]

eorðe (weak f) = EARTH [§3.4]

finger (m) = FINGER [§2.7]

for ðām (adverb) = therefore [§6.9]

forcel (m) = pitch-FORK [§2.7]

forð-bringan (strong verb 3) = to BRING FORTH, cast up [§8.6]

for-þȳ (adverb) = therefore, for this reason [§6.9]

fōt (m) = FOOT [§10.4.2]

fram (preposition + dat) = FROM [§6.15]

fȳr (n) = FIRE [§2.9]

gǣst (m) = spirit, GHOST [§2.7]

ġif (conjunction) = IF [§5.1.1]

gōd (adjective) = GOOD [§6.1]

God (m) = GOD, the Deity [§2.7]

habban (weak verb III) = to HAVE [§4.1]

hafað = pres 3 sing of *habban*

hāliġ (adjective) = HOLY, sacred [§6.1]

hand (f) = HAND [§10.6]

hangian (weak verb II) = to HANG, be suspended [§3.12]

hāt (adjective) = HOT [§6.1]

hēafod (n) = HEAD [§2.9]

hēah (adjective) = HIGH [§6.1]

hēhstan = see *hēah*

hell (f) = HELL [§2.8]

heofon (m or n) = HEAVEN, the sky [§2.7, §2.8]

heorte (weak f) = HEART [§3.4]

blūtor (adjective) = pure, clear, bright [§6.1]

hrōf (m) = ROOF; top, summit [§2.7]

hū (adverb) = HOW [§6.9]

hund (m) = dog, HOUND [§2.7]

hund (number) = a HUNDred

hund-tēontiġ (number) = a HUNDred (usually + partitive gen.) [§2.11.3.c]

hūs (n) = HOUSE, dwelling place [§2.9]

hwā (indefinite pronoun) = WHO, whoever [§7.6, §7.8]

hwæt (interjection) = indeed! lo!

hwylċ (adjective) = any; which, what [§7.8]

hȳhstan = see *hēah*

hȳra = 3 gen pl personal pronoun [§7.1]

(ġe)hȳran (weak verb I) = to HEAR; *ġe-hȳran secgan* = to hear tell [§3.11]

lāðlic (adjective) = hateful, ghastly [§6.1]

lang (adjective) = LONG, tall [§6.1]

lengest = see *lang*

lēof (adjective) = dear, beLOVed; (compare

lēofre = "preferable") [§6.1, §6.4]

leornian (weak verb II) - to teach; LEARN [§3.12]

luflīċe (adverb) = willingly, gladly [§6.9]

mǣre (adjective) =famous, illustrious [§6.1]

magan (preterite-present verb) = be able, have the ability to [§4.4]

mann (m) = MAN, person [§10.4.2]

meahte = see *magan*

miċel (adjective) = great, huge, large [§6.1]

mid (preposition + dat) = with, along with [§6.15]

mōd (n) = mind, heart, MOOD [§2.9]

mōtan (preterite-present verb) = to be able [§4.3]

mūð (m) = MOUTH [§2.7]

myċel (adjective) = much; great, large [§6.1]

(ġe)mynd (f) = MIND, memory (pl with sing sense); thought [§2.8]

nā (adverb) = not at all [§6.9]

nǣdre (weak f) = ADDER, snake, serpent (i.e., with sharp fangs) [§3.4]

nǣfre (adverb) = NEVER [§6.9]

næġl (m) = NAIL, fingernail [§2.7]

nama (weak m) = NAME [§3.3]

nān (adjective and pronoun) = NO, none [§6.1]

ne (adverb) = not [§6.9]

niht (f) = NIGHT [§10.4.2]

nis = see *bēon*

nū (adverb) = NOW [§6.9]

oððe (conjunction) = or

of-dūn-rihte (adverb) = DOWNward, upside-down [§6.9]

ofer (preposition + dat/acc) = OVER [§6.16.2]

on (preposition) = (dat) in, ON; (acc) into, onto [§6.15]

ond (conjunction) = AND, but

on-gristliċ (adjective) = GRISLY, ghastly [§6.1]

on-wari(ġ)an (weak verb II) = to guard oneself against, be WARY against [§3.12]

sǣ (m or f) = SEA [§10.11.1 or 2]

sǣ-clif (n) = SEA-CLIFF, cliff by the sea [§2.9]

sagað = pres 3 sing of *secgan*

sāwol (f) = SOUL [§2.8]

sculan (preterite-present verb) = SHALL, must [§4.3]

(ġe)scyran (weak verb I) = to allot, apportion [§3.11]

(ġe)sēċan (weak verb I) = to SEEK out, visit; attack [§3.11]

secgan (weak verb III) = to SAY [§4.1]

seofon (adjective or number) = SEVEN

(ġe)sēon (strong verb 5) = to SEE [§9.1]

(ġe)sewen = past participle of *ġe-sēon*

sīe = see *bēon*

sīġan (strong verb 1) = to descend, rush down [§8.4]

sīo = see *sēo*

sōðlīċe (adverb) = truly, in truth [§6.9]

standan (strong verb 6) = to STAND [§9.2]

stōw (f) = place [§2.8]

strǣl (f) = arrow, dart [§2.8]

swā = (adverb) thus, SO [§6.9]; (conjunction) as; *swā . . . swā* = as . . . as, so . . . as [§5.1.1]

(ġe)swīcan (strong verb I) = to cease from, stop (+ gen) [§8.4]

swīðe (adverb) = very, exceedingly [§6.9]

swylċ (pronoun) = the same, SUCH [§7.8]

sȳ = see *sīe*

symle (adverb) = constantly, continually [§6.9]

sȳn = see *bēon*

synn (f) = SIN, crime [§2.8]

telga (weak m) = branch, bough [§3.3]

(ġe)teodde = past participle of *ġe-teohhian*

(ġe)teohhian (weak verb II) = to judge, determine [§3.12]

tō (infinitive marker) = TO

tō (preposition + dat) = TO; as [§6.15]

torr (m) = rock [related to ModE *TOWER*; §2.7]

trēow (n) = TREE [§2.9]

twā (number) = TWO, twice as

ðǣr (adverb) = THERE [§6.9]

þæt (conjunction) = THAT [§5.1.1]

þanon (adverb) = from there, THENce [§6.9]

þe (relative pronoun) = who, which [§7.5]

ðe (comparative marker) = THE (as in "*the* smaller *the* better")

þēah (adverb) = yet, moreover; nevertheless [§6.9]

þearf (f) = need, necessity [see German *Bedurfnis* "need"; §2.8]

(ġe)þenċean (weak verb I) = to consider, THINK about carefully (note: in this case, the infinitive is probably passive: "the name is to be thought about carefully") [§3.11]

þēs (adjective and demonstrative pronoun) = THIS [§7.7]

þis = see *þēs*

þonne (adverb) = yet; THEN [§6.9]

þrōwian (weak verb II) = to suffer, tolerate [§3.12]

þurh (preposition with acc) = THROUGH [§6.15]

þurh-wrecan (strong verb 5) = to pierce, thrust THROUGH [§9.1]

þūsend (number) = THOUSAND

ufe-weard (adjective) = ascending, higher up [§6.1]

un-wīd (adjective) = narrow, UN-WIDE [§6.1]

ūp-rihte (adverb) = UPward, to the top [§6.9]

ūr (pronoun & adjective) = OUR [§7.2 and §6.1]

ūt (adverb) = OUT [§6.9]

uton = let us (+ infinitive)

wā (interjection) = WOE!, alas!

weorc (n) = WORK, deed [§2.9]

weorðan (strong verb 3) = to be, become [§8.6]

willan (irregular verb) = to be willing, to wish, desire [§4.5.3.2]

winter (m) = WINTER; year [§2.7]

wīs-dōm (m) = WISDOM [§2.7]

wīse (weak f) = way, manner, fashion [§3.4]

wīte (n) = punishment, torment [§10.2.2]

wið-ðon-þe (conjunction) = provided that [§5.1.1]

woruld (f) = WORLD; *in ealra worulda woruld* = world without end, for ever and ever [§10.11.2]

wunian (weak verb II) = to dwell, live [§3.12]

ȳð (f) = wave, billow [§2.8]

yfel (adjective and n) = EVIL, evil thing [§6.1, §2.9]

Lessons Learned

Before leaving this chapter you should . . .
- be able to recognize and look up rarer noun forms.

ELEVEN

Contract Verbs, Impersonal Constructions

11.1   Lesson One: Contracted Verbs

This section introduces a small but important sub-class of strong verbs, usually called "contract" verbs, that can be hard to find in the glossary unless you know some basic facts about them. The main difference between these verbs and regular strong verbs is that the infinitive form ends in an *–on* rather than the regular *–an*, and an *h* (or *g*) appears or disappears in various positions.

The best way to understand such verbs is to have a brief look at their evolution. Let's take one of the most important of the contracted verbs as an example, *tēon* "to pull, tug." In the earliest stage of Prehistoric Old English (PrehistOE is ca. 500-700 CE), the infinitive *tēon* must have looked (or, more accurately, sounded) something like **tēhan*. The sequence of sound changes that produced the recorded forms of *tēon* ran something like this:

- The *h* in **tēhan* caused the preceding vowel to "break" into the diphthong *ēo*.
  *tēhan > *tēohan

- Next, late in the PrehistOE period or early OE, *h* was lost when it occurred between two vowels.

  *tēohan > *tēoan

- Finally, the sequence of vowels was simplified or contracted—hence the label "contracted verbs."

  *tēoan > tēon

For the various sound changes you will find in the contracted verbs, see Appendix Two (§16).

CONTRACTED VERBS BY STRONG VERB CLASSES   11.1.2

Class	Infinitive	Present 3 Singular	Past Singular	Past Plural	Past Participle
1	ðēon "to prosper"	þīehþ	þāh	þigon	(ġe)þiġen
	wrēon "to conceal"	wrīehþ	wrāh	wrigon	(ġe)wriġen
2	flēon "to flee"	flīehþ	flēah	flugon	(ġe)floġen
	tēon "to pull"	tīehþ	tēah	tugon	(ġe)toġen
5	sēon "to see"	sīehþ	seah	*sāwon	*(ġe)sewen
6	slēan "to strike"	slīehþ	slōg	slōgon	(ġe)slæġen
	ðwēan "to cleanse"	ðwīehþ	ðwōg	ðwōgon	(ġe)ðwæġen
7	fōn "to seize, grasp"	fēhþ	fēng	fēngon	(ġe)fangen
	hōn "to hang"	hēhþ	hēng	hēngon	(ġe)hangen

CONJUGATION OF CONTRACTED VERBS   11.1.3

The conjugation of the personal endings for contracted verbs is similar to the strong verbs that you studied in Chapters Eight and Nine. The main differences between contracted verbs and other strong verbs appear in the present indicative, present subjunctive, and the imperative. In all other ways, the personal endings of contracted verbs follow those of the strong verbs of like class. We conjugate here a few representative verbs from several strong verb classes (ðēon, "to thrive, flourish" Class 1; tēon, "to draw, pull" Class 2; sēon, "to see" Class 5; fōn, "to seize, take" Class 7).

* To understand how the present tense verbs and imperatives vary in their form from other strong verbs of the same class, see Appendix Two (§16).

** See Appendix Two (§17).

Infinitive		þēon		tēon		SUMMARY	
		Present	Past	Present	Past	Present	Past
Indicative Sing	1	ðēo	ðāh	tēo	tēah	-	-
	2	ðīehst*	ðiġe*	tīehst*	tuġe*	-st	-e
	3	ðīehþ*	ðāh	tīehþ*	tēah	-þ	-
Indicative Plural	1, 2, 3	ðēoþ	ðigon**	tēoþ	tugon**	-þ	-on
Subjunctive Sing	1, 2, 3	ðēo	ðiġe	tēo	tuge	-	-e
Subjunctive Plural	1, 2, 3	ðēon	ðiġen	tēon	tugen	-n	-en
Participles		ðēonde	(ġe)þiġen	tēonde	(ge)togen	-ende	-en
Imperative Sing		ðēoh	*****	tēoh	*****	-	**
Imperative Plural		ðēoþ	*****	tēoþ	*****	-þ	**
Inflected Infin. (Gerund)		tō ðēonne	*****	tō tēonne	*****	-nne	**

Infinitive		sēon		fōn		SUMMARY	
		Present	Past	Present	Past	Present	Past
Indicative Sing	1	sēo	seah	fō	fēng	-	-
	2	sīehst*	sāwe*	fēhst*	fēnge*	-st	-e
	3	sīehþ*	seah*	fehþ*	fēng*	-þ	-
Indicative Plural	1, 2, 3	sēoþ	sāwon**	fōþ	fēngon**	-þ	-on
Subjunctive Sing	1, 2, 3	sēo	sāwe	fō	fēnge	-	-e
Subjunctive Plural	1, 2, 3	sēon	sāwen	fōn	fēngen	-n	-en
Participles		sēonde	(ġe)sewen	fōnde	(ġe)fangen	-ende	-en
Imperative Sing		sēoh	*****	fōh	*****	-	**
Imperative Plural		sēoþ	*****	fōþ	*****	-þ	**
Inflected Infin. (Gerund)		tō sēonne	*****	tō fōnne	*****	-nne	**

Exercise 11.1: UNDERSTANDING THE FORMS OF CONTRACTED VERBS

Instructions. *In the spaces provided, identify the mood, tense, person, and number of the listed verbs. Where the verb form has more than one possible answer, identify them.*

	Mood	Tense	Person	Number
1. ðēo				
2. sīehst				
3. seah				
4. sēon				
5. ðigon				
6. fōh				
7. fengen				
8. flīehþ				
9. fēhþ				
10. tēoþ				

READING OLD ENGLISH: CHAPTER ELEVEN

[1] The subject of *ġe-fliemde* is *sēo* fierd.

[2] Notice the shift to the plural here—the subject is now "they" rather than "army."

[3] The subject, "she" or "Grendel's mother," is carried over from the previous sentence.

Exercise 11.2: INFINITIVES

Instructions. *For each of the verbs listed in Exercise 11.1, give the infinitive form.*

1. _____   6. _____

2. _____   7. _____

3. _____   8. _____

4. _____   9. _____

5. _____   10. _____

Exercise 11.3: TRANSLATING CONTRACTED VERBS

Instructions. *Translate the following sentences using the glossary at the end of this exercise.*

1. Þā hīe ġe-fēngon micle here-hȳð and þā woldon ferian norþweardes ofer Temese, in on Ēastseaxe on-ġēan þā scipu. Þā for-rād sēo fierd hīe foran and him wið ġe-feaht æt Fearnhamme, ond þone here ġe-flīemde[1] and þā here-hȳþa ā-hreddon,[2] and hīe flugon ofer Temese buton ælcum forda, þā ūp be Colne on ānne iggað.

2. Of-sæt[3] þā þone sele-gyst   ond hyre seax ġe-tēah,
   brād, brūn-ecg;   wolde hire bearn wrecan,
   āngan eaferan.

3. Nū is ǣġ-hwonan hrēam ond wōp. Nu is hēaf ǣġ-hwonan ond sibbe tō-lȳsnes; nū is ǣġ-hwonan yfel ond sleġe, ond ǣġ-hwonan þes middan-ġeard flȳhþ from ūs mid myċelre biternesse, ond wē him[4] flēondum fylġeaþ ond hine feallendne[5] lufiaþ.

4. Ġe-syhð[6] sorh-ċeariġ   on his suna būre.
    wīn-sele wēstne,   windġe reste[7]
    rēote be-rōfene.

5. On þā ēa hī tugon ūp hira scipu oþ þone weald iiii mīla fram þǣm mūþan ūte-weardum and þǣr ā-brǣcon ān ġe-weorc; inne on þǣm fæstene sǣton fēawa ċirlisce menn on, and wæs sām-worht.

6. (Beowulf resolves not to use a sword to fight Grendel. To do so, the hero explains, would be too easy since Grendel doesn't know the skills (gōda) of the warrior.)

    Nāt[8] hē þāra gōda,   þæt hē mē on-ġēan slēa,
    rand ġe-hēawe,[9]   þēah ðe hē rōf sīe
    nīþ-ġeweorca.[10]

7.   Þā þǣr sōna wearð
    ed-hwyrft eorlum   siþðan inne fealh
    Grendles mōdor.

[4] *Him* and *hine* refer back to *middan-geard*.

[5] Note the adjectival *–ne* ending on the present participle *feallendne*.

[6] The subject of *ġe-syhð* is implied (the context reveals that he is a father who has lost a son).

[7] The preposition *on* carries over to both *win-sele westne* and *windge reste*.

[8] The subject is "Grendel."

[9] Both *slēa* and *ġe-heawe* are subjunctive: translate "might strike" and "might hew."

[10] *Nīþ-ġeweorca* depends on *rōf* in the previous line (the Genitive Rule).

VOCABULARY FOR EXERCISE 11.3

ā-brecan (strong verb 4) = to capture [§8.7]

ǣġ-hwonan (adverb) = everywhere [§6.9]

ǣlċ (adjective) = any [§6.2.1]

ā-hreddan (weak verb I) = to rescue, set free [§3.11]

ān (adjective) = a, an [§6.1]

ānga (adjective) = sole, only [§6.1]

be (preposition + dat) = along [§6.15]

bearn (n) = child [§2.9]

bēon (irregular verb) = to BE [§4.5.1]

be-rōfen (adjective + dat) = deprived of, BEREFt [originally a strong past participle; §6.3]

biterness (f) = grief, BITTERNESS [§2.8]

brād (adjective) = BROAD [§6.1]

brūn-ecg (adjective) = bright [§6.1]

būr (n) = dwelling, chamber; BOWER [§2.9]

būtan (preposition + dat) = without [§6.15]

Colne = the River Colne (Essex)

ċirlisc (adjective) = common ["churlish"; §6.1]

ēa (f) = river [§10.4.2]

eafera (weak m) = offspring [§3.3]

Ēast-seaxe (weak m pl) = ESSEX, the people of Essex [§3.3]

ed-hwyrft (m) = change, turn, reversal [§3.11]

eorl (m) = warrior, nobleman [§2.7]

fæsten (m) = stronghold [§10.2.1]

(ġe)*feohtan* (strong verb 3) = to FIGHT [§8.6]

fealh = see *fēolan*

feallan (strong verb 7) = to FALL, fall headlong; fail, die [§9.3]

Fearnham (m) = FARNHAM [§2.7]

fēaw (adjective) = FEW [§6.1]

fēolan (strong verb 3) = to enter [§8.6]

ferian (weak verb I) = to carry [§3.11]

fierd (f) = army (in the *Chronicle*, usually reserved to designate the Anglo-Saxon army) [§10.11.2]

flēon (contract verb, strong verb 2) = to fly, flee [§11.1]

(ġe)*flīeman* (weak verb I) = to put to flight [§3.11]

flugon = see *flēon*

flyhþ = see *flēon*

(ġe)*fōn* (contract verb, strong 7) = to capture, seize [§11.1] *foran* (adverb) = beFORE, in front of [§6.9]

ford (m) = FORD [§10.6]

for-rīdan (strong verb 1) = to intercept [§8.4]

from, fram (preposition + dat) = FROM [§6.15]

fylgan (weak verb I, + dat object) = to follow [§3.11]

gōd (n) = lit., GOOD thing(s); here, skills [§2.9]

Grendel (m) = monster in *Beowulf* [§2.7]

hē (personal pronoun) = HE [§7.1]

hēaf (m) = mourning [§2.7]

(ġe)*hēawan* (strong verb 7) = to cut, HEW [§9.3]

here (m) = army (in the *Chronicle*, usually reserved to designate the Danish army) [§10.2.1]

here-hȳð (f) = booty; lit., army-plunder [§3.4]

hīe, hine, him (personal pronouns) [§7.1]

hrēam (m) = cry, lamentation [§2.7]

iggað (m) = island [§2.7]

inne (adverb) = INside [§6.9]

in . . . on (preposition) = into [§6.15]

is = see *bēon*

lufian (weak verb II) = to LOVE [§3.12]

miċel (adjective) = great [§6.1]

mid (preposition + dat, inst) = with [§6.15]

middan-ġeard (m) = world, MIDdle earth; fig., earthly things [§2.7]

mīl (f) = MILE [§2.8]

mōdor (f) = MOTHER [§10.5]

monn (m) = MAN [§2.9]

mūþa (weak m) = MOUTH of a river, estuary [§3.3]

myċelre = see *miċel*

nāt = see *nytan*

nīð-ġeweorc (n) = hostile deeds, WORKs of violence [§2.9]

nū (adverb) = NOW [§6.9]

norþ-weardes (adverb) = NORTHWARD [§6.9]

nytan (preterite-present verb = *ne witan*) = not to know; (+ gen) not to know of or about [§4.3 and 4.3.2.1]

ofer (preposition + acc) = OVER [§6.15]

of-sittan (strong verb 5) = to hem in, besiege; SIT on? [§9.1]

on (adverb) = inside [§6.9]

on (preposition) = (+ dat) ON, in; (+ acc) ONto, into [§6.15]

ond (or *and*, conj) = AND

on-ġēan (adverb) = in return, back [§6.9]

on-ġēan (preposition + dat or acc) towards [§6.15]

oþ (preposition + acc) = as far as [§6.15]

rand (m) = shield [§2.7]

rēote = see *rētu*

rest (f) = RESTing place, bed [§2.8]

rētu (f) = joy [§3.4]

rōf (adjective) = famous, renowned; brave [§6.1]

sǣton = see *sittan*

sām-worht (adjective) = unfinished [§6.1]

scip (n) = SHIP [§2.9]

seax (n) = knife [§2.9]

sele-gyst (m) = hall GUEST [§10.11.1]

ġe-sēon (contract verb, strong 5; the prefix ġe- is always affixed to the verb *sēon* and suggests specific meanings beyond the more usual *to see*) = to SEE, perceive, understand, know, observe [§11.1]

sibb (f) = peace [§2.8]

sīe = see *bēon*

sittan (strong verb 5) = to SIT [§9.1]

siþðan (adverb) = afterwards [§6.9]

siþðan (conjunction) = after [§5.1.1]

slēan (contract verb, strong 6) = to strike, hit [see ModE *SLAY*; §11.1]

sleġe (m) = beating, stroke; death-blow; murder, SLAYing [§10.11.1]

sōna (adverb) = immediately [§6.9]

sorh-ċeariġ (adjective) = sad, SORROWful [§6.1]

sunu (m) = SON [§10.6]

ġe-sēon (contract verb, strong 5; the prefix ġe- is always affixed to the verb *sēon* and suggests specific meanings beyond the more usual *to see*) = to SEE, perceive, understand, know, observe [§11.1]

(ġe)tēon (contract verb, strong verb 2) = to draw, pull [§11.1]

tugon = see *tēon*

Temese (f) = River THAMES [§2.8]

tō-lȳsnes (f) = to destruction, loss [§3.11]

ðā (adverb) = then [§6.9]

ðǣm (definite article) = the [§2.5]

þǣr (adverb) = THERE [§6.9]

ðæt (conjunction) = THAT [§7.5]

ðēah ðe (conjunction) = although [§5.1.1]

ðēs (demonstrative pronoun) = THIS [§7.7]

ūp (adverb) = UP [§6.9]

ūs (personal pronoun) = US [§7.1]

ūte-weard (adjective) = OUTWARD, outer, external [§6.1]

wē (personal pronoun) = WE [§7.1]

weald (m) = forest [§10.6]

(ġe)weorc (n) = fortification, earthWORK [§2.9]

weorðan (strong verb 3) = to happen, become [§8.6]

wēsten (adjective) = deserted, desolate [§6.1]

willan (irregular verb) = to wish, desire [§4.5.3]

windiġ (adjective) = WINDY [§6.1]

wīn-sele (n) = WINE hall [§2.9]

wið (preposition + gen, acc, and dat) = WITH; against [§6.15]

woldon = see *willan*

wōp (m) = WEEPing, crying [§2.7]

wrecan (strong verb 5) = to avenge, WREAK vengeance [§9.1]

yfel (n) = EVIL [§2.9]

Lesson Two: Impersonals   11.2

Impersonal constructions use "it" as a kind of dummy noun in statements about natural processes, time, mental and physical states, etc. Since this "it" doesn't function like a normal subject, grammarians have called this construction an "impersonal."

It is raining.

It is half past two.

It seems to me . . .

It says in books . . .

In each of these cases, the "it" does not function like a normal pronoun (which must usually refer back to a noun, and in this case a neuter noun). These impersonal constructions do not occur randomly and in fact are often associated with certain verbs that describe conditions of the body, mental states (such as desire, belief, and the like), natural processes, etc., where the doer of the action of the verb is in some way "impersonal." Strangely, the *to be* verb can also appear as an impersonal. Since Modern English has such constructions, they should not be particularly difficult to translate.

*Hit rīnþ, **hit** ðunrað, **hit** liht, **hit** sniwð, **hit** hagelað, **hit** fryst.*
(It is raining; it is thundering; it is lightening; it is snowing; it is hailing; it is frosting.)

Hit is wyrse nū.
(It is worse now.)

*Ġif **hit** sīe willa þīn . . .*
(If it be your will/desire . . .)

*swā **hit** on bōcum cwiþ . . .*
(As it says in books . . .)

Hit ðyncð him wōh.
(It seems to him wrong.)

*Eal **hit** mē of-ðincð.*
(I regret it completely.) (lit., It is regretful to me.)

OE impersonal constructions can appear, however, without *hit* "it," and in fact such constructions seem to lack a subject at all. In these cases, you must supply the subject (an implied or understood "it") in your translation.

Hwīlum of heofnum hāte scīneð.
(Sometimes from heaven [it] shines hotly.)

Eaðe is tō understandenne.
([It] is easy to understand.)

Forþan ūs dafeneþ ðæt wē waċien symle.
(Therefore [it] is appropriate for us that we always stay awake [i.e., hold vigils].)

Ðonne him ðyncð ðæt hē ryhte lade funden hæbbe.
(Then [it] seems to him that he has found the right way.)

Eft ġe-lamp þæt hīe ā-fyrde eft fēond in firenum.
(Again [it] happened that the devil frightened them back into sin.)

Mē bet licað tō for-lǣtenne nū þisne hwīlwendlican wurðmynt.
([It] pleases me better to leave now this temporary honor.)

Some impersonals with missing *hit*'s are not so easy to translate literally since they are not idiomatic in Modern English. In fact, some of the most challenging forms combine an implied impersonal subject with a reflexive (§7.4). In such sentences, it is often advisable to translate the reflexive pronoun as the subject (after changing it into its nominative form).

*Ðonne **him** hingrað, hē yt grǣdilīċe.*
(When he is hungry, he eats ravenously [lit., when [it] hungers for him].)

*Ðonne **him** ðyrst, hē drincð.*
(When he is thirsty, he drinks [lit., when [it] thirsts for him].)

*Ðonne **him** cælð, hē cēpð him hlȳwðe.*
(When he is cold, he keeps himself in a covering [lit., when [it] is cold for him].)

Mē lyste slǣpan.
(I want to sleep [lit., [it] pleases me to sleep].)

[11] Note that *fæste* has a collapsed past tense ending: see §3.11.1.

[12] xxx = 300

[13] Think carefully about what information the *–að* ending gives you.

*Wē nabbað þone hlāf þe **ūs** lyste etan.*

(We do not have the bread which we want to eat [lit., which [it] pleases us to eat].)

Exercise 11.4: RECOGNIZING IMPERSONAL CONSTRUCTIONS

Instructions. *Translate the following sentences with the aid of the glossary following the exercise. One of the sentences is not a true impersonal. Please identify which one.*

1. Ac hit mē wyrse ġe-lomp.

2. Ēalā, ċīld, hū līcaþ ēow þēos spǣċ?

3. Hē ðā fæste[11] fēowertiġ daga and fēowertiġ nihta, ac syþðan him hingrode.

4. Mē þūhte ful oft þæt hit wǣre xxx[12] þūsend wintra tō þīnum dēað-dæġe.

5. Mē hingrode, and ġē mē ǣtes for-wyrndon; mē ðyrste, and ġē mē drincan ne sealdon.

6. For-ðȳ mē ðynċð betre, ġif ēow swā ðynċð, ðæt wē sume bēċ on Englisc wenden.

7. Langað[13] hine hearde, ðynceð him ðæt sīe xxx ðūsend wintra ǣr hē dōm-dæġes dyne ġe-hȳre.

8. He cuðe ānne mann, sē wolde drincan on lenctene þonne hine lyste.

9. Sum sāre on-ġeald æfen-ræste, swā him ful oft ġe-lamp.

10. Næs þæt herliċ dæd, þæt hine swelċes gamenes ġilpan lyste.

11. Ðonne of-ðyncð him ðæs ilcan¹⁴ þe hē ær for-bær.

12. Ġyf þē wæteres ġe-nēodiġe, þonne dō þū swylċe þū þīne handa þwēan wille.
    (An original sentence from reading VII.ii, describing monastic sign language.)

VOCABULARY FOR EXERCISE 11.4

ac (conjunction) = but

æfen-ræst (f) = EVENing REST [§2.8]

ǣr (conjunction) = before, ERE [§5.1.1]

ǣt (m or n) = EATables, food [§2.7, §2.9]

ān (adjective and pronoun) = a/an; ONE, a certain (person or thing) [§6.1, §7.8]

betre (comparative adjective) = BETTER [§6.4]

bōc (f) = BOOK (nom/acc pl: *bēċ*) [§10.4.2]

ċīld (n) = CHILD [§10.8]

cuðe = see *cunnan*

cunnan (preterite-present verb) = to know, be acquainted with; to know how (to do something) [§4.3]

ðā = (adverb) then; (conjunction) when [§6.9]

dæd (f) = DEED [§2.7]

dæġ (m) = DAY [§2.7]

dēað-dæġ (m) = DEATH-DAY [§2.7]

dōm-dæġ (m) = DOOMsDAY, the Last Judgment [§2.7]

dōn (irregular verb) = to DO; put, place; make [§4.5.3.1]

drincan (strong verb 3) = to DRINK [§8.6]

dyne (m) = DIN, noise [§10.2.1]

ēalā (interjection) = oh!, alas!; hey! (an interjection for getting the attention of an interlocutor or for expressing regret and sorrow)

Englisc (n) = the ENGLISH language [§10.11.1]

ēow = see *ġē*

fæstan (weak verb I) = to FAST, to abstain from food—usually for religious reasons (past sing: *fæste*) [§3.11]

fēowertiġ (number) = FORTY

for-beran (strong verb 4) = to tolerate, put up with, FORBEAR [§8.7]

for-ðȳ (adverb) = thereFORe [§6.9]

for-wyrnan (weak verb I) = to refuse, deny (+ acc of thing, + dat of person) [§3.11]

ful (adverb) = very, FULL [§6.9]

gamen (n) = sport, GAME [§2.9]

ġē (pronoun) = you (pl) [§7.1]

ġif (conjunction) = IF [§5.1.1]

ġilpan (strong verb 3) = to brag about, boast of (+ gen) [§8.6]

hē, hēo, hit (pronoun) = HE, she, IT [§7.1]

hand (f) = HAND [§10.6]

hearde (adverb) = HARD, severely, very much [§6.9]

herliċ (adjective) = splendid, noble [§6.1]

hingrian (weak verb II) = to HUNGER, be hungry (impersonal) [§3.11, §11.2]

hū (interrogative) = HOW

(ġe)hȳran (weak verb I) = to HEAR [§3.11]

ilca (adjective) = the same, the very (person or thing) [§6.1]

langian (weak verb II) = to LONG for, desire, yearn (impersonal with reflexive) [§3.12, §11.2]

lencten (m) = LENT, a season in the spring during which Christians are to fast and practice penance [§2.7]

līcian (weak verb II) = to please [ModE *LIKE*; §3.12]

ġe-limpan (strong verb 3) = to happen, take place [§8.6]

lystan (weak verb I) = to desire, be desirous (impersonal with reflexive) [§3.11]

mann (m) = MAN, person [§10.4.2]

mē = see *iċ* [§7.1]

næs = see *bēon*

ne (adverb) = not [§6.9]

(ġe)nēodian (weak verb II) = to be necessary; to need, require (impersonal + gen) [§3.11, §11.2]

niht (f) = NIGHT [§2.8]

of-ðyncan (weak verb I) = to be irritated or
vexed by something (impersonal; *by* =
gen) [§3.11, §11.2]

oft (adverb) = OFTen [§6.9]

on (preposition) = (+ acc) into; (+ dat) in,
on [§6.15]

on-ġieldan (strong verb 3) = to be
punished for, pay (the penalty) for
[§8.6]

sāre (adverb) = SOREly, grievously; painfully [§6.9]

se(a)llan (weak verb I) = to give [ModE
SELL; §3.11]

sīe = see *bēon*

spǣċ, sprǣċ (f) = SPEECH [§2.8]

sum (adjective) = (a) certain, SOME [§6.1]

swā = (adverb) SO, thus; (conjunction) as
[§6.9]

swelċ (adjective) = SUCH [§6.1]

swylċe (adverb) = such as, in a manner
similar to [§6.9]

syþðan (adverb) = afterwards [§6.9]

tō (preposition + dat) = TO, up to, until
[§6.15]

þæt (conjunction) = THAT [§5.1.1]

þe (relative pronoun) = who, which [§7.5]

þē = see §7.1

þēos = see *þis*

þīn (adjective) = THINE, your [§6.1]

þis, þēos, þis (demonstrative pronoun and
adjective) = THIS [§7.7]

þūhte = see *þyncan*

þūsend (n) = THOUSAND [§2.9]

þwēan (strong verb 6, contract verb) = to
wash, clean [§9.2, §11.1]

þyncan (weak verb I) = to seem, appear
[§3.11]

ðyrstan (weak verb I) = to be THIRSTy
(impersonal with reflex) [§3.11]

wǣre = *bēon*

wæter (n) = WATER [§2.9]

wendan (weak verb I) = to turn, translate
[§3.11]

willan (irregular verb) = to wish, want,
will [§4.5.3.2]

winter (m or n) = WINTER, year [§2.7,
§2.9]

wolde = see *willan*

wyrse = see *yfel*

yfel (adjective) = bad, EVIL (comparative:
wyrse) [§6.8]

Reading XI: THE HUMAN FETUS

The following excerpt comes from one of several Anglo-Saxon medical texts. For a discussion of medical lore in Anglo-Saxon England, see Stephanie Hollis's article "Scientific and Medical Writings" in A Companion to Anglo-Saxon Literature *(Eds. Phillip Pulsiano and Elaine Treharne. Oxford: Blackwell, 2001. pp. 188-208).*

Hēr on-ginð secgan ymbe mannes ġe-cynde hū hē on his mōdor innoþe tō men ġe-wyrðeð. Ǣrest þæs mannes bræġen bið ġe-worden on his mōder innoþe, þonne bið þæt bræġen ūtan mid rēoman bewefen on þǣre syxtan wucan. On ōðrum mōnþe þā ǣdran bēoð ġe-worden, on lxv ond þrēo hundred[15] scytran ond lengran hī bēoð tō-dǣlede ond

5 þæt blōd þonne flōweð on þā fēt ond uppan þā handa, ond hē þonne byþ on limum tō-dǣled ond tō-somne ġearwað. On þām þriddum mōnþe hē bið man būtan sāwle. On þām feorþan mōnþe hē bið on limum staþol-fæst. On þām fiftan mōnþe hē biþ cwica ond weaxeð, ond sēo modor līð witlēas ond þonne þā ribb bēoð ġe-worden, þonne ġe-limpð þǣr maniġ-feald sār þonne þæs byrþres līċ on hire innoþe scypiġende bið. On þām syxtan

10 mōnþe hē byþ ġe-hȳd ond bān bēoð weaxende. On þām seofoþan mōnþe þā tān ond þā fingras bēoð weaxende. On þām eahtoþan mōnþe him bēoð þā brēost-þing wexende ond heorte ond blōd ond hē bið eall staþol-fæstlīċe ġe-seted. On þām niġoþan mōnþe witodlīċe wīfum[16] bið cūð hwæþer hī cennan magon. On þām tēoþan mōnþe þæt wīf ne ġe-dīgð hyre feore ġif þæt bearn ā-cenned ne biþ, for þām þe hit in þām magan wyrð hire

15 tō feorh-ādle, oftost on Tīwes-niht.

VOCABULARY FOR READING XI

ā-cennan (weak verb I) = to bring forth, give birth to [§3.11]

ǣdre (weak f) = vein, artery [§3.4]

ǣrest (adverb) = first [§6.9]

bān (n) = BONE [§2.9]

bearn (n) = child, offspring; son [§2.9]

bēon (irregular verb) = to BE [§4.5.1]

be-wefan (strong verb 6) = to cover over [§9.3]

bið = see *bēon*

blōd (n) = BLOOD [§2.9]

bræġen (n) = BRAIN [§2.9]

brēost-þing (n) = area around the chest and heart, BREAST [§2.9]

būtan (preposition + dat) = without, lacking [§6.15]

byrþor (n) = what is BORn, the fetus, a child; the act of child birth [§2.9]

byþ = see *bēon*

cennan (weak verb I) = to give birth, bring forth [§3.11]

cūð (adjective) = known, revealed, apparent [§6.1]

cwic (adjective) = alive [see ModE *the QUICK and the dead*, §6.1]

(ġe)cynd (f or n) = birth, origin [§2.8/9]

(ġe)dīgan (weak verb I) = to survive, endure [§3.11]

eahtoþa (adjective) = EIGHTH [§6.1]

eall (adverb) = completely, ALL [§6.9]

feorh (m or n) = life [§2.7, §2.9]

feorh-ādl (f) = fatal disease; (lit.,) life-sickness [§2.8]

feorþa (adjective) = FOURTH [§6.1]

fīfta (adjective) = FIFTH [§6.1]

finger (m) = FINGER [§2.7]

flōwan (strong verb 7) = to FLOW, run [§9.3]

for þām þe = (adverb) therefore, for that reason [§6.9]; (conjunction) because [§5.1.1]

fōt (m) = FOOT [§10.4.2]

ġearwian (weak verb II) = to equip, prepare, construct, make ready [§3.11]

ġif (conjunction) = IF [§5.1.1]

hand (f) = HAND [§10.6]

heorte (f) = HEART [§2.8]

hēr (adverb) = HERE [§6.9]

hī = see *hē, hēo, hit*

hū (conjunction) = HOW [§5.1.1]

hundred (number) = HUNDRED

hwæþer (conjunction) = WHETHER [§5.1.1]

ġe-hȳdan (weak verb I) = to furnish with skin or HIDE [§3.11]

innoþe (m) = womb, INsides [§2.7]

lang (adjective) = LONG (comp: *lengra*) [§6.7]

lengran = see *lang*

līċ (n) = body, corpse [see German *Leiche* "corpse"; §2.9]

līcgan (strong verb 5) = to LIE, lie down, recline; lie prostrate [§9.1]

limpan (strong verb 3) = to happen, occur, exist [§8.6]

lim (n) = LIMB, member [§2.9]

maga (weak m) = stomach, womb [see German *Magen* "stomach" §3.3]

magan (preterite-present verb) = to be allowed, be able [§4.4]

maniġ-feald (adjective) = numerous,

MANIFOLD [§6.1]

mann (m) = man, human being (*men* = dat sing) [§10.4.2]

mid (preposition + dat) = with [§6.15]

mōdor (f) = MOTHER [§10.5]

mōnaþ (m) = MONTH [§2.7]

ne (adverb) = not [§6.9]

nigoþa (adjective) = NINTH [6.1]

ōðer (adjective) = OTHER; second [§6.1]

oft (adverb) = OFTen (superl = *oftost*) [§6.9]

on (preposition) = (+ dat) in; (+ acc) into [§6.15]

on-ġinnan (strong verb 3) = to beGIN, start (impersonal) [§8.6, §11.2]

rēama (weak m) = membrane, ligament [§3.3]

ribb (n) = RIB [§2.9]

sār (n) = pain, SOREness; SORRow, distress [§2.9]

sāwol (f) = SOUL, spirit [§2.8]

scort (adjective) = SHORT (comp: *scytra*) [§6.4]

scypian (strong verb 6) = to take SHAPE, form [§9.2]

scytran = see *scort*

secgan (weak verb III) = to SAY, tell, relate, describe [§4.1]

seofoþa (adjective) = SEVENTH [§6.1]

(ġe)settan (weak verb I) = to SET, establish; create, make [§3.11]

staþol-fæst (adjective) = steadFAST, firm, fixed [§6.1]

staþol-fæstlīċe (adverb) = firmly, securely [§6.9]

syxta (adjective) = SIXTH [§6.1]

tā (weak f) = TOE (pl: *tān*) [§3.4, but see Campbell §619.3]

tēoþa (adjective) = TENTH [§6.1]

Tīwes-niht (f) = Monday NIGHT, the night before TUESday [§2.8]

tō (adverb, intensifier) = TOO, excessively [§6.9]

tō (preposition + dat) = TO, into; as [§6.15]

tō-dǣlan (weak verb I) = to separate [§3.11]

tō-somne (adverb) = together [§6.9]

þǣr (adverb) = THERE [§6.9]

þonne = (adverb) then [§6.9]; (conjunction) when [§5.1.1]

þrēo (number) = THREE

þridda (adjective) = THIRD [§6.4]

uppan (preposition ı acc) = UP, up to [§6.15]

ūtan (adverb) = on the OUTside [§6.9]

weaxan (strong verb 7) = to grow; see ModE phrase *to wax and wane* [§9.3]

(ġe)weorðan (strong verb 3) = to become, develop, come into being; to be [§8.6]

wīf (n) = woman [§2.9]

witleas (adjective) = WITLESS, mad, insane; unconscious? [§6.1]

witodlīċe (adverb) = certainly [§6.9]

(ġe)worden = see *(ġe)weorðan*

wuca (weak f) = WEEK [§3.4]

ymbe (preposition + dat) = about, concerning [§6.15]

Lessons Learned

Before leaving this chapter you should . . .
- be able to recognize and look up the contract verb forms (§11.1).
- be able to translate impersonal constructions (§11.2).

APPENDIX ONE

A Basic Introduction
to Traditional Grammar

Introduction

This appendix will outline briefly the basic grammatical concepts of the English language, particularly those concepts (and their terminology) that we refer to as we explain how Old English works. It should be noted at the outset of this appendix that the grammar which it describes is not a linguistically technical grammar; it is not designed to analyze in depth the system or rules by which a speaker communicates. Rather, it is what is generally called a "school" grammar or a "traditional" grammar, "traditional" in that it follows a grammatical system ancient in its origins which is used to explain more recent, often contemporary languages. When Ælfric wrote his *Latin Grammar* (circa 1000), for example, he based his approach on that of his Latin forebears, Priscian and Donatus, oftentimes translating their Latin into his Old English. When students read the sidebars from Ælfric's *Grammar* in this text, they can enter into that venerable tradition. They will recognize many of the definitions which Ælfric offered his students as identical to those that they remember from their own "school" grammars. In this regard, our students are not too distant from Ælfric's. Like his students who were asked to learn something of their own grammar that they might learn how to read Latin, our students are asked to understand the basic principles of their own grammar that they may understand how to read Old English.

1.1 The Sentence

A sentence is traditionally defined as containing two components: (1) it includes a *subject* and a *predicate*, and (2) it makes a complete statement. In the following examples, the first group of words is a sentence; the second group is not.

1. The scop sings.
2. as the scop sings

1. He slays the monster.
2. because he slays the monster

1. The bold warrior has been standing quietly at the door.
2. the bold warrior standing quietly at the door

1. The hero's faithful thane discovered the dragon's treasure.
2. discovered the dragon's treasure

Despite the signals that we have added to all the word groups that are sentences—they begin with a capital and they end with a period—we can recognize each word group, almost intuitively, as being complete. In the same way, we recognize all the incomplete word groups as leaving out a crucial bit of information. In each instance, the phrase of words in (2) does not finish what it starts out to say. We will begin our discussion by defining *subject* and *predicate*; in the next section (§2) we will discuss how the subject and predicate function to make a complete grammatical statement.

THE SUBJECT   1.2

The subject is what the rest of the sentence is talking about. We can describe the subject in two ways: first, as the **simple subject**, that is, the main **noun** or **pronoun**, without its modifiers: (*scop, He, warrior, thane*); second, as the **complete subject**, that is, the main noun or pronoun and all its modifiers (*the scop, He, the bold warrior, the hero's faithful thane.*) In the last example, the article *the* modifies the noun *thane*, as does the possessive noun *hero's* and the adjective *faithful*. (More about parts of speech and modifiers at §3.)

If the sentence has two or more simple subjects of the same verb, the subjects are said to be **compound**.

> Beowulf and Wiglaf gazed on the treasure. [*Beowulf* and *Wiglaf* are compound subjects of the verb *gazed*.]

The Danish king and the Geatish hero discuss Grendel's bloody feud. [*King* and *hero* are compound subjects of the verb *discuss*.]

1.3   THE PREDICATE

The predicate is the part of the sentence that makes a statement about the subject. The predicate includes a verb as its main word. In the sentences at the outset of this section, the predicates are: *sings, slays the monster, has been standing quietly at the door, discovered the dragon's treasure.* Like the subject, the predicate can be described in two ways, as a **simple predicate** and as a **complete predicate**. A **simple predicate** is the verb (or verb phrase) which is the main element of the predicate: in the above sentences, *sings, slays, discovered,* and *has been standing* are the simple predicates. Note that *has been standing* is a **verb phrase**. A verb phrase is made up of the main verb and its auxiliary or helping verb or verbs. In the above sentence, *standing* is the main verb and *has* and *been* are the auxiliary verbs. The main verb carries the lexical information about the verb; the auxiliary verb gives information about things like number and tense.

The **complete predicate** is the verb plus all of its modifiers and complements. In the predicate *has been standing quietly at the door,* the adverb *quietly* modifies the verb phrase; the prepositional phrase *at the door* also modifies the verb phrase. (More on prepositional phrases and modifiers at §4.) In the predicate *discovered the dragon's treasure,* the noun *treasure* functions as the direct object of the verb *discovered* (and therefore *completes* the action of the verb); the article *the* and the possessive noun *dragon's* modify *treasure*.

Finally, like the subject, the predicate can be **compound**; that is, the predicate can have two or more verbs that are governed by the same subject.

The Viking taunted the Saxons and brandished his spear.
[*Taunted* and *brandished* are governed by the subject *Viking*.]

Sentence Types and Complements 2

The following sentence types represent the basic forms that we use to create sentences in Modern English (ModE). Although some of these patterns are different from those we'll find in Old English, those very differences will help us to understand how Old English sentences are put together. As we will find out, however, the complements themselves are virtually identical to those we will find in Old English (OE).

SENTENCE TYPE #1: Subject + Intransitive Verb 2.1

> The scop sings.
> Grendel was growling.
> The warriors trembled.

Type 1 sentences are the most basic of sentence structures mainly because the verb does not need a *complement* to finish its meaning. In §1 we defined a complete predicate as constituting a verb plus its modifiers and complements. In the case of Type 1 sentences, the verb may take modifiers, but it does not take a complement; that is to say, the verb's action is complete in itself and does not pass on to another word that completes its meaning. Compare, for example, these two sentences:

(A) The warriors trembled.
(B) The warriors crushed the monster.

In (A) the action of the verb does not pass on to a complement; the meaning of the sentence is finished with the verb. In (B) the action of the verb does pass over to a complement (*monster*). The difference between these two verbs, in part, is that one (A) is *intransitive* and the other (B) is *transitive*. The definition of an *intransitive* verb, then, is simply a verb whose action does not "pass over" to a complement.

2.2   SENTENCE TYPE #2: Subject + Transitive Verb + Direct Object

> The warrior carried his spear.
> The Vikings tested the hero's strength.
> Every good queen seeks wisdom.

In each of these examples, the verb's action is ***transitive***; that is, it "passes over" to a complement, in this case a **direct object** (*spear, strength,* and *wisdom*). Finding the direct object is simple: first, find the simple **subject** (it answers "who?" or "what?" did the action of the verb), then find the **verb**, then the **direct object** (it answers "whom?" or "what?" received the action of the verb). Therefore, *warrior* + *carried* what? whom? = *spear*. Note: When we look for the subject, verb, and direct object in a sentence, we look for the simple form, that is, the form without its modifiers. Therefore, in the second example: *Vikings* + *tested* what? whom? = *strength*. In the third, *queen* + *seeks* what? whom? = *wisdom*.

2.3   SENTENCE TYPE #3: Subject + Linking Verb + Subject Complement

> Grendel is a monster. [The noun *monster* is the subject complement.]

> Grendel is he. [The pronoun *he* is the subject complement.]

> Grendel was fierce. [The adjective *fierce* is the subject complement.]

In Type 3 sentences, the subject complement, as its name suggests, completes the predicate's statement about the subject. In the first example, the subject *Grendel* is linked to the **subject complement** *monster* by the linking verb *is*. Since the linking verb *is* means something like "equals," we could say that the sentence reads *Grendel* "equals" *monster*. Or, we could describe the function of the subject complement in another way: as a noun the complement *monster* **renames** the subject.

In the second example, the subject complement is the pronoun *he* and functions like the noun subject complement. In the third example, the subject *Grendel* is linked to the subject complement *fierce*. In this instance, the subject complement is an adjective and therefore its function is not to "rename" but to modify, that is, to describe the subject.

The most commonly used linking verbs are the *be* verbs: **be, is, am, are, was, were,** and **been**. Other less common verbs are those that are connected to the senses: **appear, become, feel, look, seem, smell, sound, taste.**

The thane becomes a coward. [The noun *coward* is the subject complement.]

The cake smells delicious. [The adjective *delicious* is the subject complement.]
Full of beer, Unferth seemed addled. [The adjective *addled* is the subject complement.]

ONE CAVEAT: These less common verbs of senses can operate in several different ways in a sentence. They can function as intransitive verbs, transitive verbs, or linking verbs. Note the following examples:

After the accident, the thane could barely taste. [The verb *taste* is intransitive.]

The young child tasted the cake greedily. [The verb *tasted* is transitive, followed by the direct object *cake*.]

The cake tasted delicious. [The verb *tasted* is a linking verb, followed by the subject complement *delicious*.]

SENTENCE TYPE #4: Subject + Transitive Verb + Indirect Object + Direct Object   **2.4**

Wealhtheow offered the thane a jeweled cup.

The subject of the sentence is *Wealhtheow*; the verb is *offered*. The verb is followed by two nouns—both complements, one an **indirect object** and one a **direct object**. As pointed out in Type 3, we can discover the direct object by asking the question *Wealhtheow offered* whom? or what? The direct object is *cup* since it receives the action of the verb *offered*. We know too that the sentence describes "to whom" or "for whom" that action was performed, the indirect object *thane*. We know that information "indirectly" because the sentence identifies that person without using the preposition "to" or "for" to indicate "to whom" or "for whom" (or "to what" or "for what") the action of the verb was directed.

Note, for example, what happens if we rephrase our example sentence to use the preposition *to*:

The battle-weary warrior gave the sword to his kinsman.

In this case, *kinsman* becomes the object of the preposition *to* and does not function as an indirect object. It is a part of a prepositional phrase that serves as an adverb, modifying the verb (more on phrases at §4).

An indirect object can be a noun or pronoun.

The battle-weary warrior gave his kinsman the sword. [The noun *kinsman* is the indirect object; *sword* is the direct object.]

The battle-weary warrior gave him the sword. [The pronoun *him* is the indirect object.]

In Modern English [but not Old English] the indirect object usually appears between the verb and the direct object. In OE the position of the indirect object in the sentence is not so crucial since the complement takes the dative case ending, and that suffix identifies the indirect object.

SENTENCE TYPE #5: Subject + Passive Verb   **2.5**

The sleeping warrior was eaten by Grendel.

The subject is *warrior*; the verb is the verb phrase *was eaten*. The meaning of the sentence is complete with the verb; put another way, the verb does not require a complement to complete the meaning of the sentence. In its basic structure, then, Type 5 sentences look very much like those of Type 1: both have a subject and a verb only; neither require a complement to finish the meaning of the sentence. But the two patterns differ in a crucial way: Type 1 sentences use an *intransitive* verb; Type 5, like Type 2 sentences, uses a *transitive verb*.

We defined a transitive verb as one whose action "passes over" to a complement (more specifically, a direct object). In the case of the Type 5 sentence the action of the verb "passes over" to the subject: in the example sentence, it is the subject *warrior* that receives the action of the verb *was eaten*. In this sentence the actual (that is to say, the narrative agent of the action—*Grendel*) is, in grammatical terms, the object of the preposition. If we were to turn the sentence around and change the "actual" subject into the grammatical subject, the sentence would look like this:

Grendel ate the sleeping warrior.

Now the sentence has a Type 2 structure: *Grendel* is the subject; *ate* is the verb; and *warrior* is the direct object.

When we speak of a verb as a passive verb, we are describing its property of *voice*. A verb has one of two voices: *active* or *passive*. In a passive verb sentence, the subject receives the action of the verb. In an *active* verb sentence, the subject performs the action of the verb.

> The monster drank the blood from the warrior's veins. [*Drank* is an active verb; the subject *monster* performs the action.]

> The blood was drunk from the warrior's veins by the monster. [*Was drunk* is a passive verb; the subject *blood* receives the action of the verb.]

Therefore, a passive verb sentence has the following characteristics:

(1) The subject of the sentence receives the action of the verb.

(2) The verb is a verb phrase made up of a "be" verb—*be, is, am, are, was, were, been*—plus a past participle (the verb form that appears after the helping verb *have, has,* or *had*: for example, *has rung, has written, has skipped*; in those phrases, *rung, written,* and *skipped* are past participles).

(3) On occasion, a passive verb sentence will include the "actual" subject of the verb, and when it does, the subject appears in a prepositional phrase. In the sample passive verb sentence above (*The blood was drunk from the warrior's veins by the monster*), the "actual" subject of the sentence, that is, the agent who did the "actual" drinking, is the *monster*. But in grammatical terms, the *monster* is the object of a prepositional phrase (*by the monster*). The grammatical subject of the sentence is *blood*.

3 Parts of Speech

3.1 NOUN

A word that names a person, place, thing, or idea.

- **Person:** *mother, child, athlete, president, poet*

- **Place:** *campus, home, stadium, city, theater*
- **Thing:** *coffee, elephant, book, department, mountain*
- **Idea:** *charity, knowledge, illusion, loyalty*

A noun is classified as either a ***common*** or ***proper*** noun. ***Common*** nouns refer to general types or categories. ***Proper*** nouns refer to a particular person, place, or thing.

	Common Nouns	Proper Nouns
Person:	king	Hrothgar
	hero	Beowulf
Place:	country	England
	city	New York
Thing:	poem	"To Autumn"
	dog	Lassie

PRONOUN   3.2

A word that is used in place of a noun. Pronouns can be classified as follows:

- **Personal:** *I, you, he, she, it, we, they, me, him, her, us, them, my, mine, our, ours, your, yours, his, her, hers, its, their, theirs*

The personal pronouns in ModE, much like those of OE, take case forms, depending upon their number and how they are used in a sentence. The nominative case forms are used for pronouns that function as a subject or a subject complement. The accusative case forms are used for pronouns that function as a direct object, an indirect object, or an object of a preposition. Note: In OE the indirect object takes the dative case and the object of the preposition can take dative, accusative, or genitive depending on the preposition; In ModE all these endings collapse into a simplified accusative [objective] form. The genitive case forms are used to modify nouns, in particular to show possession.

	First Person	Second Person	Third Person
Nominative Singular	I	you	he, she, it
Plural	we	you	they
Accusative Singular	me	you	him, her, it
Plural	us	you	them
Genitive Singular	my, mine	your, yours	his, her, hers, its
Plural	our, ours	your, yours	their, theirs

• **Reflexive/Intensive:** *myself, yourself, himself, herself, itself, oneself, themselves, ourselves, yourselves*

Reflexive pronouns are used as direct objects, indirect objects, and objects of a preposition. They are used only when the subject of the sentence is the antecedent of the pronoun. Example: *The Vikings prided* **themselves** *in their nautical skills.*

Intensive pronouns, in form the same as reflexive pronouns, are used to emphasize a noun. In its grammatical function, the intensive pronoun serves as an appositive, that is, it renames the noun it emphasizes. Example: *Beowulf* **himself** *saw the strange sea beasts in the mere.*

In OE there are no separate forms for the reflexive/intensive pronouns. The personal pronoun forms are used to indicate the reflexive and intensive.

• **Demonstrative:** *this, that, these, those*

Demonstrative pronouns function in both ModE and OE either as pronouns or as adjectives (in OE as a definite article), depending on how they function in the sentence. Example: *That wise prince rode a magnificent horse.* [The demonstrative modifies the noun *prince;* therefore, it would be classified as a demonstrative adjective.] Example: *That was a wise prince.* [The demonstrative takes the place of the noun *prince* and therefore would be classified as a pronoun.]

- **Interrogative:** *who, whose, whom, which, what, whoever, whomever, whichever, whatever*

These pronouns function in two ways: first, they introduce either a direct question (the sentence ends with a question mark) or an indirect question (the sentence does not end with a question mark); second, they function within the sentence usually as a *substantive* (subject, direct object, object of a preposition, etc.) or as a modifier. Examples:

> **Who** *killed those sea monsters from the deep?* [The interrogative *Who* introduces a direct question and functions as the subject of the sentence.]

> *Beowulf asked* **who** *killed the sea monster.* [The interrogative pronoun introduces an indirect question and serves as the subject of the verb *killed.*]

> **Whose** *sword was named Hrunting?* [The interrogative pronoun *Whose* is the genitive form of *who;* the pronoun functions as a possessive modifier of the noun *sword.* (Some grammarians would classify *whose* in this instance as an interrogative adjective—since it modifies a noun.)]

For our purposes, however, *whose* functions as an interrogative pronoun, its genitive form expressing the possessive (see OE *hwǣs*).

- **Indefinite:** *any, anyone, anybody, anything, some, someone, somebody, something, one, none, no one, nobody, each, several, all, both, neither, either, everyone, everybody, everything*

  As their name suggests, these pronouns do not refer to a specific person, place, thing, or idea.

- **Relative Pronouns:** *who, whom, whose, which, that, where, what, whoever, whomever*

  Because relative pronouns introduce dependent clauses and function as a substantive within those clauses, we will delay discussion of the relative pronoun until we take up dependent clauses at §5.

3.3   VERB

A word or group of words that indicates action or state of being (see §2.3 for "state of being," i.e., linking verbs). Verbs are usually discussed in terms of the following characteristics:

- **Voice:** A verb will be either active or passive (see §2.5).
- **Person:** A verb indicates who is speaking: the first person (*I, we*), the second person (*you*), the third person (*he, she, it, they*).
- **Number:** A verb indicates whether the speaker is singular (*I, you, he, she, it*) or plural (*we, you, they*).
- **Tense:** A verb indicates the time of the action described—present, past, future. See example paradigms below.
- **Aspect:** A verb indicates the duration of the action described. There are two aspects in ModE: *progressive* and *perfect*.

Progressive: The verb indicates that the action it describes is in progress. Example: *The edge of the sword **is gleaming** in the sunlight.* The progressive aspect is formed by the auxiliary verb *be* plus the present participle (verb plus the *-ing* suffix).

Notice that the progressive aspect may indicate different tenses. The verb in the example sentence is **present progressive** (the action continues in the present). **Past Progressive:** *The edge of the sword **was gleaming** in the sunlight.* (The action continues sometime in the past.) **Future progressive:** *The edge of the sword **will be gleaming** in the sunlight.* (The action continues sometime in the future.)

Perfect: The verb indicates that the action started in the past. Example: *The warrior **has tested** his courage against fierce competitors.* The perfect aspect is formed by the auxiliary verb *has*, *have*, or *had* plus the past participle. The verb in the example sentence is in the ***present perfect tense***. (That is, the action began in the past and continues into the present.) **Past perfect:** *The warrior **had tested** his courage against fierce competitors.* (The action began sometime in the past and it was concluded at a later time in the past.) **Future perfect:** *The warrior **will have tested** his courage against fierce competitors.* (The action began in the past and will be completed at some future time.)

- **Mood:** Indicates the manner of the verb, that is, whether the verb is ***indicative***, ***imperative***, or ***subjunctive***.

Indicative: The verb states a fact or asks a question. Example: *The monster grabbed the hero in her terrible claws.*

Imperative: The verb states a command or makes a request. Example: *Bring me my armor.* The subject of the verb, *you*, is understood. The imperative mood verb almost always uses the second person pronoun, and generally that pronoun is omitted.

Subjunctive: The verb expresses an idea contrary to fact or a desire or a requirement. See §3.10.1 for an explanation and examples.

- **Principal Parts:** All forms of a verb can be generated from the principal parts. In ModE there are three principal parts: the present (infinitive form), the past (first person, singular), and the past participle (the verb form that follows *have, has, had*). Example: *walk, walked, have walked.* In this case *walk* is a **weak** verb, that is, it forms its past tense and past participle by adding *-d* or *-ed* to the present. See §3.1, §3.7, and §8.1. A strong verb forms its principal parts by changing the internal vowel of the present verb. Example: *sing, sang, have sung.*

- Note: OE verbs use the same principal parts as ModE; the only difference is that OE strong verbs add a fourth part—the past plural. Therefore, the OE strong verb has the following principal parts: present (infinitive form), past (first person singular), past plural, and past participle.

3.4   ADJECTIVE

A word that modifies a noun. The adjective answers the questions:

What ones?: *this warrior, that hero, these Vikings, those warriors* (in these cases the adjectives are demonstratives); *most warriors, many heroes, much joy, several battles, some swords* (in these cases the adjectives are indefinite adjectives)

How many?: *one* monster, *two* swords, *first* battle, *second* warrior.

What kind of thing?: *bright* sword, *angry* champion, *strongest* man, *shining* light (the adjectives are descriptive)

ADVERB   3.5
A word that modifies a verb, adjective, or another adverb. The adverb answers the questions:

How?: The monster toppled *quickly* to the ground. [modifies the verb *toppled*]
The elders spoke *quietly* about the hero. [modifies the verb *spoke*]

When?: The thanes *immediately* saw the churning water. [modifies the verb *saw*]
They left the battle *soon.* [modifies the verb *left*]
The warriors will return *tomorrow.* [modifies the verb *will return*]

Where?: Several of the brave warriors found their leader *inside.* [modifies the verb *found*]
The monster drew *near.* [modifies the verb *drew*]

To What Degree?: They left the battle *too* soon. [modifies the adverb *soon*]
The elders spoke *very* quietly about the hero. [modifies the adverb *quietly*]
The brave warriors gazed upon the *gruesomely* bloody waters. [modifies the adjective *bloody* which modifies the noun *waters*]

PREPOSITION   3.6
A word or group of words that shows the relationship between its object and another word in the sentence. Example:

The warriors dragged Grendel's head to the hall.

The preposition *to* functions in two ways. First, it introduces a phrase of words (*to the hall*) called a ***prepositional phrase***. The phrase begins with a preposition and ends with a noun or pronoun (*hall*) that functions as the object of the preposition. (Note: The term preposition itself indicates something about its position in the phrase—it occupies the pre-position.) Second, the preposition shows the relationship between its object *hall* and another word in the sentence. Note that the phrase answers the adverbial question ***where***? That is, the *warriors dragged the head* where? The prepositional phrase functions as an adverb, modifying the verb *dragged*.

The gold hilt was the work of giants.

In this sentence, the preposition is *of*; the prepositional phrase is *of giants*. The prepositional phrase functions as an adjective, modifying the noun *work*. To put it another way, the prepositional phrase answers the adjectival question ***which?*** Which *work*? (The work) *of giants*.

Common Prepositions:

above	according to	after
around	at	behind
below	beneath	beside
by	down	for
in	in spite of	into
of	on	out of
over	through	to
under	upon	with

CONJUNCTION

A word or group of words that connects words, phrases, or clauses. The types of conjunctions:

- **Coordinating Conjunction:** Joins words, phrases, and clauses of equivalent use in the sentence; the common coordinating conjunctions are *and, but, or, nor, for, so, yet.*

  a bright but ancient sword [*but* joins *bright* and *ancient,* adjectives that modify the subject *sword*]

  the old work of giants and ancient smithies [*and* joins *giants* and *smithies,* nouns that function as the objects of the preposition *of*]

  Hrothgar or Beowulf will face the monster. [*or* joins *Hrothgar* and *Beowulf,* nouns that function as the subject of the verb *will face*]

  Beowulf did not use the sword Hrunting, for God sent him another in Grendel's den. [*for* joins two independent clauses]

- **Subordinate Conjunction:** Joins a subordinate clause to an independent clause. As the definition suggests, our understanding of the subordinate conjunction depends necessarily on our understanding of how subordinate and independent clauses work. Therefore, the present treatment will be abbreviated, and we urge the reader to look at §4 for a fuller treatment.

- **Common subordinate conjunctions** simply join the subordinate clause to the main clause. Examples:

after	if	until
although	since	when
as	that	where
because	though	whether
before	unless	while

As Hrothgar spoke, he examined the hilt of the sword. [The subordinate conjunction *As* introduces the subordinate clause *As Hrothgar spoke*. The conjunction also links the subordinate clause to the main clause of the sentence (*he examined the hilt of the sword*), the conjunction signaling an adverbial connection (*As* indicates a time relationship) to the action of the main clause.]

Although God had granted King Heremod great strength, the king turned blood-thirsty. [The subordinate conjunction *Although* introduces the subordinate clause *Although God had granted King Heremod great strength* and links the subordinate clause to the main clause (*although* indicates the adverbial idea of "with what reservations?").]

- **Functional subordinate conjunctions** (including *relative pronouns*, *adjectives*, and *adverbs* [see §4] not only link a subordinate clause to the main clause, but they also perform a grammatical function within the subordinate clause. Examples:

who	whoever	what
which	whomever	when
whosoever	whatsoever	where
whose	whatever	why
that	whichever	how

Heremod was a king *who did not reward his warriors with rings.* [The relative pronoun *who* links the subordinate clause *who did not reward his warriors with rings* to its antecedent *king,* which the clause modifies. The relative pronoun also functions within the subordinate clause as the subject of the verb *did reward.*]

The king's son was honored in those battles *where he showed his courage.* [The relative adverb *where* links the subordinate clause *where he showed his courage* to its antecedent *battles,* which the clause modifies. The relative adverb *where* also functions as an adverb within the subordinate clause as a modifier of the verb *showed.*]

- **Correlative Conjunction:** Coordinating conjunctions used in pairs to link words, phrases, and clauses of equivalent use in a sentence. Examples: *both . . . and*; *either . . . or*; *neither . . . nor*; *not only . . . but also.*

The good king is both generous and wise. [The correlative conjunctions connect the adjectives *generous* and *wise*, which function as subjective complements of the linking verb *is.*]

The warrior carried either a sword or a spear into the fray. [The correlative conjunctions connect the nouns *sword* and *spear* which function as the direct objects of the verb *carried.* Several correlative conjunctions are used mainly to connect a subordinate clause to a main clause. Examples: *although . . . still*; *as . . . as*; *if . . . then*; *so . . . as*; *so . . . that*; *the . . .the*; *when . . . then*; *where . . . there.*]

When the company quieted down, then the scop began his song. [*When* is the subordinate conjunction that introduces the subordinate clause and links that clause to the main clause *then the scop began his song,* the subordinate clause modifying the verb *began* in the main clause. The second part of the conjunction *then* also functions as an adverb that modifies the verb *began* in the main clause. Some grammarians would add that *when* is a relative adverb and therefore modifies the verb *quieted* in the subordinate clause.]

The harder Beowulf grappled with the monster, the faster the hero's strength ebbed. [The two *the* correlatives are in fact correlative adverbs and a modern descendant of the Old English instrumental *þȳ* of the demonstrative pronoun *þæt.* In comparisons like the ones above, the OE sense of the instrumental *þȳ* would have been something like "by that much" in the first case, and "by that much" in the second. Therefore, in the sentence above, the first phrase could be reworded: *When by that much harder Beowulf grappled with the monster then by that much faster did the hero's strength ebb.*]

3.8   INTERJECTION

A word or group of words used to express strong emotion. Examples: Wow! Goodness! Alas! Oh no! How awful!

4   Clauses

By definition a clause is a group of words that has a subject and a verb. If the clause makes a complete idea, it is called an ***independent clause.*** If the clause does not make a complete idea, it is called a ***dependent clause*** (or ***subordinate clause***); that is, it depends on an independent clause to complete its idea.

Therefore, a group of words like *when he gave the queen a golden necklace* is a dependent clause: it has a subject and a verb, which makes it a clause, but it cannot stand alone; rather, it depends on an independent clause to make full sense. Therefore, if we link *when he gave the queen a golden necklace* to an independent clause, such as *he bowed before her throne*, we have a complete sentence. All we have to do is dress it up a bit with a capital at the beginning and a period at the end: *When he gave the queen a golden necklace, he bowed before her throne.*

In the following examples, the dependent clause is in boldface; the independent clause (or ***main clause*** of the sentence) is in italics.

Because Beowulf seemed slack in his youth, *he received little honor from the court.*

Beowulf became king **when Hygelac died.**

In both instances, the main clause can stand alone as a sentence. The dependent clause, however, depends on the main clause to complete the idea that it begins. The dependent clause also reflects a particular kind of relationship to the main clause; in the first sentence, the dependent clause answers the adverbial question "why?" That question speaks to the idea that the main clause expresses, that is, *he received little honor from the court* "why?" **Because Beowulf seemed slack in his youth.** In the second sentence, the subordinate clause answers the adverbial question "when?" which speaks to the idea that the main clause expresses, that is, *Beowulf became king* "when?" **When Hygelac died.** In short, both of the subordinate clauses function as adverbs; both modify the verb in the main clause.

There are three types of subordinate clauses—***adverb***, ***adjective***, and ***noun***—each functioning as a single part of speech.

ADVERB CLAUSES

Like single-word adverbs, adverb clauses modify verbs, adjectives, and adverbs. Like single-word adverbs, the clauses also answer distinctive questions: How? When? Where? Why? To what extent? Under what conditions? The ***subordinate conjunctions*** that introduce

4.1

the adverb clauses express what question and therefore what relationship the adverb clause has to the clause that it modifies. The most common subordinate conjunctions are listed with each question.

How? *as, as if, as though*

The hero entered the dragon's lair **as if** *he were fearless*. [In most instances, the adverb clause modifies the verb of the main clause, in this case *entered*.]

When? *after, before, since, until, when, while*

When *the thief seized into the dragon's lair*, terror seized him. [The adverb clause modifies the verb *looked*.]

Where? *where, wherever*

The thief cautiously stepped **wherever** *he would not disturb the sleeping dragon*. [The adverb clause modifies the verb *stepped*.]

Why? *as, because, in that, in order that, since, so that*

The dragon sought revenge **because** *someone had disturbed his treasured hoard*. [The adverb clause modifies the verb *sought*.]

To What Extent? *as . . . as; so . . . as; than*

The dragon's flames destroyed the land **as** far **as** *the hero could see*. [The subordinate conjunctions in this case are the correlative adverbs **as . . . as**.

The first *as* functions within the main clause, modifying the adverb *far*. The second *as* modifies the first *as*, that is, as an adverb modifying another adverb. The second *as* also links the adverb clause to the main clause.]

ADJECTIVE CLAUSES   4.2

Adjective clauses are introduced by relative pronouns (*who, whom, whose, which, that*) or a relative adverb (*when, where, why*). Like adverb clauses, an adjective clause functions like a single-word modifier; it modifies either a noun or pronoun. In the following examples, the adjective clause is in italics; the relative pronoun is in boldfaced italics.

Beowulf was a brave king ***who*** *planned revenge against the dragon*.
[The adjective clause ***who*** *planned revenge against the dragon* modifies the noun *king*. The adjective clause is introduced by the relative pronoun ***who*** which relates (as its name suggests) to the noun or pronoun in the main clause that the adjective clause modifies. In this case, ***who*** relates back to the noun *king*, the ***antecedent***, which, as its name suggests, "goes before" the relative pronoun. Finally, the relative pronoun ***who*** functions within the adjective clause as the subject of the verb *planned*. Note: The relative pronoun takes the nominative form of the pronoun since it functions as a subject. If the pronoun had functioned as a direct object, it would have used the accusative form *whom*. If you have difficulty deciding what is the function of the relative pronoun in the adjective clause, substitute the relative with its antecedent: the clause would read *the king planned revenge against the dragon*.]

A king ***whose*** *wisdom grows with age* never suffers from arrogance or avarice.
[The adjective clause modifies the noun *king*, the antecedent of the relative pronoun

whose. In turn, *whose* functions in the adjective clause as the possessive modifier of the noun *wisdom.* Again, if you have difficulty deciding how the relative pronoun functions within the clause, replace it with its antecedent: *a king's wisdom grows with age.*]

The dragon's flames destroyed Beowulf's home *where the king housed the gift-throne.* [The relative adverb *where* introduces the adjective clause *where the king housed the gift-throne* which modifies the noun *home* in the main clause. The relative adverb has *home* as its antecedent and functions as an adverb in the subordinate clause, modifying the verb *housed.*]

4.3   NOUN CLAUSES

Like single-word nouns, noun clauses function most frequently as the subject of a sentence, a direct object, an indirect object, a subject complement, an object of a preposition, or an appositive. Noun clauses are introduced by two kinds of connectives—a *subordinate conjunction* (*if, that, whether*) or a *functional connective*: a relative pronoun such as *what, who, whom, which*; a relative adjective such as *what, which*; a relative adverb such as *how, when, where, why.* Subordinate conjunctions (like those that introduce adverb clauses) simply introduce the clause. Functional connectives, in addition to introducing the subordinate clause, also serve a grammatical function inside the subordinate clause.

The king of the land granted *that the warrior avenge himself.* [The noun clause *that the warrior avenge himself* functions as the direct object of the verb *granted* in the main clause.]

Whether death was better than shame was a principle clear to the Germanic warrior. [The subordinate conjunction *whether* introduces the noun clause *whether death was better than shame* which functions as the subject to the verb *was* of the main clause.]

The fact ***that** Beowulf was dead and the Geats without a king* emboldened the Swedes. [The noun clause ***that** Beowulf was dead and the Geats without a king* is an appositive, in apposition with the noun *fact.*]

The hearth-companions sang about ***how** his people mourned this best of kings.* [The noun clause ***how** his people mourned this best of kings* is the object of the preposition *about.* The relative adverb ***how*** introduces the noun clause and functions as an adverb modifying the verb *mourned.*]

The Geatish woman sang at the pyre ***what** she most feared from the invading enemy.* [The noun clause ***what** she most feared from the invading enemy* is the direct object of the verb *sang.* The relative pronoun ***what*** introduces the noun clause and functions as the direct object of the adjective clause: *she most feared **what** from the invading enemy.*]

Phrases 5

A phrase is a group of related words that function together as a single part of speech. Unlike the clause, the phrase does not include a subject and verb. In this section we will deal with those phrases that are of particular interest to our study of Old English: **noun phrases, verb phrases, prepositional phrases, appositive phrases, gerund phrases, participial phrases, infinitive phrases,** and *absolute phrases.*

NOUN PHRASES 5.1

The noun phrase consists of the main noun or pronoun (some grammarians call it the headword) and all of its modifiers. The noun phrase functions within a sentence as does a single-word noun or pronoun; that is, as a subject, direct object, subject complement, object of a preposition, indirect object, and the like. When we spoke of the **complete subject** of a sentence in §1.2, we were in fact describing the noun phrase in one of its functions—that of a subject. In the following examples, the main word or headword is in boldface:

the *dragon*
the fire-breathing *dragon*
the ancient fire-breathing *dragon*
the ancient fire-breathing *dragon* hot with rage

Note: The modifiers may appear both before and after the noun.

5.2   VERB PHRASES

The verb phrase consists of a main verb, which is a finite verb, and its helping verbs. A finite verb is a verb that is inflected for features such as person, number, and tense. Therefore, the verb in the predicate of a sentence is a finite verb. In the following examples, the main verb is in boldface:

is *diving*
has *dived*
would *dive*
would have *dived*
had been *diving*
must have been *diving*

Note: The *verb phrase* includes only the auxiliary verbs and the main verb. A *predicate phrase*, however, which is synonymous with the **complete predicate** of a sentence, would also include modifiers and the complements of the verb. Example (the predicate phrase is in italics): The enraged dragon *swiftly destroyed the houses of Beowulf's people.*

PREPOSITIONAL PHRASES   5.3

See §3.6 for an introduction to the preposition and the prepositional phrase. A prepositional phrase functions as either an adjective or an adverb. In the following examples, the prepositional phrases are in italics; the preposition in boldface:

Beowulf and twelve thanes traveled **to** *the dragon's lair*. [The prepositional phrase functions as an adverb, answering the adverbial question, "Where?" and modifying the verb *traveled*.]

The famous hero **in** *his mail shirt* slashed the dragon **with** *his sword*. [The first prepositional phrase functions as an adjective, modifying the noun *hero*; the second functions as an adverb, modifying the verb *slashed* and answering the adverbial question, "How?"]

Angry **about** *the sword stroke*, the dragon spat flames **at** *the brave warrior*. [The first prepositional phrase functions as an adverb, modifying the adjective *angry;* the second functions as an adverb, modifying the verb *spit* and answering the question, "Where?"]

The famous king did not boast happily **about** *his sword*. [The prepositional phrase functions as an adverb, modifying the adverb *happily*.]

APPOSITIVE PHRASES   5.4

An appositive phrase is a noun phrase (see §5.1) that repeats, renames, or identifies a noun or pronoun that it follows. In rare occasions an appositive may precede the substantive it identifies, but in that case, the substantive is usually a pronoun. In the following sentences the appositive phrase is in italics, the main noun or headword is in boldface.

Beowulf, *the son of Ecgtheow*, ruled his people for fifty years. [The appositive is set off by commas because it repeats the information given by the noun it follows and, therefore, in grammatical terms simply adds extra, non-essential information.]

The thane Wiglaf, *a loyal shield-warrior and prince of the Scylfings*, came to Beowulf's aid. [The appositive has a compound headword *shield-warrior* and *prince*.]

Wiglaf grasped his sword, *an ancient weapon crafted by giants*. [Note that one can test whether the appositive phrase is an appositive or not by substituting it for the noun or pronoun that it renames, in this case, *sword*. If the sentence remains complete with the substitution, the phrase is an appositive. However, if we were to rewrite the sentence with an adjective clause, we would have: *Wiglaf grasped his sword, which was an ancient weapon crafted by giants*. In this case, if we were to try to substitute the adjective clause for the antecedent *sword,* the substitution would not result in a complete sentence.]

5.5   VERBAL PHRASES

A verbal phrase consists of a verbal, that is, a non-finite verb and all its modifiers and complements. A non-finite verb is a verb that is not inflected to indicate the person, number, and tense of a verb (§5.2). Therefore, a non-finite verb cannot function as the predicate verb of a sentence. As its name suggests, a verbal is "like a verb" in its form and its ability to take a subject, adverbial modifiers, and complements. However, a verbal functions not as a verb, but as another part of speech such as noun, adjective, or adverb.

There are three types of verbals: *participles* (which function as an adjective), *gerunds* (which function as a noun), and *infinitives* (which function as an adjective, adverb, or noun).

PARTICIPLES   5.5.1

There are two kinds of participles: *present participles* and *past participles*.

Present participles consist of a **verb** plus the suffix *-ing* (*diving, planning, complaining, shouting*). When the present participle functions as a verb, it always appears as the headword in a verb phrase (*was diving, has been planning, is complaining, could have been shouting*). When the present participle functions as an adjective, it appears without auxiliary verbs, but it may appear with modifiers and complements (*the diving plane, our original planning committee, the complaining child in the restaurant, the victorious team shouting insults*).

Past participles consist of a verb plus the suffixes *-ed, -d, -t, -en, or -n,* that is, those verb forms that appear with the auxiliary verbs *have, has, had* (*discouraged, fed, caught, shaven, seen*). When the past participle functions as a verb, it always appears as the headword in a verb phrase (*had dived, were fed, has been caught, was shaven, has seen*). When the past participle functions as an adjective, it appears without auxiliary verbs, but it may appear with modifiers and complements (*the discouraged father, the well-fed puppies, the villain caught by his own vices, a shaven head, a seldom seen event*).

When the participle functions as a verbal, it may function like any adjective: it may modify a noun or a pronoun or it may act as a subject complement or an object complement. The participle may function as a **single-word adjective** or as a part of a *participial phrase*.

The *single-word participle:* [The participle is in boldface.]

The **coiling** dragon sought battle with the hero. [The participle *coiling* modifies the noun *dragon* which is the subject of the sentence.In ModE the single-word participle invariably appears before the noun it modifies.]

Beowulf's companions looked **grieved**. [The participle functions as a subject complement.]

Wiglaf found his lord *wounded*. [The participle functions as an object omplement.]

The *participial phrase*: The phrase consists of the participle as headword and all of its modifiers and complements. In the following examples, the participial phrase is in italics and the headword in boldface.

Coiling its scaly tail, the dragon attacked the Geatish king. [The noun *tail* is the direct object of the participle *coiling*. Unlike the single-word participle which invariably comes before the noun it modifies, the participial phrase can move around the sentence without losing its clarity as the modifier. In the above example, the participial phrase clearly refers to and therefore modifies *dragon*, the subject of the sentence. But, the phrase can also appear after the subject: The dragon, *coiling its scaly tail*, attacked the Geatish king.]

Quickly **bracing** *himself against the dragon's attack*, Beowulf slashed the monster with his sword. [The participial phrase modifies *Beowulf*, the subject of the main clause. The adverb *quickly* modifies the participle *bracing*; the pronoun *himself* is the direct object of the participle; the prepositional phrase *against the dragon's attack* functions as an adverb modifying the participle.]

Beowulf appeared **braced** *for the dragon's onslaught*. [The participial phrase *braced for the dragon's onslaught* functions as the subject complement of the verb *appeared*. The prepositional phrase *for the dragon's onslaught* functions as an adverb modifying the participle braced.]

Wiglaf found the old warrior **braced** *for battle with the dragon*. [The participial phrase *braced for battle with the dragon* functions as an object complement modifying the direct object *warrior* and completing the action started by the verb *found*.]

GERUNDS

Gerunds consist of a *verb* plus the suffix *–ing*. Although the form of the gerund is like that of the participle, its function is that of a noun: it can function as a subject, direct object, object of a preposition, subject complement, or appositive.

The *single-word gerund:* [The gerund is in boldface.]

We heard their **wailing**. [The gerund *wailing* functions as the direct object of the verb *heard*.]

The **roaring** was heard throughout the land of the Geats. [The gerund *roaring* functions as the subject of the verb *was heard*.]

The warriors did not object to his **boasting**. [The gerund *boasting* functions as the object of the preposition *to*.]

The *gerund phrase:* the gerund phrase consists of the gerund as the headword and all its modifiers and complements. In the following examples, the headword gerund is in boldface; the gerund phrase is in italics.

We heard *the **wailing** of the mourners*. [The gerund phrase functions as the direct object of the verb *heard*. The gerund **wailing** is the direct object; it is modified by the article *the* and the prepositional phrase *of the mourners* which functions as an adjective modifier of the gerund.]

*The **roaring** of the funeral pyre* was heard throughout the land of the Geats.
[The *-ing* phrase functions as the subject of the verb *was heard.*]

The warriors mourned about ***losing*** *their beloved king.* [The *-ing* phrase functions as the object of the preposition *about*. The gerund ***losing*** is the simple object of the preposition; it takes *king* as its direct object which, in turn, is modified by the possessive pronoun *their* and the adjective *beloved.*]

The warriors' only consolation was *the **celebrating** of their king's courage and generosity.*
[The *-ing* phrase functions as the subject complement of the verb *was.*]

The warriors' only consolation, ***celebrating*** *their king's courage,* offered little solace.
[The *-ing* phrase functions as an appositive; the phrase is in apposition with the noun *consolation.*]

5.5.3   INFINITIVES

Infinitives typically consist of a verb plus the sign *to* (*to dive, to plan, to complain, to shout*). The infinitive functions as a noun, adjective, or adverb.

The *simple infinitive*: In the following examples, the infinitive is in boldface.

The scop selected an appropriate song ***to sing***. [The infinitive *to sing* functions as an adjective modifying the noun *song.*]

To sing is the scop's chief role in the beer hall. [The infinitive *to sing* functions as the subject of the verb *is.*]

The scop came to the beer hall ***to sing***. [The infinitive *to sing* functions as an adverb, modifying the verb *came.*

The *infinitive phrase*: The infinitive may also serve as the headword of an infinitive phrase which, like other verbal phrases, includes the headword, all its modifiers, and complements. In the following examples, the infinitive headword is in boldface, the infinitive phrase in italics.

Infinitive phrases functioning as nouns:

To capture the mead-benches of an enemy won high honors for a warrior. [The infinitive phrase functions as the subject of the verb *won*. The infinitive takes the noun *mead-benches* as its direct object. The prepositional phrase *of an enemy* functions as an adjective modifying the direct object *mead-benches*.]

The king commanded *the scop to sing the song about the victory*. [The infinitive phrase functions as the direct object of the verb *commanded*. In the infinitive phrase, the accusative noun *scop* functions as the subject of the infinitive *to sing*; the noun *song* functions as the direct object of the infinitive; the prepositional phrase *about the victory* modifies the noun *song*.]

Beowulf's plan was *to fight without his sword or shield*. [The infinitive phrase functions as the subject complement of the verb *was*. In the infinitive phrase, the prepositional phrase *without his sword or shield* functions as an adverb modifying the infinitive.]

Beowulf's plan, *to fight without his sword or shield*, worried his thanes. [The infinitive phrase functions as an appositive, in apposition with the noun *plan*.]

The plan was for *him to fight without his sword or shield*. [The infinitive phrase functions as the object of the preposition *for*. In the infinitive phrase, the pronoun *him* is the subject of the infinitive. Note: The subject of the infinitive takes the accusative case. In both OE and ModE, the subject of a finite verb takes the nominative case; however, the subject of the infinitive takes the accusative.]

Infinitive phrases functioning as adjectives:

The thane performed his duty *to fill the warriors' flagons with mead*. [The infinitive phrase functions as an adjective modifying the noun *duty*.]

Beowulf's strategy *to swim with swords drawn* protected them from the sea-beasts. [The infinitive phrase functions as an adjective, modifying the noun *strategy*.]

Infinitive phrases functioning as adverbs:

Unferth stood *to speak to the young hero*. [The infinitive phrase functions as an adverb, modifying the verb *stood*.]

Breca and Beowulf swam together *to protect themselves from the sea monsters*. [The infinitive phrase functions as an adverb, modifying the adverb *together*. The pronoun *themselves* is the direct object of the infinitive. The prepositional phrase *from the sea* functions as an adverb, modifying the infinitive.]

The two young heroes were happy *to see at last the windy headland*. [The infinitive phrase functions as an adverb, modifying the adjective *happy*. The prepositional phrase *at last* modifies the infinitive *to see*, and the noun *headland* functions as the direct object of the infinitive.]

NOTE: On certain occasions the sign "to" disappears from the infinitive construction. In the following examples, the infinitive phrase is in italics.

Example: We heard *the scop sing a poem about the king's courage.* [The noun *scop* functions as the subject of the infinitive *sing.* The problem is that because the sign "to" is omitted, *sing* appears to be a finite verb with the noun *scop* as its subject. However, *sing* is not a finite verb, since it does not take the expected affix that would indicate tense or person (*the scop sings a poem* or *the scop sang a poem*). Rather, *sing* is an infinitive in its form, but the infinitive sign "to" has been omitted (that is, the sentence intends: *We heard the scop* **to** *sing a poem about the king's courage*).]

The sign "to" will be absent in certain circumstances:

(1) after the verbs *to hear, to see, to feel*

They heard *the monster* (to) *burst the door.*
Beowulf saw *Grendel* (to) *rip the warrior apart.*
Grendel felt *the hero* (to) *grab his fingers in a fearful grip.*

(2) after the verbs *to dare, to help, to let, to make*

The scop helped *me* (to) *sing the poem about the king's courage.*
None of the warriors dared (to) *defend their comrades.*
The hero's attack made *the monster* (to) *flee the hall without delay.*

(3) after the subjunctive constructions *need not, had better, had rather, would rather, had as soon, would as soon*

The warriors need *not* (to) *grieve for Grendel's hurried flight.*
The monster would *rather* (to) *hide in his dark fen.*

(4) as the object of a preposition

The warrior had done all that he was asked except (to) *find the gold hoard.*

(5) as an appositive

Hrothgar offered Beowulf a final piece of advice, (to) *reward generously your faithful thanes.*

5.5.4   ABSOLUTE PHRASES

In this section, we will concentrate especially on the absolute phrase traditionally named a *nominative absolute*. But, the reader should be aware that an absolute construction is any word, phrase, or clause that is used in a sentence without having any grammatical connection with any other word, phrase, or clause in the sentence. In many cases, the absolute construction is an idiom that over time has become little more than a sentence-filler. For example, the infinitive phrase *to tell you the truth* can be inserted into a sentence without grammatical purpose: *To tell you the truth, I have often wondered about his politics.* The phrase is used absolutely; that is, it has no grammatical function within the main clause *I have often wondered about his politics.*

The *nominative absolute* is an absolute construction that consists of two parts, a substantive (either a noun or pronoun) and a participial modifier. In the following examples, the absolute phrase is in italics, the substantive in boldface.

*The **ball** having been cleansed of the gore*, the king called for his warriors. [Although the nominative absolute has something of an adverbial sense about it, the phrase has no real grammatical function in the main clause; it neither modifies any element in the main clause, nor does it provide a connection to the main clause.]

*The king's **strength** having waned*, the thanes worried for their kingdom.

*The king's favorite **thane** having been slaughtered by Grendel's mother*, Hrothgar mourned his loss.

Summary of
Sound Changes

Introduction

This appendix explains those sound changes that will help you to understand some of the apparent spelling and inflectional oddities in Old English. "Apparent" is used advisedly, since in almost every instance where an OE word seems at variance with the other words in the same class, that difference can be usually explained by examining how the class of words developed systematically from an earlier period of the language. We present the sound changes chronologically in order to give the student a sense of how OE developed from its earlier stages of development. We discuss only those sound changes that are relevant to our larger purpose of introducing the language to beginning readers. (For a more complete treatment of the sound changes from Indo-European to Old English, the student should consult Richard M. Hogg, *A Grammar of Old English, Vol.1: Phonology.* Oxford: Blackwell, 1992; Alistair Campbell, *Old English Grammar.* Oxford: Clarendon P, 1959.)

1   Indo-European (IE) to Germanic (Gmc)

GRIMM'S LAW: THE FIRST CONSONANT SHIFT

Grimm's Law demonstrates that certain Indo-European consonants differ from the way that they were sounded in Germanic cognates of other IE words. All the consonants described in Grimm's Law are stops. The changes can be described as follows:

I.

IE voiceless stops	[p]	[t]	[k]
	⌄	⌄	⌄
Gmc voiceless fricatives	[f]	[θ]	[h]

[Examples: Latin represents the IE sounds; OE gives the Gmc cognate: (L) pater "father" > (OE) fæder; (L) tres "three" > (OE) þríe; (L) cornu "horn" > (OE) horn.]

II.

IE voiced stops	[b]	[d]	[g]
	⋎	⋎	⋎
Gmc voiceless stops	[p]	[t]	[k]

[Examples: Latin represents the IE sounds; OE gives the Gmc cognate: (L) *turba* "crowd" > (OE) *þorp* "village"; (L) *dentis* "tooth" > (OE) *tōþ*; (L) *genu* "knee" > (OE) *cnēow*.]

III.

IE voiced aspirated stops	[bh]	[dh]	[gh]
	⋎	⋎	⋎
Gmc unaspirated voiced stops	[b]	[d]	[g]

[In IE [bh] and [dh] become [f] in Latin; [gh] becomes [h] in Latin. Therefore, (L) *frater* "brother" > (OE) *brōðor*; (L) *foris* "door" > (OE) *dor*; (L) *hortus* "garden" > (OE) *ġeard* "yard".]

Verner's Law

2

In some instances the consonant changes that Grimm describes do not occur as one would expect. For example, the Latin *centum* (hundred) corresponds with its Gmc cognate OE *hund* with the expected change of the IE [k] to the Gmc [h]. But one would expect that the medial [t] seen in *centum* would change to [θ] to yield OE **hunþred*. Grimm's Law seems not to apply in this instance, and it is this kind of apparent irregularity that Karl Verner explains.

* [The two examples are taken from A. H. Marckwardt and James L. Rosier, *Old English Language and Literature,* New York: Norton, 1972, p. 79, and Bruce Mitchell and Fred C. Robinson, *A Guide to Old English,* Oxford: Blackwell, 1986, p. 42.]

Verner points out that when the IE voiceless stops—[p], [t], [k] and the voiceless fricative [s]—appear in the middle of a word or at its end, preceded by an unaccented vowel and in a voiced environment, the voiceless stops become voiced. Thus, [p] did not change to [f] but to [v] (but spelled *f*); [t] did not change to [θ] but to [d]; [k] did not change to [h] but to [g]; and [s] changed to [r].

Verner's Law helps us understand some of the apparent anomalies in certain strong verbs. For example, the strong verb 1 *scrīpan* "to go, glide" has the following principle parts: *scrāþ* (past sing), *scridon* (past pl), and *scriden* (past participle). The past singular form is what we would expect for a Class 1 strong verb, given the infinitive *scrīpan*. But the **d** in the past plural and past participle do not follow Grimm's Law. The voiced **d** can be accounted for by Verner. First, it is probable that the stress in the word shifts from the first syllable (in the infinitive and present tense) to the second syllable in the past plural and past participle form. A similar shift and change from voiceless to voiced sound is attested in Modern English. Compare, for example*:

$$/\qquad\qquad /$$
dissolute with *dissolve*

and

$$/\qquad\qquad /$$
absolute with *absolve*

When the stress falls on the first syllable, the fricative [s] is voiceless; when the stress falls on the second syllable, the fricative is voiced [z]. Something very similar must have occurred in the case of *scrīpan*: the voiceless fricative in *scrāþ* changes to a voiced stop [d] in the past plural and the past participle, according to Verner's rule **þ > d.**

Germanic to West Germanic (WGmc)   3

PRIMITIVE GERMANIC E > I

The PrimGmc **e** fronts to **i** in several cases, among them:

a.   **e** before a nasal plus a consonant fronts to **i** (compare Latin *gemma* with OE *gimm*; Latin *ventus* with OE *wind*).

b.   **e** before **i, ī,** or **j** fronts to **i** (compare Latin *medius* with OE *midd* and OE infinitive *helpan* with its second and third person present forms *hilpist* and *hilpiþ* caused by the PrimGmc forms for the second and third person [*-is* and *-iþ*]). In this connection, see below §15.

c.   Present tense forms.

Gemination   4

In Germanic (Gmc) all consonants (except **r**) following a short vowel and, in turn, followed by a **j**, were lengthened in WGmc. The lengthened consonant is indicated in writing by doubling the consonant, that is, by **gemination** (L. *gemini*, "twins"). In almost every instance, the **j** that produces gemination also produces *i-mutation* in the root vowel.

For example, the infinitive form of the Gmc Class I weak verb **framjan* undergoes the following stages: Gmc **framjan* > WGmc *frammjan* [gemination] > Prehist OE **fræmmjan* [the WGmc vowel **a** changed to **æ** in most closed syllables, as in this case, when followed by two consonants; see below §5] > Prehist OE **fremmian* [the **j** changes to an **i** after a long syllable which ends in a consonant; the **i** is lost before OE, that is about CE 700; see below §8], and the root vowel undergoes *i-mutation* (see below §11) > OE *fremman*.

4.1   **GEMINATION** and the accompanying *i-mutation* appear most frequently in Class I weak verbs and Classes 5 and 6 strong verbs. Examples:

1. Class I Weak Verbs:

    a.   *settan* "to set"
         Gmc **satjan* > WGmc **sattjan* > Prehist OE **sættjan* > Prehist OE **settian* > OE *settan*

    b.   *sellan* "to give"
         Gmc **saljan* > WGmc **salljan* > Prehist OE **sælljan* > Prehist OE **sellian* > OE *sellan*

2. Class 5 Strong Verbs:

    a.   *biddan* "to ask"
         Gmc **bidjan* > WGmc **biddjan* > Prehist OE **biddian* > OE *biddan*

    b.   *sittan* "to sit"
         Gmc **setjan* > WGmc **settjan* > Prehist OE **sittian* > OE *sittan*

    c.   *licgan* "to lie down"
         Gmc **legjan* > WGmc **leggjan* > Prehist OE **liggian* > OE *licgan*
    (In OE the WGmc geminated consonant **gg** is spelled **cg**. The change in spelling indicates that the WGmc sound for **g** [ɤ], a voiced velar fricative, was palatalized by the following **j** to an alveolo-palatal.)

3. Class 6 Strong Verbs:

   a. *hebbun* "to raise"

   Prim Gmc **havjan* > Gmc **habbjan* > Prehist OE **hæbbjan* > Prehist OE
   *hebbian > OE hebban

   In Primitive Germanic the voiceless bilabial fricative [f] was voiced to a bilabial
   fricative [β], a sound similar to Modern English [v]. We give the Prim Gmc
   infinitive as *havjan for that reason. When the bilabial fricative [β] underwent
   gemination, it "acquired stop articulation," which is rendered [bb] in OE. See
   Richard M. Hogg, *A Grammar of Old English*, Vol. 1: Phonology, Oxford:
   Blackwell, 1992, pp. 68-73.

   b. *hliehhan* "to laugh"

   Gmc **hlahjan* > WGmc **hlahhjan* > Prehist OE **hlæhhjan* > Prehist OE
   *hleahhjan > * Prehist OE **hliehhian* > OE *hliehhan*

   After the change of **a > æ** in Prehist OE, the **æ** broke to **ea** before the geminated **h**;
   then, the **ea** umlauted to **ie**.

   c. *scieppan* "to create"

   Gmc **skapjan* > WGmc **skappjan* > Prehist OE **skæppjan* > Prehist OE
   *skeppian > Prehist OE **scieppian* > OE *scieppan*

   The change in Prehist OE from **skeppian* to **scieppian* is the result of the
   palatalization of **sk** by a front vowel. See §1 and Hogg, *A Grammar of Old English*,
   vol. 1, pp. 261 ff.

d. *steppan* "to step"

Gmc *stapjan* > WGmc *stappjan* > Prehist OE *stæppjan* > Prehist OE *steppian*
> OE *steppan*

5   Change of WGmc a > æ:
This change takes place in one instance that is relevant to our purposes. The **a** becomes
æ when it appears in a closed syllable, that is when it is followed by two consonants. This
is particularly true in Class I weak verbs (see above §4.1, #1) and Class 6 strong verbs (see
above §4.1, #3).

6   Change of WGmc e > i:
When the WGmc **e** was followed by **m**, it became **i** in OE. Therefore, the OE *niman*
appeared in WGmc as *neman*.

7   Change of WGmc a > o:
When followed by a nasal, the WGmc **a** either stayed **a** or changed to **o**. The change
took place in Prehist OE (that is, between 500 and 700), more regularly in some dialects
than others. In Early West Saxon the **o** appears in most cases; in Late West Saxon, the **a**
is the usual form.

8   Medial WGmc j:
a. Medial **j** after a long syllable ending in a consonant changed to **i** (see example
below §4 [OE *fremman*] and §4.1 [OE *settan, biddan,* etc.]). Later, the **i** was lost
about 700 CE.

b. Medial **j** after a short syllable ending in **r** changed to **i, g, ig, gc,** or **ige** (see OE
weak I verb *nerian: *nærjan* > *nerjan* > nerian;* see also OE weak II verb *lufi(ge)an*
in which the several different changes are attested).

West Germanic to Old English 9
PRIMITIVE OLD ENGLISH (PRIMOE): BEFORE 500 CE
PRE-HISTORIC OLD ENGLISH (PREHISTOE): 500-700 CE

WGMC SK > SC

Like diphthongization by initial palatals (see Appendix Two, §11), where the palatalized sound **sc** affected the front vowels (**e**, **æ**, and **æ**) the **sc** could also affect back vowels. In West Saxon, both early and late, when **sc** was followed by a back vowel, an **e** was inserted between the **sc** and the following vowel. Therefore, *scacan* and *scafan* in Early West Saxon (EWS) and Late West Saxon (LWS) dialect may appear as *sceacan* and *sceafan*. The same insertion may appear in the case of the past tenses and the past participles of those verbs. Hogg (*A Grammar of Old English*, p. 118, paragraph 5.69) offers the following rule of thumb: In WS the sequence **sca** and **sco** sometimes remain **sca** and **sco** and sometimes are spelled **scea** and **sceo**. Generally, the **e** is more likely to be inserted before the **a** than the **o**; the insertion is more likely to take place in LWS than EWS.

BREAKING 10

The front vowels **æ**, **e**, and **i** were changed into diphthongs before certain consonants:

> Before **r** + a consonant (but not the semi-vowel **j**)
>> **l** + a consonant
>> **h**

> The front vowel **æ** changed to **ea** (examples: *hælp > healp, æld > eald, wærm > wearm*)
> Before **r** + a consonant (but not the semi-vowel **j**)
>> **l** + the consonants **h** and **c**
>> **h**

The front vowel **e** changed to **eo** (examples: *feh > feoh, werpan > weorpan, melc > meolc*)

The front vowel **i** changed to **io** (examples: **tīhis > *tīohis* [see below §15], **wirþiþ >*wiorþiþ* later **wierþiþ* [i-mutation]).

Note: The long front vowels, that is, **ǣ**, **ē**, and **ī**, change to **ēa**, **ēo**, and **īo** respectively.

11 DIPHTHONGIZATION BY INITIAL PALATALS

In Prehistoric Old English, the simple vowels **æ**, **ǣ**, and **e** were changed into diphthongs when preceded by an initial palatal—**ġ**, **ċ**, or **sc**.

1. **æ** changed to **ea**   examples: **ġæf > ġeaf, *ġæt > ġeat*
2. **ǣ** changed to **ēa**   examples: **ġǣfon > ġēafon, *ġǣton > ġēaton*
3. **e** changed to **ie**   examples: **ġefan > ġiefan, *ġetan > ġietan*

See also §8.7, Class 4 strong verbs where the OE ablaut series is **e**, **æ**, **ǣ**, **o**. The initial palatal **sc-** in the infinitive *scieran* (to shear) produces the following principal parts: *scieran, scear, scēaron,* and *scoren* [the **o** of the past participle is not changed by the initial palatal].

12 I-MUTATION

See §8.11, §8.11.1, and §8.11.2 for a full discussion of i-mutation.

13 SYNCOPATION

Vowels that appeared between two consonants, especially vowels in an unstressed position, were frequently syncopated, that is, "cut out" between the two consonants, the consonants falling together. Syncopation is particularly found in the second and third person singular present tense of strong verbs and weak I verbs. For example, in the second person singular form of the weak verb *dēman* (*dēmest*), the syncopated form is *dēmst*. The third person present form (*dēmeþ*) syncopates to *dēmþ*. Generally, syncopation occurs in West Saxon and Kentish dialects; unsyncopated forms occur in Anglian. See §8.10 and, below in Appendix Two, §15.4 and §15.5.

LOSS OF INTERVOCALIC H

14

About 700 CE, the **h** that appears between two vowels or between a vowel and a diphthong disappears. The first vowel or diphthong, if short, is lengthened. Therefore, in the case of contract verbs, for example (see Chapter Eleven and §16 below), the Prehistoric OE verb **tēhan* undergoes several changes, beginning with breaking (see above §10): **tēhan* > **tēohan* > *tēon* (loss of intervocalic **h**). The contract verb *sēon* undergoes a similar process: **sehan* > **seohan* [breaking] > *sēon* [loss of intervocalic **h** and note that the short diphthong **eo** is lengthened].

Sound Changes and Verbs in Old English

WEAK VERBS AND POTENTIALLY CONFUSING SOUND CHANGES

15

(see Chapter Three)

[-**ede**] or [-**de**, -**te**]. In order to distinguish whether a verb will use the suffix -**ede** or -**de**, -**te**, you must determine whether the verb's *original* stem was long or short. Verbs that had originally short stems form the first person singular past tense by adding -**ede** to the stem [for example, *fremman* > *fremede*]. Verbs that had originally long stems form the first person past singular by adding either -**de** or -**te** to the stem.

15.1

[-**de**] or [-**te**]. We said at the outset of Chapter Three that a weak verb is distinguished by its use of the dental suffix [d] or [t] to signal the past tense. We noted above that the

15.2

original short stem verb uses the suffix **-ede**. Original long stem verbs may use either **de-** or **-te** in the following circumstances: the dental suffix [d] is used when the stem of the verb ends in voiced consonant [*dēman* "to judge" > *dēmde* (first person singular past)]; the suffix [t] is used when the stem of the verb ends in a voiceless consonant [*lǣfan* (to leave) > *lǣfte* (first person singular past)].

15.3   **Long or Short?** We can offer some general principles here about how to judge whether the original stem of a Class I weak verb was long or short. One caveat: These principles apply to most, but not all of those verbs. There are a few exceptions to these rules, which are beyond our present needs.

Verbs with original *short* stems have OE stems that have a short vowel or diphthong followed by a doubled consonant [for example, *fremman*] or by a single **r** [for example, *nerian*]. (The doubled consonant is the result of a Germanic [Gmc] sound change called **gemination** [see §4].) Briefly, gemination occurs when a single consonant (except **r**) follows a short vowel and is followed in turn by a **j** (typically the sound that begins the infinitive suffix in Gmc **-jan**). (In that case, the single consonant is lengthened, indicated by doubling the consonant. For example, the Gmc Class I weak verb **framjan* changes in WGmc to **frammjan*.) Verbs with original *long* stems have OE stems that have either a long vowel [*dēman*] or diphthong [*dēlan*] or stems that have a short vowel or diphthong followed by two consonants [*sendan*] or by a doubled consonant that is not caused by gemination. (This last principle—whether the doubled consonant is the result of gemination or not—requires some understanding of the etymological history of the verb and is beyond our present interests. For our purposes it is sufficient to say that most doubled consonants in weak verbs are the result of gemination.)

15.4   SYNCOPATION

Verbs which have stems that end in a **d** or **t**, whether the stem is long or short, drop (*syncopate*) the first **e** of the **-ede** suffix so that the ending is **-de** or **-te**. If the stem ends in a doubled **d** or **t** the first person singular past form ends in -**dde** or -**tte** [*hreddan* "to save" > *hredde*; *lettan* "to hinder" > *lette*]. See §8.10. Verbs which have stems that end in two consonants, the second of which is a **d** or **t**, syncopate one of the dentals in the past tense [*sendan* "to send" > *sende*; *fæstan* "to fast" > *fæste*].

SYNCOPATION AND ASSIMILATION   **15.5**

These two sound changes often occurred in EWS Class I weak verbs. When it occurred, it did so usually in the past tense and past participle, and in the second and third person singular of the present indicative. In the past participial forms the suffix -**ed** undergoes sound changes similar to those of the past tense mentioned in #4 above. For example, in the case of stems that end with a double **d** or **t**, the vowel of the past participle is sometimes syncopated: therefore, *hreddan* > *hreded* or *hredd*. In some cases, where the stem ends in a dental, the syncopation creates an odd combination of sounds; therefore, in the instance of *settan,* the past participle form will appear as *seted* or it may appear in EWS as *sett.* In the latter case, the word undergoes two changes: first, the medial vowel is syncopated, leaving the verb with the odd combination of sounds—**td**. In such a case, the two sounds are blended together (***assimilated***), in this instance to *sett.* See §8.10. Syncopation and assimilation also appear in class I weak verbs which have long stems. Note, for example, in the conjugation at §3.11 above the verbs *dēman* and *sēċan* indicate syncopation in the second and third person present singular: *dēmest* and *dēmeþ* > *dēmst* and *dēmþ*; *sēċest* and *sēċeþ* > *sēċst* and *sēċþ*. In some instances, the verbs may undergo both syncopation and assimilation. For example, in the EWS third person singular present indicative of *mētan: mēteþ* undergoes syncopation > *mētþ* and then because the combination **tþ** is awkward to pronounce, the consonant sounds assimlate to *mēt.* For the combinations of consonants and how they assimilate, see §8.10.

GEMINATION AND SPELLING   **15.6**

We noted at §3.11.4 that in the conjugation of *fremman* the verb is sometimes spelled with two **m**'s and sometimes with one. In the case of *nerian* sometimes the **i** is attached to the endings and sometimes not. What is interesting is that where *fremman* is spelled with two **m**'s, so too does *nerian* add the **i** to the suffix. The reason for the difference of spelling has to do with the Gmc suffix for the infinitive form **–jan**. Where the Gmc verb form includes the **j** of the infinitive suffix, gemination takes place and the OE verb will be spelled with a doubled consonant. The **j** later disappears. In the case of *nerian* the same thing takes place with two exceptions: (1) because an **r** does not undergo gemination, no doubling occurs, and (2) the **j**, instead of disappearing, changes to an **i**. Therefore, in the case of the first person present indicative, the present subjunctive, imperative plural, infinitive, gerund, and present participle, the geminated vowel occurs, but does not elsewhere. So, too, the **i** of *nerian* appears in those forms but not elsewhere.

16   CONJUGATION OF CONTRACT VERBS: PRESENT TENSE FORMS

(See Chapter Eleven)

Each of the following explanations offers a single but generally applicable example that should help the student understand the apparent irregularities of the verb forms of the contract verbs. Each of the sound changes mentioned in this section is treated above.

The *first person singular present indicative* of the infinitive *tēon* is *tēo*. The first person form is from Prehist OE **tēhu*, which is the root form of the Prehist OE infinitive **tēhan* plus the suffix **–u**. The sequence of sound changes that produced *tēo* ran something like this:

Prehist OE **tēhu* > **tēohu* [breaking before intervocalic –h] > *tēo* [loss of intervocalic **h**]

The *second person singular present indicative* of the infinitive *tēon* is *tīehst*. The sequence of sound changes:

Primitive Gmc **tēhis* [the suffix -**is** is an early form; later –**est** is used universally] > PrehistOE **tīhis* [the mutation from PGmc **e** to PrehistOE **i** is a Gmc change that precedes the later OE i-mutation by several centuries] > *tīohis* [breaking before –**h**] > *tīehis* [OE i-mutation] > *tīehes*(*t*) [change of unstressed **i** to **e**; the –**est** suffix is universal in historical OE] > *tīehst* [syncopation; note that syncopation occurs before loss of intervocalic **h**; therefore, since the **h** is no longer intervocalic, it is not lost].

The ***third person singular present indicative*** of the infinitive *tēon* is *tīehþ*. The sequence of sound changes:

Primitive Gmc *tēhiþ* > PrehistOE *tīhiþ* [Gmc mutation] > *tīohiþ* [breaking before **h**] > *tīehiþ* [i-mutation] > *tīeheþ* [change of unstressed **i** to **e**] > *tīehþ* [syncopation]

CONJUGATION OF CONTRACT VERBS:
PAST TENSE FORMS AND THE PAST PARTICIPLE

17

As we mentioned in Chapter Eight, strong verbs change the root vowel to form the past tense and the past participle. This change of the root vowel, sometimes called an ablaut, depends on what class of strong verb the verb belongs to since each class has a distinctive set or sets of ablaut series that define the class. In the case of our model contract verb *tēon*, a Class 2 strong verb, the ablaut series is **ēo** (infinitive), **ēa** (past singular), **u** (past plural), and **o** (past participle). In the case of the past singular, we would expect an OE form of *tēah*; in the past plural, we would expect an OE form something like **tuhon* and a past participle form of **tohen*. In the case of the past singular, the form *tēah* is the received OE form. However, in both the past plural and the past participle forms the **h** changes to **g**: **tuhon* comes down as *tugon* and **tohen* as *togen*.

The change of **h** to **g** is the result of the Primitive Germanic change called **Verner's Law** (see above §2).

Thus, the winking in and out of **h** and **g** in the past tense and the past participle, though it may at first glance seem random, is regular. In the present singular forms, the **h** is retained because the **h** is lost only when it is intervocalic, that is, between vowels.

Similarly, the past singular forms listed below, **h** is retained because it did not occur between two vowels in either instance. The appearance of -**g**- in the past plural and past participle forms is also regular once you understand the evolution of such verbs.

18   APPARENT ANOMALIES IN THE PRONUNCIATION OF [ċ] AND [ġ]

In Prehistoric Old English, before the palatalizing of [sk] (see §9) and breaking (see §10), the [k] and [g] sounds were palatalized (that is, fronted) when they appeared in a front vowel environment. The "specific rules" for the pronunciation of [ċ] and [ġ] in Chapter One, in fact, summarize under what conditions these two consonant sounds underwent palatalization. What is problematic about these sound changes and of sound changes in general is that the history of the word under discussion may well result in a form that apparently contradicts the usual rules of change.

For example, the first "specific rule" for how both velar consonants [k] and [g] change to the palatals [ċ] and [ġ] explains that palatalization occurs when the consonant appears before a front vowel or diphthong. However, in the case of *cemban* "to comb," *cēpan* "to seize," or *gēs* (plural of *gōs*), neither [k] nor [g] undergoes palatalization even though it appears before a front vowel. The reason for the anomaly lies in the history of the words' pronunciation. In West Germanic the vowel before the initial consonant was not originally a front vowel but a back vowel that was later fronted by i-mutation, but the consonant remained a velar when i-mutation took place. Examples: WGmc *cōpyan* > Prehist OE *cēpian* (the back vowel [ō] fronts to [ē] because of i-mutation, see §8.11) > OE *cēpan*. Or, in the case of *gēs*: WGmc *gōsiz* (nominative plural of *gōs*) > *gēsiz* > OE *gēs*.

Another dimension of the "apparent" exception to the "specific rules" occurs when the consonant appears in the medial position. When the medial consonant preceded an *i* or *j* (that is, the sounds [I] or [i] or [y] as they are spelled), in Prehistoric OE, the consonant may undergo palatalization. (It should be noted that in WGmc the *j* is pronounced as semi-vowel [y]; later in Prehistoric OE the *j* is spelled and apparently pronounced [i].) For instance, all three of the following examples—*sēċan* "to seek," *tǣċan* "to teach," and *þenċan* "to thank"—seem to resemble the form of *cēpan* above, but in this case the [k] palatalizes to [ċ] in all three words.

The OE *sēċan* provides an example: WGmc **sōkjan* > Prehist OE **sōċjan* > **sēċian* (root vowel umlauts) > OE *sēċan* (see §8 above, the *i* is lost about 700 CE).

We know why the [k] does not palatalize before the front vowel in the instance of *cemban* above; the question now is why it does in the second example. Richard M. Hogg explains that when the velar consonant appears before a front vowel, palatalization will occur, "provided that it [the consonant] is in the same syllable" as the vowel [Hogg, *A Grammar of Old English*, 7.16, p. 259]. Therefore, in the case of *sēċan*, in its Prehistoric OE form, the velar consonant heads the second syllable of the word (*sō-kjan*), the velar [k] fronting to (*so-ċjan*) because of the *j*.

Hogg summarizes the principle, noting that palatalization depends at least in part on where the consonant appears in the "syllable structure" of the word: "namely that a velar consonant was palatalized provided not only that it was adjacent to a front vowel or /j/, but also that it was in the same syllable as the palatalizing segment" [Hogg, 7.16, p. 259].

The same principle obtains when the velar consonant [k] is in the final position, that is, when the consonant appears after an [ɪ] or [i] in which case the consonant would come right after the front vowel and in the same syllable. Examples: *dīċ* "ditch," *piċ* "pitch." In the case of the velar [g], when the same positioning occurs, the consonant palatalizes. Examples: *byriġ* "town," *hāliġ* "holy." But, note that when the consonant moves to another syllable where it is next to a back vowel, the rule changes. For example, if we add the accusative plural suffix to the noun *dīċ*, we have the word *dīcas*. Hogg explains that in this instance the velar consonant remains a velar because it apparently heads the second syllable, "assigning priority to the vowel of the second syllable rather than that of the first" [Hogg, 7.16, p. 259]. That is, the velar consonant remains a velar because it is influenced by the back vowel of the second syllable.

In the case of the noun forms for the noun *here* "army" (§10.2.1), the forms of the noun in the genitive, dative, and instrumental singular cases is *her(i)ġes* or *her(i)ġe*; the palatalization of the [g] sound is clear since the consonant appears before a front vowel. In the plural cases, however, the consonant appears before a back vowel: *her(i)ġas* (nominative, accusative), *her(i)ġa* (genitive), and *her(i)ġum* (dative), but it remains the palatalized [ġ]. Hogg points out that in the case of [ċ], [ġ], and [sc], a front vowel is often placed between the consonant and a back vowel. For example, *heriġeas* "armies," *seċean* "to seek," and *þenċean* "to think." Hogg goes on to explain that "it is extremely difficult to determine whether or not this [inserted] vowel was purely diacritic [that is, an informative symbol merely] or indicated a genuine sound change . . ." [Hogg, 2.68, p. 38]. Therefore, one can assume that in such instances, the loss of the inserted vowel is a spelling shift that does not influence the palatalized consonant.

CAVEAT: The preceding material takes up only *some* of the principles that might explain a *few* of the anomalies that the student of OE might confront in only *one* of the "specific rules" for the palatalization of [k] and [g]. You are not to be daunted by all of the details outlined here, nor are you to despair. It is not necessary to worry through such anomalies, nor is it important to understand fully "why" they happened. What is important is to understand the general principles of how Old English might have been pronounced and how you might pronounce it. However, if you are interested in the history of OE phonology and some of the mechanics of sound change, and in particularly of the present issue, you might consider the following texts:

A. Campbell, *Old English Grammar* (Oxford: Oxford University Press, 1959; repr. 1977), pp. 173-79, §426-443.

Richard M. Hogg, *A Grammar of Old English*, Vol. 1: Phonology (Oxford: Blackwell, 1992), pp. 257-76, 7.15-7.43.

A. H. Marckwardt and James L. Rosier, *Old English Language and Literature* (New York: W.W. Norton, 1972), p. 79.

Bruce Mitchell and Fred C. Robinson, *A Guide to Old English* (Oxford: Basil Blackwell, 1986), p. 42.

The Old English Gloss for
Ælfric's Latin *Colloquy*

The opening lines of Ælfric's *Colloquy*, with Latin text and interlinear glosses in Old English (London, British Library, Ms. Cotton Tiberius A.iii, fol. 60v).

Abbot Ælfric or Ælfric of Eynsham (circa 950-circa 1010) wrote the following colloquy or conversation to help children (novices in a monastery) learn Latin. Though originally composed in Latin, the *Colloquy* was provided with an English gloss, perhaps by Ælfric Bata, a student of his namesake Abbot Ælfric. The main subject matter of the colloquy is work and various professions, and for years historians have attempted to use it as a source of information about labor in late Anglo-Saxon England. More recently, however, Nicholas Howe has suggested that the *Colloquy* is not so much a reliable reflection of working conditions in the period in which it was written as a text reflecting the ideology of the monastery vis-à-vis outside workers.[1]

Using the gloss to the *Colloquy* as a learning text has both advantages and disadvantages. Since it was written for beginning Latin students, its sentences are relatively simple and the style conversational—thus it is ideally suited for beginning students of Old English. On the other hand, since the Old English text is actually an interlinear gloss of the Latin (not an independent translation), it preserves Latin, not native word order, and often attempts to gloss the Latin literally rather than fluently or idiomatically. In the following edition, the OE gloss appears above the Latin, though not as an interlinear gloss. In the original, the Latin text appeared in a normal book hand while the OE gloss was written much smaller above the line.

As a late text, the *Colloquy* contains a number of post-classical OE spellings: for example, *-um* (for dative plural) frequently appears in the manuscript as *–on*, while *–on* (for past plurals) and *–an* (for infinitives and weak nouns and adjectives) sometimes appears as *-en*.[2] We have regularized these spellings to their classic forms. A few peculiarities have been preserved in this text—note for example that the syllable spelled *–ing* in standard OE appears here consistently as *–incg*.

This edition is based on that of G. N. Garmonsway (London: Methuen, 1967).

---

[1] See Howe's essay on "Historicist Approaches" in *Reading Old English Texts*, ed. Katherine O'Brien O'Keefe (Cambridge: Cambridge UP, 1997), pp. 79-100.

[2] In general, the spelling of late OE texts reveals that final unstressed vowels (particularly those in inflectional endings) were changing to *schwa*.

STUDENTS: Wē ċildra[3] biddaþ þē, ēalā lārēow, þæt þū tǽċe ūs sprecan for-
þām un-ġelǽredc wē syndon ond ge-wæmmodlīċe wē sprecaþ.

*Nos pueri rogamus te, magister, ut doceas nos loqui latialiter[4]
recte, quia idiote sumus et corrupte loquimur.*

TEACHER: Hwæt wille[5] ġē sprecan?   5

Quid vultis loqui?

STUDENTS: Hwæt reċe wē[6] hwæt wē spreċen, būton hit riht sprǽċ sȳ ond
be-hēfe, næs īdel oþþe fracod?

*Quid curamus quid loquamur, nisi recta locutio sit et utilis, non
anilis aut turpis?*   10

TEACHER: Wille be-swungen[7] on leornunge?

Vultis flagellari in discendo?

STUDENTS: Lēofre[8] ys ūs bēon be-swungen for lāre þonne hit ne cunnan.
Ac wē witon þē bilewitne wesan ond nellan on-belǽdan
swincgla ūs,[9] būton þū bēo tō-ġenȳdd fram ūs.   15

---

[3] An alternative form for the nominative plural—see §10.8.

[4] The OE text does not gloss the word *latialiter* "in Latin."

[5] Normally, the second person plural form of *willan* should be *willaþ*, but here the ending is reduced to *-e* because the personal pronoun follows immediately (see §7.1.7).

[6] The verb *reċe*, like *wille* of note 3, is a reduced form (= *reċaþ*) conditioned by the immediately-following personal pronoun *wē*.

[7] Supply the understood verb *bēon*.

[8] A comparative form of the adjective *lēof*—see the glossary and §6.5.

[9] Because of the underlying Latin, the syntax of this phrase is abnormal for OE. Literally, it reads "we know you to be . . . and know you not to want to. . . ."

Carius est nobis flagellari pro doctrina quam nescire. Sed scimus te
mansuetum esse et nolle inferre plagas nobis, nisi cogaris a nobis.

TEACHER: Iċ āxie þē, hwæt sprycst þū? Hwæt hæfst þū weorkes[10]?

Interrogo te, quid mihi loqueris? Quid habes operis?

20   MONK: Iċ eom ġe-andwyrde monuc, ond iċ sincge ælċe dæġ seofon tīda
mid ġe-brōþrum, ond iċ eom bysgod[11] ond on sange, ac þēah-
hwæþere iċ wolde be-twēnan leornian sprecan on Lēden ġe-reorde.

Professus sum monachus, et psallam omni die septem sinaxes cum
fratribus, et occupatus sum lectionibus et cantu, sed tamen vellem
25   *interim discere sermocinari latina lingua.*

TEACHER: Hwæt cunnon þās þīne ġe-fēran?

Quid sciunt isti tui socii?

MONK: Sume synt yrþlincgas, sume scēp-hyrdas, sume oxan-hyrdas,
sume ēac swylċe huntan, sume fisceras, sume fuġeleras, sume
30   ċȳp-menn, sume scēo-wyrhtan, sealteras, bæċeras.

Alii sunt aratores, alii opiliones, quidam bubulci, quidam etiam
venatores, alii piscatores, alii aucupes, quidam mercatores,
quidam sutores, quidam salinatores, quidam pistores, coci.

---

[10] *weorces* = "for work"

[11] The OE text does not gloss the word *lectionibus* "readings." Translate: "I am occupied with [readings and] singing."

TEACHER: Hwæt sæġest þū, yrþlingc? Hū be-gǣst þū weorc þīn?

             Quid dicis tu, arator? Quomodo exerces opus tuum?   35

PLOWMAN: Ēalā, lēof hlāford, þearle iċ deorfe. Iċ gā ūt on dæġ-ræd,
             þǣwende[12] oxan tō felda,[13] ond iugie hiġ tō sȳl. Nys hit swā
             stearc winter þæt iċ durre lūtian æt hām for eġe hlāfordes
             mīnes, ac ġe-iukod*um* ox*um*, ond ġe-fæstnod*um* sceare ond
             cultre[14] mi*d* þǣre sǣl, ǣlċe dæġ iċ sceal erian fulne æcer oþþe   40
             mǣre.

             O, mi domine, nimium laboro. Exeo diluculo, minando boves
             ad campum, et iungo eos ad aratrum. Non est tam aspera hiems
             ut audeam latere domi pro timore domini mei, sed iunctis bobus,
             et confirmato vomere et cultro aratro, omni die debeo arare   45
             integrum agrum aut plus.

TEACHER: Hæfst þū ǣniġne ġe-fēran?

             Habes aliquem socium?

PLOWMAN: Iċ hæbbe sumne cnapan þǣwende[15] oxan mid gād-īsene, þe
             ēac swilċe nū hās ys for ċylde ond hrēame.   50

---

[12] The present participle *þēwende* comes from the verb *þȳwan*.

[13] *Felda* is an irregular dative singular form.

[14] The phrases *ge-iukodum oxum* and *gefæstnodum sceare ond cultre* do not make much sense in OE but are intended as glosses for a construction peculiar to Latin—the ablative absolute. The phrases are best translated as follows: "the oxen having been yoked" and "the plowshare and coulter having been fastened."

[15] This use of the present participle is relatively unusual in native OE texts.

Habeo quendam puerum minantem boues cum stimulo,
qui etiam modo raucus est pro frigore et clamatione.

TEACHER: Hwæt māre dēst þū on dæġ?

Quid amplius facis in die?

55   PLOWMAN: Ġe-wīslīċe, þænne, māre iċ dō. Iċ sceal[16] fyllan binnan
oxena mid hīeġ, ond wæterian hiġ, ond scearn heora
beran ūt. Hiġ! Hiġ! Miċel ġe-deorf ys hyt! Ġe, lēof,
miċel ġe-deorf hit ys, for-þām iċ neom frēo.

Certe, adhuc, plus facio. Debeo implere presepia bovum feno,
60   *et adaquare eos, et fimum eorum portare foras. O! O! Magnus*
labor! Etiam, magnus labor est, quia non sum liber.

TEACHER: [Hwæt sæġst þū,] scēap-hyrde? Hæfst þū æniġ ġe-deorf?

Quid dicis tu, opilio? Habes tu aliquem laborem?

SHEPHERD: Ġēa, lēof, iċ hæbbe. On fore-werdne morgen iċ drīfe scēap
65   mīne tō heora læse, ond stande ofer hiġ on hæte ond on ċyle
mid hundum, þē læs wulfas for-swelġen hiġ, ond iċ āġēan-
læde hiġ on heora loca, ond melke hiġ tweowa on dæġ, ond

---

[16] *sceal* = "must"

heora loca iċ hæbbe, on þǣr-tō[17] ond ċȳse ond buteran iċ dō.
And ic eom ġe-trȳwe hlāforde mīn*um*.

Etiam, habeo. In primo mane mino oves meas ad pascua, et sto   70
super eas in estu et frigore cum canibus, ne lupi devorent eas, et
reduco eas ad caulas, et mulgeo eas bis in die, et caulas earum
moveo, insuper et caseum et butirum facio. Et fidelis sum domino
meo.

TEACHER: Ēalā, oxan-hyrde, hwæt wyrkst þū?   75

O, bubulce, quid operaris tu?

OXHERD: Ēalā, hlāford mīn, miċel iċ ġe-deorfe. Þænne sē yrþlingc un-
scenþ þā oxan, iċ lǣde hiġ tō lǣse, ond ealle niht iċ stande ofer
hiġ waċiende for þēof*um*, ond eft on ǣrne-merġen iċ be-tǣċe
hiġ þām yrþlincge wel ġe-fylde ond ġe-wæterode.   80

O, domine mi, multum laboro. Quando arator disiungit boves, ego
duco eos ad pascua, et tota nocte sto super eos vigilando propter fures,
et iterum primo mane adsigno eos aratori bene pastos et adaquatos.

TEACHER: Ys þēs[18] of þȳnum ġe-fērum?

Est iste ex tuis sociis?   85

---

[17] *on þǣr-tō* = "in addition"
[18] Pointing to one of the boys.

OXHERD: Ġēa, hē ys.

Etiam, est.

TEACHER: Canst þū ǣniġ þing?

Scis tu aliquid?

90   HUNTER: Ǣnne cræft iċ cann.

Unam artem scio.

TEACHER: Hwylċne?

Qualem?

HUNTER: Hunta iċ eom.

95   *Venator sum.*

TEACHER: Hwæs?

Cuius?

HUNTER: Cincges.

Regis.

TEACHER: Hū be-gǣst þū cræft þīnne?   100

             Quomodo exerces artem tuam?

HUNTER: Iċ brede mē max ond sette hiġ on stōwe ġe-hæppre, ond ġe-
             tihte hundas mīne þæt wild-dēor hiġ ēhten, oþ-þæt hiġ be-
             cumen tō þām nettum un-for-scēawodlīċe ond þæt hiġ swā
             bēon be-grynodu, ond iċ of-slēa hiġ on þām maxum.   105

             *Plecto mihi retia et pono ea in loco apto, et instigo canes meos ut
             feras persequantur, usque quo perveniunt ad retia inprovise et sic
             inretientur, et ego iugulo eas in retibus.*

TEACHER: Ne canst þū huntian būton mid nettum?

             Nescis venare nisi cum retibus?   110

HUNTER: Ġēa, būtan nettum huntian iċ mæġ.

             Etiam, sine retibus venare possum.

TEACHER: Hū?

             Quomodo?

HUNTER: Mid swiftum hundum iċ be-tǣċe wild-dēor.   115

             Cum velocibus canibus insequor feras.

TEACHER: Hwilċe wild-dēor swīþost[19] ġe-fēhst þū?

Quales feras maxime capis?

HUNTER: Iċ ġe-fēo heortas ond bāras ond rān ond rǣgan[20] ond hwīl*um*
120   haran.

Capio cervos et apros et dammas et capreos et aliquando lepores.

TEACHER: Wǣre þū tō-dæġ on huntnoþe?

Fuisti hodie in venatione?

HUNTER: Iċ næs, for-þām Sunnan-dæġ ys, ac ġyrstan-dæġ iċ wæs on
125   huntunge.

Non fui, quia dominicus dies est, sed heri fui in venatione.

TEACHER: Hwæt ġe-lǣhtest þū?

Quid cepisti?

HUNTER: Twēġen heortas ond ǣnne bār.

130   *Duos cervos et unum aprum.*

TEACHER: Hū ġe-fēncge þū hiġ?

Quomodo cepisti eos?

HUNTER: Heortas iċ ġe-fēngc on nettum ond bār iċ of-slōh.

Cervos cepi in retibus et aprum iugulavi.

TEACHER: Hū wǣre þū dyrstiġ of-stikian bār?   135

Quomodo fuisti ausus iugulare aprum?

HUNTER: Hundas be-drifon hyne tō mē, ond iċ þǣr tō-ġēanes[21]
                      standende fǣrlīċe of-stikode hyne.

*Canes perduxerunt eum ad me, et ego econtra stans subito
iugulavi eum.*   140

TEACHER: Swȳþe þrȳste þū wǣre þā.

Valde audax fuisti tunc.

HUNTER: Ne sceal hunta forht-full wesan, for-þām misliċe wild-dēor
                      wuniað on wudum.

*Non debet venator formidolosus esse, quia varie bestie morantur   145
in silvis.*

---

[19] *Referred from page 424, line 117:* Translate "most of all."
[20] *Referred from page 424, line 119:* The Latin text has *capreos* "goats" for the OE *rēġan* "roes."
[21] Translate *þǣr tō-ġēanes* as "in opposition to" or "facing."

TEACHER: Hwæt dēst þū be þīnre huntunge?

Quid facis de tua venatione?

HUNTER: Iċ sylle cynċge swā hwæt swā iċ ġe-fō, for-þām iċ eom hunta
150   hys.

Ego do regi quicquid capio, quia sum venator eius.

TEACHER: Hwæt sylþ hē þē?

Quid dat ipse tibi?

HUNTER: Hē scrȳt mē wel ond fētt[22] ond hwīlum sylþ mē hors oþþe
155   bēah, þæt þē lustlīcor cræft mīnne iċ be-ganċge.

*Vestit me bene et pascit, aliquando dat mihi equum aut armillam,
ut libentius artem meam exerceam.*

TEACHER: Hwylċne cræft canst þū?

Qualem artem scis tu?

160   FISHER: Iċ eom fiscere.

Ego sum piscator.

---

[22] *scryt = scrudeð; fētt = fēdeð* (see §8.10, §8.10.2)

TEACHER: Hwæt be-gyst þū of þīnum cræfte?

             Quid adquiris de tua arte?

FISHER: Bīġleofan ond scrūd ond feoh.

             Victum et vestitum et pecuniam.   165

TEACHER: Hū ġe-fēhst þū fixas?

             Quomodo capis pisces?

FISHER: Iċ ā-stīġie mīn scyp ond wyrpe max mīne on ēa, ond ancgil
             oððe ǣs iċ wyrpe on spyrtan, ond swā hwæt swā hiġ ġe-hæftað
             iċ ġe-nime.   170

             *Ascendo navem et pono retia mea in amne, et hamum proicio et
             sportas, et quicquid ceperint sumo.*

TEACHER: Hwæt ġif hit un-clǣne bēoþ fixas?

             Quid si inmundi fuerint pisces?

FISHER: Iċ ūt-wyrpe þā un-clǣnan ūt, ond ġe-nime mē clǣne tō   175
             mete.

             Ego proiciam inmundos foras, et sumo mihi mundos in escam.

TEACHER: Hwǣr cǣpst þū fixas þīne?

Ubi vendis pisces tuos?

180   FISHER: On ċeastre.

In civitate.

TEACHER: Hwā biġþ hī?

Quis emit illos?

FISHER: Ċeaster-waran. Iċ ne mæġ [fōn] swā fela swā iċ mæġ ġe-syllan.

185   *Cives. Non possum tot capere quot possum vendere.*

TEACHER: Hwilċe fixas ġe-fēhst þū?

Quales pisces capis?

FISHER: ǢLAS ond hacodas, mynas ond æle-pūtan, sceotan ond lampredan, ond swā *h*wylċe swā on wætere swymmaþ, sprote.

190   *Anguillas et lucios, menas et capitones, tructas et murenas, et qualescumque in amne natant, saliu.*

TEACHER: For-hwī ne fixast þū on sǣ?

Cur non piscaris in mari?

FISHER: Hwīl*um* iċ dō, ac seldon, for-þām miċel rēwyt mē ys tō sǣ.

Aliquando facio, sed raro, quia magnum navigium mihi est ad   195
mare.

TEACHER: Hwæt fēhst þū on sǣ?

Quid capis in mare?

FISHER: Hǣrincgas ond leaxas, mere-swǣn ond stirian, ostran ond
crabban, muslan, wine-winclan, sǣ-coccas, fagc ond flōc ond   200
lopystran ond fela swylċes.

Alleces et isicios, delfinos et sturias, ostreas et cancros, musculas,
torniculi, neptigalli, platesia et platissa et polipodes et similia.

TEACHER: Wylt þū fōn sumne hwæl?

Vis capere aliquem cetum?   205

FISHER: N'iċ![23]

_____   *Nolo.*

[23] *N'iċ* is a contraction of *ne* + *iċ*, a fairly colloquial translation of the Latin *nolo* "I do not want to."

	TEACHER:	For-hwī?
		Quare?
210	FISHER:	For-þām plyhtliċ þingc hit ys ġe-fōn hwæl. Ġe-beorhliċre ys mē faran tō ēa mid scype mīn*um*, þænne faran mid manegum scypum on huntunge hranes.
		Quia periculosa res est capere cetum. Tutius est mihi ire ad amnem cum hamo meo, quam ire cum multis navibus in venationem ballene.
215	TEACHER:	For-hwī swā?
		Cur sic?
	FISHER:	For-þām lēofre ys mē ġe-fōn fisc þone iċ mæġ of-slēan, þonne fisc, þe nā þæt ān[24] mē ac ēac swylċe mīne ġe-fēran mid ānum sleġe mæġ be-senċean oþþe ġe-cwylman. Ond þēah mæniġe ġe-fōþ hwælas, ond æt-berstaþ frēcnysse, ond miċelne sċēat þanon be-ġytaþ.
220		
		Quia carius est mihi capere piscem quem possum occidere, quam illum, qui non solum me sed etiam meos socios uno ictu potest mergere aut mortificare. Et tamen multi capiunt cetos, et evadunt pericula, et magnum pretium inde adquirunt.
225		

---

[24] Translate *nā þæt ān* as "not only"—a literal, but not very idiomatic, gloss of the Latin *non solum*.

TEACHER: Sōþ þū seġst, ac iċ ne ġe-þrīstġe for mōdes mīnes nyten*nesse*.

             Verum dicis, sed ego non audeo propter mentis meae ignaviam.

TEACHER: Hwæt sæġst þū, fuġelere? Hū be-swīcst þū fuġelas?

             Quid dicis tu, auceps? Quomodo decipis aves?

FOWLER: On feala wīsan iċ be-swīċe fugelas, hwīl*um* mid net*um*,   230
             mid grīnum, mid līme, mi*d* hwistlunge, mid hafoce, mid
             treppan.

             Multis modis decipio aues, aliquando retibus, aliquando laqueis,
             aliquando glutino, aliquando sibilo, aliquando accipitre, aliquando
             decipula.   235

TEACHER: Hæfst þū hafoc?

             Habes accipitrem?

FOWLER: Iċ hæbbe.

             Habeo.

TEACHER: Canst þū temian hiġ?   240

             Scis domitare eos?

FOWLER: Ġēa, iċ cann. Hwæt sceoldon hiġ mē,[25] būton iċ cūþe temian hiġ?

Etiam, scio. Quid deberent mihi, nisi scirem domitare eos?

245 TEACHER: Syle mē ǣnne hafoc.

Da mihi unum accipitrem.

FOWLER: Iċ sylle lustlīċe, ġyf þū sylst mē ǣnne swiftne hund. Hwilċne hafoc wilt þū habban, þone māran hwæþer þe[26] þone lǣssan?

Dabo libenter, si dederis mihi unum velocem canem. Qualem
250 *accipitrem vis habere, maiorem autminorem?*

TEACHER: Syle mē þone māran. Hū ā-fēdst þū hafocas þīne?

Da mihi maiorem. Quomodo pascis accipitres tuos?

FOWLER: Hiġ fēdaþ hiġ sylfe ond mē on wintra, ond on lencgten iċ lǣte hiġ æt-windan tō wuda, ond ġe-nyme mē briddas on
255 hærfæste, ond temiġe hiġ.

Ipsi pascunt se et me in hieme, et in vere dimitto eos avolare ad silvam, et capio mihi pullos in autumno, et domito eos.

---

[25] Literally, this phrase means "what would they [be] to me," but the sense is, "what good are they to me."
[26] *hwæþer þe* = "or"

TEACHER: And for-hwī for-lǣtst þū þā ġe-temedan æt-windan fram þē?

             Et cur permittis domitos avolare a te?

FOWLER: For-þām iċ nelle fēdan hiġ on sumera, for-þām-þe hiġ þearle etaþ.   260
             Ond maniġe fēdaþ þā ġe-temodan ofer sumor, þæt eft hiġ habben
             ġearuwe. Ġēa, swā hiġ dōþ, ac iċ nelle o þæt ān[27] deorfan ofer hiġ,
             for-þām iċ cann ōþre, nā þæt ænne, ac ēac swilċe maniġe ġe-fōn.

             Quia nolo pascere eos in estate, eo quod nimium comedunt. Et
             multi pascunt domitos super estatem, ut iterum habeant paratos.   265
             Etiam, sic faciunt, sed ego nolo in tantum laborare super eos,
             quia scio alios, non solum unum, sed etiam plures capere.

TEACHER: Hwæt sæġst þū, mancgere?

             Quid dicis tu, mercator?

MERCHANT: Iċ secge þæt be-hēfe iċ eom ġe cingce ond ealdor-mannum   270
             ond weligum ond eallum folce.

             Ego dico quod utilis sum et regi et ducibus et divitibus et omni populo.

TEACHER: And hū?

             Et quomodo?

---

[27] The phrase *o þæt ān* "on that only" is a "mechanical gloss" according to Garmonsway (see note to l. 146, p. 32). Translate "so much."

275 MERCHANT: Iċ ā-stīġe mīn scyp mid hlæstum mīnum, ond rōwe ofer sǣliċe dǣlas, ond ċȳpe mīne þingc, ond bicge þincg dǣr-wyrðe, þā[28] on þisum lande ne bēoþ ā-cennede, ond iċ hit tō-ġelǣde[29] ēow hider mid miċċlan plihte ofer sǣ, ond hwȳl*um* for-lidenesse iċ þolie mid lyre ealra þinga mīnra, un-ēaþe cwiċ æt-berstende.

280 *Ego ascendo navem cum mercibus meis, et navigo ultra marinas partes, et vendo meas res, et emo res pretiosas, quae in hac terra non nascuntur, et adduco vobis huc cum magno periculo super mare, et aliquando naufragium patior cum iactura omnium rerum mearum, vix vivus evadens.*

285 TEACHER: Hwylċe þinc ġe-lǣdst þū ūs?

Quales res adducis nobis?

MERCHANT: Pællas ond sīdan, dēor-wyrþe ġymmas ond gold, sel-cūþe rēaf ond wyrt-ġe-mangc, wīn ond ele, ylpes-bān ond mæstlingc, ǣr ond tin, swefel ond glæs, ond þylċes fela.

290 *Purpuram et sericum, pretiosas gemmas et aurum, varias vestes et pigmenta, vinum et oleum, ebur et auricalcum, aes et stagnum, sulfur et vitrum, et his similia.*

TEACHER: Wilt þū syllan þingc þīne hēr eal swā[30] þū hī ġe-bohtest þǣr?

Vis vendere res tuas hic sicut emisti illic?

---

[28] See §7.5.3.

[29] The word *tō-ġelǣēde*, otherwise unknown in OE, is probably a direct translation of the Latin word *ad-duco* (with *ad-* meaning "to" and *duco* "to lead"); the native form is simply *ġe-lǣdan*.

MERCHANT: Iċ nelle; hwæt þænne mē fremode ġe-deorf mīn? Ac iċ wille heora   295
ċypan hēr luflīċor þonne ġe-bicge þǣr, þæt sum ġe-strēon mē iċ
be-ġyte, þanon iċ mē ā-fēde ond mīn wīf ond mīnne sunu.

Nolo; quid tunc mihi proficit labor meus? Sed volo vendere hic
carius quam emi illic, ut aliquod lucrum mihi adquiram, unde
me pascam et uxorem et filios.   300

TEACHER: Þū, scēo-wyrhta, hwæt wyrcst þū ūs nyt-wyrþnesse?

Tu, sutor, quid operaris nobis utilitatis?

SHOEMAKER: Ys, witodlīċe, cræft mīn be-hēfe þearle ēow ond nēod-þearf.

Est, quidem, ars mea utilis valde vobis et necessaria.

TEACHER: Hū?   305

Quomodo?

SHOEMAKER: Iċ bicge hȳda ond fell, ond ġearkie hiġ mid cræfte mīnum, ond
wyrċe of him ġe-scȳ mistliċes cynnes, swyftlēras ond scēos,
leþer-hosa ond buter-icas, brīdel-þwancgas ond ġe-rǣda,
flaxan *oððe* pinnan ond hīgdi-fatu, spur-leþera ond hælf-tra,   310
pusan ond fætelsas; ond [nān] ēower nele ofer-wintran būton
mīnum cræfte.

---

[30] *Referred from page 434, line 293:* Literally, *eal swā* means "just as," but it could be translated "for the same price" in this context.

315

Ego emo cutes et pelles, et preparo eas arte mea, et facio ex eis calciamenta diversi generis, subtalares et ficones, caligas et utres, frenos et falera, flascones et casidilia, calcaria et chamos, peras et marsupia; et nemo vestrum vult hiemare sine mea arte.

TEACHER: Sealtera, hwæt ūs fremaþ cræft þīn?

O salinator, quid nobis proficit ars tua?

SALTER: Þearle fremaþ cræft mīn ēow eallum. Nān ēower blisse brȳcð on

320   ġe-rerduncge oþþe mete, būton cræft mīn ġist-līþe him bēo.

Multum prodest ars mea omnibus. Nemo vestrum gaudio fruitur in prandio aut cena, nisi ars mea hospita ei fuerit.

TEACHER: Hū?

Quomodo?

325   SALTER: Hwylċ manna þurh-werodum[31] þurh-brǣcþ mettum būton swæċċe sealtes? Hwā ġe-fylþ cleafan his oþþe hēdd-erna būton cræfte mīn*um*? Efne, buter-ġeþwēor ǣlċ ond ċȳs-ġerunn losaþ ēow būton iċ hyrde[32] æt-wese ēow, þe ne fur-þum þæt ān[33] wyrtum ēowrum būtan mē brūcaþ.

---

[31] The adjective *þurh-werodum* "very sweet" modifies the noun *mettum* "foods," the dative object of *þurh-brǣcþ*.
[32] Translate *hyrde* "as a protector."
[33] Translate *þe* "you who." The phrase *ne furþum þæt ān* is either corrupt or confused. Judging from the Latin *non saltem*, it must mean "not even." Literally the phrase could be read as "you who not even that only."

Quis hominum dulcibus perfruitur cibis sine sapore salis? Quis   330
replet cellaria sua siue promptuaria sine arte mea? Ecce, butirum
omne et caseum perit vobis nisi ego custos adsim, qui nec saltem
oleribus vestris sine me utimini.

TEACHER: [Hwæt sæġest þū,] bæcere? Hwām fremaþ [cræft þīn] oþþe
hwæþer wē būtan þē magon līf ā-drēogan?   335

Quid dicis tu, pistor? Cui prodest ars tua, aut si sine te possimus
vitam ducere?

BAKER: Ġē magon þurh sum fæċ būtan nā lancge ne tō wel. Sōþlīċe
būtan cræfte mīn*um* ælċ bēod æmtiġ byþ ġe-sewen [bēon],
ond būton[34] hlāfe ælċ mete tō wlættan byþ ġe-hwyrfed. Iċ   340
heortan mannes ġe-strangie, iċ mæġen wera [eom], ond
for-þon lītlincgas nellaþ for-bīġean mē.

Potestis quidem per aliquod spatium sine arte mea vitam
ducere sed non diu nec adeo bene. Nam sine arte mea omnis
mensa vacua videtur esse, et sine pane omnis cibus in nausiam   345
convertitur. Ego cor hominis confirmo, ego robur virorum sum,
et nec parvuli volunt preterire me.

---

[34] *būton* = "without"

TEACHER: [Hwæt secgaþ wē be þām cōce,] hwæþer wē be-þurfon on
          æniġ*um* [his] cræfte?

350   *Quid dicimus de coco, si indigemus in aliquo arte eius?*

COOK: [Sē cōc secgð̆:] Ġif ġē mē ūt ā-drīfaþ fram ēowrum ġe-fērscype,
          ġē etaþ wyrta ēowre grēne, ond flǣsc-mettas ēowre hrēawe, ond
          [ne] furþ*um* fǣtt broþ ġē magon [būton cræfte mīnum habban].

          Dicit cocus: Si me expellitis a vestro collegio, manducabitis holera
355   *vestra viridia, et carnes vestras crudas, et nec saltem pingue ius*
          potestis sine arte mea habere.

TEACHER: Wē ne reċċaþ [þīnes cræftes], ne[35] hē ūs nēod-þearf ys, for-
          þām wē sylfe magon sēoþan þā þingc þe tō sēoþenne synd,
          ond brǣdan þā þingc þe tō brǣden*ne* synd.

360   *Non curamus de arte tua, nec nobis necessaria est, quia nos ipsi*
          possumus coquere quae coquenda sunt, et assare que assanda
          sunt.

COOK: [Sē cōc secgð̆:] Ġif ġē for-þǣ mē fram ā-drǣfaþ, þæt[36] ġē þus
          dōn, þonne bēo ġē ealle þrǣlas, ond nān ēower ne biþ[37]hlāford!
365   Ond þēah-hwæþere būton [cræfte mīnum] ġē ne etaþ.

---

[35] In normal OE word order, the verb *ys* (at the end of the clause) would occur after *ne*. As usual, it is good to keep in mind that the OE text is a gloss, not a translation.
[36] *Swā* "as" might be a slightly better gloss than *þæt* for the Latin *ut*.
[37] Future sense (see §5.8).

Dicit cocus: Si ideo me expellitis, ut sic faciatis, tunc eritis omnes coci, et nullus vestrum erit dominus! Et tamen sine arte mea non manducabitis.

TEACHER:　Ēalā, munuc, þe mē tō-spycst, efne, iċ hæbbe ā-fandod þē[38] habban gōde ġe-fēran ond þearle nēod-þearfe. Ond iċ āhsie　370 þē . . .[39] [if then you have any other companions but these.]

O, monache, qui mihi locutus es, ecce, probavi te habere bonos socios et valde necessarios. [Et interrogo te, si adhuc habes aliquos tales his exceptis.]

MONK:　[Yes, I have many others very necessary and very good.]　375

[Etiam, habeo plures valde necessarios et optimos.]

TEACHER:　[Who are they?]

[Qui sunt illi?]

MONK:　Iċ hæbbe smiþas, īsene-smiþas, gold-smiþ, seolofor-smiþ, ār- smiþ, trēow-wyrhtan ond maneġra ōþra mistliċra cræfta bīġ-　380 ġenceras.

---

[38] An alternative accusative form: see §7.1.2. For the construction *hæbbe ā-fandod þē habban*, see §5.2.6.

[39] Some of the following Latin text, and thus the OE gloss, has been omitted. The missing text, with a Modern English translation, is provided in square brackets from another manuscript.

Habeo fabros, ferrarios, aurificem, argentarium, aerarium, lignarium et multos alios variarum artium operatores.

TEACHER: Hæfst [þū] ǣniġne wīsne ġe-þeahtan?

385   *Habes aliquem sapientem consiliarium?*

MONK: Ġe-wīslīċe iċ hæbbe! [Hū meahte] ūre ġe-gaderungc būton ġe-þeahtynde bēon wissod?

Certe habeo! Quomodo potest nostra congregatio sine consiliario regi?

390   TEACHER: [Hwæt sæġst þū,] wīsa? Hwilċ cræft þē ġe-þuht, be-twux þās, furþra wesan?

Quid dicis tu, sapiens? Que ars tibi videtur, inter istas, prior esse?

MONK: [Iċ secge þē,] mē ys ġe-þuht[40] Godes þēow-dōm be-tweoh þās cræftas ealdor-scype healdan, swā swā hit ġe-rǣd [bið]

395   on Godspelle: "Fyrmest sēċeað rīċe Godes ond rīht-wīsnesse Hys, ond þās þingc ealle bēoþ tō-ġehyhte ēow."

Dico tibi, mihi videtur servitium Dei inter istas artes primatum tenere, sicut legitur in evangelio: "Primum querite regnum Dei et iustitiam Eius, et haec omnia adicientur vobis."

---

[40] The glossator renders Latin *videtur* "seems" rather literally as *ys ġe-þuht* (since *videtur* resembles a passive in Latin), though *þinċeð* "seems" would be more idiomatic in OE. For *mē þinċeð* see §11.2.

TEACHER: Ond hwilċ þē ġe-þūht [is]⁴¹ be-twux woruld-cræftas heoldan   400
            ealdor-dōm?

            Et qualis tibi uidetur inter artes seculares retinere primatum?

MONK: Eorþ-tilþ, for-þām sē yrþling ūs ealle fētt.⁴²

            Agricultura, quia arator nos omnes pascit.

SMITH: Sē smiþ seċġð: Hwanon⁴³ sȳlan scear oþþe culter, þe nā gāde   405
            hæfþ būton of cræfte mīn*um*? Hwanon fiscere ancgel, oþþe sċēo-
            wyrht*an* æl, oþþe sēamere nǣdl, nis⁴⁴ hit of mīn*um* ġe-weorce?

            *Ferrarius dicit, Unde aratori vomer aut culter, qui nec stimulum
            habet nisi ex arte mea? Unde piscatori hamus, aut sutori subula,
            sive sartori acus, nonne ex meo opere?*   410

MONK: Sē ġe-þeahtend andsweraþ: Sōþ witodlīċe [þū] sæġst, ac
            eallum ūs⁴⁵ lēofre ys wīkīan mid þē, yrþlincge, þonne mid þē,⁴⁶
            for-þām sē yrþling sylð ūs hlāf ond drenċ. Þū! Hwæt sylst [þū]
            ūs on smiþþan þīnre būton īsenne fȳr-spearcan ond swēġincga
            bēatendra slecgea ond blāwendra byliġa?   415

---

⁴¹ See the preceding note.

⁴² *fētt*: see §8.10.2.

⁴³ You must supply a verb here since the Latin omits it: "from where [comes] . . ."; *sǣlan* is a genitive singular.

⁴⁴ Translate *nis* "(if it) is not."

⁴⁵ *eallum ūs* = "(to) us all" or "to all of us"

⁴⁶ i.e., the smith

Consiliarius respondit: Verum quidem dicis, sed omnibus nobis carius est hospitari apud te aratorem, quam apud te, quia arator dat nobis panem et potum, tu. Quid das nobis in officina tua nisi ferreas scintillas et sonitus tundentium malleorum et flantium follium?

420   CARPENTER: Sē trēow-wyrhta seġð: Hwilċ ēower ne notaþ cræfte mīn*um*, þonne hūs ond mistliċe fat*u* ond scyp*u* ēow eallum iċ wyrċe?

Lignarius dicit: Quis vestrum non utitur arte mea, cum domos et diversa vasa et naves omnibus fabrico?

      SMITH: Sē gold-smiþ andwyrt: Ēalā, trǣw-wyrhta, for-hwī swā
425   spryċst þū, þonne ne furþ*um* ān þyrl [būton cræfte mīnum] þū ne miht dōn?

Ferrarius respondit, O, lignarie, cur sic loqueris, cum nec saltem unum foramen sine arte mea vales facere?

      MONK: Sē ġe-þeahtend sæġþ: Ealā, ġe-fēran ond gōde wyrhtan! Uton
430   tō-wurpon hwætlīċor þās ġe-flitu, ond sȳ[47] sibb ond ġe-þwǣrnyss be-tweoh ūs, ond framiġe ānra ġe-hwylċ[48] ōþr*um* on cræfte hys, ond ġe-ðwǣrian symble mid þām yrþlinge þǣr[49] wē biġleofan ūs, ond fōddor horsum ūrum habbaþ. And þis ġe-þeaht iċ sylle eallum wyrhtum, þæt ānra ġe-hwylċ cræft his ġeornlīċe
435   be-gange, for-þām sē þe cræft his for-lǣt, hē byþ for-lǣten fram

---

þām cræfte. Swā hwæðer þū sȳ, swā mæsse-prēost, swā munuc, swā ċeorl, swa kempa,[30] be-gā oþþe be-hwyrf þē sylfne on þisum, ond bēo þæt þū eart, for-þām miċel hȳnð ond sceamu hyt is menn nellan wesan[51] þæt þæt hē ys ond þæt þe hē wesan sceal.

Consiliarius dicit: O, socii et boni operarii. Dissolvamus citius has   440
contentiones, et sit pax et concordia inter vos, et prosit unusquisque
alteri arte sua. Et conveniamus semper apud aratorem, ubi victum
nobis et pabula equis nostris habemus. Et hoc consilium do omnibus
operariis, ut unusquisque artem suam diligenter exerceat quia qui
artem suam dimiserit, ipse dimittatur ab arte. Sive sis sacerdos sive   445
monachus, seu laicus, seu miles, exerce temet ipsum in hoc, et esto
quod es, quia magnum dampnum et verecundia est homini nolle esse
quod est et quod esse debet.

TEACHER: Ēalā, ċild[52] hū ēow līcaþ þēos spǣċ?

O pueri, quomodo vobis placet ista locutio?   450

STUDENTS: Wel hēo līcaþ ūs, ac þearle dēoplīċe spryċst ond ofer mæþe ūre þū forþ-tȳhst sprǣċe, ac spreċ ūs æfter ūrum and-ġyte, þæt wē magon under-standan þā þing þe þū sprecst.

---

[48] *Referenced from page 442, line 431:* Translate *ānra ġe-hwylċ* "each one"(*ānra* is a genitive plural that defies translation!). Similarly, translate the subjunctive *framiġe* "let . . . benefit."

[49] *Referenced from page 442, line 432:* þær = "from where, from whom"

[50] *swā hwæðer . . . swā . . . swā* = "whichever . . . whether . . . or"

[51] *nellan wesan* = "not to want to be"

[52] Here *ċild* behaves like a regular neuter strong noun (§2.9), probably by analogy. The expected plural form would be *ċildru –ra* (see §10.8).

<table>
<tr><td>455</td><td></td><td>*Bene quidem placet nobis, sed valde profunde loqueris et ultra etatem nostram protrahis sermonem, sed loquere nobis iuxta nostrum intellectum, ut possimus intelligere que loqueris.*</td></tr>
</table>

TEACHER: Iċ āhsiġe ēow, for-hwī swā ġeornlīċe leorne ġē?[53]

Interrogo vos, cur tam diligenter discitis?

STUDENTS: For-þām wē nellaþ wesan swā stunte nǣtenu, þā nān þing
460   witaþ, būton gærs ond wæter.

Quia nolumus esse sicut bruta animalia, quae nihil sciunt, nisi herbam et aquam.

TEACHER: And hwæt wille ġē?

Et quid vultis vos?

465 STUDENTS: [Wē] wyllaþ wesan wīse.

Volumus esse sapientes.

TEACHER: On hwilċum wīsdōme? Wille ġē bēon prættiġe oþþe þusent-
                     hīwe on lēasungum, lȳtiġe on sprǣċum, on-glǣwliċe, hinder-
                     ġēape, wel spreċende ond yfele þenċende, swǣsum wordum

---

[53] *leorne ġē*: normally, the verb would appear as *leornaþ*, but since the personal pronoun *ġē* follows immediately, the ending has been reduced (see §7.1.7). See previous note.

under-þēodde, fācen wið-innan tȳddriende, swā swā bergyls　470
mēttum[54] ofer-ġeweorke, wiþinnan fūl stenċe?

*Qua sapientia? Vultis esse versipelles aut milleformes in mendaciis,
astuti in loquelis, astuti, versuti, bene loquentes et male cogitantes,
dulcibus verbis dediti, dolum intus alentes, sicut sepulchrum
depicto mausoleo, intus plenum fetore?*　475

STUDENTS:　Wē nellaþ swā wesan wīse, for-þām hē nys wīs, þe mid
dydrunge hyne-sylfne be-swīcð.

*Nolumus sic esse sapientes, quia non est sapiens, qui simulatione
semet ipsum decipit.*

TEACHER:　Ac hū wille ġē?　480

Sed quomodo vultis?

STUDENTS:　Wē wyllaþ bēon bylewite būtan līċetunge, ond wīse þæt wē
būgon fram yfele ond dōn gōda. Ġȳt þēah-hwæþere dēoplīcor
mid ūs þū smēagst, þonne yld ūre on-fōn mæġe; ac spreċ ūs
æfter ūrum ġe-wunan, næs swā dēoplīċe.　485

*Volumus esse simplices sine hipochrisi, et sapientes ut declinemus
a malo et faciamus bona. Adhuc tamen profundius nobiscum*

---

[54] *mēttum* = "painted," dative plural past participle of the verb *mētan* "to paint"

*disputas, quam etas nostra capere possit; sed loquere nobis nostro
more, non tam profunde.*

490   TEACHER: And iċ dō[55] eal swā ġē biddaþ. –Þū, cnapa, hwæt dydest [þū]
tō-dæġ?

Et ego faciam sicut rogatis. –Tu, puer, quid fecisti hodie?

BOY: Maneġa þing iċ dyde. On þisse niht,[56] þā þā cnyll iċ ġe-
hǣrde, iċ ā-rās on mīn*um* bedde ond ēode tō ċyrċean ond
495   sang ūht-sang mid ġe-brōþrum. Æfter þām[57] wē sungon be
eallum hālgum ond dæġ-rēdliċe lof-sangas. Æfter þysum [wē
sungon] prīm ond seofon seolmas mid letanīan ond capitol-
mæssan; syþþan [wē sungon] under-tīde, ond dydon mæssan
be dæġe. Æfter þisum wē sungon mid-dæġ, ond ǣton ond
500   druncon ond slēpon ond eft wē ā-rison ond sungon nōn. Ond
nū wē synd hēr æt-foran þē, ġearuwe ġe-hǣran hwæt þū ūs
secge.[58]

*Multas res feci. Hac nocte, quando signum audivi, surrexi
de lectulo et exivi ad ecclesiam, et cantavi nocturnam cum
505   fratribus. Deinde cantavimus de omnibus sanctis et matutinales
laudes. Post haec primam et VII psalmos cum letaniis et
primam missam; deinde tertiam, et fecimus missam de die.*

---

[55] future sense (see §5.8)

[56] i.e., last night

[57] *Æfter þām* = "after that" or "after it" (i.e., *ūht-sang*)

[58] Garmonsway notes, "The monks eat nothing before noon, and the school is held in the late afternoon" (note to l. 274, p. 44). *Secge* is a
subjunctive form; translate "may say."

Post haec cantavimus sextam, et manducavimus et bibimus et
dormivimus, et iterum surreximus et cantavimus nonam. Et
modo sumus hic coram te, parati audire quid nobis dixeris.   510

TEACHER: Hwænne wylle ġē syngan, æfen oþþe niht-sangc?

     Quando vultis cantare, vesperam aut completorium?

BOY: Þonne hyt tīma byþ.

     Quando tempus erit.

TEACHER: Wǣre þū tō-dæġ be-swuncgen?   515

     Fuisti hodie verberatus?

BOY: Iċ næs, for-þām wærlīċe iċ mē heold.

     Non fui, quia caute me tenui.

TEACHER: And hū þīne ġe-fēran?[59]

     Et quomodo tui socii?   520

BOY: Hwæt mē āhsast be þām, iċ ne dear yppan þē dīġla ūre.[60]

     Quid me interrogas de hoc; non audeo pandere tibi secreta nostra.

---

[59] This sentence lacks a verb as does the Latin original. It probably means "How did your companions behave themselves?"

[60] Garmonsway notes, "In one of Bata's colloquies . . . two boys who have been stealing apples from the monastery orchard are shamelessly betrayed by their fellows, when the master asks the class for information" (note to 1. 282, p. 45).

TEACHER: Ānra ġe-hwylċ wāt ġif hē be-swuncgen wæs oþþe nā. —Hwæt ytst þū on dæġ?

525   *Unusquisque scit si flagellatus erat an non. —Quid manducas in die?*

BOY: Ġæt flæsc-mettum iċ brūce, for-ðām ċild iċ eom under ġyrda drohtniende.[61]

Adhuc carnibus vescor, quia puer sum sub virga degens.

TEACHER: Hwæt māre ytst þū?

530   *Quid plus manducas?*

BOY: Wyrta ond æiġra, fisc ond ċӯse, buteran ond bēana ond ealle clæne þingc iċ ete mid miċelre þancunge.

Holera et ova, pisces et caseum, butirum et fabas et omnia munda manduco cum gratiarum actione.

535   TEACHER: Swæþe wax-ġeorn eart þū, þonne þū ealle þingc etst þe þē tō-foran [ġe-sette synd].

Valde edax es, cum omnia manducas que tibi apponuntur.

---

[61] Novices and the sick were allowed to eat meat.

BOY: Iċ ne eom swā miċel swelġere þæt iċ ealle cynn metta on ānre
ġe rcordunge etan mæġe.

Non sum tam vorax ut omnia genera ciborum in una refectione   540
edere possim.

TEACHER: Ac hū?

Sed quomodo?

BOY: Iċ brūċe hwīlum þisum mettum, [hwīlum] ōþrum mid
sȳfernysse, swā swā dafnað[62] munuce, næs mid ofer-hropse,   545
for-þām iċ eom nān gluto.

Vescor aliquando his cibis, et aliquando aliis cum sobrietate, sicut
decet monachum, non cum voracitate, quia non sum gluto.

TEACHER: Ond hwæt drincst þū?

Et quid bibis?   550

BOY: Ealu, ġif iċ hæbbe, oþþe wæter ġif iċ næbbe ealu.

Cervisam, si habeo, vel aquam si non habeo cervisam.

---

[62] An impersonal construction—supply an "it" in translation. See §11.2.

TEACHER: Ne drincst þū wīn?

Nonne bibis vinum?

555   BOY: Iċ ne eom swā spēdiġ þæt iċ mæġe bicgean mē wīn. Ond wīn nys drenċ ċildra ne dysgra, ac ealdra ond wīsra.[63]

Non sum tam dives ut possim emere mihi vinum. Et vinum non est potus puerorum sive stultorum, sed senum et sapientium.

560   TEACHER: Hwǣr slǣpst [þū]?

Ubi dormis?

BOY: On slǣp-ern mid ġe-brōþrum.

In dormitorio cum fratribus.

TEACHER: Hwā ā-weċþ þē tō ūht-sancge?

Quis excitat te ad nocturnos?

565   BOY: Hwīlum iċ ġe-hǣre cnyll ond iċ ā-rīse. Hwīlum lārēow mīn ā-weċþ mē stiþlīċe mid ġyrde.

Aliquando audio signum et surgeo. Aliquando magister meus excitat me duriter cum virga.

---

[63] a series of genitive plurals, depending on *drenċ.*

TEACHER: Ēalā, ġē ċildra ond wynsume leorneras, ēow manaþ ēower lārēow
           þæt ġē hǣrsumian godcundum lārum ond þæt ġē healdan ēow   570
           sylfe ænlīċe on ælċere stōwe. Gāþ þēawlīċe þonne ġē ġe-hǣran
           ċyriċean bellan, ond gāþ intō ċyrċean, ond ā-būgaþ ēad-mōdlīċe tō
           hālgum wēfodum, ond standaþ þēawlīċe, ond singað ān-mōdlīċe,
           ond ġe-biddaþ for ēowrum synnum ond gāþ ūt būtan hyġe-lēaste
           tō claustre oþþe tō leorninga.

           O, probi pueri et venusti mathites, vos hortatur vester eruditor   575
           ut pareatis divinis disciplinis et observetis vosmet eleganter
           ubique locorum. Inceditis morigerate cum auscultaveritis ecclesie
           campanas, et ingredimini in orationem et inclinate suppliciter ad
           almas aras, et state disciplinabiliter et concinite unanimiter et
           intervenite pro vestris erratibus, et egredimini sine scurrilitate in   580
           claustrum vel in gimnasium.

Four *Lives* of
St. Æðeldrȳð

A portrait of St. Ætheldreda from the Benedictional of St. Æthelwold (London, British Library, Ms. Additional 49598, fol. 90v). The Latin reads: "Imago S[an]c[t]e Æðeldryðe abbatissa ac perpetue uirginis" ("The image of St. Ætheldreda, abbess and perpetual virgin").

Four Lives of St. Æðeldryð

St. Æðeldryð (d. 679) or St. Audrey, as she was later called, was one of a group of prominent 7th-century royal women saints. Founder of the monastery at Ely, she was the daughter of King Anna and Queen Bertha of East Anglia, and her four sisters (Erconwald, Ethelburga, Sexburga, and Withburg) also came to be recognized as saints. Though twice married, she remained a virgin. After a distinguished career serving as abbess at Ely, she died of a neck tumor in 679. Her sister Sexburga (who succeded her as abbess) was instrumental in promoting her sister's cult. The Venerable Bede first recorded her life in his *Historia ecclesiastica gentis Anglorum* (*The Ecclesiastical History of the English People*), adding an extensive poem in praise of her saintly virtues. Bede's account (reproduced here in Latin with a Modern English translation) served as the basis for three vernacular lives of Æðeldryð provided below: 1) the OE translation of Bede's *Ecclesiastical History*, produced as part of a program of translations in King Alfred the Great's educational reform in the 9th century, 2) her entry in the *Old English Martyrology*,[1] probably also composed in the 9th century, and 3) Ælfric's version of her life from his collection, *The Lives of The Saints*.

An extensive life of Æðeldryð forms the first book of the late 12th-century *Liber Eliensis* (*Book of Ely*), providing a full biography of the saint and founder of the monastery, and perhaps drawing details from a lost version of her life.[2]

In the early modern period, the celebration of Æðeldryð's (St. Audrey's) feast day in Ely was accompanied by a fair in which lace necklaces were sold. These became known as *tawdry* laces, a contraction of "Saint Audrey laces." Later on, *tawdry* came to mean "showy or gaudy without real value" and, even later, "untidy, slovenly, or ungraceful" (OED). Though the word *tawdry* is directly related to the saint's name, it refers to the cheap souvenirs sold at her fair rather than to her character, which was heroically chaste.

The following collection of texts should allow you to trace the evolution of an Anglo-Saxon saint's life from its Latin sources through its various vernacular adaptations.

---

[1] A collection of brief lives or *passiones* of saints in the vernacular, organized in calendar form by the feast days of the saints.

[2] For a translation of the *Liber Eliensis*, see Janet Fairweather's *Liber Eliensis: A History of the Isle of Ely from the Seventh to the Twelfth Century* (Cambridge: Boydell, 2004).

I. Account of St. Æðeldryð in Bede's *Ecclesiastical History of the English People* (8th century)

XVII

Accepit autem rex Ecgfrid coniugem nomine Aedilthrydam, filiam Anna regis Orientalium Anglorum, cuius saepius mentionem fecimus, viri bene religiosi ac per omnia mente et opere egregii; quam et alter ante illum vir habuerat uxorem, princeps videlicet Australium Gyrviorum vocabulo Tondberct. Sed illo post modicum temporis, ex quo eam accepit, defuncto, data est regi praefato. Cuius consortio cum xii annis uteretur, perpetua tamen mansit virginitatis integritate gloriosa, sicut mihimet sciscitanti, cum hoc an ita esset quibusdam venisset in dubium, beate memoriae Vilfrid episcopus referebat, dicens se testem integritatis eius esse certissimum, adeo ut Ecgfridus promiserit se ei terras ac pecunias multas esse donaturum, si reginae posset persuadere eius uti conubio, quia sciebat illam nullum virorum plus illo diligere. Nec diffidendum est nostra etiam aetate fieri potuisse, quod aevo preaecedente aliquoties factum fideles historiae narrant, donante uno eodemque Domino, qui se nobiscum usqe in finem saeculi manere pollicetur. nam etiam signum divini miraculi, quo eiusdem feminae sepulta caro corrumpi non potuit, indicio est quia a virili contactu incorrupta duraverit.

Quae multum diu regem postulans, ut saeculi curas relinquere atque in monasterio tantum vero regi Christo servire permitteretur, ubi vix aliquando impetravit, intravit monasterium Aebbae abbatissae, quae erat amita regis Ecgfridi, positum in locoquem Coludi urbem nominant, accepto velamine sanctimonialis habitus a praefato antistite Vilfrido. Post annum vero ipsa facta est abbatissa in regione quae vocatur Elge, ubi constructo monasterio virginum Deo devotarum perplurium mater virgo et exemplis vitae caelestis esse coepit et monitis. De qua ferunt quia, ex quo monasterium petiit, nunquam lineis sed solum laneis vestimentis uti voluerit, raroque in calidis balneis praeter inminentibus sollemniis maioribus, verbi gratia paschae pentecostes ephiphaniae, lavari voluerit, et tunc novissima omnium, lotis prius suo suarumque ministrarum obsequio ceteris quae ibi essent famulis Christi; raro praeter maiora sollemnia vel artiorem necessitatem plus quam semel per diem manducaverit; semper, si non non infirmitas gravior prohibuisset, ex tempore matutinae synaxeos usque ad ortum diei in ecclesia precibus intenta persteterit. Sunt etiam qui dicant, quia per prophetiae spiritum et pestilentiam, qua ipsa esset moritura, praediscerit, et numerum quoque eorum qui de suo monasterio hac essent de mundo rapiendi palam cunctis praesentibus intimaverit. rapta est autem ad Dominum in medio suorum post annos septem ex quo abbatissae gradum susceperat, et aeque, ut ipsa iusserat, non alibi quam in medio eorum iuxta ordinem quo transierat ligneo in locello sepulta.

Cui successit in ministerium abbatissae soror eius Sexburg, quam habverat in coniugem Earconberct rex Cantuariorum. Et cum sedecim annis esset sepulta, placuit eidem abbatissae levari ossa eius et in locello novo posita in ecclesiam transferri; iussitque quosdam e fratribus quaerere lapidem, de quo locellum in hoc facere possent. Qui ascensa navi (ipsa enim regio Elge undique est aquis ac paludibus circumdata, neque lapides maiores habet) venerunt ad civitatulam quandam desolatam non procul inde sitam, quae linga Anglorum Grantacaestir vocatur, et mox invenerunt iuxta muros civitatis locellum de marmore albo pulcherrime factum, operculo quoque similis lapidis aptissime tectum. Vnde intellegentest a Domino suum inter esse prosperatum gratias agentes rettulerunt ad monasterium.

Cumque corpus sacrae virginis ac sponsae Christi aperto sepulchro esset prolatum in lucem, ita incorruptum inventum est, ac si eodem die fuisset defuncta sive humo condita, sicut et praefatus antistes Vilfred et multi allii qui novere testantur; sed certiori notitia medicus Cynifrid, qui et morienti illi et elevatae de tumulo adfuit, qui referre erat solitus quod illa infirmata habuerit tumorem maximum sub maxilla. "Iusseruntque me," inquit, "incidere tumorem illum, ut efflueret noxius umor qui inerat. Quod dum facerem, videbatur illa per biduum aliquanto levius habere, ita ut milti putarent quia sanari posset a languore. Tertia autem die prioribus adgrauata doloribus et rapta confestim de mundo, dolorem omnem ac mortem perpetua salute ac vita mutavit. Cumque post tot annos elevanda essent ossa de sepulchro, et extento desuper papilione omnis congregatio, hinc fratrum inde sororum, psallens circumstaret, ipsa autem abbatissa intus cum pacis ossa elatura et dilutura intrasset, repente audivimus abbatissam intus clare voce proclamare: 'Sit gloria nomini Domini.' Nec multo post clamaverunt me intus, reserato ostio papilionis, vidique elevatum de tumulo et positum in lectulo corpus sacrae Deo virginis quasi dormientis simile. Sed et discooperto vultus indumento monstraverunt mihi etiam vulnus incisurae, quod feceram, curatum, ita ut mirum in modum pro aperto et hiante vulnere, cum quo sepulta erat, tenuissima tunc cicatricis vestiga parerent. Sed et linteamina omnia, quibus involutum erat corpus, integra apparuerunt et ita nova, ut ipso die viderentur castis eius membris esse circumdata." Ferunt autem quia, cum praefato tumore ac dolore maxillae sive colli premeretur, multum delectata sit hoc genere infirmitatis, ac solita dicere: "Scio certissime quia merito in collo pondus languoris porto, in quo iuvenculam me memini superuacua moniliorum pondera portare; et credo quo ideo me superna pietas dolore colli uoluit grauiari, ut sic absoluar reatu superuacuae leuitatis, dum mihi nunc pro auro et margaretis de collo rubor tumoris ardorque promineat." Contigit autem tactu indumentorum eorundem et daemonia ab obsessis effugata corporibus et infirmitates alias aliquoties esse curatas. Sed et loculum, in quo primo sepulta est, nonnullis oculos dolentibus saluti fuisse perhibent, qui cum suum caput eidem loculo adponentes orassent, mox doloris siue caliginis incommodum ab oculis amouerent. Laurent igitur uirgines corpus, et nouis indutum uestibus intulerunt in ecclesiam, atque in eo quod adlatum erat sarcofago posuerunt, ubi usque hodie in magna ueneratione habetur. Mirum uero in modum ita aptum corpori uirginis sarcofagum inuentum est, ac si ei specialiter praeparatum fuisset, et locus quoque capitis seorsum fabrefactus ad mensuram capitis illius aptissime figuratus apparuit.

Est autem Elge in prouincia Orientalium Anglorum regio familiarum circiter sexcentarum, in similitudinem insulaeuel paludibus, ut diximus, circumdata uel aquis, unde et a copia anguillarum, quae in eisdem paludibus capiuntur, nomen accepit; ubi monasterium habere disiderauit memorata Christ famula, quoniam de prouincia eorundem Orientalium Anglorum ipsa, ut praefati sumus, carnis originem duxerat.

King Ecgfrith married a wife named Æthelthryth, the daughter of Anna, king of the East Angles, who has often been referred to, a very religious man and noble both in mind and deed. She had previously been married to an alderman of the South Gyrwe, named Tondberht. But he died shortly after the marriage and on his death she was given to King Ecgfrith. Though she lived with him for twelve years she still preserved the glory of perfect virginity. When I asked Bishop Wilfrid of blessed memory whether this was true, because certain people doubted it, he told me that he had the most perfect proof of her virginity; in fact Ecgfrith had promised to give him estates and money if he could persuade the queen to consummate their marriage, because he knew that there was none whom she loved more than Wilfrid himself. Nor need we doubt that this which often happened in our time too through the help of the Lord, who has promised to be with us even to the end of the age. And the divine miracle whereby her flesh would not corrupt after she was buried was token and proof that she had remained uncorrupted by contact with any man.

For a long time she had been asking the king to allow her to relinquish the affairs of this world and to serve Christ, the only true King, in a monastery; when at length and with difficulty she gained his permission, she entered the monastery of the Abbess Æbbe, Ecgfrith's aunt, which is situated in a place called Coldingham, receiving the veil and the habit of a nun from Bishop Wilfrid. A year afterwards she was herself appointed abbess in the district called Ely, where she built a monastery and became, by the example of her heavenly life and teaching, the virgin mother of many virgins dedicated to God. It is related of her that, from the time she entered the monastery, she would never wear linen but only woollen garments and would seldom take a hot bath except just before the greater feasts, such as Easter, Pentecost, and Epiphany, and then last of all, after the other handmaidens of Christ who were present had washed themselves, assisted by herself and her attendants. She rarely ate more than once a day except at the greater festivals or because of urgent necessity; she always remained in the church at prayer from the time of the office of Matins until dawn, unless prevented by serious illness. There are indeed some who say that, by the spirit of prophecy, she not only foretold the plague that was to be the cause of her death but also openly declared, in the presence of all, the number of those of the monastery who were to be taken from the world by the same pestilence.

She was taken to the Lord in the midst of her people, after holding the rank of abbess for seven years. When she died she was buried by her own command in a wooden coffin, in the ranks of the other nuns, as her turn came.

She was succeeded in the office of abbess by her sister Seaxburh, who had been the wife of Eorcenberht, king of Kent. After Æthelthryth had been buried for sixteen years, the abbess decided that her bones should be raised and placed in the church in a new coffin; she therefore ordered some of the brothers to look for some blocks of stone from which to make a coffin for this purpose. So they got into a boat (for the district of Ely is surrounded on all sides by waters and marshes and has no large stones) and came to a small deserted fortress not far away which is called *Grantacæstir* (Cambridge) in English, and near the walls of the fortress they soon found a coffin beautifully made of white marble, with a close-fitting lid of the same stone. Realizing that the Lord had prospered their journey, they brought it back to the monastery.

When the tomb of the sacred virgin and bride of Christ was opened and the body brought to light, it was found to be as uncorrupt as if she had died and been buried that very day. Bishop Wilfrid and many others who knew about it testify to this; but more certain proof is given by a doctor named Cynefrith, who was present at her death-bed and at her elevation from the tomb. He used to relate how, during her illness, she had a very large tumour beneath her jaw. "I was ordered," he said, " to cut this tumour so as to drain out the poisonous matter within it. After I had done this she seemed to be easier for about two days and many thought that she would recover from her sickness. But on the third day she was attacked by her former pains and was soon taken from life. When, some years later, her bones were to be taken out of the sepulchre, a tent was erected over it and the whole congregation stood round singing, the brothers on one side and the sisters on the other. The abbess herself had gone inside with a few others, for the purpose of raising and washing the bones, when we suddenly heard the abbess cry out from within in a loud voice, 'Glory be to the name of the Lord!' Shortly afterwards they called me in, lifting the entrance to the tent; then I saw the body of God's holy virgin raised from the tomb and laid on a bed like one asleep. They drew back the cloth which covered her face and showed me the wound I had made by my incision, now healed, so that instead of the open gaping wound which she had when she was buried, there now appeared marvellous to relate, only the slightest traces of a scar. Besides this, all the linen clothes in which her body was wrapped appeared as whole and fresh as on the very day when they had been put around her chaste limbs." It is also related that when she was afflicted with this tumour and by the pain in her neck and jaw, she gladly welcomed this sort of pain and used to say, "I know well enough that I deserve to bear the weight of this affliction in my neck, for I remember that when I was a young girl I used to wear an unnecessary weight of necklaces; I believe that God in His goodness would have me endure this pain in my neck in order that I may thus be absolved from the guilt of my needless vanity. So, instead of gold and pearls, a fiery red tumour now stands out upon my neck." It happened also that, by the touch of the linen clothes, devils were expelled from the bodies of those who were possessed by them, and other diseases were healed from time to time. The coffin also in which she was first buried is said to have healed some who suffered from eye troubles; after they had prayed with their heads resting on the coffin, they were quickly relieved of the pain and dimness of their eyes. So the maidens washed her body, wrapped it in new robes, carried it into the church, and placed it in the sarcophagus which they had brought, where it is held in great veneration to this day. This sarcophagus was found to fit the virgin's body in a wonderful way, as if it had been specially prepared for her; and the place for the head, which was cut out separately, seemed to be exactly shaped to its size.

Ely is a district of about 600 hides in the kingdom of the East Angles and, as has already been said, resembles an island in that it is surrounded by marshes or by water. It derives its name for the large number of eels which are caught in the marshes. This servant of Christ wished to have her monastery here because, as has also been said, she sprang from the race of the East Angles.

—Bertram Colgrave and R.A.B. Mynors, eds. *Bede's Ecclesiastical History of the English People* (Oxford: Clarendon, P, 1969), pp. 390-97.

II. Account of St. Æðeldryð in the OE Translation of Bede's *Ecclesiastical History* (9th century)

On-fēng Ecgfrið sē cyning ġe-mæccan ond wīf, þǣre noma wæs Æðeldryð, Annan dohtor Ēast-engla cyninges, þæs wē oft ǣr ġe-myndgodon. Brōhte hēo ǣr ōðer wer[3] him tō wīfe Sūð-gyrwa aldormon, þæs noma wæs Tondberht, ac æfter med-miclum fæċe, þæs þe hē hȳ tō wīfe on-fēng, hē forð-fērde. Þā wæs hēo seald ond for-ġifen þǣm fore-spreċenan cyninge.

5

Þæs ġe-mānan myd þȳ hēo wæs twelf winter brūcende,[4] hwæðre hēo mid ēċre on-wealhnesse mæġð-hādes[5] wuldorlīċe ā-wunade; swā swā mē seolfum friġnendum[6]—mid þȳ sumum monnum cwōm[7] in twēon hwæðer hit swā wǣre— þā þǣre ēadgan ġe-mynde Wilferþ biscop sæġde, ond cwæð þæt hē wǣre sē cūðesta ġe-weota hire clǣnnisse ond hire mæġð-hādes, tō ðon þætte Ecgfrið sē cyning him ġe-hēht ġe lond ġe miċel feoh tō ġe-syllenne, ġif hē ðā cwēne ġe-spanan ond ġe-lǣran meahte, þæt hēo brūcan wolde his ġe-synscypes; for-þon hē ġeare wiste þæt hēo nǣniġne wǣpned-mon mā lufode þonne hine.

10

Nis þæt tō ġe-ortrȳwanne þæt in ūsse ielde þæt bēon meahte, þætte [in] forð-gangendre ielde oft ġe-worden [is, swā] ġe-trēow spell cȳðað ond secgað, þurh ānes Drihtnes ġife ond þæs ilcan, sē ðe hine ġe-hātende wæs mid ūs ēac wunian āa oð weorulde ende.[8]

15

---

[3] Hint: Normal word order here is reversed (*hēo* = accusative).

[4] The translation here follows the word order of the Latin closely (*Cuius consortio cum xii annis uteretur*), making for difficult reading in OE. In normal word order, the clause would run, *Mid þȳ hēo wæs þæs ġe-mānan twelf winter brūcende*.

[5] *Mæġð-hādes* depends on *on-weulhnesse* (see §5.4.3).

[6] *Swā swā mē seolfum friġnendum*. Again, this construction is a close translation of the Latin, but not very idiomatic in OE. Translate "just as I learned . . . when (*þā*)" or more literally, "just as with me learning."

[7] Supply an "it" as the subject of *cwōm*, and be careful with *sumum monnum* (be sure to check the case)!

[8] A difficult sentence, mainly because it misrepresents the Latin slightly. Translate "Nor is it to be doubted that in our age that (i.e., a chaste marriage) could be, which in a previous age often occurred, as true histories make known and say, through the gift of one and the same Lord who promised to remain with us forever until the end of the world."

Wæs ēac swilċe þæs godcundan wundres sweotol tācnung, þæt þǣre ilcan
fǣmnan līċ-homa, be-byrġed, brosnian ne meahte, þæt[9] hēo fram werliċre
hrinenesse un-ġewemmed ā-wunade.   20

Bæd hēo swīðe longe þone cyning, þæt hēo mōste weoruld-sorge ond ġe-
mǣnne for-lǣtan, ond [hē] hēo for-lǣte[10] in mynstre þǣm sōðan cyninge Crīste
þēowian.

Þæt hēo þā æt nēhstan mā þurh-tēah, ðā ēode hēo in Æbban mynster, þǣre
abbudissan, sēo wæs Ecgfrīðes faðe þæs cyninges; þæt is ġe-seted in þǣre stōwe,   25
þe mon nemneð Coludis-byriġ.

Ond hēo þǣr hāliġ-refte on-fēng ond Godes þēow-hāde fram þǣm fore-
spreċenan biscope Wilferðe. Þā wæs emb ān ġēr æfter þissum þæt hēo wæs
abbudisse ġe-worden, in þǣm þēod-londe þe is ġe-cēġed Eliġe, þǣr hēo mynster
ġe-timbrode Gode wilsumra fǣmnena.[11]   30

Ond hēo fǣmna moniġra mōdor on-gōn bēon, ġe mid bysenum heofonlīċes
līfes ġe ēac mid manungum. Secgað men be hire, seoðþan hēo mynster ġe-sōhte,
þæt hēo nǣfre līnnum[12] hræġlum brūcan wolde ac wyllenum. Ond seldan in
hātum baðum hēo baðian wolde, būton [on] þām hȳhstan symbelnessum ond
tīdum æt Ēastran ond æt Pentecosten ond þȳ twelftan dæġe ofer Ġeochol. Ond   35
þonne hēo [ðēnode] ǣrest þurh hire þeġnunge ond hire þīnenna þā ōðre Crīstes
þēowas, þā ðe þǣr wǣron, ond on-þwēġne,[13] þonne wolde hēo ealra nȳhst hȳ[14]
baþian ond þwēan.

---

[9] *þæt* = "since, because"

[10] Note that this sentence uses *for-lǣtan* in two different senses: "to abandon, leave behind" in the first instance, and "to permit, allow" in the second.

[11] *Wilsumra fǣmnena* is a genitive plural depending on *mynster* (see §5.4.3).

[12] A syncopated form of *linenum*.

[13] The past participle *on-þwēġne* (plural nominative) represents a Latin construction, not very idiomatic in OE, that should be translated "and [once they were] washed . . ."

[14] *Hȳ* = "herself" (see §7.4)

40 Ond seld*a*n, būton [on] māran symbelnessum ond tīdum oðþe māran nȳd-
þearfe, mā þonne ǣne sīðe on dæġe þæt hēo wolde mete þycgan. [15] Ond symle, ġif
hire hefiġre untrymnesse ne be-were, of þǣre tīde ūht-sanges oð hlūttorne dæġ
in ċiriċan [hēo] in hālgum ġe-bedum stōd.

Sume men ēac swylċe sæġdon, þæt hēo þurh wīte-dōmes gāst þa ādle fore-
cwǣde, þe hēo on forð-fērde, ond swelċe ēac þāra Godes þēowa rīm,[16] þā ðe of
45 heora mynstre of middan-ġearde wǣron tō ġe-lēorenne,[17] þæt hēo sweotolīċe
eallum cȳðde.

Þā ġe-lēorde hēo tō Drihtne on middum hire hīwum æfter seofon ġēarum,
þæs þe hēo abbudessan hād on-fēng. Ond þā, ġe-līċe swā swā hēo be-bēad, nales
in ōðre stōwe būtan in middum hire hīwum æfter ende-byrdnesse, þe hēo ġe-
50 lēorde, in trēowenre þrȳh wæs [hēo] be-byrġed.[18]

Þā fēng æfter hire in þā þeġnunge abbudissan[19] Seaxburh hire sweostor, þā[20]
hæfde tō wīfe Ærconbyrht Cantwara cyning. Ond mid þȳ Æðeldrȳð wæs syx-tȳne
ġēar be-byrġed, þā līcode[21] þǣre abbudissan hire mǣgan, þæt hēo hire bān ūp ā-
dyde ond in nēowe þrūh ġe-sette ond in ċircan ġe-dyde.

55 Þā hēht hēo sume brōðor faran ond þone stān sēċan, þæt mon meahte þā
ðrūh of ġe-hēawan ond ġe-wyrċan. Þā ēodon hēo in scip, for-þon Elia lond is
ǣġ-hwonan mid wætrum ond mid fennum ymb-seald, ne hit miċele stānas hafað.
Þā cwōmon hēo tō sumre ċeastre ġe-hrorenre noht feor þonon, sēo is on Englisc
Granta-ċester ġe-ċēġed. Ond hēo sōna ġe-metton bi þǣre ċeastre wallum þrūh of

---

[15] Translate "[It was] rare that she would consume food . . ."

[16] *Þāra Godes þēowa rīm* means "the number of God's servants" (literally, "number of the servants of God"). Note that you must supply "she predicted" from the earlier part of the clause

[17] *wǣron tō ġe-lēorenne* = "were to depart" (i.e., die)

[18] The order of clauses here is confusing, but if you patiently move the elements around, you should arrive at an intelligible translation. Note that the main subject and verb of this sentence appear at the very end (*wæs hēo be-byrġed*).

[19] *Abudissan* is a genitive singular depending on *þeġnunge.*

[20] *þā* = "whom" (feminine accusative singular of the definite article: see §7.5.3)

[21] An impersonal construction: see §11.2.

hwītum stāne fæġere ġe-worht, ond sēo wæs swilċe ēac ġe-risenlīċe ġe-hleodad 60
mid ġe-līċe stūne. Þā on-ġeton hēo sōna, þæt heora ærende wæs ond heora sīð-
fæt from Drihtne seolfum ġe-hradod ond ġe-syndgad; ond hēo þæs[22] Gode þanc
sæġdon, ond þā þrūh to þǣm mynstre ġe-læddon.

Mid þȳ þā sē līċ-homa þǣre hālgan fǣmnan ond þǣre Crīstes brȳde openre þǣre
byrġenne[23] wæs forð on lēoht ġe-læded, þā wæs hē ġe-meted swā un-ġebrosnad 65
ond swā un-ġewemmed, swā hēo þȳ ylcan dæġe forð-fēred ond be-byrged wǣre—
swā swā sē fore-spreċena biscop Wilferð ond moniġe ōðre, þā ðe hit cūðon,
cȳðdon ond sæġdon. Ac hwæðre cūðran ġe-witnesse Cyneferð lǣċe,[24] sē æt hire
wæs þā hēo forð-fērde ond eft þā hire līċ-homan mon of byrġenne ūp-hōf.

Wæs his ġe-wuna þæt hē sæġde,[25] þā hēo un-trumu wæs, þæt hēo hæfde 70
miċelne swile on hire swēoran: "Þā hēht mē mon," cwæð he, "þæt iċ þone swile
ġe-sticade,[26] þætte sēo sceðþende wǣte ūt flēowe, sēo þǣr-in wæs. Mid þȳ iċ þæt
þā dyde, þā wæs hēo ge-seġen[27] þurh tweġen dagas þæt hire lēohtor[28] ond wel
wǣre, swā þætte moniġe tealdon, þæt hēo ġe-hǣled bēon meahte from þǣre un-
trymnesse. Þā þȳ þriddan dæġe hēo wæs eft hefiġad mid þǣm ǣrrum sārum, ond 75
sōna wæs ġe-risen ond ġe-numen of middan-ġearde, ond eal þæt sār ond þone
dēað mid ēċre hǣlo ond līfe[29] on-wende."

"Mid þȳ þā æfter swā monegum ġēarum hire līċ-homa wæs of byrġenne ūp
ā-hæfen, þā ā-þennedon hēo ond ā-slōgon ġe-teld ofer, ond eal sēo ġe-somnung

---

[22] In OE, one generally says thanks to someone (dative) for something (genitive).
[23] *openre þǣre byrġenne* = "[from] the opened grave" (dative rule)
[24] The OE translation of the Latin is a bit difficult here: "But of more noted testimony still [was] Cyneferð the physician, who . . ."
[25] This phrase is a direct translation of the Latin *referre erat solitus* "he was accustomed to say . . ." and merely indicates the past tense rather than a habit. In OE, the phrase "it was his custom to say" sounds a bit odd in context. It must mean "he used to say that . . ."or simply "he said that . . ."
[26] *Ġe-sticade* = past subjunctive; translate "should lance."
[27] *Wæs hēo ġe-seġen* is a literal translation of the Latin *videtur* "seemed." As a result, the OE is awkward: "then she seemed over two days that it was more comfortable for her." The meaning is, "then she seemed more comfortable and well over the course of two days."
[28] An impersonal construction: "so that [it] was more comfortable for her."
[29] *Ēċre* applies to *life* as well as *hǣlo*.

80   brōðra ond sweostra on twā healfe singende ymb-stōdon. Ond sēo abbudisse in
þæt ġe-teld ēode ond fēa monna mid hēo,[30] þæt hēo þā bān woldon ūp ā-dōn ond
on-þwēan ond ġe-feormian æfter monna ġe-wunan."

"Þā samnunga ġe-hȳrdon wē þā abbudissan inne hlūdre stefne cleopian: 'Sēo
wuldor,' cwæð hēo, 'Drihtnes noman!' Ðā æfter med-miċlum fæċe þā cleopode mē
85   mon ond ċegde in. On-wrēogon[31] þā duru þæs ġe-teldes; þā ġe-seah iċ līċ-homan
þære hālgan Godes fǣmnan ūp ā-hefenne of byrġenne ond on bedde ġe-setedne:[32]
ond [hēo] wæs slǣpendum men ġe-līċra[33] þonne dēadum. Þā on-wrēogon hēo ēac
hire ond-wlitan ond ēowdon mē[34] ðā wunde þæs snides, þe iċ ġēo ǣr dyde."

"Ðā wæs hēo[35] fæstlīċe ġe-hālod—þætte wundorlīċe ġe-mete.[36] For openre
90   wunde ond ġēoniendre, mid þām hēo be-byrġed wæs, þā sēo þynneste dolg-swæð
ond sēo lǣsseste æt-ēawde; ġe ēac ealle þā scȳtan, þe sē līċ-homa mid be-wunden
wæs, swā on-wealge ond swā nēowe ond swā clǣne æt-ēawdon, swā swā þȳ seolfan
dæġe hire þǣm clǣnum leomum[37] ymb-seald wǣron.

Secgað ēac men, þā hēo þryċċed wæs ond swenċed mid swile ond sāre [on]
95   hire swīran, þæt hēo wǣre swīðe lust-fulliende þisse un-trymnesse cynne,[38] ond
hēo ġe-wuneliċe cwæde oft: "Iċ wāt cūðlīċe, þæt iċ be ġe-wyrhtum on mīnum
swēoran bere þā byrðenne þisse āðle ond þisse un-trymnesse, in þǣm[39] iċ ġe-
mon meċ ġēo beran,[40] þā iċ ġeong wæs, þā īdlan byrðenne gyldenra siġila. Ond iċ

---

[30] *Mid* generally takes a dative object, but here *hēo* is accusative.

[31] The subject of this plural verb must be an understood "they."

[32] Notice that *ā-hefenne* and *ġe-setedne* are past participles with a masculine accusative adjectival ending *-ne* (see §6.3). They agree with the masculine noun *līċ-boman.*

[33] A comparative form—see §6.5: "more like a sleeping man / person."

[34] The speaker is still Cyneferð, Æðelðryd's physician.

[35] *Hēo* refers more plausibly to *wund,* a feminine noun, than to Æðelðryð herself. (See §7.1.5.)

[36] *Þætte wundorlīċe ġe-mete* means "and that in a miraculous way." Like the Latin original, the OE employs the dative case without a preposition.

[37] *Hire* is dative of possession: translate "her chaste limbs" (§2.11.4.e).

[38] *Þisse untrymnesse* is a genitive depending on the dative *cynne.*

[39] Translate *in þǣm* literally as "in that" or "since."

[40] See §5.2.6.

ġe-lȳfe *mē þætte* for-ðon sēo ūpliċe ār-fæstnis wolde meċ hefiġade bēon mid sāre mīnes swēoran, þæt iċ swā wære on-līesed þære scylde þære swīðe īdlan lēasnisse, mid þȳ mē[41] nū for golde ond for ġimmum of swīran forð-hlīfað sēo rēadnis ond bryne þæs swiles ond wærces."

Hwæt, þā ġe-lomp mid þā ġe-hrinenisse þāra ilċena ġe-gyrelena, þe mon of hire līċ-homan dyde, þætte dēoful-sēoċe men ond moniġe oðerre un-trymnesse oft ġe-hælde wæron. Swelċe ēac sēo þrūh in þære hēo ærest be-byrġed wæs monegum monna þe heora ēagan sārġedon ond hefiġodon wearð tō hælo, þonne hēo heora hēafod ond heora ēagan tō on-hieldon ond him tō ġe-bædon: ond sōna sēo un-ġescrēpnes þæs sāres ond þære hefiġnesse from heora ēagan ġe-wāt.

Ono hwæt hēo þā þwōgon ond baðodon þone līċ-homan þære hālgan fæmnan, ond mid nēowum hræġlum ġe-gyredon ond in ċiriċan bæron ond in þā stænenan þrūh ġe-setton, þe ðyder ġe-læded wæs; ond þær nū ġēna oð þisne ond-weardan dæġ in miċelre ār-wyrðnesse is hæfd.

Wæs þæt ēac miċel wundor, þæt sēo þrūh wæs swā ġe-screpe þære fæmnan līċ-homan ġe-meted, swā swā hēo synderlīċe hire ġe-ġearwod wære. Swelċe ēac sēo heafod-stōw, wundor-cræftiġlīċe ġe-worht ond ġe-screpelīċe ġe-hēowod, æt-ēowde tō þām ġe-mete hire heafdes.

Is Elia lond in Ēast-engla mæġðe hū-hugu syx hund hīda in ēa-londes ġe-līċnesse. Is eal, swā swā wē cwædon, mid fenne ond mid wætre ymb-seald: ond mid ġe-nihtsumnesse æla, þā ðe in þæm ilcan fennum fongne bēoð, hit noman on-fēng.

Þær wilnode mynster habban sēo[42] ġe-myndgode Crīstes þēowe, for-ðon hēo of þære ylcan mæġðe Ēast-engla līċ-homan frymþe lædde,[43] swā swā wē fore-spreċende wæron.

---

[41] Another dative of possession with body part: *swiran* (l. 96).

[42] A relative pronoun "who," referring to Seaxburg: see §7.5.3.

[43] *Līċ-homan frymð lædde* means "(she) derived the origin of her body"; i.e., "she was born in. . . ."

100

105

110

115

120

III. The Brief Life of St. Æðeldryð from the Old English Martyrology for June 23 (9th century)

On ðone ðrēo ond twēnteġþan dæġ þæs mōnðes bið þære hālgan cwēne ġe-leornes Sancte Æþeldryþe. Sēo wæs twām werum ġe-brȳdod, ond hwæþre hēo wæs clǣne fǣmne. Ǣrest hēo wæs ġe-brȳdad Tondberhte, Sūð-ġerwa ealdormen, ond æfter þǣm hēo wæs seald Ecgferðe tō cwēne, Norðan-hymbra cyninge, for-þon þe hēo

5   wæs Onnan dohter, Ēast-engla cyninges. Ond hēo þā wæs twelf ġēar mid Ecgferð þone cyning, ond hē mid nǣngum ðingum mihte hire ġe-þōht on-ċerran. Þā on-fēng hēo hāliġ-ryfte[44] on þǣm mynstre ðe is nemned Colodes-burh. Þæs æfter ānum ġēare hēo timbrede fǣmnena mynster on ðǣm londe þe wē nemneð æt Elie. Ond hēo wæs þǣr abbodysse ond brēac sið ðan wyllenra hræġla, ond seldon

10   hēo baðode on hātum bæþe, būtan foran tō Ēastrum ond foran tō þǣm fiftiġan dæġe[45] ond foran tō Crīstes fullwihtes dæġe. Ond seldon on dæġe hēo ēode oftor tō ġe-reordum þonne ǣne, ond fram ūht-sanges tīde hēo ā wunode on ċiereċean on hire ġe-bede oð dæġ ond þurh Godes gāst hēo self ǣr fore-sæġde hwonne hēo sceolde of middan-ġearde lēoran, ond hēo þā ġe-lēorde. Ond hēo wæs siextēne

15   ġēar on eorðan be-byrġed, ond þā mon eft þone līċ-homan ūpp dyde,[46] þā wæs hē[47] swā un-ġebrosnad ġe-mēted, swā hēo ðȳ ilcan dæġe wǣre forð-fēred. Ond hire wæs miċel wund open on ðǣm swȳran ðā hēo mon on byrġenne dyde, ond þā hī mon eft ūp dyde of þære byrġenne, ðā wæs hit ġe-batod þæt þær næs būtan sēo swaðu on.

---

[44] i.e., she became a nun

[45] The so-called *Quinquagesima*. "Properly the period of fifty days preceding Easter which begins on the Sunday before Ash Wednesday; but the word came to be generally applied only to the Sunday mentioned. In earlier times a new stage in the pre-Lenten discipline, e.g. abstinence from flesh-meat, began on this day" (*Oxford Dictionary of the Christian Church*).

[46] *mon eft þone līċ-homan upp dyde*: this construction, with *mon* "one, someone" as the subject, is a substitute for the passive voice. Translate, "the body was brought up, disinterred."

[47] *Hē* refers back to *līċ-homan* (§7.1.5).

IV. Ælfric's Life of St. Æðeldryð (late 10th century)

[VIIII KALENDAS JULII, NATALE SANCTE ÆÐELDRYÐE VIRGINIS]

Wē wyllað nū ā-wrītan, ðēah ðe hit wundorliċ sȳ, be ðǣre halgan Sancte Æðeldryðe þām Engliscan mǣdene, þe wæs mid twām werum and swa-ðēah wunode mǣden, swā swā þā wundra[48] ġe-swuteliað þe hēo wyrcð ġe-lōme.

Anna hātta hyre fæder Ēast Engla cynincg, swīðe Crīsten man swā swā hē cȳdde mid weorcum, and eall his tēam wearð ġe-wurðod þurh God. Æðeldryð   5
wearð þā for-ġifen ānum ealdormenn tō wīfe, ac hit nolde sē æl-mihtiga God þæt hire mægð-hād wurde mid hǣmede ā-dȳlegod, ac hēold hī on clǣnnysse, for-ðan þe hē is æl-mihtiġ God and mæġ dōn eall þæt hē wile, and on manegum wīsum his mihte ġe-swutelað.

Sē ealdorman ġe-wāt þā ðā hit wolde God, and hēo wearð for-ġifen Ecfride   10
cynincge, and twelf ġēar wunode un-ġewemmed mǣden on þæs cynincges synscype, swā swā swutele wundra hyre mǣrða cȳðaþ and hire mægð-hād ġe-lōme.

Hēo lufode þone Hǣlend, þe hī[49] hēold un-wemme, and Godes ðēowas wurðode; ān þæra wæs Wilfrid bisceop þe hēo swȳðost lufode, and hē sǣde Bedan þæt sē cyning Ecfrid him oft be-hēte myċel on lande and on feo, ġif hē lǣran   15
mihte Æðeldryðe his ġe-beddan, þæt hēo brūċe[50] his synscipes.

Nu cwæð sē hālga Beda þe þās bōc ġe-sette þæt sē æl-mihtiga God mihte ēaðe ġe-dōn, nū on ūrum dagum, þæt Æðeldryð þurh-wunode[51] un-ġewemmed mǣden, þēah ðe hēo wer hæfde, swā swā on ealdum dagum hwīlum ǣr ġe-tīmode þurh þone ylcan God þe ǣfre þurh-wunað mid his ġe-corenum hālgum, swā swā hē sylf be-hēt.   20

---

[48] *Wundor*, normally a neuter noun, is behaving here like a feminine (see §2.8).

[49] *Hī* is an accusative: *þe* "who" is the subject of this clause.

[50] *Bruce* is a subjunctive form (see §3.10.1).

[51] *Þurh-wunode* is a past subjunctive. Translate "would remain."

Æðeldryð wolde ðā ealle woruld-þincg for-lǣtan, and bæd ġeorne þone cynincg þæt hēo Crīste mōste þēowian on mynsterliċre drohtnunge, swā hire mōd hire tō spēon. Þā lȳfde hire sē cynincg, þēah þe hit embe lang wǣre þæs þe hēo ġe-wilnode, and Wilfrid bisceop þā hī ġe-hādode tō myneċene, and hēo syððan on

25   mynstre wunode sume twelf mōnað swā, and hēo syððan wearð ġe-hādod eft tō abudissan on Eliġ mynstre, ofer manega myneċena, and hēo hī mōdorlīċe hēold mid gōdum ġe-bysnungum tō þām gāstliċan līfe.

Be hire is ā-wrȳten þæt hēo wel drohtnode tō ānum mǣle fæstende, būtan hit frēols-dæġ wǣre, and hēo syndriġe ġe-bedu swȳðe lufode and wyllen weorode,

30   and wolde seld-hwænne hire līċ baðian būtan tō hēah-tīdum, and ðonne hēo wolde ǣrest ealle ðā[52] baðian þe on ðām mynstre wǣron, and wolde him ðēnian mid hire þīnenum, and þonne hī sylfe baðian.

Þā on þām eahtēoðan ġēare siððan hēo abbudisse wæs, hēo wearð ġe-untrumod swā swā hēo ǣr wītegode, swā þæt ān ġe-swel wēox on hire swūran myċel under

35   þām cynn-bāne, and hēo swīðe þancode Gode þæt hēo on þām swūran sum ġe-swinc þolode. Hēo cwæð, "iċ wāt ġeare þæt iċ wel wyrðe eom þæt mīn swūra bēo ġe-swenċt mid swylċere un-trumnysse, for-ðan þe iċ on *geogoðe* frætwode mīnne swūran mid mæniġ-fealdum swūr-bēagum, and mē is nū ġe-þūht[53] þæt Godes ār-fæstnyss þone gylt ā-clǣnsiġe, þonne mē nū þis ġe-swel scȳnð for[54] golde, and

40   þæs hātan bryne for hēalicum ġym-stānum."

Þā wæs þǣr sum lǣċe on ðām ġe-lēaffullum hēape, Cynefryð ġe-hāten, and hī cwǣdon þā sume þæt sē lǣċe sceolde ā-scēotan þæt ġe-swell; þā dyde hē sōna swā, and þǣr sāh ūt wyrms. Wearð him þā ġe-ðūht swilċe[55] hēo ġe-wurpan mihte ac hēo ġe-wāt of worulde mid wuldre tō Gode on þām ðriddan dæġe syððan sē dolh

---

[52] *ðā*: an accusative plural pronoun

[53] *Mē is nū ġe-þūht* is a literal tranlsation of the Latin *videtur*: translate "(it) seems to me."

[54] *for* = "instead of, in exchange for"

[55] *Wearð him þā ġe-ðūht swilċe* = "(It) seemed to him (i.e., the physician) as if. . . ."

wæs ġe-openod, and wearð be-byrġed swā swā hēo bæd sylf and hēt, betwux hire   45
ġe-swustrum on trēowenre ċyste.

Þā wearð hire swustor Sexburh ġe-hādod tō abbudissan æfter hire ġe-
endunge, sēo ðe ǣr wæs cwēn on Cantware-byrig. Þā wolde sēo Sexburh æfter
syx-tȳne ġēarum dōn hire swustor bān of ðǣre byrġene ūp, and beran intō þǣre
ċyrcan, ond sende þā ġe-brōðra tō sēċenne sumne stān tō swilċere nēode, for-ðan   50
þe on þām fen-lande synd fēawa weorc-stāna.

Hī rēowon þā tō Grantanċeastre, and God hī sōna ġe-hradode, swā þæt hī þǣr
ġe-mētton āne mǣre þrūh wið[56] þone weall standende, ġe-worht of marm-stāne
eall hwītes blēos, bufan þǣre eorðan, and þæt hlyd ðǣr-tō ġe-limplīċe ġe-fēged,
ēac of hwītum marm-stāne swā swā hit macode God.   55

Þā nāmon ðā ġe-brōðra blȳðelīċe þā ðrūh and ġe-brōhton tō mynstre, myċclum
ðanciġende Gode; and Sexburh sēo abbudisse hēt slēan ān ġe-teld bufan ðā byrġene,
wolde þā bān gaderian. Hī sungon ðā ealle sealmas, and līċ-sang þā hwīle þe man ðā
byrġene bufan ġe-openode. Þā læġ hēo on ðǣre ċyste, swilċe hēo læġe on slǣpe hāl
eallum limum, and sē lǣċe wæs ðǣr ðe þæt ġe-swell ġe-openode, and hī[57] sċēawode   60
ġeorne. Þā wæs sēo wund ġe-hǣled, þe sē lǣċe worhte ǣr; ēac swilċe þā ġe-wǣda, þe[58]
hēo be-wunden wæs mid, wǣron swā an-sunde swylċe hī eall nīwe wǣron.

Sexburh þā hyre swuster swīðe þæs fæġnode, and hī þwōgon ðā syððan þone
sāwl-lēasan līċ-haman, and mid nīwum ġe-wǣdum be-wundon ār-wurðlīċe, and
bǣron intō ðǣre ċyrcan, blyssigende mid sangum, and lēdon hī on ðǣre þrȳh,   65
þǣr ðǣr hēo līð oð þis on myċelre ār-wurðnysse, mannum tō wundrunge. Wæs
ēac wundorlīċ, þæt sēo ðrūh wæs ġe-worht þurh Godes fore-sċēawunge hire swā
ġe-mǣte, swylċe hēo hyre sylfre swā ġe-sceapen wǣre, and æt hire heafde wæs ā-
hēawen sē stān, ġe-mǣte þām heafde þæs hālgan mǣdenes.

---

[56] wið = "against"

[57] hī = feminine accusative singular

[58] þe = "with which"

70   Hit is swutol þæt hēo wæs un-ġewemmed mæden, þonne hire līċ-hama ne
mihte for-molsnian on eorðan, and Godes miht is ġe-swutelod sōðlīċe þurh hī,
þæt hē mæġ ā-ræran ðā for-molsnodan līċ-haman, sē ðe hire līċ hēold hāl on
ðære byrġene ġit oð þisne dæġ; sȳ him ðæs ā wuldor. Þær wæron ġe-hǣlede þurh
ðā hālgan fǣmnan fela ādliġe menn, swā swā wē ġe-fyrn ġe-hȳrdon; and ēac ðā

75   þe hrepodon þæs rēafes æniġne dæl þe hēo mid be-wunden wæs, wurdon sōna
hāle; and manegum ēac fremode sēo ċyst miċċlum þe hēo ærest on læġ, swā swā
sē lārēow Beda on ðære bēċ sæde, þe hē ġe-sette be ðȳsum.

Oft woruld-menn ēac hēoldon, swā swā ūs bēċ secgað, heora clænnysse on
synscipe for Crīstes lufe, swā swā wē mihton reċċan ġif ġē rōhton hit tō ġe-

80   hȳrenne. Wē secgað swā-ðēah be sumum ðeġne, sē wæs þrȳttiġ ġēara mid his wīfe
on clænnysse. Þrȳ suna hē ġe-strȳnde,[59] and hī siððan būtu ðrittiġ ġēara wæron
wuniġende būtan hǣmede and fela ælmyssan worhton, oð þæt sē wer fērde tō
munuc-liċere drohtnunge, and Drihtnes englas cōmon eft on his forð-sīðe, and
feredon his sāwle mid sange tō heofonum, swā swā ūs secgað bēċ.

85   Manega bysna synd on bōcum be swylcum, hū oft weras and wīf wundorlīċe
drohtnodon, and on clænnysse wunodon, tō wuldre þām Hǣlende, þe þā
clænnysse ā-stealde, Crīst ūre Hǣlend, þām is ā wurð-mynt and wuldor on
ēċnysse. AMEN.

---

[59] The man and woman had a chaste marriage *after* they gave birth to three sons.

V. Æðeldryð in the News

NEWS

Remains of Saxon town discovered

David Keys, Archaeology Correspondent

11/05/1999

The Independent - London

(Copyright 1999 Newspaper Publishing PLC)

A PREVIOUSLY unknown Anglo-Saxon town which owed its existence to a princess famous for her virginity has been discovered by archaeologists near Ely, in Cambridgeshire.

Excavations suggest that at its peak it covered 60 acres and had a population of up to 400.

The site, a mile from Ely town centre, probably developed due to an East Anglian princess called Aethelthryth, later known as Saint **Etheldreda** or Saint Audrey. Famous for preserving her virginity, despite being married twice, she was championed by one of the country's leading churchmen—much to the annoyance of her second husband. She went on to become a nun and to found an abbey around which the town probably developed.

Investigations show that the town was founded in the late 7th century, reached a peak in the 10th and 11th centuries, shrank to village proportions in the 12th century as medieval Ely developed, and disappeared in the early 15th century. Over recent months an archaeological team, directed by Richard Mortimer and Roddy Regan of Cambridge University archaeological unit, unearthed at least four substantial long houses and 35,000 Anglo-Saxon artefacts—pottery shards, spindle whirls, nails and knives. They also found thousands of sheep, cattle and pig bones, and the remains of 30 dogs and cats.

Mr Mortimer said the site was of "national importance" because it provided a rare opportunity to examine how an Anglo-

Saxon town came into existence, flourished and declined.

The find came as archaeologists examined the site prior to its development for housing. From the Fifties to the Seventies, developers built on 75 per cent of the lost town and the current housing development will cover a further 15 per cent.

Garden gives up its secret unearthed in a quiet village, the lost monastery of a Virgin Queen from the Dark Ages
CHRIS BROOKE; MICHAEL HANLON

08/16/2001
Daily Mail
Associated Newspapers Ltd.
(Copyright 2001)

THE story began with the discovery of a few bones in the back garden of a house on Humberside.

Anxious resident Susan Sibborn called in police but they soon concluded the remains were far too old to warrant criminal investigation.

Now, 14 years on, the mother of two has been told she is sitting on an archaeological treasure which could solve a 1300-year-old Anglo Saxon mystery.

The house, in the village of Whitton, is believed to stand on the site of a monastery built by **Etheldreda,** the 7th century 'Virgin Queen', whose celibate state survived two husbands and who later became a revered Catholic saint.

Mrs Sibborn initially all but forgot about her find, but over the years her intrigue was reawakened as she developed an interest in local history.

She called in an archaelogical team from Sheffield University and their excavations have unearthed dozens of skeletons and Anglo Saxon artefacts.

Generations of historians have puzzled over the location of a monastery the Virgin Queen is reputed to have established near the Humber estuary in the late 600s.

It was rumoured to have been in the

village of West Halton, two miles from the excavation, where a church is dedicated to the saint.

But Dr Dawn Hadley, of the Sheffield University archaeology department, believes her team has found the site in Whitton.

'We think there was an Anglo Saxon monastery on this site,' she said. 'That would be the most plausible explanation for a large cemetery with elaborate coffin fittings in such a rural environment.

'There is also quite a bit of history that says St **Etheldreda** crossed the Humber and founded a monastery in the marshes. West Halton wasn't in the marshes and Whitton was.' Carbon dating tests will be carried out later this year to confirm the age of the remains.

Although it will be impossible conclusively to prove a link to St **Etheldreda**, the episode offers an opportunity to reopen the archive on one of English history's most colourful characters.

Etheldreda was a beacon of light in the period that became known as the Dark Ages, an Anglo Saxon heroine whose virtues guaranteed a fast-track into sainthood after her death, and a woman who inspired others to follow her into the religious life.

What little we know of her originates in the writings of the famous chronicler of his time, the Venerable Bede.

Her story begins in 597 when St Augustine, the Roman missionary, came to Kent to convert the local pagans to Christianity.

The new religion took root in England and within a few decades religious fervour gripped the land. Monasteries and nunneries were founded from the Scottish borders to the Channel.

One of the most fervent converts was **Etheldreda**, an East Anglian princess, daughter of the Suffolk King Anna, who lived at Exning, a village close to present-day Newmarket.

She wanted to become a nun but her family insisted upon marriage, and she was betrothed to Tonbert, the Prince of East Anglia. In 652, the reluctant princess was wed.

Tonbert died three years later leaving **Etheldreda** a rich young widow and with her virginity (so she claimed) intact.

For five years she lived on her inheritance, but once again local dynastic politics necessitated her marriage, this time to Northumbrian Prince Egfrith.

Etheldreda and Egfrith, who was only 15 and 12 years her junior, did not make a happy couple. She insisted on remaining chaste and refused to wash more than once every three months.

Keeping the body clean, she insisted, was vanity, and vanity was a sin.

After 12 years he requested that she sleep with him. **Etheldreda** refused.

The king tried to bribe Wilfred, Bishop of Northumbria, to release her from her vow of virginity.

Instead the bishop helped **Etheldreda** to a promontory called Colbert's Head.

The king gave chase, but a seven-day high tide considered divine intervention kept them apart and he gave up.

The existence of the monastery is alluded to in writings of the time but no trace of it has ever been found and it has remained one of the great mysteries of the Virgin Queen's life. Until now.

Etheldreda lived out the rest of her life in piety and penance in Ely, consecrated as Abbess by Bishop Wilfred. She died in 662 from a tumour on the neck, reputedly God's punishment for her vanity in wearing necklaces in her younger days.

In reality, she succumbed to a plague that killed several of her fellow nuns and monks.

Her sainthood status was confirmed when, 17 years after her death, her body was exhumed and found not to have decayed.

Wilfred and her doctor were among the 'witnesses' when the tumour in her neck was cut out and found to be healed.

Linen cloths in which her body had been wrapped were fresh as the day she was buried. Now **Etheldreda's** life and works survive only in legend and in writing and perhaps in her newly-discovered monastery.

The unlikely custodian of the ancient site, Mrs Sibborn said: 'Not everybody has something like this in the back garden. I will probably put up a plaque at the site.

'The remains will be left where they are and we will respect the cemetery part of the garden.'

A Quick Guide to
Old English Poetry

A Quick Guide to OE Poetry

The Germanic peoples shared an ancient alliterative verse form that survived in Old Norse, Old High German, Old Saxon, and OE. The basics of this system are explained below for the beginner.[1]

In the surviving manuscripts, OE poetry appears exactly as prose, with no line divisions or extra spaces for caesura as in modern printed versions of OE verse, though the line and half-line boundaries are sometimes marked with points. The only contemporary discussion of native Germanic meter and poetics comes from thirteenth-century Iceland in the form of Snorri Sturluson's handbook on a very specialized form of Old Norse poetry, skaldic verse.[2]

The main rules:

1. *Two Half-Lines.* A line of OE verse is divided into two half-lines separated by a break or caesura (represented in print by blank spaces). Normally each half-line has two stressed syllables and any number of unstressed syllables (though there's a natural limit, of course). The first half-line is called either the a-verse or the "on" verse, while the second half-line is the b-verse or the "off" verse.

2. *Stress.* Any analysis of an OE metrical line should begin with the b-verse (the second half-line), the one that fixes the alliteration for the entire unit. You will need to find the first *stressed* syllable. Determining stress may be a bit difficult for beginners. The main rule of thumb is that only "content" words normally receive stress—nouns, adjectives, and verbs, for the most part, since these carry the main semantic weight of a sentence. Function words (definite articles, conjunctions, prepositions, etc.) that

---

[1] For more advanced treatments of meter and poetics, see "Old English Versification" in *Eight Old English Poems*, ed. John C. Pope and R.D. Fulk (New York: Norton, 2001), pp. 129-58, and "Old English Poetry" in *Bright's Old English Grammar and Reader*, eds. Frederic G. Cassidy and Richard N. Ringler (New York: Holt Rinehart Winston, 1971), pp. 264-288.

[2] The *Prose Edda* consists of three parts, 1) the "Deception of Gylfi" (giving a summary of pagan mythological stories that underly poetic metaphors), 2) the "Language of the Skalds" (describing the formation of kennings or metaphors), and 3) the "Key to meters" (describing and exemplifying a number of different meters). The *Prose Edda* is sometimes called *Snorri's Edda* or *The Younger Edda*.

carry relatively light semantic content are usually unstressed. Pronouns (*I, me,* etc.), adjectives (*blue, light,* etc.), and adverbs (*easily, quickly,* etc.) can carry stress in some cases. Also important is the fact that as a Germanic language, OE tends to put the stress on the first syllable of a word, unless the first syllable is a prefix like *be-, ġe-,* etc. Syllables containing inflectional endings (*eteð* or *mīdre*) are never stressed. Secondary stress (see below) for the most part falls on the second element of a compound (think of the word *doghouse,* where the first syllable receives the main stress, while the second syllable receives a strong, but not equally strong, stress).

3. *Alliteration.* The two half-lines of OE verse are cemented together by alliteration or assonance, rather than rhyme.[3] (Alliteration must be fairly exact, though any vowel "alliterates" with any other vowel.) The alliterating sound is established by the first stressed syllable in the *second* half-line. At least one of the stressed syllables from the first half-line must alliterate with this sound, and sometimes both do (double alliteration).

Let's look at a few examples.

> *Hwæt, iċ swefna ċyst   secgan wylle . . .*
> (Listen, I of dreams the choicest   want to tell . . .)

Here, the second half-line is fairly easy to interpret. Since OE, like other Germanic languages, puts the stress on the first syllable of a multi-syllabic word, the pattern would be *SECGan WYLLe,* so that the first stressed syllable in the second half-line would be *SECG,* thus making *S* the alliterating sound for the entire line. Clearly, *swefna* (the first stressed syllable in the first half line) is the alliterative

---

[3] OE poetry may contain some sporadic rhyming, though rhyme occurs systematically only in "The Rhyming Poem" and the OE *Judith.*

counterpart. Remember that *at least one* of the stressed syllables in the first half-line must alliterate with the first stressed syllable of the second half-line.

> *Hwæt mē ġe-mǣtte*   *tō midre nihte.*
> (What I dreamed   in the middle night.)

In the second half-line of this verse, *tō* does not receive stress because it is a function word; the first syllable of *midre*, since it is an adjective with semantic content, can bear primary stress: *tō MIDre NIHTe*. *M* then is the alliterative sound for this line. Going back to the first half-verse, the alliterating words must be *mē* and *ġe-MǢTte* (note that the *ġe-* prefix receives no stress)—in this case, double alliteration since both stressed syllables in the first half line alliterate with the first stressed syllable in the second half-line.

> *Hū hēo þone atolan*   *ēaðost mihte . . .*
> (How she the horrible one   most easily might . . .)

Here, the second half-line is best interpreted this way: *ĒAÐost MIHTe*, thus establishing *E* as the linking sound (assonance). Since any vowel can alliterate with any other vowel, *ATOLan* (an adjective) must be the alliterative counterpart in the first half-line.

4. *Sievers' Types.* Though there are many complex systems for analyzing OE verse patterns, you should probably start with one of the oldest and most widely used, that devised by Eduard Sievers and modified by A. J. Bliss.[4] In the Sievers system, half-lines are classified by the relative positions of stressed and unstressed elements:

---

[4] The main competitor to Sievers's system is that championed by John C. Pope. It uses a system of musical notation and assumes a pattern of regular beats, dividing unstressed syllables into fractions of a beat. See also Geoffrey Russom's word-foot theory of OE meter in *Old English Meter and Linguistic Theory* (Cambridge: Cambridge UP, 1987).

LEGEND

/ = Stressed syllable (usually a long syllable in a "content word"—noun, adjective, or verb).

\ = A syllable with secondary stress, as *house* in *doghouse* (/ \ ).

x = Any number of unstressed syllables (function words usually receive no stress at all). Note that an *x* may represent several unstressed words.

TYPE A	/ x / x	/ x x / x x FISC sceal on WÆTere
TYPE B	x / x /	x / x / þīn ĀĠen BEARN
TYPE C	x / / x	x / / x on FLŌT FĒRan
TYPE D1	/ (x) / \ x	/ x / \ x FEORres FOLC-*land*es [5]
D2	/ (x) / x \	/ / x \ BLŌD ĒDRum *dranc*
TYPE E	/ x \ x /	/ x \ x / OND-*long*ne DÆĠ

---

[5] Syllables with secondary stress are italicized—they generally occur in compounds. Note that the symbol "(x)" represents an optional unstressed syllable or syllables.

Note that types A and D can add an additional unstressed syllable or two to the beginning of the verse, almost always a verb prefix or negative particle *ne* (a process known as *anacrusis*).

		(x) / x x / x
TYPE A	(x) / x / x	ā-HWEARF nū fram SYNNum
		(x) / x x / x x
		ne HYRDe iċ CYMlicor
		(x) / / \ x
TYPE D	(x) / / \ x	ġe-SÆGD SŌÐlīċe

HYPER-METRICAL VERSES. Old English verse lines can sometimes contain more than the usual four stressed syllables, and these so-called hypermetrical verses often appear in groups within poems whose meter is otherwise "normal." Metrical theorists have not agreed on how to describe these verses on the deep level, but they are relatively easy at least to identify on the page.

Eall þæt bēacen wæs

be-goten mid golde;   *ġimmas stōdon*

fæġre æt foldan scēatum,   *swelċe þær fīfe wǣron*

uppe on þām eaxl-ġespanne   *(be-hēold on þām engel dryhtnes)*

In this example from the "Dream of the Rood," the last two lines are hypermetrical. Notice that each of the hypermetrical half-lines contains at least one more stressed syllable than usual: *FÆĠre æt FOLDan SCĒATum* (3); *SWELċe þēr FĪFe WǢRon* (3); *UPpe on þām EAXL-ġeSPANne* (3); *beHEOLD on þām ENGel DRYHTnes* (3).

VARIATION. For compositional and poetic reasons, OE verse often repeats various sentence elements (noun and verb phrases mainly), sometimes separated from each other by several lines; each of these repetitions or appositions usually has the same grammatical form. Once you begin to appreciate the subtleties of variation, you'll see that it's a bit like jazz. Each repetition may bring out different qualities of the person, thing, or action under poetic scrutiny. (Variation is different from *enumeration*, where the list of noun or verb phrases represents separate and distinct persons, things, or actions.)

The following example contains two cases of variation: the first on the subject of the sentence, "the braided-hair" (with the variation "God's maiden") and the second on the adjective "sharp" (with the variation "hard in battle showers").

> *ġe-nam ðā wunden-locc,*
> *Scyppendes mæġð,   scearpne mēċe*
> *scūrum heardne,   and of sċēaðe ā-brǣd.*

(The braided-hair [woman] took, / God's maiden, the sharp sword, / hard in [battle] showers, and pulled [it] from the sheath.)

Note that both *wunden-locc* and *mæġð* are nominative nouns while the adjectives *scearp-ne* and *heard-ne* are masculine accusative singulars (agreeing with *mēċe*).

In the next example, variation has the effect of making a rather general description, "mindful of hardships," more and more concrete and powerful (the effect is something like a crescendo):

> *Swā cwæð eard-stapa   earfeþa ġe-myndiġ,*
> *wrāþra wæl-sleahta,   wine-mǣga hryre.*

(So said the earth-wanderer, mindful of hardships / [mindful] of fierce slaughters, of the fall of near kinsmen.)

Notice that each of the preceding variations is a genitive depending on *ġe-myndiġ*.

The next example, taken from the OE *Judith*, shows a more complex kind of variation in which the repeated structure is a past participle (functioning as an adjective) and a dative noun (though the last variation substitutes an adverb for the dative):

> *and ðǣr ġe-nyðerad wæs,*
> *sūsle ġe-sǣled   syððan ǣfre,*
> *wyrmum bewunden,   wītum ġe-bunden,*
> *hearde ġe-hæfted   in helle-bryne.*

(And [Holofernes] was brought low, fettered in torture ever after, / wound with snakes, bound in punishments, / severely restrained in hell fire.)

All of these variations repeat the idea of tying and restraint.

The following passage from *Cædmon's Hymn* contains rather complex patterns of variation. To help you see them, variations on the names of the creator are in boxes, on the words for earth, shaded; and words for human beings, in bold.

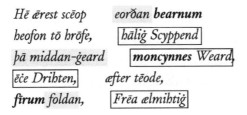

> *Hē ǣrest scēop   eorðan **bearnum***
> *heofon tō hrōfe,   hāliġ Scyppend*
> *þā middan-ġeard   moncynnes Weard,*
> *ēċe Drihten,   æfter tēode,*
> ***firum** foldan,   Frēa ælmihtiġ*

(He first created for the sons of the earth / heaven as roof, holy Creator, / then middle earth mankind's Guardian, eternal Lord, afterwards established / the ground for men, Lord almighty.)

Again, it is good to notice the grammatical nature of the variation, where the repetitions fulfill the same syntactic function in the sentence: words for the creator are all nominatives, while those for mankind are dative and those for the earth are accusative. The verb phrases look like potential variations (they have the same grammatical form), but they are probably enumerations—that is, descriptions of separate and sequential events: 1) *ǣrest scēop* "first created" and 2) *æfter tēode* "afterwards established." Note that *heofon* is not a variation on *middan-ġeard*, since it represents a different part of creation. God creates first heaven, then earth afterwards.

COMPOUNDS. The constraints of OE meter favor compounds, one of the glories of OE verse, since they create a rich store of vocabulary fitting different alliterative environments. Many compounds in fact are not free formations but part of a system of compounding that combines typical elements. Take, for example, compounds whose second element is *rinc* "warrior."

> *fyrd-rinc* "army warrior"
> *gūð-rinc* "battle warrior"
> *heaðu-rinc* "battle warrior"
> *here-rinc* "army warrior"
> *hilde-rinc* "battle warrior"
> *mago-rinc* "young warrior"
> *sǣ-rinc* "sea warrior, sailor"

By varying the first element in such compound systems, poets could find synonyms fitting different metrical environments. Although compounds like *gūð-rinc* are repeated verbatim in many poems, and are thus part of the common poetic stock, compound systems themselves are essentially generative—they provide a structure for creating new words.

Some poets more than others (and the *Beowulf* poet in particular) create compounds that go beyond the typical.

Have a look at the following groups to begin to get a feel for the way compounding works in OE poetry:

bēag-ġifa "ring-giver," i.e., "lord, king, generous chief"
blǣd-ġifa "glory-giver," i.e., "giver of prosperity"
gold-ġifa "gold-giver"
symbel-ġifa "feast-giver"

hin-fūs "eager/ready [to go] hence," i.e., "to depart or die"
ellor-fūs "eager/ready [to go] elsewhere," i.e., "to depart or die"
ūt-fūs "eager/ready [to go] out," i.e., "to depart"
wæl-fūs "eager/ready for slaughter, death"
grund-fūs "eager/ready for the bottom," i.e., "hastening to hell"

bēag-hroden "ring-adorned" (often used to describe royal women)
gold-hroden "gold-adorned"
sinc-hroden "treasure-adorned"

æsc-plega "ash-play," i.e., "play of ash spears, battle"
ecg-plega "edge-play," i.e., "sword-play, battle"
gūð-plega "battle-play"
lind-plega "linden-play," i.e., "play of linden-wood shields, battle"
nīð-plega "strife-play," i.e., "battle"

bēor-sele "beer hall"
bēag-sele "ring hall"

dēað-sele "death hall," i.e., "hell"

driht-sele "troop hall"

eala-sele "ale hall"

eorð-sele "earth hall," i.e., "cave"

gold-sele "gold hall," i.e., "hall in which gold is distributed"

gūð-sele "battle hall," i.e., "hall of warriors"

horn-sele "horn hall," i.e., "hall with antlers hung in the gables"

hring-sele "ring hall"

nīð-sele "strife hall," i.e., "a hall as a site of battle"

wind-sele "wind hall," i.e., "windy hall, hell"

wīn-sele "wine hall"

wyrm-sele "worm/serpent/dragon hall," i.e., "hell"

bēag-hord "ring hoard," i.e., "treasure"

bōc-hord "book hoard," i.e., "a library"

brēost-hord "chest hoard," i.e., "thought, mind"

flǣsc-hord "flesh hoard," i.e., "the body"

gold-hord "gold hoard," i.e., " treasure"

līċ-hord "body hoard," i.e., "interior of the body"

mōd-hord "thought hoard," i.e., "secret thoughts"

sāwl-hord "soul hoard," i.e., "life or body"

word-hord "word hoard," i.e., "a treasury of words, a speech"

brēost-wylm "breast surge," i.e., "teat or emotion, sorrow"

flod-wylm "flood surge"

hēafod-wylm "head surge," i.e., "tears"

sǣ-wylm "sea surge"

sorh-wylm "sorrow surge"

dryht-lēoð "troop song," i.e., "battle cry"

fyrd-lēoð "army song," i.e., "battle cry"

gūð-lēoð "war song," i.e., "battle cry"

gryre-lēoð "terror song," i.e., "wail"

sorh-lēoð "sorrow song," i.e., "sob"

aldor-ġedāl "life separation," i.e., "death"

gǣst-ġedāl "spirit separation," i.e., "death"

līf-ġedāl "life separation," i.e., "death"

sāwul-ġedāl "soul separation," i.e., "death"

þēoden-ġedāl "prince separation," i.e., "separation from one's prince (through his death)"

weġ-ġedāl "way separation," i.e., "a crossing, dividing of roads"

brim-rād "sea-road," i.e. "the sea"

hran-rād "whale road," i.e., "the sea"

hwēol-rād "wheel road," i.e., "rut, orbit"

seġl-rād "sail road," i.e., "the sea"

setl-rād "setting road," i.e., "the sinking (of the sun)"

strēam-rād "stream road," i.e., "sea path, course"

swān-rād "swan road," i.e., "the sea"

KENNINGS. Simply put, kennings[6] are metaphors. In OE poetry, they usually appear in the form of compounds (or they consist of a base noun and a dependent noun) and, more

---

[6] The word *kenning* "name" or "description" comes from Snorri Sturluson's book on the skaldic poetry.

importantly, the metaphor must be "pure"—that is, a full kenning mentions no literal or direct attribute of the thing it refers to. Some famous OE kennings are:

hran-rād "whale road" = sea
bēag-ġifa "ring giver" = king, lord
Godes candel "God's candle" = the sun

The first two kennings work by *metonymy*—that is, their first elements consist of a thing closely associated with the object that the kenning describes (whales live in the sea, and treasure is part of court life). The second element in the first and third kennings contains the actual metaphors. They are like the object being described in one way but radically unlike it in others. A *road* for example is a means of transportation (as the sea can be) but unlike the sea, it is not built, has no particular shape, is not solid, etc.

Half-kennings mention directly some part of the thing being described (usually in the first element) in unmetaphorical language. Take the following examples:

bān-hūs "bone-house," i.e., "body"
strēam-rād "stream-road," i.e., "sea path"
flǣsc-hord "flesh hoard," i.e., "the body"

In each of these examples, the first element describes directly a part or attribute of the object of the kenning (by synecdoche—where the part stands for the whole), while the second element contains the actual metaphor.

To provide you with the opportunity to observe some of these poetic features at first hand, we have included the following edition of the "The Wife's Lament."

The Wife's Lament

The following poem, "The Wife's Lament," appears at the end of the first cluster of riddles in the late tenth-century *Exeter Book*, the sole source for a much-studied genre of Old English verse, the elegy (a short lyric of loss and often of consolation). The other elegies, often anthologized, are "The Wanderer," "The Seafarer," "Deor," "Wulf and Eadwacer," "Resignation," "The Husband's Message," and "The Ruin."[7] The poem has many riddle-like features, and some commentators have suggested mythological "solutions" for the identity of the speaker or declared her a ghost. Note that the voice of the poem is clearly female (see the adjectival endings on *ġeomor-re* and *mīn-re*, for example).

Iċ þis ġiedd wreċe   bi mē ful ġeomorre,[8]
mīnre sylfre[9] sīð.   Iċ þæt secgan mæġ,
hwæt[10] iċ yrmþa ġe-bād,   siþþan iċ ūp wēox,
nīwes oþþe ealdes,[11]   nō mā þonne nū.

5 Ā iċ wīte wonn   mīnra wræc-sīþa.[12]
Ǣrest mīn hlāford ġe-wāt   heonan of lēodum
ofer ȳþa ġe-lāc;   hæfde iċ ūht-ċeare
hwǣr mīn lēod-fruma   londes wǣre.[13]
Þā iċ mē fēran ġe-wāt   folgað sēcan,[14]

10 winelēas wræcċa,   for mīnre wēa-þearfe.
On-gunnon þæt þæs monnes   māgas hycgan

---

[7] Note that all these titles are editorial—*The Exeter Book* provides no titles, instead signaling the beginning of a new poem with a prominent capital letter.

[8] The adjective *ġeomorre* agrees with *mē* in case (dative) but takes its gender from the speaker (f.). See §6.1.

[9] Note that *mīnre sylfre* is a feminine genitive singular phrase depending on *sīð*: literally, "the journey of my self" or (more loosely) "my own journey." *Sīð* itself is accusative, a variation on *ġiedd*.

[10] This sentence has two objects: the first is *þæt* and the second, the *hwæt* clause. You may omit the *þæt* for a smoother translation.

[11] The phrase *nīwes oþþe ealdes* appears in the genitive because both adjectives are functioning as adverbs—translate "recently or long ago" (see §10.11.3.g and §10.11.4.f).

[12] *Mīnra wræc-sīþa* depends on *wīte* (see §54.3).

[13] *Londes* is a so-called genitive of respect: translate "with respect to country." Translate the subjunctive form *wǣre* as "could be" or "might be" (see §3.10.1 and §4.5.2).

[14] *Mē* is a hard-to-translate reflexive required by the *ġe-witan* construction (see §74.1): "I betook myself to travel to seek a troop."

þurh dyrne ġe-þōht,   þæt[15] hȳ tō-dǣlden[16] unc,

þæt wit ge-wīdost   in woruld-rīċe

lifdon lāðlīcost,   ond meċ longade.[17]

Hēt meċ hlāford mīn   her-eard niman,   15

āhte iċ lēofra lȳt   on þissum lond-stede,

holdra frēonda.   For-þon is mīn hyġe ġeomor,

ðā[18] iċ mē ful ġe-mæcne   monnan funde,

heard-sǣliġne,   hyġe-ġēomorne,

mōd mīþendne,   morþor hycgendne.[19]   20

Blīþe ġe-bǣro[20]   ful oft wit bēotedon

þæt unc ne ġe-dǣlde   nemne dēað āna

ō-wiht elles.   Eft is þæt on-hworfen.

Is nū [samnung þēos]   swā hit nō wǣre[21]

frēondscipe uncer.   Sceal iċ fēor ġe nēah   25

mīnes fela-lēofan[22]   fǣhðu drēogan.

Hēht meċ mon wunian   on wuda bearwe,

under āc-trēo   in þām[23] eorð-scræfe.

Eald is þēs eorð-sele,   eal iċ eom of-longad;

sindon dena dimme,   dūna ūp-hēa,   30

---

[15] This sentence has a double *þæt* construction—you may omit the first one.

[16] Note that *tō-dǣlden* is a past subjunctive form (see §3.10.1 and §3.11).

[17] The verb phrase *meċ longade* contains both an impersonal and a reflexive pronoun (see §11.2).

[18] Translate *ðā* as "since."

[19] This series of adjectives (*heard-sǣliġne*, *hycendne*, *mīþendne*, and *hycgendne*) all agree with the object of the sentence, *monnan*, and thus each have the masculine accusative singular ending *-ne*.

[20] Translate as "in a happy mood"—the phrase appears to be in the instrumental case.

[21] This line has defective meter in that the first half-line lacks two stressed syllables: we supply the noun *sēo samnung*, since it seems that a variation on *frēondscipe uncer* has dropped out here. Other editors have provided different emendations: Bernard J. Muir, for example, reads *is nu [fornumen]* "now is taken away" in his edition, *The Exeter Anthology of Old English Poetry*, 2nd ed. (Exeter, Exeter UP, 2001).

[22] *Mīnes fela-lēofan* is a genitive phrase dependent on *fēhðu*.

[23] *Þām* here probably has a demonstrative sense: translate as "this."

bitre burg-tūnas   brērum be-weaxne,
wīċ wynna lēas.   Ful oft meċ hēr wrāþe be-ġeat
from-sīþ frēan.   Frēond sind on eorþan,
lēofe lifġende,   leġer weardiað,
35   þonne²⁴ iċ on ūhtan   āna gonge
under āc-trēo   ġeond þās eorð-scrafu.
Þǣr iċ sittan mōt   sumor-langne dæġ,
þǣr iċ wēpan mæġ   mīne wræc-sīþas,
earfoþa fela;   for-þon iċ ǣfre ne mæġ
40   þǣre mōd-ċeare   mīnre ġe-restan,
nē ealles þæs longaþes   þe meċ on þissum līfe be-ġeat.
Ā scyle ġeong mon   wesan ġēomor-mōd,
heard heortan ġe-þōht,²⁵   swylċe habban sceal
blīþe ġe-bǣro   ēac þon²⁶ brēost-ċeare,
45   sin-sorgna ġe-drēag,   sȳ æt him sylfum ġe-long
eal his worulde wyn,   sȳ ful wīde fāh
feorres folc-londes,   þæt mīn frēond siteð
under stān-hliþe   storme be-hrīmed,
wine wēriġ-mōd,   wætre be-flōwen
50   on drēor-sele.   Drēogeð sē mīn wine²⁷
micle mōd-ċeare;   he ġe-mon tō oft
wynlicran wīċ.   Wā bið þām þe sceal
of langoþe   lēofes ā-bīdan.

---

²⁴ þonne = "when" or "although"
²⁵ *Heard* modifies *ġe-þoht*, while *heortan* is a genitive singular.
²⁶ *ēac þon* = "besides" or "in addition to"
²⁷ *sē mīn wine* = *mīn wine*

Two
Beheadings

The following two excerpts depict the battle between good and evil on the brute level of bodies.

The first comes from the Old English *Judith*, a poem that adapts rather loosely the events in a book of the Vulgate Bible by the same name, considered apocryphal after the Reformation. The poem appears after *Beowulf* in the Nowell Codex (copied circa C.E. 1000) and lacks both the beginning and end. In the section of the poem that survives, Judith takes on Holofernes, the Assyrian general sent to destroy the Jewish people. She assassinates him and then leads her people into battle against his leaderless forces. In the section immediately preceding the excerpt given here, Holofernes has held a lavish and wine-soaked feast and returns to his pavilion drunk, where the dazzling Judith is brought to him supposedly for his pleasure. To compare the poem with the Vulgate version, see the on-line Douay-Rheims translation of *Judith*, particularly chapters 12 and 13 (http://www.drbo.org/chapter/18013.htm).

The second excerpt comes from *Beowulf* and recounts the hero's battle with Grendel's mother in her under-water lair. Grendel's mother, bent on revenge for the killing of her son, proves a treacherous enemy for the usually invincible Beowulf.

1. Judith (46-117)

		þǣr wæs eall-gylden
	flēoh-net fæġer[1]	ymbe þæs folc-togan
	bed a-hongen,	þæt sē bealo-fulla
	mihte wlītan þurh,	wīġena baldor,
50	on ǣġ-hwylċne	þe ðǣr inne cōm
	hæleða bearna,	ond on hyne nǣniġ
	monna cynnes,	nymðe sē mōdiga hwæne

---

[1] See the Vulgate *Judith* 10:19.

nīðe rōfra   him þe nēar hēte[2]

rinca tō rūnc ġe-gangan.   Hīe ðā on reste[3] ġe-brōhton

snūde ðā snoteran idese;   ēodon ðā sterced-ferhðe,   55

hæleð heora hearran cȳðan   þæt wæs sēo hāliġe mēowle

ġe-brōht on his būr-ġetelde.   þā wearð sē brēma on mōde

blīðe, burga ealdor,   þōhte ðā beorhtan idese

mid widle ond mid womme be-smītan.   Ne wolde þæt wuldres dēma

ġe-ðafian, þrymmes hyrde,   ac hē him þæs ðinges ġe-styrde,   60

dryhten, dugeða waldend.   Ġe-wāt ðā sē dēoful-cunda,

gāl-ferhð gumena ðrēate

bealo-full his beddes nēosan,   þǣr hē sceolde his blǣd for-lēosan

ǣdre binnan ānre nihte;   hæfde ðā his ende ġe-bidenne[4]

on eorðan un-swǣsliċne,   swylcne hē ǣr æfter worhte,   65

þearl-mōd ðēoden gumena,   þenden hē on ðysse worulde

wunode under wolcna hrōfe.   Ġe-fēol ðā wīne swā[5] druncen

sē rica on his reste middan,   swā hē nyste rǣda nānne

on ġe-wit-locan.   Wiġġend stōpon

ūt of ðām inne   ofstum miclum, [6]   70

weras wīn-sæde,   þe ðone wǣr-logan,

lāðne lēod-hatan,   lǣddon tō bedde

nehstan sīðe.   þā wæs nergendes

þēowen þrymful,   þearle ġe-myndiġ

hū hēo þone atolan   ēaðost mihte   75

---

[2] Note that *þe nēar* is a comparative form of *nēah* and could be translated "the closer, nearer."

[3] *rest* = bed, resting place.

[4] The participle *ġe-bidenne* (see §6.3), the adjective *un-swǣslicne* (l. 65a), and pronoun *swylcne* (l. 65b) are masculine acc singular adjectives (note the –ne endings) that modify *ende*. Translate, "(he) had experienced his end, a cruel (one) on earth, such (a one) as he before worked towards (or, deserved)."

[5] Translate *swā* as "that."

[6] Translate as a singular, "with great speed"

	ealdre be-niman	ǣr sē un-sȳfra,
	womfull, on-wōce.	Ġe-nam ðā wunden-locc
	scyppendes mægð	scearpne mēċe,
	scūrum heardne,	ond of sċēaðe ā-bræd
80	swīðran folme;	on-gān ðā sweġles weard
	bē naman nemnan,	nergend ealra
	woruld-būendra,	ond þæt word ā-cwæð:
	"Iċ ðē, frymða god	ond frōfre gǣst,
	bearn al-waldan,	biddan wylle
85	miltse þīnre	mē þearfendre,
	ðrynesse ðrym.	Þearle ys mē nū ðā
	heorte on-hǣted	ond hiġe ġeomor,
	swȳðe mid sorgum ġe-drēfed.	For-ġif mē, sweġles ealdor,
	sigor ond sōðne ġe-lēafan,	þæt iċ mid þys sweorde mōte
90	ġe-hēawan þysne morðres bryttan;	ġe-unne mē mīnra ġe-synta,[7]
	þearl-mōd þēoden gumena.	Nāhte iċ þīnre[8] nǣfre
	miltse þon māran þearfe.	Ġe-wrec nū, mīhtiġ dryhten,
	torht-mōd tīres brytta,	þæt mē ys þus torne on mōde,
	hāte on hreðre mīnum."	Hī ðā sē hēhsta dēma
95	ǣdre mid elne on-bryrde,[9]	swā hē dēð ānra ġe-hwylċne
	hēr-būendra	þe hyne him tō helpe sēċeð
	mid rǣde ond mid rihte ġe-lēafan.	Þā wearð hyre rūme on mōde,
	hāliġre hyht ġe-nīwod;	ġe-nām ðā þone hǣðenan mannan
	fæste bē feaxe sīnum,	tēah hyne folmum wið hyre weard[10]

---

[7] ġe-synta = gen plural in a singular sense (see mīnra). Note that ġe-unnan takes a dative of person and genitive of thing: "grant me my salvation."

[8] þīnre modifies miltse (gen) in the following line. Translate þīnre miltse þearf as "need of your mercy."

[9] For this form, see §3.11.1.

[10] wið hire weard = "toward her"

bysmerlīċe,   ond þone bealo-fullan   100
liꝣtum ā-lēde,   lāðne mannan,
swā hēo ðæs un-lǣdan[11]   ēaðost mihte
wel ġe-wealdan.   Slōh ðā wunden-locc
þone fēond-sceaðan   fāgum mēċe,
hete-þoncolne,   þæt hēo healfne for-ċearf   105
þone swēoran him,[12]   þæt hē on swīman læġ,
druncen ond dolh-wund.   Næs ðā dēad þā ġyt,
ealles or-sāwle;   slōh ðā eornoste
ides ellen-rof   ōðre sīðe
þone hǣðenan hund,   þæt him þæt hēafod wand   110
forð on ðā flōre.   Læġ sē fūla lēap
gǣsne be-æftan,   gǣst ellor hwearf
under neowelne næs   ond ðǣr ġe-nyðerad wæs,
sūsle ġe-sǣled   syððan æfre,
wyrmum be-wunden,   wītum ġe-bunden,   115
hearde ġe-hæfted   in helle bryne
æfter hin-sīðe.

II. Beowulf (1518-70)

On-ġeat þā sē gōda   grund-wyrġenne,
mere-wīf mihtiġ;   mæġen-rǣs for-ġeaf
hilde-bille,   hond sweng ne of-tēah   1520
þæt hire on hafelan   hring-mǣl ā-gōl

---

[11] *ðæs un-lǣdan* is the gen object of *ġe-wealdan*. See also §6.2.3.
[12] *healfne for-ċearf / þone swēoran him*: note that *healfne* modifies *swēoran* and that *him* is a dative of possession. Translate "hacked through half his neck."

        grǣdiġ gūð-lēoð.   Ðā sē ġist on-fand

        þæt sē beado-lēoma   bītan nolde,

        aldre sceþðan,   ac sēo ecg ġe-swāc

1525   ðēodne æt þearfe;   ðolode ǣr fela

        hond-ġemōta,   helm oft ġe-scær,

        fǣġes fyrd-hræġl;   ðā wæs forma sīð

        dēorum madme, þæt his dōm ā-læġ.

        Eft wæs ān-rǣd,   nalas elnes læt,

1530   mǣrða ġe-myndiġ   mǣġ Hȳlāces.

        Wearp ðā wunden-mǣl   wrǣttum ġe-bunden

        yrre ōretta,   þæt hit on eorðan læġ,

        stīð ond stȳl-ecg;   strenge ġe-trūwode,

        mund-gripe mæġenes.   Swā sceal man dōn,

1535   þonne hē æt gūðe   ġe-gān þenċeð

        long-sumne lof,   nā ymb his līf ċearað.

        Ġe-fēng þā be eaxle   (nalas for fǣhðe mearn)

        Ġuð-Ġēata lēod   Grendles mōdor;

        Brægd þā beadwe heard,   þā hē ġe-bolgen wæs,

1540   feorh-ġenīðlan,   þæt hēo on flet ġe-bēah.

        Hēo him eft hrāþe   and-lēan for-ġeald

        grimman grāpum   ond him tō-ġeanes fēng;

        ofer-wearp þa wēriġ-mōd   wīgena strengest,

        fēþe-cempa,   þæt hē on fylle wearð.

1545   Of-sæt þā þone sele-ġyst   ond hyre seax ġe-teah,

        brad ond brūn-ecg,   wolde hire bearn wrecan,

        āngan eaferan.   Him on eaxle læġ

---

[16] *sceal* = "must"

brēost-net brōden;   þæt ġe-bearh fēore,
wið ord ond wið ecge   in-gang for-stōd.
Hæfde ðā for-sīðod   sunu Ecg-þēowes   1550
under ġynne grund,   Ġēata ċempa,
nemne him heaðo-byrne   helpe ġe-fremede,
here-net hearde,   ond hāliġ god
ġe-wēold wīġ-sigor;   wītiġ drihten,
rodera rǣdend,   hit on ryht ġe-scēd: 1555
ȳðelīċe,   syþðan hē eft ā-stod.
Ġe-seah ðā on searwum   siġe-ēadiġ bil,
eald sweord eotenisc,   ecgum þȳhtiġ,
wiġena weorð-mynd;   þæt wæs wǣpna ċyst,
būton hit wæs māre   ðonne ǣniġ mon ōðer   1560
tō beadu-lāce   æt-beran meahte,
gōd ond ġeatolīċ,   gīganta ġe-weorc.
Hē ġe-fēng þā fetel-hilt,   freca Scyldinga.
hrēoh ond heoro-grim   hring-mǣl ġe-brǣġd,
aldres or-wēna,   yrringa slōh,   1565
þæt hire wið halse   heard grāpode,
bān-hringas brǣc. Bil eal ðurh-wōd
fǣġne flǣsc-homan;   hēo on flet ġe-crong.
Sweord wæs swatiġ,   secg weorce ġe-feh.

The Making of Books

We owe the existence of the texts we study to the scribes, artists, and makers of books working in the monastic scriptoria of Anglo-Saxon England. The following texts give a sense of the motives and concerns of those involved in the making of books and allow a rare window into the world of book and text production. The majority of these texts mention the names of their creators in order to ask the reader to pray for them. The Benedictine Rule enjoined monks to engage in daily manual labor, and the making of books, an incredibly expensive and meticulous undertaking, would have formed an important part of the labor of monasteries with scriptoria.

The first two prose excerpts are colophons or epilogues composed by scribes detailing how two gospel books were copied and came to be glossed in English. The colophon to the Lindisfarne Gospels (circa 680–720), one of the most lavish and beautiful books produced in Anglo-Saxon England, was written much later (around 940) by a scribe named Aldred, who provided an interlinear English gloss to the Latin text of the gospels, but who tells of the much earlier makers and illuminators of the book. For a careful analysis of this text, see Lawrence Nees's "Reading Aldred's Colophon for the Lindisfarne Gospels," *Speculum* 78 (2003): 333-77. To see a full online facsimile of the Lindisfarne Gospels, connect to the British Library's virtual book gallery: http://www.bl.uk/onlinegallery/virtualbooks/viewall/index.html#.

The Rushworth Gospels, whose Latin text is nearly identical to that of the Lindisfarne Gospels, appears to have been copied in the eighth century and, like the Lindisfarne Gospels, was glossed in Mercian English much later, probably in the second half of the tenth century. The English colophon documents the work of two scribes, Farman (a priest) and Owun who were responsible for the English glosses, while the Latin colophon states that a Macregol, presumably the eighth-century artist and scribe, created the book. Interestingly, Macregol appears to be an Irish name, while Farman and Owun are Welsh.

The "Metrical Epilogue to MS. 41, CCCC" was written into an eleventh-century manuscript (Cambridge, Corpus Christi College Library, MS. 41) containing a copy of the OE translation of Bede's *Ecclesiastical History* as well as a number of marginal texts in English and Latin, including charms and a version of the "Solomon and Saturn" poem. Though the scribe does not mention his name, he does ask readers for prayer so that he may be able to copy more books.

The next three poems have a more pronounced literary character.

The first is the runic "signature" from the epilogue to Cynewulf's poem, "The Fates of the Apostles." Cynewulf, a poet of the ninth or tenth centuries about whom we otherwise know very little, named himself with runes in four poems: "The Fates of the Apostles," "Elene" (both in the Vercelli Book), "Christ II," and "Juliana" (in the Exeter Book). Like the authors of the colophons, Cynewulf apparently wants readers to remember his name, though perhaps not as a full-blown "author."

The last two poems, both riddles from the Exeter Book (copied around 975), emerge from the culture of books and book making, which involved the treatment of animal skins, cutting them into pages, mixing of ink, ruling of pages, and of course the copying and illuminating of the texts themselves, as well as binding. See if you can solve these two riddles.

I. Colophon to Lindisfarne Gospels

Eadfrið Biscop Lindisfearnensis Ecclesiæ,[1] hē ðis bōc ā-wrat æt fruma, Gode ond Sancte Cuðberhte[2] ond eallum ðæm hālgum ġe-mænelīċe, ðā ðe in ēalonde sint. Ond Eðilwald,[3] Lindisfearneolondinga biscop, hit ūtan

---

[1] *Lindisfearnensis Ecclesiæ* = "of the church of Lindisfarne."
[2] St. Cuthbert
[3] Eadfrith was bishop from 698-721, and Æthelwald, the prior of Melrose.

ġe-ðrȳde ond ġe-belde,[4] swā hē wel cūðe. Ond Billfrið sē āncre, hē ġe-

5   smioðade ðā ġe-hrino, ðā ðe ūtan on sint, ond hit ġe-hrinade mid golde
ond mid ġimmum, ēac mid seolfre of-gylded fācon-lēas fēh.[5] Ond Aldred
[presbyter indignus ond misserrimus][6] mid Godes fultume ond Sancti
Cuðberhtes hit of-glēsade on englisc ond hine ġe-hāmade[7] mid ðǣm
ðrīm dǣlum: Matheus dǣl, Gode ond Sancte Cuðberhti; Marc dǣl, ðǣm

10   biscope; ond Lucas dǣl, ðǣm hīrede, ond eaht ora seolfres mid to in-lāde;
ond Sancti Johannes dǣl for hine seolfne, fore his sāwle, ond feower ora
seolfres mid, Gode ond Sancti Cuðberti, þætte hē hæbbe and-fang ðurh
Godes miltse on heofnum, sǣl ond sibb on eorðan, forð-geong ond ġe-
ðyngo, wīs-dōm ond snyttru ðurh Sancti Cuðberhtes earnunga. *Eadfrið,*

15   *Æðilwald, Billfrið, [et] Aldred hoc euangelium deo Cuthberhto construxerunt*
et ornauerunt.[8]

II. Colophon From The Rushforth Gospels

Ðe mīn brūce,[9] ġe-bidde fore Owun ðe ðās bōc gloesde [ond] Færmen
ðǣm preoste æt Harawuda, [þe] hæfe nū bōc ā-writne. Brūca mid willan
symle mid sōðum ġe-leofa. Sibb is æġ-hwǣm lēofost. *Macregol depinxit*
hoc euangelium. Quicunque legerit et intelligerit istam narrationem oret pro
Macreguil scriptori.[10]

---

4   See §3.11.1.
5   The word *fēh* is either a form of the word *feoh* "treasure" or related to *ġe-fēg* "binding, joint"; Nees glosses it as "metal" (341).
6   *presbyter indignus ond misserrimus* = "an unworthy and most wretched churchman." Aldred, a priest of Chester-le-Street, glossed the Lindisfarne Gospel from between 950 and 970.
7   This unique verb is most probably derived from *hām* "home."
8   "Eadfrith, Æðelwald, Billfrith, and Aldred made and ornamented this Gospel-Book."
9   The book itself speaks here "Whoever might use me . . ." *Mīn* is the gen object of *brūcan.*
10   "Macregol illuminated this Gospel-Book. Whoever may read and understand this narrative, pray for Macreguil the scribe."

III. Metrical Epilogue to MS. 41, CCCC

Bidde iċ ēac   æġ-hwylċne mann,
brego, rīċes weard,   þe þās bōc ræde
and þā bredu be-fō,   fira aldor,
þæt ġe-fyrðrige[11] þone writre   wynsum cræfte
þe ðās bōc ā-wrāt   bām handum twām,   5
þæt hē mōte maneġa[12] ġȳt   mundum sȳnum
ġe-endigan,   his aldre tō willan,
and him þæs ġe-unne   sē ðe āh ealles ġe-weald,
rodera waldend,   þæt hē[13] on riht mōte
oð his daga ende   drihten herigan.   10
          Amen.
          Ġe-weorþe[14] þæt.

IV. Runic Signature for Cynewulf's
"Fates of the Apostles"

Hēr mæġ findan   fore-þances glēaw,[15]
sē þe hine lysteð   lēoð-ġiddunga,
hwā þās fitte fēgde: .ᚠ. (fēoh) þær on ende standeþ,
eorlas þæs[16] on eorþan brūcaþ;   ne mōton hīe[17] āwa æt-somne
woruld-wuniġende.   .ᚹ. (wynn) sceal ġe-drēosan   100

---

[11] The subject of *ġe-fyrðrige* must be the "each man" of l. 1 that the scribe has called upon God to inspire to pray for the writer of the book.

[12] I.e., many more books.

[13] I.e., the writer.

[14] *Ġe-weorþe* = 3 present subjunctive: translate, "let that come to pass."

[15] See §6.2.3.

[16] *þæs* is the gen object of *brūcaþ*, referring back to *fēoh*. Translate as "it."

[17] Supply *brūcan* from l. 99a.

.ᚢ. (ūr) on ēðle,   æfter tō-hweorfan
lǣne līċes frætewa,[18]   efne swā ᚠ. (lagu) tō-glīdeð.
Þonne .ᚢ. (cēn) ond .ᚢ. (ȳr)   cræftes nēotað
nihtes nearowe,[19]   on him .ᚾ. (nēod) liġeð,

105   cyninges þēow-dōm.   Nū ðū cunnan miht
hwā on þām wordum wæs   werum on-cȳðiġ.
        Sīe þæs ġe-myndiġ,   mann sē ðe lufiġe
þisses galdres be-gang,   þæt hē ġēoce mē
ond frōfre fricle.   Iċ sceal feor hēonan[20]

110   ān elles forþ   eardes nēosan,
sīð ā-settan,[21]   nāt iċ sylfa hwær,
of þisse worulde;   wīċ sindon un-cūð
eard ond ēðel.   Swā bið ǣlcum menn,
nemðe hē god-cundes   gāstes brūce.

115   Ac utu wē þē ġeornor   tō Gode cleopigan,
sendan usse bēne   on þā beorhtan ġe-sceaft,
þæt wē þæs botles   brūcan mōton,
hāmes in hēhðo;   þǣr is hihta mǣst
þǣr cyning engla   clǣnum ġildeð

120   lēan un-hwīlen.   Nū ā his lof standeð
myċel ond mǣre,   ond his miht seomaþ,
ēċe ond ed-ġiong,   ofer ealle ġe-sceaft.   *Finit.*[22]

---

18   *lǣne* modifies *frætewa*.
19   No matter which of many interpretations of these two runes one chooses, the idea is difficult. Translate, "the torch and the horn (sharp weapon? pen?) require skill because of the hardship of night." This line might refer to the skill and effort required for night-time fighting or perhaps copying at night, the sequence of ideas is obscure.
20   The verb of motion is implied: supply "go." See §5.2.2.
21   *ā-settan* depends on *sceal* in l. 109.
22   *Finit* = "It ends" or "the end."

V. Exeter Book Riddle 24

Meċ fēonda sum   feore[23] be-snyþede,
woruld-strenga bi-nom,   wǣtte[24] siþþan,
dȳfde on wǣtre,   dyde eft þonan,
sette[25] on sunnan,   þǣr iċ swīþe be-lēas
hǣrum þām þe iċ hæfde.   Heard[26] meċ siþþan   5
snāð seaxses ecg,   sindrum be-grunden;
fingras feoldon,   ond meċ fugles wyn
ġeond spēd-dropum   spyrede ġe-nēahhe,
ofer brūnne brerd,   bēam-telge swealg,
strēames dǣle,   stōp eft on meċ,   10
sīþade sweart-last.   Meċ siþþan wrāh
hæleð hlēo-bordum,   hȳde be-þenede,
ġierede meċ mid golde;   for-þon mē glīwedon
wrǣtliċ weorc smiþa,   wīre bi-fongen.
Nū þā ġe-rēnu   ond sē rēada telg   15
ond þā wuldor-ġesteald   wīde mǣren[27]
dryht-folca helm,   nales dol wīte.[28]
Ġif mīn[29] bearn wera   brūcan willað,
hȳ bēoð þȳ ġe-sundran   ond þȳ siġe-fæstran,
heortum þȳ hwætran   ond þȳ hyġe-blīþran,   20

---

[23] *feore = feorhe.*
[24] *wǣtte = wǣtede*; see §3.11.1. Note that the object *meċ* (l. 1) is carried over for this and the series of verbs that follow.
[25] See §3.11.1.
[26] *Heard* modifies *ecg* in l. 6.
[27] *mǣre* = subjunctive form of *mǣran* "to glorify, celebrate." Translate "Let [these] ornaments, the read ink, and the glorious possessions honor the protector of peoples."
[28] *nales dol wīte* = "do not at all let a fool find fault with (him or them)."
[29] *mīn* is the gen object of *brūcan*: translate as "me."

       ferhþe þȳ frōdran,   habbaþ frēonda þȳ mā,
       swǣsra ond ġe-sibbra,   sōþra ond gōdra,
       tilra ond ġe-trēowra,   þā hȳra tȳr ond ēad
       ēstum ȳcað   ond hȳ ār-stafum
25   lissum bi-lecgað   ond hī lufan fæþmum
       fæste clyppað.   Frīġe hwæt iċ hātte,
       niþþum tō nytte.   Nama mīn is mǣre,
       hæleþum ġifre   ond hāliġ sylf.

VI. Exeter Book Riddle 51

       Iċ seah wrǣtlīċe   wuhte fēower
       samed sīþian;   swearte wǣron lāstas,
       swaþu swīþe blācu.   Swift[30] wæs on fōre,
       fuglum framra[31];   flēag on lyfte,
5   dēaf under ȳþe.   Drēag un-stille
       winnende wīġa   sē him[32] weġas tācneþ
       ofer fǣted gold   fēower eallum.

---

[30] Note the shift to the singular here, either referring to the four creatures as a collective entity or singling out one.
[31] Note that *framra* "bolder" is a comparative and that the dative of the previous word *fuglum* stands in for "than."

Glossary

In the following glossary, *æ* appears between *ad-* and *af-* within the letter *A* and is so alphabetized within words. Words beginning with *ð,Ð* or *þ,Þ* appear in a separate letter entry after *T*. Otherwise, *ð* and *þ* are alphabetized like *th* when they occur in the middle or end of a word. A word's *ġe-* prefix is ignored in the alphabetical ordering, so that (for example) *ġe-wyrcan* appears under *W*. If a form requires the *ġe-* prefix, it appears simply as *ġe-*, but if the prefix is optional, it appears in parentheses *(ġe)*.

A

ā- (prefix) = adds the sense of "up," "out," "forward," or "away" to verbs, though it often merely intensifies the base meaning without adding any sense of direction, or in many cases seems to add no discernable meaning

ā, āa (adverb) = always, forever [§6.9]

ā-bīdan (strong verb 1 + gen object) = to wait, wait for, await [§8.4]

ā-bisġian (weak verb II) = to BUSY, occupy [§3.12]

ā-brecan (strong verb 4) = to capture [§8.7]

ā-bregdan (strong verb 3) = to draw out, pull out [§8.6]

abbudisse, abudisse, -ese (weak f) = prioress, abbess, female leader of a double monastery [§3.4]

ā-būgan (strong verb 2) = to BOW to, do reverence to [§8.5]

ac (conjunction) = but; and

ā-cennan (weak verb I) = to give birth to, produce, bring forth; be brought forth, born [§3.11]

ā-clǣnsian (weak verb II) = to CLEANSE, wipe clean [§3.12]

āc-trēo (n) = OAK TREE [§10.3.2]

ā-cweðan (strong verb 5) = to speak out, say [§9.1]

ādl, āðl (f) = sickness, disease [§2.8]

ādliġ (adjective) = sick, ill, diseased [§6.1]

ā-dōn (irregular verb) = to bring, take away, remove [§4.5.3]

ā-drēogan (strong verb 2) = to survive, endure, put up with (something) [§8.5]

ā-drīfan (strong verb 1) = to DRIVE away, banish [§8.4]

ā-drincan (strong verb 3) = to drown [§8.6]

ā-dūne (adverb) = DOWN, downward [§6.9]

ā-dȳleġian (weak verb II) = to destroy, stain [§3.12]

Æbbe (weak f, a name) = Abbe, an abbess [§3.4]

æcer (m) = field; ACRE [§2.7]

ǣdre (weak f) = vein, artery [§3.4]

ǣdre (adverb) = at once, instantly [§6.9]

ǣfen (m or n) = EVENing [§2.7, §2.9]

ǣfen-ræst (f) = EVENing REST [§2.8]

ǣfre (adverb) = EVER, always [§6.9]

æfter (preposition + dat) = AFTER; according
to [§6.15]

æfter-fyġiend (adjective) = FOLLOWing
AFTER (originally a present participle)
[§6.1]

ǣġ- (prefix) adds a generalizing or universal
sense to pronouns and adverbs: *hwilċ* =
"any," *ǣġ-hwylċ* = every

ǣġ-hwonan (adverb) = everywhere [§6.9]

ǣġ-hwylċ (adjective or indefinite pronoun,
usually + gen) = each, every [§6.1, §7.8]

ǣglæċa (weak m) = fierce fighter [§3.3]

ǣġðer ġe . . . ġe (conjunction) = both . . . and

æht (f) = property, possessions (usually pl)
[§10.11.2]

ǣiġ (n) = EGG (pl: *ǣiġra*) [§10.8]

æl (m) = AWL, tool to punch holes in leather
[§2.7]

ǣl (m) = EEL [§2.7]

ǣlċ (adjective or pronoun) = any; EACH, every
(person or thing) (often + gen) [§6.1, §7.8]

ælednyss (m) = fire; burning, burning down
[§2.7]

ǣle-pūta (weak m) = EEL-POUT, burbot
(freshwater fish) [§3.3]

ælmesse, ælmysse (f) = ALMS, charity [§2.8]

æl-mihtiġ (adjective) = ALMIGHTY (as a m
noun) the ALMIGHTY (one) [§6.1]

ǣmette (weak f) = ant [§3.4]

ǣmtiġ (adjective) = EMPTY, bare [§6.1]

ǣn, ǣne = see *ān*

ǣniġ (adjective or pronoun) = ANY [§6.1, §7.8]

ǣnlīċe (adverb) = ONLY; fittingly,
appropriately [§6.9]

ǣr (adjective) = earlier, previous, first [§6.1]

ǣr (adverb) = before, ERE [§6.9]

ǣr (conjunction) = before, ERE [§5.1.1]

ǣr (preposition + dat and instr) = before
[§6.15]

ǣr (n) = ORE, brass, copper [§2.9]

erċ-biscop (m) = ARCHBISHOP [§2.7]

Ærconbyrht (m) = king of Kent (died 664),
husband of Seaxburh [§2.7]

ǣrende (n) = mission, ERRAND; message
[§10.2.2]

ǣrest (adverb) = first [§6.9]

ǣrne-merġen (n) = early morning, dawn [§2.9]

ǣs (n) = meat, carrion, bait [§2.9]

æt (preposition + dat) = AT, by, next to
[§6.15]

ǣt (m or n) = EATables, food [§2.7, §2.9]

æt-beran (strong verb 4) = to carry to, bring
[§8.4]

æt-berstan (strong verb 3) = to escape, get
away [§8.6]

æt-ēawede, æt-ēowede, -on = past sing and pl
forms of *æt-īewan*

æt-foran (preposition + dat) = beFORE, in the
presence of [§6.15]

æt-brīnan (strong verb 1) = to touch (+ gen
object) [§8.4]

æt-īewan (weak verb I) = to reveal, show,
display [§3.11]

ǣton = past pl form of *etan*

æt-somne (adverb) = together [§6.9]

æt-wesan (irregular verb) = to be present
[§4.5.1]

æt-windan (strong verb 3) = to escape [§8.6]

Æðeldryð (f) = queen of Northumbria (ca. 630-679 C.E.), founder of the monastery at Ely, revered as a saint

æðele (adjective) = noble, fine [§6.1]

æþeling (m) = nobleman, retainer [compare German *edel* "noble"; §2.7]

ǣw-fæst (adjective) = upstanding, devout [§6.1]

ā-fandian (weak verb II) = to put to the test, prove [§3.12]

ā-fēdan (weak verb I) = to FEED [§3.11]

ā-fēst = *ā-fēdest* (pres 2 sing of *ā-fēdan*)

ā-festigian (weak verb II) = to become or be envious [§3.12]

Affrica-land (n) = Africa [§2.9]

ā-fyllan (weak verb I) = to FILL up [§3.11]

ā-fyrhtan (weak verb I) = to terrify, make afraid (past tense: *ā-fyrde*) [§3.11]

ā-galan (strong verb 6) = to sing, chant out [§9.2]

āgan (preterite-present verb) = to own, possess [§4.3.1]

āgēan-lēdan (weak verb I) = to LEAD back [§3.11]

ā-ġētan (weak verb I) = to destroy [§3.11]

āglǣca (weak m) = monster, prodigious creature [§3.3]

ā-bæfen = past participle of *ā-hebban*

ā-bangen = past participle of *ā-bōn*

ā-bēawan (strong verb 7) = to cut out, carve [§9.3]

ā-hebban (strong verb 6) = to lift, raise, cast, HEAVE up (past participle = *ā-hæfen, -hefen*) [see German *heben* "to lift"; §9.2]

ā-hof = past sing of *ā-hebban*

ā-hōn (strong verb 7) = to HANG up [§9.3, 11.1.2]

ā-breddan (weak verb I) = to rescue, set free [§3.11]

ābsie, ābsast, etc. = pres 1 and 2 sing of *āscian*

āhte = past sing of *āgan*

āhton = past pl of *āgan*

aldorman = see *ealdormon*

aldre, aldor = see *ealdor*

ā-lēde = past participle of *ā-lecgan*

ā-lecgan (weak verb I) = to LAY down, put down, conquer, destroy [§3.11]

ā-licgan (strong verb 5) = to fail, cease, stop [§9.1]

al-walda (weak m) = ALL-WIELDer, the Almighty, God [§3.3]

ān (adjective) = sole, lone; alone; a certain (person or thing) (note that when it means "alone" *ān* usually takes weak adjective endings: see §6.4; *ān* can occasionally function like the indefinite article *a/an* in Modern English, though "one" or "alone" is its more usual meaning in OE) [§6.1]

ān (adverb) = alone, only; *þæt ān* = "only that" [§6.9]

ān (number) = ONE

āna (adverb) = alone, ONly [§6.9]

an-bidian (weak verb II) to await, wait for [§3.12]

ancgel, ancgil (m) = hook, fishing hook [§2.7]

āncra (weak m) = ANCHORite, hermit, advanced monk [§3.3]

and- = see also *an-, ond-*; generally adds a sense of opposition, reciprocation, or negation

and (conjunction) = AND

and-fang (n) = acceptance [§2.9]

and-ġit, -ġyt (f) = understanding, insight [§2.8]

and-lang (preposition + gen) = ALONG [§6.15]

and-lēan (n) = reward, repayment [§2.9]

and-swarian, answarian (weak verb II) = (+ dat of person) to ANSWER [§3.12]

(ġe)and-weard (adjective) = present, existing, actual [§6.1]

and-wlita (m) = face, countenance [§3.3]

and-wyrde = past tense of *and-swarian*

(ġe)and-wyrdan (weak verb I) = to answer [§3.11]

and-wyrt = *and-wyrdeð* [see §8.10.2]

āne (adverb) = alone, singly, only [§6.9]

ānga (adjective) = sole, only [§6.1]

Angel-cyn (n) = English, the tribe of the ANGLES [§2.8]

angnes (f) = anxiety, trouble; pain [§2.8]

ān-mōdlīċe (adverb) = together, with a single mind [§6.9]

Anna (weak m) = king of East Anglia 635-654, father of St. Æðeldryð [§3.3]

ānne = m acc sing of *ān*

ān-rǣd (adjective) = resolute, single minded (lit., one-counsel) [§6.1]

an-sīen (f) = presence, sign [§2.8]

an-sund (adjective) = healthy, whole, sound [§6.1]

an-weald = see *on-weald*

(ġe)anwyrd = see *(ġe)and-weard*

apostol (m) =APOSTLE [§2.7]

ā-priccan (weak verb I) = to PRICK, gouge [§3.11]

ā-rǣran (weak verb I) = to REAR up, raise [§3.11]

ār-fæstnis, -nys (f) = piety, devoutness; honor, grace; virtue, goodness [§2.8]

Archoboleta = proper name

ā-rīsan (strong verb 1) = to ARISE [§8.4]

ār-smið (m) = ORE-SMITH, coppersmith, brass-smith [§2.7]

ār-stæf (m) = help-STAFF, support, assistance, grace [§2.7]

ār-wurðlīċe (adverb) = honorably [§6.9]

ār-wurðnys, -wyrðnes (f) = reverence, honor [§2.8]

ā-sċēotan (strong verb 2) = to lance, pierce; SHOOT out [§8.5]

āscian (weak verb II) = to ASK, question [§3.12]

ā-scyrpan (weak verb I) = to SHARPEN [§3.11]

ā-secgan (weak verb III) = to speak about, describe; tell, relate [§4.1]

ā-send = collapsed past participle of *ā-sendan* [see §3.11.1]

ā-sendan (weak verb I) = to SEND [§3.11]

ā-settan (weak verb I) = to SET, put; get out on (past tense: *ā-sette*) [§3.11]

ā-singan (strong verb 3) = to SING out, sing, compose verse [§8.6]

ā-slēan (strong verb 6) = to strike; pitch, erect, set up [§9.2, §11.1]

ā-slīdan (strong verb 1) = to SLIDE, slip, fall [§8.4]

ā-slōgon = past pl of *ā-slēan*

ā-springan (strong verb 3) = to SPRING up, break forth, spread [§8.6]

ā-ste(a)llan (weak verb I) = to establish, set up, create [§3.11] *ā-standan* (strong verb 6) = to STAND, get up [§9.2]

ā-stīgan (strong verb 1) = to climb onto, board (a ship) [§8.4]

ā-stingan (strong verb 3) = to put out, pierce out [§8.6]

ā-styrian (weak verb I) = to STIR, move, raise [§3.11]

ā-sungen = past participle of *ā-singan*

atol (adjective) = hateful, repulsive, deformed, debauched [§6.1]

āttor (n) = poison [§2.9]

ā-þennan (weak verb I) = to spread out, extend [§3.11]

āðl = see *ādl*

ā-þrēotan (strong verb 2) = to grow weary or tired [§8.5]

āwa (adverb) = forever [§6.9]

ā-wacian (weak verb II) = to WAKE up [§3.12]

ā-wæcnian (weak verb II) = to AWAKE, revive [§3.12]

ā-weccan (weak verb I) = to wake up, awaken [3.11]

ā-weġ (adverb) = AWAY [§6.9]

ā-wendan (weak verb I) = to turn; translate [§3.11]

ā-wendednes (f) = change, mutability [§2.8]

ā-wiergan (weak verb I) = to curse, condemn; outlaw, banish [§3.11]

ā-wiht (n) = anything, something, aught [§10.11.1]

ā-wrītan, -wrȳtan (strong verb 1) = to write down, record [§8.4]

ā-wunian (weak verb II) = to remain, continue [§3.12]

ā-wyrged = past participle of *ā-wiergan*

axie = see *āscian*

B

bacan (strong verb 6) = to BAKE [§9.2]

(ġe)bād = past sing of *(ġe)bīdan*

bæcere (m) = BAKER [§10.2.1]

bæd = past sing of *(ġe)biddan*

(ġe)bædon = past pl of *(ġe)biddan*

(ġe)bǣr (n) = spirits, demeanor; behavior, BEARing [§10.3.2]

bærnan (weak verb I) = to BURN, set on fire [§3.11]

bǣron = past pl of *beran*

bæð (n) = BATH (pl forms in *bað-*) [§2.9, §2.10.3]

baldor, bealdor (m) = lord, master, commander [§2.7]

bām = dat plural of *beġen*

bān (n) = BONE [§2.9]

bana (weak m) = murderer, slayer [see ModE *BANE*; §3.3]

bān-fæt (n) = BONE-VAT, bone container; body, corpse (pl = *-fatu*) [§2.9]

bān-bring (m) = BONE-RING, vertebra [§2.7]

bān-loca (weak m) = BONE-LOCKer, body [§3.3]

bannan (strong verb 7) = to summon [§9.3]

bār (m) = BOAR [§2.7]

bāt = *bītan*

(ġe)batian (weak verb II) = to heal, get better [§3.12]

bað- = pl stem of *bæð*

baðian (weak verb II) = to BATHE, take a bath [§3.12]

be- (prefix) = 1) adds the sense of the prepostion *be*; 2) often makes an intransitive verb transitive (*gān* "to go," *be-gān* "to start, accomplish [something]"), or 3) indicates loss or deprivation (to *be-head*)

be (preposition + dat) = BY, by means of; with; about, concerning; in [§6.15]

beado-lēoma (weak m) = battle-light, i.e., a (flashing) sword [§3.3]

beadu (f) = battle [§10.3.3]

beadu-lāc (n) = battle-sport, battle [§2.9]

be-æftan (adverb, preposition + dat) = AFTER, behind [§6.15]

bēag, bēah (m) = ring, necklace [Yiddish *BAGel* "little ring," §2.7]

bēag-ġiefa (weak m) = ring-GIVEer [§3.3]

(ġe)bēah = see *(ġe)būgan*

bealo-ful (adjective) = BALEFUL, wicked, malicious, [§6.1]

bealwa (n) = evil [ModE *BALEful*; §10.3.2]

bēam-telg (m) = wood dye, ink [§2.7]

bean (f) = BEAN [§2.8]

beard (m) = BEARD [§2.7]

(ġe)bearh = see *(ġe)beorgan*

bearm (m) = lap; embrace [§2.7]

bearn (n) = child, offspring; son [Scots *BAIRN*; §2.9]

bearu –o (m) = wood, grove [§10.3.1]

bearwe = see *bearu*

bēatan (strong verb 7) = to BEAT, strike, hit [§9.3]

be-bēodan (strong verb 2) = to command, order, instruct [§8.5]

be-bīode = pres 1 sing of *be-bēodan*

be-bod (n) = command, decree [§2.9]

be-byrgan, -byrian (weak verb I) = to BURY, inter [§3.11]

bēċ = see *bōc*

be-clȳsan (weak verb I) = to enCLOSE, lock [§3.11]

be-cuman (strong verb 4) = to COME [§8.7]

(ġe)bed (n) = prayer, supplication [ModE *BEAD* derives from the practice of saying one prayer or "bead" for each section of a rosary neckclace; §2.9]

Beda (proper name) = (672/3-735) English churchman [§3.3]

bed(d) (n) = BED, cot [§2.9]

(ġe)bedde (weak f) = BEDmate, wife [§3.4]

beden = past participle of *(ġe)biddan*

be-drīfan (strong verb 1) = to drive [§8.4]

be-fæstan (weak verb I) = to apply; to establish, strengthen; entrust [§3.11]

be-fangen = past participle of *be-fōn*

be-flēon (strong verb 2) = to FLEE [§8.5]

be-flōwan (strong verb 7) = to FLOW, flow around, surround [§9.3]

be-fōn (strong verb 7) = to catch, seize; envelop, clasp, surround; contract [§9.3]

be-foran (preposition + dat) = BEFORE, in front of [§6.15]

be-gǣst = pres 2 sing of *be-gān*

be-gān (irregular verb) = to BEGIN, start; do, perform, accomplish [§4.5.3]

be-gang (m) = circuit, course; practice; drift (of a poem) [§2.7]

be-gang(c)an (strong verb 7) = to chase, pursue; practice [§9.3]

be-ġeat = past sing of *be-ġytan*

bēġen (adjective) = both

be-ġeondan (preposition + acc/dat) = on the other side of, BEYOND [§6.15]

be-ġietan (strong verb 5) = to GET, find, receive; beget, give birth to [§9.1]

be-grindan (strong verb 3) = to GRIND, polish, sharpen [§8.6]

be-grynian (weak verb II) = to ensnare, trap [§3.12]

be-ġȳman (weak verb I) = to observe, attend to [§3.11]

be-ġytan (weak verb I) = to get, obtain, acquire; take, seize [§3.11]

be-hātan (strong verb 7) = to promise, vow [§9.3]

be-healdan (strong verb 7) = TO BEHOLD [§9.3]

be-hēfe (adjective) = useful, necessary [§6.1]

be-hēt = past sing of *be-hātan*

be-hrīman (weak verb I) = to cover with frost [§3.11]

be-hwyrfan (weak verb I) = to exercise, perform; turn, change; instruct [§3.11]

(ġe)beldan (weak verb I) = to cover, bind (a book?) [§3.11]

be-lecgan (weak verb I) = to be encircled, covered [§3.11]

belg (m) = a pair of BELLOWs [§2.7]

belgan (strong verb 3) = to be angry, to swell with rage [§8.6.b]

belle (weak f) = BELL [§3.4]

be-lēosan (strong verb 2) = to LOSE, be deprived of (+ dat) [§8.5]

be-lūcan (strong verb 2) = TO LOCK [§8.5]

be-lȳfan (weak verb I) = to BELIEVE [§3.11]

be-lȳfdest = past 2 sing of *be-lȳfan*

bēn (f) = prayer, request [related to ModE *BOON*: §10.11.2]

benċ (f) = BENCH [§2.8]

be-niman (strong verb 4) = to take away, deprive of, rob [§8.7]

benn (f) = wound, injury [§2.8]

be-nom = be-nam; see *be-niman*

bēo (f) = BEE [§3.4]

bēo = 1 pres sing, pres subjunctive sing, or imperative sing of *bēon* [§4.5.2]

bēod (n) = table, board [§2.9]

bēodan (strong verb 2) = to offer; to command [compare German *bieten* "to offer"; §8.5]

bēon (irregular verb) = to BE [§4.5.1]

bēor (n) = BEER [§2.9]

(ġe)beorgan (strong verb 3) = to protect, save [§8.6]

(ġe)beorhliċ (adjective) = safe, prudent; fitting [§6.1]

beorht (adjective) = BRIGHT, beautiful, dazzling [§6.1]

beorn (m) = man; warrior, hero, chief [§2.7]

bēor-sele (m) = BEER hall [§2.7]

(ġe)bēotian (weak verb II) = to boast, vow, promise; to threaten [§3.12]

bēoð = pres pl or imperative pl of *bēon*

Bēowulf (m) = Beowulf (a proper name)

bera (weak m) = BEAR (the animal) [§3.3]

beran (strong verb 4) = to BEAR, to carry; bring forth, produce, give birth to; wear; endure, survive [§8.7]

bergyls (m) = tomb, grave, sepulchre [§2.7]

be-rōfen (adjective + dat) = deprived of,

BEREFt [originally a strong past participle; §3.12]

berstan (strong verb 3) = to BURST, break into pieces [§8.6]

be-sencan (weak verb I) = to submerge, immerse, cause to SINK [§3.11]

be-smītan (strong verb 1) = to make dirty or filthy, degrade, dishonor [§8.4]

be-snyðian (weak verb II) = to rob, deprive of, cut short [§3.12]

be-swīcan (strong verb 1) = to deceive, trick [§8.4]

be-swin(c)gan (strong verb 3) = to whip, flog, smack [§8.6]

be-tǣċan (weak verb I) = to hand over; entrust; pursue, hunt [§3.11]

betera (adjective) = BETTER (comparative form of *gōd* "good") [§6.8]

bet, betst (adverb) = BETter, in the BEST way (comparative, superlative forms of *wel*) [§6.9, §6.14]

be-tweoh, betwux (preposition + dat) = between, among, amidst [§6.15]

be-twē(o)nan (adverb) = in BETWEEN, in the meantime [§6.9]

betst (adjective) = BEST (superlative form of *gōd* "good") [§6.8]

be-twȳnum (preposition + dat) = BETWEEN, among [§6.15]

be-tȳnan (weak verb I) = to imprison; enclose [§3.11]

be-þenian (weak verb II) = to cover, stretch on, spread over [§3.12]

be-þurfan (preterite-present) = to need to, be obliged to, to need, require (+ infinitive) [§4.4]

be-weaxan (strong verb 7) = to begrow, grow over, cover over with growth [§9.3]

be-wēfan, -wǣfan (strong verb 6) = to cover over §9.2]

be-werian (weak verb I) = to pre*vent*, forbid; defend [§3.11]

be-windan (strong verb 3) = to WIND around, wrap, encircle [§8.6]

bi = see *be*

bicgdon = past pl of *bycgan*

bicnian (weak verb III) = to signify, betoken [§4.1]

(ġe)bīdan (strong verb 1) = wait, endure; to wait for, expect (+ gen object) [§8.4]

(ġe)biddan (strong verb 5) = TO BID, ask for, pray, implore [§9.1]

bieldu (f) = BOLDness [§10.7]

biernan (strong verb 3) = to BURN [§8.6]

biġ-ġencere, bī-ġengere (m) = worker [from OE *be-gān*; §10.12.1]

biġ-leofa (weak m) = sustenance, food [§3.3]

biġþ = pres 3 sing of *bycgan*

bilewit, bylewit (adjective) = gracious, kind [§6.1]

bil(l) (n) = sword [§2.9]

(ġe)bindan (strong verb 3) = to BIND, tie [§8.6]

binnan (preposition + acc or dat) = within, before the end of [§6.15]

binne (weak f) = BIN, feed-trough [§3.4]

biscop, bisceop (m) = BISHOP [§2.7]

bītan (strong verb 1) = to BITE [§8.4]

biter (adjective) = BITTER, painful [§6.1]

biterlīċ (adjective) = BITTER [§6.1]

biternys (f) = BITTERNESS [§2.8]

biþ = pres 3 sing of *bēon*

blāc (adjective) = BLACK, dark [§6.1]

blæc-horn (n) = ink HORN, container of ink [§2.9]

blēd (m) = success, prosperity, riches; mind; glory, reputation, dignity [§10.11.1]

blandan (strong verb 7) = to mix, BLEND [§9.3]

blāwan (strong verb 7) = to BLOW [§9.3]

blēo (n) = color; appearance, form [§10.3.2]

blētsian (weak verb II) = to BLESS [§3.12]

blind (adjective) = BLIND [§6.1]

blindlīċe (adverb) = BLINDLY [§6.9]

bliss (f) = happiness, enjoyment [§2.8]

blissian (weak verb II) = to be glad, rejoice [§3.12]

blīþe (adjective) = BLITHE, joyful, cheerful [§6.1]

blōd (n) = BLOOD [§2.9]

blōtan (strong verb 7) = to sacrifice [§9.3]

blōwan (strong verb 7) = to bloom [§9.3]

blȳðelīċe (adverb) = joyfully, happily, BLITHELY [§6.9]

bōc (f) = BOOK (nom/acc pl: *bēċ*) [§10.4.2]

bodian (weak verb II) = to announce, proclaim, preach [§3.12]

boga (weak m) = BOW (for shooting arrows) [§3.3]

bohte, (ġe)bohtest = past sing of *bycgan*

(ġe)bolgen (adjective) = enraged, swollen with anger (originally a past participle) [§6.1]

borian (weak verb I) = to BORE a hole through [§3.11]

bōt (f) = remedy [§2.8]

botl (n) = dwelling, house, building [§2.9]

brād (adjective) = BROAD, vast [§6.1]

brāde (adverb) = BROADly, widely, expansively [§6.9]

brādlinga (adverb) = flat, with the palm spread out [§6.9]

brǣdan (weak verb I) = to spread out, cast; to roast, bake, or broil [§3.11]

brǣġd = see *breġdan*

brǣġen (n) = BRAIN [§2.9]

brastlian (weak verb II) = to roar, crackle [§3.12]

brēac = see *brūcan*

brecan (strong verb 4) = to BREAK [§8.7]

bred (n) = board, plank; tablet, (writing) surface [compare German *Brett* "board, plank"; §10.11.1]

brēde = *brǣde* (see *brǣdan*)

brēdo (f) = breadth, extent [§10.7.1]

breġdan (strong verb 3) = to pull, draw, move quickly; to throw, toss, wrestle with [§8.6]

brego (m) = ruler, king, lord [§10.3.1]

brēme (adjective) = famous, glorious [§6.1]

brēost (m, f, or n pl noun) = chest; stomach, mid-section [ModE *BREAST*; §2.7-9]

brēost-ċearu (f) = sorrow of heart, BREAST-CARE [§2.8]

brēost-net (n) = BREAST-NET, corslet, ring mail [§2.9]

brēost-þing (n) = area around the chest and heart [§2.9]

brēotan (strong verb 2) = to break [§8.5]

brēr (m) = BRIAR, bramble [§2.7]

brerd (m) = surface [§2.7]

bridd (m) = BIRD [§2.7]

brīdel-þwan(c)g (m) = BRIDLE THONG, rein [§2.7]

brim (n) = surf, sea, ocean [§2.9]

(ġe)bringan (strong verb 3, weak verb 1) = to BRING [§8.6, §3.11]

Brixonte (f) = proper name for a river

broc (n) = misery, toil, affliction adversity [§2.9]

broden = see *bregdan*

brōhte, brōhton = see *bringan*

brosnian (weak verb II) = to fall apart, crumble, disintegrate; rot, decay [§3.12]

broþ (n) = BROTH, soup [§2.9]

brōðor (m) = BROTHER [§10.5]

(ġe)brōðor (m) = BROTHER monk, brethren [§10.5]

brūcan (strong verb 2) = to enjoy, have the use of; eat, consume; wear (+ gen or dat object) [§8.5]

brūn (adjective) = BROWN, dark, dusky; with metallic luster, shiny [§6.1]

Brūnanburg (f) = unidentified fort, site of the Battle of Brunanburg (937 C.E.) [§10.4.2]

brūn-ecg (adjective) = bright [§6.1]

brȳcð = see *brūcan*

brȳd (f) = BRIDE, newly married woman; wife [§2.8]

(ġe)brȳdian (weak verb II) = to marry, be married to [from *brȳd* "bride"; §3.12]

bryne (m) = BURNing, fire; inflammation [§10.11.1]

brytta (weak m) = distributor, sharer, giver [§3.3]

bryttan (weak verb I) = to distribute [§3.11]

būan, būġian (weak verb III) = to dwell (in), inhabit [§4.1]

bufan (preposition + dat) = aBOVE, over [§6.15]

būgan (strong verb 2) = to bend, bow; flee, leave [§8.5]

ġe-bunden = see *(ġe-)bindan*

būr (n) = dwelling, chamber; BOWER [§2.9]

burh, burg (f) = fortification, castle; town [ModE *BOROUGH*; §10.4.2]

būr-ġeteld (n) = BOWER-tent, pavillion, quarters [§2.9]

burg-tūn (m) = fortification, fortified place or TOWN [§2.7]

būtan, būton (conjunction) = except, except that, unless [§5.1.1]

būtan (preposition + dat, instr) = except; without; lacking [§6.15]

butere (weak f) = BUTTER [§3.4]

buteriċ (m) = leather bottle [§2.7]

buter-ġeþwēor (n) = BUTTER-curd, butter [§2.9]

būton = see *būtan*

bū-tu (indeclinable adjective) = both [§6.1]

(ġe)bycgan (weak verb I) = to BUY [§3.11]

byġe (m) = bend, curve [related to *būgan*; §10.2.1]

bylewit = see *bilewit*

byliġ (m) = BELLows [§2.7]

byrd (f) = BIRTH, parentage; nature [§10.11.2]

Byrhtnōð (m) = proper name

byrġels (m) = tomb [§2.7]

byrġen (f) = grave, tomb [§2.8]

byriġ = f dat form of *burh*

byrne (weak f) = mail coat, BYRNIE [§3.4]

byrst (m) = loss [§10.11.1]

byrðen (f) = BURDEN, load, weight [§2.8]

byrþor (n) = what is born, given BIRTH to, the fetus, a child; the act of child birth [§2.9]

bysen (f) = example, model, pattern; parable [§2.8]

(ġe)bysenung, -bysnung (f) = example, pattern, model [§2.8]

bysġian (weak verb II) = to occupy, BUSY; afflict, burden [§3.12]

bysmerlīċe (adverb) = contemptuously, shamefully, disgracefully [§6.9]

byst, byþ = pres 2, 3 sing of *bēon*

C

cælð = pres 3 sing of *calan*

calan (strong verb 6) = to be cold, grow cold [§9.2]

cann, cannst = pres 1/2, 3 sing of *cunnan*

Cant-ware (m pl) = the inhabitants of Kent [§10.11.3]

Cantware-byriġ (f) = CANTERBURY [§2.8]

Capi = river name

capitol-mæsse (weak f) = first or early MASS [§3.4]

carc-ern (n) = prison [§2.9]

caru = see *ċearu*

ċealf (n) = CALF [§10.8]

ċēap-mann (m) = merchant, tradesman, CHAPMAN [§10.4.2]

ċearian (weak verb II) = to CARE, be anxious, worry about [§3.12]

ċearu (f) = CARE, concern [§2.8]

ċeastre (f) = city, Roman garrison town, walled city [from Latin *castrum* "fort"; see ModE placenames ending in –*CHESTER*; §2.8]

ċeaster-waran (weak m, pl only) = inhabitants, city dwellers [§3.3]

ċēgan, (ġe)ċeged = see *ċīegan*

ċempa (weak n) = soldier, fighter [§3.3]

ċēn (m) = torch, name of the C rune [§2.7]

cennan (weak verb I) = to bear, produce; bring forth, be born (past participle = "born") [§3.11]

ċeorfan (strong verb 3) = to cut, CARVE [§8.6]

ċeorl (m) = freeman (of the lowest class), layman, peasant [ModE *CHURL*; §2.7]

(ġe)ċēosan (strong verb 2) = to CHOOSE, select, elect [§8.5]

ċēowan (strong verb 2) = to CHEW [§8.5]

ċēpan (weak verb I) = to KEEP [§3.11]

ċiele (m) = CHILL, cold, coolness [§10.2.1]

Ciconia = proper name

(ġe)ċīegan, ċēgan (weak verb I) = to call, summon, call out; name, call [§3.11]

ċierreċe = see *ċirċe*

ċierran (weak verb I) = to turn, to convert [compare German *kehren* "to turn"; §3.11]

ċild (n) = CHILD [§10.8]

cin(c)g = see *cyning*

ċirċe (weak f) = CHURCH [§3.4]

ċirlisc (adjective) = common ["churlish"; §6.1]

ċist (f) = box [§2.8]

clæmman (weak verb I) = to CLAM, press [§3.11]

clǣne (adjective) = CLEAN, pure, chaste [§6.1]

clǣne (adverb) = entirely, completely [§6.9]

clǣnnes, -nys (f) = purity, chastity [§2.8]

clāð (m) = CLOTH, CLOTHing [§2.7]

clauster, clūstor (n) = CLOISTER [§2.9]

cleafa (weak m) = cellar, chamber; cave [§3.3]

clēofan (strong verb 2) = to CLEAVE, split apart [§8.5]

clipian, cleopian (weak verb II) = to cry out, shout; speak loudly [§3.12]

clyccan (weak verb I) = to clutch, clench [§3.11]

clyf (n) = CLIFF [2.9]

clyne (n) = lump [§10.11.1]

clyppan (weak verb I) = to embrace, hug [ModE *CLIP*; §3.11]

cnafa, cnapa (weak m) = servant; boy [compare German *Knabe* "boy" ModE KNAVE; §3.3]

cnāwan (strong verb 7) = to KNOW [§9.3]

cnēoris(s) (f) = family [§2.8]

cnēow (n) =KNEE [§10.3.2]

cniht (m) = boy, young man; servant [§2.7]

cnyll (m) = sound of a bell, KNELL [§2.7]

cōc (m) = COOK [§2.7]

Coludis-byriġ, Colodes-burh (f) = Coldingham, in the Scottish borders [§2.8]

cōm = past 1, 3 sing of *cuman*

conophenas = probably a muddled version of *coeno-cephalus* [Greek: "dog" + "head"]

(ġe)corene = past participle (adjective) of *(ġe) ċēosan*

costung (f) = testing; temptation [§2.8]

crabba (weak m) = CRAB [§3.3]

cræft (m) = skill, ability, profession, CRAFT; deceit, trick, fraud [§2.7]

cræftiġ (adjective) = skillful; CRAFTY [§6.1]

crāwan (strong verb 7) = to CROW [§9.3]

crēopan (strong verb 2) = to CREEP, crawl [§8.5]

(ġe)cringan (strong verb 3) = to fall in battle, die [§8.6]

Crīst (m) = CHRIST [§2.7]

culter (m) = COULTER [§2.7]

cuman (strong verb 4) = to COME [§8.7]

cunnan (preterite-present verb) = to know, be acquainted with; to know how (to do something); CAN, be able to [§4.3.1]

cunnian (weak verb II) = to attempt, try; explore (imperative sing = *cunna!*) [§3.12]

cūð (adjective) = known, well-known; excellent, noted; revealed, apparent [§6.1]

cūðe, cūðon = past 3 sing, pl of *cunnan*

cūþlīċe (adverb) = certainly, clearly, evidently [§6.9]

cwǣde, cwǣdon, cwǣð = past 3 sing, pl of *cweþan*

cweartern (n) = prison [§2.9]

cweccan (weak verb I) = to QUAKE, shake, tremble [§3.11]

cwelan (strong verb 4) = to die [ModE *QUELL*; §8.7]

cwēn (f) = QUEEN [§2.8]

cweþan (strong verb 5) = to say, speak ["QUOTH the raven, 'Nevermore.'"; §9.1]

cwic (adjective) = alive ["the QUICK and the dead"; §6.1]

cwide (m) = saying [§10.11.1]

cwild (f) = death [§10.11.2]

cwiþ = pres 3 sing of *cweþan*

cwōm, cwōmon = past 3 sing, pl of *cuman*

(ġe)cwylman (weak verb I) = to kill, destroy; torment, afflict [§3.11]

ċyld, ċeald (n) = COLD, coldness [§2.9]

ċyle, ċiele (m) = cold, coldness, CHILL [§10.2.1]

cynd (f or n) = KIND, nature; birth, origin [§2.8, §2.9]

Cyneferð (m) = physician attending St. Æðeldryð [§2.7]

cyning, cyningc, cyncge (m) = KING [§2.7]

cynn (n) = KINd, sort; family, people, nation [§10.2.2]

ċynn-bān (n) = CHIN-BONE [§2.9]

ċȳpan (weak verb I) = to sell, bargain for; buy [related to ModE *CHEAP*; §3.11]

ċȳp-mann = see *ċēap-mann*

ċyrċe (weak f) = CHURCH [§3.4]

ċyrrednysse (f) = conversion [see *ċierran*; §2.8]

ċȳse (m) = CHEESE [§10.2.1]

ċyst (f) = choice, the best [§2.8]

ċyst, ċist (f) = CHEST, basket, box [see modern German *Kiste* "box, crate"; §2.8]

ċȳs-ġerunn (n) = curd-like mass, RUNNy CHEESE [§2.9]

cyssan (weak verb I) = to KISS [§3.11]

(ġe)cȳðan (weak verb I) = to make known, announce, publish, reveal; inform [see *cūð* "known"; §3.11]

D

dǣd (f) = DEED, action [§10.11.2]

dæġ (m) = DAY (pl forms in *dag-*) [§2.7, §2.10.3]

dæġ-rēd (n) = DAYbreak, dawn [see ModE *RED*; §2.9]

dæġ-rēdliċ (adjective) = morning, belonging to the morning, early [§6.1]

dǣl (m) = portion, part, DEAL [compare German *Teil* "part, share"; §2.7, 2.10.3]

dæl (n) = DALE, valley (pl forms in *dal-*) [§2.9, §2.10.3]

dǣlan (weak verb I) = to share, divide, DEAL out [§3.11]

dafenian (weak verb II) = to be right, proper, appropriate (often impersonal) [§3.12, §11.2]

dagum = dat pl of *dæġ*

dēacon (m) = DEACON, minister (late Latin loan) [§2.7]

dēad (adjective) = DEAD, not alive [§6.1]

dēadliċ (adjective) = DEADLY [§6.1]

dēaf = past 3 singular of *dūfan*

dear(r) = pres 1, 3 sing of *durran*

dēað (m) = DEATH [§2.7]

dēað-dæġ (m) = DEATH-DAY [§2.7]

delfan (strong verb 3) = to dig, excavate [ModE *DELVE*; §8.6]

dēma (weak m) = judge [§3.3]

dēman (weak verb I) = to judge, ascertain, DEEM [§3.11]

demm (m) = misfortune, loss [§2.7]

Dene (noun, m pl only) = DANES [§10.11.1]

denu (f) = valley, glen [§2.8]

dēofol (m or n) = DEVIL [§2.7, §2.9]

dēofol-cund (adjective) = fiendish, diabolical [§6.1]

dēofol-sēoc (adjective) = possessed (by devils), crazy, insane [lit., *DEVIL-SICK*; §6.1] *dēop* (adjective) = DEEP; profound [§6.1]

dēope (adverb) = DEEPly; profoundly, seriously [§6.9]

dēoplīċe (adverb) = DEEPLY, profoundly, with deep meaning [§6.9]

dēore (adjective) = precious, beloved [§6.11]

(ġe)deorf (n) = hard work, labor; hardship, trouble, danger [§2.9]

deorfan (strong verb 3) = to exert oneself, work hard, labor [§8.6]

dēor-wurðe, -wyrðe (adjective) = precious, DEAR; expensive [§6.1]

dēst, dēþ = pres 2, 3 sing of *dōn*

dīegol, dīgol (adjective) = secret, hidden [§6.1]

dīegollīċe (adverb) = secretly [§6.9]

dierne, dyrne (adjective) = secret, hidden [§6.1]

dīgan (weak verb I) = to survive, endure [§3.11]

dīgol = see *dīegol*

dimm (adjective) = DIM, dark, gloomy [§6.1]

dohtor (f) = DAUGHTER [§10.5]

dol (adjective) = silly, foolish; (as noun) fool [§6.1]

dolg, dolh (n) = wound, cut, tumour, sore [§2.9]

dolg-swæð (n) = scar [lit., wound-path; §2.9]

dolh-wund (adjective) = cut-WOUNDed, wounded, injured [§6.1, see OE *dolg* "wound, cut, scar"]

dōm (m) = judgment; glory [ModE *DOOM*; §2.7, 2.10.3]

dōm-dæġ (m) = DOOMsDAY, the Last Judgment [§2.7]

(ġe)dōn (irregular verb) = to DO, act, behave; make, produce, bring about, cause to happen; put, place, move [§4.5.3]

dorste = past sing of *durran*

draca (weak m) = dragon, fire-DRAKE [§3.3]

drǣdan (strong verb 7) = to be afraid of, DREAD [§9.3]

dragan (strong verb 6) = to draw, DRAG [§9.2]

dranc = past 3 sing of *drincan*

(ġe)drēag (n) = multitude, army [§2.9]

drēag = past 3 singular of *drēogan*

drēam (m) = joy, ecstasy, mirth; melody, music, song [§2.7]

(ġe)drēfan (weak verb I) = to disturb, trouble, vex; stir up [§3.11]

drēfan (strong verb 5) = to stir up, agitate; excite [§9.1]

drenċ (m) = a DRINK, drinking [§2.7]

drēogan (strong verb 2) = to survive, endure (something) [§8.5]; to be busy, be employed; to work, do, perform

drēor-sele (m) = desolate hall, bloody hall [see OE *drēor* "blood" and ModE *DREARY*; §10.11.1]

(ġe)drēosan (strong verb 2) = to fall [§8.5, §8.5.3]

drepan (strong verb 5) = to strike, strike down, kill [§9.1]

drīfan (strong verb 1) = to DRIVE, force [§8.4]

driht (f) = troop, military band [§2.8]

drihten = see *dryhten*

driht-guma (weak m) = troop-man, warrior [§3.3]

drincan (strong verb 3) = to DRINK [§8.6]

drinc-fæt (n) = DRINKing vessel, cup [§2.9, §2.10.3]

drohtnian, drohtian (weak verb II) = to behave; to live, lead a life [§3.12]

drohtnung (f) = condition, way of life; conduct [§2.8]

dropian (weak verb II) = to DROP [§3.12]

druncen (adjective) = DRUNK, intoxicated [§6.1, originally past participle of *drincan*]

druncon = past pl of drincan

drȳġe (adjective) = DRY, parched [6.4]

dryht-folc (n) = troop-FOLK, people [§2.9]

dryhten, drihten (m) = lord, leader; God [§2.7]

dryhtenliċ (adjective) = lordly, glorious, divine [§6.1]

dūfan (strong verb 2) = to DIVE; sink, go down [§8.5]

dugan (preterite-present verb) = to thrive, do well, be effective, avail [§4.3.1]

duguð (f) = body of noble retainers; people, men [§2.8]

dum (adjective) = DUMB, incapable of speech; silent [§6.1]

dūn (f) = hill, mountain; DOWN [ModE *sand-DUNE*; §2.8]

durran (preterite-present verb) = to DARE (to do something) (+ infinitive) [§4.3.1]

duru (f) = DOOR [§10.6.1]

dwelian (weak verb II) = to deceive, lead astray [§3.12]

(ġe)dyde, dydon = past 3 sing, pl of *dōn*

dydrung (f) = delusion, illusion [§2.8]

dȳfan (weak verb I) = to dip, immerse, dunk [§3.11; related to ModE *dive*]

dȳleġian (weak verb II) = to blot out, erase (text) [§3.12]

dyne (m) = DIN, noise [§10.2.1]

dȳpan (weak verb I) = to DIP [§3.11]

dyrne (adjective) = hidden, mysterious, secret; enchanted [§6.1]

dyrstiġ (adjective) = adventurous, DARing [§6.1]

dȳr-wyrðe = see *dēor-wurðe*

dysiġ (adjective) = foolish, silly [ModE *DIZZY*; §6.1]

E

ēa (f) = river (usually indeclinable except in the dat pl) [§10.4.2]

ēac (adverb) = also, likewise [compare German *auch*, Middle English *EKE*; §6.9]

ēadiġ (adjective) = blessed, happy [§6.1]

ēad (n) = riches, prosperity, happiness [§2.9]

ēad-mōdlīċe (adverb) = humbly, lowly [§6.9]

eafora (weak m) = son, offspring [§3.3]

ēage (weak n) = EYE [compare German *Auge* "eye"; §3.5]

eahta (number & adjective) = EIGHT (indeclinable) [§6.1.1]

eahtian (weak verb II) = to consider, deliberate [§3.12]

eahtoþa, eahtēoþa (adjective) = EIGHTH [§6.1]

ēa-lā (interjection) = oh!, alas!; hey! (an interjection for getting the attention of a interlocutor or for expressing either regret and sorrow)

ēa-land, ēa-lond (n) = isLAND [§2.9]

eald (adjective) = OLD, aged, ancient [§6.1]

ealdor (m) = ELDER; chief, greatest, foremost person or thing [§2.7] *ealdor* (n) = life, life force; age, old age [§2.9]

ealdor-dōm (m) = superiority, pre-eminence; power, authority [§2.7]

ealdor-lang (adjective) = life long, eternal [§6.2]

ealdor-mon (m) = ruler, chief; nobleman [ModE *ALDERMAN*; §10.4.2]

ealdor-scype (m) = seniority, superiority [§10.2.1]

eal(l) (adjective or pronoun) = ALL, every; whole, entire; everyone, all people [§6.1, §7.8]

eal(l) (adverb) = ALL, completely; *eal swā* = "just as" [§6.9]

eall-gylden (adjective) = pure gold, completely golden [§6.1]

eallunga (adverb) = entirely, completely, utterly [§6.9]

ealu (n) = ALE [§10.9]

ealu-wēġe (n) = ALE-cup [§10.2.2]

eard (m) = dwelling, home, homeland [§2.7]

eardian, eardigan (weak verb II) = to dwell, live; inhabit, make a home in [§3.12]

ēare (weak n) = EAR [§3.5]

earfoþe (n) = trouble, hardship [§10.3.2]

earm (adjective) = poor, wretched, miserable [compare German *arm* "poor"; §6.1]

earm (m) = ARM [§2.7]

earn (m) = eagle [§2.7]

earnung (f) = merit [§2.8]

eart = pres 2 sing of *bēon*

ēast (adverb) = EAST [§6.9]

Ēast-engle (m, pl) = EAST-ANGLians; inhabitants of East Anglia [§10.11.3]

Ēastre (f weak) = the Christian holdiay of EASTER (often appears in the pl); spring [§3.4]

ēaþe (adjective) = easy, not difficult [§6.1]

ēaþe (adverb) = easily, without difficulty [§6.9]

ēaþelīċe (adverb) = easily, without difficulty [§6.9]

eāð-mōd (adjective) = benevolent, humble [§6.1]

eaxl (f) = shoulder [ModE *AXLE*, German *Achse* shoulder; §2.8]

ēċe (adjective) = eternal, lasting forever [§6.1]

ēċeliċ (adjective) = eternal, lasting forever [§6.1]

ēċelīċe (adverb) = eternally, forever [§6.9]

ecg (f) = EDGE [§2.8]

Ecgferð (m) = king of Northumbria, 670-685 [§2.7]

Ecg-þēow (m) = a Geatish warrior, father to Beowulf

ēċ-nes, -nys (f) = eternity, forever [§2.8]

ed-ġeong, -ġiong (adjective) forever YOUNG, ageless [§6.1]

ed-hwyrft (m) = change, turn, reversal [§2.7]

edre = see *ǣdre*

efne (adverb) = EVEN [§6.9]

efne (interjection) = indeed!, in fact!

efsian (weak verb 2) = to trim, cut (the hair) [§3.12]

eft (adverb) = again; back; therefore, afterwards [§6.9]

eġe (m) = AWE, fear, terror [§2.7]

eġes-ful (adjective) = terrifying, FULL of horror [§6.1]

Ēgypt (m or n) = EGYPT [§10.11.1]

ēhtan (weak verb I) = to chase, follow, pursue [§3.11]

ēhtend (m) = pursuer, persecuter [§10.10]

ele (m or n) = OIL [§10.2.1/2]

Ēliġ, Ēlia = Ely, Cambridgeshire

ellen (n) = courage, fervor; strength (dat singular = *elne*) [§2.9]

ellen-rōf (adjective) = courage-famous, famed for courage or strength [§6.1]

elles (adverb) = ELSE, in another way or manner; elsewhere; another kind [§6.9]

ellor (adverb) = ELsewhere, to some other place [§6.9]

el-reordiġ (adjective) = foreign, of strange speech, barbarous [see OE *el-* "strange, ALien" + *reord* "language"; §6.1]

el-þēodiġ (adjective) = foreign, alien; (used as a noun) foreigner, alien [§6.1]

emb(e), ymbe (preposition + acc, dat) = around, about, in regard to; *embe lang* = "a long time" [§6.15]

ende (m) = END [§10.2.1]

ende-byrdnes (f) = rank, degree, class; arrangement, rule; order, succession [§2.8]

(ġe)endian (weak verb II) = to END, finish [§3.12]

(ġe)endung (f) = ENDING, end, death [§2.8]

engel (m) = ANGEL, angelic being [compare German *engel* "angel"; §2.7]

engel-cynn (n) = order, rank of angels [§10.2.2]

Englisc (adjective) = ENGLISH; (as noun) the ENGLISH language [§6.1]

ēode = past 3 sing of *gān*

eofor (m) = wild boar [compare German *Eber*; §2.7]

eom = pres 1 sing of *bēon*

eorl (m) = nobleman, EARL [§2.7]

eorl-ġewǣde (n) = EARL-WEEDs, noble attire; i.e., armor [§10.2.2]

eorðe (weak f) = EARTH, ground [§3.4]

eorð-liċ (adjective) = EARTHLY [§6.1.1]

eorð-rīċe (n) = EARTH-kingdom, earthly realm [§10.2.2]

eorð-scræf (n) = EARTH cave, cave dwelling; grave [§2.9, §2.10.2]

eorð-sele (m) = EARTH hall, dwelling in the earth, cave [§10.11.1]

eorð-tilþ (f) = agriculture, TILLing of the EARTH [§2.8]

eorð-ware (m, pl only) = EARTH dwellers, inhabitants of the earth (f pl = *-waru*) [§10.11.1]

eornoste (adverb) = EARNESTly, seriously; courageously, fiercely [§6.9]

eosel (m or f) = ass; donkey [compare German *Esel*; §2.7]

eotenisc (adjective) = giantish, made by giants [§6.1]

ēow = acc, dat sing of *ġē*

ēowdon = past 3 pl of *īewan*

erian (weak verb II) = to plow [§3.12]

ernian, earnian (weak verb II) = to deserve, gain, EARN (+ gen object) [§3.12]

ēst (f) = favor, grace, kindness, love [§2.8]

etan (strong verb 5) = to EAT, consume [§9.1]

etst = pres 2 sing of *etan*

ēþel (n) = home, dwelling [§2.9]

ēþel-turf (f) = home TURF, homeland (dat = *ēþel-tyrf*) [§10.4.2]

Eugenīa (f) = proper name [Latin form]

F

fācen (n) = deceit, fraud, treachery, crime [§2.9]

fācen-lēas (adjective) = without deceit; pure, genuine [§6.1]

fæċ (n) = space, period of time, interval [§2.9]

fæder (m) = FATHER [§10.5]

fæġ (adjective) = fated, doomed to die [§6.1]

fæġer (adjective) = FAIR, beautiful, lovely; pleasant [§6.1]

fæġnian (weak verb II) = to be glad, happy about (+ gen object); to rejoice [see ModE *FAIN*; §3.12]

fǣhð (f) = feud, fight; hostility, emnity [§10.7]

fǣmne (weak f) = maiden, virgin; woman [§3.4]

fǣr-gryre (m) = sudden terror [§10.2.1]

fǣrlīċe (adverb) = suddenly, quickly [§6.9]

fæst (adjective) = firm, secure; quick [ModE color-*FAST*; §6.1]

fæstan (weak verb I) = to FAST, to abstain from food, usually for religious reasons (past sing = *fæste*) [§3.11]

fæste (adverb) = firmly, securely, steadfastly; quickly [§6.9]

fæsten (n) = FASTness, stronghold, fortification [§10.2.2]

fæstende = present participle of *fæstan*

fæstlīċe (adverb) = completely, truly [§6.9]

(ġe)fæstnian (weak verb II) = to FASTEN, fix, secure [§3.11]

fæt (n) = VAT, container (pl = *fatu*) [§2.9, §2.10.3]

fǣtan (weak verb I) = to load, cram, stuff [§3.11]

fǣted (adjective) = ornamented, applied [§6.1]

fǣtels (m) = vessel; bag, pouch [§2.7]

fǣtt (adjective) = FAT, fatty [§6.2]

fæðm (m) = outstretched arms, embrace [§2.7]

fāg (adjective) = patterned, stained, marked; shining gleaming [§6.1]

fagc, facg (f) = plaice, loach (freshwater fish) [§2.8]

fāh (adjective) = outlawed, hostile, guilty [§6.1]

fann (f) = a winnowing FAN (usually a broad shovel or a wide basket used to toss grain into the air in order to separate it from the chaff) [§2.8]

(ġe)faran (strong verb 6) = to travel, go, FARE [§9.2]

faroð (m) = stream, flood [§2.7]

faru (f) = journey, way [§2.8]

fat- = pl forms of *fæt*

faðe (weak f) = father's sister, paternal aunt [§3.4]

fēa (adjective) = FEW [§6.1]

(ġe)fēa (weak m) = joy related to [§3.3]

feala = see *fela*

fealdan (strong verb 7) = to FOLD, wrap up, roll [§9.3]

(ġe)fēaliċ (adjective) = joyous, pleasant [§6.2.2]

(ġe)feallan (strong verb 7) = to FALL, fall headlong; fail, die [§9.3]

fēaw- = see *fēa*

feax (n) = head of hair, hair [§2.9]

feċċan, fetian (weak verb II) = to FETCH [§3.12]

fēdan (weak verb I) = to FEED [§3.11]

(ġe)fēgan (weak verb I) = to join, fix; compose [§3.11]

(ġe)fēhst = pres 2 sing of *(ġe)fōn*

fela (adverb) = very much, many [§6.9]

fela (fixed or indeclinable noun form) = many, much (+ gen) [see §2.11.3.d]

fela-lēof (adjective) = much beLOVEd, very dear [§6.1]

feld (m) = FIELD (*felda* = dat sing) [§10.6]

fell (n) = skin, hide [§2.9]

(ġe)feng = see *ġe-fōn*

(ġe)fēn(c)g = past 1, 3 sing of *fōn*

fen-land (n) = FENLAND, marsh, swampy terrain [§2.9]

fenn (n) = FEN, marsh, moor [§2.9]

(ġe)fēo = pres 1 sing of *(ġe)fōn*

feo = see *feoh*

feoh (n) = money; prosperity, wealth (dat sing = *feo*) [§2.9]

(ġe)feoht (n) = FIGHT, battle [§2.9]

feohtan (strong verb 3) = to FIGHT, do battle against [§8.6]

(ġe)feol = see *(ġe)feallan*

fēolan (strong verb 3) = to enter [§8.6]

feoldon = see *fealdan*

(ġe)fēon (strong verb 5, contract verb) = to rejoice [§9.1, §11.1.2]

fēond (m) = FIEND; enemy [§10.10]

fēond-sceaða (weak m) = enemy-SCATHEr, enemy, nemesis [§3.3]

feor (adjective) = distant, far away [§6.1]

feor (adverb) = FAR (+ *fram* = far from) [§6.9]

feorh (m or n) = life, life-force, principle of life [§2.7, §2.9]

feorh-ādl (f) = fatal disease, (lit., life-sickness) [§2.8]

feorh-ġe-nīðla (weak m) = deadly foe, life enemy [§3.3]

(ġe)feormian (weak verb II) = to clean, scour [§3.12]

feorþa (adjective) = FOURTH [§6.1]

fēower (number) = FOUR

fēowertiġ (number) = FORTY

(ġe)fēra (weak m) = companion, friend [§3.3]

fēran (weak verb I) = to go, travel, depart [§3.11]

ferhð (n) = mind, soul, spirit [§2.9]

ferian (weak verb I) = to carry [related to ModE *FERRY*; §3.11]

(ġe)fērscype (f) = companionship, fellowship, society [§2.8]

fēt = see *fōt*

fetel-hilt (n, f) = belted or ringed sword HILT [§2.9]

fētt = pres 3 sing of *fēdan* [§8.10.2]

fēðe-ċempa (weak m) = foot-warrior, infantry soldier [§3.3]

feþer (f) = FEATHER; (quill) pen [§2.8]

fierd (f) = army (in the *Chronicle*, usually reserved to designate the Anglo-Saxon army) [§10.11.2]

fierr, fierrest (adverb) = farther away, farthest (comparative, superlative forms of *feor* "far") [§6.9, §6.14]

fīf (number) = FIVE

fīfel-cynn (n) = race of monsters [§2.9]

fīfta (adjective) = FIFTH [§6.1]

fīftēne (indeclinable number) = FIFTEEN

fīftiġ (number) = FIFTY

fīftyne (number) = FIFTEEN (+ partitive gen §2.11.3.c)

findan (strong verb 3) = to FIND [§8.6]

finger (m) = FINGER [§2.7]

firen (f) = crime, sin [§2.8]

fisc (m) = FISH (pl = *fixas*) [§2.7]

fiscere (m) = FISHERman [§10.2.1]

fiscian, fixian (weak verb II) = to FISH [§3.11]

fitt (f) = song, short poem; section of a poem [§2.8]

flǣsc (n) = FLESH, body [§10.11.1]

flǣsc-homa (weak m) = FLESH-covering, corpse, carcass [§3.3]

flǣsc-mette (m) = FLESH-MEAT, meat [§10.2.1]

flasce, flaxe (weak f) = FLASK, bottle [§3.4]

flēag = past 3 singular of *flēogan*

flēogan (strong verb 2) = to FLY [compare German *fliegen* "to fly"; §8.5]

flēoh-net (n) = FLY-NET, curtain [§2.9]

flēon (strong verb 2, contract verb) = to FLEE, escape [§8.5, §11.1]

flēowe = past 3 subjunctive sing of *flōwan*

flet(t) (n) = floor, hall [§2.9]

flet-werod (n) = hall-troop, retainers [§2.9]

(ġe)flīeman (weak verb I) = to put to flight [§3.11]

(ġe)flit (n) = argument, bickering; strife [§2.9]

flōc (n) = flounder, flat fish [§2.9]

flōd (m) = FLOOD, sea [§2.7]

flōde (weak f) = channel, stream [§3.4]

flōr (f) – FLOOR, ground [§2.8]

flota (weak m) = FLEET; ship [§3.3]

flot-mann (m) = sailors (pl: *flot-menn*) [§10.4.2]

flōwan (strong verb 7) = to FLOW, run [§9.3]

(ġe)fōn (strong verb 7, contract verb) = to seize, catch, grasp [§9.3, §11.1]

fōddor (n) = FODDER, food for animals [§2.9]

fola (weak m) = FOAL, colt [§3.3]

folc (n) = FOLK, people [§2.9]

folc-lond (n) = FOLK-LAND, (Clark-Hall:) "land held by freemen according to tribal rules of family inheritance" [§2.9]

folc-toga (weak m) = leader, chieftain, commander [§3.3]

folgian (weak verb II) = to FOLLOW (+ dat object) [§3.12]

folgoþ, folgaþ (m) = group of FOLLOWers, body of retainers, retinue; employment, service [§2.7]

folm (f) = hand, palm [§2.8]

fongeð = pres 3 sing of see *(ġe)fōn*

fongne = past participle of *(ġe)fōn*

for- (prefix) = 1) often either intensifies the meaning of verbs, 2) adds a sense of destruction or loss, sometimes best translated with "apart," "to pieces," "up" or "away" (*grindan* "to grind"; *for-grindan* "to grind apart"; *swelgan* "to swallow"; *for-swelgan* "to devour, swallow up"), 3) adds a negative or pejorative sense (*sēċan* "to seek out"; *for-sēċan* "to torture, punish"), or 4) = *fore-* "before, ahead of" in either a spatial or temporal sense *for* (preposition + dat/acc) = FOR, because of; in spite of [§6.15]

fōr (f) = course, journey, going [§2.8]

foran (adverb) = beFORE, in front of; *foran tō* = in preparation for, before [§6.9]

foran (preposition + dat) = beFORE [§6.15]

for-beran (strong verb 4) = to tolerate, put up with, FORBEAR [§8.7]

for-bīġean (weak verb I) = to despise; humiliate, degrade [§3.11]

forcel (m) = pitch-FORK [§2.7]

for-ċeorfan (strong verb 3) = to CARVE apart, cut off, hack through [§8.6]

fore-cweðan (strong verb 5) = to predict, FOREtell (past subjunctive sing: *fore-cwæde*) [§9.1]

fore-sċēawung (f) = providence, FOREsight [§2.7]

fore-secgan (weak verb III) = to FOREtell, SAY beforehand, predict [§4.1]

fore-sprecan (strong verb 5) = to say or mention before (past participle as adjective = *fore-spreċen* "previously mentioned") [§9.1]

fore-þanc (m) = FORE-thought, deliberation [§2.6]

fore-we(a)rd (adjective) = FORWARD, early [§6.2]

fore-wearde (adverb) = in the front [§6.9] "to abandon"; §9.3]

for-lēosan (strong verb 2) = to LOSE, abandon [§8.5]

for-ġiefan, -ġifan (strong verb 5) = to GIVE, grant; give (in marriage); FORGIVE [§9.1]

for-ġieldan (strong verb 3) = to repay, pay for, reward (+ gen = "for") [§8.6]

for-ġietan (strong verb 5) = to FORGET [§9.1]

for-grindan (strong verb 3) = to GRIND to pieces, destroy [§8.6]

forht (adjective) = afraid, terrified, timid [§6.1]

forht-full (adjective) = afraid, fearful [§6.1]

for-hwī (interrogative) = WHY?

for-lǣtan (strong verb 7) = to abandon, leave behind; banish; allow, permit [compare German *verlassen* "to abandon"; §9.3]

for-lǣtt = pres 3 sing of *for-lǣtan* [§8.10.2]

for-lēosan (strong verb 2) = to LOSE, let go, forfeit; destroy ruin [§8.5]

for-lēt = past 1, 3 sing of *for-lǣtan*

for-lēton = past pl of *for-lǣtan*

for-lidenesse, for-liðenesse (f) = shipwreck [§2.8]

forma (adjective) = first [§6.1]

for-molsian (weak verb II) = to rot away, decay, fall apart [§3.12]

for-rīdan (strong verb 1) = to intercept (by riding ahead of) [*for-* = *fore-*; §8.4]

for-sċēawodlīċe, fore- (adverb) = with forethought, thoughtfully [§6.9]

for-scrīfan (strong verb 1) = to condemn, damn, judge [§8.4]

for-sēċan (weak verb I) = to afflict, torture [§3.11]

for-sīðian (weak verb 2) = to journey amiss, go astray, perish [§3.12]

for-standan (strong verb 6) = to withSTAND, prevent [§9.2]

for-swelgan (strong verb 3) = to SWALLOW up, devour, consume [§8.6]

forð (adverb) = FORTH, ahead; forward [§6.9]

for-þǣm, for-þām, for-þon (*þe*) = (adverb)

therefore, for this reason [§6.9];
(conjunction) because, for the reason that
[§5.1.1]

forð-bringan (strong verb 3) = to BRING
FORTH, cast up [§8.6]

forð-ēode = past sing form of *forð-gān*

forð-fēran (weak verb I) = to travel FORTH;
depart, die [§3.11]

forð-gān (irregular verb) = to GO FORTH, to
proceed, pass by; go away; succeed [§4.5.3]

forð-geong, -gang (m) = progress, advance,
success [§2.7]

forð-blīfian (weak verb II) = to be prominent,
to stand out [§3.12]

forð-sīð (m) = journey FORTH, departure;
death [§2.7]

forð-tēon (strong verb 2) = to bring forth,
come out with [§8.5, §11.1]

forð-tȳhst = pres 2 sing of *forð-tēon*

fore-þanc (m) = wisdom, FOREthought [§2.7]

for-þȳ (adverb) = therefore, for this reason
[§6.9]

for-wyrnan (weak verb I) = to refuse, deny (acc
of thing, dat of person) [§3.11]

fōt (n) = FOOT (the body part); foot (unit of
measurement) [§10.4.2]

fōt-mǣl (n) = FOOT-measure, foot (as a unit
of measurement) [§2.9]

(ġe)fōð = pres 3 sing of *(ġe)fōn*

(ġe)fō = pres 1 sing of *(ġe)fōn*

fracod (adjective) = evil, vile, wicked [§6.1]

frætewa (f. plural) = treasures, money;
trappings, appurtenances; ornaments
[§10.3.3]

frætwian (weak verb II) = to adorn, decorate
[§3.12]

fram (adjective) = bold, courageous [§6.1]

fram, from (preposition + dat) = by, FROM,
away from [§2.11.4c, §6.15]

fram (adverb) = away [§6.9]

framian (weak verb II) = to benefit, be good
for (+ dat object) [§3.12]

frēa (weak m) = lord, master [§3.3]

freca (weak m) = warrior, bold one [§3.3]

frēcnes -nys, frēcennes (f) = harm, danger;
avarice, greediness [§2.8]

fremman (weak verb I) = to do, undertake;
benefit, help [§3.11]

freō (adjective) = FREE [§6.1]

frēo-dōm (m) = FREEDOM [§2.7]

frēols-dæġ (m) = feast-DAY, holy day [§2.7]

frēond (m) = FRIEND; lover [§10.10]

frēondscip (m) = FRIENDSHIP, love;
romantic love [§2.7]

frēosan (strong verb 2) = to FREEZE [§8.5,
§8.5.3]

fretan (strong verb 5) = to devour, consume,
gobble up [compare German *fressen* "to
gobble"; §9.1]

friclan (weak verb I) = to ask for, implore, seek
(+ gen object) [§3.11]

Frīdæġ (m) = FRIDAY [§2.7]

friġnan (strong verb 3) = to inquire, find out
by asking [§8.6]

frīnan (strong verb 2) = to find out, ask, learn,
guess [§8.5]

frōd (adjective) = wise; old [§6.1]

frōfor (f, m) = comfort, consolation [§2.8]

from = see *fram*

from-sīþ (m) = "forth-journey," departure [§2.7]

fruma (weak m) = beginning [§3.3]

frum-cyn(n) (n) = origin, beginning [§10.2.2]

frymð (m) = beginning, origin [§2.7]

frystan (weak verb I) = to FROST (impersonal) [§3.11]

fuġel, fugol (m) = bird, FOWL [§2.7]

fuġelere (m) = bird catcher [§10.2.1]

ful (adverb) = very, FULL [§6.9]

ful (adjective) = FULL [§6.1]

fūl (adjective) = FOUL, repulsive; evil [§6.1]

fulliċ (adjective) = FULL, complete; large, main [§6.5]

fullwiht, fulluht (m) = the Christian rite of baptism [§2.7]

fultum (m) = help, assistance [§2.7]

fultumian (weak verb II) = to help, assist, come to the aid of (+ dat object) [§3.12]

funde = past subjunctive sing of *findan*

funden = past subjunctive pl or past participle of *findan*

furþra (comparative adjective) = superior, greater [§6.5]

furþum (adverb) = even, quite [§6.9]

fylgan (weak verb I + dat object) = to follow [§3.11]

(ġe)fyllan (weak verb I) = to FILL up, fulfill [§3.11]

fylle (m) = fall [§10.11.1]

fȳr (n) = FIRE [§2.9]

fyrd-bræġl (n) = war-garment, armor [§2.9]

fȳren-ful (adjective) = FIERy, FULL of FIRE [§6.1]

fyrmest (superlative adjective) = FOREMOST, most prominent, chief [from OE *forma*; §6.1]

(ġe)fyrn (adverb) = once, a long time ago [§6.9]

fȳr-spearca (weak m) = FIRE SPARK [§3.3]

(ġe)fyrðran, -fyrðian (weak verb I, II) = to promote, advance, FURTHER [§3.11, §3.12]

G

gā = imperative sing of *gān*

gād (f) = GOAD, spear point; plow point [§2.8]

gād-īsen, -īren (n) = GOAD-IRON, a goad with an iron tip [§2.9]

(ġe)gad(e)rian, gædrian (weak verb II) = to GATHER, collect, bring together [§3.12]

(ġe)gaderung(c) (f) = GATHERING, assembly, group [§2.8]

gærs (n) = GRASS [§2.9]

gǣsne (adjective) = dead; deprived of, lacking (something) [§6.1]

gǣst, gāst (m) = spirit, GHOST [§2.7]

galan (strong verb 6) = to sing [§9.2]

galdor (m) = song, incantation [§2.7]

gāl-ferhð (adjective) = debauched, filled with lust [§6.1]

Gallia = proper name

gamen (n) = sport, GAME [§2.9]

(ġe)gān (irregular verb) = to GO [§4.5.3]

gāng = past sing of *gān*

(ġe)gangan (strong verb 7) = to go [§9.3]

gār (m) = spear [§2.7]

gārsecg (m) = ocean, sea [§10.2.1]

gast, gæst (m) = spirit, soul; spiritual being (good or evil), angel, devil [§2.7]

gāst-dōm (m) = spirituality, spiritual devotion [OE *-dōm*, as in *Christendom* §2.7]

gāstliċ (adjective) = spiritual, GHOSTLY [§6.1]

gat = see *ġeat*

(ġe)- (prefix) = in this and most other OE glossaries, the *ġe-* prefix is ignored in the alphabetical arrangement of words so that closely related forms appear together. For example, to find *ġe-fera*, look under the letter *f.*

   With nouns, the *ġe-* prefix often adds a collective or group sense (*brōðor* "brother"; *ġe-brōðor* "group of brothers"). With verbs, *ġe-* often signals either success or completion of an action (*winnan* "to fight"; *ġe-winnan* "to win [a fight]"). As in modern German, the *ġe-* prefix often occurs in past participles where it generally signals a sense of a completed action. In many other cases however, it is difficult to detect any differences in meaning between a word with or without the *ġe-*.

ġē (pronoun) = you (pl) [§7.1]

ġe . . . ġe (conjunction) = both . . . and [§5.1.1]

ġēa (interjection) = yes, indeed

ġēar (n) = YEAR [§2.9]

ġeare = see *ġearwe*

ġearkian (weak verb II) = to prepare; to supply [§3.12]

ġearu, ġearo (adjective) = ready [§6.1.3]

ġearwe, ġeare (adverb) = full, entirely; well [§6.9]

ġearwian (weak verb II) = to equip, prepare, supply, adorn [§3.12]

(ġe)ġearwian (weak verb II) = to prepare, equip, make, make ready; GEAR oneself up, clothe (often + reflexive) [§3.12]

ġeat (n) = GATE [§2.9]

ġeatoliċ (adjective) = equipped, ready [§6.1]

ġēna (adverb) = still, now [§6.9]

ġēo (adverb) = once, some time ago; before, already [§6.9]

Ġeochol (n) = YULEday, the holiday of Christmas [§2.9]

ġēocian (weak verb II) = to help, rescue, save [§3.12]

ġeogoð, ġeoguð (f) = YOUTH, early age, young troop [§2.8]

ġēomor (adjective) = sad, troubled, miserable [§6.1]

ġēomor-mōd (adjective) = "sad-minded"; mournful, gloomy; sober-minded [§6.1]

ġēomrian (weak verb II) = to sorrow, mourn [§3.12]

ġēomrung (f) = moaning, grief [ModE *YAMMER*; §2.8]

ġeond (adverb) = here, thither [§6.15]

ġeond (preposition + acc) = throughout, through, over [§6.15]

ġeong (adjective) = YOUNG [§6.1, §6.5]

ġēonian (weak verb II) = to YAWN, gape [§3.12]

ġeorne (adverb) = eagerly, gladly (comparative = *ġeornor*) [§6.9] *ġeornlīċe* (adverb) = eagerly, diligently, zealously [§6.9]

ġeornnes (f) = desire, zeal, industry, YEARNing [§2.8]

ġēotan (strong verb 2) = to pour [§8.5]

ġēr = see *ġēar*

ġiedd (n) = song, poem; saying, proverb [§2.9]

ġiefan (strong verb 5) = to GIVE, bestow [§9.1]

ġiefu, ġifu (f) = GIFt, present [§2.8]

ġield (n) = idol, pagan god [§2.9]

ġieldan (strong verb 3) to pay, YIELD [§8.6]

ġiellan (strong verb 3) = to YELL [§8.6]

ġierede = see *ġearwian*

ġiese (interjection) = YES

ġīet = see *ġȳt*

ġietan (strong verb 5) = to GET [§9.1]

ġif, ġyf (conjunction) = IF [§5.1.1]

ġifre (adjective) = useful [§6.1]

ġifu = see *ġiefu*

ġīgant (adjective) = giant [§2.1]

ġildan, ġieldan (strong verb 3) = to reward, render; grant, YIELD, pay [§8.6]

ġilpan (strong verb 3) = to brag about, boast of (+ gen object) [§8.6]

ġimm (m) = GEM, jewel [§2.7]

ġingra, ġingest = comparative, superlative of *ġeong*

ġist (m) =guest, visitor [§2.7]

ġist-līþe (adjective) = welcoming, hospitable [§6.10]

ġīt = see *ġȳt*

ġītsiend (adjective) = greedy for, longing for (+ gen), present participle of *ġītsian*, a weak verb II [§3.12]

glæs (n) = GLASS [§2.9]

glēaw (adjective) = wise, intelligent [§6.1]

glēd (f) = flame, fire, ember [§2.8]

glīdan (strong verb 1) = to GLIDE [§8.4]

glīwian (weak verb II) = to adorn; make merry, play (music) [§3.12]

gloesan (weak verb I) = to GLOSS, provide with glosses [§3.11]

gluto (a Latin word) = GLUTTON (the OE word for glutton is *swelġere* "swallower") [§8.4]

gnīdan (strong verb 1) = to grind, rub together [§8.4]

gōd (adjective) = GOOD; (noun) GOOD, good thing, good one; (pl) goods, wares [§6.1 or §2.7]

god (n) = (pagan) god [§2.9]

God (m) = GOD (note: names for the deity are only very rarely capitalized in contemporary manuscripts) [§2.7]

god-cund (adjective) = divine, GODly [§6.1]

gōdliċ (adjective) = GOODLY, good [§6.1]

god-spell (n) = GOSPEL, the first four books of the Christian New Testament [§2.9]

gold (n) = GOLD [§2.9]

gold-smith (m) = GOLDSMITH, artisan working with gold [§2.7]

gong, gang (m) = path, passage; flow [§2.7]

Gorgoneus = place name

grǣdiġ (adjective) = GREEDY, hungry, fierce [§6.1]

grǣdlīċe (adverb) = GREEDILY, voraciously [§6.9]

græs-hoppa (weak m) = GRASS-HOPPer [§3.3]

grafan (strong verb 6) = to dig [§9.2]

Granta-ċester (f) = Grantchester, Cambridgeshire

grānung (f) = GROANING, lamentation [§2.8]

grāp (f) = claw, grasp, GRIP [§2.9]

grāpian (weak verb 2) = to grasp [§3.12]

grēat (adjective) = GREAT, tall, thick, massive [§6.1]

Grendel = a monster in *Beowulf*

grēne (adjective) = GREEN [§6.10]

grētan (weak verb I) = to GREET, visit; touch, handle; attack [§3.11]

grim(m) (adjective) = GRIM, cruel; horrible [§6.1]

grimful (adjective) = fierce, violent [§6.1]

grin (n) = snare, trap [§2.9]

grōwan (strong verb 7) = to GROW [§9.3]

grund (m) = depth [§2.7]

grund-wyrgen (f) = monster of the deep, sea wolf

guma (weak m) = man [§3.3]

gūð (f) = battle, combat [§2.8]

Gūð-Ġēat (m) = battle-Geat, member of the Geat tribe

gūð-lēoð (n) = war song, battle cry [§2.9]

ġydd = *ġiedd*

ġyf = see *ġif*

gylden (adjective) = GOLDEN [§6.1]

gylt (m) = GUILT, crime, sin [§10.11.1]

ġymm (m) = GEM stone, precious stone [§2.7]

ġym-stān (m) = GEMSTONE [§2.7]

ġyn, ġin (adjective) = spacious, wide; yawning, deep [§6.1]

ġyrd (f) = stick, rod (as an instrument of punishment), cudgel [§2.8]

(ġe)gyrla (weak m) = clothing, dress, apparel [§3.3]

ġyrw(i)an = see *ġearwian*

ġyrstan-dæġ (m) = YESTERDAY [§2.7]

ġȳt, ġīt, ġīet (adverb) = YET, still [§6.9]

H

habban (weak verb III) = to HAVE; possess, hold; keep [§4.1]

hacod (m) = HAKE, pike, mullet, a food fish resembling cod [the name may mean "hooked" since the hake has a hooked lower jaw; §2.7]

hād (m) = office, rank [§2.7, originally §10.6]

(ġe)hādian = (weak verb II) = to ordain, consecrate [§3.12]

hæfd = past participle of *habban*

hæfde = past 3 sing of *habban*

(ġe)hæftan (weak verb I) = to fetter, bind; arrest, imprison [§3.11]

(ġe)hǣlan (weak verb I) = to HEAL, cure; save; say hello to, greet [§3.11]

hæle (m) = warrior, hero; man [§10.2.1]

hǣlend (m) = savior, one who saves [§10.10]

hæleþ (m) = man, hero [§10.9]

hælf-ter (f) = HALTER, a device made of leather straps to fit around an animal's head or neck [§2.8]

hǣlo, hǣlu (f) = HEALth, prosperity; salvation [§10.7]

hǣmed (n) = sex, fornication, adultery; marriage [§2.9]

(ġe)hæp (adjective) = fitting, appropriate, convenient [§6.1]

hærfest (m) = HARVEST, fall, autumn [§2.7]

hǣr (n) = HAIR, a hair [§2.9]

hērin(c)ġ (m) = HERRING [§2.7]

hǣtu (f) = HEAT [§2.8]

hǣðen (adjective) = HEATHEN [§6.1]

hafað = present 3 sing of *habban*

hafela (weak m) = head [§3.3]

hafoc (m) = HAWK, a hunting bird and generally a symbol of aristocratic privilege [§2.7]

hagolian (weak verb II) = to HAIL (impersonal) [§3.12]

hāl (adjective) = WHOLE, healthy; not wounded or injured [§6.1]

hālga, hālgan, hālgum = see *hāliġ*

hālga (weak m) = saint, HOLY one [§3.3]

hāliġ (adjective) = HOLY, sacred [§6.1]

hāliġ-reft, -ryft (n) = veil [§2.9]

(ġe)hālġian (weak verb II) = to HEAL, get well [§3.12]

(ġe)hālod = past participle of *(ġe)hālġian*

hals = see *heals*

hām (m) = HOME, dwelling (dat sing: *hām*) [§2.7]

hām (adverb) = HOMEwards, at home, home [§6.9]

ġe-hamian (weak verb II) = to make (one's self) a home, establish a home; "to make [one's self] familiar with?" (Bosworth-Toller) [§6.1]

hamor (m) = HAMMER [§2.7]

hand, hond (f) = HAND [§10.6]

hangian (weak verb II) = to HANG, be suspended [§3.12]

hara (weak m) = HARE, a creature similar to a rabbit but with longer ears and legs [§3.3]

Hara-wudu = probably Harewood in West Yorkshire [§10.6]

Harold (m) = Harold Godwinson

hās (adjective) = HOARSE, having a sore or raspy throat [compare German *heiser* "hoarse"; §6.1]

hāt (adjective) = HOT, fiery [§6.1]

(ġe)hātan (strong verb 7) = to call, name; be called, named; order, command; promise, vow [§9.3]

hāte (adverb) = HOTly [§6.9]

(ġe)hāten = past participle of *hātan*

hātte = past 3 sing of *hātan*, present 1 sing of *hatan*

hē, hēo, hit (personal pronoun) = HE, she, IT [§7.1]

hēaf (m) = mourning [§2.7]

hēafod (n) = HEAD [§2.9]

hēafod-stōw (f) = place for the HEAD [§10.3.3]

hēa(h) (adjective) = HIGH, lofty, tall [§6.1]

hēah-tīd (m) = HIGH-TIDE, holy day [§10.11.1]

healdan (strong verb 7) = to HOLD, keep; (+ reflexive) to behave, act [§9.3]

healf (f) = HALF; side, region [§2.8]

healf-hunding (m) = HALF-HOUND or *cynocephalus*, creature with the head of a dog [§2.7]

hēaliċ (adjective) = HIGH, excellent; lofty, sublime [§6.1]

hēan (adjective) = miserable, despised; (also appears as a variation of *hēah*) [§6.2] *hēap* (m or f) = crowd, group, assembly, host [§2.7, §2.8]

heard (adjective) = HARD, harsh; strong, cruel [§6.1]

hearde (adverb) = HARD, severely, very much [§6.9]

heard-sǣliġ (adjective) = unfortunate, unlucky, someone with hard luck [§6.1]

hearra (weak m) = master, lord [compare German *Herr*; §3.3]

heaðo-rinc (m) = battle warrior [§2.7]

heaðo-byrne (weak f) = war-BYRNIE, corslet [§3.4]

healf (adjective) = HALF [§6.1]

heals (m) = neck [§2.7]

(ġe)hēawan (strong verb 7) = to HEW, hack, cut [§9.3]

hebban (strong verb 6) = to lift, raise, HEAVE up [§9.2]

hēdd-ern (n) = storehouse, store-room, bARN [§2.9]

hefiġ (adjective) = HEAVY; oppressive, painful; important, grave [§6.1]

hefiġian (weak verb II) = to make HEAVY, weigh down; oppress, subjugate, afflict [§3.12]

hefiġnes (f) = HEAVINESS, weight; suffering, affliction [§2.8]

hēhsta = superlative form of *hēah*

(ġe)hēht = past 3 sing of *(ġe)hātan*

hēhðo (f) = HEIGHts, heaven [§10.7]

hel(l) (f) = HELL [§2.8]

hēla (weak m) = HEEL [§3.3]

help (f) = HELP, aid [§2.8]

(ġe)helpan (strong verb 3) = to HELP (+ dat or gen object) [§8.6]

(ġe)hende (adjective) = near, close to; HANDy [§6.1]

helm (m) = protection, covering, HELMet; protector, lord [§2.7]

heofon, heofen (m, f, often pl) = HEAVEN; the heavens, the sky [§2.7, §2.8]

heofon-cund (adjective) = divine, of a heavenly nature [§6.1]

heofonliċ (adjective) = HEAVENLY [§6.1]

hēold = past 3 sing of *healdan*

hēoldon = past pl of *healdan*

heonan (adverb) = HENCE, from here [§6.9]

heonu, ono (interjection, adverb) = behold!, see!; moreover, therefore; *ono hwæt* = "indeed, moreover" [§5.1.1]

heora, hyra = their (3 gen pl personal pronoun) [§7.1]

heoro-grim (adjective) = sword-GRIM, fierce, savage [§6.1]

Heorot (n) = the name of Hrothgar's hall in *Beowulf*

heort, heorot (m) = HART, stag [§2.7]

heorte (weak f) = HEART [§3.4]

hēow, hīw (n) = HUE, color; beauty [§2.9, §10.3.2]

hēowod = a weak past participle of the strong verb *(ġe)hēawan* (the normal strong form would be *[ġe]heawen*)

hēr (adverb) = HERE [§6.9]

hēr-būend (m) = HERE-dweller, dwellers on this earth [§10.10]

here, herġe (m) = army (in the *Anglo-Saxon*

Chronicle usually reserved to designate the Danish army) [§10.2.1]

berġe = see *here*

her-eard, hearg-eard (m) = dwelling in a (sacred or pagan) grove [§2.7]

here-bȳð (f) = booty; lit., army-plunder [§3.4]

here-net(t) (n) = army-NET, corslet, mail coat [§2.9]

herian, hergian (weak verb I) = to praise, compliment, extol [§3.11]

herliċ (adjective) = splendid, noble [compare German *herrlich* "splendid"; §6.1]

hēt = past 3 sing of *hātan*

hēte = past 3 sing subjunctive of *hātan*

hete-þoncol (adjective) = hostile, scheming violence [§6.1]

hēton = past pl of *hātan*

hī, hīe, hȳ (personal pronoun) = f nom / acc sing OR pl nom / acc; see *hē, hēo, hit* [§7.1]

hider (adverb) = HITHER, to that place [§6.9]

hīe = f acc sing or n acc 3 pl of *hē, hēo, hit*

hiene, hine = m acc 3 sing of *hē, hēo, hit*

hīeġ (n) = HAY (as an animal feed) [§10.2.2]

hīera (pronoun) = their [§7.1]

hīeran (weak verb I) = to HEAR [§3.11]

hierde (m) = HERDsman, shepherd [§10.2.1]

hīerra, hīest = comparative, superlative of *hēah*

hiġ (personal pronoun) = *hīe*

hiġ (interjection) = oh!, ah!

hiġe = see *hyġe*

hīgdi-fæt (n) = bottle or vessel made of leather [§2.9]

hiht = see *hyht*

hilde-bill (n) = battle sword [§2.9]

hinder-ġēap (adjective) = crafty, wily, deceitful [see ModE *underhanded* and *backhanded* for similar formations; §6.1]

hingrian (weak verb II) = to HUNGER, be hungry (impersonal) [§3.12, §11.2]

hin-sīð (m) = journey HENce, departure; death [§2.7]

hire (personal pronoun) = HER, hers, theirs [§7.1]

hīred (m) = household, family, community [§2.7]

his (personal pronoun) = HIS, its [§7.1]

hit (personal pronoun) = IT [§7.1]

hīw = see *hēow*

hīwan (pl m weak) = household, members of a family or religious house [§3.3]

hladan (strong verb 6) = to LOAD [§9.2]

hlǣfdiġe (weak f) = LADY [§3.4]

hlæst (n) = load, cargo, burden, balLAST [§2.9]

hlāf (m) = bread, LOAF [§2.7]

hlāford (m) = LORD [originally *hlāf-weard* "guardian of the loaf"; §2.7]

hlēapan (strong verb 7) = to LEAP, jump [§9.3]

hlēo(w) (m) = protection; lord [§10.3.1]

hlēo-bord (n) = protection-BOARD, i.e., book cover [§2.9]

hliehhan (strong verb 6) = to LAUGH [§9.2]

hlīfian (weak verb II) = to tower, rise up [§3.12]

hlūtor (adjective) = pure, clear, bright [§6.1]

hlystan (weak verb I) = to LISTEN, hear (past tense = *hlyste*) [§3.11]

(ġe)bleodad (adjective) = having a LID
  (originally a past participle) [§6.1]

blēowð (f) = covering, protection; warmth [§2.8]

blūd (adjective) = LOUD, resounding [§6.1]

blūttor (adjective) = pure, clear, bright; broad
  (day) [§6.1]

blyd, blid (n) = LID, top, cover [§2.9]

bold (adjective) = kind, loyal, friendly [§6.1]

Homodubii (m pl noun) = DUBIous
  HUMANs, human-like monsters [Latin
  ending]

bōn (strong verb 7, contract verb) = to hang
  [§9.3, §11.1]

bond = see *hand*

bond-ġe-mōt (n) = HAND-MEETing, battle
  [§2.9]

bond-wyrm (m) = a kind of insect (literally,
  HAND-WORM or –serpent) [§2.7]

bopian (weak verb II) = to HOPE [§3.12]

bors (n) = HORSE [§2.9]

Hostes = proper name, Latin for "enemies"

(ġe)bradian (weak verb II) = to hasten, further
  (an enterprise) [§3.12]

brǣd (adjective) = quick, nimble; ready, alert
  [§6.1]

brǣdlīċe (adverb) = quickly, suddenly, nimbly
  [§6.9]

brǣġl (n) = clothing, clothes; garment [§2.9]

bran (m) = whale [§2.7]

brāðe (adverb) = quickly [§6.9]

brēam (m) = cry, scream; sob [§2.7]

brēaw (adjective) = RAW, uncooked [§6.1]

brēob (adjective) = rough, fierce, savage [§6.1]

(ġe)brēosan (strong verb 2) = to fall, sink;

decay, go to ruin (*ġe-hroren* = "abandoned,
  ruined, in ruins") [§8.5]

brēow (f) = sorrow, regret, penitence, RUE (as
  in "you'll rue the day") [§2.8]

brepian (weak verb II) = to touch; deal with,
  have to do with (+ gen object) [§3.12]

brepung (f) = touching, examination [§2.8]

breðer (m) = chest, breast; heart, mind
  [§2.7]

(ġe)brinenes (f) = touch, touching, contact
  [§2.8]

ġe-brīnian (weak verb II) = to decorate,
  ornament [§3.12]

bring-mǣl (n) = sword with RING ornaments
  [§2.9]

ġe-brīno (n plural) = ornaments [§10.11.1]

brōf (m) = ROOF; top, summit [§2.7]

(ġe)broren = past participle (functioning as an
  adjective) of *(ġe)brēosan*

Hroðgar (m) = character in *Beowulf*
  ["ROGER" in ModE]

brycg (m) = back (part of the human body)
  [ModE *RIDGE*, compare German *Rücken*
  "back"; §2.7]

bū (adverb) = HOW [§6.9]

bū (conjunction) = HOW [§5.1.1]

bū (interrogative) = HOW?

bū-bugu (adverb) = somewhere about,
  approximately [§6.9]

bund (m) = dog, HOUND [§2.7]

bund (n) = HUNDred, a hundred (+ partitive
  gen) [§2.9, §2.11.3.c]

bund-tēontiġ (number) = a HUNDred (usually
  + partitive gen)

hunel (adjective) = wanton, lascivious; impudent [§6.1]

hungor (m) = HUNGER [§2.7]

huniġ (m) = HONEY [§2.7]

hunta (weak m) = HUNTer [§3.3]

huntian (weak verb II) = to HUNT [§3.12]

huntoþ (m) = HUNTing; game, prey, what is hunted [§2.7]

huntung (f) = HUNTING, a hunt, chase [§2.8]

hūs (n) = HOUSE, dwelling place [§2.9]

hwā (indefinite, interrogative pronoun) = WHO, whoever [§7.6, §7.8]

(ġe)hwēde (adjective) = slender, slight [§6.1]

hwæl (m) = WHALE [§2.7, §2.10.3]

hwæne = m acc sing of *hwā*

hwænne (adverb) = WHEN [§6.9]

hwēr (adverb) = WHERE [§6.9]

hwærf = past 3 sing of *hweorfan*

hwæt (adjective) = bold, brave; quick, active [§6.1]

hwæt (indefinite, interrogative pronoun) = WHAT; something [§7.6]

hwæt (interjection) = indeed!, hey!, listen!

hwæt-līċe (adverb) = quickly, briskly, promptly [§6.9]

hwæþer (conjunction) = WHETHER, whether or not; (*hwæþer* often introduces a question but is itself not translated); *swā hwæðer* = whichever; *hwæðer þe* = or [§5.1.1]

hwæþ(e)re (adverb) = nevertheless, however, yet, still [§6.9]

hwām = dat sing of *hwā*

hwanon (adverb) = how, whence, from where [§6.9]

hwelċ = see *hwilċ*

hweorfan (strong verb 3) = to change, transform; turn (to go), depart [§8.6]

hwēsan (strong verb 7) = to WHEEZE [§9.3]

hweðer (indefinite pronoun) = whichever (of two) [§7.8]

hwierfan = see *hweorfan*

hwīl (f) = time, hour, WHILE [§2.8]

(ġe)hwilċ, (ġe)hwylċ (adjective) = any, which, what, what kind of; *ānra ġe-hwilċ* = "each one, each and every person" [§6.1]

(ġe)hwilċ (indefinite pronoun) = each, everyone, someone [§7.8]

hwīlum (adverb) = sometimes, at times [originally the dat pl of *hwīl*; §6.9]

hwīl-wendlīċ (adjective) = temporary [§6.1]

hwistlung (f) = WHISTLING [§2.8]

hwīt (adjective) = WHITE [§6.1]

hwonne (adverb) = then, at some time, at any time [§6.9]

hwonne (conjunction) = when [§5.1.1]

hwylċ = see *hwilċ*

(ġe)hwyrfan, hweorfan (strong verb 3) = to turn [§3.11]

hȳ = *hīe*

hycgan (weak verb III) = to think, consider, intend [§4.1]

hȳd (f) = HIDE, animal skin [§2.9, §10.11.2]

hȳdan (weak verb I) = to furnish with skin or HIDE [§3.11]

(ġe)hygd (n) = thought, mind [§2.9]

hyġe (m) = thought, mind, heart [§10.11.1]

hyġe-blīþe (adjective) = BLITHE of heart, happy, glad, joyful [§6.1] *byġe-ġeomorne* (adjective) = "thought-sad," sad, mournful [§6.1]

byġe-lēast (f) = nonsense, horseplay, folly ["thought-lessness"; §2.8]

byhstan = superlative of *hēah*

byht (f) = joy [§2.8]

Hȳlāc (m) = Hygelac, the chieftain of the Geats, and Beowulf's lord

byne = *hine*, m acc 3 sing of *hē, hēo, hit*

byne-sylfne = m acc sing of *him-seolf*

bȳnð (f) = humiliation, oppression; damage, harm, loss [§2.8]

byra (pronoun) = their [§7.1]

(ġe)bȳran (weak verb I) = to HEAR; obey; *bȳran secgan* = to hear tell [§3.11]

byrde, bierde (m) = HERDsman, shepherd [§10.2.1]

bȳrsumian (weak verb II) = to obey, be obedient to (+ dat object) [§3.12]

I

Iacinctus (m) = a proper name [Latin form]

iċ, wē (personal pronoun) = I, WE (1 dat pl: *ūs*) [§7.1]

īdel (adjective) = IDLE, empty, useless [§6.1]

ides (f) = queen, lady; woman; maiden [§2.8]

īeġ-land = see *ēa-lond*

ield, ieldo (f) = age, old age; [from the adjective *eald* "old," showing i-mutation; §10.7]

ielde (m, pl) = men, people [§10.2.1]

ieldra, ieldest = comparative, superlative forms of *eald*

iermð, iermðu (f) = misery, hardship [§2.8]

ierðling (m) = ploughman, farmer, "earthling" [§2.7]

(ġe)īewan = to show, display, reveal, disclose [§3.11]

iggað (m) = island [§2.7]

ilca, ilċe, ilċe (adjective) = the same, the very (person or thing) [almost always weak, regardless of environment; §6.4]

in (adverb) = IN [§6.9]

in (preposition) = (+ dat) IN, on; (+ acc) INto, onto [§6.16.2]

Indeum (proper noun) = INDIA

in-gang (m) = entrance [§2.7; compare German *Eingang* "entrance"]

in-lād (f) = (f) = induction, entrance fee [§2.8]

inn (adverb) = IN [§6.9]

inn (n) = apartment, chamber, room [§2.9]

innan (preposition + acc, dat, or gen) = IN, INto; from within, within [§6.15]

inne (adverb) = inside, within [§6.9]

inne-weard (adjective) = INWARD, inner [§6.1]

innoþe (m) = womb, INsides [§2.7]

intō (preposition + dat) = INTO [§6.15]

Iobannes (m) = John [with Latin ending in the nom]

is = pres 3 sing of *bēon*

īsen (n, also adjective) = IRON, made of iron [compare German *Eisen* "iron"; §2.9]

(ġe)iukian, ġeocian = to YOKE, join together [§3.12]

K

(OE, for the most part, uses *c* rather than *k*).

kempa = see *cempa*

L

(ġe)lāc (n) = play, tossing, tumult [§2.9]

lād (f) = path, way [§2.8]

(ġe)læċċan (weak verb I) = to catch, seize, LATCH onto; get, obtain [§3.11]

lēċe (m) = physician, doctor, LEECH [§10.2]

(ġe)lædan (weak verb I) = to LEAD; take, bring, carry [§3.11]

lædde = past sing of *(ġe)lædan*

lǣfan (weak verb I) = to LEAVE [§3.11]

læġ = past sing of *licgan*

(ġe)læhte = past 3 sing of *(ġe)læccan*

(ġe)læhtest = past 2 sing of *læccan*

lǣne (adjective) = temporary, fleeting, on LOAN [§6.1]

(ġe)lǣran (weak verb I) = to teach, advise, give advice to [§3.11]

(ġe)lǣrede (adjective) = learned, educated [originally the past participle of *lǣran*; §6.1]

lǣs (conjunction) = LESt, for fear that (sometimes appears as *þȳ lǣs* or *þē lǣs*) [§5.1.1]

lǣs (f) = pasture [§10.3.4]

lǣsest, lǣst (adjective, superlative of *lȳtel*) = smallest, least [§6.7]

lǣssa, lǣsse, lǣsse (adjective, comparative of *lȳtel*) = LESS, smaller, fewer [as a comparative form, it always takes weak endings; §6.7]

lǣstan (weak verb I) = to accomplish, perform, carry about; do [§3.11]

læt (adjective) = LATE [§6.1]

lǣtan (strong verb 7) = to LET, allow [§9.3]

lǣwede (adjective and noun) = unlearned, lay (person) [compare ModE *LEWD*; §6.1]

lagu (m) = water, sea; name of the L rune [§10.3.1]

lamb (n) = LAMB [§10.8]

lamprede (weak f) = LAMPREY eel [§3.4]

land (n) = LAND, country [§2.9]

land-here (m) = LAND-army, infantry [§10.2.1]

landscip (m) = region, area of land (ModE *landscape* borrowed much later from Dutch) [§10.11.1]

lang, lancg, long (adjective) = LONG; tall (comparative: *lengra*) [§6.7]

langoþ (m) = LONGing, desire [§2.7]

lār (f) = teaching, LORE [§2.8]

lāst (m) = footprint, track, trail (left behind) [§2.7]

lārēow (m) = teacher [§10.3.1]

lāð (adjective) = hateful, LOATHsome [§6.1]

laðian (weak verb II) = to invite, call, summon [§3.12]

lāðliċ (adjective) = LOATHLY, loathsome, hateful, repulsive, horrific [§6.1]

lāðlīċe (adverb) = wretchedly, miserably, unpleasantly [§6.9]

lēac (n) = LEEK, onion [§2.9]

(ġe)lēafa (weak m) = beLIEF, faith [§3.3]

(ġe)lēafful (adjective) = believing, orthodox [§6.1]

lēan (n) = LOAN, compensation [§2.9]

lēap (m) = trunk, carcass, body [§2.7]

lēas (adjective) = false, lying; of LOOSE morals [§6.1]

lēase (adverb) = falsely, deceitfully [§6.9]

lēasnes, -nis (f) = frivolity; lying [§2.8]

lēasung (f) = lie, falsehood, deceit [§2.8]

leax (m) = salmon [see Yiddish *LOX*; §2.7]

lecgan (weak verb I) = to lay, place, put; bury [causative form of *licgan*; §3.11]

Lēden (adjective) = LATIN [§6.1]

lēdon = past pl of *lecgan*

lēġ, līġ (m or n) = flame [§10.11.1]

leġer (n) = bed; resting, lying; illness [related to OE *licgan*; see ModE *LAIR*; §2.9]

lencten, lencgten (m) = springtime; LENT, a season in the spring during which Christians are to fast and practice penance [§2.7]

leng, lengra = comparative of *lang*

leng (f) = LENGth, height [§10.11.2]

lengest = superlative form of *lang*

lengþo (f) = LENGTH [§10.7]

lēod(e) (f) = people, nation [compare German *Leute* "people"; §10.11.2]

lēod-fruma (weak m) = lord, leader [§3.3]

lēof (adjective) = dear, beLOVed; (as noun) friend, companion, lover; (as form of address) sir, dear sir; (+ dat) dear to, loved by; *lēofre* (comparative) = "preferable" [§6.1, §6.5]

lēoð-gidding (f) = song-poem, poetry [§2.8]

lēod-hata (weak m) = people-HATer, tyrant, torturer [§3.3]

lēogan (strong verb 2) = to LIE, lie down, recline [§8.5]

lēoht (adjective) = LIGHT, bright, illuminated; not heavy; comfortable [§6.1]

lēoht (n) = LIGHT, source of illumination [§2.9]

leom = see *lim*

lēoma (weak m) = light, radiance, beam of light [§3.3]

lēon (m) = LION [§2.7]

(ġe)lēoran (weak verb I) = to go, leave, depart; die [§3.11]

leornere (m) = LEARNER, student, scholar [§10.2.1]

(ġe)lēornes, -lēorednes (f) = departure, death; anniversary of a death [§2.8]

leornian (weak verb II) = to teach; LEARN [§3.12]

leornung, leorning (f) = LEARNING, teaching [§2.8]

lēosan (strong verb 2) = to LOSE [§8.5, §8.5.3]

lēoð (n) = song, poem [§2.9]

Lertices = proper name [Latin form]

lesan (strong verb 5) = to collect [§9.1]

letanīa (weak m) = LITANY, a liturgical prayer that enlists the aid of various apostles, saints, and confessors in list-like fashion [§3.3]

lettan (weak verb I) = to hinder, prevent; LET [§3.11]

leþer-hosu (f) = leggings made of LEATHER [compare German *Lederhose* "leather trousers"; §2.8]

libban (weak verb III) = to LIVE [§4.1.2]

liblāc (n) = witchcraft, magic spell, occult art

[OE *lybb* "poison, charm, drug"; §2.9]

(ġe)līċ (adjective) = like, aLIKE, similar (often + dat: "similar to") [compare German *gleich* "similar, like"; §6.1]

līċ (n) = body, corpse; LIKEness, form [compare German *Leiche* "corpse," ModE *LICH-gate*; §2.9]

(ġe)līċe (adverb) = as, like, equally, similarly; like as if; *ġe-līċe swā swā* = exactly as [§6.9]

līċetung (f) = hypocrisy, deceit [§2.8]

licgan (strong verb 5) = to LIE, lie down, recline; lie prostrate [§9.1]

līċ-hama, -homa (weak m) = body; lit., body-HOME [§3.3]

līċian (weak verb II) = to please, be pleasant to (+ dat, often impersonal) [§3.12, §11.2]

(ġe)līcnes (f) = LIKENESS, appearance, form [§2.8]

līċ-sang (m) = dirge, "corpse-SONG" [§2.7]

(ġe)līefan, lȳfan (weak verb I) = to beLIEVE (sometimes + reflexive), trust in [§3.11]

līf (n) = LIFE [§2.9]

lifdon = past pl of *libban*

liġ, lieġ (m) = flame [compare German *Lohe* "blaze, flame"; §10.11.1]

līhtan (weak verb I) = to LIGHTen [§3.11]

lim, leom (n) = LIMB, member [§2.9]

līm (m) = LIME, a sticky substance used to catch birds [§2.7]

(ġe)limpan (strong verb 3) = to happen, take place (impersonal) [§8.6, §11.2]

(ġe)limplīċe (adverb) = fittingly, suitably [§6.9]

līnen (adjective) = made of flax, LINEN [§6.1]

liss (f) = grace, love, mercy [§2.8]

list (f) = cunning, skill; clever deception [§2.8]

lītlincg (m) = child [§2.7]

līð = present 3 sing of *licgan*

līþan (strong verb 1) = to travel, go, traverse [§8.4]

līþeliċ (adjective) = soft, gentle, LITHE [§6.1]

loc (n) = fold, pen [§2.9]

lof (n) = praise, glory [§2.9]

lofian (weak verb II) = to praise [§3.12]

lof-sang (m) = SONG of praise; lauds, one of the canonical hours of the divine office [§2.7]

(ġe)lōme (adverb) = often, frequently [§6.9]

(ġe)lomp = past 3 sing of *(ġe)limpan*

lond-stede (m) = plot of LAND [§10.11.1]

long- = see *lang*

(ġe)long (adjective) = beLONGing to, dependent on [§6.1]

longaþ- = see *langoþ*

longian, langian (weak verb II) = to LONG for, desire, yearn (impersonal, with reflexive) [§3.12, §11.2]

long-sum (adjective) = long, long lasting, enduring [§6.1]

lopystre (f weak) = LOBSTER [§3.4]

losian (weak verb II) = to go bad, mould, perish [ModE *LOSE*; §3.12]

lūcan (strong verb 2) = to LOCK [§8.5]

Lucifer (m) = the devil (before his fall from grace: literally, "bearer of light") [§2.7]

lufe = see *lufu*

lufian (weak verb II) = to LOVE [§3.12]

luflīċe (adverb) = willingly, gladly; *luflīcor* = more expensively, for more money, dearer [§6.9] *lufu* (f) = LOVE (unattested form) [§2.8, §3.4]

Lunden (n) = LONDON [§2.9]

lust (m) = desire, appetite; pleasure [§2.7]

lust-fullian (weak verb II) = to enjoy, celebrate; desire; *lust-fulliende* (present participle) = "happy for, desirous of" (+ dat) [§3.12]

lustlīċe (adverb) = willingly, gladly [§6.9]

lūtian (weak verb II) = to hide, lurk [§3.12]

(ġe)lȳfan, -lȳfe = see *(ġe)līefan*

lyft (f or m) = air, sky [§2.8, §2.7; compare German Luft "sky"]

lyre (m) = loss [§10.11.1]

lystan (weak verb I) = to desire, be desirous (impersonal, + reflexive) [§3.11, §11.2]

lȳt (indeclinable substantive, often + partitive genitive) = a few, LITtle, small number of [§2.11.3.c]

lȳtel (adjective) = LITTLE, small, simple (comparative: *læssa*; superlative: *læst*) [§6.1]

lȳtiġ (adjective) = crafty, sneaky [§6.1]

lȳtlian (weak verb II) = to lessen, decrease, diminish [§3.12]

M

mā (adjective, noun, indeclinable comparative of *miċel*, often + partitive gen) = more [§6.9]

mā (adverb, comparative of *miċel*) = more; hereafter [§6.9]

macian (weak verb II) = to MAKE, form [§3.12]

mādm- = see *māðum*

mādme = see *māðum*

(ġe)mæċ (adjective) = appropriate, suitable, MATCHing, similar [§6.1]

(ġe)mæċċa (weak m) = mate, equal, one of a pair [§3.3]

(ġe)mæċċe (weak f) = mate, equal, one of a pair [ModE *MATCH*; §3.4]

mǣd (f) = MEADow [§10.3.4]

mǣden (n) = MAIDEN, virgin [§2.9]

mǣġ (m) = (male) kinsman (pls in *mag-*) [§2.7, §2.10.3]

mǣġe, māġe (weak f) = kinsman, relative [§3.4]

mæġ = pres 1, 3 sing of *magan*

mæġe = pres subjunctive sing of *magan*

mæġen (n) = might, strength [§2.9]

mæġen-rǣs (m) = troop-RUSH; onslaught, attack [§2.7]

mæġen-ðrym (m) = grandeur, grand majesty [§10.11]

mæġð, mæġeð (f) = maiden, girl [§10.9]

(ġe)mǣġð (f) = family, tribe, province [§2.8]

mæġð-hād (m) = virginity [§10.6, §2.7]

mǣl (n) = MEAL; occasion, time [§2.9]

mænego (f) = multitude, MANY [§10.7]

mæniġ, maniġ (adjective) = MANY [§6.1.1]

mæniġ-feald- = see *maniġ-feald*

mǣran (weak verb I) = to celebrate, honor, glorify [§3.11]

mǣre (adjective) = famous, illustrious [§6.1]

mǣrðu (f) = glorious thing, holy relic, glory [§2.8]

mæsse (weak f) = MASS, Christian celebration of the eucharist [§3.4]

mæss(e)-prēost (m) = PRIEST [§2.7]

mǣst = superlative of *miċel* [see §6.8]

mæstlingc (n) = brass [§2.9]

(ġe)mēnelīċe (adverb) = generally, universally [§6.9]

(ġe)mētan (weak verb I) = to dream (impersonal) [§3.11]

(ġe)mēte (adjective) = suitable, MEET, fitted [§6.1]

mǣð (f) = measure, ability, level [§10.11.2]

mæðel (n) = council, meeting [§2.9]

mæðelian (weak verb II) = to speak (formally), make a speech [§3.11]

maga (weak m) = stomach, womb [see German *Magen* "stomach"; §3.3]

magan (preterite-present verb) = be able, have permission or ability (to do something) [§4.3.1]

man (indefinite pronoun) = one, a person [compare German *man* "one"; §7.8]

man = see *mann*

mān (f) = MANE [§2.8]

(ġe)māna (weak m) = companionship, company [§3.3]

manna (weak m) = MAN [§3.3]

mancgere (m) = MONGER (as in *ironmonger*), trader, merchant [§10.2.1]

māne (adjective) = MANEd, with a mane [§6.1]

maneġ = see *maniġ*

manian (weak verb II) = to remind, exhort, admonish [§3.12]

maniġ, mæniġ (adjective) = MANY [§6.1]

maniġ-feald (adjective) = many, various, numerous, MANIFOLD [§6.1]

ġe-mēn(n)e (n) = relationship; intercourse [§2.9]

mānliċ (adjective) = wicked, evil [§6.1]

man(n), mon(n) (m) = MAN, human being (dat sing = *men*) [§10.4.2]

mann-cyn (n) = MAN-KINd, human beings (as a collective) [§2.8]

man-sleġe (m) = MANslaughter, murder [§10.2.1]

manung (f) = admonition, reprimand; discipline [§3.4]

man-þwǣre (adjective) = mild, gentle, humane [§6.1]

māra (adjective) = "greater, larger"; comparative of *miċel* [see §6.8]

marm-stān (m) = marble STONE [§2.7]

martyrian (weak verb II) = to MARTYR, torture (to death) [§3.12]

māðum (m) = treasure, jewel, valuable (gen sing = *maðmes*) [§2.7]

māwan (strong verb 7) = to MOW [§9.3]

max (n) = net, MESH [§2.9]

mē, meċ = 1 acc sing of *iċ, wē*

mēċe (m) = sword, blade [§10.2]

meaht, meahte = past 1, 3 sing of *magan*

(ġe)mearcian (weak verb II) = to MARK, set down, describe, seal [§3.12]

mearc-stapa (weak m) = haunter of desolate land, MARCH prowler [§3.3]

mearn = see *murnan*

mēd (f) = reward, MEED [§2.8]

med-miċel (adjective) = little, small [§6.1]

medo (m) = MEAD [§2.7]

melcan, melkan (strong verb 3) = to MILK [§8.6]

meltan (strong verb 3) = to MELT [§8.6]

men = see *man(n)*

meniġu (f, usually indeclinable in sing) = crowd, multitude [compare German *Menge*; §10.7]

mennisc (adjective) = human [§6.1]

meolc (f) = MILK [§10.11.2]

mēowle (weak f) = woman; maiden, virgin [§3.4]

mere (weak f) = MARE [§3.4]

mere (m) = sea, ocean; lake [§10.2.1]

mere-grota (weak m) = pearl, sea-GROAT [§3.3]

mere-swȳn (n) = porpoise, dolphin, sea-SWINE [§2.9]

mere-wīf (n) = sea-woman, water witch [§2.9]

(ġe)met (n) = manner, way; measure, limit, size; *wundoriċe ġe-mete* = "in a miraculous way" [§2.9]

metan (strong verb 5) = to measure [§9.1]

(ġe)mētan (weak verb I) = to MEET with, find, encounter [§3.11]

mētan (weak verb I) = to paint [§3.11]

mete, mette (m) = food, sustenance; MEAT [§10.2]

(ġe)metliċ (adjective) = fitting, proper, MEET [§6.1]

(ġe)metton = past pl of *mētan*

miċċlum (adverb) = greatly, very much [§6.9]

miċel (adjective) = big, large, great [§6.1]

miċelnesse (f) = greatness, size [§2.8]

mid (preposition + dat) = with, along with, among; with respect to [compare German *mit*; §6.15]

mid þȳ (þe) (conjunction) = when, while, after, since [§5.1.1]

middan (preposition + dat) = amidst, in the middle of [§6.15]

middan-ġeard = (m) = earth; lit., MIDDle-YARD, middle earth [§2.7]

midd (adjective) = center, MIDDle [§6.1]

mid-dæġ (m) = MID-DAY; sext, a canonical hour in the divine office, about 12pm [§2.7]

midde (f weak) = MIDst, MIDDle, center [§3.4]

midemesta (adjective) = MIDDleMOST [§6.1]

midlen (n) = MIDst, presence [§2.9]

Mierċe (m, pl only) = MERCian people, inhabitants of Mercia (a kingdom in Anglo-Saxon England) [§10.11.3]

miht (f) = MIGHT, power [§10.11.2]

miht, mihte = see *magan*

mīl (f) = MILE [§2.8]

mild (adjective) = MILD, kind [§6.1]

milts (f) = mercy, compassion, grace [§10.3.4]

mīn (personal pronoun) = MY [§7.1]

misliċ (adjective) = various, many kinds of [§6.1]

mislīċe (adverb) = variously [§6.9]

mīðan (weak verb I) = to conceal, hide [§3.11]

mōd (n) = mind, heart, spirit [ModE MOOD; §2.9]

mōdiġ (adjective) = brave, courageous; (as noun) the brave one [§6.1]

mōd-ġeþonc (m) = mind-thought, thought [§2.7]

mōdor (f) = MOTHER [§10.5]

mōdorlīċe (adjective) = MOTHERLY, as a MOTHER [§6.1]

mon = see *man*

(ġe)mon = present 1, 3 sing of *(ġe)munan*

mōna (weak m) = MOON [§3.3]

mōnaþ (m) = MONTH [§10.9]

moniġ, moneġ (adjective) = MANY [§6.1]

monn = see *man(n)*

monna (weak m) = MAN, person [§3.3]

Mōnnan-dæġ (m) = MONDAY [§2.7]

monn-cynn (n) = MANKINd [§2.9]

mōnð- = see *monaþ*

monuc, munuc (m) = MONK [§2.7]

mōr (m) = MOOR [§2.7]

morġen (m) = MORNing [§2.7]

morðor (n, m) = act of violence; crime, sin; MURDER, manslaughter [§2.9]

moste = past sing of *mōtan*

mōtan (preterite-present verb) = be able, have the power (to do something) [§4.3.1]

(ġe)munan (preterite-present verb) = to remember, recall, think about [§4.3.1]

mund (f) = hand, palm [§2.8]

mund-grip (m) = hand-GRIP [§10.11.1]

munt (m) = MOUNT, mountain [§2.7]

munuc-liċ (adjective) = monastic [§6.1]

murnan (strong verb 3) = to MOURN, be sorrowful about [§8.6]

musle, muscule (weak f) = MUSSLE [§3.4]

mūð (m) = MOUTH [§2.7]

mūþa (weak m) = MOUTH of a river, estuary [§3.3]

myċel (adjective) = much, great, large, immense [§6.1]

myne (m) = minnow [§10.2.1]

(ġe)mynd (f) = MIND, recollection, memory (often pl with sing sense); thought [§2.8]

(ġe)myndiġ (adjective) = MINDful, aware of (often + gen) [§6.1]

(ġe)myndġian (weak verb II) = to remember, be mindful of, mention [§3.12]

myneċen (f) = female monk, nun [§10.3.5]

(ġe)myneġian (weak verb II) = to warn, mention, remind [§3.12]

mynster (n) = monastery, MINSTER; see placenames such as *West-MINSTER* [§2.9]

mynsterliċ (adjective) = monastic [§6.1]

mȳre (weak f) = MARE [§3.4]

N

nā (adverb) = not at all [§6.9]

nabban (weak verb III) = not to HAVE (= *ne* + *habban*); lack [§4.1]

naca (weak m) = boat, ship, vessel [§3.3]

nǣdl (f) = NEEDLE [§2.8]

nǣdre (weak f) = ADDER, snake, serpent (i.e., with sharp fangs) [§3.4]

nǣfre (adverb) = NEVER [§6.9]

næġl (m) = NAIL, fingernail [§2.7]

nǣniġ (adjective or indefinite pronoun) = NONE, no [§6.1, §7.8]

nǣre, næs = *ne* + *wesan* [§4.5.3b]

næss (m) = cliff, headland [§2.7]

nafað = *ne* + *habban*

nafola (weak m) = NAVEL [§3.3]

nāht (adverb) = not, not at all [§6.9]

nāht (n) = nothing, NAUGHT [§2.9]

nāhte = *ne ahte*, from *āgan*

nalas, nales, nalæs = (adverb, *ne* + *ealles*) = not at all, not, by no means [§6.9]

nām = past 1,3 sing of *niman*

nāmon = past pl of *niman*

nama (weak m) = NAME [§3.3]

nān (adjective or pronoun) = NO, none (pronoun often + gen) [§7.8, 6.3]

(ġe)nāp = past sing of *(ġe)nīpan*

nāse (weak f) = NOSE [§3.4]

nāt = *ne wāt*. See *witan*.

Nazareniscan (adjective) = NAZARENE [§6.1]

ne (adverb) = not [§6.9]

ne . . . ne (conjunction) = neither . . . nor [§5.1.1]

nēah (adjective) = close, near, NIGH to [§6.1, §6.14]

nēah (adverb) = near; almost, nearly [§6.9]

ġe-nēahhe (adverb) = often, frequently; sufficiently, enough [§6.9]

nēahst = see *nīehst*

nēar (adjective) = closer, NEARer (comparative form of *nēah*) [§6.1, §6.14]

nearu (n) = hardship, distress [§10.3.2]

nearwe (adverb) = closely, tightly, forcefully [§6.9]

nēawest, -wist (f) = neighborhood, vicinity; nearness, presence [related to OE *nēah*; §2.8]

neb (n) = nose, face [§2.9]

nēhst = see *nīehst*

nele = 1, 3 pres sing of *nyllan*

nemnan (weak verb I) = to NAME, called; be named, be called [§3.11]

nemne, nefne, nemðe (conjunction) = unless, except, only [§5.1.1]

nēodian (weak verb II) = to be necessary; to need, require (impersonal + gen object) [§3.11, §11.2]

nēod- = see *nīed-*

neom = *ne + eom*; 1 pres sing of *bēon* [§4.5.1, §4.5.2b]

nēosan (weak verb I) = to seek out, go to, visit (+ gen object) [§3.11]

nēotan (strong verb 2) = to use, employ, enjoy (+ gen object) [§8.5]

neowel (adjective) = precipitous, vast, steep [§6.1]

nergend (m) = savior, redeemer [§10.10.1]

nerian (weak verb I) = to save [§3.11]

nesan = *ne + wesan*

nett (n) = NET [§2.9]

nīed, nēod (f) = NEED, duty, necessity; errand; compulsion; force, violence; name of the N-rune [§2.8]

nīed-gripe (m) = coercive, forceful grip [§10.2]

nīed-þearf (adjective) = necessary, essential [§2.8]

nīed-þearf (f) = need, necessity; force, compulsion; distress, poverty [§6.1]

nīehst, nēxt, nēst (adjective, superlative form of *nēah*) = NEXT, last, closest [§6.1, §6.14]

nīehst (adverb) = NEXT; closest; last, final [originally, the superlative form of *nēah*; §6.9]

niġen-hund (number) = NINE HUNDred (+ partitive gen)

niġoþa (adjective) = NINTH [6.1]

niht (f) = NIGHT [§10.4.2]

-niht (f) = NIGHT (when it appears in a compound like *Mōnan-niht*, *niht* refers to the night before the specified day) [§10.4.2]

niht-helm (m) = cover of night [§2.7]

niht-hwīl (f) = NIGHT-time [§2.8]

niht-sang(c) (m) = compline, the last of the canonical hours in the divine office [§2.7]

(ġe)niht-sum-nes (f) = abundance, plenty [§2.8]

Nīl (f proper noun), = Nile [§2.8]

nillan = see *nyllan*

(ġe)niman (strong verb 4) = to take; capture; keep, retain [compare German *nehmen* "to take"; §8.7]

(ġe)nīpan (strong verb 1) = to grow dark [§8.4]

nis = *ne + is*, pres 3 sing of *bēon*

nīð (m) = attack, war; animosity, spite, hatred [§2.7]

nīð-ġeweorc (n) = hostile deeds, WORKs of
violence [§2.9]

nīððas (m, pl only) = men, human beings
[§2.7]

(ġe)nīwian (weak verb II) = to reNEW, restore
[§3.12]

nīwe (adjective) = NEW, recent, novel [§6.10]

nō = see *nā*

noht = see *naht*

nolde = past sing of *nyllan*

noldon = past pl of *nyllan*

noma = see *nama*

nōn (n) = nones, one of the canonical hours in
the divine office [§2.9]

norð-dǣlas (m, pl) = NORTHern parts,
regions [§2.7]

norþern (adjective) = NORTHERN [§6.1]

Norð-hymber (adjective) = Northumbrian;
Northumbrian (people) [§6.1]

norþ-weardes (adverb) = NORTHWARD
[§6.9]

nōsa (f) = NOSE [§ 10.6]

notian (weak verb II) = (+ dat object) to enjoy,
use, make use of; use up [§3.4]

nū (adverb) = NOW [§6.9]

(ġe)numen = past participle of *(ġe)niman*

nunne (f) = NUN [§3.4]

nȳd- = see *nīed-*

nȳhst = see *nīehst*

nyle = see *nyllan*

nyllan (irregular verb *ne+willan*) = WILL not,
not to want, not to wish or desire [§4.5.3]

nymðe = see *nemne*

nys = *ne* + *is*, pres 3 sing of *bēon*

nyste = pres. 3 sing. of *nytan*

nytan (pret-pres) = *ne* + *witan*; not to know;
(+ gen) not to know of or about [§4.3,
4.1.3]

nȳten (n) = beast, small animal; cattle [§2.9]

nytennes (f) = cowardice; ignorance [derived
from *nytan* "not to know"; §2.8]

nytenyssæ = see *nytennes*

nytt (f) = use, advantage, utility; duty, office,
employment [§2.8]

nyt-wyrþnes (f) = utility, usefulness [§2.8]

(ġe)nyðerian (weak verb II) = to bring low,
throw down, humble, oppress [§3.12]

O

o = *on*

of- (prefix) = intensifies verbs to which it is
attached, sometimes adding to verbs the
sense of "off," "away," or "down"; with verbs
that describe an attack, *of-* often can add
the sense "to death"

of (preposition + dat) = from, OFF [§6.15]

of-ālǣdan (weak verb I) = to LEAD OFF, to
carry off [§3.11]

of-dūn-rihte (adverb) = DOWNward, upside-
down [§6.9]

ofer (preposition) = (+ dat) OVER; (+ acc)
from over [§6.16.2]

ofer-gān (irregular verb *gan*) = to over-run
[§4.5.3]

ofer-ġeweork, -ġeweorc (n) = superstructure;
sepulcher [§2.9]

ofer-hrops (f) = greediness, voracity [§2.8]

ofer-swīðan (weak verb I) = to OVERcome,
overpower, conquer [§3.11]

ofer-urnen = pl subjunctive of *ofer-gān*

ofer-weorpan (strong verb 3) = to fall, stumble; to throw OVER, throw down, overturn [§8.6]

ofer-wintrian (weak verb I) = to OVER WINTER, live through the winter [§3.11]

of-glēsian (weak verb II) = to GLOSS, provide a gloss [§3.12]

of-gyldan (weak verb I) = to apply GILDing or metal enamel [§3.11]

of-langian, -longian (weak verb II) = to LONG, give (oneself) over to LONGing, oppress with LONGing [§3.12]

ofost (f) = speed, haste, hurry [§2.8]

of-sittan (strong verb 5) = to hem in, besiege; SIT on? [§ 9.1]

of-slægen = past participle of *of-slēan*

of-slēan (strong verb 6, contract verb) = to SLAY OFF, kill [§9.2, §11.1]

of-slog, of-slogon = past sing and past pl of *of-slēan*

of-stikian, -stician (weak verb II) = to stab, pierce, to death [§3.12]

of-stingan (strong verb 3) = to stab (to death) [§8.6]

oft (adverb) = OFTen, frequently (comparative = *oftor*; superlative = *oftost*) [§6.9]

of-tēon (strong verb 2, contract verb) = to deny, deprive, withhold [§8.5, §11.1.2]

of-ðyncan (weak verb I) = to be irritated or vexed (by something), to regret (impersonal; *by* = + gen) [§3.11, §11.2]

olfende (m or f) = camel [apparently a form of Latin *elefantem*; §3.3, 3.4]

on-, an- (prefix) = often adds no detectable meaning to a word, though it can add the meaning of the preposition (see below), the sense of "in return" or "in response to," or the sense of *un-*.

on (preposition) = (+ dat) in, ON; (+ acc) into, ONto [§6.16.2]

on-ǣlan (weak verb I) = to ignite, set on fire, burn; see ModE *ANNEAL* "to temper" and *Hamlet*'s "unannealed" [§3.11]

on-belǣdan (weak verb I) = to inflict upon, LOAD down with [§ 3.11]

on-bryrdan (weak verb I) = to incite, inspire, encourage; ignite [§3.11]

on-ċ(i)erran (weak verb I) = to change, turn [§3.11]

on-cnāwan (strong verb 7) = to KNOW, recognize [§9.3]

on-cnēowon = past pl of *on-cnāwan*

on-cȳðiġ (adjective) = revealed, made known [§6.1]

ond, and (conjunction) = AND; *ond . . . ond* = both . . . and [§5.1.1]

ond- = see *and-*

on-drēdan (weak verb I *and* strong verb 7) = to fear, DREAD (+ reflexive) [§3.11, §74.1, §9.3]

onemn-þrōwigan (weak verb I) = to sympathize, suffer along with [§3.11]

on-fēng = past 3 sing of *on-fōn*

on-findan (strong verb 3) = to discover, come upon, FIND out [§8.6]

on-fōn (strong verb 7) = to begin, start something; meddle with [§9.3, §11.1]

on-ġēan (adverb) = in return, back [§6.9]

on-ġēan (preposition + dat and acc) = towards [§6.15]

on-ġetan = see *on-ġietan*

on-ġieldan (strong verb 3) = to be punished for, pay (the penalty) for [§8.6]

on-ġietan, -ġetan (strong verb 5) = to see, perceive [§9.1]

on-ġinnan (strong verb 3) = to beGIN, start (often impersonal), start to do something (+ infinitive) [§8.6, §11.2]

on-glēwliċ (adjective) = artful, cunning [see *glēaw*; §6.1]

on-gon = past sing of *on-ġinnan*

on-gunnon = past pl of *on-ġinnan*

on-gristliċ (adjective) = GRISLY, ghastly [§6.1]

on-hǣtan (weak verb I) = to HEAT, inflame, set ablaze [§3.11]

on-hieldan (weak verb I) = to bend down, recline, decline [§3.11, §3.11.1]

on-hweorfan (strong verb 3) = to change, turn, reverse [§8.6]

on-liċ (adjective) = ALIKE, similar to [§6.1]

on-līesan (weak verb I) = to set free, loose, release [§3.11]

Onna (weak m) = Anna, King of East Anglia

on-sittan (strong verb 5) = to SIT ON, mount [§9.1]

on-stāl (m) = supply [§2.7]

on-þwēan, -þwēon (strong verb 6) = to wash (past participle = *on-þwēġen*) [§9.2, §11.1]

on-wacan (strong verb 6) = to AWAKEn, wake up; be born, originate [§9.2]

on-wari(ġ)an (weak verb I) = to guard oneself against, be WARY of, against [§3.11]

on-weald (n) = power [related to ModE *WIELD*; §2.9]

on-wealg, -wealh (adjective) = whole, sound, healthy [§6.1]

on-wealh-nes (f) = WHOLENESS, integrity; health; purity, chasitity [§2.8]

on-weġ (adverb) = AWAY, out, onward [§6.9]

on-wendan (weak verb I) = to change, exchange, take the place of [§3.11, see §3.11.1]

ō-wiht (n) = see *ā-wiht*

on-wrēon (strong verb 1, contract verb) = to cover, envelop; explain, reveal [§8.4, §11.1]

open (adjective) = OPEN, exposed [§6.1]

(ġe)openian (weak verb II) = to OPEN [§3.12]

ora = ounces (partitive gen)

ord (m) = point, front [§2.7]

ōret-mæcg (m) = warrior, champion [§2.7]

ōretta (weak m) = warrior [§3.3]

ormǣtnys (f) = excess, immensity [§2.8]

oroð (n) = breath [§2.9]

or-sāwle (adjective) = lifeless, dead, without a SOUL [§6.1]

(ġe)ortrȳwian (weak verb II) = to doubt, be skeptical of [§3.12]

or-wēna (weak adjective) = despairing [§6.1]

ostre (weak f) = OYSTER [§3.4]

oþ (preposition + acc, rarely dat) to, as far as; until [§6.15]

ōþer (pronoun) = anOTHER (person, thing) [§6.1, 7.8]

ōþer (adjective) = OTHER, another; second in a sequence [§6.1]

oþ-brīnan (strong verb 1) = to touch [§8.4]

oþ-þæt (conjunction) = until [§5.1.1]

oððe (conjunction) = or
oxa (weak m) = OX [§3.3]
oxan-hyrde (m) = oxherd [§10.2.1]

P

(In OE, for the most part, only borrowed
words begin in *p*.)

pæll (m) = silk robe, purple garment [§2.7]
papol-stān (m) = PEBBLE-STONE [§2.7]
pening (m) = PENNY [§2.7]
Pentecosten (m) = the seventh Sunday after the
Christian holiday of Easter, the fiftieth day
after Easter
Pētrus (m) = a proper name [Latin form]
pinne (weak f) = leather flask, bottle [§3.4]
pleġ-scyld (m) = PLAY-SHIELD, a particular
toy [§2.7]
pliht (m) = danger, peril, risk; PLIGHT [§2.7]
plyhtliċ (adjective) = dangerous, hazardous
[§6.1]
prættiġ (adjective) = sly, cunning [§6.1]
prēost (m) = PRIEST [§2.7]
prica (weak m) = PRICK, point [§3.3]
prīm (n) = prime, the first canonical hour of
the divine office, about 6 a.m. [§2.9]
prūt (adjective) = PROUD [§6.1]
pusa (weak m) = bag, scrip [§3.3]
Prōtus (m) = a proper name [Latin form]

Q

quinque vocales = Latin for "five vowels"

R

rǣd (m) = counsel, advice [§2.7]

rǣdan (strong verb 7) = to READ (a text)
[§9.3]
(ġe)rǣde (n) = trappings, armor, ornaments
[§10.2.2]
rǣdend (m) = ruler, i.e., God [§10.11.1]
rǣġe (weak f) = female deer, doe, ROE deer
[§3.4]
rān (m) = roebuck [§10.8]
rand (m) = shield [2.7]
rēad (adjective) = RED [§6.1]
rēadnis (f) = REDNESS, irritation [§2.8]
rēaf (n) = plunder, booty; garment, armor
[§2.9]
rēama (weak m) = membrane, ligament [§3.3]
reċ(ċ)an (weak verb I) = to care for, to care, be
concerned with (+ gen object); RECKON
with [§3.11]
(ġe)reċċan (weak verb I) = to explain, explicate;
tell about, narrate; judge, decide [§3.11]
regol (m) = RULE, code of monastic laws
[§2.7]
rēn (m) = RAIN [§2.7]
ġe-rēn (n) = ornament [§10.11.1]
reordian (weak verb II) = to speak, talk [§3.12]
(ġe)reord (f) = language, voice, speech; meal,
food [§3.4]
(ġe)reordung, rerduncg (f) = meal [§3.4]
rēowon = past pl of *rōwan*
rest (f) = REST; resting place, bed [§2.8]
(ġe)restan (weak verb I) = to REST; rest from,
find relief from (+ gen object) [§3.11]
rētu (f) = joy [§3.4]
rēwyt (n) = rowing [§2.9]
ribb (n) = RIB [§2.9]
rīce (adjective) = powerful, RICH [§6.1]

rīċe (n) = rule, reign, empire, realm; power, might, authority [compare German *Reich* "empire"; §10.2.2]

rīdan (strong verb 1) = to RIDE [§8.4]

riht (adjective) = RIGHT, correct [§6.1]

rihtlīċe (adverb) = RIGHTLY, properly, virtuously, correctly [§6.9]

riht-wīs-nes (f) = RIGHTeousness [§2.8]

rīm (n) = number, count, reckoning [§2.9]

rīnan (strong verb 1) = to RAIN (impersonal, see §11.2) [§8.4]

rinc (m) = warrior, soldier [§2.7]

rīpan (strong verb 1) = to REAP, harvest [§8.4]

rīsan (strong verb 1) = to RISE, get up; seize, carry off [§8.4]

rixian (weak verb II) = to rule, govern [§3.12]

rodor (m) = sky, heaven [§2.7]

rōf (adjective) = famous, renowned, celebrated; brave [§6.1]

rōhton = past pl of *reċċan*

rōwan (strong verb 7) = to ROW (a boat) [§9.3]

rūm (adjective) = ROOMy, spacious, large; noble, unfettered, open [§6.1]

rūn (f) = secret, mystery; advice, consultation, counsel; RUNE [§2.8]

ryht = see *riht*

(ġe)rӯne (n) = mystery, secrets [ModE *RUNE*; §10.2.2]

S

sacan (strong verb 6) = to quarrel, feud [§9.2]

sacu (f) = disagreement, quarrel, feud [§10.7]

sǣ (m or f, often indeclinable) = SEA [§10.11.1, §10.11.2]

sæċċe (f) = battle, strife, contest [§2.8]

sǣ-clif (n) = SEA-CLIFF, cliff by the sea [§2.9]

sǣ-cocc (m) = COCKLE [§2.7]

sǣde, sǣġde = past 1,3 sing of *secgan*

sǣġdon = past pl of *secgan*

sǣġest = present 2 sing of *secgan*

sǣl (m) = happiness, prosperity [§2.7]

sǣlan (weak verb I) = to tie, fetter; chain [compare German *Seil* "rope"; §3.11]

sǣ-liċ (adjective) = of the SEA, marine [§6.1]

sǣliġ (adjective) = blessed; fortunate, lucky [§6.1]

Sæternes-dæġ (m) = SATURDAY [§2.7]

saga = imperative sing of *secgan*

sagað = pres 3 pl of *secgan*

sāh = past 3 sing of *sīgan*

(ġe)samnian (weak verb II) = to gather, assemble, call up [§3.12]

samnung, somnung (f) = congregation, meeting, council; union, marriage [§2.8]

samnunga (adverb) = suddenly, immediately [§6.9]

samod, samed (adverb) = simultaneously, together, at the same time [$6.9]

sām-worht (adjective) = unfinished [§6.1]

sanct (m) = SAINT, holy person [from Latin *sanctus* "holy"; §2.7]

sang (m) = SONG [§2.7]

sār (adjective) = sad, SORRowful [§6.1]

sār (n) = pain, SOREness; SORRow, distress [§2.9]

sāre (adverb) = SORELy, grievously; painfully [§6.9]

sārġian (weak verb II) = to cause pain, wound, afflict; suffer [§3.12]

sārliċ (adjective) = painful, dreadful, bitter; sad, SORrowful, SORELY [§6.1]

sāwan (strong verb 7) = to SOW, plant seed [§9.3]

sawe = see *sēon*

sāwol, sāwl (f) = SOUL, spirit [§2.8]

sāwol-lēas (adjective) = SOULLESS, lifeless, dead [§6.1]

scacan (strong verb 6) = to SHAKE, quiver [§9.2]

(ġe)scādan (strong verb 7) = to decide [§9.3]

scǣnan (weak verb 1) = to wrench open [§3.11]

ġe-scær = see *ġe-scieran*

scafan (strong verb 6) = to SHAVE [§9.2]

scand (f) = shame, disgrace, SCANDal [§2.8]

sceadu (f) = SHADOW [§10.3.3]

ġe-sceaft (f) = creature, created thing; creation [§2.8]

sceal, scealt = pres 1, 3 sing and pres 2 sing of *sculan*

scealc (m) = servant, retainer [compare German *Schalk* "scoundrel"; §2.7]

sceamu (f) = SHAME, disgrace, modesty [§2.8]

sceap (n) = SHAPE, form [§2.9]

scēap (n) = SHEEP [§2.9]

(ġe)sceapen = past participle of *(ġe)scieppan*

scēap-hyrde (m) = SHEPHERD [§10.2.1]

ġe-scær = *see ġe-scieran*

scear (m) = plowSHARE, pointed blade (of a plough) [§2.7]

scearn (n) – dung, muck [§2.9]

scearp (adjective) = SHARP, shrewd; bright; rough, severe [§6.1]

scearpliċ (adjective) = painful, SHARP [§6.1]

scearplīċe (adverb) = painfully, sharply [§6.9]

scēarra (f, pl only) = SHEARs, scissors [§2.8]

sceatt (m) = coin, money, wealth [§2.7]

scēað (f) = SHEATH, scabbard, holder [§2.8]

scēawian (weak verb II) = to see, view, look upon, gaze at, examine [compare German *schauen* "to look"; §3.12]

ġe-scēd = see *(ġe)scādan*

scēob, scheob (m) = SHOE [§2.7]

sceoldon = past pl of *sculan*

sceota (weak m) = trout [§3.3]

scēotan (strong verb 2) = to SHOOT [§8.5]

scēp-hyrde = see *scēap-hyrde*

sceþþan (strong verb 6) = to injure, harm (+ dat object) [§9.2]

sceolde = past sing of *sculan*

scield (f, m) = guilt, offense, sin [compare German *Schuld* "guilt, fault"; §2.7, §2.8]

sciell (f) = SHELL, shell fish; oyster [§2.8]

(ġe)scieppan (strong verb 6) = to form, shape; create [compare German *schaffen* "to create"; §9.2]

scieran (strong verb 4) = to SHEAR, cut [§8.7]

ġe-scieran (strong verb 4) = to cut, hew, split [§8.7]

scild (m) = SHIELD [§2.7]

scīnan (strong verb 1) = to SHINE [§8.4]

scinn (n) = spectre, ghoul, evil spirit [§2.9]

scip (n) = SHIP [§2.9]

scip-here (m) = SHIP-army, fleet [§10.2.1]

scolu (f) = SCHOOL [§2.8]

sconca (weak m) = leg, SHANK [§3.3]

scop (m) = singer, minstrel, poet [§2.7]

scort (adjective) = SHORT, not tall (comp: *scytra*) [§6.7]

(ġe)screpan (strong verb 5) = to SCRAPE, scratch; prepare [§9.1]

(ġe)screpe (adjective) = suitable, fit, adapted to [§6.1]

(ġe)screpelīċe (adverb) = suitably, fittingly [§6.9]

scrift (m) = confessor [§2.7]

scrīðan (strong verb 1) = to go, glide [§8.4]

scrūd (n) = clothing, dress, garment [ModE *SHROUD*; §2.9]

scrȳdan (strong verb 1) = to clothe, dress [see *scrūd*; §8.4]

scrȳt = *scrȳdeð* [§8.10.2]

scūfan (strong verb 2) = to SHOVE, push [§8.5]

sculan (preterite-present verb) = must, be obliged, be bound to [§4.3.1]

scūr (m) = SHOWER; storm, tempest; storm of battle? shower of blows? [§2.7]

(ġe)scȳ (n pl noun) = pair of SHOEs [§2.9]

scyldiġ (adjective) = guilty (of); liable, responsible (for) (+ gen, dat) [compare German *schuldig* "guilty"; §6.1]

Scylding (m) = Son of Shield, i.e., a Dane [§2.7]

scȳnð = present 3 sing of *scīnan* (showing i-mutation)

scyp = see *scip*

scypian (strong verb 6) = to take SHAPE, form [§9.2]

scyppend (m) = creator [§10.10]

scyran (weak verb I) = to allot, apportion [§3.11]

scȳte (f) = SHEET, cloth, linen [§3.4]

scyte-finger (m) = index FINGER, SHOOTing finger [§2.7]

scytra = comparative from of *scort*

sē, sēo, þæt (definite article, adjective, or pronoun) = the; that (one), that (thing) [§2.5, §7.7]

(ġe)seah = past 1, 3 sing of *(ġe)sēon*

se(a)llan (weak verb I) = to give something (acc) to someone (dat), furnish, lend; entrust, deliver to [ModE *SELL*; §3.11]

sealm (m) = song, PSALM [§2.7]

sealt (n) = SALT [§2.9]

sealtere (m) = SALTER, saltmaker [§10.2.1]

sēamere (m) = tailor [see the ModE feminine form *SEAMSTRESS*; §10.2.1]

(ġe)sēne, -siene (adjective) = SEEN, visible [§6.1]

searu –o (n) = war gear, armor; contrivance, trick; wiliness, cunning [§10.3.2]

seax (n) = knife [§2.9]

Seaxburh = Queen of Kent, Abbess of Ely (679-ca. 700), and sister of Etheldreda

(ġe)sēċ(e)an (weak verb I) = to SEEK out, go to, move to; attain; visit; attack [§3.11]

secg (m) = man [§10.2.1]

secgan (weak verb III) = to SAY; relate, tell about, describe [compare German *sagen* "to say"; §4.1]

seft (adverb) = comparative form of *softe* [§6.14]

(ġe)seġen = past participle of *(ġe)sēon*

seġl (m) = SAIL; pillar of cloud [§2.7]

sel-cūþ (adjective) = rare, strange, novel [§6.1]

seldan, seldon (adverb) = SELDOM, not frequently [§6.9]

seld-hwænne (adverb) = SELDom, rarely [§6.9]

sele (m) = hall, house [compare German *Saal* "hall"; §10.11.1]

sele-ġyst (m) = hall GUEST [§10.11.1]

sēlest (adjective) = best (superlative form of *gōd* "good") [§6.8]

sellan = see *se(a)llan*

sēlra (adjective) = better (comparative form of *gōd* "good") [§6.8]

senċean (weak verb I) = to sink, cause to sink, drown [§3.11]

sendan (weak verb I) = to SEND [§3.11]

sēoc (adjective) = SICK, ill [§6.1]

seofon (adjective or number) = SEVEN [§6.1]

seofoþa (adjective) = SEVENTH [§6.1]

sēoh = see *sēon*

se(o)lf (adjective) = the same, the very [§6.1]

se(o)lf (pronoun, strong and weak) = SELF, mySELF, himSELF [§7.4]

seolfor (n) = SILVER [§2.9]

seolofor-smiþ (m) = SILVERSMITH [§2.7]

seolm (m) = psalm [§2.7]

seomian (weak verb II) = to remain, lie, rest [§3.12]

sēon (strong verb 5, contract verbs) = to SEE [§9.1, §11.1]

sēoþan (strong verb 2) = to SEETHE, boil [§8.5]

seoðþan = see *siþþan*

setl (n) = seat, place [§2.9]

(ġe)settan (weak verb I) = to SET, establish, place; create, make [§3.11]

se þe (pronoun phrase) = "he who"

(ġe)sewen = past participle of *(ġe)sēon*

Sexburh = see *Seaxburh*

(ġe)sibb (m or f) = kinsman; relationship, peace [§2.8]

(ġe)sibb (adjective) = peaceful; related, akin [§6.1]

sib-sum (adjective) = peace-loving, friendly [§6.1]

sīd (adjective) = broad, ample, large; wide [§6.1]

sīde (weak f) = SIDE, torso [§3.4]

sīde (weak f) = silk [compare German *Seide* "silk"; §3.4]

sīe = "be" (present, subjunctive sing form of *bēon*)

sīe = see *bēon*

siex (indeclinable number) = SIX

siex-tēne (indeclinable number) = SIXTEEN

sīgan (strong verb 1) = to descend, rush down, come out; sink [§8.4]

siġe-ēadiġ (adjective) = victory-prosperous, victorious [§6.1]

siġe-fæst (adjective) = victory-FAST, firm in victory, victorious, triumphant [§6.1]

siġil, siġl (n) = brooch, gem; buckle [§2.9]

sigor (m) = victory, triumph, success [§2.7]

sihð = sees (present 3 sing of the strong verb 5 *sēon* "to see") [§9.1, §11.1]

sihðe (f) = SIGHT, vision [§2.8]

simble (adverb) = always, continuously [§6.9]

sīn (reflexive pronoun) = his, her, its, or their

sinc (n) = treasure, riches, valuables [§2.9]

sincan (strong verb 3) = to SINK [§8.6]

sinc-fāh (adjective) = treasure-decorated, decorated with treasure [§6.1]

sincge = see *singan*

sinder (n) = CINDER (for scouring) [§2.9]

sindon = see *bēon*

singal (adjective) = continual, perpetual, everlasting [§6.1]

singan (strong verb 3) = to SING [§8.6]

(ġe)sin-scipe, syn-scipe (m) = marriage; sex, cohabitation; married couple [§2.7]

sin-sorg (f) = perpetual sorrow, grief [§2.8]

sīo = *sēo*

sīð (m) = journey, expedition, exploit; time [§2.7]

(ġe)sīð (m) = companion [§2.7]

sīð-fæt (m, n) = journey, voyage [§2.7, 2.9]

sittan (strong verb 5) = to SIT [§9.1]

sīþ (adverb, conjunction) = after

sīþian (weak verb 2) = to go, depart, travel, wander [§3.12]

sīþþan (adverb) = afterwards, from that point on [§6.9]

slǣp (m) = SLEEP [§2.7]

slǣpan (strong verb 7) = to SLEEP [§9.3]

slǣp-ern (n) = dormitory, sleeping quarters [see ModE *bARN*, from OE *bere-ærn* "barley building"; §2.9]

slāt = past sing of *slītan*

slēan (strong verb 6, contract verb) = to strike, hit; pitch (a tent) [see ModE *SLAY*; §9.2, §11.1]

slecg (f) = SLEDGEhammer [§2.8]

sleġe (m) = beating, stroke; death-blow; murder [§10.11.1]

slēp = see *slǣpan*

slit (n) = bite, sting [§2.7]

slītan (strong verb 1) = to SLIT, tear to pieces, bite [§8.4]

slītung (f) = bite, sting [§2.8]

slōb = see *slēan*

smæl, smal (adjective) = narrow, thin [§6.1]

smēagan (weak verb III) = to think, examine, investigate [see *Smeagol*, the human name of Tolkien's Gollum; §4.1]

smēocan (strong verb 2) = to SMOKE [§8.5]

smeoru (n) = lard or other spread (for SMEARing on bread) [§10.3.2]

smið (m) = maker, workman [ModE blackSMITH; §2.7]

(ġe)smiðian (weak verb I) = to forge, fabricate, design [§3.11]

smiþþe (weak f) = SMITHY, workshop [§3.4]

snæġl (m) = SNAIL [§2.7]

snid (m) = slice, incision, cut [compare German *Schnitt* "cut" and *Schnitzel* "cutlet"; §2.7]

snīðan (strong verb 1) = to cut [compare German *schneiden* "to cut"; §8.4]

snottor (adjective) = wise, knowing [§6.1]

snūde (adverb) = quickly, right away [§6.9]

snyttru (f) = intelligence, cleverness, prudence [§10.6.1]

softe (adverb) = SOFTly, gently [§6.9, §6.14]

(ġe)sōhte = past 1,3 sing of *(ġe)seċ(e)an*

somnung = see *samnung*

sōna (adverb) = immediately [§6.9]

sorg, sorh (f) = SORROW, pain [§2.8]

sorh-ċearig (adjective) = sad, sorrowful [§6.1]

sorġian (weak verb II) = to SORROW, mourn [§3.12]

sōð (adjective) = true [§6.1]

sōþ (n) = the truth [see early ModE *forSOOTH*; §2.9]

sōðlīċe (adverb) = truly, in truth [§6.9]

spǣċ = see *sprǣċ*

spǣtan (weak verb I) = to SPIT [§3.11]

(ġe)spanan (strong verb 7) = to persuade, urge; seduce [§9.3]

spannan (strong verb 7) = to fasten [§9.3]

spēd (f) = capacity, power; means [§2.8]

spēd-dropa (weak m) = useful drop, i.e., ink [§3.3]

spēdiġ (adjective) = wealthy, rich [§6.1]

spell (n) = news, information [§2.9]

spēon = past 3 sing of *spannan*

spere (n) = SPEAR [§10.2.2]

sprǣċ = see *sprecen*

sprǣċ, spǣċ (f) = SPEECH, talk [§2.8]

sprecan (strong verb 5) = to speak [§9.1]

sprycst = see *sprecan*

sprot (f) = a small food fish, SPRAT [§2.8]

spur-leþer (f) = SPUR strap [§2.8]

spurnan (strong verb 3) = to kick, trample on [see ModE *SPURN*; §8.6]

spyrian (weak I) = to track, go, travel (on) [§3.11]

spyrte (weak f) = basket, wicker basket [§3.4]

stæf (m) = letter, character (dat pl = *stafum*) [§2.7]

stǣnen (adjective) = made of STONE, stone [§6.1]

stān (m) = STONE, rock [§2.7]

standan (strong verb 6) = to STAND [§9.2]

stān-hliþ (n) = rocky slope, cliff [§2.9]

staþol-fæst (adjective) = steadFAST, firm, fixed [§6.1]

staþol-fæstlīċe (adverb) = firmly, securely [§6.9]

staþol-fæstnes (f) = steadFASTNESS, stability [§2.8]

stearc (adjective) = hard, stiff, rough [§6.1]

stēda (weak m) = (male) camel; STEED [§3.3]

stede (m) = place, site, location [§10.2]

stefn (f) = voice [compare German *Stimme* "voice"; §2.8]

stelan (strong verb 4) = to STEAL [§8.7]

stemne, stefne (f) = voice [compare German *Stimme* "voice"; §2.8]

stenċ (m) = smell, fragrance, scent; stink, odor, STENCH [§10.11.1]

steorra (weak m) = STAR [§3.3]

stēoran (weak verb I) = to guide, direct, STEER (+ dat or gen object) [§3.11]

steorfan (strong verb 3) = to die [compare German *sterben* "to die", ModE *STARVE*; §8.6]

Stēphan (m) = proper name

steppan (strong verb 6) = to STEP, take a step, walk [§9.2]

sterced-ferþð (adjective) = stout of heart, determined, resolute [§6.1]

(ġe)stician, stikian (weak verb II) = to STICK, stab, kill; to lay open [§3.12]

stīeran (weak verb I) = to STEER, guide [§3.11]

stīgan (strong verb 1) = to climb, ascend [compare German *steigen* "to climb"; §8.4]

(ġe)stik- = see *(ġe)stician*

stincan (strong verb 3) = to smell, sniff
(something) [§8.6]

stiria (weak m) = sturgeon [§3.3]

stīð (adjective) = firm, strong, unbending
[§6.1]

stiþlīċe (adverb) = sternly, strongly, harshly
[§6.9]

stōd = past sing of *standan*

stōl (m) = STOOL, seat [§2.7]

stondan, stondeþ = see *standan*

stōp = see *steppan*

stōpon = see *steppan*

storm (m) = STORM [§2.7]

stōw (f) = place, locality; see place names like
Padstow and *Felixstowe* [§10.3.3]

strǣl (f) = arrow, dart [§2.8]

strand (m) = shore [§2.7]

strang, strong (adjective) = STRONG;
superlative = *strengest* [§6.1]

(ġe)strangian (weak verb II) = to strengthen,
make STRONG [§3.12]

strēam (m) = STREAM [§2.7]

streġdan (strong verb 3) = to STREW, spread
[§8.6]

strengra, strengest = see *strang*

strengð, strengðu (f) = STRENGTH [§2.8]

strengu (f) = strength [§2.8]

(ġe)strēon (n) = treasure [§2.9]

strīcan (strong verb 1) = to spread, rub lightly
over the surface, rub [§8.4]

stroccian (weak verb II) = to STROKE
[§3.12]

strȳdan (weak verb I) = to rob, steal [§3.11]

stunt (adjective) = foolish, dull, stupid [§6.1]

stȳl-ecg (adjective) = STEEL-EDGed [§6.1]

(ġe)styrian (weak verb I) = to restrain, prevent
(from = gen); STIR, move, rouse [§3.11]

sulh (f) = plow [§10.4.2]

sum (adjective) = SOME, (a) certain; (+
number) = about, approximately [§6.1.1]

sumor (m) = SUMMER [§10.6]

sumor-lang (adjective) = SUMMER LONG,
(lasting) the length of a summer's day [§6.1]

suncon = see *sincan*

ġe-sund (adjective) = healthy, sound,
prosperous [§6.1; compare German *gesund*
"healthy"]

Sunnan-dæġ (m) = SUNDAY [§2.7]

sunne (weak f) = SUN [§3.4]

sunu (m) = SON, male offspring [§10.6]

sūsl (f) = torment, torture; misery [§2.8]

sūð (adjective, adverb) = SOUTH [§6.1, 6.9]

Sūð-ġerwe, -gyrwe (m) = fen dwellers,
Southern Angles [§2.7, 10.11.1]

suwiende = present participle of *swīġian*

swā (adverb) = as , so, thus, in this way, to
such an extent [§6.9]

swā (conjunction) = as, like, just like; *swa swa*
= "just as, just as if"; *swā . . . swā* = "so . . .
as," "whether . . . or"; *eal swā* = "completely
as, just as"; *swā hwæðer . . . swā . . . swā* =
"whichever . . . whether
. . . or" [§5.1.1]

swæċċ (m) = taste, flavor [§2.7]

swǣs (adjective) = intimate, close, favorite,
dear; gentle [§6.1]

swǣtan (weak verb I) = to SWEAT, exude
(+ dat object) [§3.11]

swā hwæt swā (pronoun phrase) – WHATSOever, whatever [§7.8.1]

swā hwylċ swā (pronoun phrase) = whatever, whoever [§7.8.1]

swān (m) = swineherd, herdsman, peasant [§2.7]

swātiġ (adjective) = SWEATY, bloody [§6.1]

swa-ðēah (adverb) = however, nevertheless, yet [§6.9]

swaðu (f) = track, footstep, path; SWATH [§2.8]

swealh = see *swelgan*

sweart (adjective) = black, dark [ModE SWARThy; §6.1]

sweart-lāst (adjective) = with black tracks, trailing black [§6.1]

swefan (strong verb 5) = to sleep [§9.1]

swefel (m) = sulphur [§2.7]

(ġe)swef(n)ian (weak verb II) = to put to sleep, cause to fall asleep [§3.12]

swefn (n, often pl) = sweep; dream [§2.9]

swēġincg, swēgung (f) = sound, roar, clamor [§2.8]

sweġl (n) = sky, heavens [§2.9]

swelċ (adjective, pronoun) = SUCH [§6.1/4]

swelgan (strong verb 3) = to SWALLOW [§8.6]

swelġere (m) = glutton, SWALLOWER [see *swelgan*; §10.2.1]

(ġe)swell (n) = SWELLing, boil, tumor [§2.9]

swellan (strong verb 3) = to SWELL [§8.6]

sweltan (strong verb 3) = to die [ModE SWELTer; §8.6]

swenċ(e)an (weak verb I) = to afflict, oppress, distress, cause pain [from OE *swinc* "labor, pain"; §3.11]

sweng (m) = blow, stroke, cut [§2.7]

sweoloð (m) = flame, fire, glowing heat [§2.7]

swēor (m) = pillar, column [§2.7]

swēora (weak m) = neck [§3.3]

swēor-bēag (m) = "neck-ring"; necklace, torque, collar [§2.7]

sweord (n) = SWORD [§2.9]

sweostor (f) = SISTER [§10.5]

(ġe)sweostra (f pl noun) = sisters [§10.5]

sweotol (adjective) = clear, distinct, open [§6.1]

sweotole, sweotolīċe (adverb) = clearly, distinctly [§6.9]

(ġe)sweotolian, swutolian (weak verb II) = to show, reveal, make clear; explain, prove [§3.12]

swerian (strong verb 6) = to SWEAR, curse [§9.2]

swēt (adjective) = SWEET, delicious [§6.1]

swētnys (f) = SWEETNESS [§2.8]

(ġe)swīcan (strong verb 1) = to cease from, stop (+ gen object); deceive, trick ; fail, prove useless [§8.4]

swift (adjective) = SWIFT, quick, fast [§6.1, §6.5]

swīġe (weak f) = silence [§3.4]

swīġian (weak verb II) = to be quiet, silent, to become silent [compare German *schweigen* "to be quiet"; §3.12]

swilċ, swelċ, swylċ (adjective) = such, the same (*swelċe . . . swā = such . . . as*) [§6.1]

swilċe, swylċe (adverb) = such as, in a manner similar to, similarly, likewise [§6.9] *swilċe, swylċe* (conjunction) = just as if; *swilċe . . . swilċe* = "as much . . . as" [§5.1.1]

swile (m) = tumor, swelling [§10.2.1]

swīma (weak m) = vertigo, dizziness; swoon, faint [§3.3]

swimman (strong verb 3) = to SWIM, float [§8.6]

(ġe)swinc (n) = hardship, affliction, suffering; labor, hard work, effort [§2.9]

swingan (strong verb 3) = to beat, strike, whip [§8.6]

swin(c)gell (f) = stroke, blow, stripe [§2.8]

swīran = see *swēora*

swīð (adjective) = strong, powerful [§6.1]

swīðe (adverb) = violently, powerfully; quickly, swiftly [§6.9]

swīðe (intensifier) = very, very much, exceedingly [§6.9]

swīð-ferhð (adjective) – stout-hearted, brave [§6.1]

swīðor (adjective) = right (as opposed to left) [§6.1, originally the comparative of *swīð* "stronger"]

swu- = see also *sweo-*

swulte = see past 2 sing *sweltan*

swut- = see *sweot-*

swūra = see *swēora*

swustor = see *sweostor*

swyftlēre (m) = slipper [§10.11.1]

swylċ = see *swilċ*

swylċe = see *swilċe*

swymð = pres 3 sing of *swimman*

swȳðe = see *swīðe*

sȳ, sȳn, synd, syndon = subj forms of *wesan*

sȳ . . . sȳ = whether (it) be... or whether (it, he) be

sȳfernys (f) = moderation, cleanliness, sobriety [§2.8]

(ġe)sybð (f) = SIGHT, thing seen, vision [§2.8]

sȳl = dat sing of *sulh*

sȳla (weak m) = ploughman §3.3]

sylf, seolf (pronoun) = SELF [§7.4]

(ġe)syllan, sylle, sylð = see *se(a)llan*

symbel-nes (f) = festival, festivity [§2.9]

symble, symle (adverb) = constantly, continually; always [§6.9]

syn- = see also *sin-*

synd, syndon = see *bēon*

syndriġlīċe, syndriġe (adverb) = separately, specially, alone [§6.9]

synn (f) = SIN, crime [§2.8]

synnful (adjective) = SINFUL, wicked [§6.1]

syn-snǣd (f) = large piece [§2.8]

(ġe)synto (f) = salvation, welfare; health, prosperity [§10.3.3]

syððan = see *siððan*

syx- = see *siex-*

syxta (adjective) = SIXTH [§6.1]

T

tā (f) = TOE (pl: *tān*) [§2.8]

tācen (n) = sign, TOKEN [§2.9]

(ġe)tācnian (weak verb II) = to symbolize, beTOKEN [§3.12]

tācnung (f) = sign, signification, TOKEN, type [§2.8]

tǣċan (weak verb I) = to TEACH [§3.11]

tæġl (n) = TAIL [§2.9]

tēah = past 3 sing of (ġe)teon

teald (n) = number, count [§2.9]

tealdon = past pl of *tellan*

tēam (m) = family, band, descendant; offspring, progeny [§2.7]

tēar (m) = TEAR; drop [§2.7]

teld (n) = tent [§2.9]

telga (weak m) = branch, bough [§3.3]

tellan (weak verb I) = to count, reckon; to relate, TELL [see ModE *bank TELLer*; §3.11]

(ġe)temian (weak verb II) = to TAME, train [§3.12]

temiġe = see *temian*

tempel, templ (n) = TEMPLE, (pagan) place of worship [§2.9]

teodde = past participle of *teohhian*

(ġe)teohhian (weak verb II) = to judge, determine, assign; intend [§3.12]

(ġe)tēon (strong verb 2, contract verb) = to pull, TUG; create, prepare [§8.5, §11.1]

tēoþa (adjective) = TENTH [§6.1]

teran (strong verb 4) = to TEAR, rip [§8.7]

tīd (f) = time; hour, canonical hour [ModE *Christmas TIDE, Yule TIDE*; §10.11.2]

(ġe)tihtan (weak verb I) = to draw, pull; incite, instigate; teach, train [§3.11]

til (adjective) = good, fitting [§6.1]

tīma (weak m) = TIME [§3.3]

timbran (weak verb I) = to build, erect [§3.11]

(ġe)tīmian (weak verb II) = to happen, occur, take place [§3.12]

tin (n) = TIN [§2.9]

tintreġ (n) = torment [§2.9]

tīr (m) = glory [§2.7]

Tīwes-dæġ (m) = TUESDAY [§2.7]

Tīwes-niht (f) = Monday NIGHT, the night before TUESday [§2.8]

tō- (prefix) = can add the meaning of the preposition (see below) as well as the sense of "to pieces" or "apart" (*drīfan* "to drive"; *tō-drīfan* "to drive apart, disperse")

tō (adverb, intensifier) = TOO [§6.9]

tō (infinitive marker) = TO (as in "to be or not to be")

tō (preposition + dat, gen, instr) = as, TO, into, until; for [§6.15, §2.11.4c]

tō-dæġ (adverb) = TODAY [§6.9]

tō-dǣlan (weak verb I) = to separate, divide [§3.11]

tō-foran (preposition + dat) = before, in front of [§6.15]

tō-gædere (adverb) = TOGETHER [§6.9]

tō-ġēanes (preposition + acc, dat) = for, in preparation for; in opposition to, toward [§6.15]

tō-ġēanes (adverb) = opposite, toward, in front; in the way, in the path [§6.9]

tō-ġe-lædan (weak verb I) = to LEAD to, bring, transport, carry [§3.11]

tō-ġe-hyht = past participle of *tō-ġe-ȳcan*

tō-ġe-nȳdan (weak verb I) = compel, force [§3.11]

tō-ġe-ȳcan (weak verb I) = to add, give (past participle = *tō-ġehȳht*) [related to *ēac*; §3.11]

tō-glīdan (strong verb 1) = to GLIDE away, vanish [§8.4]

tō-hweorfan (strong verb 3) = to move apart, disperse [§8.6] *tō-lēsan* (weak verb I) = to dissolve, destroy [§3.11]

tō-lȳsnes (f) = to destruction, loss [§3.11]

tollere (m) = tax collector [§10.2.1]

Tondberht (proper name) = Prince of the South Gyrwas

torht (adjective) = bright [§6.1]

torhte (adverb) = brightly [§6.9]

torht-mōd (adjective) = bright of mind or heart, resplendent [§6.1]

torn (adjective) = angry, enraged [§6.1, compare German *Zorn* "rage"]

torr (m) = rock [related to ModE *TOWER*; §2.7]

tō-scēadednes (f) = separation [§2.8]

tō-specan (strong verb 5) = to address, SPEAK TO [§9.1]

tō-somne (adverb) = TOgether [§6.9]

tō-ðām (idiom) = to that extent, so

tō þon = see *þon*

tō-weard, tō-werd (adjective) = approaching, coming, imminent [§6.2.2]

tō-weorpan (strong verb 3) = to cast away, stop, destroy, dismiss [§8.6]

tō-wurpon = past pl of *tō-weorpan*

tredan (strong verb 5) = to step, TREAD on, trample [§9.1]

(ġe)trēowe, trȳe (adjective) = TRUE, loyal, faithful [§6.10]

trēo(w) (n) = TREE [§10.3.2]

trēowen (adjective) = wooden, made of wood [§6.1]

trēow-wyrhta, trȳ- (weak m) = carpenter, TREE-WRIGHT [§3.3]

treppe (weak f) = TRAP, snare [§3.4]

trum (adjective) = firm, strong, resolute [§6.1]

ġe-trūwian (weak verb II) = to trust, believe in; conclude [§3.12]

trymman, trymian (weak verb I) = to strengthen, encourage, make firm [from *trum*, with i-mutation; §3.11]

tūn (m) = TOWN, enclosure, fort [§2.7]

tunge (weak f) = TONGUE [§3.4]

tungol (n) = star [§2.9]

tūx (m) = grinder, TUSK [§2.7]

twā (adjective or number) = TWO (+ partitive gen) [§6.1]

twēġen (adjective) = two [ModE *TWAIN*; §6.1]

tweġen (number) = two

twelf (number) = TWELVE

twelfte (adjective) = TWELFth [§6.1]

twēntegoþa (adjective) = TWENTieth [§6.1]

twēo-mann, twi-men (m) = lit., doubt MAN, or a doubtfully human creature; OE *twēo* "doubt, confusion" is related to *twā* "TWO." Having doubts means not being able to decide between two alternatives. See the phrase "to be of two minds" about something. [§10.4.2]

twēo (m) = doubt, uncertainty [§3.3]

twēo (number) = TWO

tweowa (adverb) = twice [§6.9]

twȳlic (adjective) = doubtful, ambiguous, belonging to TWO different categories [§6.1.1]

tȳdran (weak verb I) = to abound in, to produce, to be prolific [§3.11]

tȳhst = 2 pres sing of *tēon*

tȳr = see *tīr*

Þ, Ð

þā = (adverb) then, at that time [§6.9]; (conjunction) when [§5.1.1]

þā . . . þā (conjunction) = then . . . when [§5.1.1]

þā, ðām = see *sē, sēo, þæt*

þænne = see *þonne*

þǣr (adverb) = THERE, in that place; *þǣr þǣr* = "there where" [§6.9]

þǣr (conjunction) = where [§5.1.1]

þǣre = see *sē, sēo, þæt*

þǣr-inne (adverb) = THERE-IN, in there [§6.9]

þǣr-tō (adverb) = to THERE, thither [§6.9]

þæs (adverb) = therefore, because; the more; afterwards (originally, the gen sing of *þæt*) [§6.9]

þæs þe (conjunction) = since, after [§5.1.1]

þæt (conjunction) = THAT, so that; since, because [§5.1.1]

þæt = see *sē, sēo, þæt*

þæt þæt (pronoun phrase) = THAT which [§7.5]

þætte (conjunction) = THAT [§5.1.1]

(ġe)þafian (weak verb II) = to grant, allow [§3.12]

þām = see *sē, sēo, þæt*

þām līċe swylċe (conjunction) = in a similar way, as if, just as if [§5.1.1]

þām mete þe (conjunction) = in a similar way as, just as if [§5.1.1]

þancian (weak verb II) = to THANK (+ gen of person + dat of person) [§3.12]

þancung (f) = THANKS, THANKSgiving [§2.8]

þanon (adverb) = from there, from that place, THENce [§6.9]

þāra = see *sē, sēo, þæt*

þās = see *þēs, þēos, þis*

þe (relative pronoun) = who, which, that [§7.5]

þē = see *þū*

þē, þȳ (comparative marker) = THE (as in "*the* bigger *the* better") [§6.4]

þēah (adverb) = nevertheless [§6.9]

þēah (conjunction) = THOUGH, although [§5.1.1]

þēah-hwæðre (adverb) = however, nevertheless [§6.9]

(ġe)þeaht (n) = THOUGHT; plans, advice [§2.9]

(ġe)þeahta (weak m) = counselor, advisor [§3.3]

(ġe)þeahtend, -ynd (m) = counselor, advisor [originally a present participle: "thinking (one)"; §10.10]

þearf (f) = need, necessity [compare German *Bedurfnis* "necessity"; §2.8]

þearfan, þurfan (preterite-present verb) = to need, have need of (+ gen object) [§4.4.1]

þearfendre = f dat sing of the present participle *þearfan* "needing, in need of"

þearle (adverb) = very much, vigorously; heavily, excessively [§6.9]

þearl-mōd (adjective) = stern-minded, severe; cruel; mighty [§6.1]

þēaw (m) = custom, practice, habit [§10.3.1]

þēawlīċe (adverb) = obediently, decently; customarily [§6.9]

þeġn (m) = THANE, servant, retainer [§2.7]

þeġnian, þēnian (weak verb II) = to serve, wait

upon, attend to, minister to (often + dat object) [derived from OE *þeġn*; §3.12]

þeġnung (f) = attendants; service, ministry; divine service; office [§2.8]

þel, þell (n) = (metal) plate; board, plank [§2.9]

þē lǣs = see *lǣs* (conjunction)

(ġe)þenċ(e)an (weak verb I) = to consider, THINK about carefully; intend [§3.11]

þenden (conjunction) = as long as, while; when [§5.1.1]

þēnian = see *þeġnian*

ðēodan, þȳdan (weak verb I) = to join, associate with; come to, be near [§3.11]

þēoden (m) = prince, lord, leader [§2.7]

þēod-lond (n) = "people-LAND"; inhabited land; world, country, the continent [§2.9]

þēof (m) = THIEF [§2.7]

þēon (strong verb 1, contract verb) = to prosper [§8.4, §11.1]

þēos = see *þēs*

þēostru, þȳstru, -o (f) = darkness, gloom (often in pl) [§10.7]

þēow (m) = servant, slave [§10.2.1]

þēowa (weak m) = servant, slave [§3.3]

þēow-dōm (m) = slavery, servitude, vassaldom; service (to God) [§2.7]

ðēowe(n) (weak f) = servant, handmaid [§3.3]

þēow-hād (m) = service [§2.7]

þēowian (weak verb II) = to serve, be subject to (+ dat object) [§3.12]

ðerscan (strong verb 3) = to THRESH [§8.6]

þēs, þēos, þis (demonstrative pronoun, adjective) = THIS; this (person), this (thing) [§7.7]

þiċċe (adjective) = THICK [§6.10]

þiċċe (adverb) = THICKLY [§6.9]

þicgan (strong verb 5) = to consume, eat or drink [§9.1]

þider (adverb) = THITHER, there, to that place [§6.9]

þīn (adjective) = your, THINE [§7.1]

þincan = see *þyncan*

ðing, ðinc, ðincg (n) = THING, matter, concern [§2.9.2]

þīnen (f) = maid servant, handmaiden [§10.3.4]

þis = see *þēs, þēos, þis*

(ġe)þōht (m) = thought, purpose, idea [§2.7]

(ġe)þōhte = past 3 sing of *(ġe)þenċan*

þolian (weak verb II) = to suffer, endure, put up with [§3.12]

þon (adverb), *tō þon* = "to that extent" [§6.9]; (conjunction) *tō þon þætte* = "since, because" [§5.1.1]

þonan = *þonon*

þonc (m) = THANKs [§2.7]

þone = see *sē*

þonne (adverb) = then, immediately [§6.9]

þonne (conjunction) = when [§5.1.1]

þonon (adverb) = from there, THENCE [§6.9]

þrǣll (m) = slave, THRALL [§2.7]

þrāg (f) = time, period, space of time [§2.8]

þrēagan (weak verb I) = to torment; correct, punish [§3.11]

ðrēat (m) = troop, crowd, gang, host [§2.7]

þrēo (number) = THREE

þrī, þrȳ (adjective) = THREE [§6.1]

þridda (weak adjective) = THIRD [§6.4]

þringan (strong verb 3) = to press [compare German *dringen* "to press"; §8.6]

(ġe)þrīstian (weak verb II) = to dare, be bold enough [§3.12]

þrītiġ, ðrittiġ (number) = THIRTY

þrōwian (weak verb II) = to suffer; tolerate [§3.12]

þrūh, þrȳh (f) = chest, coffin, tomb [§2.8]

þrȳ = see *þrī*

þryċċan (weak verb I) = to crush, oppress, afflict [§3.11]

þrȳh = see *þrūh*

þrym-ful (adjective) = FULL of glory, magnificent [§6.1]

þrymliċ (adjective) = magnificent, glorious [§6.1]

þrymm (m) = glory, majesty; army, troop, host [§2.7]

ġe-ðrȳn (weak verb I) = to bind, press [§3.11]

ðryness (f) = trinity, THREENESS [§2.7]

þrȳste (adjective) = daring, bold [§6.10]

þū (personal pronoun) = you, THOU [§7.1]

(ġe)þūht, þūhte = see *þynċan*

Þunres-dæġ (m) = THURSDAY [§2.7]

ðunrian (weak verb I) = to THUNder [§3.11]

þurfan = see *þearfan*

þurh (adverb or preposition + acc) = THROUGH [§6.15]

þurh-brūcan (strong verb 2) = to enjoy thoroughly (+ dat object) [§8.5]

þurh-tēon (strong verb 2, contract verb) = to finish, fulfill, undergo [§11.1]

þurh-wādan (strong verb 6) = to go through, penetrate, pierce [§9.2]

þurh-werod (adjective) = thoroughly sweet, very sweet [§6.1]

þurh-wrecan (strong verb 5) = to pierce, thrust THROUGH [§9.1]

ðurh-wunian (weak verb II) = to remain, continue [§3.12]

þurst, þyrst (m) = THIRST [§10.11.1]

þus (adverb) = THUS [§6.9]

þūsend (n, number) = THOUSAND

þūsent-bīwe (adjective) = multi-form, shifty, protean [lit., THOUSAND-formed, glossing Latin *milleformis*; §6.1]

(ġe)ðwērian (weak verb I) = to consent, agree, be in agreement with [§3.11]

(ġe)þwērnys (f) = peace, agreement, harmony [§10.3.3]

þwēan (strong verb 6, contract verb) = to wash, clean [§9.2, §11.1]

þwōgon = past pl of *þwēan*

þȳ = see *þē*

þyder = see *þider*

þȳhtiġ (adjective) = strong, mighty, firm [§6.1]

þylċ (pronoun) = such, of that sort [§7.8]

þynċan (weak verb I) = to seem, appear (impersonal, + reflexive); *is ġe-þūht* = "seems" (a literal translation of Latin *videtur* "seems") [§3.11, §11.2]

ġe-ðyngo = promotion, progress [§10.3.2]

þynne (adjective) = THIN, lean, not dense [§6.1]

þyrl (n) = hole [see ModE nosTRIL, from OE *nos-þyrl* (lit.) "NOSE-hole"; §2.9]

ðyrstan (weak verb I) = to be THIRSTy (impersonal, + reflexive) [§3.11, §11.2] *þys, þysne, þyssum* = see *þēs, þēos, þis*

þȳwan (weak verb I) = to urge, drive [§3.11]

U

ufan (adverb) = from above, above [§6.9]

ufe-weard (adjective) = ascending, higher up [§6.9]

ufor (adjective) = higher, greater (comparative) [ModE *OVER*; §6.1.1]

ūht, ūhte (m, weak f) = dawn, early morning [§3.3]

ūht-ċearu (f) = grief at dawn, anxiety before dawn [§2.8]

ūht-san(c)g (m) = morning-SONG; matins, one of the canonical hours of the divine office [§2.7]

un- (prefix) = has the negative force of modern *un-*, occasionally adding a negative or pejorative sense (*dǣd* "deed, act"; *un-dǣd* "evil act")

unc = see wit (dual pronoun)

un-clǣne (adjective) = UNCLEAN [§6.10]

un-cūð (adjective) = unknown [§6.1]

under (preposition + dat/acc) = UNDER [§6.15]

under-brǣdan (weak verb I) = to spread under [§3.11]

under-standan (strong verb 6) = to UNDERSTAND, comprehend [§9.2]

under-tīd (f) = morning time; Tierce, one of the canonical hours of the divine office [§10.11.2]

under-þēodan (weak verb I) = to be addicted to, be subject to, reduce to [§3.11]

un-dyrne (adverb) = openly, widely, UN-secretly [§6.9]

un-ēaþe (adverb) = not easily, barely, with difficulty [§6.9]

un-for-sċēawodlīċe (adverb) = unawares, not forewarned [§6.9]

un-ġe-brosnad (adjective, derived from past participle) = not decomposed, incorrupt, not withered [§3.12]

un-ġe-frǣġelīċ (adjective) = unheard of, strange [§6.1]

un-ġe-lǣred (adjective) = UNLEARned, unschooled, ignorant (originally a past participle) [§6.1]

un-ġelīċ (adjective) = UNLIKE, un-alike, not similar to [§6.1]

un-ġe-scrēpnes (n) = inconvenience [§2.9]

un-ġe-wemmed (adjective, derived from past participle) = unblemished, unspotted, undefiled; pure [§3.11]

un-hēanlīċe (adverb) = bravely, UN-cowardly [§6.9]

un-hwīlen (adjective) = timeless, eternal [§6.1]

un-lǣd (adjective) = accursed, wicked, damned; poor, miserable, wretched

un-lifiġend (adjective) = UNLIVing, dead (originally a present participle) [§6.1]

(ġe)unnan (preterite-present verb) = to grant, allow, give (dat of person, gen of thing) [§4.3]

un-ofer-hrēfed (adjective) = not ROOFED OVER (originally a past participle) [§6.1]

un-rōtnes (f) = sadness, contrition [OE *rōtnes* "gladness"; §2.8] *un-scennan* (weak verb I) = to unyoke, unharness [§3.11]

un-spediġ (adjective) = POOR, unprosperous [§6.1]

un-stille (adverb) = moving, restless, never stopping [§6.9]

un-swǣsliċ (adjective) = cruel, ungentle [§6.1]

un-sȳfre (adjective) = filthy, impure, defiled [§6.1]

un-trum (adjective) = sick, infirm [see OE *trum* above; §6.1]

un-trumnys (f) = lack of strength, weakness, illness, infirmity [§2.8]

(ġe)un-trumod (adjective, derived from past participle) = weakened, lacking strength [§6.1]

un-wǣre (adjective) = UNAWARE [§6.1]

un-wearnum (adverb) = suddenly, in a moment [§6.9]

un-wemme(d) (adjective, derived from past participle) = unblemished, pure, inviolate [§6.1]

un-wīd (adjective) = narrow, UN-WIDE [§6.1]

ūp (adverb) = UP, UPward [§6.9]

ūp-bēah (adjective) = uplifted, tall, high; elevated, sublime [§6.1]

ūp-hebban (strong verb 6) = to raise up, lift [§9.2]

ūp-hōf = past 3 sing of *ūp-hebban*

ūpliċ (adjective) = UPper, lofty; sublime, heavenly, celestial [§6.1]

uppan (preposition + acc) = UP, up to [§6.15]

ūp-rihte (adverb) = UPward, to the top [§6.9]

ūr (pronoun) = OURs; name of the U rune

ūr, ūre, ūsse (pronoun) = OUR [§7.1]

ūs = see *iċ*

ūsse = see *ūr*

ūt (adverb) = OUT [§6.9]

utu = see uton

ūtan (adverb) = from the outside, on the outside [§6.9]

utan = see *uton*

ūt-ēode = 1, 3 past sing of *ūt-gān*

ūte-weard (adjective) = OUTWARD, outer, external [§6.1]

ūt-gān (irregular verb) = to GO OUT [§4.5.3]

uton, uta(n), wutan (special verb) = let us (+ infinitive)

ūt-weorpan, -wyrpan (strong verb 3) = to throw away, throw OUT [compare German *werfen* "to throw"; §8.6]

W

wā (interjection) = WOE ; usually + to be verb and dative: "woe be unto them"

wacian (weak verb II) = to stay aWAKE, be awake; to WATCH, keep watch [§3.12]

wadan (strong verb 6) = to go, traverse, WADE [§9.2]

(ġe)wǣd (f) = garment, dress [§2.8]

wæl-ċyrie (weak f) = witch, sorceress, VALKYRIE [lit., chooser of the slain; §3.4]

wæl-kyrging (f) = VALKYRIE [§3.4]

wæl-stōw (f) = slaughter-place, battlefield [§3.4]

(ġe)wæmmodlīċe (adverb) = badly, in a faulty

way, with blemishes; ungrammatically [from OE *wamm* "stain, blemish, spot"; §6.9]

wǣpen (n) = WEAPON [§2.9]

wǣpned-mann, -monn (m) = man, male, a beWEAPONED person (perhaps in the Freudian sense) [§10.4.2]

wær (adjective) = aWARe, astute [§6.1]

wærĉ (m) = pain, suffering (frequently confused with *weorc*) [§2.7]

wære, wēron, wæs = see *bēon, wesan*

wærlīĉe (adverb) = carefully, WARILY [§6.9]

wǣr-loga (weak m) = truce-breaker, traitor, liar [§3.3, see ModE *WARLOCK*]

wær-wyrde (adjective) = cautious in speech, aWARE of WORDs [§6.1]

wæstm (m) = growth, stature, form (pl in sing sense) [§2.7]

wǣtan (weak verb I) = to WET, moisten [§3.11]

wǣte (f) = liquid, moisture [§3.4]

wæter (n) = WATER [§2.9]

(ġe)wæterian (weak verb II) = to water (an animal), bring water [§3.12]

wall = see *weall*

waldend = see *wealdend*

wamb, womb (f) = belly, stomach [ModE *WOMB*; §2.8]

wan = see *winnan*

wand = see *windan*

(ġe)wanian (weak verb II) = to diminish, make less, WANE [§3.12]

wann = past sing of *winnan*

wascan (strong verb 6 or 7) = to WASH [§9.2, §9.3]

wāt = present 1, 2 sing of *witan*

(ġe)wāt = past 3 sing of *(ġe)wītan*

wax-ġeorn (adjective) = very greedy, ravenous; "eager to grow"? [related to OE *weaxan* "to grow"; §6.1]

wē (personal pronoun) = WE [§7.1]

wealcan (strong verb 7) = to toss, roll [§9.3]

weald (m) = forest, wood [compare German *Wald* "forest"; §2.7]

(ġe)weald (n) = power, might, control [compare German *Gewalt* "power"; §2.9]

(ġe)wealdan (strong verb 7) = to govern, rule, control (+ dat or gen object) [§9.3]

wealdend (m) = ruler, leader [§10.10]

weall, wall (m) = WALL, earthwork; rocky cliff [§2.7]

weard (m) = guardian, keeper [ModE *WARDen*; §2.7]

weard (adverb) = toWARD, to [§6.9]

weardian (weak verb II) = to guard, protect; occupy, inhabit [§3.12]

wearð = see *wēorðan*

wēa-þearf (f) = WOEful need, sad necessity [§2.8]

weaxan (strong verb 6 or 7) = to grow [see ModE phrase "to WAX and wane"; §9.2, §9.3]

weax-bred (n) = writing board, WAX tablet [§2.9]

wecgan (weak verb I) = to move back and forth [§3.11]

wefan (strong verb 5) = to WEAVE [§9.1]

wēfod (m) = altar [§2.7]

weġ (m) = WAY, path [§2.7]

wel (adverb) = WELL [§6.9]

wela (weak m) = WEALth, riches; happiness [§3.3]

weliġ (adjective) = prosperous, rich [§6.1]

wēn (f) = belief, expectation [§2.8]

wēnan (weak verb I) = to imagine, believe, think (+ gen or acc object); fancy; hope, WEEN [§3.11]

wendan (weak verb I) = to transform, change; turn, translate; WEND, go (+ reflexive) [§3.11]

wēnliċ (adjective) = comely, good-looking [§6.1]

(ġe)weorc (n) = WORK, deed, labor; fortress, fortified encampment [§2.9]

weorc-stān (m) = hewn STONE [§2.7]

weorode = past 3 sing of *werian*

weorpan, wyrpan (strong verb 3) = to throw, cast [§8.6]

weorþ (adjective) = WORTHy, deserving [§6.1]

(ġe)weorðan (strong verb 3) = to be, become; to turn (into) something; happen, come to pass; develop, come into being (often used interchangeably with *bēon* and *wesan*, but also often in passive constructions) [compare German *werden* "to become"; §8.6]

weorðian (weak verb II) = to honor, value [see ModE *WORTH*; §3.12]

weorð-mynd (f, m) = WORTH-memory, honor, glory [§2.8]

weorpan (strong verb 3) = to throw, cast down, expel [§8.6]

weoruld = see *woruld*

(ġe)weota = see *(ġe)wita*

wēox = see past 3 sing of *weaxan*

wēpan (strong verb 7) = to WEEP, cry [§9.3]

wer (m) = man, male; husband; hero [see ModE *WEREwolf*; §2.7]

werian (weak verb I) = to defend, protect; to clothe; put on, WEAR [compare German *wehren* "to defend"; §3.11]

weriġ (adjective) = WEARY [§6.1.1]

weriġ-mōd (adjective) = weary, dis-heartened [§6.1]

werliċ (adjective) = male, manly [§6.1]

wesan (irregular verb) = to be [§4.5.1]

wēsten (adjective) = deserted, desolate [§6.1]

wīċ (n) = dwelling place, settlement, lodging [§2.9]

wiċċa (weak f) = WITCH [§3.4]

(ġe)wīcian, wīkian (weak verb II) = to dwell, rest in; encamp; lay at anchor [§3.12]

wīcing (m) = VIKING [§2.7]

wīd (adjective) = WIDE, spacious [§6.1]

(ġe)wīde (adverb) = WIDEly, far apart [§6.9]

widl (m) = filth, sullying, defilement [§2.7]

(ġe)wierpan, wurpan (weak verb I) = to recover from illness, get better [§3.11]

wiers, wyrrest (adverb) = WORSE, most badly (comparative, superlative forms of *yfle* "badly") [§6.9, §6.14]

wiersa, wierrst (adjective) = WORSE, WORST (comparative, superlative of *yfel* "bad") [see §6.8]

wīf (n) = woman, female; WIFE [§2.9]

wif-mann (m) = WOMAN, female [§10.4.2]

wīġ (n) = war [§2.9]

wīġa (weak m) = warrior, soldier [§3.3]

wīġ-hēap (m) = battle band, war troop [§2.7]

wīġend (m) = warrior, soldier, fighter [§10.10.1, originally a past participle]

wīġ-sigor (m) = battle-victory, victory [§2.7]

wiht (f) = creature, being [ModE *WIGHT*; §2.8]

wīkian = see *wīcian*

wild-dēor (n) = WILD animal [compare German *Tier* "animal"; §2.9]

Wilferð = Wilfrid, Bishop of York (died 709)

willa (weak m) = WILL, desire; pleasure [§3.3]

willan (irregular verb) = to want, wish, desire (+ infinitive) [§4.5.3]

wilnian (weak verb II) = to wish, desire, long for [§3.12]

wil-sum (adjective) = desireable, delightful; ready, willing, voluntary; devoted [§6.1]

wilt = see *willan*

wind (m) = WIND [§2.7]

wīnestra (adjective) = left [§6.1]

wīn (n) = WINE [§2.9]

windan (strong verb 3) = to WIND, twist [§8.6]

windiġ (adjective) = WINDY [§6.1]

wine (m) = friend, confidant; lover [§10.2]

wine-lēas (adjective) = friendless, lordless [§6.1]

wine-wincle (weak f) = periWINKLE, a small, edible sea-snail [§3.4]

(ġe)winn (n) = profit, gain; war, conflict [§10.11.2]

winnan (strong verb 3) = to struggle, fight (with); experience, suffer; conquer, WIN, gain [§8.6]

wīn-sæd (adjective) = WINE-filled, satiated with wine, drunk [§6.1]

wīn-sele (n) = WINE hall [§2.9]

winsian, wynsumian (weak verb I) = to revel, rejoice, be WINSOME [§3.11]

winter (m or n) = WINTER, year [§2.7, §2.9]

wīr (m) = WIRE, metal thread, wire ornament [§2.7]

wīs (adjective) = WISE [§6.1]

wīs-dōm (m) = WISDOM [§2.7]

wīse (weak f) = way, manner, fashion [§3.4]

wīs-fæst (adjective) = WISE, knowledgeable [§6.1]

(ġe)wīslīċe (adverb) = certainly, truly [§6.9]

wissian (weak verb II) = to direct, instruct [compare German *weisen* "to guide"; §3.12]

wit (personal pronoun, dual number) = we two [§7.1.1]

wita (weak m) = counsellor, wise man, seer; witness [§2.3]

witan (preterite-present verb) = to know [§4.4.1]

(ġe)wītan (strong verb 1) = to depart, leave; pass away, die; to find fault with, blame; to betake, undertake to do something (+ reflexive + infinitive) [§8.4]

wīte (n) = torture, punishment; pain [§10.2.2]

wīte(g)-dōm (m) = prophecy, prediction [§2.7]

wīteġian (weak verb II) = to prophesy, predict, foretell [§3.12] *wītega* (weak m) = wise man; seer, prophet [§3.3]

witlēas (adjective) = WITLESS, mad, insane; unconscious? [§6.1]

ġe-wit-loca (weak m) = WIT-LOCKer, mind, thought [§3.3]

(ġe)witnes (f) = WITNESS, testimony [§2.8]

witodlīċe (adverb) = truly, certainly [§6.9]

wiþ (preposition + gen, acc, dat, instr) = WITH, against, in opposition to, as a remedy for [§6.15]

wið-innan (adverb) = WITHIN [§6.9]

wið-ðon-þe (conjunction) = provided that [§5.1.1]

wlǣtta (weak m) = loathing, disgust, object of loathing [§3.3]

wlītan (strong verb 1) = to gaze, observe, look at [§8.4]

wlitiġ, wliteġ (adjective) = beautiful, lovely; bright [§6.1]

Wōdnes-dæġ (m) = WEDNESDAY [§2.7]

wob (adjective) = wrong; crooked [§6.1]

wolcen (n) = cloud, WELKIN [§2.9]

wolde = past 1, 3 sing of *willan*

wom-ful (adjective) = full of blemishes; evil, criminal [§6.1]

womm, wamm (m) = spot, blotch, stain, disgrace; sin, evil, crime [§2.7]

wonn = see *wann*

won-sēliġ (adjective) = unhappy, miserable, wretched [§6.1]

wōp (m) = cry, scream; WEEPing, crying [§2.7]

word (n) = WORD [§2.9]

(ġe)worden = past participle of *weorðan*

(ġe)worhte = past 3 sing of *wyrcan*

woruld (f) = WORLD; *in ealra worulda woruld* = world without end, for ever and ever [§10.11.2]

woruld-būend (m) = world-dweller, inhabitant of the earth [§10.10.1]

woruld-cræft (m) = WORLDly CRAFT, occupation [§2.7]

woruld-mann (m) = human being; layman, lay person [§10.4.2]

woruld-rīċe (n) = this WORLD, earthly kingdom [§2.9]

woruld-sorg (f) = WORLDly care, SORrow [§3.4]

woruld-strengu (f) = WORLD-STRENGth, physical strength, life strength [§2.8]

woruld-þin(c)g (n) = worldly affair, (pl) worldly riches [§2.9]

woruld-wunigende (adjective) = world-living, dwelling on earth [§6.1]

wræċċa (m weak) = outcast, exile, fugitive, WRETCH [§3.3]

wræc-sīþ (m) = "exile-journey," hardship, exile [§2.7]

wrǣtliċ (adjective) = wondrous, beautiful, rare; ornamental [§6.1]

wrǣtlīċe (adverb) = woundrously, marvelously, curiously [§6.9]

wrǣtt (f) = ornament, work of art [§2.8]

wrāh = see *wrēon*

wrāþe (adverb) = cruelly, fiercely [§6.9]

wrāð-mōd (adjective) = angered, in a WRATHful MOOD [§6.1]

(ġe)wrecan (strong verb 5) = to avenge, WREAK vengance; to utter, relate, tell [§9.1]

wrēon (strong verb 1, contract verb) = to cover, envelop [§8.4, §11.1]

wringan (strong verb 3) = to WRING; squeeze, press out [§8.6]

wrītan (strong verb 1) = to WRITE [§8.4]

wrītere (m) = WRITER, scribe, author, painter [§10.2.1]

wrōht (f) = blame, reproach [§2.8]

wuca (weak f) = WEEK [§3.4]

wudu (m) = WOOD, forest [§10.6]

wuhte = f plural of *wiht*

wuldor (n) = glory [§2.9]

wuldor-ful (adjective) = full of glory, glorious [§6.1]

wuldor-ful-līċe (adverb) = gloriously [§6.9]

wuldor-ġe-steald (n plural) = realms of glory, glorious possessions [§2.9]

wuldorlīċ (adjective) = glorious [§6.1]

wulf (m) = WOLF [§2.7]

wull (f) = WOOL [§2.8]

(ġe)wuna (weak m) = habit, practice, custom [§3.3]

wund (f) = WOUND [§2.8]

wunden-locc (adjective) = with braided LOCKs [§6.1]

wunden-mǣl (n) = sword with WOUND or twisted ornaments [§2.9]

wundor (n) = WONDER, marvel, miracle [§2.9]

wundor-cræftiġ-līċe (adverb) = with WONDRous skill [§6.9]

wundor-līċ (adjective) = strange, marvellous, miraculous, inspiring amazement or WONDER [§6.1.]

wundrian (weak verb II) = to marvel, WONDER [§3.12]

wundrung (f) = WONDER, admiration [§2.8]

(ġe)wunelīċe (adverb) = accustomed to, habitually, usually [§6.9]

wunian (weak verb II) = to dwell, live, reside; remain, stay [compare German *wohnen* "live, reside"; §3.12]

wunne = see *winnan*

(ġe)wurpan = see *(ġe)wierpan*

wurðaþ, wurde, wurdon = see *weorðan*

wurð-mynt (m) = honor [§2.7]

wyllaþ, wylle, wylt, etc. = see *willan*

Wyllelm bastard (m) = William the Conquerer

wyllen (adjective) = WOOLEN, made of wool [§6.1]

wyn(n) (n) = joy, pleasure, delight [§10.11.1]

wynliċ (adjective) = pleasant, agreeable [§6.1]

wynsum (adjective) = WINSOME, pleasing, delightful, pleasant [§6.1]

wynsumnes (f) = joyfulness, delight, loveliness; WINSOMENESS [OE *wynn* "joy"; §2.8]

(ġe)wyrċan (weak verb I) = to perform, do; WORK [§3.11]

(ġe)wyrht (f) = merit, deserving; transgression; *be (ġe)wyhrtum* = "deservedly" [§2.8]

wyrhta (weak m) = worker, WRIGHT [§3.3]

wyrm (m) = WORM, serpent, snake; dragon [§10.11.1]

wyrpan = see *weorpan* or *wierpan*

wyrse (adjective) = WORSE (comparative of *yfel* "bad, evil") [§6.7]

wyrsta (adjective) = WORST (superlative of *yfel* "bad, evil") [§6.7]

wyrt (f) = plant, vegetable, root, herb [§2.8]

wyrt-ġemang(c) (n) = mixture of herbs and spices; perfume [§2.9]

wyrt-tūn (m) = "plant-enclosure"; garden [§2.7]

(ġe)wȳslīċe = see *(ġe)wīslīċe*

Y

ȳcan (weak verb I) = to increase, enlarge, add to [§3.11]

yfel (adjective) = bad, EVIL (comp: *wyrse*) [§6.7]

yfel (n) = EVIL, evil thing [§6.1, §2.9]

yfel-wyrde (adjective) = EVIL-tongued, accustomed to evil speech or WORDs [§6.1]

ylċ- = see *ilċ*

yld = see *ieldo*

ylpes-bān (n) = ivory [§2.9]

ymb(e) (preposition + acc / dat) = around, near; about, concerning [§6.15]

ymb-līgan, -licgan (strong verb 5) = to surround, enclose [§9.1]

ymb-sellan (weak verb I) = to surround, enclose, clothe [§3.11]

ymb-settan, emb- (weak verb I) = to SET about or around, surround [§3.11]

ymb-standan (strong verb 6) = to STAND around; surround [§9.3]

ymb-tȳnan, emb- (weak verb I) = to enclose, surround [from OE *tūn* "walled TOWN, enclosure" with i-mutation; §3.11]

yppan (weak verb I) = to utter, reveal, betray, open; disclose, mention [§3.11]

yrfe (n) = inheritance, bequest; heritage [§10.2.2]

yrnan, iernan (strong verb 3) = to run [§8.6]

yrmð- = see *iermð*

yrre (adjective) = angry [§6.1]

yrringa (adverb) = angrily [§6.9]

yrþlin(c)g (m) = farmer, plowman [§2.7]

ys = *is*, pres 3 sing of *bēon*

yt, ytst = see *etan*

ȳð (f) = wave, billow [§2.8]

ȳðe = see *ēaðe*

ȳðelīċe (adverb) = easily, with no difficulty [§6.9]